Apache Server Bible

Apache Server Bible

Mohammed J. Kabir

IDG Books Worldwide, Inc.
An International Data Group Company

Foster City, CA ✦ Chicago, IL ✦ Indianapolis, IN ✦ New York, NY

Apache Server Bible

Published by
IDG Books Worldwide, Inc.
An International Data Group Company
919 E. Hillsdale Blvd., Suite 400
Foster City, CA 94404
`www.idgbooks.com` (IDG Books Worldwide Web site)

Library of Congress Catalog Card No.: 98-071158

ISBN: 0-7645-3218-9

Printed in the United States of America

10 9 8 7 6 5 4 3 2 1

1E/SV/QW/ZY/FC

Distributed in the United States by IDG Books Worldwide, Inc.

Distributed by Macmillan Canada for Canada; by Transworld Publishers Limited in the United Kingdom; by IDG Norge Books for Norway; by IDG Sweden Books for Sweden; by Woodslane Pty. Ltd. for Australia; by Woodslane (NZ) Ltd. for New Zealand; by Addison Wesley Longman Singapore Pte Ltd. for Singapore, Malaysia, Thailand, Indonesia, and Korea; by Norma Comunicaciones S.A. for Colombia; by Intersoft for South Africa; by International Thomson Publishing for Germany, Austria, and Switzerland; by Toppan Company Ltd. for Japan; by Distribuidora Cuspide for Argentina; by Livraria Cultura for Brazil; by Ediciencia S.A. for Ecuador; by Ediciones ZETA S.C.R. Ltda. for Peru; by WS Computer Publishing Corporation, Inc., for the Philippines; by Unalis Corporation for Taiwan; by Contemporanea de Ediciones for Venezuela; by Computer Book & Magazine Store for Puerto Rico; by Express Computer Distributors for the Caribbean and West Indies. Authorized Sales Agent: Anthony Rudkin Associates for the Middle East and North Africa.

For general information on IDG Books Worldwide's books in the U.S., please call our Consumer Customer Service department at 800-762-2974. For reseller information, including discounts and premium sales, please call our Reseller Customer Service department at 800-434-3422.

For information on where to purchase IDG Books Worldwide's books outside the U.S., please contact our International Sales department at 650-655-3200 or fax 650-655-3297.

For information on foreign language translations, please contact our Foreign & Subsidiary Rights department at 650-655-3021 or fax 650-655-3281.

For sales inquiries and special prices for bulk quantities, please contact our Sales department at 650-655-3200 or write to the address above.

For information on using IDG Books Worldwide's books in the classroom or for ordering examination copies, please contact our Educational Sales department at 800-434-2086 or fax 317-596-5499.

For press review copies, author interviews, or other publicity information, please contact our Public Relations department at 650-655-3000 or fax 650-655-3299.

ABOUT IDG BOOKS WORLDWIDE

Welcome to the world of IDG Books Worldwide.

IDG Books Worldwide, Inc., is a subsidiary of International Data Group, the world's largest publisher of computer-related information and the leading global provider of information services on information technology. IDG was founded more than 25 years ago and now employs more than 8,500 people worldwide. IDG publishes more than 275 computer publications in over 75 countries (see listing below). More than 90 million people read one or more IDG publications each month.

Launched in 1990, IDG Books Worldwide is today the #1 publisher of best-selling computer books in the United States. We are proud to have received eight awards from the Computer Press Association in recognition of editorial excellence and three from *Computer Currents'* First Annual Readers' Choice Awards. Our best-selling *...For Dummies®* series has more than 50 million copies in print with translations in 38 languages. IDG Books Worldwide, through a joint venture with IDG's Hi-Tech Beijing, became the first U.S. publisher to publish a computer book in the People's Republic of China. In record time, IDG Books Worldwide has become the first choice for millions of readers around the world who want to learn how to better manage their businesses.

Our mission is simple: Every one of our books is designed to bring extra value and skill-building instructions to the reader. Our books are written by experts who understand and care about our readers. The knowledge base of our editorial staff comes from years of experience in publishing, education, and journalism — experience we use to produce books for the '90s. In short, we care about books, so we attract the best people. We devote special attention to details such as audience, interior design, use of icons, and illustrations. And because we use an efficient process of authoring, editing, and desktop publishing our books electronically, we can spend more time ensuring superior content and spend less time on the technicalities of making books.

You can count on our commitment to deliver high-quality books at competitive prices on topics you want to read about. At IDG Books Worldwide, we continue in the IDG tradition of delivering quality for more than 25 years. You'll find no better book on a subject than one from IDG Books Worldwide.

John Kilcullen
CEO
IDG Books Worldwide, Inc.

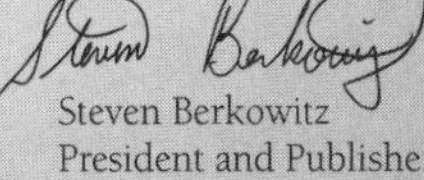

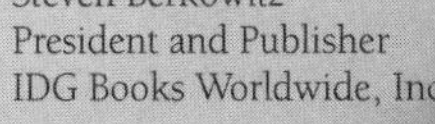

Steven Berkowitz
President and Publisher
IDG Books Worldwide, Inc.

Eighth Annual Computer Press Awards 1992

Ninth Annual Computer Press Awards 1993

Tenth Annual Computer Press Awards 1994

Eleventh Annual Computer Press Awards 1995

IDG Books Worldwide, Inc., is a subsidiary of International Data Group, the world's largest publisher of computer-related information and the leading global provider of information services on information technology. International Data Group publishes over 275 computer publications in over 75 countries. More than 90 million people read one or more International Data Group publications each month. International Data Group's publications include: **ARGENTINA:** Buyer's Guide, Computerworld Argentina, PC World Argentina; **AUSTRALIA:** Australian Macworld, Australian PC World, Australian Reseller News, Computerworld, IT Casebook, Network World, Publish, Webmaster; **AUSTRIA:** Computerwelt Osterreich, Networks Austria, PC Tip Austria; **BANGLADESH:** PC World Bangladesh; **BELARUS:** PC World Belarus; **BELGIUM:** Data News; **BRAZIL:** Annuário de Informática, Computerworld, Connections, Macworld, PC Player, PC World, Publish, Reseller News, Supergamepower; **BULGARIA:** Computerworld Bulgaria, Network World Bulgaria, PC & MacWorld Bulgaria; **CANADA:** CIO Canada, Client/Server World, ComputerWorld Canada, InfoWorld Canada, NetworkWorld Canada, WebWorld; **CHILE:** Computerworld Chile, PC World Chile; **COLOMBIA:** Computerworld Colombia, PC World Colombia; **COSTA RICA:** PC World Centro America; **THE CZECH AND SLOVAK REPUBLICS:** Computerworld Czechoslovakia, Macworld Czech Republic, PC World Czechoslovakia; **DENMARK:** Communications World Danmark, Computerworld Danmark, Macworld Danmark, PC World Danmark, Techworld Denmark; **DOMINICAN REPUBLIC:** PC World Republica Dominicana; **ECUADOR:** PC World Ecuador; **EGYPT:** Computerworld Middle East, PC World Middle East; **EL SALVADOR:** PC World Centro America; **FINLAND:** MikroPC, Tietoverkko, Tietoviikko; **FRANCE:** Distributique, Hebdo, Info PC, Le Monde Informatique, Macworld, Reseaux & Telecoms, WebMaster France; **GERMANY:** Computer Partner, Computerwoche, Computerwoche Extra, Computerwoche FOCUS, Global Online, Macwelt, PC Welt; **GREECE:** Amiga Computing, GamePro Greece, Multimedia World; **GUATEMALA:** PC World Centro America; **HONDURAS:** PC World Centro America; **HONG KONG:** Computerworld Hong Kong, PC World Hong Kong, Publish in Asia; **HUNGARY:** ABCD CD-ROM, Computerworld Szamitastechnika, Internetto online Magazine, PC World Hungary, PC-X Magazin Hungary; **ICELAND:** Tolvuheimur PC World Island; **INDIA:** Information Communications World, Information Systems Computerworld, PC World India, Publish in Asia; **INDONESIA:** InfoKomputer PC World, Komputek Computerworld, Publish in Asia; **IRELAND:** ComputerScope, PC Live!; **ISRAEL:** Macworld Israel, People & Computers/Computerworld; **ITALY:** Computerworld Italia, Macworld Italia, Networking Italia, PC World Italia; **JAPAN:** DTP World, Macworld Japan, Nikkei Personal Computing, OS/2 World Japan, SunWorld Japan, Windows NT World, Windows World Japan; **KENYA:** PC World East African; **KOREA:** Hi-Tech Information, Macworld Korea, PC World Korea; **MACEDONIA:** PC World Macedonia; **MALAYSIA:** Computerworld Malaysia, PC World Malaysia, Publish in Asia; **MALTA:** PC World Malta; **MEXICO:** Computerworld Mexico, PC World Mexico; **MYANMAR:** PC World Myanmar; **NETHERLANDS:** Computer! Totaal, LAN Internetworking Magazine, LAN World Buyers Guide, Macworld Netherlands, Net, WebWereld; **NEW ZEALAND:** Absolute Beginners Guide and Plain & Simple Series, Computer Buyer, Computer Industry Directory, Computerworld New Zealand, MTB, Network World, PC World New Zealand; **NICARAGUA:** PC World Centro America; **NORWAY:** Computerworld Norge, CW Rapport, Datamagasinet, Financial Rapport, Kursguide Norge, Macworld Norge, Multimediaworld Norge, PC World Ekspress Norge, PC World Nettverk, PC World Norge, PC World ProduktGuide Norge; **PAKISTAN:** Computerworld Pakistan; **PANAMA:** PC World Panama; **PEOPLE'S REPUBLIC OF CHINA:** China Computer Users, China Computerworld, China InfoWorld, China Telecom World Weekly, Computer & Communication, Electronic Design China, Electronics Today, Electronics Weekly, Game Software, PC World China, Popular Computer Week, Software Weekly, Software World, Telecom World; **PERU:** Computerworld Peru, PC World Profesional Peru, PC World SoHo Peru; **PHILIPPINES:** Click!, Computerworld Philippines, PC World Philippines, Publish in Asia; **POLAND:** Computerworld Poland, Computerworld Special Report Poland, Cyber, Macworld Poland, Networld Poland, PC World Komputer; **PORTUGAL:** Cerebro/PC World, Computerworld/Correio Informático, Dealer World Portugal, Mac*In/PC*In Portugal, Multimedia World; **PUERTO RICO:** PC World Puerto Rico; **ROMANIA:** Computerworld Romania, PC World Romania, Telecom Romania; **RUSSIA:** Computerworld Russia, Mir PK, Publish, Seti; **SINGAPORE:** Computerworld Singapore, PC World Singapore, Publish in Asia; **SLOVENIA:** Monitor; **SOUTH AFRICA:** Computing SA, Network World SA, Software World SA; **SPAIN:** Communicaciones World España, Computerworld España, Dealer World España, Macworld España, PC World España; **SRI LANKA:** Infolink PC World; **SWEDEN:** CAP&Design, Computer Sweden, Corporate Computing Sweden, Internetworld Sweden, it.branschen, Macworld Sweden, MaxiData Sweden, MikroDatorn, Nätverk & Kommunikation, PC World Sweden, PCaktiv, Windows World Sweden; **SWITZERLAND:** Computerworld Schweiz, Macworld Schweiz, PCtip; **TAIWAN:** Computerworld Taiwan, Macworld Taiwan, NEW ViSiON/Publish, PC World Taiwan, Windows World Taiwan; **THAILAND:** Publish in Asia, Thai Computerworld; **TURKEY:** Computerworld Turkiye, Macworld Turkiye, Network World Turkiye, PC World Turkiye; **UKRAINE:** Computerworld Kiev, Multimedia World Ukraine, PC World Ukraine; **UNITED KINGDOM:** Acorn User UK, Amiga Action UK, Amiga Computing UK, Apple Talk UK, Computing, Macworld, Parents and Computers UK, PC Advisor, PC Home, PSX Pro, The WEB; **UNITED STATES:** Cable in the Classroom, CIO Magazine, Computerworld, DOS World, Federal Computer Week, GamePro Magazine, InfoWorld, I-Way, Macworld, Network World, PC Games, PC World, Publish, Video Event, THE WEB Magazine, and WebMaster; online webzines: JavaWorld, NetscapeWorld, and SunWorld Online; **URUGUAY:** InfoWorld Uruguay; **VENEZUELA:** Computerworld Venezuela, PC World Venezuela; and **VIETNAM:** PC World Vietnam. 5/7/98

Credits

Acquisitions Editors
Anne Hamilton
Tracy Thomsic

Development Editor
Jennifer Rowe

Technical Editor
John Dupuy

Copy Editors
Larisa North
Nicole Fountain
Ami Knox
Brian MacDonald

Project Coordinator
Tom Debolski

Graphics and Production Specialist
Jude Levinson

Quality Control Specialists
Mark Schumann
Mick Arellano

Graphics Technicians
Hector Mendoza
Linda Marousek

Proofreader
Nancy Reinhardt

Indexer
Liz Cunningham

Cover Design
Murder By Design

About the Author

Mohammed J. Kabir specializes in Internet software development. Over the last few years, he has managed Internet software development projects for many companies. He studied Computer Engineering at California State University, Sacramento. His current interests are operating systems, network hardware, and microcontrollers. When he is not working toward a deadline, he designs simple and often silly hardware and software. Recently he has been trying to get a vending machine hooked up to the Ethernet he runs from his home. Kabir is also the author of *CGI Primer Plus for Windows*. Kabir's e-mail address is kabir@nitec.com.

To the memory of my mother, Nazma Bathen.

Preface

Welcome to *Apache Server Bible*. Chances are you have already heard about Apache Server. In fact, more than 50 percent of Internet-based Web administrators are using Apache all around the world. However, despite its widespread use, there aren't many books on administering Apache Server. Yes, I have been to the bookstores, and having seen what is out there, I feel that none of the available titles are geared toward Web administrators. I have seen one that talks more about the internals of Apache (C code) than how to make use of Apache itself; another book devotes a large portion to HTML. This book is meant for anyone who is interested in administering Apache and focused on getting the most out of Apache. So if you want to become a master Apache administrator, you found the magic wand. Use it!

Is This Book for You?

This book will benefit anyone interested in learning how to administer an Apache Web Server. Because the book does not assume any previous Web administration experience, it is suitable for just about anyone. Unlike many Web server books, this book only deals with a single topic — the Apache Web Server.

The text focuses on the administration aspects of the Apache Web Server. It walks you through source compilation, binary installations, and configuration issues in the early chapters, so you can get the server up and running right away and at the same time understand what is being done each step of the way.

The book then focuses on more advanced issues such as the SSI, CGI, and FastCGI configurations and their impact on the server and its security model. You will be introduced to the risks involved and how to minimize these risks using various techniques. More advanced topics include Web server performance enhancement, user authentication, monitoring, and issues such as URL rewriting techniques, embedding Perl interpreter within Apache, and using the Secured Socket Layer.

How This Book Is Organized

I organized the book into five parts, as follows:

Part I: Getting Started

After a brief introduction to the world's number one Web server, you are guided through the process of obtaining and compiling Apache. You learn how to get Apache up and running with minimal changes to the default configuration files — to get it up and running on your system as quickly as possible. This part ends by providing complete references to the Apache core directives and standard modules so you can get ready for serious Apache administration tasks.

Part II: Administering Your Web Sites

This section of the book is going to turn you into a pro administrator. Typical Web administration topics such as virtual Web sites, Server Side Includes (SSI), and the Common Gateway Interface (CGI) are discussed. Here you learn everything there is to know about creating and managing virtual Web sites, including how to create virtual e-mail addresses to give your virtual Web sites the professional look and feel expected only from Internet service providers. You learn to master Server Side Includes (SSI) through numerous examples; these examples not only show you how to do the usual stuff, but also how to do cool things such as displaying HTML content based on the flow-control decisions you make, and injecting custom environment variables to give external SSI/CGI programs clues about what to do. The CGI chapters show you how to create a powerful CGI platform with your Apache server; configure your server to support CGI functionality; and boost your server's CGI performance many times by using the emerging FastCGI technology.

Part III: Playing It Safe

Any computer on the Internet is subject to abuse or attempts at misuse. It is always a good idea to play it safe and take precautionary measures. In this part of the book, you first learn how to use various authentication techniques based on the standard Web authentication scheme — the basic HTTP authentication. You learn to create restricted access areas in your Web sites based on user name/password pairs, host addresses, or IP addresses. Here, I go beyond the basics by introducing external authentication programs and demonstrating how to use databases for managing large-scale user-access control. The next logical step after learning how to control access is discovering who is accessing what on your sites. You learn to monitor your Web server via the Web, analyze your server log files, and create custom logs for both security and marketing needs. I also introduce you to the potential risks of running SSI and CGI programs, and cite various preventive measures you can take to avoid these risks.

Part IV: Implementing Advanced Features

This part of the book discusses advanced topics that are bound to come up in any discussion of Apache. Here, you learn how Apache can embed the most widely used CGI programming language — Perl; how it can act as a proxy server; how secured transactions can be implemented in Apache; and how you can have it rewrite URLs. Once you have mastered these techniques, consider yourself a wizard administrator.

Part V: Using Apache Today and Tomorrow

In this part, I discuss how you can use Apache for tomorrow's needs as well as today's. First, I point out general performance issues you should be aware of. Paying attention to these issues and implementing recommended solutions will ensure your Apache server is ready to handle its workload now and in the future. Next, I introduce you to such concepts as the Web cycle, which will enable you to develop manageable Web sites for the future. You learn the importance of standards when it comes to your Web site development. I discuss how you can create a set of policies to control the quality of your Web site. Because most successful Web sites will require future expansion, I show you how Apache, along with other Internet technologies, can create large-scale, multihost Web networks. Finally, you get to take a peek at the upcoming version of Apache for the Windows platform. Using the latest Apache beta for Windows, you will be able to turn your Windows system into an Apache Server! After reading this part, you will have only one thought in your mind — Apache is here to stay!

Conventions Used in This Book

You won't have to learn any new conventions to read this book. Just remember, when you are asked to enter a command, press the Enter or Return key after you type the command at your command prompt. Also, pay attention to the following icons:

The Note icon is used whenever something needs additional explanation.

The Tip icon is used to tell you something that is likely to save you time and effort.

The Caution icon is used to make you aware of a potential danger.

The Cross-reference icon is used to tell you that related information exists somewhere else in the book.

Tell Us What You Think

Both IDG Books Worldwide and I would like to know what you think of this book. Please register this book online at the IDG Books Worldwide Web site (http://www.idgbooks.com) and give us your feedback. If you are interested in communicating with me directly, send e-mail messages to kabir@nitec.com. I will try my best to respond promptly.

Acknowledgments

First of all, I would like to thank the Apache Group for creating the most powerful, extensible, and modular Web server in the world. I would like to give special thanks to the following people in the Apache Group:

Ralf S. Engelschall, the author of mod_rewrite module, provided a great deal of support in the development of the chapter on URL rewriting rules. The practical examples in that chapter are derived from his personal collection, which keeps growing at his Web site (http://www.engelschall.com/pw/apache/rewriteguide/). Brian Behlendorf responded quickly to my queries regarding Apache software distribution and other general matters. And Tyler Allison helped me understand quite a few things about the external authentication module.

Next, I would like to thank the IDG team that made this book a reality. It is impossible to list everyone involved, but I must mention the following kind individuals:

Jennifer Rowe, development editor, kept this project going. I don't know how I could have done this book without her generous help and suggestions every step of the way. Larisa North, copy editor, made sure the book is readable. She, with the help of Nicole Fountain, regularly reworded many of my "machine language" sentences to plain, readable English. John Dupuy, technical reviewer, provided numerous technical suggestions, tips, and tricks — many of which have been incorporated in the book. And, finally, thanks to Tracy Thomsic and Anne Hamilton, acquisitions editors. Anne provided me with this book opportunity, and Tracy made sure I followed through to the end. I am very grateful to both of them.

A few other important people played unique roles in making this book happen:

Sheila Kabir, my wife, had to put up with many long work hours during the few months it took to write this book. She also contributed a great deal of time in helping me draw the figures. And Purok, Purni, Lisa, and Sohel made sure I got my daily dose of encouragement via e-mail and electronic postcards.

Contents at a Glance

Contents

Getting Started

PART I

✦ ✦ ✦ ✦

In This Part

✦ ✦ ✦ ✦

Apache – The Number One Web Server

In This Chapter

A brief history of Apache

Features of Apache

Apache architecture

The future of Apache

Understanding the Apache license

Exactly who uses Apache?

Welcome to Apache — the number one Web server in the world. More than 50 percent of the Web servers in the world use Apache, according to a prominent Web server survey company called Netcraft (www.netcraft.co.uk/Survey/). If you are toying with the idea of running Apache, you are in the right place! This chapter will introduce to the Apache way of running a Web server.

In the early days of the Web, the National Center for Super Computing Applications (NCSA) created a Web server that became the number one Web server in early 1995. However, the primary developer of the NCSA Web server left NCSA about the same time, and the server project began to stall. In the meantime, people who were using the NCSA Web server began to exchange their own patches for the server and soon realized that a forum to manage the patches was necessary. The Apache Group was born. The group used the NCSA Web server code and gave birth to a new Web server called Apache. Originally derived from the core code of the NCSA Web server and a bunch of patches, the Apache server is now the talk of the Web server community. In three short years, it has acquired the lead server role in the market.

The very first version (0.6.2) of publicly distributed Apache was released in April 1995. The 1.0 version was released on December 1, 1995. Since the beginning, the Apache Group has expanded and incorporated as a non-profit group. The group operates entirely via the Internet. However, the development of the Apache server is not limited in any way by the group. Anyone who has the know-how to participate in the development of the server or its component modules is welcome to do so, although the group is the final authority on what gets included in the standard distribution of what is known as the Apache Web server. This allows literally thousands of developers around the world to come up with new features, bug fixes, ports to new platforms, and more. When new code is submitted to the Apache Group, the group members investigate the details, perform tests, and do quality control checks. If they are satisfied, the code is integrated into the main Apache distribution.

Now that you know a little bit more about the history of Apache, let's look at the features that make it so good.

The Apache Feature List

One of the greatest features that Apache offers is that it runs on virtually all widely used computer platforms. At the beginning, Apache used to be primarily a UNIX-based Web server, but that is no longer true. Apache not only runs on most (if not all) flavors of UNIX, but it also runs on Windows 95/NT and many other desktop and server-class operating systems such as Amiga, and OS/2.

There are many other features Apache offers such as fancy directory indexing, directory aliasing, content negotiations, configurable HTTP error reporting, SetUID Execution of CGI Programs, resource management for child processes, server-side image maps, URL rewriting, URL spell checking, and online manuals.

The other major features of Apache are:

- Support for the latest HTTP/1.1 protocol — Apache is one of the first Web servers to integrate the HTTP/1.1 protocol. It is fully compliant with the new HTTP/1.1 standard and at the same time it is backward compatible with HTTP/1.0. Apache is ready for all the great things that the new protocol has to offer. For example, before HTTP/1.1, a Web browser had to wait for a response from the Web server before it could issue another request. With the emergence of HTTP/1.1, this is no longer the case. A Web browser can send requests in parallel, which saves bandwidth by not transmitting HTTP headers in each request. This is likely to provide a performance boost at the end-user side because files requested in parallel will appear faster on the browser.
- Simple, yet powerful file-based configuration — The Apache server does not come with a graphical user interface for administrators. It comes with three plain-text configuration files that you can use to configure Apache to your liking. All you need is your text editor of choice. It is also possible to simplify configuration tasks further by aggregating three configuration files into one.
- Support for Common Gateway Interface (CGI) — Apache supports CGI using the mod_cgi module. It is CGI/1.1 compliant and offers extended features such as custom environment variables and debugging support that are hard to find in other Web servers. See Chapter 8 for details.
- Support for virtual hosts — Apache is also one of the first Web servers to support both IP-based and named virtual hosts. See Chapter 6 for details.

✦ Support for HTTP authentication—-Web-based basic authentication is supported in Apache. It is also ready for message-digest-based authentication, which is something the popular Web browsers have yet to implement. Apache can implement basic authentication using either standard password files, DBMs, SQL calls, or calls to external authentication programs. See Chapter 10 for details.

✦ Integrated Perl—Perl has become the de facto standard for CGI script programming. Apache is surely one of the factors that made Perl such a popular CGI programming language. Apache is now more Perl-friendly then ever. Using its mod_perl module, you can load a Perl-based CGI script in memory and reuse it as many times as you want. This process removes the start-up penalties that are often associated with an interpreted language like Perl. See Chapter 13 for details.

✦ Integrated Proxy server—You can turn Apache into a caching (forward) proxy server. However, the current implementation of the optional proxy module does not support reverse proxy or the latest HTTP/1.1 protocol. There are plans for updating this module soon. See Chapter 14 for details.

✦ Server status and customizable logs—Apache gives you a great deal of flexibility in logging and monitoring the status of the server itself. Server status can be monitored via a Web browser. You can also customize your log files to your liking. See Chapter 11 for details.

✦ Support for Server Side Includes (SSI)—Apache offers an extended set of server side includes that add a great deal of flexibility for the Web site developer. Using the eXtended Server Side Includes commands in Apache, you can do everything you could do with SSI and more. See Chapter 7 for details.

✦ Support for Secured Socket Layer (SSL)—Because of copyright laws and restrictions on export and import by U.S. law, Apache is not SSL compliant by itself. However, you can either get a set of patches for Apache (Apache-SSL) or buy a commercial Apache derivative to meet your SSL needs. See Chapter 15 for details.

✦ User session tracking capabilities—Using HTTP cookies, an Apache module called mod_usertrack can track users as they browse an Apache Web site. See Chapter 11 for details.

✦ Support for FastCGI —Not everyone writes their CGI in Perl, so how can they make their CGI applications faster? Apache has a solution for that as well. Use the mod_fcgi module to implement a FastCGI environment within Apache and make your FastCGI applications blazing fast. See Chapter 9 for details.

✦ Support for Java Servlets—An experimental Java Servlet (alpha) module called mod_jserv is available for Apache. When this module is officially released, it will allow Apache to run server-side Java applications that can take advantage of multithreading and other Java features.

Apache Architecture 101

The official Apache server consists of the core Apache code and the standard modules that are compiled into the server by the default configuration. If you choose to remove one of these standard modules, you can easily do so by editing the Configuration file and reconfiguring Apache using the nifty Configure script. This process is extremely simple and only requires you to remove a single line from a text file. Once you recompile your Apache server, the module is no longer in the executable.

For example, if you had no need for CGI script support in your server, you can comment out the following line from the Configuration file found in the source subdirectory of the Apache distribution:

```
Addmodule modules/standard/mod_cgi.o
```

Apache also supports an Application Programming Interface (API) that allows developers to build modules to plug into the Apache server to add new functionality. Figure 1-1 shows an example scenario where three Apache servers have three different levels of functionality.

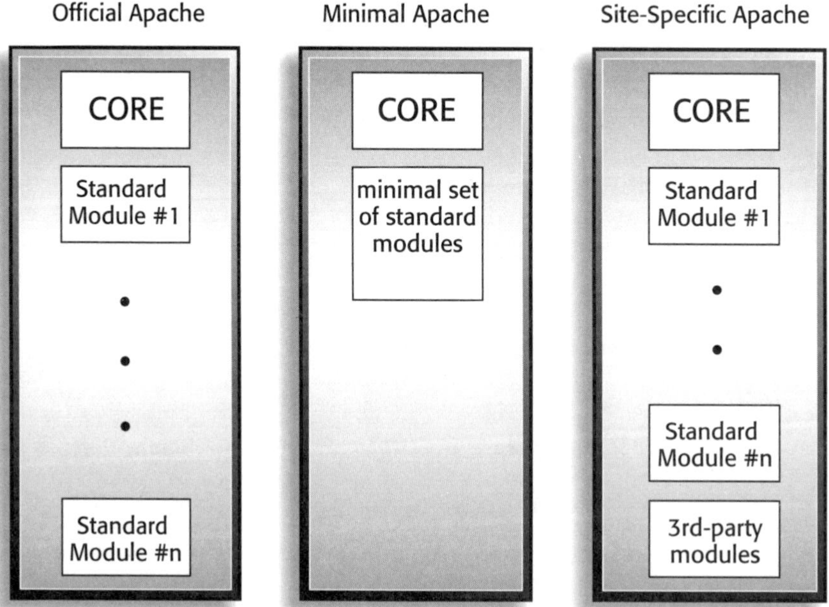

Figure 1-1: Apache's modular architecture

This way you can construct an Apache server that suits your needs. The minimal Apache server in Figure 1-1 is one such server. However, if you need a module that is not present in the standard Apache distribution, you can add one from a third party or develop one yourself. Figure 1-1 shows this as a site-specific Apache server.

The advantage of being able to add and remove modules in Apache is fantastic. It means you can compile an Apache server that is specialized for your site's needs. The module developers also enjoy a great deal of flexibility. They can develop their modules using the API provided by Apache and not worry about the core Apache at all. Because adding a new module does not mean applying a patch to the core Apache source, it makes the developer's life a bit easier as well.

The Future of Apache

Apache's future looks very bright for several reasons. The free software movement on the Internet is very strong; even companies like Netscape Communications realized it eventually. Until the recent waves of commercial Internet software, the Internet used to be run primarily by free software. It is a good time to instill faith in the free software movement. Ask yourself this question: how many times did I hear about Linux, Perl, FreeBSD, or Apache? You are hearing more and more about free software because it is good and does its job well.

However, it is not the end of the world for commercial software. There is room for both commercial and free software in the world. In fact, most free software encourages commercialization of the core technology it has to offer. If you are now convinced (at least in spirit) that Apache is here to stay, perhaps you are concerned about the technical future of Apache. In the next sections, I will discuss two frequently expressed technical concerns about Apache.

The missing GUI link

Whenever Apache gets compared by a so-called "fair" Web server comparison, entities such as magazines or third-party server benchmark outfits are always eager to point out that Apache does not come with a graphical user interface (GUI) for the administrator. Well, the days of missing GUI are numbered!

Apache developers are working on a project called the Apache GUI Configuration Project. Its goal is to develop a back-end configuration server that will interact with Java- and tcl/tk-based front-end configuration clients. They are very close to completion of the first public release. You can visit the project's home page at the URL:

```
www.esi.us.es/~ridruejo/gui/home.html
```

A Java-based configuration client that is almost ready is available for download from the URL:

```
http://butler.disa.mil/ApacheConfigClient/
```

Figure 1-2 shows the main configuration window for an Apache server running on the localhost.

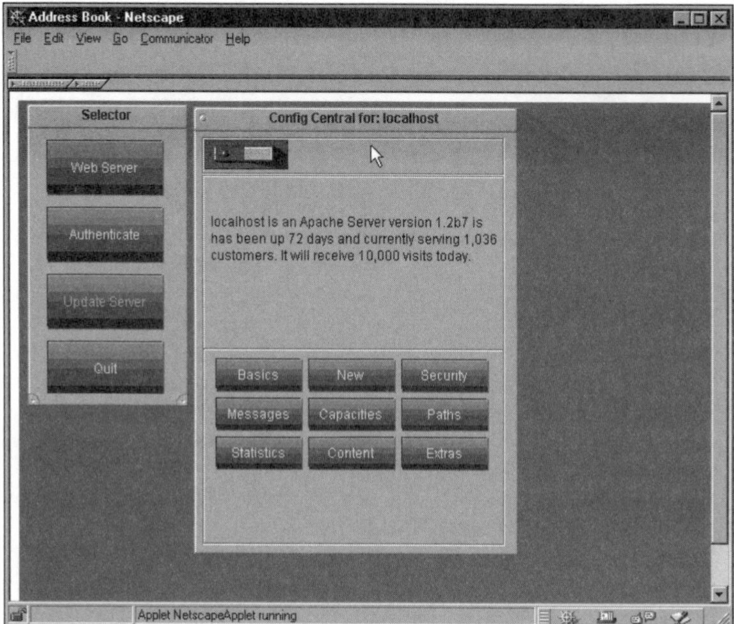

Figure 1-2: Main configuration window for localhost

Figure 1-3 shows the basic server configuration window for localhost.

Check the site for updates to the project. However, if you must have a GUI for your Apache server now, you can buy one. A product called Warpaint is available at the URL:

```
www.rovis.com/warpaint/
```

One other concern that is sure to surface soon (if it hasn't already) is the year-2,000 issue.

Getting ready for the next millennium

As the year 2,000 comes closer many IT managers are (just) beginning to wonder about software failure issues associated with it. Because a Web server is usually an organization's front-end to the Internet, it is likely that before you deploy a new Web server, you are likely to be asked: is Apache year-2,000-bug-proof?

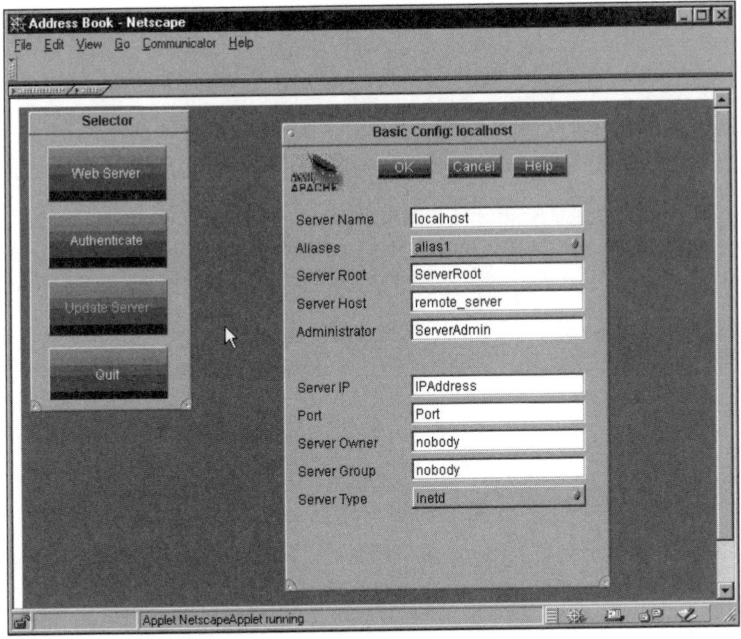

Figure 1-3: Basic configuration window for localhost

The answer is not an easy one because there are too many things involved in it. Apache code does not store years in two digits, so it is internally year-2,000-bug-free. However, problems could surface from external sources such as your operating system or even the protocols. To cope with external problems, Apache tries its best to protect itself from the famous bug. For example, if Apache encounters a year prior to 1970 (the magical year for many computer date/time functions) it assumes the century to be 2,000 instead of 1,900.

Technically speaking, Apache itself is year-2,000-compliant but if your external software environment is not, Apache's being compliant does not do you much good. If you are concerned about year-2,000 issues, make sure you investigate all the software and even hardware components in your computing environment.

Understanding the Apache License

Recently, free software such as Apache, Perl (Practical Extraction and Reporting Language), and Linux (a x86-based UNIX clone O.S.) is getting a great deal of press because of Netscape's decision to make Netscape Communicator, one of the most popular Web browsers, available for free. Unfortunately, free software such as Apache, Perl, and Linux does not share the same licensing agreements and therefore the media has created some confusion by associating these packages in the same licensing category.

All free software is intended to be free for all. However, there are some legal restrictions that the individual software licenses enforce. For example, Perl licensing terms do not require an organization that modifies Perl to release their changes to the world. Linux, which is made free by GNU Public License (GPL), requires that any changes to Linux be made public. Apache, on the other hand, does not require that changes to Apache be made public by anyone.

In short, think of Apache as free, copyrighted software published by the Apache Group. It is neither in the public domain nor is it shareware. Also note that Apache is not covered by GPL. See the CD-ROM for the full text of the Apache license.

Now that you understand the Apache license a little better, are you ready to use Apache? Maybe you are ready but still want to know who runs Apache as their Web server.

Exactly Who Uses Apache?

As I mentioned before, over 50 percent of Web servers are Apache. However, if you want to put faces to the numbers, you can visit the URL:

```
www.apache.org/info/apache_users.html
```

There you can get a partial listing of who runs Apache. Ever wonder how all these site administrators live without any technical support hot lines from the Apache Group? Although there isn't any toll-free 800 numbers (or even regular phone numbers) that you can call, what Apache users have is access to a set of Web sites and newsgroups that deal with Apache. Most of the time these forums are more than enough to get problems solved. However, if you must have commercial support for a free product, you can arrange a support agreement with one of the many Internet consulting companies who offer Apache support services around the world. See Appendix C for a list of Internet resources for Apache.

Are You Ready?

I hope you are ready to get started. This book will help you become a proficient Apache administrator in no time. Soon you will realize the power of Apache, which has proven itself a winner in only three years of existence.

✦ ✦ ✦

Obtaining and Installing Apache

In This Chapter

Where to find the latest Apache source

System requirements for Apache

How to download the software

How to compile the source

How to install binaries on your system

Creating directories in Apache

Keeping up with Apache developments

I like Apache for all the reasons I discussed in Chapter 1, but one of the most important reasons I like it so much is that the source code is freely available to anyone! This gives me a chance to browse the source code and see how things are being done, and even tweak the code if I want to. For people who are not C programmers but who still need a powerful, free Web server, however, playing around with a lot of ANSI C code may not exactly be a favorite pastime. Fortunately, there's nothing to worry about — Apache comes in both source code and prebuilt binary packages. In this chapter, I discuss installing Apache from both source code and prebuilt binaries.

The Official Source for Apache

Whenever you obtain free software (source code or binary files), make sure you're not getting it from an unknown, faraway place. What I mean by "an unknown, faraway place" can be better understood in the following example. Say you want to obtain free Java-based Web browser software developed by Sun Microsystems. You don't want to get it from an FTP site called troyzon.horse.getitnow.com.sg. You should probably look for it somewhere on the java.sun.com site instead. You need to be able to do some sort of authenticity check, which is often difficult on the Internet; therefore, you should stick with sites that are widely used. For example, if you obtain a utility for your Windows machine from ftp.cdrom.com (a well-known freeware/shareware resource archive), you can't be sure that cdrom.com has completely checked the software for any hidden dangers. Chances are, if there's any history of a problem with the software, then the software won't be there. You get the idea. If you are ever in doubt, ask around on the USENET; post a question in an appropriate newsgroup regarding the official location for the software you seek.

Lucky for us, Apache developers and supporters made sure an official place was set up for obtaining Apache software. The official Apache Web site is:

```
http://www.apache.org
```

This site contains the latest stable version of Apache, the latest release version of Apache, patches, contributed Apache modules, and so on. This is where you want to go for all your Apache needs — although you might be directed to a mirror site that is geographically near you to help cut down on bandwidth and network congestion.

System Requirements

Before you can display the Powered by Apache logo (shown in Figure 2-1) on your Web server, you want to make sure your Web server has enough "power" to run it.

Figure 2-1: Powered by Apache logo

Apache does not require massive computing resources to run. It runs fine on a Linux system with 6–10MB of hard disk space and 8MB of RAM. However, just being able to run Apache is probably not what you had in mind. Most likely, you want to run Apache to serve Web pages, launch CGI processes, and take advantage of all the wonderful stuff the Web has to offer. In that case, you want to come up with some disk space and RAM size figures that reflect your load requirements. You can go about this in two ways: you can ask someone who runs a similar site with Apache and find out what type of system resources they're using; or, you can try to figure out your realistic needs after you've installed Apache on your system.

In the latter case, you can use system utilities such as ps, top, and so on to display memory usage by an Apache process. You can then determine the total memory needed by multiplying a single process's memory usage by the total number of Apache processes that will be running at peak hours (see the MaxSpareServers directive in Chapter 4). This should give you a reasonable estimate of your site's RAM requirements for Apache. Note that if you plan to run several CGI programs on your Apache server, you will have to determine memory usage for these programs as well, and take this additional need into account.

The disk requirements for Apache source or binary files shouldn't be a concern with most systems, since Apache binaries take no more than 1MB of space and the source file is about 5MB. You should really pay attention, however, to the log files Apache creates, because each log entry takes up approximately 80 bytes of disk space. If you expect to get about 100,000 hits in a day, for example, your Apache access log file may be 8,000,000 bytes.

In Chapter 11, you'll learn how to rotate the log files in the "Log Maintenance" section.

Downloading the Software

Before you download the Apache software for the first time, you should note a few things. There's a good chance you will find two versions of Apache available: one is an official release version, and one is a beta release version that has the latest code and features. For example, if you see an Apache version 1.2.4 and a version called 1.3b3, then the first one is an official release and the latter is a beta version. A third beta such as 1.3b3 (1.3b1 and 1.3b2 came before it) is likely to be stable, but is not recommended for use in a production Web server. To download the version you want, just find a link to download the software, or use

```
www.apache.org/dist/
```

to go to the distribution directory of the site. Here, you will find both the release and the beta versions of the software in multiple compression packages. For example:

```
apache_1.2.4.tar.Z
apache_1.2.4.tar.gz
apache_1.3b3.tar.gz
apache_1.3b3_win32.exe
```

Listed above are a few examples of the various types of compression format used to distribute source code. You need to choose the compression format your system can handle (in other words, make sure you have a utility to decompress the code). Typically, all you need are the tar, gnuzip, or gzip utilities to decompress the files. For example, to decompress the Apache 1.2.4.tar.gz file on a Linux (RedHat 4.2) system, I use the following command:

```
tar xvzf apache_1.2.4.tar.gz
```

Or, I could use:

```
gzip -d apache_1.2.4.tar.gz
tar xvf apache_1.2.4.tar
```

which will decompress and extract all the files in a subdirectory while keeping the relative path for each file intact.

Some self-extracting compressed files may exist for the Windows NT/95 version of Apache. Any such file can be extracted by simply running the downloaded file. For Windows 95/NT-specific installation and configuration details, you should skip the rest of this chapter and read Chapter 20.

The binaries are usually kept in a different directory where each operating system has a subdirectory of its own. Note that if your operating system does not appear in the binaries directory, this does not necessarily mean the operating system is not supported. All it means is that no one in the Apache development group or contribution groups have compiled a binary file for your system yet. You are likely to find binaries for the following systems:

- AIX
- FreeBSD
- HPUX
- IRIX
- Linux NetBSD
- OS2, Solaris
- SunOS
- Ultrix

If you decide to download a prebuilt binary version of Apache, you can skip the following sections and go to the "Using Downloaded Binaries" section later in this chapter.

Configuring the Source for Your System

In this section, I discuss how to compile Apache for a Linux system. The steps should be virtually the same for almost all UNIX systems.

Once the source is extracted in a directory of its own, you'll see an src subdirectory with all the Apache source code in it. Follow these steps:

1. Read the README file in the main distribution directory (that is, the directory one level outside of the src directory).
2. Change the directory to the src directory of the Apache source distribution.
3. Read the text file named INSTALL. Note any specifics about your system.
4. Copy the configuration template file (Configuration.tmpl) to a file called Configuration in the same directory.

Now you can use a text editor (such as vi) to take a look at the configuration options in the Configuration file.

Configuration options

Five types of information are available in the Configuration file. They are as follows:

- ✦ Comments — lines with a # (hash) symbol as the first character
- ✦ Makefile options — lines such as CC=gcc, EXTRA_CFLAGS, and so on
- ✦ Rules options — lines that begin with the word *Rules*
- ✦ AddModule options — lines that begin with *AddModule*
- ✦ Optional module options — lines that begin with *%Module*

For a typical installation, you do not need to change any of these lines. If you do change them, however, make sure you know what you're doing.

Makefile configuration options

These option lines enable you to specify various elements of the Makefile that will be created later by the Configure script. For most systems, you would not need to modify any of these elements. The Configure script will try to figure out which C compiler you use on your system. In case you think it might fail to find your compiler for some reason, you can tell the Configure script what your compiler is by assigning your compiler's binary name in the following line:

```
CC=
```

For example:

```
CC = gcc
```

Now, if you need to specify extra flags (parameters) to your C compiler for compiling code, you can use the following lines:

```
EXTRA_CFLAGS=
EXTRA_LFLAGS=
```

If your system requires special libraries or include files, you can specify them here:

```
EXTRA_LIBS=
EXTRA_INCLUDES=
```

Note that the Configure script automatically sets code optimization to -O2. If you want a different setting, uncomment the following line:

```
#OPTIM=-O2
```

Then, change the value to whatever you desire, and your C compiler supports it. For most installations, the default settings work just fine, as they did for me on a RedHat Linux system.

Rules configuration

Next, you have to decide what functionality you want to tell Configure about. The configuration options are as follows:

- `Rule STATUS=yes`
- `Rule SOCKS4=no`
- `Rule WANTHSREGEX=default`
- `Rule IRIXNIS=no`

The first rule specifies that you want the STATUS functionality in the server. This means you want to use the status_module in Apache, which enables the server to display performance-related information. For this rule to be effective, you need to make sure you include the status_module in the module configuration area.

The SOCKS4 functionality is turned off by default. For those who do not know what SOCKS is, it is a control system where all TCP/IP network application data flows through the SOCKS daemon. This enables SOCKS to collect, audit, screen, filter, and control the network data. Most people use it as a software-based firewall. If you want to make Apache SOCKS4-compliant, you need to turn this feature on by setting it to Yes. Also make sure you modify the EXTRA_LIBS setting, in the Makefile configuration area, to point to your SOCKS4 library file. The Configure script will otherwise set it to -L/usr/local/lib -lsocks.

The WANTHSREGEX option is automatically set to Default. This specifies that you want to use the regular expression package included with Apache. If you'd rather use your own system's regular expression package, however, you can set this option to No.

The IRIXNIS option is for people who want to use Apache on a Silicon Graphics system running IRIX and NIS.

Modules configuration

A module is a component software for Apache that adds new functionality to the core of Apache. Using module configuration, you can define what functionality you want in the Apache server. The module configuration line looks like the following:

```
AddModule modules/standard/mod_env.o
```

This line adds the mod_env module found in the src/modules/standard subdirectory to Apache.

Older versions of Apache (1.2.x or below) use the following format for module lines:

```
Module module_name  module_object_file
```

The default modules provided are listed in Listing 2-1. These should be sufficient for a typical installation of Apache. You should note that each module adds more memory and space requirement on the final Apache executable (httpd), and therefore you should carefully go through the list to see if any module can be removed from this default list. If you can remove a module, your Apache server will be lighter and possibly a bit faster. On the other hand, if you find a module to be useful but commented out, you can just remove the comment character (#) to enable it. Similarly, disabling a module only requires the insertion of a comment character in a module specification line.

Listing 2-1: Default module list in the Configuration file

```
AddModule modules/standard/mod_env.o
AddModule modules/standard/mod_log_config.o
AddModule modules/standard/mod_mime.o
AddModule modules/standard/mod_negotiation.o
AddModule modules/standard/mod_include.o
AddModule modules/standard/mod_autoindex.o
AddModule modules/standard/mod_dir.o
AddModule modules/standard/mod_cgi.o
AddModule modules/standard/mod_asis.o
AddModule modules/standard/mod_imap.o
AddModule modules/standard/mod_actions.o
AddModule modules/standard/mod_userdir.o
AddModule modules/standard/mod_alias.o
AddModule modules/standard/mod_access.o
AddModule modules/standard/mod_auth.o
AddModule modules/standard/mod_setenvif.o
```

If you elected to set the STATUS rule to Yes, you need to uncomment the status_module line to look like this:

```
AddModule modules/standard/ mod_status.o
```

If you said Yes for the STATUS rule, but you didn't uncomment the status_module line to look like the preceding line, the rule will be ignored. Now you are ready to run the Configure script.

Running Configure

To run the Configure script, you need to be in the src directory (as you should already be, if you are following the instructions). Simply enter the following:

```
./Configure
```

at your shell prompt. Configure runs and creates the Makefile. Now you are ready to compile the source file.

Compiling Apache

You need to run the make utility to compile the source file. From your shell prompt, enter:

```
make
```

The make utility will use the Makefile created by the Configure script and will run your C compiler to create the Apache executable (httpd).

The amount of time it takes to compile Apache depends on how fast and resourceful your computer is. A powerful CPU and lots of RAM helps. If the make utility fails to compile for some reason, note the error message carefully and see if you can make any sense out of it. Most likely, any errors will be due to missing system library files or your compiler needing more flags. In either case, you will have to fiddle with the Makefile options in the Configuration file (unless you want to modify the Configure-generated Makefile itself), and then run Configure (if you didn't modify Makefile yourself) and the make utility again. If the problem persists, find someone who knows your operating system and C compiler better than you do, and ask for assistance.

If that is not an option, post a message in an appropriate newsgroup (see Appendix D) explaining your problem. Include the error message in its entirety.

If everything went well, on the other hand, you should now have the httpd executable in your src directory. If you have been holding your breath all this time, breathe!

Testing the newborn Apache

Well, it's time to make sure your executable is indeed "executable." First you need to do a directory listing to show the permission setting. For example:

```
ls -l httpd
```

Typing this in the src directory will show you the file permission settings. Make sure the httpd is readable and executable by you. Test your version of Apache by typing:

```
./httpd -v
```

This will print out the version number of your Apache server. If the version matches your downloaded version number, you're in business! Congratulations!

Now, you may also want to compile the support utility programs. Apache comes with a few utilities that may be useful in managing the program itself. You can compile these from the support directory by running the following command:

```
make all
```

This compiles all the utilities and creates executables such as htpasswd, htdigest, httpd_monitor, rotatelogs, logresolve, and so on. Note that the suexec program is not compiled by the preceding command. You will learn about this program in Chapter 12.

You can now skip the next section and go to the "Creating Apache Directories" section.

Using Downloaded Binaries

It's a good idea to compile the Apache source yourself instead of using someone else's binary. When you use a downloaded binary file, you are letting someone else (possibly someone you don't know) decide which modules and features are enabled in your Web server. Occasionally, downloaded binary files may not work at all on your system, because there could be incompatibilities between the library files required by the binary and what is available on your system. If this is acceptable, or if compiling is not an option for you, make sure the site from which you download the binaries is reputable. You can get many common operating systems specific binaries from the www.apache.org or its mirror sites.

Extract the downloaded binaries in a directory. Locate the httpd executable, and set file permissions to enable you to run it. Use the following command to get the version number:

```
./httpd -v
```

If this version matches the one you thought you downloaded, you are ready to create the directory structure for your Apache server. Proceed to the next section.

Linux RedHat users can download an RPM version of Apache distribution found in ftp://ftp.redhat.com/ to simplify the Apache installation process.

Creating Apache Directories

You can keep your Apache executable anywhere you want, but it might be a good idea to get organized from the start; following are some suggestions for doing this.

Create a directory called Apache in a convenient location such as /usr/local or /usr/home. I will refer to this directory as %ApacheRoot%. Create the following subdirectories:

```
%ApacheRoot%/bin
%ApacheRoot%/conf
%ApacheRoot%/logs
```

Copy the httpd executable and all compiled utilities into %ApacheRoot%/bin. Copy the sample configuration files (in the conf directory) to the %ApacheRoot%/conf directory.

It's a good idea to create a new user and group for Apache. This gives you better control over which areas of your disk are accessible by Apache. I created user httpd and group httpd for this purpose. Now, you can set up the permission settings for the directories and the executables.

You should not allow anyone but the root user to access the executables and configuration files. Using the chown command, you only allow the root user and anyone in the root group to access these files. The commands are:

```
chown -R root.root %ApacheRoot%/bin
chown -R root.root %ApacheRoot%/conf
```

The logs directory should only be readable by the Apache user, as well. Again, you can use the chown command to set permission for it, as follows:

```
chown -R httpd.httpd %ApacheRoot%/logs
```

All the chown commands have set up the proper ownership permissions, but you still need to set the access permission. You want the root user to have full access (read, write, and execute) in the bin and conf directory, and you want the httpd user to have full access in the logs directory, so you should use the following chmod command to accomplish this all in one command:

```
chmod -R 700 %ApacheRoot%
```

This command sets up access permission so that only the owner of each directory has access to the directory, which is what was intended.

It is very important that the logs directory under %ApacheRoot% be readable and writable only by the user account that will be used to run the Apache process. Since the root user, when in the standalone mode (you will learn about this in Chapter 3), has to run the primary Apache server process, the directory settings I have recommended here should be sufficient.

Installing Apache

Before you install the httpd binary in the desired location, it might be a good idea to strip out any extra symbols that might be left (in the binary) by the linker. You can use the following command:

```
strip httpd
```

This command removes the extra information from the binary, and most likely will make it a bit smaller in size.

Now, you are ready to install Apache. Follow these steps:

1. Copy the httpd binary to the %ApacheRoot%/bin directory.
2. If you have compiled the support utilities, you can copy them to the %ApacheRoot%/bin directory as well.
3. Copy the distribution version of Apache configuration files (such as (access.conf-dist, httpd.conf-dist, mime.types, and srm.conf-dist) to the %ApacheRoot%/conf directory.

This completes your Apache software installation.

Keeping Up with Apache Development

Do you ever wonder if, by the time you get around to installing the downloaded Apache source or binaries, a new version is out or perhaps a security patch is available? That's how I feel about a lot of software. Software changes very quickly these days, and there's always one update after another — which is good, but not always easy to keep up with if you have a real job to do. Anyway, you can rid yourself of such worries, at least for Apache. Just subscribe (for free) to the great Apache resource called Apache Week, and all the Apache news will be e-mailed directly to you. The Apache Week Web site is at:

```
http://www.apacheweek.com/
```

This is a great information resource for Apache administrators who want to be on top of Apache development news. You can also read many helpful articles on how to get the best out of your server. I highly recommend checking out this Web site.

Summary

In this chapter, I discussed the installation details of Apache server. Although compiling your own Apache binaries may seem like a bit of work, it's worth the effort. As you become more familiar with Apache, you will learn that it is probably the only Web server in the world that provides virtually all (if not more) of the functionalities of a full-blown commercial server, and at the same time lets you take a look at how these functionalities are implemented in the source. I find this aspect of Apache fascinating.

In the next chapter, you learn how to get your Apache server up and running.

✦ ✦ ✦

Getting Apache Up and Running

In This Chapter

Basics of Apache server configuration

Stating, stopping, and restarting Apache server

Testing a running Apache server

In the last chapter, you learned how to compile and install the Apache Web server on your UNIX system. Now you are ready to get it up and running! Before you run the server, however, you need to edit a few runtime configuration files so the server runs properly. This chapter covers the basic configuration details to get your server up and running.

Apache reads four configuration files: httpd.conf, access.conf, srm.conf, and mime.type. The last one usually needs no changes for typical sites, and is therefore ignored in this chapter. The three other files tell Apache how to behave as a Web server. All these files are normally read during the server startup process.

In this chapter I discuss how to configure each of these files. I also cover different methods of running the server, and what's involved in starting and stopping the server. At the end of the chapter, I'll also show you how to test your server.

Configuring the Server

Every Apache source distribution comes with a set of sample configuration files. In the standard Apache source distribution, you will find a directory called conf, which contains sample configuration files with the -dist extension.

The very first step you need to take before you modify these sample files is to copy the files as follows:

httpd.conf-dist to httpd.conf

access.conf-dist to access.conf

srm.conf-dist to srm.conf

Although there are three files, they all share the same structure. These text files have two types of information: optional comments and server directives. Lines that contain a # symbol as the very first character are comments; these comments have no purpose for the server software, but serve as a form of documentation for the server administrator. You can add as many comment lines as you want; the server simply ignores all comments when it parses these files.

Except for the comments and blank lines, the server treats all other lines as either complete or part of directives. A directive is like a command for the server. It tells the server to do a certain task in a particular fashion. While editing these files, you need to make certain decisions regarding how you want the server to behave. In the following sections, you will learn what these directives mean and how you can use them to customize you server.

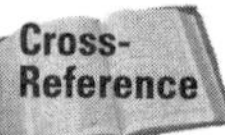

You will find an in-depth explanation of all the core directives in Chapter 4.

httpd.conf

httpd.conf is the primary configuration file. It is used to tell the server how it is run. Listing 3-1 shows the default httpd.conf created from httpd.conf-dist.

Listing 3-1: Default httpd.conf created from httpd.conf-dist

```
# This is the main server configuration file. See URL
http://www.apache.org/
# for instructions.

# Do NOT simply read the instructions in here without
understanding
# what they do, if you are unsure consult the online docs. You
have been
# warned.

# Originally by Rob McCool

# ServerType is either inetd, or standalone.

ServerType standalone

# If you are running from inetd, go to "ServerAdmin".

# Port: The port the standalone listens to. For ports < 1023,
you will
# need httpd to be run as root initially.
```

```
Port 80

# HostnameLookups: Log the names of clients or just their IP
numbers
#   e.g.   www.apache.org (on) or 204.62.129.132 (off)
# You should probably turn this off unless you are going to
actually
# use the information in your logs, or with a CGI.  Leaving
this on
# can slow down access to your site.
HostnameLookups on

# If you wish httpd to run as a different user or group, you
must run
# httpd as root initially and it will switch.

# User/Group: The name (or #number) of the user/group to run
httpd as.
#  On SCO (ODT 3) use User nouser and Group nogroup
#  On HPUX you may not be able to use shared memory as nobody,
and the
#  suggested workaround is to create a user www and use that
user.
User nobody
Group #-1

# The following directive disables keepalives and HTTP header
flushes for
# Netscape 2.x and browsers which spoof it. There are known
problems with
# these

BrowserMatch Mozilla/2 nokeepalive

# ServerAdmin: Your address, where problems with the server
should be
# e-mailed.

ServerAdmin you@your.address

# ServerRoot: The directory the server's config, error, and log
files
# are kept in

ServerRoot /usr/local/etc/httpd

# BindAddress: You can support virtual hosts with this option.
This option
# is used to tell the server which IP address to listen to. It
can either
```

(continued)

Listing 3-1 *(continued)*

```
# contain "*", an IP address, or a fully qualified Internet
domain name.
# See also the VirtualHost directive.

#BindAddress *

# ErrorLog: The location of the error log file. If this does
not start
# with /, ServerRoot is prepended to it.

ErrorLog logs/error_log

# TransferLog: The location of the transfer log file. If this
does not
# start with /, ServerRoot is prepended to it.

TransferLog logs/access_log

# PidFile: The file the server should log its pid to
PidFile logs/httpd.pid

# ScoreBoardFile: File used to store internal server process
information.
# Not all architectures require this.  But if yours does
(you'll know because
# this file is created when you run Apache) then you *must*
ensure that
# no two invocations of Apache share the same scoreboard file.
ScoreBoardFile logs/apache_status

# ServerName allows you to set a host name which is sent back
to clients for
# your server if it's different than the one the program would
get (i.e. use
# "www" instead of the host's real name).
#
# Note: You cannot just invent host names and hope they work.
The name you
# define here must be a valid DNS name for your host. If you
don't understand
# this, ask your network administrator.

#ServerName new.host.name

# CacheNegotiatedDocs: By default, Apache sends Pragma: no-
cache with each
```

```
# document that was negotiated on the basis of content. This
asks proxy
# servers not to cache the document. Uncommenting the following
line disables
# this behavior, and proxies will be allowed to cache the
documents.

#CacheNegotiatedDocs

# Timeout: The number of seconds before receives and sends time
out

Timeout 300

# KeepAlive: Whether or not to allow persistent connections
(more than
# one request per connection). Set to "Off" to deactivate.

KeepAlive On

# MaxKeepAliveRequests: The maximum number of requests to allow
# during a persistent connection. Set to 0 to allow an
unlimited amount.
# We recommend you leave this number high, for maximum
performance.

MaxKeepAliveRequests 100

# KeepAliveTimeout: Number of seconds to wait for the next
request

KeepAliveTimeout 15

# Server-pool size regulation.  Rather than making you guess
how many
# server processes you need, Apache dynamically adapts to the
load it
# sees -- that is, it tries to maintain enough server processes
to
# handle the current load, plus a few spare servers to handle
transient
# load spikes (e.g., multiple simultaneous requests from a
single
# Netscape browser).

# It does this by periodically checking how many servers are
waiting
# for a request. If there are fewer than MinSpareServers, it
creates
```

(continued)

Listing 3-1 *(continued)*

```
# a new spare.  If there are more than MaxSpareServers, some of
the
# spares die off.  These values are probably OK for most sites
---

MinSpareServers 5
MaxSpareServers 10

# Number of servers to start --- should be a reasonable
ballpark figure.

StartServers 5

# Limit on total number of servers running, i.e., limit on the
number
# of clients who can simultaneously connect --- if this limit
is ever
# reached, clients will be LOCKED OUT, so it should NOT BE SET
TOO LOW.
# It is intended mainly as a brake to keep a runaway server
from taking
# Unix with it as it spirals down...

MaxClients 150

# MaxRequestsPerChild: the number of requests each child
process is
#  allowed to process before the child dies.
#  The child will exit so as to avoid problems after prolonged
use when
#  Apache (and maybe the libraries it uses) leaks.  On most
systems, this
#  isn't really needed, but a few (such as Solaris) do have
notable leaks
#  in the libraries.

MaxRequestsPerChild 30

# Proxy Server directives. Uncomment the following line to
# enable the proxy server:

#ProxyRequests On

# To enable the cache as well, edit and uncomment the following
lines:

#CacheRoot /usr/local/etc/httpd/proxy
#CacheSize 5
#CacheGcInterval 4
```

```
#CacheMaxExpire 24
#CacheLastModifiedFactor 0.1
#CacheDefaultExpire 1
#NoCache a_domain.com another_domain.edu joes.garage_sale.com

# Listen: Allows you to bind Apache to specific IP addresses
and/or
# ports, in addition to the default. See also the VirtualHost
command

#Listen 3000
#Listen 12.34.56.78:80

# VirtualHost: Allows the daemon to respond to requests for
more than one
# server address, if your server machine is configured to
accept IP packets
# for multiple addresses. This can be accomplished with the
ifconfig
# alias flag, or through kernel patches like VIF.

# Any httpd.conf or srm.conf directive may go into a
VirtualHost command.
# See alto the BindAddress entry.

#<VirtualHost host.some_domain.com>
#ServerAdmin webmaster@host.some_domain.com
#DocumentRoot /www/docs/host.some_domain.com
#ServerName host.some_domain.com
#ErrorLog logs/host.some_domain.com-error_log
#TransferLog logs/host.some_domain.com-access_log
#</VirtualHost>
```

Note that the goal of this chapter is to get your server up and running with minimal configuration, so the chapter does not provide in-depth details of the three configuration files discussed.

The first directive you need to configure is:

```
ServerType standalone | inetd
```

This directive specifies how the Web server is run. The server can be run using two methods: standalone and inetd-run. It may appear that both the standalone and the inetd methods are virtually identical in their functionality (which I discuss in the following sections), but there's a big difference. The difference lies in the performance of the server. An inetd-run server process exits as soon as it finishes servicing a request. In the standalone mode, the child Web server processes hang out for a certain amount of time before they cease to exist. This gives them a chance to be reused by future requests. Because the overhead of launching a new process per request is absent in the standalone mode, this mode is more efficient.

There are some advantages to running in inetd mode as well, however. For example, running in inetd mode is considered more secure than the standalone mode. Many system administrators use TCP wrapper programs to validate requests before inetd can launch a server process. If you are concerned about security and have a low traffic expectation for your Web site, you may want to consider setting the ServerType directive to inetd instead of standalone.

Let's explore how each of these methods works and look at some of their common directives.

Standalone Apache server

In the standalone method (the default), the ServerType directive is set to standalone so that the primary Web server listens to a particular port for connection requests. When a request to connect to that particular port address is made by a client machine, the primary server launches a child Web server process to service the request. Figure 3-1 shows the standalone method.

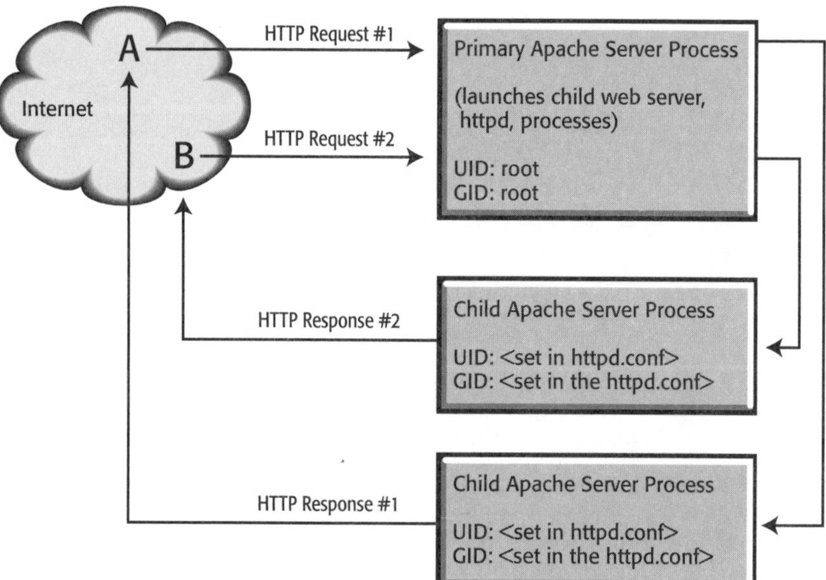

Figure 3-1: Standalone server

Port for the standalone Apache server

The directive that tells the primary Apache server process to listen to a particular port address is:

```
Port [number]
```

The default HTTP port is 80, and this should be used in typical Web sites. If you are not the root user of the system, however, and you want to run the Web server, you need to use a port number greater than 1023 and lower than 32768. All ports below 1024 are considered standard reserved ports and require inetd-level (root-level) access to start a service on these ports. If you are just experimenting with Web servers on a non-root account on a system, you can use a port higher than the mentioned range, as long as it has not already been taken. If you try to use a port address that is already in use by another server, you will get an error message when you try to start the server. Also, note that if you use any port other than the standard HTTP port 80, you will have to supply a port number along with all URL requests to the server. For example, if you set this directive as follows:

```
Port 8080
```

you need to request resources (such as a page called mypage.html) on this server as follows:

```
http://www.yourcompany.com:8080/mypage.html
```

If you decide to run Apache servers using the standalone method, you also need to tell Apache what its user and group names are.

User and group names for the standalone Apache server

The two directives that tell Apache the user and group names are:

```
User [username| #UID]
Group [group name| #GID]
```

These two directives are very important for security reasons. When the primary Web server process launches a child server process to fulfill a request, it changes the child's UID and GID according to the values set for these directives. Refer back to Figure 3-1 to see how the primary Web server process that listens for the connection runs as a root user process, and how the child processes run as different user/group processes. If the child processes are run as root user processes, a potential security hole will be opened for attack by hackers. Allowing the capability to interact with a root user process would maximize a potential breach of security in the system; hence, this is not recommended. Rather, I highly recommend that you choose to run the child server processes as a very low-privileged user belonging to a very low-privileged group. In most UNIX systems, the user named nobody (usually UID = -1) and the group named nogroup (usually GID = -1) are low-privileged. You should consult your /etc/group and /etc/passwd files to determine these settings.

If you plan to run the primary Web server as a non-root (regular) user, it will not be able to change the UID and GID of child processes, because only root user processes can change the UID or GID of other processes. Therefore, if you run your primary server as the user named foobar, then all child processes will have the same privileges of foobar. Similarly, whatever group ID you have will also be the group ID for the child processes.

Note that if you plan on using the numeric format for user and/or group ID, you need to insert a # symbol before the numeric value, which can be found in /etc/passwd and in /etc/group files.

inetd Apache server

The other way to run Apache server is using the inetd method. In this case, the ServerType directive is set to inetd, which changes the entire process. Figure 3-2 shows how this works. inetd is the Internet daemon (a server process) that listens for connection requests on all ports less than 1024. Unlike the previous method, inetd controls which requests are serviced by which processes. When requests for a connection to the Web server are made by a client system, inetd launches a Web server process, which services the request and then exits.

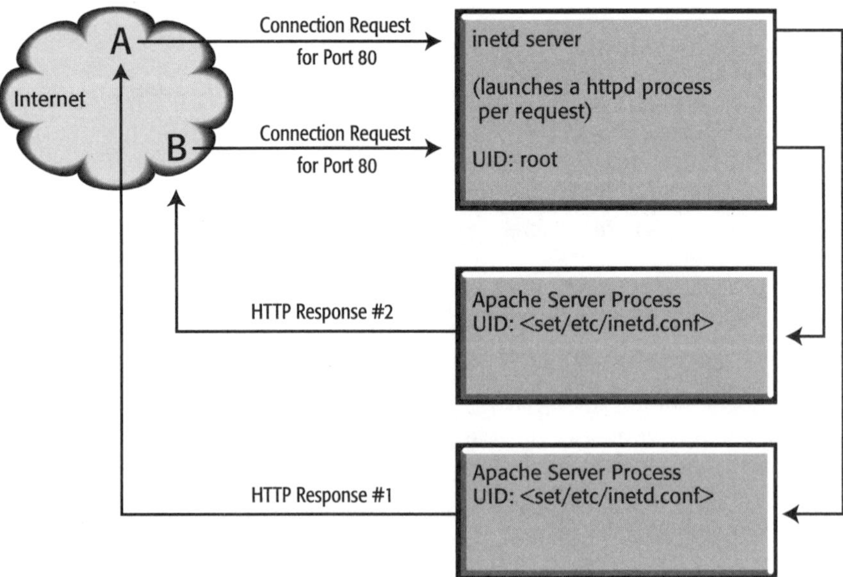

Figure 3-2: inetd-run server

If you choose to run Apache via the inetd server, you need to edit your /etc/inetd.conf file to add a new record for Apache. This text file has a specific record format which you should be able to determine by looking at the entries in the file. Unless you have an unusual UNIX system, however, you will probably have an inetd.conf file that uses the following record definition:

```
<service_name> <sock_type> <proto> <flags> <user> <server_path>
<args>
```

As you can see in the preceding line, the service is run as a particular user. You need to decide which user you want to run the Apache server as. The simplest method is either to use the nobody user or to create a special user named httpd to run the server process. If you use the nobody user for other services, then don't use it again for Apache. Reusing nobody for Web service might affect what is accessible to the Web server when you modify a directory/file setting for the other service using the nobody account. I recommend creating a special httpd account and using it as follows:

```
httpd stream tcp nowait httpd /usr/sbin/httpd -f
/etc/httpd/conf/httpd.conf
```

Once you have modified the inetd.conf file, you need to modify the /etc/services file, which has a record structure as follows:

```
<service name>  <port number>/<protocol name>    <service entry
in inetd.conf>
```

So the line to add in the /etc/services is:

```
httpd 80/tcp httpd
```

The preceding entry describes the httpd service available and used by the inetd server. It specifies that the HTTP service is available on port 80. If you want to use a different port for your Web (HTTP) service, replace 80 with a port number that is not already being used by another service. Since all port numbers below 1024 are reserved for standard services, you want to use a port address higher than 1024 (for example, 8080) and lower than 32768.

Now you need to restart your inetd process. First, you need its process ID (PID), which you can obtain using the following commands:

```
ps auxw | grep inetd
```

Note that depending on your UNIX system, you may have to use different arguments for the ps utility (see the man pages for ps, if necessary). Piping the output of ps to the grep utility enables grep to search the lines for any line that matches the word *inetd*, and print out the line on the screen (standard output.) Although ps output format varies on different systems, usually the first numeric column in the output is the process ID for the process on that line. Now, use the kill utility as follows:

```
kill -HUP <PID of inetd>
```

Don't forget to replace the <PID of inetd> part with the actual process ID. The kill utility sends a HUP signal to the named PID. This restarts your inetd server and enables it to re-read the configuration files you modified. Now your inetd configuration is complete.

Once you assign the Apache directive ServerType to inetd and configured the /etc/inetd.conf and the /etc/services files, the User and Group directives in the httpd.conf file have no effect. However, make sure the user name you used in the /etc/inetd.conf file has access privileges both to your Web directories and where you store the log files for the server. You will define the Web directories, as well as the log file locations, in a later section of this chapter.

I recommend that you only use the inetd option for Apache if your system has very little RAM to spare, or if you do not expect to have a high-traffic Web site.

Common directives

The standalone and inetd-run methods share some common directives. The first one I'll talk about is a directive that tells the server to display an error page with an e-mail address whenever it detects a problem. This gives the visitors a chance to report any problem via e-mail. To set this up, use the e-mail address for the person responsible for maintaining the server in the following syntax:

```
ServerAdmin [email address]
```

Another common directive is ServerRoot, which specifies where the server's configuration, error, and log files are kept. This is the parent directory for all server-related files. The default directory for the server is /usr/local/etc/httpd. If you have installed the server in a different location, change the path to reflect your changes. The syntax is:

```
ServerRoot [fully qualified path name]
```

Two directives specify files the server uses to record errors and access information. The first directive tells the server the path and name of the error log file:

```
ErrorLog [fully qualified path name or error log file]
```

The second directive states the path and the name of the access information:

```
TransferLog [fully qualified path name or access log file]
```

The default error log file location and filename is logs/error_log, which means that the log file is called error_log and it is stored in a subdirectory called logs under the directory specified by ServerRoot. If you wish to keep the error log file in a different location, enter the full path of the file and make sure you start the path name with a / (forward slash) character. Similarly, the default transfer log is stored in the logs directory, and it is called access_log.

Whatever directory you keep the logs in, make sure that only the primary server process has write access in that directory. This is a major security issue, because allowing other users or processes to write to the log directory can potentially mean someone unauthorized might be able to take over your primary Web server process UID, which is normally the root account.

Another common directive is one that Apache uses to write its primary server's process ID (PID) in a file. You can tell it where to write this file using the PidFile directive as follows:

```
PidFile [fully qualified path name of the pid file]
```

Note that the security concerns stated for the ErrorLog and TransferLog directive also apply for the PidFile directive.

The very last directive you need to configure in the httpd.conf file is the server's Internet host name:

```
ServerName [host name]
```

Normally, you want to enter a host name such as www.yourcompany.com. Be sure, however, that the host name you enter here has proper domain name server records that point it to your server machine. The next configuration file we look at is the srm.conf file.

srm.conf

srm.conf is the resource configuration file. It is used to tell the server what resources you want to offer from your Web site, and where and how to offer them. Listing 3-2 shows the default srm.conf file.

Listing 3-2: Default srm.conf created from srm.conf-dist

```
# With this document, you define the name space that users see
of your http
# server.  This file also defines server settings that affect
how requests are
# serviced, and how results should be formatted.

# See the tutorials at http://www.apache.org/ for
# more information.

# Originally by Rob McCool; Adapted for Apache

# DocumentRoot: The directory out of which you will serve your
# documents. By default, all requests are taken from this
directory, but
# symbolic links and aliases may be used to point to other
locations.

DocumentRoot /usr/local/etc/httpd/htdocs

# UserDir: The name of the directory which is appended onto a
user's home
# directory if a ~user request is recieved.

UserDir public_html

# DirectoryIndex: Name of the file or files to use as a pre-
written HTML
# directory index.  Separate multiple entries with spaces.

DirectoryIndex index.html

# FancyIndexing is whether you want fancy directory indexing or
standard

FancyIndexing on

# AddIcon tells the server which icon to show for different
files or filename
# extensions

AddIconByEncoding (CMP,/icons/compressed.gif) x-compress x-gzip

AddIconByType (TXT,/icons/text.gif) text/*
AddIconByType (IMG,/icons/image2.gif) image/*
AddIconByType (SND,/icons/sound2.gif) audio/*
AddIconByType (VID,/icons/movie.gif) video/*

AddIcon /icons/binary.gif .bin .exe
AddIcon /icons/binhex.gif .hqx
AddIcon /icons/tar.gif .tar
AddIcon /icons/world2.gif .wrl .wrl.gz .vrml .vrm .iv
```

```
AddIcon /icons/compressed.gif .Z .z .tgz .gz .zip
AddIcon /icons/a.gif .ps .ai .eps
AddIcon /icons/layout.gif .html .shtml .htm .pdf
AddIcon /icons/text.gif .txt
AddIcon /icons/c.gif .c
AddIcon /icons/p.gif .pl .py
AddIcon /icons/f.gif .for
AddIcon /icons/dvi.gif .dvi
AddIcon /icons/uuencoded.gif .uu
AddIcon /icons/script.gif .conf .sh .shar .csh .ksh .tcl
AddIcon /icons/tex.gif .tex
AddIcon /icons/bomb.gif core

AddIcon /icons/back.gif ..
AddIcon /icons/hand.right.gif README
AddIcon /icons/folder.gif ^^DIRECTORY^^
AddIcon /icons/blank.gif ^^BLANKICON^^

# DefaultIcon is which icon to show for files which do not have
an icon
# explicitly set.

DefaultIcon /icons/unknown.gif

# AddDescription allows you to place a short description after
a file in
# server-generated indexes.
# Format: AddDescription "description" filename

# ReadmeName is the name of the README file the server will
look for by
# default. Format: ReadmeName name
#
# The server will first look for name.html, include it if
found, and it will
# then look for name and include it as plaintext if found.
#
# HeaderName is the name of a file which should be prepended to
# directory indexes.

ReadmeName README
HeaderName HEADER

# IndexIgnore is a set of filenames which directory indexing
should ignore
# Format: IndexIgnore name1 name2...
IndexIgnore */.??* *~ *# */HEADER* */README* */RCS

# AccessFileName: The name of the file to look for in each
directory
# for access control information.
```

(continued)

Listing 3-2 *(continued)*

```
AccessFileName .htaccess

# DefaultType is the default MIME type for documents which the
server
# cannot find the type of from filename extensions.

DefaultType text/plain

# AddEncoding allows you to have certain browsers (Mosaic/X
2.1+) uncompress
# information on the fly. Note: Not all browsers support this.

AddEncoding x-compress Z
AddEncoding x-gzip gz

# AddLanguage allows you to specify the language of a document.
You can
# then use content negotiation to give a browser a file in a
language
# it can understand.  Note that the suffix does not have to be
the same
# as the language keyword -- those with documents in Polish
(whose
# net-standard language code is pl) may wish to use
"AddLanguage pl .po"
# to avoid the ambiguity with the common suffix for perl
scripts.

AddLanguage en .en
AddLanguage fr .fr
AddLanguage de .de
AddLanguage da .da
AddLanguage el .el
AddLanguage it .it

# LanguagePriority allows you to give precedence to some
languages
# in case of a tie during content negotiation.
# Just list the languages in decreasing order of preference.

LanguagePriority en fr de

# Redirect allows you to tell clients about documents which
used to exist in
# your server's namespace, but do not anymore. This allows you
to tell the
# clients where to look for the relocated document.
# Format: Redirect fakename url
```

```
# Aliases: Add here as many aliases as you need (with no
limit). The format is
# Alias fakename realname

# Note that if you include a trailing / on fakename then the
server will
# require it to be present in the URL. So "/icons" isn't
aliased in this
# example.

#Alias /icons/ /usr/local/etc/httpd/icons/

# ScriptAlias: This controls which directories contain server
scripts.
# Format: ScriptAlias fakename realname

#ScriptAlias /cgi-bin/ /usr/local/etc/httpd/cgi-bin/

# If you want to use server side includes, or CGI outside
# ScriptAliased directories, uncomment the following lines.

# AddType allows you to tweak mime.types without actually
editing it, or to
# make certain files to be certain types.
# Format: AddType type/subtype ext1

# AddHandler allows you to map certain file extensions to
"handlers",
# actions unrelated to filetype. These can be either built into
the server
# or added with the Action command (see below)
# Format: AddHandler action-name ext1

# To use CGI scripts:
#AddHandler cgi-script .cgi

# To use server-parsed HTML files
#AddType text/html .shtml
#AddHandler server-parsed .shtml

# Uncomment the following line to enable Apache's send-asis
HTTP file
# feature
#AddHandler send-as-is asis

# If you wish to use server-parsed imagemap files, use
#AddHandler imap-file map

# To enable type maps, you might want to use
#AddHandler type-map var
```

(continued)

Listing 3-2 *(continued)*

```
# Action lets you define media types that will execute a script
whenever
# a matching file is called. This eliminates the need for
repeated URL
# pathnames for oft-used CGI file processors.
# Format: Action media/type /cgi-script/location
# Format: Action handler-name /cgi-script/location

# MetaDir: specifies the name of the directory in which Apache
can find
# meta information files. These files contain additional HTTP
headers
# to include when sending the document

#MetaDir .web

# MetaSuffix: specifies the file name suffix for the file
containing the
# meta information.

#MetaSuffix .meta

# Customizable error response (Apache style)
#  these come in three flavors
#
#    1) plain text
#ErrorDocument 500 "The server made a boo boo.
#  n.b.  the (") marks it as text, it does not get output
#
#    2) local redirects
#ErrorDocument 404 /missing.html
#  to redirect to local url /missing.html
#ErrorDocument 404 /cgi-bin/missing_handler.pl
#  n.b. can redirect to a script or a document using server-
side-includes.
#
#    3) external redirects
#ErrorDocument 02
http://some.other_server.com/subscription_info.html
#
```

The directives that need to be configured in srm.conf are discussed in the sections that follow. These directives are needed to create directory configuration for the primary Web site.

Web directory configuration

Like all other Web servers, Apache needs to know the path of the top-level directory where Web pages will be kept. This directory is typically called the document root directory. Apache provides a directive called DocumentRoot, which can be used to specify the path of the top-level Web directory.

This directive instructs the server to treat the supplied directory as the root directory for all documents, using the following syntax:

```
DocumentRoot [fully qualified path to your Web document
directory]
```

This is a very important decision for you to make. For example, if the directive is set as follows:

```
DocumentRoot /
```

then every file on the system becomes accessible by the Web server. Of course, you can protect files by providing proper file permission settings, but setting the document root to the physical root directory of your system is definitely a major security risk. Instead, you want to point the document root to a specific subdirectory of your file system. The default setting is as follows:

```
DocumentRoot /usr/local/etc/httpd/htdocs
```

A potentially better option, however, would be to create a Web directory structure for your organization. Figure 3-3 shows the Web directory structure I prefer for a multiuser, multidomain system.

As you can see in the figure, I chose to create a partition called /www, and under it there are subdirectories for each Web site hosted by my system. /www/www.mycompany.com/ has three subdirectories: public, stage, and development. Each of these three subdirectories has two subdirectories: htdocs and cgi-bin. The htdocs subdirectory is the document root directory, and the cgi-bin subdirectory is used for CGI scripts. So, the DocumentRoot setting for the www.mycompany.com Web site is:

```
DocumentRoot /www/www.mycompany.com/public/htdocs
```

The advantage of this directory structure is that it keeps all the Web documents and applications under one partition (/www.) This allows for easy backups, and the partition can be mounted on different systems via the Network File System (NFS) in case another machine in the network is given the task to provide Web services.

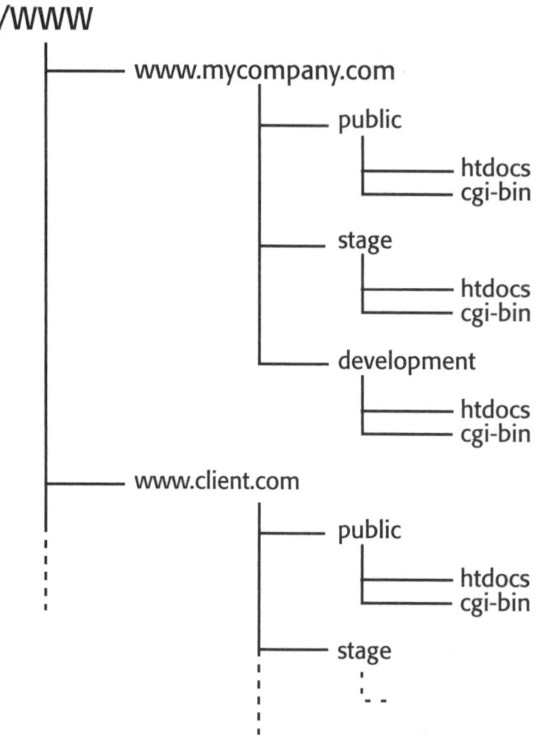

Figure 3-3: My preferred Web directory structure

Cross-Reference

You will learn more about well-designed Web directory structures in Chapter 18.

Note that just because your document root points to a particular directory, this does not mean the Web server cannot access directories outside your document tree. You can easily enable it to do so using symbolic links (with proper file permission) or using aliases (I talk about aliases in the next chapter). From an organization and security perspective, I don't recommend using a lot of symbolic links or aliases to access files and directories outside your document tree. Nonetheless, it is sometimes necessary to keep a certain type of information outside the document tree, even if you need to keep the contents of such a directory accessible to the server on a regular basis.

If you have to add symbolic links to other directory locations outside the document tree, make sure that when you back up your files, your backup program is instructed to back up symbolic links properly.

cgi-bin directory configuration

If you plan on running CGI scripts, you'll want to store these scripts in a directory other than the one pointed to by DocumentRoot (or one of its subdirectories.) You need to do this for security reasons. Keeping scripts in the document tree might enable someone to take a look at your scripts and find vulnerabilities in them. That's why in Figure 3-3 the directory structure includes a script directory called cgi-bin, which is outside the document tree for each site.

To keep this directory outside the document tree, you can use the ScriptAlias directive to create an alias for the directory as follows:

```
ScriptAlias [/alias/] [fully qualified path for script
directory]
```

The alias is just a name that you arbitrarily assign to the physical directory that stores the scripts, applets, and so on. The standard alias for the CGI script directory is cgi-bin; however, you are free to call it anything you like. The default setting is:

```
ScriptAlias /cgi-bin/ /usr/local/etc/httpd/cgi-bin/
```

For the www.mycompany.com site in the Figure 3-3, the alias would be as follows:

```
ScriptAlias /cgi-bin/ /www/www.mycompany.com/public/cgi-bin/
```

So, when you want to refer to a script in a URL or an HTML file in your document tree, you should use the alias instead of the physical file location. For example:

```
http://www.mycompany.com/cgi-bin/finger.cgi
```

requests the finger.cgi script in the /www/www.mycompany.com/public/cgi-bin/ directory. Another way to look at this directive would be:

```
ScriptAlias fakename realname
```

The next directive you need to look at is the UserDir directive, which has the following syntax:

```
UserDir [directory name]
```

This directive is used to tell Apache which directory to consider as the DocumentRoot for users on your system. This only applies if you have multiple users on the system and want to allow each one to have his very own Web directory. The default setting is:

```
UserDir public_html
```

which means that if you set up your Web server's name to be www.yourcompany.com, and you have two users (joe and jenny) their personal Web site URLs would be as shown in Table 3-1.

Table 3-1
Personal Web Directory for Users

URL	***Web Directory***
`http://www.yourcompany.com/~joe`	`~joe/public_html`
`http://www.yourcompany.com/~jenny`	`~jenny/public_html`

Note that on UNIX systems, ~ (tilde) expends to a user's home directory. The directory specified by the UserDir directive resides in each user's home directory, and Apache must have read and execute permissions to read files and directories within the public_html directory. This can be accomplished using the following commands on a UNIX system:

```
chown -R <user>.<Apache server's group name>
  ~<user>/<directory assigned in UserDir>
chmod -R 770 ~<user>/<directory assigned in UserDir>
```

For example, if the user name is joe and Apache's group is called httpd, and public_html is assigned in the UserDir directive, the preceding commands will look like this:

```
chown -R joe.httpd  ~joe/public_html
chmod -R 2770 ~joe/public_html
```

The first command, chown, changes ownership of the ~joe/public_html directory (and that of all files and subdirectories within it) to joe.httpd. In other words, it gives the user joe and the group httpd full ownership of all the files and directories in the public_html directory. The next command, chmod, sets the access rights to 2770 — in other words, only the user (joe) and the group (httpd) have full read, write, and execute privileges in public_html and all files and subdirectories under it. It also ensures that when a new file or subdirectory is created in the public_html directory, the newly created file has the group ID set. This enables the Web server to access the new file without the user's intervention.

If you create user accounts on your system using a script (such as /usr/sbin/adduser script on Linux systems), you may want to incorporate the Web site creation process in this script. Just add a mkdir command to create a default public_html directory (if that's what you assign to the UserDir directive) to create the Web directory. Add the chmod and chown commands to give the Web server user permission to read and execute files and directories under this public directory.

The last directive you need to set up is the DirectoryIndex directive, which has the following syntax:

```
DirectoryIndex [filename1, filename2, filename3, … ]
```

This directive specifies which file the Apache server should consider as the index for the directory being requested. For example, when a URL such as www.yourcompany.com/ is requested, the Apache server determines that this is a request to access the / (document root) directory of the Web site. If the DocumentRoot directive is set as follows:

```
DocumentRoot /www/www.yourcompany.com/public/htdocs
```

then the Apache server looks for a file named /www/www.yourcompany.com/public/htdocs/index.html; if it finds the file, Apache services the request by returning the content of the file to the requesting Web browser. If the DirectoryIndex is assigned welcome.html instead of the default index.html, however, the Web server will look for /www/www.yourcompany.com/public/htdocs/welcome.html instead. If the file is absent, Apache returns the directory listing by creating a dynamic HTML page. Figure 3-4 shows such a case, where index.html is missing in a directory and the server has generated a directory listing for the requesting browser.

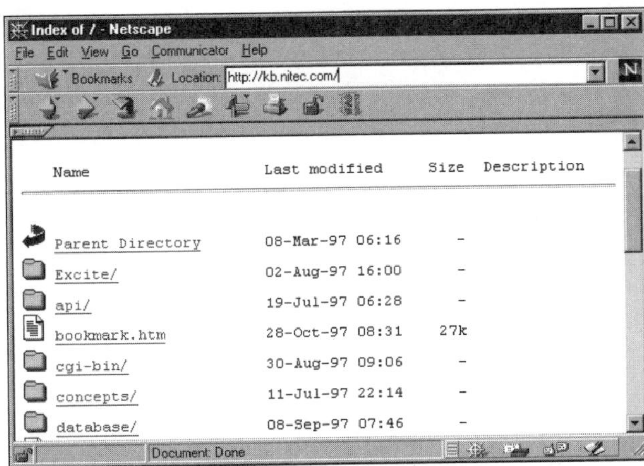

Figure 3-4: Dynamic directory listing in the absence of index.htm

You can specify multiple index filenames in the DirectoryIndex directive. For example:

```
DirectoryIndex index.html index.htm welcome.htm
```

tells the Web server that it should check for the existence of any of the three files, and if any one is found, it should be returned to the requesting Web client.

Note that listing many files as the index may create two problems. First, the server will now have to check for the existence of many files per directory request; this could potentially make it a bit slower than usual. Second, having multiple files as indexes could make your site a bit difficult to manage from the organization point of view. If your Web site content developers use various systems to create files, however, it might be a practical solution to keep both index.html and index.htm as index files. For example, a Windows 3.*x* machine is unable to create filenames with extensions longer than three characters, so a user working on such a machine may need to manually update all of his or her index.htm files on the Web server. Using the recommended index filenames eliminates this hassle.

access.conf

The final configuration file you need to modify is the access.conf file. The access.conf file is used to set access permissions for items such as files, directories, and scripts on your Web site. Listing 3-3 shows the default access.conf file.

Listing 3-3: Default access.conf created from access.conf-dist

```
# access.conf: Global access configuration
# Online docs at http://www.apache.org/

# This file defines server settings which affect which types of
services
# are allowed, and in what circumstances.

# Each directory to which Apache has access, can be configured
with respect
# to which services and features are allowed and/or disabled in
that
# directory (and its subdirectories).

# Originally by Rob McCool

# This should be changed to whatever you set DocumentRoot to.

<Directory /usr/local/etc/httpd/htdocs>

# This may also be "None", "All", or any combination of
"Indexes",
# "Includes", "FollowSymLinks", "ExecCGI", or "MultiViews".

# Note that "MultiViews" must be named *explicitly* -- "Options
All"
# doesn't give it to you (or at least, not yet).

Options Indexes FollowSymLinks

# This controls which options the .htaccess files in
directories can
# override. Can also be "All", or any combination of "Options",
"FileInfo",
```

```
# "AuthConfig", and "Limit"

AllowOverride None

# Controls who can get stuff from this server.

order allow,deny
allow from all

</Directory>

# /usr/local/etc/httpd/cgi-bin should be changed to whatever
your ScriptAliased
# CGI directory exists, if you have that configured.

<Directory /usr/local/etc/httpd/cgi-bin>
AllowOverride None
Options None
</Directory>

# Allow server status reports, with the URL of
http://servername/server-status
# Change the ".your_domain.com" to match your domain to enable.

#<Location /server-status>
#SetHandler server-status

#order deny,allow
#deny from all
#allow from .your_domain.com
#</Location>

# There have been reports of people trying to abuse an old bug
from pre-1.1
# days.  This bug involved a CGI script distributed as a part
of Apache.
# By uncommenting these lines you can redirect these attacks to
a logging
# script on phf.apache.org.  Or, you can record them yourself,
using the script
# support/phf_abuse_log.cgi.

#<Location /cgi-bin/phf*>
#deny from all
#ErrorDocument 403 http://phf.apache.org/phf_abuse_log.cgi
#</Location>

# You may place any other directories or locations you wish to
have
# access information for after this one.
```

This is the only configuration file in which you need to modify directives that span multiple lines. The first directive you need to modify has following syntax:

```
<Directory directory> ... </Directory>
```

`<Directory>` and `</Directory>` are used to enclose a group of directives. The scope of the enclosed directive is limited to the named directory (with subdirectories.); however, you may only use directives that are allowed in a directory context (you will learn about these directives in detail in the next chapter).

The named directory is either the full path to a directory, or a wild-card string. The default access.conf file comes with the following directive setting:

```
<Directory /usr/local/etc/httpd/htdocs>
Options Indexes FollowSymLinks
AllowOverride None
order allow,deny
allow from all
</Directory>
```

You need to change the directory /usr/local/etc/httpd/htdocs to whatever you set earlier as the argument for the DocumentRoot directive in the httpd.conf file. The default setting, which includes multiple directives such as Options and AllowOverride, tells the server the following:

✦ The named directory and all subdirectories under it can be indexed. In other words, if there is an index file, it will be displayed; in absence of one, the server will create a dynamic index for the directory. The Options directive specifies this.

✦ The named directory and all subdirectories under it can have symbolic links that the server can follow (that is, use as a path) to access information. The Options directive also specifies this.

✦ No options specified in the Directory directive can be overridden by a local access control file (specified by the AccessFileName directive in srm.conf; the default is .htaccess). This is specified using the AllowOverride directive.

✦ Access is permitted for all.

The default setting should be sufficient at this early stage. If your server is going to be on the Internet, however, you may want to remove the FollowSymLinks option from the Options directive line. Leaving this option creates a potential security risk. For example, if a directory in your Web site does not have an index page, the server displays an automated index that shows any symbolic links you may have in that directory. This could cause sensitive information to be displayed, or may even allow anyone to run an executable that resides in a carelessly linked directory.

Starting and Stopping the Server

Now that you have completed all the necessary basic configuration, you are ready to run the server. I mentioned earlier that you can run the server in two ways. Lets take a look at each method.

Standalone server

If you set up your server to run as a standalone, the following sections tell you how to run, stop, and restart the server.

Running Apache as a standalone server

To run your standalone server, just run the httpd server program you installed previously on your system. If you installed the httpd program in the /usr/sbin/ directory, log in as the root user and run the program from anywhere using the following:

```
/usr/sbin/httpd
```

This launches httpd, the primary Web server process, which looks for configuration files in the default location (specified at compilation time), such as /usr/local/apache/conf/. If you installed your configuration files in another directory, you need to tell httpd where to find them using the following:

```
/usr/sbin/httpd -f /path/to/httpd.conf
```

where /path/to should be the actual path to the httpd.conf configuration file.

In either case, if there are no error messages on the screen and you are back to the shell prompt, the server is running successfully. The quickest way to check whether the server is running is to try the following command:

```
ps auxw | grep httpd
```

This uses the ps utility to list all the processes that are in the process queue, and then pipes this output to the grep program. grep searches the output for lines that match the keyword httpd, and then displays each matching line. If you see one line with the word *root* in it, that's your primary Apache server process. Note that when the server starts, it creates a number of child processes to handle the requests. If you started Apache as the root user, the parent process continues to run as the root, while the children change to the user as instructed in the httpd.conf file.

If httpd complains about being unable to "bind" to an address, then either another process is already using the port you have configured Apache to use, or you are running httpd as a normal user but trying to use a port below 1024 (such as the default port 80).

If the server is not running, read the error message displayed when you run httpd. You should also check the server error_log for additional information (with the default configuration, this is located in the file error_log in the logs directory).

If you want your server to start up automatically after a system reboot, you should add a call to httpd to your system startup files (typically rc.local or a file in an rc.N directory). The httpd.sh script in Listing 3-4 can be used in a startup file to automatically launch the Web server at system startup or after a reboot.

Listing 3-4: The httpd.sh script

```
#!/bin/sh
#
# httpd   This shell script starts and stops the Apache server
# It takes an argument 'start' or 'stop' to receptively start
and
# stop the server process.
#
# Notes: You might have to change the path information used
# in the script to reflect your system's configuration.
#
[ -f /usr/sbin/httpd ] || exit 0

# See how the script was called.
case "$1" in
  start)
        # Start daemons.
        echo -n "Starting httpd: "
        /usr/sbin/httpd
        touch /var/lock/subsys/httpd
        echo
        ;;
  stop)
        # Stop daemons.
        echo -n "Shutting down httpd: "
        kill -TERM 'cat /usr/local/etc/httpd/httpd.pid'

        echo "done"
        rm -f /var/lock/subsys/httpd
        ;;
  *)
        echo "Usage: httpd {start|stop}"
        exit 1
esac
exit 0
```

To start the Apache server, run the preceding script as follows:

```
httpd.sh start
```

To stop the Apache server, run the script as follows:

```
httpd.sh stop
```

You need to include these commands in appropriate rc files on your system. You can use the start command in your rc.local file to autostart the server when your system boots up.

Stopping a standalone Apache server

To stop the standalone version of the Apache server, you can use the UNIX kill command to send a TERM signal. The TERM signal tells the server program (httpd) to terminate gracefully. Before you can send a TERM signal to the primary Web server process, however, you need to know the process ID (PID) of the httpd process that is running as a root process.

Apache makes it convenient to find the PID of the primary Web server process. The PID is written into a file assigned to the PidFile directive. This PID is for the primary httpd process. Do not attempt to kill the child processes because the parent will renew them. A typical command to stop the server is:

```
kill -TERM `cat /usr/local/etc/apache/logs/httpd.pid`
```

If you specified a different path, then the default is PidFile, so use that instead.

Restarting a standalone Apache server

If you change one or more Apache configuration files and want the running servers to re-read the configuration files, you do not need to terminate the server processes. All you need is to restart the primary Web server process using the HUP signal as follows:

```
kill -HUP `cat /usr/local/etc/apache/logs/httpd.pid`
```

This forces the primary Web server process to re-read the configuration files.

inetd Apache server

If you set up your server to run via inetd, the following sections tell you how to run, stop, and restart the server.

Running Apache as an inetd-run server

If you properly set up the inetd configuration for httpd, you don't need to do anything to run the Apache server, because inetd runs it when it receives a request for access on the HTTP port.

Stopping an inetd-run Apache server

Normally, you shouldn't need to terminate an inetd-run Apache server, because it disappears as soon as a request is processed. However, if for some reason you have to force it to exit due to an unusual situation (perhaps the server is hung), you can first determine the PID of the process as follows:

```
ps auxw | grep httpd
```

Note that you may have to use a different set of arguments for the ps utility on your system (see the ps man pages for details). The first command (ps) shows all the processing that exists in the process queue of your system, and passes this list to the grep utility. The grep utility searches for lines matching the keyword httpd, and displays any line that matches.

Now you can determine the PID from the output of the grep. If you're unable to determine this yet, just run the ps part of the command, and the very first line in the ps output should tell you which column represents the PID of each process. Once you locate the PID, simply run the following command:

```
kill -TERM [PID]
```

Restarting and inetd-run Apache server

Restarting an inetd-run server is not necessary, because inetd launches a new server process per request. If you just updated the configuration files, the next request you or someone else makes will be affected by the changes you made in the configuration file.

Testing the Apache Server

Now you are ready to test your running Apache server. The first test is simple.

Run your favorite Web browser and point it to the Web site running your newly configured Apache server. If you are running the Web browser on the same system running Apache, you can use the following URL:

```
http://localhost/
```

In all other cases, however, you need to specify the exact host name (such as www.yourcompany.com.

If you have not made any changes to the default htdocs directory, you will see a page such as the one shown in Figure 3-5.

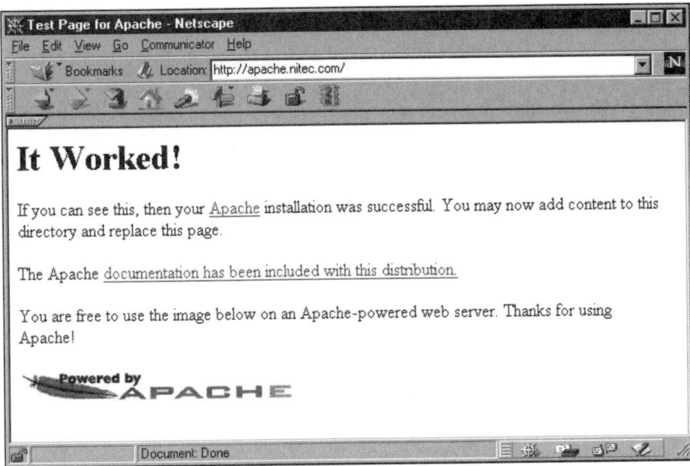

Figure 3-5: Default Apache home page

This page is shipped with the Apache distribution and needs to be changed with your own content.

Finally, you want to make sure the log files are updated properly. To check your log files, enter the log directory and run the following UNIX command:

```
tail -f  [name of access log]
```

The tail part of the command is a UNIX utility that enables viewing of a growing file (when the -f option is specified). Now, use a Web browser to access the site, or if you are already there, simply reload the page you currently have on the browser. You should see an entry added to the listing on the screen. Press the reload button a few more times to ensure the access file is updated accordingly. If you see the updated records, your access log file is working. Press Control+C to exit from the tail command session. If you do not see any new records in the file, you should check the permission settings for the log files and the directory in which they are kept.

Another log to check is the error log file. Use:

```
tail -f  [name of error log]
```

to view the error log entries as they come in. Simply request nonexistent resources (such as a file you don't have) on your Web browser, and you will see entries being added. If you observe this, the error log file is properly configured.

If all of these tests were successful, then you have successfully configured your Apache server. Congratulations!

Summary

In this chapter, you learned the basics of Apache configuration. My goal was to keep the details to a minimum so you could get your Apache server up and running in a short time. You learned how to run Apache as an inetd or standalone Web server. You also learned to configure the httpd.conf, srm.conf, and access.conf files to get Apache up and running.

The next chapter discusses the core Apache directives.

✦ ✦ ✦

C H A P T E R

The Core Directives

✦ ✦ ✦ ✦

In This Chapter

Understanding directive contexts

The Apache core directives

✦ ✦ ✦ ✦

A directive is simply a command for Apache to act on. Apache reads the directives from the configuration files you learned about in Chapter 3. Using directives, an Apache administrator can control the behavior of the Web server. Many directives are available for Apache, which makes it a highly configurable Web server. The directives that are part of the base Apache installation are called the core directives. These directives are always available. Several other directives are also available from the standard modules that are part of the standard distribution of Apache.

I discuss the standard module-based directives in Chapter 5. In this chapter, I discuss the standard contexts in which directives (core and all others) apply, and I also provide in-depth coverage of the core directives. Instead of providing an alphabetical listing of all the possible core directives, I've grouped them according to their usage; the categories include general configuration, performance and resource configuration, standard container, virtual host specific, logging, and authentication and security. Each directive description provides you with the following information:

✦ Syntax — Shows the name of the directive and all possible arguments or values it takes.

✦ Context — Specifies the context (or scope) at which a directive applies.

✦ Default — This line shows the default value for a directive. This is only shown where applicable.

✦ AllowOverride — Value needed to enable the directive in per-directory access configuration file (.htaccess by default). This is only shown where applicable.

✦ Compatibility — This line tells you Apache version-specific details for a directive.

Before we get to the core directive reference sections, let's look at the contexts in which you can use directives.

Apache Directive Contexts

Before you decide to use any of the core directives, it is important that you understand in which context a directive is usable; in other words, you need to know the scope of a directive. Once you understand the terminology needed to discuss the core directives, you'll learn about the core directives themselves.

There are three major contexts for using a directive. A directive can appear anywhere in the primary server configuration files (server config context) outside any containers (which look very much like HTML tags), between containers (container context), or in per-directory configuration files (per-directory context).

Server config context

Directives may appear anywhere in the primary server configurations files outside any containers. You can think of this context as the global context or scope. Directives that apply in this context affect all other contexts by default. A rule of thumb is to treat a directive that is not enclosed in a container as a global directive. These directives may be used anywhere in the server configuration files (such as httpd.conf, srm.conf, and access.conf), but not within any containers or a per-directory configuration file (.htaccess.)

Container context

To limit the scope of a directive, you can use containers. A container tag pair encloses a set of directives and thus restricts the scope of the directives within itself. Apache offers the following standard containers:

✦ <VirtualHost ...> ... </VirtualHost> is used to apply one or more directives to the virtual host specified in the opening tag of the container.

✦ <Directory ...> ... </Directory> is used to apply one or more directives to a certain directory. Note that if you specify one or more directives for a directory using this container tag, the directives automatically apply to all the subdirectories as well. If this is not a desirable side effect, however, you can create a separate directory container for each subdirectory and control the server's behavior differently in each sublevel of the directory.

✦ <DirectoryMatch regex> ... </DirectoryMatch> is exactly same as the <Directory> container; however, it takes a regular expression (regex) as an argument instead of a regular directory name.

A regular expression is typically composed of both normal and special characters to create a pattern. This pattern is used to match one or more substrings or an entire string. To learn more about regular expressions, see Appendix C.

- ✦ <Files ...> ... </Files> is used to apply one or more directives to a certain file or group of files.
- ✦ <FilesMatch regex> ... </FilesMatch regex> is exactly same as the <Files> container; however, it takes a regular expression (regex) as an argument instead of one or more filenames.
- ✦ <Location ...> ... </Location> is used to apply one or more directives to a certain URI.
- ✦ <LocationMatch regex> ... </LocationMatch regex > is exactly same as the <Location> container; however, it takes a regular expression (regex) as an argument instead of a URI.
- ✦ <Limit ...> ... </Limit> is used to apply one or more directives to control access to certain areas of a Web site or a particular HTTP request method. This container has the narrowest scope of all containers.

Note

URI (Uniform Resource Identifier) is the generic term for the family of Uniform Resource Identifiers, of which URL is but one member. The others are Uniform Resource Names (URN), Uniform Resource Characteristics (URC), and Location Independent File Names (LIFN). Only URL is widely used, however.

Let's look at an example of container scope. The following shows a segment of an httpd.conf file:

```
<VirtualHost 206.171.50.50>

ServerName www.nitec.com
DocumentRoot /www/nitec/public/htdocs
DirectoryIndex welcome.html

<Location /secured/>
         DirectoryIndex login.html
</Location>

</VirtualHost>
```

In this example, a virtual host called www.nitec.com is defined using the <VirtualHost> container. The three directives, ServerName, DocumentRoot, and DirectoryIndex, are in the virtual host context and therefore apply to the entire virtual host. The DirectoryIndex directive specifies that if a request is made to access a directory in this virtual server, a file named welcome.html should be returned if available. However, the Location container specifies that a different file, login.html, be returned when someone tries to access the www.nitec.com/secured/

URL. The directives in a narrower scoping container always override the directives in a higher scoping container.

You should keep a few rules in mind when using any of the containers to define a behavior for a section of your Web space:

✦ A <VirtualHost> container can not be nested within another container of any kind.

✦ There can be no container within the narrowest context container <Limit>.

✦ A <Files> container can have only the narrowest container <Limit> within itself.

✦ The <Location> and the <Directory> containers do not mix, so do not use one inside another.

Per-directory context

You can also include directives in per-directory configuration files. A per-directory configuration file (the default filename is .htaccess) is a text file containing one or more directives that apply only to the current directory. These directives can also be enclosed in containers such as <Files ...> or <Limit ...>. Using this file, you can control how Apache behaves when a request is made for a file in a directory. If a directive is valid in this context, it means that it appears inside per-directory access configuration files.

Note that it is possible to disable all or part of what can be overridden in a per-directory configuration file in the server config or virtual host context. Therefore, all directives in this context may not be processed, depending on the overrides currently active.

General Configuration Directives

These directives are fundamental in nature and generally apply to both the primary server (server config context) and the virtual servers (virtual host context.)

AccessConfig

```
Syntax: AccessConfig filename
Default: AccessConfig conf/access.conf
Context: server config, virtual host
```

You may remember from Chapter 3 that Apache server reads a set of configuration files during startup. One of these files is the global access configuration file called access.conf. This file is located by default in the conf directory under the server's root directory, which is specified by the ServerRoot directive.

Using the AccessConfig directive, you can instruct Apache to read a different file than the default conf/access.conf file. For example, if you want to load global access information from a file called conf/globalaccess.conf, you need to use the following directive in the httpd.conf file:

```
AccessConf conf/globalaccess.conf
```

The filename has to be relative to the ServerRoot path name.

If you like to have a single configuration file for each Apache server you run, you can disable loading of conf/access.conf file by setting AccessConfig as follows:

```
AccessConfig /dev/null
```

You also need to disable loading of the conf/srm.conf file using the ResourceConfig directive in a similar fashion. See the ResourceConfig directive for details.

Until recently, the access.conf file contained only <Directory> sections; now, it can contain any server directive allowed in the server config context. It is also valid in virtual host contexts, so you can use it to load a configuration file from within the <VirtualHost> directive. However, only one instance of AccessConfig is permitted in a <VirtualHost> section. This can come in handy if you have many virtual hosts to support. Use this directive to load a separate virtual host configuration file, and thus increase the readability of your primary server configuration file.

Note that the file specified by the AccessConfig directive is read after the file specified by the ResourceConfig directive is read.

AccessFileName

```
Syntax: AccessFileName filename filename ...
Default: AccessFileName .htaccess
Context: server config, virtual host
Compatibility: more than one filename option is available in
Apache 1.3 and later.
```

This directive specifies the name of the per-directory access control file. The default setting (.htaccess) makes Apache look for the .htaccess file each time an access request is made by a client system. For example, let's say the DocumentRoot directive of an Apache-powered Web site called www.mycompany.com is set as follows:

```
DocumentRoot /www/mycompany/public/htdocs
```

and a Web browser requests the following URL:

```
www.mycompany.com/ feedback.html
```

This causes Apache to search for the following access control files:

- `/.htaccess`
- `/www/.htaccess`
- `/www/mycompany/.htaccess`
- `/www/mycompany/public/.htaccess`
- `/www/mycompany/public/htdocs/.htaccess`

After Apache has checked for all these files, it looks for the feedback.html file. If this seems like a lot of disk I/O, it is! If you do not make use of the per-directory access control file and would like Apache to stop checking for it, simply use the <Directory> directive to disable privileges to override options as follows:

```
<Directory />
AllowOverride None
</Directory>
```

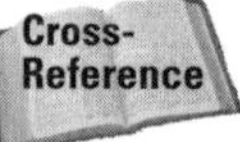

See the sections on the <Directory> and AllowOverride directives in this chapter for more details.

BindAddress

```
Syntax: BindAddress IP address
Default: BindAddress *
Context: server config
```

Apache running on a UNIX system can listen for connections on one or more IP addresses. This directive enables you to specify an IP address, which Apache will service. The default value of this directive is * (wildcard), which means that Apache listens on all IP addresses attached to a server machine. For example,

```
BindAddress 206.171.50.50
```

will make Apache listen to only the given IP address. Only one BindAddress directive can be used. For more control over which addresses and ports Apache listens to, use the Listen directive instead of BindAddress. BindAddress can be used as an alternative method for supporting virtual hosts using multiple independent servers, instead of using <VirtualHost> sections.

CoreDumpDirectory

```
Syntax: CoreDumpDirectory directory
Default: the same location as ServerRoot
Context: server config
```

If you are capable of exploring a core dump file and want Apache to dump core in a certain file in case of a crash, set this directive to the location where you want the core dump file to reside. The default is in the ServerRoot directory; however, since your ServerRoot should not be writable by the user that the server runs as, core dumps won't get written there. Therefore, the default value is likely to be wrong.

DocumentRoot

```
Syntax: DocumentRoot directory
Default: DocumentRoot /usr/local/apache/htdocs
Context: server config, virtual host
```

The directory specified by this directive becomes the top-level directory for all the documents serviced by Apache. For example, if

```
DocumentRoot /www/mycompany/public/htdocs
```

is set for the server www.mycompany.com, then an access request for www.mycompany.com/corporate.html makes the server look for the following file:

```
/www/mycompany/public/htdocs/corporate.html
```

If the file is found, it is returned to the client (that is, the Web browser). Similarly, an access request for www.mycompany.com/info/corporate.html makes the server look for

```
/www/mycompany/public/htdocs/info/corporate.html
```

A bug in one of the core modules (mod_dir) causes a problem when the DocumentRoot has a trailing slash (for example, DocumentRoot /usr/web/), so you should avoid entering a / character at the end of any path for any directive.

Note that it is possible to have the server look for files in a directory outside the DocumentRoot directory. In other words, if you want to access some files outside the DocumentRoot tree, you can use the Alias directive to create a virtual directory name that can point to a physical directory anywhere in your server's file system.

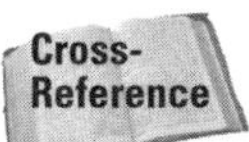

See Chapter 5 for details on the Alias directive.

ErrorDocument

```
Syntax: ErrorDocument error-code filename | error message | URL
Context: server config, virtual host, directory, per-directory
Override: FileInfo
Compatibility: the directory and per-directory (.htaccess)
contexts are available in Apache 1.1 and later.
```

When the server encounters a problem, it generates a standard error message with the error code in it. This is not very user-friendly for most people, however, so a more customized version of the error message or possibly a recovery measure is more desirable. If you need such customization, use the ErrorDocument directive to override standard error messages.

The directive requires two arguments. The first one is the standard HTTP error code, which you can find in Appendix B, and the second one is the action item for the error. Depending on your needs, you can define what action you want the server to take for a particular error condition.

For example, if you want to provide a custom message for all requests that result in a standard "file not found" message, all you have to do is find the server status code for that error condition and use the ErrorDocument directive. Since the server status code for missing files is 404, the following directive setting enables Apache to display a custom message:

```
ErrorDocument 404 "Sorry, this is an invalid request since %s "
```

Notice that the entire message is quoted, and the server replaces %s with whatever information is available regarding the error. If you find this a bit limiting, however, you can use a file as your error message response. For example:

```
ErrorDocument 404 /errors/404.html
```

Whenever the missing file error occurs, the 404.html file found in the errors directory under the DocumentRoot directory is returned to the client (the Web browser). If you want to do more than just return a static page, you can use a CGI script to perform some specific action. In such a case, you replace the filename with a call to your CGI script:

```
ErrorDocument 404 /cgi-bin/missingurl.cgi
```

This calls a CGI script called missingurl.cgi every time a 404 error occurs. You can also redirect the client to another site using a URL instead of a filename:

```
ErrorDocument 404 http://www.newsite.com/we.moved.html
```

This can be used when a page or an entire site has moved to another location.

You cannot point the client to a remote server if an error 401 (unauthorized) occurs. The value of this directive must be a local file or a message.

Include

```
Syntax: Include filename
Context: server config
Compatibility: available in Apache 1.3 and later.
```

If you want to include other configuration files from within the server configuration files, use this directive.

Listen

```
Syntax: Listen [IP address:] port number
Context: server config
```

By default, Apache responds to requests on all the IP addresses attached to the server machine, but only to the port address specified by the Port directive. The Listen directive can be used to make this situation more configurable. You can use the Listen directive to tell Apache to respond to a certain IP address, an IP address and port combination, or just a port by itself.

Although Listen can be used instead of BindAddress and Port, you may have to use the Port directive if your Apache server generates URLs that point to itself.

Multiple Listen directives may be used to specify a number of addresses and ports to listen to. The server will respond to requests from any of the listed addresses and ports. For example, to make the server accept connections on both port 80 and port 8080, use:

```
Listen 80
Listen 8080
```

The following examples make Apache accept connections on two IP addresses and port numbers:

```
Listen 11.22.3311.22.33.1:80
Listen 11.22.3311.22.33.2:8080
```

Port

```
Syntax: Port number
Default: Port 80
Context: server config
```

This directive assigns a port number in the range of 0 to 65535 to a host. In the absence of any Listen or BindAddress directives specifying a port number, the Port directive sets the network port on which the server listens. If any Listen or BindAddress directives specify a port number, then the Port directive has no effect on which address the server listens at. The Port directive sets the SERVER_PORT environment variable (for CGI and SSI), and is used when the server must generate a URL that refers to itself.

Although you can specify a port number between 0 and 65535, there is one restriction you should keep in mind. All the port numbers below 1024 are reserved for standard services such as TELNET, SMTP, POP3, HTTP, and FTP. You can locate all the port number assignments to standard services in your /etc/services file. Or, if you want to be safe, use any port number other than 80 for your Apache server (use a high address such as 8000, for example).

If you are a non-root user and want to run Apache for experimentation or some other noble cause, you need to use ports higher than 1024, because only root users can run services such as Apache on these restricted ports.

Note

The <VirtualHost> container can also be used to set up which port is used for a virtual host.

User

```
Syntax: User unix-userid
Default: User #-1
Context: server config, virtual host
```

This directive sets the user ID that is used by the child Apache server processes that respond to requests. In order to use this directive, Apache must be configured to run as a standalone server (see the ServerType directive), and the standalone server must be run initially by the root. Once the Apache server is started, it launches child processes to respond to requests. However, these child processes are not run as a root. The parent Apache process (often called the daemon) changes the child process user ID to whatever is set in the User directive, as long as it is a valid user ID.

If you start the server as a non-root user, it fails to change to the user ID specified by the User directive, and instead continues to run as the original user. If you do start the server as a root, then it is normal for the parent Apache process to remain running as a root; however, it runs the child processes as the user specified by the User directive.

You can also employ user ID numbers, which you can usually find in your /etc/password file. If you plan on using a numeric value instead of the actual user name, the number should be preceded by a # sign.

Many Apache administrators use the default nobody user for their sites. This user is not available on all UNIX systems, and is not always desirable. I highly recommend that you employ a unique user and group ID (see the Group directive) for your Apache server. Doing so will give you better control of what the server can or cannot access. The user ID you decide to use for Apache child processes should have very few access privileges. It should not be able to access files that are not intended to be visible to the outside world, and similarly, the user should not be able to execute applications that are not meant for HTTP requests.

Use of this directive in the <VirtualHost> container requires a properly configured suEXEC wrapper. When the wrapper is used inside a <VirtualHost> container in this manner, only the user that CGIs are run as is affected. Non-CGI requests are still processed with the user specified in the main User directive. So, the primary User directive is not completely overridable.

Finally, never set the User (or Group) directive to root unless you know exactly what you are doing and what the dangers are.

Group

```
Syntax: Group Unix-group
Default: Group #-1
Context: server config, virtual host
```

The Group directive should be used in conjunction with the User directive. Group determines the group under which the standalone server answers requests. In order to use this directive, the standalone server must be run initially as root. The group directive can be assigned a group number as well. Look up group names and their corresponding numeric values in your /etc/group file.

All the warnings and recommendations I provide for the User directive apply to this directive as well. Make sure you read the User directive details.

<IfModule>

```
Syntax: <IfModule [!]module-name> ... </IfModule>
Default: None
Context: all
Compatibility: only available in 1.2 and later.
```

Use this directive if you have directives that are available from a custom module that may not always be present in your Apache installation. For example, if you want to use certain directives only if a module is available, then you can use the following conditional construct:

```
<IfModule module-name>
# assign the following directives their respective value
# your directives goes here
</IfModule>
```

On the other hand, if you need a conditional statement that is the exact reverse of the above, all you need to do is insert a ! (bang or exclamation symbol) before the module name. Note that the module name argument is the filename of the module at the time it was compiled (for example, mod_rewrite.c). <IfModule> sections are nestable; this is a method that can be used to implement simple multiple-module condition tests.

Options

```
Syntax: Options [+|-]option [+|-]option ...
Context: server config, virtual host, directory, .htaccess
Override: Options
```

The Options directive controls which server features are available in a particular directory. When this directive is set to None, none of the extra features are enabled for the context in which the directive is used. All the possible settings for this directive are:

✦ None — No options.

✦ All — All options except for MultiViews.

✦ ExecCGI — Execution of CGI scripts is permitted.

✦ FollowSymLinks — The server follows symbolic links in the directory. However, the server does not change the path name used to match against <Directory> sections.

✦ Includes — Server Side Include (SSI) commands are permitted.

✦ IncludesNOEXEC — A restricted set of Server Side Include (SSI) commands can be embedded in the SSI pages. The SSI commands that are not allowed are #exec and #include.

✦ Indexes — If a URL that maps to a directory is requested, and there is no DirectoryIndex (for example, index.html) in that directory, then the server returns a formatted listing of the directory.

✦ SymLinksIfOwnerMatch — The server only follows symbolic links for which the target file or directory is owned by the same user as the link.

✦ MultiViews — Enables content negotiated based on a document's language.

Use the + and - signs to enable or disable an option in the Options directive. Let's look at an example to make this a bit clearer. The following configuration segment shows two directory containers in a single configuration file such as access.conf:

```
<Directory /www/myclient/public/htdocs >
Options Indexes MultiViews
</Directory>

<Directory /www/myclient/public/htdocs>
Options Includes
</Directory>
```

The /www/myclient/public/htdocs will only have the Includes option set. However, if the second <Directory> section uses the + and - signs as follows:

```
<Directory /www/myclient/public/htdocs>
Options +Includes -Indexes
</Directory>
```

then the options MultiViews and Includes are set for the specified directory.

When you apply multiple Options, be aware that the narrowest context always takes precedence over the broader ones. For example:

```
ServerName
Options ExecCGI Includes
<VirtualHost 11.22.3311.22.33.1>
ServerName www.myclient.com
Options -ExecCGI -Includes
```

```
<Directory /www/myclient/public/htdocs/ssi >
        Options Includes
</Directory>
</VirtualHost>
```

In this example, the main server enables both CGI execution and Server Side Includes by setting the Options directive to ExecCGI and Includes. The virtual host www.myclient.com disables both of these options, however, using the -ExecCGI and -Includes settings in its own Options directive. Finally, the virtual host has another Options directive for the /www/myclient/public/htdocs/ssi directory, that enables the Server Side Include execution. Note that Includes is the only option that is set for the /www/myclient/public/htdocs/ssi directory.

As you can see, if the Options directive uses the + or - signs, then the values are added or subtracted from the current Options list. On the other hand, if the Options directive does not use the relative + or - signs, then the values for that container will completely override any previous Options directives.

ResourceConfig

```
Syntax: ResourceConfig filename
Default: ResourceConfig conf/srm.conf
Context: server config, virtual host
```

This directive is exactly same as the AccessConfig directive. If you want to disable loading of the default conf/srm.conf file, just set it as follows in your httpd.conf file:

```
ResourceConfig /dev/null
```

ServerAdmin

```
Syntax: ServerAdmin email-address
Context: server config, virtual host
```

This directive assigns an e-mail address that appears in conjunction with many error messages issued by the server. If you host a large number of virtual Web sites, you may want to use a different e-mail address for each virtual host so you can immediately figure out which server a problem reporter is talking about.

In order to give your virtual sites the professional look and feel they deserve, do not use an e-mail address that does not include the virtual site as the host part of the address. For example, if your company is an Internet Service Provider (ISP) named mycompany.net, and you have a client site called www.myclient.com, then set the www.myclient.com site's ServerAdmin to a user@myclient.com address such as webmaster@myclient.com, instead of webmaster@mycompany.net. This way, when the server displays an error message to someone visiting www.myclient.com, the visitor will see an e-mail address that belongs to myclient.com. This would be considered a bit more professional.

To find out how you can configure your mail server to provide SMTP mail support for virtual hosts, see Chapter 6.

ServerName

```
Syntax: ServerName fully qualified domain name
Context: server config, virtual host
```

The ServerName directive sets the host name of the server. When this directive is not used, Apache tries to determine the host name by doing a DNS request at startup. Depending on your DNS setup, however, this may not be desirable because the lookup done by Apache may choose an undesirable name for your server, if you have canonical name records for your server. Therefore, it is best to just set this to whatever host name you prefer.

Make sure you enter a fully qualified domain name instead of just a shortcut. For example, if you have a host called wormhole.mycompany.com, you should not set the ServerName to wormhole. The valid choice is:

```
ServerName wormhole.mycompany.com
```

ServerRoot

```
Syntax: ServerRoot directory-filename
Default: ServerRoot /usr/local/apache
Context: server config
```

The ServerRoot directive sets the directory in which the server files reside. Do not confuse this with DocumentRoot directive, which is used for pointing the server to your Web contents. The ServerRoot directory is used for locating all the server configuration files and log files. The standard distributions include conf, src, and logs directories under the ServerRoot directory. If you do not specify the ServerRoot directive, however, you can use the -d command line option to tell Apache what your ServerRoot directory is.

Note that the AccessConfig and ResourceConfig directives use the ServerRoot directory to locate configuration files. For example, if you have the directives set as follows:

```
ServerRoot /usr/local/httpd
AccessConfig conf/access.conf
ResourceConfig conf/srm.conf
```

then AccessConfig and ResourceConfig will tell Apache to load the /usr/local/httpd/conf/access.conf and /usr/local/httpd/conf/srm.conf files, respectively.

DefaultType

```
Syntax: DefaultType mime-type
Default: DefaultType text/html
Context: server config, virtual host, directory, .htaccess
Override: FileInfo
```

This directive is used to establish a default content type, so when Apache receives a request for a document whose file type is unknown (in other words, it cannot be determined from the MIME type map available to the server), it uses the predetermined default type.

For example, if you have a directory in which you keep a lot of text files with no extensions, you can use the DefaultType directive inside a <Directory> container that points to this directory. In this case, setting the DefaultType to text/plain would enable the server to tell the other side (the Web browser) that these are plain text files. Here's an example:

```
<Directory /www/mycompany/public/htdocs/plaindata>
DefaultType plain/text
</Directory>
```

Here, all the files in the /www/mycompany/public/htdocs/plaindata/ directory are treated as plain text files.

Performance and Resource Configuration Directives

These directives enable you to fine-tune Apache for higher performance and better control. You can fine-tune the Apache processes in many ways. Note that almost all of these directives require a clear understanding of how your system works in terms of the operating system, hardware, and so on; therefore, it would be helpful to browse your operating system manuals and/or man pages to learn how your system limits system resources to processes, how it controls TCP/IP connectivity, and so on.

The directives in this section are further divided into subfunctions.

Controlling Apache processes

The following directives are used to control how Apache executes in your system. Using these directives also enables you to control how Apache uses resources on your system. For example, you can decide how many child server processes to run on your system, or how many threads you should allow Apache to use on a Windows platform.

A few things to remember when configuring these directives:

✦ The more processes you run, the more load your CPU(s) experiences.

✦ The more processes you run, the more RAM you need.

✦ The more processes you run, the more operating system resources (such as file descriptors, shared buffers) are used.

Of course, more processes also could mean more requests serviced, and thus more hits for your site. So, setting these directives should be based on a combination of experimentation, requirements, and available resources.

ServerType

```
Syntax: ServerType inetd | standalone
Default: ServerType standalone
Context: server config
```

The ServerType directive tells Apache how it should be run by a UNIX system. There are two values for this directive: inetd and standalone.

Use the inetd value to run your server by the system process called -inetd. In this system, for each HTTP connection received, a new copy of the Apache server is started; after the connection is serviced by the Apache server, it exits. This increases the amount of work the system must do to service a request, and therefore is not efficient performance-wise. However, inetd has been around for a long time, and various security options (such as TCP wrappers) are available for it. Many Internet server administrators prefer running services this way. For low-traffic sites, the difference in performance may not be noticeable.

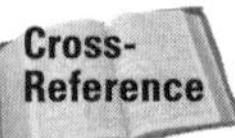

If you are interested in setting up your server this way, read Chapter 3, which covers this option in detail.

Running Apache as an inetd-run server does not automatically make it more secure than running it in standalone mode. Since inetd has been around for a long time, many veteran administrators consider it less prone to attack.

Use the standalone value to run your system in standalone mode, in which Apache runs as a daemon process. In other words, a primary Apache server listens for a connection request to the specified ports, and as new connection requests come, it launches child Apache processes to service the requests; it never services any HTTP request by itself. The child processes are run with the user ID and the group ID specified in the User and Group directives. You should consult these directives to learn more about their settings. For busy, high-traffic sites, this option is recommended.

StartServers

```
Syntax: StartServers number
Default: StartServers 5
Context: server config
```

The StartServers directive is useful only when the Apache server is running as a standalone server. In other words, you need to have ServeType set to standalone for this directive to be effective.

This directive sets the number of child Apache server processes that are created on startup. Note that the number of Apache child processes needed for a certain time period is dynamically controlled. The primary Apache server (the daemon process) launches new child processes as it encounters a higher load of requests. The actual number of child processes is controlled by the MinSpareServers, MaxSpareServers, and the MaxClients directives. Therefore, you have little to gain by adjusting this parameter.

Note that when running with Microsoft Windows, this directive sets the total number of child processes running. Because the Windows version of Apache is multithreaded, one process handles all the requests. The rest of the processes are held in reserve until the primary process dies.

ThreadsPerChild

```
Syntax: ThreadsPerChild number
Default: ThreadsPerChild 50
Context: server config  (Windows)
Compatibility: only with Apache 1.3 and later with Windows
```

The Windows NT/95 version of Apache is a multithreaded server. The ThreadsPerChild directive tells the server how many threads it should use. It also decides the maximum number of connections the server can handle at any given time. Therefore, this value should be set reasonably high to allow the maximum number of possible hits.

SendBufferSize

```
Syntax: SendBufferSize bytes
Context: server config
```

This directive sets the TCP send buffer size to the number of bytes specified. On a high-performance network, setting the directive to a higher value than the operating system defaults may increase server performance.

ListenBacklog

```
Syntax: ListenBacklog backlog
Default: ListenBacklog 511
Context: server config
Compatibility: only available in Apache versions after 1.2.0.
```

This directive enables you to take defensive action against a known security attack called Denial of Service (DOS) by enabling you to set the maximum length of the queue of pending connections. Increase this if you detect that you are under a TCP SYN flood (DOS) attack; otherwise, you can leave it alone.

TimeOut

```
Syntax: TimeOut number
Default: TimeOut 300
Context: server config
```

As you may already know, the Web is really a client/server system where the Apache server responds to requests. The requests and responses are transmitted via packets of data. Apache must know how long to wait for a certain packet. This directive enables you to configure the time in seconds. The time you specify here is the maximum time Apache will wait before it breaks a connection. The default setting allows Apache to wait for 300 seconds before it disconnects itself from the client. If you are on a slow network, however, you may want to increase the time out value to decrease the number of disconnects.

Currently, this time out setting applies to:

- ✦ The total amount of time it takes to receive a GET request
- ✦ The amount of time between receipt of TCP packets on a POST or PUT request
- ✦ The amount of time between ACKs on transmissions of TCP packets in responses

MaxClients

```
Syntax: MaxClients number
Default: MaxClients 256
Context: server config
```

This directive limits the number of simultaneous requests that Apache can service. Because Apache uses one child server for each request, this is also the effective limit for the number of child servers that can exist at the same time. The default limit is really the hard limit set in the httpd.h file in the Apache source distribution. This setting should be fine for most typical-to-moderate load sites. The Apache programmers put the hard limit there for two reasons: they do not want the server to crash the system by filling out some kernel table, and this maximum limit keeps the scoreboard file small enough to be easily readable.

If you have a high-performance server system and have the necessary bandwidth, however, you can recompile the server with a higher hard limit by modifying the httpd.h file. Look for the following conditional define statements. Change the number 256 to a higher number.

```
#ifndef HARD_SERVER_LIMIT
#define HARD_SERVER_LIMIT 256
#endif
```

So, what happens when the server reaches the maximum request count? Well, it puts the incoming requests in a wait state until it is free to service them.

MaxRequestsPerChild

```
Syntax: MaxRequestsPerChild number
Default: MaxRequestsPerChild 0
Context: server config
```

Apache launches a child server process to service a request; however, a child server can process multiple requests. The number of requests a child server can process is limited by the MaxRequestsPerChild directive. After servicing the maximum number of requests, the child process terminates.

If the MaxRequestsPerChild is 0, then the process will never expire. If you suspect there are libraries on your operating system (for example, Solaris) that have memory-leaking code, you may want to set this directive to a non-zero value. This enables you to define a life cycle for a child process, and therefore reduces the chances of a process consuming leaked memory and slowly eating up all available memory. It also provides you with a small load average number for your system, since the Apache-related load is reduced as your Web server becomes less busy.

MaxSpareServers

```
Syntax: MaxSpareServers number
Default: MaxSpareServers 10
Context: server config
```

This directive lets you set the number of idle Apache child processes you want on your server. If the number of idle Apache child processes exceeds the maximum number specified by the MaxSpareServers directive, then the parent process kills off the excess processes. Tuning of this parameter should only be necessary for very busy sites. Unless you know what you are doing, do not change the default.

MinSpareServers

```
Syntax: MinSpareServers number
Default: MinSpareServers 5
Context: server config
```

The MinSpareServers directive sets the desired minimum number of idle child server processes. An idle process is one that is not handling a request. If there are fewer idle Apache processes than the number specified by the MinSpareServers directive, , then the parent process creates new children at a maximum rate of 1 per second. Tuning of this parameter should only be necessary on very busy sites. Unless you know what you are doing, do not change the default.

Making persistent connections

Using the KeepAlive directives discussed in this section, you can instruct Apache to use persistent connections so that a single TCP connection can be used for multiple transactions. Normally, every HTTP request and response uses a separate connection. This means that every time the server gets a request, it opens a connection to retrieve the request and then closes it. Once the server has received the request, it opens another TCP connection to respond, and finally closes the connection after completing the service. This method increases the toll on high performance. Reuse of a single connection for multiple transactions reduces the overhead needed for setting up and closing a TCP connection repeatedly, and thereby increases performance.

To establish a persistent connection, however, both the server and the client need to have the persistent connection facility. Most popular browsers, such as Netscape Navigator and Microsoft Internet Explorer, have KeepAlive features built in.

Note that not all transactions can take advantage of the persistent connections. One of the requirements for a persistent connection is that the resources being transmitted must have a known size. Because many CGI scripts, SSI commands, and other dynamically generated contents do not have a known length before transmission, they are unable to take advantage of this feature.

KeepAlive

```
Syntax: (Apache 1.2) KeepAlive On | Off
Default: (Apache 1.2) KeepAlive On
Context: server config
Compatibility: only available in Apache 1.1 and later
```

This directive enables you to activate/deactivate persistent use of TCP connections in Apache.

Older Apache servers (prior to version 1.2) may require a numeric value instead of On/Off. This value corresponds to the maximum number of requests you want Apache to entertain per request. A limit is imposed to prevent a client from taking over all your server resources. To disable KeepAlive in the older Apache versions, use 0 (zero) as the value.

KeepAliveTimeout

```
Syntax: KeepAliveTimeout seconds
Default: KeepAliveTimeout 15
Context: server config
```

If you have the KeepAlive directive set (on), you can use this directive to limit the number of seconds Apache will wait for a subsequent request before closing a connection. Once a request has been received, the timeout value specified by the Timeout directive applies.

MaxKeepAliveRequests

```
Syntax: MaxKeepAliveRequests number
Default: MaxKeepAliveRequests 100
Context: server config
Compatibility: only available in Apache 1.2 and later.
```

The MaxKeepAliveRequests directive limits the number of requests allowed per connection when KeepAlive is on. If it is set to 0 (zero), unlimited requests will be allowed. I recommend that this setting be kept to a high value for maximum server performance.

Controlling system resources

Apache is quite flexible in allowing you to control the amount of system resources (such as CPU time, and memory) it consumes. These control features come in handy for making your Web server system more reliable and responsive. Many typical hacking attempts try to make a Web server consume all system resources like a hog, and thus try to make the system nonresponsive and virtually halted. Apache provides a set of directives to combat such a situation. These directives are discussed below.

RLimitCPU

```
Syntax: RLimitCPU  n | 'max' [ n | 'max']
Default: Unset; uses operating system defaults
Context: server config, virtual host
Compatibility: only available in Apache 1.2 and later
```

This directive enables you to control Apache's CPU usage. The directive takes two parameters. The first parameter sets a soft resource limit for all processes, and the second parameter sets the maximum resource limit. Raising the maximum resource limit requires that the server be running as a root, or in the initial startup phase. The second parameter is optional.

For each of these parameters, there are two possible values:

- ✦ n is the number of seconds per process
- ✦ max is the maximum resource limit allowed by the operating system

RLimitMEM

```
Syntax: RLimitMEM  n | 'max' [ n | 'max']
Default: Unset; uses operating system defaults
Context: server config, virtual host
Compatibility: only available in Apache 1.2 and later
```

This directive limits the memory (RAM) usage of Apache processes. The directive takes two parameters. The first parameter sets a soft resource limit for all processes, and the second parameter sets the maximum resource limit. Raising the maximum resource limit requires that the server be started by the root user. The second parameter is optional.

For each of these parameters, there are two possible values:

✦ n is the number of bytes per process

✦ max is the maximum resource limit allowed by the operating system

RLimitNPROC

```
Syntax: RLimitNPROC  n | 'max' [ n | 'max']
Default: Unset; uses operating system defaults
Context: server config, virtual host
Compatibility: only available in Apache 1.2 and later
```

This directive sets the maximum number of simultaneous processes per user. It takes one or two parameters. The first parameter sets the soft resource limit for all processes, and the second parameter sets the maximum resource limit. Each parameter can be either of the following:

✦ n is the number of bytes per process

✦ max is the maximum resource limit allowed by the operating system

Raising the maximum resource limit requires that the server be running as a root, or in the initial startup phase.

If your CGI processes are run under the same user ID as the server process, use of this directive limits the number of processes the server can launch (or "fork"). If the limit is too low, you will see a message similar to the following:

```
"Can not fork process"
```

in your server error log file. In such a case, you should increase the limit or just leave it as the default.

Using dynamic modules

Apache loads all the precompiled modules when it starts up; however, it also provides a dynamic module loading and unloading feature that may be useful on certain occasions. When you use the following dynamic module directives, you can change the list of active modules without recompiling the server.

ClearModuleList Directive

```
Syntax: ClearModuleList
Context: server config
Compatibility: only available in Apache 1.2 and later
```

You can use this directive to clear the list of active modules and enable the dynamic module-loading feature. Then, use the AddModule directive to add modules that you want to activate.

AddModule

```
Syntax: AddModule module module ...
Context: server config
Compatibility: only available in Apache 1.2 and later
```

This directive can be used to enable a precompiled module that is currently not active. The server can have modules compiled that are not actively in use. This directive can be used to enable these modules. The server comes with a preloaded list of active modules; this list can be cleared with the ClearModuleList directive. Then, new modules can be added using the AddModule directive.

Standard Container Directives

In this section, I discuss the standard containers that are part of the base Apache server. These containers are widely used to apply a group of other directives to a certain directory, file, or location.

Note

The <VirtualHost> container is discussed in a separate section, later in this chapter.

You can not randomly mix and match the containers. The general guidelines are:

✦ Use the <Directory> or <Files> containers to specify directives for file system objects such as files and directories. You can not use <Directory> inside an .htaccess file, because an .htaccess file applies only to the directory where it is found.

✦ Use the <Location> container for matching URL objects. You cannot use this directive inside an .htaccess file.

✦ When using the regular expression version of a directive (for example, <DirectoryMatch>), follow the same guidelines as for the regular version. Use the regular expression version of the containers only if you are confident that your regular expressions are tightly expressed.

Due to a mistake in the early stage of Apache, the proxy control is still done with the <Directory> container, whereas the <Location> container is more appropriate for it. This may be corrected in a future version. However, this really doesn't cause any harm, other than making things a bit more difficult to conceptualize.

<Directory>

```
Syntax: <Directory directory> ... </Directory>
Context: server config, virtual host
```

<Directory> and </Directory> are used to enclose a group of directives that apply only to the named directory and its subdirectories.

Any directive that is allowed in a directory context may be used. The argument can be a fully qualified path name. For example:

```
<Directory /www/mycompany/public/htdocs/download>
Options +Indexes
</Directory>
```

Here, the directory /www/mycompany/public/htdocs/download is used as a fully qualified path name. This example enables directory indexing in this directory. You can also use wildcard characters in specifying the path. For example:

```
<Directory /www/mycompany/public/htdocs/downloa?>
Options +Indexes
</Directory>
```

Here, the ? will match any single character; therefore, directories such as /www/mycompany/public/htdocs/download and /www/mycompany/public/htdocs/downloaD will be matched. You can also use * (asterisk) to match any sequence of characters other than the / (slash) character. Extended regular expressions can also be used, with the addition of the ~ (tilde) character. For example:

```
<Directory ~ "^/www/.*/">
```

would match any subdirectory under /www/.

Note that regular expression-based <Directory> containers may not be applied until all normal (that is, without regular expression) <Directory> containers and .htaccess files have been applied. Then, all the regular expressions are tested in the order in which they appeared in the configuration file.

Cross-Reference For a detailed explanation of the regular expressions, see Appendix C.

Note that if you specify more than one <Directory> container for the same directory space, the <Directory> container with the narrowest scope is applied first. For example:

```
<Directory /www>
AllowOverride None
</Directory>

<Directory ~ "/www/mycompany/public/htdocs/*">
AllowOverride FileInfo
</Directory>
```

According to this, when a request for /www/mycompany/public/htdocs/somefile.cvs arrives, Apache disables the per-directory access control file (.htaccess) for /www and then enables it for /www/mycompany/public/htdocs. It also accepts any FileInfo directive such as DefaultType from within the /www/mycompany/public/htdocs/.htaccess file.

<DirectoryMatch>

```
Syntax: <DirectoryMatch regex> ... </DirectoryMatch>
Context: server config, virtual host
Compatibility: only in Apache 1.3 and later
```

This is exactly the same as the <Directory> container, except that it takes a regular expression as the argument and does not require the ~ (tilde) character. <DirectoryMatch> and </DirectoryMatch> are used to enclose a group of directives that apply only to the named directory and its subdirectories. For example:

```
<DirectoryMatch "^/www/mycompany/pubic/htdocs/[A-Z]{8}/*">
```

would match all subdirectories of /www/mycompany/public/htdocs that have exactly eight uppercase letters as a name; therefore, /www/mycompany/public/htdocs/AAAABBBB/ would match the preceding regular expression. For more details on regular expressions, see Appendix C.

<Files>

```
Syntax: <Files filename> ... </Files>
Context: server config, virtual host, .htaccess
Compatibility: only available in Apache 1.2 and above.
```

To control access by filename, you need to use this directive. <Files> sections are processed in the order in which they appear in the configuration file, after the <Directory> sections and .htaccess files are read, but before the <Location> sections are read. The filename argument should include a filename, or a wild-card string, where ? matches any single character, and * matches any sequence of characters except the / character. Using the ~ (tilde) character, you can enable extended regular expression checking on the argument. For example:

```
<Files ~ "\.(zip|tar|tgz|arj|zoo)$">
```

would match any file with the .zip, .tar, .tgz, .arj, and .zoo extensions. Unlike <Directory> and <Location> sections, <Files> sections can be used inside .htaccess files. When using these from within an .htaccess file, you don't need to append the path name, because an .htaccess file only applies to the directory where it is found.

<FilesMatch>

```
Syntax: <FilesMatch regex> ... </Files>
Context: server config, virtual host, .htaccess
Compatibility: only available in Apache 1.3 and above.
```

This is exactly the same as the <Files> directive, except that it takes a regular expression as its argument. For example:

```
<FilesMatch "\.( zip|tar|tgz|arj|zoo)$">
```

would match any file with the .zip, .tar, .tgz, .arj, and .zoo extensions. Notice that you do not need the ~ (tilde) character in this directive to use a regular expression.

<Location>

```
Syntax: <Location URL> ... </Location>
Context: server config, virtual host
```

This directive provides access control by URL. <Location> containers are processed in the order in which they appear in the configuration file, after the <Directory> containers and .htaccess files are read.

The URL argument does not need the http://servername. It can use wildcard characters such as ? (matches any single character) or * (matches any sequence of characters except for the / character). You can also use an extended regular expression using the ~ character before the expression. For example:

```
<Location ~ "/(my|your)/file">
```

would match URLs such as /my/file or your/file.

<LocationMatch>

```
Syntax: <LocationMatch regex> ... </LocationMatch>
Context: server config, virtual host

Compatibility: Location is only available in Apache 1.3 and
later
```

This directive is identical to the <Location> directive except that its argument (URL) is a regular expression, and it does not require a ~ (tilde) before the expression. For example:

```
<LocationMatch "/(my|your)/file">
```

would match URLs such as /my/file or your/file.

Virtual Host Specific Directives

These directives are used for creating virtual hosts. By default, Apache services only the Web site host specified by the ServerName directive. It is possible, however, to make Apache serve other Web sites using a virtual host container directive. Note that many directives I discussed in the General Configuration Directives section are also applicable to virtual hosts.

<VirtualHost>

```
Syntax: <VirtualHost addr[:port] ...> ... </VirtualHost>
Context: server config
Compatibility: multiple address support only available in
Apache 1.2 and later.
```

This container directive specifies a virtual host configuration. All the enclosed directives found within the <VirtualHost> and the closing </VirtualHost> apply only to the named virtual host. Any directive that is allowed in a virtual host context may be used. When the server receives a request for a document on a particular virtual host, it uses the configuration directives enclosed in the <VirtualHost>.

To specify which IP address or IP name is to be used for a particular virtual host, you can use any of the following:

✦ An IP address. Example: <VirtualHost 11.22.33.44> ... </VirtualHost>

✦ An IP address with a port number. Example: <VirtualHost 11.22.33.44:8080> ... </VirtualHost>

✦ Multiple IP addresses. Example: <VirtualHost 11.22.33.1 11.22.33.2> ... </VirtualHost>

✦ Multiple IP addresses with port numbers. Example: <VirtualHost 11.22.33.1:8000 11.22.33.2:10000> ... </VirtualHost>

You can replace IP addresses with IP names, but this is not recommended; if the DNS lookup necessary to determine the address fails for some reason, the server may get confused and not service the virtual site at all.

The special name _default_ can be specified, in which case this virtual host will match any IP address that is not explicitly listed in another virtual host. In the absence of any _default_ virtual host, the primary server config, which consists of all the definitions outside any VirtualHost section, is used when no match occurs.

If a port is unspecified, then it defaults to the same port as the most recent Port directive of the primary server. You may also specify :* to match all ports on that address.

NameVirtualHost

```
Syntax: NameVirtualHost addr[:port]
Context: server config
Compatibility: only available in Apache 1.3 and later
```

If you plan on using name-based virtual hosts, you need to use this directive. Although addr can be the host name, I recommend that you always use an IP address.

For example, for a virtual host named www.mycompany.com that uses the IP address 11.22.33.44, the directive and virtual host definition will be:

```
NameVirtualHost 11.22.33.44
<VirtualHost 11.22.33.44>
ServerName www.mycompany.com
</VirtualHost>
```

If you have multiple name-based hosts on multiple addresses, repeat the directive for each address. For example:

```
NameVirtualHost 11.22.33.44

# First virtual host that corresponds to the above directive
<VirtualHost 11.22.33.44>
ServerName www.mycompany.com
</VirtualHost>

# Second virtual host that corresponds to the above directive
<VirtualHost 11.22.33.44>
ServerName www.friendscompany.com
</VirtualHost>

#  Another NameVirtualHost directive for a new set of name-
based virtual hosts that
#  use a different IP.
NameVirtualHost 11.22.33.55>

<VirtualHost 11.22.33.55>
ServerName www.myclient.com
</VirtualHost>
<VirtualHost 11.22.33.55>
ServerName www.herclient.com
</VirtualHost>
```

Here, the first NameVirtualHost directive is used for the www.mycompany.com and www.friendscomany.com virtual hosts. The second one is used for the www.myclient.com and the www.herclient.com virtual hosts. Optionally, you can specify a port number on which the name-based virtual hosts should be used. For example:

```
NameVirtualHost 11.22.33.44:8080
```

ServerAlias

```
Syntax: ServerAlias host1 host2 ...
Context: virtual host
Compatibility: only available in Apache 1.1 and later.
```

When you have a name-based virtual host with multiple IP names (CNAME records in the DNS database), you can use a single virtual host definition to service all of them. For example:

```
NameVirtualHost 11.22.33.55>

<VirtualHost 11.22.33.55>
ServerName www.myclient.com
ServerAlias www.sac-state.edu  www.csu.sacramento.edu
</VirtualHost>
```

Here, www.sac-state.edu and www.csu.sacramento.edu are aliases for the www.csus.edu virtual host. You can also use wildcard characters such as * in defining aliases.

ServerPath

```
Syntax: ServerPath pathname
Context: virtual host
Compatibility: only available in Apache 1.1 and later.
```

This directive sets the legacy URL path name for a host, for use with name-based virtual hosts. Typically, this is used to support browsers that are not HTTP/1.1-compliant.

See Chapter 6 for details about supporting non-HTTP/1.1 browsers.

Logging Directives

Logging server transactions is a must for any system running Apache. Server logs provide you with valuable information, such as who accesses your Web site(s), which pages are accessed, and which errors are generated by the server.

ErrorLog

```
Syntax: ErrorLog filename
Default: ErrorLog logs/error_log
Context: server config, virtual host
```

This directive specifies the log filename used to log error messages that the server produces. If the filename does not begin with a slash (/), then it is assumed to be relative to the ServerRoot.

If you need to disable error logging, you can use the following:

```
ErrorLog /dev/null
```

It is very important that the permission settings for your server log directory indicate that only the Apache user (specified by the User directive) is allowed read/write access. Allowing anyone else to write in this directory could potentially create security holes.

ScoreBoardFile

```
Syntax: ScoreBoardFile filename
Default: ScoreBoardFile logs/apache_status
Context: server config
```

This directive sets the path to the file used for storing internal process data. If the filename does not begin with a slash (/), then it is assumed to be relative to the ServerRoot.

This file is used by the primary server process to communicate with the child processes. If you want to find out if your system requires this file, just run the Apache server and see if a file gets created in the specified location. If your system architecture requires the file, then you must ensure that this file is not used at the same time by more than one invocation of Apache. Also, make sure that no other user has read or write access to this file, or even to the directory in which it is kept.

Because the processes have to perform disk I/O to communicate, this could potentially cause a performance bottleneck; therefore, you should create a RAM disk for this file, if possible. Consult your operating system manuals for details.

PidFile

```
Syntax: PidFile filename
Default: PidFile logs/httpd.pid
Context: server config
```

Using this directive, you can tell Apache to write the primary server (that is, the daemon process) process ID (PID) in a file. If the filename does not begin with a slash (/), then it is assumed to be relative to the ServerRoot. The PidFile is used only in standalone mode.

Note that its primary use is to make it convenient for the Apache administrator to find the primary Apache PID, which is needed to send signals to the server. For example, if the PID file is kept in the /usr/local/httpd/logs directory, and its name is httpd.pid, an administrator can force Apache server to reread its configuration by sending a SIGHUP signal from the shell prompt (as root) as follows:

```
kill -HUP `cat /usr/local/httpd/logs/httpd.pid`
```

The same command makes Apache reopen the ErrorLog and TransferLog,

As with any other log files, make sure the PID file is not writeable or even readable by anyone other than the server process. For better security, you should make the log directory read/write-able only by the Apache server user.

LockFile

```
Syntax: LockFile filename
Default: LockFile logs/accept.lock
Context: server config
```

If Apache is compiled with the USE_FCNTL_SERIALIZED_ACCEPT or USE_FLOCK_SERIALIZED_ACCEPT options, a lock file is used. You can use this directive to set the path to the filename of the lock file. Make sure that only the Apache server has read and write access to the file.

Storing the lock file on a Network File System (NFS) mounted partition is not be good idea because NFS is known to be problematic when it comes to file locking and security.

Authentication and Security Directives

The authentication and security directives discussed below enable you to define access policies for your server.

AllowOverride

```
Syntax: AllowOverride override override ...
Default: AllowOverride All
Context: directory
```

This directive tells the server which directives declared in an .htaccess file (as specified by AccessFileName) can override earlier directives found in configuration files.

When Override is set to None, the server does not read the file specified by AccessFileName (default .htaccess). This could speed up the response time of the server, because the server does not have to look for an AccessFileName specified file for each request (see the AccessFileName section for details).

If you do want to allow AccessFileName-based control, however, you can specify one or more of the options. The override options are:

✦ AuthConfig — Allows use of the authorization directives (such as AuthDBMGroupFile, AuthDBMUserFile, AuthGroupFile, AuthName, AuthType, AuthUserFile, and require)

✦ FileInfo—Allows use of the directives controlling document types (such as AddEncoding, AddLanguage, AddType, DefaultType, ErrorDocument, and LanguagePriority)

✦ Indexes—Allows use of the directives controlling directory indexing (such as AddDescription, AddIcon, AddIconByEncoding, AddIconByType, DefaultIcon, DirectoryIndex, FancyIndexing, HeaderName, IndexIgnore, IndexOptions, and ReadmeName)

✦ Limit—Allows use of the directives controlling host access (allow, deny, and order)

✦ Options—Allows use of the directives controlling specific directory features (Options and XBitHack)

AuthName

```
Syntax: AuthName label
Context: directory, .htaccess
Override: AuthConfig
```

This directive sets a label for a resource (such as a directory) that requires authentication. The label is usually displayed by a Web browser in a pop-up dialog window when prompting for a user name and password to access the requested (controlled) resource. There is no default label. The primary purpose of this label is to inform users on the client side about what resource they are trying to access. For example:

```
AuthName Secured Game Zone
```

informs users that they are requesting to enter the Secured Game Zone area of a site.

Note that in order for this directive to work, it must be accompanied by AuthType, require directives, and directives such as AuthUserFile, and AuthGroupFile.

AuthType

```
Syntax: AuthType type
Context: directory, .htaccess
Override: AuthConfig
```

This directive selects the user authentication type for a directory. Currently, only basic HTTP authentication type is implemented in Apache. This type of authentication should not be used for serious needs; the password and user name are transmitted in clear (plain) text. The password and user name is retransmitted for each subsequent request that maps in the same restricted directory or its subdirectories.

This directive must be accompanied by AuthName, and requires other directives such as AuthUserFile, and AuthGroupFile to work.

require

```
Syntax: require entity-name entity entity...
Context: directory, .htaccess
Override: AuthConfig
```

Using this directive, Apache determines which users or group can access a restricted directory. There are three types of entity-names available:

- ✦ user
- ✦ group
- ✦ valid-user

For example, this line:

```
require user joe jenny
```

tells Apache to allow only joe or jenny to enter the area after successful authentication. Only the named users can access the directory. An example of a group-based access requirement would be as follows:

```
require group my-group your-group his-group her-group
```

Only users in the named groups can access the directory.

```
require valid-user
```

With the preceding line, all valid users can access the directory.

If the require directive appears in a <Limit> section, then it restricts access to the named methods; otherwise it restricts access for all methods. For example:

```
AuthType Basic
AuthName Game Zone Drop Box
AuthUserFile /www/netgames/users
AuthGroupFile /web/ntgames/groups
<Limit GET>
require group coders
</Limit>
```

If the preceding configuration is found in an .htaccess file in a directory, only a group called coders is allowed access to the directory to retrieve files via the HTTP GET method. In order to work correctly, the require directive must be accompanied by AuthName and AuthType directives, and directives such as AuthUserFile and AuthGroupFile.

See Chapter 10 for details on authentication.

Satisfy

```
Syntax: Satisfy 'any' | 'all'
Default: Satisfy all
Context: directory, .htaccess
Compatibility: only available in Apache 1.2 and later
```

If you have created a basic HTTP authentication configuration where both allow and require directives are used, you can use this directive to tell Apache what will satisfy the authentication requirements. The value of the Satisfy directive can be either all or any. If the value is all, then the authentication succeeds only if both allow *and* require succeed. If the value is any, then the authentication succeeds if either allow *or* require succeeds.

This directive is useful only if access to a particular area is being restricted by both the user name/password and the client host address. In this case, the default behavior (all) requires that the client pass the address access restriction and enter a valid user name and password. With the any option, the client is granted access if he either passes the host restriction or enters a valid user name and password. This directive can be used to restrict an area using passwords, and at the same time, all clients from a particular IP address pool (that is, a set of IP addresses) are let in without being required to enter passwords.

IdentityCheck

```
Syntax: IdentityCheck boolean
Default: IdentityCheck off
Context: server config, virtual host, directory, .htaccess
```

This directive tells Apache to log remote user names by interacting with the remote user's identd (identification daemon) process, or something similar and RFC1413-compliant. This is rarely a useful directive because it will not work for all systems. Most systems do not run identd processes to provide user identifications to remote servers.

If you decide to use this directive in your configuration, be aware that the information you log is not to be trusted in any way except for usage tracking. This directive can also cause major performance problems because the server has to perform checking for each request. Also, when a remote user is either not providing an identd service or is behind a firewall or proxy, the checking process has to time out.

HostNameLookups

```
Syntax: HostNameLookups on | off | double
Default: HostNameLookups off
Context: server config, virtual host, directory, .htaccess
Compatibility: double available only in Apache 1.3 and above.
```

This directive instructs Apache to enable or disable a DNS lookup for each request. When enabled, Apache stores the host name of the client in the REMOTE_HOST environment variable of each CGI and SSI process it runs.

The on and off values should be obvious. The double refers to doing a double-reverse DNS lookup — that is, after a reverse lookup is performed, a forward lookup is then performed on that result. At least one of the IP addresses in the forward lookup must match the original address. However, the CGI and SSI processes do not get the results from the double DNS lookups.

No matter what you set this directive to, when mod_access (a module I discuss in Chapter 13) is used for controlling access by host name, a double reverse lookup is performed.

I recommend that you keep the default setting for this directive. This will rid the Internet of a lot of unnecessary DNS traffic. If you want to turn it on just so your log files contain IP names instead of IP addresses, you may want to consider another option, such as running the logresolve utility to resolve IP addresses to IP names. See Chapter 11 for more details.

<Limit>

```
Syntax: <Limit method method ... > ... </Limit>
Context: any
```

This container is used to enclose a group of access control directives, which will then apply only to the specified HTTP methods. The method names listed can be one or more of the following: GET, POST, PUT, DELETE, CONNECT, and OPTIONS. If GET is used, it will also restrict HEAD requests. If you wish to limit all methods, do not include any method in the <Limit> directive at all.

Note that this container can not be nested, and a <Directory> container can not appear within it either.

Summary

In this chapter, you learned about the core directives and the contexts in which they apply. These core directives provide a great deal of functionality and flexibility in managing the highly configurable Apache Web server.

In the next chapter, I discuss the standard Apache modules.

✦ ✦ ✦

Apache Modules

✦ ✦ ✦ ✦

In This Chapter

Introduction to Apache modules

How to use various Apache modules

✦ ✦ ✦ ✦

In the previous chapter, you learned about core Apache directives. Apache offers many more directives, which are available from the modules distributed in the standard source distribution. These modules offer a great deal of functionality via the use of directives.

In this chapter, I discuss these modules and their directives. For easy reading, the modules are listed in alphabetical order.

mod_access

This module is built into the default for Apache. It provides host-based access control directives, which are discussed in Chapter 10.

See the "Host-based Access Control" section in Chapter 10 for details on mod_access directives.

mod_actions

This module is compiled by default. It enables you to run a CGI script based on MIME-type or the HTTP request method. It offers the following directives.

Action

```
Syntax: Action MIME-type cgi-script
Context: server config, virtual host,
directory, per-directory configuration
(.htaccess)
Override: FileInfo
Status: Base
```

This directive enables you to associate an action for a specific MIME-type. The action is usually a CGI script that processes the file being requested. For example:

```
Action text/html /cgi-bin/somescript.pl
```

This makes Apache run the specified script whenever an HTML file is requested. The script receives the URL and file path of the requested document via the standard CGI PATH_INFO and PATH_TRANSLATED environment variables. This can be useful in developing filter scripts. This section discusses one such filter script.

When a text file (.txt) is requested via the Web, it appears on the Web browser in a less-than-desirable format, because the line breaks are not translated by Web browsers in any manner. Usually, most text files appear as a large paragraph. Using the Action directive, you can develop a better solution. To make this example a bit more interesting, let's also say that you want to develop a solution that not only displays the text files better on the Web browser, but also inserts a copyright message at the end of each text file.

To accomplish this, you need to do two things. First, add the following directive in an Apache configuration file (such as srm.conf.):

```
Action plain/text /cgi-bin/textfilter.pl
```

Then, develop the Perl script, textfilter, that will display the text file the way you wish. Listing 5-1 shows one such script.

Listing 5-1: textfilter.pl

```
#!/usr/local/bin/perl
#
# Script: textfilter.pl
#
# Purpose: this filter script converts plain text files
#          into an HTML document but keeps the text layout
#          as-is.
#
# $Author$
# $Revision$
# $Id$
# $Status
#

# The copyright message file will be always stored on
# the server's document root
# directory and is called copyright.html.
#
my $copyright_file = $ENV{DOCUMENT_ROOT} . "/copyright.html";

# Get the requested document's path
my $path_translated = $ENV{PATH_TRANSLATED};

# Other variables needed for storing data
my $line;
my @text;
```

```
my @html;

# Store the path info and the file name of requested doc in an
array
@filename = split(/\//,$path_translated);

# Since HTML tags will be used to display the text file,
# lets print the text/html content header.
print "Content-type: text/html\n\n";

# Read the document requested and store the data
# in @text array variable
@text = &readFile($path_translated);

# Now print the following HTML document tags
# these tags will be sent before the actual document content
#
print <<HEAD;
<HTML>
<HEAD>
<TITLE>$filename[-1] </TITLE>
</HEAD>
<BODY BGCOLOR="white">

<BLOCKQUOTE>

<PRE>

<FONT FACE="Arial">

HEAD

# Now print each line stored in the @text array
# (i.e. the content of the document requested)
#
foreach $line (@text){ print $line; }

# Now read the copyright file and store the content
# in the @html array variable
#
@html = &readFile($copyright_file);

# Print each line stored in the @html array (i.e.
# the content of the copyright message file)
#
foreach $line (@html){ print $line; }

# Exit the filter
exit 0;
```

(continued)

Listing 5-1 *(continued)*

```
sub readFile{
#
# Subroutine: readFile
# Purpose: reads a file if it exists or else prints
# an error messages and exists script
#

# Get the name of the passed file name and store
# it in variable $file
 my $file = shift;

# Local buffer variable
 my @buffer;

# If the file exists then open it and read all the
# lines into the @buffer array variable
 if(-e $file){

    open(FP,$file) || die "Can not open $file.";

    while(<FP>){
      push(@buffer,$_);
      }

    close(FP);
    }

   else{
      push(@buffer,"$file is missing.");
      }

# Return the content of the buffer.
 return (@buffer);
 }
```

This script reads the requested text file and prints out the content inside a few HTML tags that enable the content to be displayed as is. This trick is done using the HTML tag <PRE>. After the content is printed, a copyright message file content is inserted at the end of the output. This enables a copyright message to be printed with each requested text file. Figure 5-1 shows an example output where a text file is being displayed on the Web browser.

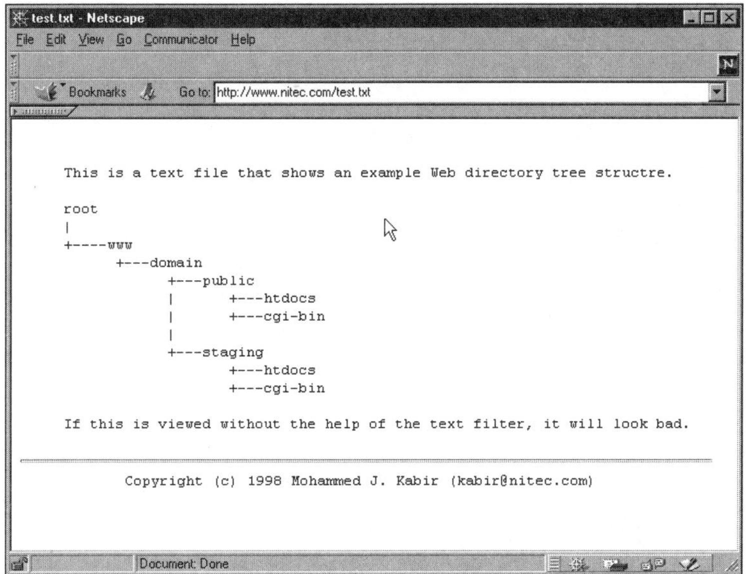

Figure 5-1: Output of textfilter.pl

As you can see, the requested filename appears as the title. The document is block quoted, and a custom copyright message is printed. The copyright message file is stored in the document root directory. The one used in this example is:

```
<BLOCKQUOTE>
<CENTER>
<HR>
Copyright ÷ 1998 Mohammed J. Kabir () ({Hyperlink
Mail to:kabir@nitec.com})
</CENTER>
</BODY>
</HTML>
```

Script

```
Syntax: Script method cgi-script
Context: server config, virtual host, directory
```

This directive is like the Action directive, but instead of associating an action with a MIME-type, it associates the action with an HTTP request such as GET, POST, PUT, or DELETE. The CGI script receives the URL and file path of the requested document using the standard CGI PATH_INFO and PATH_TRANSLATED environment variables. This directive defines default action. In other words, if you have defined the following:

```
Script POST /cgi-bin/deafult_post.pl
```

in a Apache configuration file (such as srm.conf), then whenever a request is made via the HTTP POST method, it will be processed as usual unless the default action specified by the directive needs to be used. For example, the following HTML form does not specify a CGI script as its action:

```
<FORM METHOD="POST">
Enter Name: <INPUT TYPE=TEXT NAME="name" SIZE=25>
<INPUT TYPE=SUBMIT VALUE="Click Here">
</FORM>
```

If a name is submitted by a user via this form, there is no specified CGI script to process the information, in which case the default POST action /cgi-bin/default_post.pl script is run. However, if the <FORM ...> tag is changed to:

```
<FORM ACTION="/cgi-bin/form_processor.pl" METHOD="POST">
```

then whenever the form is submitted, the /cgi-bin/form_processor.pl script will be called as usual. What you do in the default action script is up to you. In an Internet service provider setup, I recommend making the default script print out meaningful messages, so the HTML form developer user can get a clue about what he or she is not doing right.

In case of the GET request, the default action is used only if the request accompanies query data. For example, www.yoursite.com/somefile.html will be processed as usual, but if a request such as www.yoursite.com/somefile.html?some=data is received, then the default action for GET will be run.

mod_alias

This module is compiled into the default for Apache. It provides various directives that can be used to map one part of the server's file system to another, or even perform URL redirection services.

Alias

```
Syntax: Alias URL-path path
Context: server config, virtual host
```

This directive enables you to map a path to anywhere in your system's file system. For example:

```
Alias /data  /web/data
```

This maps /data to /web/data; therefore, when a request such as www.yoursite.com/data/datafile.cvs is received, the file called /web/data/datafile.cvs is returned. The aliased path does not have to reside inside your document root tree, so be careful when you create aliases — you might accidentally reveal some part of your file system to the entire world.

Note that if you use a trailing / (slash) in defining an alias, the requests that are able to access the aliased directory also need to contain a trailing /. For example:

```
Alias /data/  /web/data
```

This is only used to service www.yoursite.com/data/, and not www.yoursite.com/data. In the latter case, Apache looks for a data directory under the document tree, and not the /web/data directory.

AliasMatch

```
Syntax: AliasMatch regex path
Context: server config, virtual host
```

This is similar to the Alias directive, except it can make use of regular expressions. For example:

```
AliasMatch ^/data(.*)  /web/data$1
```

This matches www.yoursite.com/data/index.html to the /web/data/index.html file.

Redirect

```
Syntax: Redirect [status] old-URL new-URL
Context: server config, virtual host, directory, per-directory
configuration (.htaccess)
```

This directive redirects a URL request to another URL. For example:

```
Redirect /data  www.your-new-site.com/data
```

This redirects all URL requests containing the /data path to the new URL. Therefore, requests for www.yoursite.com/data/somefile.txt are redirected to www.your-new-site.com/data/somefile.txt instead.

The Redirect directive has a higher precedence over the Alias and ScriptAlias directives. By default, the status code sent to the client is Temp (HTTP status code 302). If you want to specify a different status code, use the following:

- ✦ Permanent — Tells the client that the redirect is permanent. The HTTP status code 301 is returned.
- ✦ Temp — Returns a temporary redirect status (302). This is the default.
- ✦ See other — Returns a See Other status (303), indicating that the resource has been replaced.

✦ Gone — Returns a Gone status (410) indicating that the resource has been permanently removed. When this status is used, the URL argument should be omitted.

You can provide valid HTTP status codes in numeric format as well. If the status you provide is between 300 and 399, the new-URL must be present; otherwise, it must be omitted. You may wonder about the use of different status codes. In the future, clients may be smart enough to recognize the status codes in a more meaningful manner. For example, if a proxy server receives a permanent redirect status code, it can store this information in a cache so it can directly access the new resource in a later request.

RedirectMatch

```
Syntax: RedirectMatch [status] regex URL
Context: server config, virtual host
```

This directive is similar to the Redirect directive, but it accepts regular expressions instead of the simple old-URL. For example:

```
RedirectMatch (.*)\.htm$ www.yourserver.com$1.html
```

This redirects all requests that end with .htm to a .html version of the same request. For example, the following request:

```
www.yoursite.com/some/old/dos/files/index.htm
```

is redirected to:

```
www.yoursite.com/some/old/dos/files/index.html
```

RedirectTemp

```
Syntax: RedirectTemp old-URL new-URL
Context: server config, virtual host, directory, per-directory
configuration (.htaccess)
```

This is similar to the Redirect directive. It lets the client know that the redirect is only temporary. Note that the Redirect directive also produces a temporary status by default.

RedirectPermanent

```
Syntax: RedirectPermanent old-URL new-URL
Context: server config, virtual host, directory, per-directory
configuration (.htaccess)
```

This is similar to the Redirect directive. It lets the client know that the redirect is permanent. Note that the Redirect directive produces a temporary status by default, but you can use the status code 301 or the keyword permanent, as the status does the same as this directive.

ScriptAlias

```
Syntax: ScriptAlias URL-path  path
Context: server config, virtual host
```

This directive creates an alias (URL-path) for path. Additionally, any filename supplied in the request is treated as a CGI script, and the server attempts to run the script. For example:

```
ScriptAlias /cgi-bin/ /www/nitec/public/cgi-bin/
```

This can be used to process a request such as www.nitec.com/cgi-bin/somescript.pl. The server tries to run somescript.pl if proper permission is verified. Note that the ScriptAlias directory is not browsable.

ScriptAliasMatch

```
Syntax: ScriptAliasMatch regex directory-filename
Context: server config, virtual host
Status: Base
```

This directive is equivalent to the ScriptAlias directive except it uses regular expression. For example:

```
ScriptAliasMatch ^/cgi-bin(.*)     /www/nitec/public/cgi-bin$1
```

will do exactly the same as:

```
ScriptAliasMatch  /cgi-bin/  /www/nitec/public/cgi-bin/
```

mod_asis

This module is compiled into the default for Apache. It enables you to send a document as is — in other words, the document is sent to the client without HTTP headers. This can be useful in redirecting clients without the help of any scripting. To send a file as is, you need to make sure that one of your Apache configuration files (for example, srm.conf) contains an entry such as:

```
AddType httpd/send-as-is asis
```

This assigns the MIME-type httpd/send-as-is to file extension .asis. If you create a file called foobar.asis and a client requests it, the file will be sent to the client without any HTTP header. It will be your job to include appropriate headers in the file. For example, if you want to provide a redirect mechanism via the .asis files, you can create files with headers such as:

```
Status: 301 Text Message
Location: new-URL
Content-type: text/html
```

For example, Listing 5-2 shows a file called redirect.asis, which redirects the clients to a new location.

Listing 5-2: redirect.asis

```
Status: 301 We have moved.
Location: http://www.our-new-site/
Content-type: text/html

<H1>Notice to Visitors</H1>
Please update your bookmark to point to <A HREF=" www.our-new-site/ "> www.our-new-site/ </A><BR>
<BR>
Thanks.
```

When a client requests this file, the 301 status message tells the client to use the location information to redirect the request. You do not have to add the Date: and Server: headers, because the server automatically adds them. However, the server does not provide a Last-Modified header.

mod_auth

See Chapter 10.

mod_auth_anon

See Chapter 10.

mod_auth_db

See Chapter 10.

mod_auth_dbm

See Chapter 10.

auth_external

See Chapter 10.

mod_autoindex

This module is compiled into the default for Apache. When a request for a directory is received by Apache it looks for one or more directory index files specified by the DirectoryIndex directive. Typically, this file is index.html or index.htm. In the absence of such an index file, however, Apache can generate a dynamic directory listing. This module enables you to control how Apache creates the dynamic directory listing.

Apache generates two types of dynamic directory indices. Figure 5-2 shows an example of a dynamic directory index for www.nitec.com/ski directory.

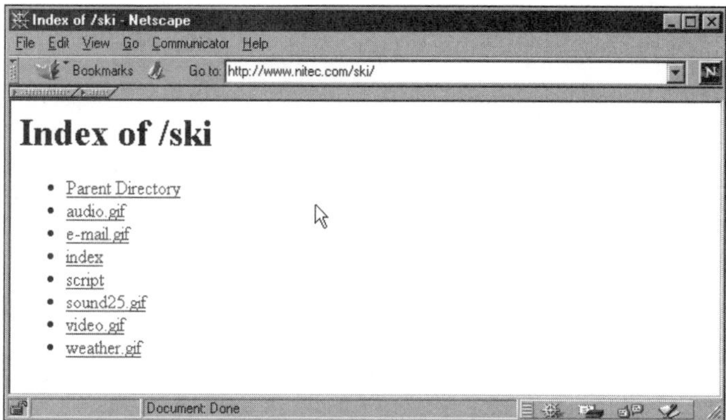

Figure 5-2: A simple directory index generated by Apache

Notice that this is a very simple index. Now take a look at Figure 5-3, which shows a very nice index of the same directory. Fancy indexing is available through either the FancyIndexing or IndexOptions directives found in this module.

This fancy index and many other indexing options are available from this module. The directives for mod_authoindex are listed as follows.

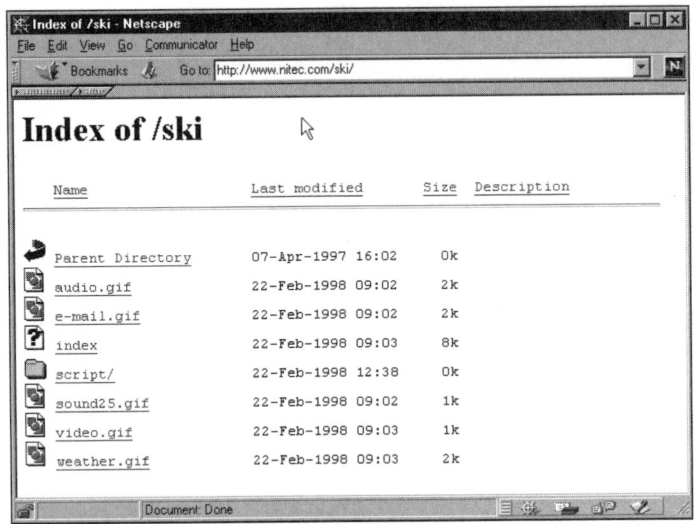

Figure 5-3: A fancy directory index generated by Apache

AddAlt

```
Syntax: AddAlt "text" file file...
Context: server config, virtual host, directory, per-directory
configuration (.htaccess)
Override: Indexes
```

When FancyIndexing is on, this directive sets the specified text as an alternative to the icon that is displayed for one or more files or file extensions specified as arguments. This is done for nongraphical browsers such as Lynx. For example:

```
AddAlt "Pictures" gif jpeg jpg bmp
```

This enables Apache to display the alternative text “Pictures” in place of the icon for each type of graphics file specified here. For graphical browsers such as Netscape Navigator or Internet Explorer, the alternative text is displayed as help text under popular Windows platforms. In such systems, users can get a tip or help about the file when they move their mouse cursor on top of the icon representing one of the file types.

AddAltByEncoding

```
Syntax: AddAltByEncoding "text" MIME-encoding MIME-encoding
Context: server config, virtual host, directory, per-directory
configuration (.htaccess)
Override: Indexes
```

If you do not like to assign alternative text to filenames or file extensions via the AddAlt directive, you can use this directive to assign such text for one or more MIME-encodings. Like AddAlt, this directive is also only usable when FancyIndexing is turned on. For example:

```
AddAltByEncoding "Compressed File" x-compress
```

AddAltByType

```
Syntax: AddAltByType "text" MIME-type MIME-type...
Context: server config, virtual host, directory, per-directory
configuration (.htaccess)
Override: Indexes
```

Like the AddAltByEncoding directive, this directive sets alternative text for a file, instead of an icon for FancyIndexing. However, it uses MIME-type instead of MIME-encoding. For example:

```
AddAltByType "HTML FILE" text/html
```

This shows the “HTML FILE” text in place of the icon for nongraphical browsers. In the case of graphical browsers, this text may appear as a tip or help.

AddDescription

```
Syntax: AddDescription "text" file file...
Context: server config, virtual host, directory, per-directory
configuration (.htaccess)
Override: Indexes
```

This directive sets the description text for a file, partial, or wild-card filename when FancyIndexing is turned on. For example:

```
AddDescription "Graphics File" *.gif *.jpeg *.jpg *.bmp
```

This displays the description for all GIF, JPEG, JPG, and BMP files.

AddIcon

```
Syntax: AddIcon icon name name ...
Context: server config, virtual host, directory, per-directory
configuration (.htaccess)
Override: Indexes
```

This directive enables you to assign icons to files and directory names that are displayed for FancyIndexing. For example:

```
AddIcon /icons/picture.gif .gif .jpg .bmp
```

This tells Apache to show /icons/picture.gif next to files that have extensions such as .gif, .jpg, and .bmp. If you also want to provide alternative text for the file extension listed, you can use a format such as:

```
AddIcon (IMG, /icons/picture.gif) .gif .jpg .bmp
```

Here, IMG is the alternative text displayed for nongraphical browsers. If you want to display an icon for a directory, you can use the directive as follows:

```
AddIcon /path/to/your/directory/icon      ^^DIRECTORY^^
```

Similarly, if you want to display an icon for each blank line displayed by the fancy indexing scheme, you can use:

```
AddIcon /path/to/your/blank/line/icon     ^^BLANKICON^^
```

AddIconByEncoding

```
Syntax: AddIconByEncoding icon mime-encoding mime-encoding ...
Context: server config, virtual host, directory, per-directory
configuration (.htaccess)
Override: Indexes
```

This directive lets you assign icons to MIME-encodings. For example:

```
AddIconByEncoding  /icons/zip.gif   x-gzip
```

AddIconByType

```
Syntax: AddIconByType icon MIME-type MIME-type ...
Context: server config, virtual host, directory, per-directory
configuration (.htaccess)
Override: Indexes
```

This directive also enables you to assign icons to MIME-types. For example:

```
AddIconByType (HTML,/icons/html.gif) text/html
```

DefaultIcon

```
Syntax: DefaultIcon url
Context: server config, virtual host, directory, per-directory
configuration (.htaccess)
Override: Indexes
```

When no AddIcon, AddIconByEncoding, or AddIconByType is matched for a file, a default icon can be displayed. This directive enables you to set that icon. For example:

```
DefaultIcon /icon/idontknow.gif
```

This shows idontknow.gif whenever a file's icon association is unknown.

FancyIndexing

```
Syntax: FancyIndexing on | off
Context: server config, virtual host, directory, per-directory
configuration (.htaccess)
Override: Indexes
```

This directive lets you enable and disable fancy indexing of directories. You can achieve the same with the IndexOptions directive as well.

HeaderName

```
Syntax: HeaderName filename
Context: server config, virtual host, directory, per-directory
configuration (.htaccess)
Override: Indexes
```

If you use FancyIndexing, you can insert a file's content at the top of the index listing. This directive lets you specify the name of the file for such an insertion. For example:

```
HeaderName welcome
```

This makes Apache look for a file called welcome or welcome.html in the directory of the listing. If such a file is found, the content is inserted before the actual listing.

IndexIgnore

```
Syntax: IndexIgnore file file ...
Context: server config, virtual host, directory, per-directory
configuration (.htaccess)
Override: Indexes
```

If you need some files or file extensions to be invisible in the directory listing, you can use this directive to accomplish this. For example:

```
IndexIgnore welcome welcome.html per-directory configuration
(.htaccess)
```

This ensures that Apache does not list welcome, welcome.html, or per-directory configuration (.htaccess) files in directory listings. The . (dot) character is automatically in the IndexIgnore list; thus, files that start with this character are not listed. However, I still prefer to add per-directory configuration (.htaccess) in the list just to feel safer.

IndexOptions

```
Syntax: IndexOptions option option ...
Context: server config, virtual host, directory, per-directory
configuration (.htaccess)
Override: Indexes
```

The IndexOptions directive specifies the behavior of the directory indexing. Options are:

FancyIndexing	This turns on fancy indexing of directories. Note that the FancyIndexing and IndexOptions directives will override each other.
IconHeight[=pixels]	This option enables Apache to include the HEIGHT=pixels attribute in the IMG tag of the icon, which makes the loading of the icon faster on most browsers. If you do not specify a pixel count, a standard default is used.
IconsAreLinks	This makes the icons part of the anchor for the filename, for fancy indexing.
IconWidth[=pixels]	This option enables Apache to include the WIDTH=pixels attribute in the IMG tag of the icon, which makes the loading of the icon faster on most browsers. If you do not specify a pixel count, a standard default is used.
ScanHTMLTitles	If you want Apache to read the title (denoted by the <TITLE> and </TITLE> tag pair) of an HTML document for fancy indexing, use this option. If you have already specified a description using the AddDescription directive, however, this option is not used. Note that reading each file's content and searching for title information is a time-consuming task that may slow down the delivery of directory listings. I do not recommend this option.
SuppressColumnSorting	By default, Apache makes clickable column headings for a fancy directory index, which enables users to sort information in that column. This option disables this feature.
SuppressDescription	If you do not want to display file descriptions in the fancy directory listing, use this option.
SuppressHTMLPreamble	If the directory actually contains a file specified by the HeaderName directive, the module usually includes the contents of the file after a standard HTML preamble (<HTML>, <HEAD>,

	and so on). The SuppressHTMLPreamble option disables this behavior.
SuppressLastModified	This suppresses the display of the last modification date in fancy indexing listings.
SuppressSize	This suppresses the file size in fancy indexing listings.

ReadmeName

```
Syntax: ReadmeName filename
Context: server config, virtual host, directory, per-directory
configuration (.htaccess)
Override: Indexes
```

If you want to insert a file at the end of the fancy directory listing, use this directive. For example:

```
ReadmeName readme
```

Apache looks for a file called readme.html or readme to insert at the end of the listing.

mod_cern_meta

This module is not compiled by default. It provides support for metainformation. This information can either be additional HTTP headers such as:

```
Expires: Saturday, 3-Oct-98 12:00:00 GMT
```

or it can be any other information such as:

```
Foo=Bar
```

The meta information is stored in a file and appears along with the HTTP response header.

MetaFiles

```
Syntax: MetaFiles on/off
Default: MetaFiles off
Context: per-directory config (.htaccess)
```

This directive enables or disables metaheader file processing.

MetaDir

```
Syntax: MetaDir directory name
Default: MetaDir .web
Context: per-directory config (.htaccess)
```

This directive specifies the name of the directory that is used to store metaheader files. For example, if you have a directory called /www/mycompany/public/htdocs and you want to store metainformation files for that directory, you need to create a subdirectory called .web if you use the default value for the MetaDir directive. The .web directory is used to store metaheader files.

MetaSuffix

```
Syntax: MetaSuffix suffix
Default: MetaSuffix .meta
Context: per-directory config (.htaccess)
```

This directive specifies the filename extension for metainformation files. For example, if you have an HTML file called mypage.html, you need to create mypage.html.meta (using the default value of this directive) to store your metaheaders. The mypage.html.metafile must reside in the directory specified by the MetaDir directive.

To enable Apache to send out metainformation for a directory called /www/mycompany/public/htdocs, you need to do the following:

1. Set the MetaFiles directive to on in the per-directory configuration file (.htaccess) for /www/mycompany/public/htdocs. You can also set the MetaDir and MetaSuffix directive in this file.
2. Create a sub directory called .web (assuming you are using the default for MetaDir directive)
3. Create a text file with extension .meta (assuming you are using the default value for MetaSuffix directive)
4. Put all the HTTP headers that you want to supply in this file.

For example, to provide metaheaders for a file named /www/mycompany/public/htdocs/mypage.html, you need to create a file called /www/mycompany/public/htdocs/.web/mypage.html.meta.

This file could include lines such as:

```
Expires: Saturday, 3-Oct-98 12:00:00 GMT
Anything=Whatever
```

mod_cgi

See Chapter 8.

mod_digest

See Chapter 10.

mod_dir

This module is compiled in the default for Apache. Using this module, Apache can redirect any request for a directive that does not include a trailing slash character. For example, this module can redirect www.yoursite.com/somedirectory to www.yoursite.com/somedirectory/. It also provides a directive called DirectoryIndex to help with indexing a directory content.

DirectoryIndex

```
Syntax: DirectoryIndex local-URL local-URL...
Default: DirectoryIndex index.html
Context: server config, virtual host, directory, per-directory
configuration (.htaccess)
Override: Indexes
```

This directive specifies the name(s) of files that Apache should look for before creating a dynamic directory index. The files can be anything from an HTML file to a CGI script. The default setting enables Apache to look for the index.html file for any request that ends with a directory name. For example, www.yoursite.com/some/directory/ causes Apache to look for a file called /some/directory/index.html. If the file exists, its content is delivered to the client. In the absence of this file, Apache creates a dynamic directory listing.

You can specify one or more files as the default directory index files. For example:

```
DirectoryIndex index.html index.htm welcome.html welcome.htm
```

This tells Apache to look for all the named files for each directory request. Note that Apache will look for files in the same order (from left to right) as they appear in the preceding configuration. In other words, if Apache finds index.html, it will no longer look for index.htm, welcome.html, or welcome.htm. You can specify a CGI script name as the default index, as well. For example:

```
DirectoryIndex /cgi-bin/show_index.cgi
```

This makes Apache run the /cgi-bin/show_index.cgi script every time Apache gets a directory request.

mod_env

This module is not compiled by default. It enables you to pass environment variables to CGI or SSI scripts. It has the following directives.

PassEnv

```
Syntax: PassEnv variable variable ...
Context: server config, virtual host
```

This directive tells the module to pass one or more environment variables from the server's own environment to the CGI and SSI scripts. For example:

```
PassEnv HOSTTYPE PATH
```

SetEnv

```
Syntax: SetEnv variable value
Context: server config, virtual host
```

This directive sets an environment variable, which is then passed on to CGI/SSI scripts. For example:

```
     SetEnv CAPITAL_CITY      SACRAMENTO
```

UnsetEnv

```
Syntax: UnsetEnv variable variable ...
Context: server config, virtual host
```

This directive removes one environment variable or more from those that are passed to CGI/SSI scripts. For example:

```
UnsetEnv PATH
```

mod_expires

This module is not compiled in Apache by default. It lets you determine how Apache deals with Expires HTTP headers in the server's response to requests. Expires HTTP headers provide you with means for telling the client about the time when the requested resource becomes invalid. This is useful when documents are cached by the client and need to be requested again. Most smart clients will determine the validity of a re-requested document by investigating the cached document's expiration time provided by Expires HTTP headers. This module enables you to control the setting of the Expires HTTP headers.

ExpiresActive

```
Syntax: ExpiresActive on | off
Context: server config, virtual host, directory, per-directory
configuration (.htaccess)
Override: Indexes
```

This directive enables or disables the generation of the Expires header. It does not guarantee that an Expires header will be generated. If the criteria are not met, no header is sent.

ExpiresByType

```
Syntax 1: ExpiresByType MIME-type  M<seconds> | A<seconds>
Syntax 2: ExpiresByType MIME-type "<base time> [plus] <num>
<years|months|weeks|days|hours|minutes|seconds>"
Context: server config, virtual host, directory, per-directory
configuration (.htaccess)
Override: Indexes
```

This directive specifies the value of the Expires HTTP header for documents of a specified MIME-type. The expiration time is specified in seconds. You can define the time in two ways. If you choose to use the M<seconds> format to specify expiration time, then the file's last modification time is used as the base time. In other words, M3600 means that you want the file to expire 1 hour after it was last modified. On the other hand, if you use the A<seconds> format, then client's access time is used as the base time. Following are some examples.

The following expires all plain text files after an hour in the client's cache:

```
ExpiresByType text/plain A3600
```

This expires all GIF files after a week from the last modified time:

```
ExpiresByType image/gif M604800
```

If you want to use the second syntax for specifying expiration times, you need to determine the appropriate value of <base time> using the following options:

- ✦ Access — Time when client accessed the file
- ✦ Now — Current time. This is the same as the access time.
- ✦ Modification — Time when the file was last changed

For example:

```
ExpiresByType text/html "access plus 7 days"
ExpiresByType image/gif "modification plus 3 hours 10 minutes"
```

ExpiresDefault

```
Syntax 1: ExpiresDefault M<seconds> | A<seconds>
Syntax 2: ExpiresDefault "<base time> [plus] <num>
<years|months|weeks|days|hours|minutes|seconds>"
Context: server config, virtual host, directory, per-directory
configuration (.htaccess)
Override: Indexes
```

This directive sets the default expiration time for all documents in the context in which it is specified. For example, if this directive is specified in the virtual host context, it will only apply to the documents accessible via the virtual host. Similarly, you can specify this directive in a per-directory context, which allows all documents in that directory to expire at a specified interval. See ExpiresByType for details on the syntax. Here are some examples:

- `ExpiresDefault M3600`
- `ExpiresDefault "access plus 2 days"`

The first example sets the expiration time to one hour after the last modification time of the documents. The second one sets the expiration time to 2 days after access by the client.

mod_headers

This module is not compiled by default. It enables you to manipulate HTTP response headers, and it offers a single directive called Header.

Header

```
Syntax 1: Header <action> <header> <value>
Context: server config, virtual host, directory, per-directory
configuration (.htaccess)
Override: FileInfo
```

This directive enables you to manipulate the HTTP response header. The allowed actions are:

- Set — Sets a header. If an old header with the same name existed, its value is changed to the new value.
- Add — Adds a header. This can cause multiple headers with the same name when one or more headers with the same name exist.
- Append — Appends the value to an existing header value.
- Unset — Removes a header.

For example:

```
Header add Author "Mohammed J. Kabir"
```

This adds the Author header with the value "Mohammed J. Kabir". The following line removes this header:

```
Header unset Author
```

mod_imap

This module is compiled in Apache by default. It provides imagemap support, which used to be provided by the CGI program called imagemap. You can use the AddHandler directive to specify the imap-file handler (built into this module) for any file extension. For example:

```
AddHandler imap-file map
```

This makes Apache treat all files with the .map extension as image maps, and Apache processes the file using this module. Note that the older format:

```
AddType application/x-httpd-imap map
```

is still supported by this module; however, it is not recommended. The lines in an imagemap file can have any of the following formats:

```
directive value [x,y ...]
directive value "Menu text" [x,y ...]
directive value x,y ... "Menu text"
```

The allowed directives are:

- base — Relative URLs used in map files are considered relative to the value of this directive. Note that the Imapbase directive setting is overridden by this directive when found in a map file. It defaults to http://server_name/. base_uri is synonymous with base.
- default — Specifies the action to take when the coordinates do not fit into any poly, circle, or rect, and no point directives are given. The default value for this directive is nocontent, which tells the client to keep the same page displayed.
- poly — Defines a polygon using at least three points to a maximum of one hundred points. If user-supplied coordinates fall within the polygon, this directive is activated.
- circle — Defines a circle using the center coordinates and a point on the circle. If user-supplied coordinates fall within the circle, this directive is activated.

✦ rect — Defines a rectangle using two opposing corner coordinates. If user-supplied coordinates fall within the rectangle, this directive is activated.

✦ point — Defines a single point coordinate. The point directive closest to the user-supplied coordinate is used when no other directives are satisfied.

The value is an absolute or relative URL, or one of the special values in the following list. The coordinates (x,y) are separated by whitespace characters. The double-quoted text is used as the text of the link if an imagemap menu is generated. Any line with a leading # character is considered a comment and is ignored.

The special imagemap file directive values are:

✦ a URL — A relative or absolute URL. Relative URLs resolve relative to the base.

✦ Map — Same as the URL of the imagemap file itself. Unless ImapMenu is set to none, a menu will be created.

✦ Menu — Same as Map.

✦ Referer — Same as the URL of the referring document. Defaults to http://servername/ if no Referer: header is present.

✦ Nocontent — A status code of 204 is sent to tell the client to keep the same page displayed. This is not valid for base.

✦ Error — A status code of 500 is sent to inform the client about a server error.

The coordinates are written in x,y format, where each coordinate is separated by a whitespace character. The quoted text string is used as the link when a menu is generated. In the absence of such a string, the URL will be the link shown in the following imagemap file example:

```
# Comments goes here
#  Version 1.0.0

base http://www.yoursite.com/some/dir
rect thisfile.html "Customer info" 0,0 100,200
circle http://download.yoursite.com/index.html 295,0 100,22
```

If this imagemap file is called imagemap.map, it can be referenced as follows from another HTML file, such as:

```
<A HREF="/path/to/imagemap.map"><IMG ISMAP
SRC="/path/to/imagemap.gif"></A>
```

ImapMenu

```
Syntax: ImapMenu {none, formatted, semi-formatted, unformatted}
Context: server config, virtual host, directory, .htaccess
Override: Indexes
```

This directive determines the action for a request for an imagemap file without any valid coordinates. It allows the following actions:

✦ none — No menu is generated, and the default action is performed.

✦ Formatted — The simplest menu is generated. Comments are ignored. A level one header is printed, and then an hrule, and then the links — each on a separate line.

✦ Semiformatted — In the semiformatted menu, comments are printed. Blank lines are converted into HTML breaks. No header or hrule is printed.

✦ Unformatted — In the unformatted menu, comments are printed. Blank lines are ignored.

ImapDefault

```
Syntax: ImapDefault {error, nocontent, map, referer, URL}
Context: server config, virtual host, directory, .htaccess
Override: Indexes
```

This defines the default action for imagemaps. This default setting can be overridden in the imagemap file using the default directive.

ImapBase

```
Syntax: ImapBase {map, referer, URL}
Context: server config, virtual host, directory, .htaccess
Override: Indexes
```

This directive sets the default base used in the imagemap files. This base setting can be overridden by using the base directive within the imagemap file. If this directive is not present, the base defaults to http://servername/.

mod_include

See Chapter 7.

mod_info

See Chapter 11.

mod_log_agent

See Chapter 11.

mod_log_config

See Chapter 11.

mod_log_referer

See Chapter 11.

mod_mime

This module is compiled in Apache by default. It is used to provide clients with metainformation about documents. It also enables you to define a handler for a document to determine how the document is processed by Apache.

AddEncoding

```
Syntax: AddEncoding MIME-encoding file-extension file-
extension...
Context: server config, virtual host, directory, per-directory
configuration (.htaccess)
Override: FileInfo
```

This directive maps one or more file extensions to a MIME-encoding scheme. For example:

```
AddEncoding x-gzip gz
AddEncoding x-tar tar
```

This causes a file called backup.gz to be mapped as an x-gzip encoded file, and a file called tarball.tar to be mapped as an x-tar encoded file.

AddHandler

```
Syntax: AddHandler handler-name file-extension file-
extension...
Context: server config, virtual host, directory, per-directory
configuration (.htaccess)
```

This directive is used to define a handler for one or more file extensions. For example:

```
AddHandler server-parsed  .shtml
```

This specifies that all .shtml files be processed by a handler called server-parsed, which is found in mod_include (see Chapter 7).

AddLanguage

```
Syntax: AddLanguage MIME-language file-extension file-
extension...
Context: server config, virtual host, directory, per-directory
configuration (.htaccess)
Override: FileInfo
```

This directive maps a list of file extensions to a MIME-language. For example:

```
AddLanguage en .en .english
```

This maps all files with extensions .en or .english to be mapped as English language files. This becomes useful in content negotiation, where the server can return a document based on the client's language preference. For example:

```
AddLanguage en .en
AddLanguage fr .fr
```

If the client prefers an English document, and both document.fr.html and document.en.html are available, the server should return document.en.html.

AddType

```
Syntax: AddType MIME-type file-extension file-extension...
Context: server config, virtual host, directory, per-directory
configuration (.htaccess)
Override: FileInfo
```

This directive maps a list of file extensions to a MIME-type. For example:

```
AddType text/html htm html. HTM HTML
```

ForceType

```
Syntax: ForceType MIME-type
Context: directory, per-directory configuration (.htaccess)
```

This directive is used to force a certain MIME-type for all files in a directory. The directory can be specified by a <Directory> or <Location> container. For example:

```
<Directory /www/nitec/public/htdocs/files/with/no/extensions>
ForceType text/html
</Directory>
```

This forces the text/html MIME-type for all files in the specified directory, regardless of their extensions.

SetHandler

```
Syntax: SetHandler handler-name
Context: directory, per-directory configuration (.htaccess)
```

This directive is used to define a handler for a directory or a URL location. For example:

```
<Location /ssi>
SetHandler server-parsed
</Location>
```

This force all files in the /ssi location to be treated as Server Side Includes, which are handled by the server-parsed handler.

TypesConfig

```
Syntax: TypesConfig filename
Default: TypesConfig conf/mime.types
Context: server config
```

This directive specifies the default MIME configuration file. The default value should be fine for most Apache installations. If you want to add your own MIME-types, use the AddType directive instead of modifying this file.

If you need additional support for handling MIME-types, you may want to look at the mod_mime_magic module. For most Apache installations this is not necessary, so it is not covered in this book.

mod_negotiation

This module is compiled by default. It provides support for content negotiations. In a typical content negotiation scenario, the client provides information about what type of content it can handle, and the server attempts to provide the most appropriate content. The server performs this with the help of type maps and the MultiViews search.

A type map provides a description of documents. Each document description contains one or more headers. It can also contain comment lines that start with a # character. Document descriptions are separated by blank lines. The document description headers are:

- ✦ Content-Encoding — This specifies the encoding type of the file. Only x-compress and x-gzip encoding are allowed at present.
- ✦ Content-Language — The language of the document.

- ✦ Content-Length — The length of the file, in bytes.
- ✦ Content-Type — The MIME type of the document. Optional key=value parameters are allowed. The allowed parameters are level and qs. The first one provides the version number (as an integer) of the MIME type, and the second one is used to indicate the quality (as a floating point number) of the document.
- ✦ URI — The path to the document relative to the map file.

A MultiViews search tries to determine the closest match for the missing document using the information it knows from the client, and returns the match if possible. When you enable the MultiViews option in the Options directive, the server is able to perform the MultiViews search when a requested document is not found.

Mod_negotiation provides the following two directives.

CacheNegotiatedDocs

```
Syntax: CacheNegotiatedDocs
Context: server config
```

This directive allows content-negotiated documents to be cached by proxy servers. Note that the new HTTP/1.1 specification provides much better control for caching negotiated documents, and CacheNegotiatedDocs has no effect in response to HTTP/1.1 requests. This directive is likely to disappear after HTTP/1.1 is widely used. Use of CacheNegotiatedDocs is not recommended.

LanguagePriority

```
Syntax: LanguagePriority MIME-language MIME-language...
Context: server config, virtual host, directory, per-directory
configuration (.htaccess)
Override: FileInfo
```

This directive specifies what language preference the server should use in a MultiViews search scenario, when the client does not provide language preference information. For example:

```
LanguagePriority en fr de
```

If the MultiViews option is turned on and the client does not provide language preference information for a file that is missing, the server first tries to serve the English version of the closest match, and then the French version, and so on. Like the CacheNegotiatedDocs directive, this directive is not effective in the HTTP/1.1 environment.

mod_rewrite

See Chapter 18.

mod_setenvif

This module is compiled in Apache by default. It enables you to create custom environment variables that can later be used to make decisions.

BrowserMatch

```
Syntax: BrowserMatch regex variable[=value] [...]
Default: none
Context: server config
Override: none
```

This directive is used to set and remove custom environment variables when a pattern is matched by the regular expression. For example:

```
BrowserMatch ^Mozilla vbscript=no javascript
```

This sets a variable called vbscript to the value no if the User-Agent HTTP request header field contains the word Mozilla, and an environment variable called javascript is set to 1 because no value was specified for this variable. Let's take a look at another example:

```
BrowserMatch IE vbscript !javascript
```

Here, the variable javascript is removed and the vbscript is set to 1 if the word IE is found in the User-Agent HTTP request header.

Note that the regular expression matches are case-sensitive.

BrowserMatchNoCase

```
Syntax: BrowserMatchNoCase regex variable[=value] [...]
Default: none
Context: server config
Override: none
```

This directive is same as the BrowserMatch directive, except that it provides case-insensitive matching for regular expressions. For example:

```
BrowserMatchNoCase ^MSIE vbscript=yes
```

This matches MSIE, msie, Msie, and so on.

SetEnvIf

```
Syntax: SetEnvIf attribute regex envar[=value] [...]
Default: none
Context: server config
Override: none
```

Like the BrowserMatch and BrowserMatchNoCase directives, this directive enables you to set and unset custom environment variables. Actually, BrowserMatch and BrowserMatchNoCase are two special versions of SetEnvIf. These two directives can only perform the regular expression on the User-Agent HTTP request header field, whereas SetEnvIf can be used for all request header fields. For example:

```
SetEnvIf Remove_Host "yourdomain\.com" local_user=true
```

Some of the other variables you can use are Remote_Addr, Remote_User, Request_Method, Request_URI, and Referer, if they are available.

SetEnvIfNoCase

```
Syntax: SetEnvIfNoCase attribute regex variable[=value] [...]
Default: none
Context: server config
Override: none
```

This is the same as SetEnvIf, but it offers case-insensitive regular expression matches.

mod_speling

This module is not compiled in Apache by default. It enables you to handle misspelled or miscapitalized URL requests. It compares the requested (misspelled or miscapitalized) document name with all the document names in the requested directory for one or more close matches.

In the case of a misspelled document request, the module allows a single spelling error, such as an extra character insertion, a character omission, or a transposition. In the case of a miscapitalized document request, it performs a case-insensitive filename comparison. Either way, if the module locates a single document that closely resembles the request, it sends a redirect request to the client. If there's more than one match, it sends the list to the client for selection.

The single directive offered by this module is called CheckSpelling.

CheckSpelling

```
Syntax: CheckSpelling on | off
Default: CheckSpelling Off
Context: server config, virtual host
```

This directive enables or disables the module. Note that when the spelling correction is on, the server may experience performance loss due to extra searches that are needed for serving a misspelled document request. You should also be aware that the module only works with file and directory names.

mod_status

See Chapter 11.

mod_unique_id

This module provides a magic token for each request that is guaranteed to be unique across "all" requests under very specific conditions. The unique identifier is even unique across multiple machines in a properly configured cluster of machines. The environment variable UNIQUE_ID is set to the identifier for each request.

mod_usertrack

See Chapter 11.

Summary

In this chapter, you learned about the many useful modules that make Apache so powerful. Most of these modules are part of the standard Apache distribution. New modules are frequently added to the standard, so you have to keep yourself updated with Apache happenings to keep on top of these changes.

In the next chapter, you learn how to host virtual Web sites.

✦ ✦ ✦

P A R T

Administering Your Web Sites

✦ ✦ ✦ ✦

In This Part

✦ ✦ ✦ ✦

C H A P T E R 6

Hosting Virtual Sites

✦ ✦ ✦ ✦

In This Chapter

Do you need a virtual Web site?

DNS configuration for a virtual Web site

How to create a virtual Web site

Virtual host examples

SMTP mail server configuration for virtual hosts

✦ ✦ ✦ ✦

In Chapter 3, you learned how to configure Apache to host a Web site. As you become more familiar with the Web, and your personal or business needs change, you may need more than just a single Web site to showcase your products, services, and so on. In such a case, you would need to set up multiple server machines running Apache servers to host these additional sites. Running each Web site on its own dedicated host machine may seem appealing to the novice system administrator, but those who have been around for a while know better. They prefer a solution called the *virtual Web site*. In this chapter you learn how to set up virtual Web sites using Apache.

Do You Need a Virtual Web Site?

Before I go into the details of virtual Web site implementation on Apache, it's important to determine whether you actually need a virtual Web site. Table 6-1 shows the advantages and disadvantages of a virtual Web solution.

If you're thinking that the virtual server solution is primarily an economic decision, you won't be far off from the point I'm making here. However, there's another point I must consider, which comes from experience. Most experienced Webmasters know that typical Web sites are neither CPU-intensive nor overly resource-hungry (*resource* meaning disk or memory). Therefore, when they are faced with a group of sites that fall in the typical category, they use virtual servers instead of dedicated servers. When traffic expectations are high, however, dedicated servers (possibly multiple servers per site) are the way to go.

Table 6-1
Pros and Cons for Virtual Web Site

Pros	*Cons*
Virtual Web sites are more manageable an than having multiple dedicated host systems running individual Web sites on them.	Dedicating one host per Web site may result in increase in server performance, because each host will only service calls pertaining to a single Web site. However, this performance gain may only be true for sites that usually experience heavy traffic. If a low-traffic site is being run on a dedicated Web server, the utility of the server's resource is not being maximized.
A single set of configuration files. You only have to administer four configuration files. Most likely, you won't have to change the mime.types file, so you really need to manage only three files: httpd.conf, srm.conf, and access.conf.	You need to administer four configuration files per server. Most likely, you won't have to change the mime.types file, but you still have to make sure this file is available in each server system.
Whenever a hardware or software upgrade is made to a single server system running one or more virtual Web sites, they all benefit from the upgrade.	When a single server system is upgraded, only the Web site hosted on that server benefits.
When a server firm (that is, more than one server system) is used to host one or more virtual Web sites, a level of fault tolerance is achieved. Typically, this type of configuration includes a round-robin DNS scheme as well as NFS file systems.	When a server hosting a Web site fails, that site becomes completely unavailable because other servers are hosting different sites.

Most sites on the Web are virtual in nature. You may have seen a number of advertisements trying to sell virtual Web space. Many organizations are using deals to establish their Web presence. Before virtual Web sites were possible, however, ISPs were left with solutions that were less than professional. For example, in the absence of a virtual Web site solution, an ISP would have to offer one of the following three options to a customer wanting a site of his or her own:

✦ www.isp.net/customer or www.isp.net/~customer, which meant that the ISP's Web site address would be part of the customer's site, therefore providing a not-so-elegant look and feel.

✦ http://<customer's domain>:<non standard port>/ is another way. For example, www.gunchy.com:8080/ can be the Web site for Gunchy Inc. Note, however, that a port address other than 80 (the default HTTP port) has to be used here.

✦ The final solution would be to use a dedicated host running an Apache server for the customer domain.

You may wonder why I'm spending so much time explaining these options. Well, the reasons are as follows.

Some of you may still want or need to implement one of the nonvirtual solutions listed above, and you should know all your options before you implement one or the other. For example, if you are just planning on hosting several user Web sites that do not have custom domain names, you can use the http://your.web.site/~user as the home page URL for the users. In fact, it is still the standard way of providing user Web sites. The second option listed is a good choice if you want to use the same IP alias for another site; for example, if you need a development site where you can try out new technologies for your primary Web site, you may want to try this option (Chapter 18 discusses this in more detail). The final option is preferred for sites with high traffic and load.

Now, if you plan on creating economical, virtual Web sites, the rest of this chapter will help you do so.

Domain Name Registration

Domain Name Service (DNS) is the name resolution service for Internet domains. For example, when you enter www.idgbooks.com/ in the Address (or URL) field of your Web browser, a DNS server (usually your ISP's DNS server) is contacted by your Web browser for resolving the IP alias www.idgbooks.com to an IP address of 206.80.51.140. For your virtual Web site, you need to have the same service enabled; in this section I tell you how to go about doing this.

To make this fairly complex concept clear to you, let me use an example. In this and the next section I discuss creating a virtual Web site called www.milkyweb.com that will actually be hosted on a domain called nitec.com. The nitec.com domain already has DNS servers configured to resolve all the host names available in its domain.

For example, if you entered www.nitec.com/ on your browser, you would be able to see Nitec's Web pages. This means your browser was able to get your local DNS server to resolve www.nitec.com. In short, nitec.com is set up properly, so now you can set up a new site on Nitec's Apache Web server running on the host www.nitec.com.

The Domain Name Dilemma

It's becoming increasingly difficult to find good domain names these days. It seems as though all English words have already been registered by someone or some company. The example domains milkyweb.com and nitec.com are both real domains owned by different organizations. Interestingly, while writing this chapter, I checked milkyweb.com to make sure it was a nonexistent domain; it was until the first draft of the chapter was complete, but later it turned out to be registered as well! I had to request permission to use the name in the example. It appears that anything you can think of as a domain name is probably taken by the time you make up your mind to register it.

So beware, and be prompt in getting a cool domain name registered.

Note that if you do not deal with DNS yourself (like many Web administrators), you may want to skip to the IP-based virtual hosts section of this chapter. Typically, your ISP deals with all DNS issues. The following example describes what to do when that is not the case.

If milkyweb.com is a new domain to be created, then all you need to do is go to the InterNIC Web site at http://rs.internic.net/, find the appropriate online domain registration form, and fill out the information.

To fill out the form, however, you need to know what nitec.com's primary and secondary domain name servers are, since these are the same DNS servers that will have to do DNS service for milkyweb.com. Finding out a domain's name servers is a fairly easy task. All you need to do is run a TCP/IP utility called whois. In Figure 6-1, the output for the whois nitec.com command is displayed. The whois utility is a query program that connects to the InterNIC domain database and queries about a domain.

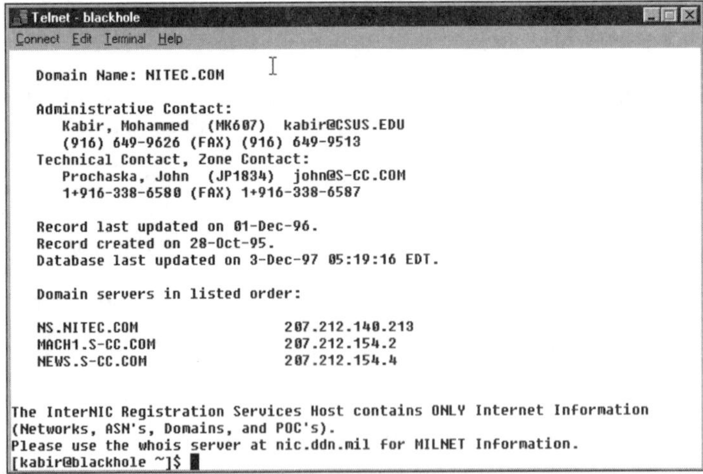

Figure 6-1: Output of the whois nitec.com command

As you can see, the DNS servers (ns.nitec.com, mach1.s-cc.com, news.s-cc.com) for nitec.com are listed in the output. In the domain registration application, then, you enter ns.nitec.com as the primary DNS server and mach1.s-cc.com as the secondary DNS server for milkyweb.com. Once you've completed the application, you need to configure Nitec's domain name servers to answer to queries regarding milkyweb.com.

Creating a new domain requires payments to InterNIC.

DNS Configuration for Your Virtual Web Site

Because the www.milkyweb.com host has a domain address milkyweb.com (not nitec.com), you must tell InterNIC (the domain name service authority) to point milkyweb.com to nitec.com. This is done in two steps: first you create the appropriate database records for the domain, and then you choose between IP-based and name-based.

Creating database records for the domain

The first step in creating a virtual host is to create domain databases. You can either create new domain databases or modify existing domain databases.

Creating new domain databases

In order for nitec.com's domain servers to provide service for milkyweb.com, nitec.com needs to know details about the milkyweb domain. Using two text files called milkyweb.db (as shown in Listing 6-1) and milkyweb.rev (as shown in Listing 6-2), you can create the DNS records necessary for the milkyweb.com domain. Note that these files employ the widely used BIND name server file format.

Listing 6-1: milkyweb.db

```
@ IN SOA milkyweb.com.   hostmaster.milkyweb.com.(
   19981110001 ; Serial YYYYMMDDXXX
   7200 ; refresh
   3600 ; (1 hour) retry
   1728000 ; (20 days) expire
   3600) ; (1 hr) minimum ttl

; Name Servers
IN NS     ns.nitec.com.
IN NS     mach1.s-cc.com.

; A Records
www IN A  206.171.50.50
```

Although a complete explanation of all DNS records is beyond the scope of this book, I want to explain the bare minimum needed to get you going. The first record is an SOA record, which specifies when a remote DNS server should refresh, retry, expire the information provided. This enables the DNS record provider to update the information and have it propagated over the Internet in a certain fashion. This record also contains an e-mail address without the @ symbol (such as hostmaster.milkyweb.com) and a serial number. The e-mail address is there for administrative purposes, and the serial number is simply there for record keeping. I like to use a special YYYYMMDDXXX format, where I use the month, day, year, and a unique 3-digit number to create a serial number. This serial number is looked up by DNS servers to see if information they have cached about a domain needs to be updated. Therefore, every time a DNS record is updated, this number needs to be incremented accordingly.

The next set of records are NS records, which specify what name servers are there to provide DNS service for a domain. In this case, the DNS servers for milkyweb.com are really the same DNS servers as for nitec.com.

Tip

A typical mistake that novice DNS administrators make is forgetting to end host aliases (such as ns.nitec.com) with a period.

The final record is an A record, or an address record. This record specifies which host has what address. You can use a shortcut record format where www is a shortcut for www.milkyweb.com. This is really what you want to achieve. You want to make a host called www.milkyweb.com, so you need all the preceding settings to tell the world that www.milkyweb.com is a host in the milkyweb.com domain, which is hosted in the nitec.com domain, and that its primary name service is provided by ns.nitec.com.

Note

The IP address I use here is not coming out of the blue. It is a valid IP address for nitec.com, and the machine connected to this IP address will service www.milkyweb.com.

The procedure for DNS settings does not end here. You still need to provide a way for other computers to do reverse name lookup. For that, you set up the milkyweb.rev database file as shown in Listing 6-2.

Listing 6-2: **milkyweb.rev**

```
@ IN SOA milkyweb.com    hostmaster.milkyweb.com.(
   19981110001 ; Serial YYYYMMDDXXX
   7200 ; refresh
   3600 ;(1 hour) retry
   1728000 ;(20 days) expire
  3600) ; (1 hr) minimum TTL
```

```
; Name Servers
IN NS     ns.nitec.com.
; PTR Records
50 IN PTR www.milkyweb.com.
```

This file has the same SOA and NS records as the file in Listing 6-1. The only new record you have in this file is the PTR record, which points an IP address to an IP alias. In this case, I only used the host part (the last octet of a class C network) of the IP address (206.171.50.50) in the PTR record to point it to www.milkyweb.com.

Now, if a server on the Internet is interested in knowing whether 206.171.50.50 is really www.milkyweb.com, it can do a reverse name lookup to confirm that.

Now you need to use these two files in the nitec.com domain's name server configuration file, stored in /etc/named.boot. The lines you need to add in this configuration file are as follows:

```
primary          milkyweb.com               milkyweb.db
primary          50.171.206.in-addr.arpa    milkyweb.rev
```

The first line states that this DNS server (ns.nitec.com) is also a primary DNS server for milkyweb.com, and the records are stored in milkyweb.db file. The second line states that the primary reverse lookup records are stored in milkyweb.rev file. Note that reverse DNS is usually handled by the ISP.

Once these lines are added to the /etc/named.boot file, the name server process needs to be restarted so it has a chance to read the files. This is done using the command:

```
/usr/sbin/named.restart
```

Typically, you need to be a root user to do the preceding task. This command is really a call to a shell script that executes the /usr/sbin/ndc command with an argument named restart. The ndc program is an interface program for the name server. Your name server software may have a different program or option to restart it, though. Consult your name server man pages for help.

Once the name server is restarted, it needs to be tested. In Figure 6-2, you can see I entered the command

```
ping www.milkyweb.com
```

at my shell prompt, and got responses from the www.milkyweb.com host.

```
Telnet - blackhole
Connect  Edit  Terminal  Help
[kabir@blackhole ~]$ ping www.milkyweb.com
PING blackhole.nitec.com (206.171.50.50): 56 data bytes
64 bytes from 206.171.50.50: icmp_seq=0 ttl=64 time=0.3 ms
64 bytes from 206.171.50.50: icmp_seq=1 ttl=64 time=0.2 ms
64 bytes from 206.171.50.50: icmp_seq=2 ttl=64 time=0.2 ms
64 bytes from 206.171.50.50: icmp_seq=3 ttl=64 time=0.2 ms
64 bytes from 206.171.50.50: icmp_seq=4 ttl=64 time=0.2 ms

--- blackhole.nitec.com ping statistics ---
5 packets transmitted, 5 packets received, 0% packet loss
round-trip min/avg/max = 0.2/0.2/0.3 ms
[kabir@blackhole ~]$
```

Figure 6-2: Pinging www.milkyweb.com

This test should be sufficient to convince me that the DNS configuration is working. However, a more robust way of checking DNS configuration needs to be discussed, because in case of a misconfiguration, ping will simply fail without providing any clues. So, lets take a look at a name server lookup utility called nslookup.

This utility, as its name indicates, is there to perform name server lookups. Figure 6-3 shows an nslookup session where I entered a few nslookup commands to determine whether the previous DNS configuration was a success.

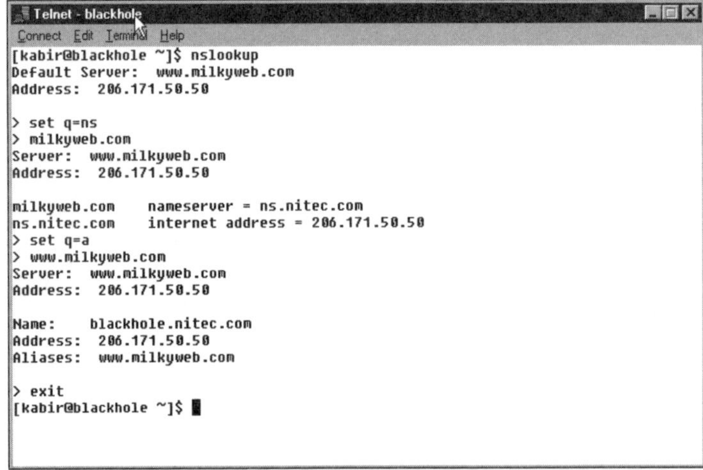

Figure 6-3: Using nslookup to test DNS configurations

The command to run from the shell prompt is as follows:

```
nslookup
```

This should open a session where a > prompt is displayed. It also displays the DNS server it is using to perform the queries. If the DNS server is not the server where new configurations are made, a command such as the following is needed to tell nslookup to communicate with the server that was just configured:

```
server <servername>
```

In my case the default server is ns.nitec.com, which has the modified DNS settings, so I didn't have to enter the preceding command. If you look at Figure 6-3, you see that the first set of commands I entered at the nslookup prompt is:

```
set q=ns
milkyweb.com
```

The first line tells nslookup to set its query type to NS (name server) records, and the next line simply tells it to look up milkyweb.com's name server record. The output shows that ns.nitec.com reported that milkyweb.com is being DNSed by ns.nitec.com. Now look at the second set of nslookup commands:

```
set q=a
www.milkyweb.com
```

The first command tells the program to set its query to A (address) records and then ask ns.nitec.com for the address of www.milkyweb.com. The output shows that the address for this IP alias is 206.171.50.50.

Finally, quit by using the following command:

```
exit
```

At this point, the primary DNS server configuration for www.milkyweb.com is complete. However, you still need to configure the secondary DNS server. You can do this by adding the following line in each secondary DNS server's /etc/named.boot file:

```
secondary          milkyweb.com               milkyweb.db
secondary          50.171.206.in-addr.arpa    milkyweb.rev
```

Note that instead of using the following A record:

```
www     IN      A       206.171.50.50
```

you could use the following CNAME record:

```
www     IN      CNAME   blackhole.nitec.com.
```

What would be the difference? Well, not much, since 206.171.50.50 is really the address of blackhole.nitec.com. By not using an A record, however, you would make milkyweb.com's DNS more manageable, because you would eliminate the need for updating milkyweb.com's DNS record whenever you needed to change the blackhole.nitec.com host's IP address to something else. Also, the A record version is needed for IP-based virtual hosting, and the CNAME version is used for name-based virtual hosting. You will learn about these two types of virtual hosting in a later section of this chapter.

Existing domain database modification

So far, I've talked about creating a virtual host name for a brand new domain (milkyweb.com.) If you already have a Web site such as www.yourcompany.com, however, and you wanted to create a virtual site called intranet.yourcompany.com, all you need to do is create an alias using the CNAME record for www.yourcompany.com in your DNS server, as follows:

```
intranet    IN    CNAME    www
```

In your reverse DNS database, you want to duplicate the entry for your www.yourcompany.com line and replace the www part with **intranet**.

For example, I set up the following:

```
apache      IN    CNAME    blackhole          ; in nitec.db file

50          IN    PTR      apache.nitec.com. ; in nitec.rev  file
```

Now, when I use the nslookup, as shown in Figure 6-4, to see what IP address apache.nitec.com has, I see that it returns the IP address of a machine called blackhole.nitec.com, as intended.

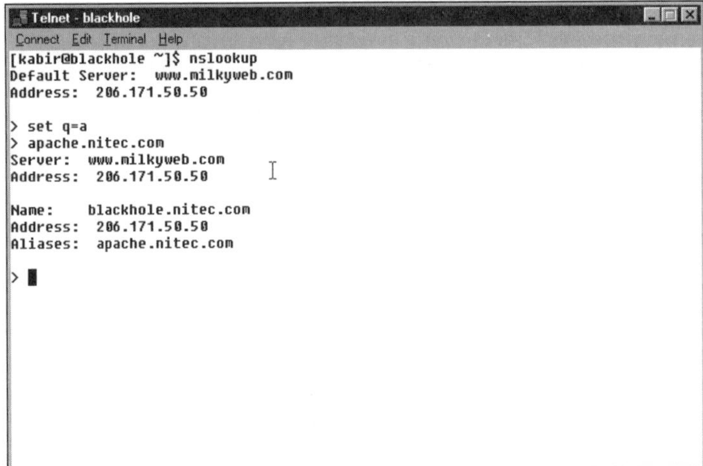

Figure 6-4: Using nslookup to verify domain record modifications

You need the preceding type of configuration when using name-based virtual hosting, but if you wanted to use IP-based virtual hosting, then you would have to use an A record instead. For example, to accomplish the same goal I could have set up the same host apache.nitec.com as follows:

```
apache    IN    A     206.171.50.50       ; in nitec.db file

50        IN    PTR   apache.nitec.com. ; in nitec.rev  file
```

However, this version can be used for the IP-based virtual hosting.

Deciding between IP-based and name-based

The next step in creating a virtual Web site is to decide whether you want an IP-based virtual host or a name-based virtual host. I discuss both in this section.

IP-based virtual hosts

An IP-based virtual host means you give each new host an IP address of its own. Figure 6-5 shows one such configuration, where each virtual host has its own IP and these IP addresses are all routed to a single machine.

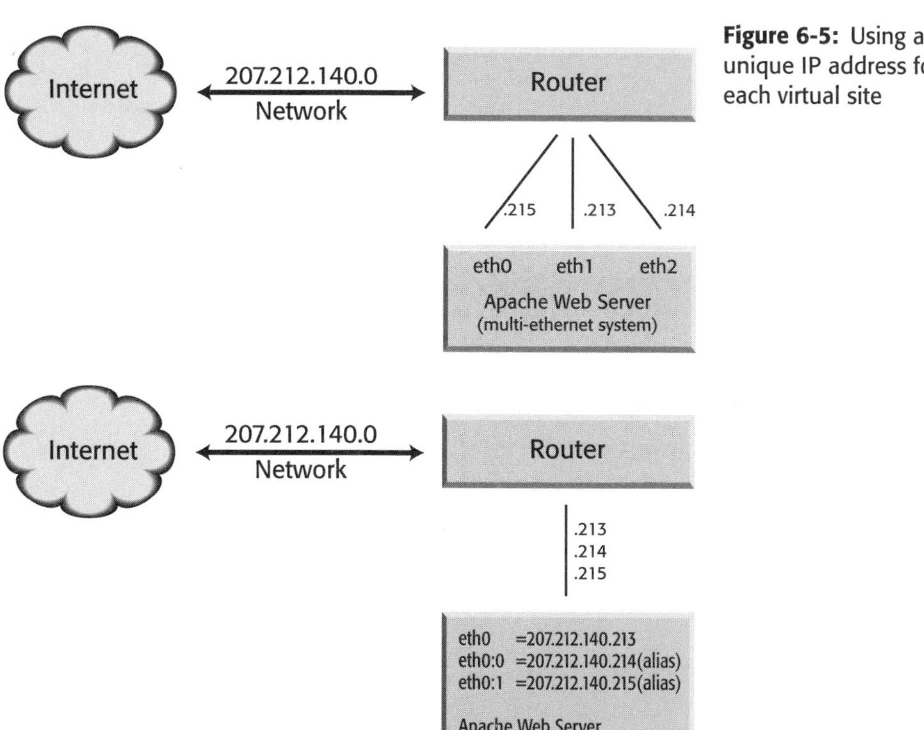

Figure 6-5: Using a unique IP address for each virtual site

Using an unique IP address for each virtual Web site means you need to create an A record for each site. For example, the configuration shown in Figure 6-5 may result in a DNS configuration such as:

```
; The following entry goes in nitec.com's DNS database
{ref hyperlink http:www.nitec.com}        IN   A 207.212.140.213
; The following entry goes in client1.com's DNS database
{ref hyperlink http:www.client1.com       IN   A 207.212.140.214
; this entry goes in client2.com's DNS database
{ref hyperlink http:www.client2.com       IN   A 207.212.140.215
```

You also need to set up appropriate routing assignments so that all the IP addresses you want to use for your Web servers (virtual and primary) are properly routed to the target server system. Depending on which operating system you use for your primary Web server, you have a choice either to create IP aliases for a single Ethernet interface, or to have a different interface for each IP address (typically by adding extra Ethernet cards to the system.)

In the following example, I discuss how aliasing can be used to link multiple IP addresses to a single Ethernet device. The example uses the Linux operating system and an ifconfig utility, which is capable of IP aliasing. If you use a different operating system, please consult your ifconfig manual pages for availability of the alias option.

Popular operating systems such as Linux, BSDI, Digital UNIX, FreeBSD, HPUX 10.x, and AIX 4.1 all have alias features available in the ifconfig utility. Some of these, however, along with many other operating systems, may require kernel patches for ifconfig to work.

Figure 6-6 shows the output of the ifconfig command run by the root user.

```
Telnet - blackhole
Connect Edit Terminal Help
[kabir@blackhole kabir]# ifconfig
lo        Link encap:Local Loopback
          inet addr:127.0.0.1  Bcast:127.255.255.255  Mask:255.0.0.0
          UP BROADCAST LOOPBACK RUNNING  MTU:3584  Metric:1
          RX packets:58684 errors:0 dropped:0 overruns:0
          TX packets:58684 errors:0 dropped:0 overruns:0

eth0      Link encap:10Mbps Ethernet  HWaddr 00:C0:F6:98:37:37
          inet addr:206.171.50.50  Bcast:206.171.50.63  Mask:255.255.255.240
          UP BROADCAST RUNNING MULTICAST  MTU:1500  Metric:1
          RX packets:353979 errors:0 dropped:0 overruns:0
          TX packets:353668 errors:0 dropped:0 overruns:0
          Interrupt:5 Base address:0x340

[kabir@blackhole kabir]#
```

Figure 6-6: Output of ifconfig before aliasing

As you can see from this figure, two devices have been set up using ifconfig: the loopback device lo and the default Ethernet device eth0. Now, to add an IP alias for the eth0 device, you would have to use the ifconfig command as follows:

```
ifconfig device:N IP_address
```

Here, N is 0, 1, 2, 3, and so on. For example, to create an alias for eth0 using the IP address 206.171.50.56, you would enter the command:

```
ifconfig eth0:0 206.171.50.56
```

Running the ifconfig command by itself produces an output similar to Figure 6-7.

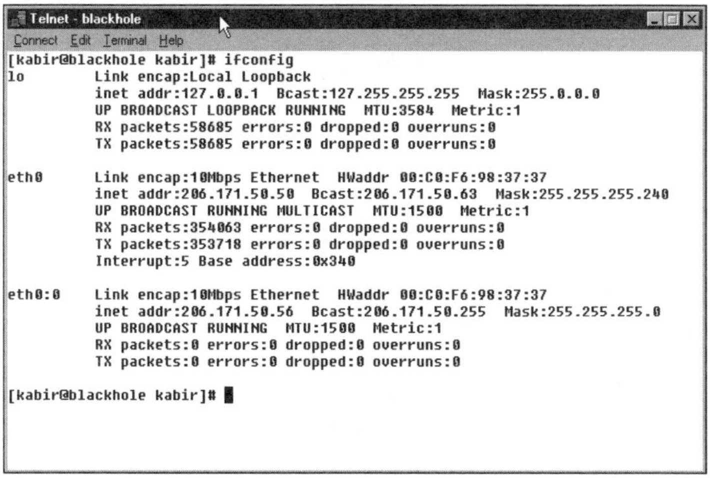

```
Telnet - blackhole
Connect  Edit  Terminal  Help
[kabir@blackhole kabir]# ifconfig
lo        Link encap:Local Loopback
          inet addr:127.0.0.1  Bcast:127.255.255.255  Mask:255.0.0.0
          UP BROADCAST LOOPBACK RUNNING  MTU:3584  Metric:1
          RX packets:58685 errors:0 dropped:0 overruns:0
          TX packets:58685 errors:0 dropped:0 overruns:0

eth0      Link encap:10Mbps Ethernet  HWaddr 00:C0:F6:98:37:37
          inet addr:206.171.50.50  Bcast:206.171.50.63  Mask:255.255.255.240
          UP BROADCAST RUNNING MULTICAST  MTU:1500  Metric:1
          RX packets:354063 errors:0 dropped:0 overruns:0
          TX packets:353718 errors:0 dropped:0 overruns:0
          Interrupt:5 Base address:0x340

eth0:0    Link encap:10Mbps Ethernet  HWaddr 00:C0:F6:98:37:37
          inet addr:206.171.50.56  Bcast:206.171.50.255  Mask:255.255.255.0
          UP BROADCAST RUNNING  MTU:1500  Metric:1
          RX packets:0 errors:0 dropped:0 overruns:0
          TX packets:0 errors:0 dropped:0 overruns:0

[kabir@blackhole kabir]#
```

Figure 6-7: Output of ifconfig after aliasing

A route for the aliased IP address is also needed, as follows:

```
route add -host 206.171.50.56 dev eth0:0
```

Adding these two commands in the rc.local file in the /etc/rc.d directory ensures that this alias is set up properly when the server is started.

An IP address is a scarce resource on the Internet, because only a finite number of IP addresses are available under the current IP addressing scheme. Until the new addressing scheme (IPNG, or IP Next Generation) is widely used, obtaining IP addresses will remain an increasingly difficult task. InterNIC, the authority for issuing IP addresses, usually does not issue IP addresses to just anyone. InterNIC recommends asking the ISP for IP addresses, which could mean paying a sum of money to the ISP for routing the IP addresses to a specific system such as your Web server.

Compatibility with Pre-HTTP/1.1 Browsers

This workaround involves using the ServerPath directive in the first virtual host configuration. Example configuration:

```
NameVirtualHost 111.222.333.444

<VirtualHost 111.222.333.444>
# primary virtual host
DocumentRoot /www/subdomain
...
</VirtualHost>

<VirtualHost 111.222.333.444>
DocumentRoot /www/subdomain/client1
ServerName www.client1.com
ServerPath /client1/
...
</VirtualHost>

<VirtualHost 111.222.333.444>
DocumentRoot /www/subdomain/client2
ServerName www.client2.com
ServerPath /client2/
...
</VirtualHost>
```

In the first virtual host's index page (/www/subdomain/index.html) you would need to establish links with a URL prefix to the name-based virtual hosts. You also need to locate all name-based virtual hosts under the first virtual host's document root directory, each in its own subdirectory. In the preceding example, the first virtual host's document root directory is /www/subdomain/. www.client1.com and www.client2.com have their document roots located in the /www/subdomain/client1 directory and the /www/subdomain/client2 directory, respectively. The final piece of discipline you need to add in this virtual Web site is that all links should be relative links (for example, file.html or ../icons/image.gif) or links containing the prefacing /domain/ (for example, www.domain.tld/domain/misc/file.html or /domain/misc/file.html).

The ServerPath directive causes a request to the URL www.client1.com/client1/ to always be served from the client1 virtual host. A request to the URL www.client1.com/ is only served from the client1 virtual host if the client sent a correct Host: header using HTTP/1.1. If no Host: header is sent, the client receives the information page from the first virtual host.

This solution may appear cumbersome and difficult to manage, but adherence to these guidelines will, for the most part, ensure that your pages work with all browsers, new and old.

Name-based virtual hosts

Due to the wide acceptance of HTTP/1.1, you can now employ another method for creating virtual Web hosts using a non-IP scheme. This enables you to use the same IP address for multiple host names.

Prior to HTTP/1.1, there was no way for a Web server to know which host name the browser user entered to request service. The new HTTP/1.1 specification adds a facility where the browser must tell the server the host name it is using, on the Host: header. Of course, if someone is using a browser that is not HTTP/1.1-compliant, it will not send the necessary Host: header information, and the server will fail to find the appropriate site. See the "Compatibility with Pre-HTTP/1.1 Browsers" sidebar to learn how to create a workaround for this situation.

To support non-IP-based virtual hosts, all you need to do is have CNAME records in appropriate DNS databases to point to an existing host with an A record. For example, if I wanted to point the www.client1.com and www.client2.com hosts to a Web server called webserver.nitec.com, then I would have to modify both client1.com and client2.com's DNS database to add the following entries, respectively:

```
; The following entry goes in client1.com DNS database
{ref hyperlink http:www.client1.com}     IN  CNAME webserver.nitec.com.
; The following entry goes in client2.com DNS database
{ref hyperlink http:www.client2.com}     IN  CNAME webserver.nitec.com.
```

In this section I discussed two ways of setting up the DNS for virtual Web sites. Based on the information you learned here, you should be able to make a decision about whether to use IP-based or name-based virtual sites.

Now, let's set up Apache to provide Web service for your virtual hosts.

Apache Configuration for Virtual Hosts

You can configure Apache in two ways to enable it to support multiple hosts (the main server and the virtual servers). You can either run multiple daemons, so that each host has a separate httpd daemon, or you can run a single daemon, which supports all the virtual hosts and the primary server host. Figure 6-8 shows both of these options.

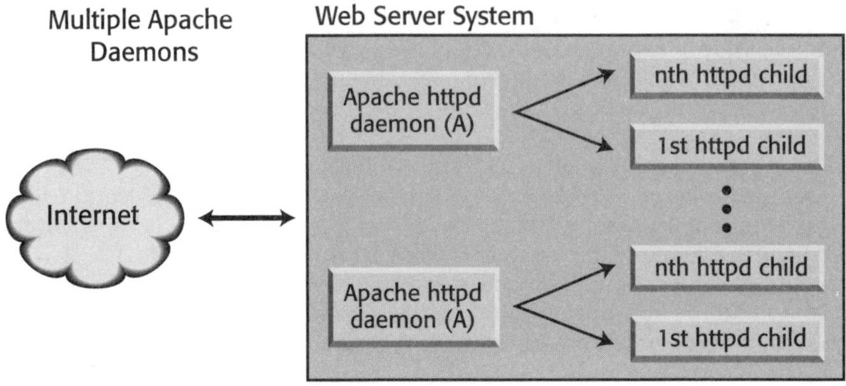

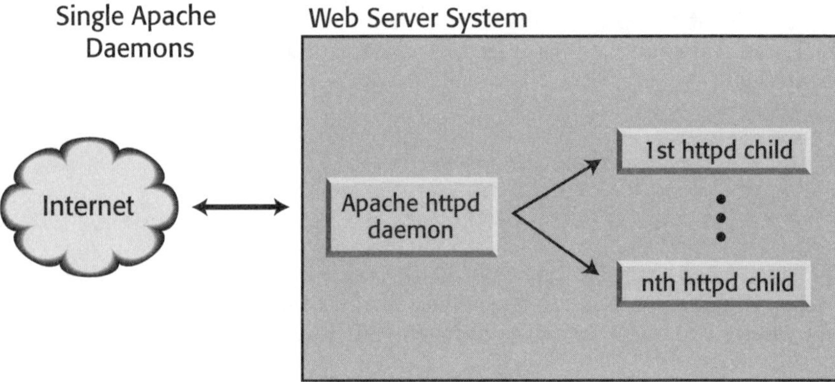

Figure 6-8: Multiple and single Apache daemons

In the figure, you can see that the multiple daemon configuration has multiple primary servers, and the single daemon configuration has only one primary server. In both methods, child processes launched by the primary server(s) service requests. For example, if a request came to server A in the multiple daemon configuration, it would spawn a child process and have it service the request. In the single primary server configuration, the primary server spawns a child as well to service the request — the difference is that in the multiple daemon configuration, several Apache daemon processes are being used to do the all work that the single Apache daemon does in the single mode.

For typical needs, you would want to run a single primary Apache daemon. If sharing httpd configuration between virtual hosts is not acceptable, however, because of differences in ServerType, user, group, TypesConfig, ServerRoot, and so on, then you need to run multiple main Apache processes. These separate primary httpd processes would require separate configuration files.

Let's take a look at how to configure each of your options: setting up multiple daemons and setting up a single daemon.

Setting up multiple Apache daemons

To set up multiple Apache daemons, you first need to create a separate httpd installation for each virtual host. Basically, you have to create a separate set of Apache configuration files for each daemon process. For each installation, use the Listen directive in the configuration file to select which IP address (or virtual host) the daemon services.

There are two ways to tell Apache which addresses and ports to listen to: you can either use the BindAddress directive to specify a single address or port, or use the Listen directive to specify any number of specific addresses or ports. For example, if you run your primary server on IP address 206.171.50.50 port 80, and a virtual host on IP 206.171.50.54 port 8080, you would use:

```
Listen 206.171.50.50:80
Listen 206.171.50.54:8080
```

It is better to use IP addresses instead of host names in Listen directives, because it reduces the domain name lookup needed to resolve the host name to the IP address at server startup.

Note that using multiple main servers for virtual Web sites puts a heavy load on the system, and is not recommended for sites that are likely to experience high traffic.

Setting up a single Apache daemon

This is the default configuration for Apache. A single httpd daemon launches child processes to service requests for the primary Web site and all the virtual sites; by default, Apache listens to port 80 on all IP addresses of the local machine, and this is often sufficient. If you have a more complex requirement, such as listening on various port numbers or listening only to specific IP addresses, the BindAddress or Listen directives can be used.

Let's look at how you can configure Apache to use a single daemon process to service all your virtual Web sites.

Apache uses the special container <VirtualHost> in the httpd.conf file to handle all the virtual host-specific configurations. An example of a minimal virtual host configuration might look as follows:

```
<VirtualHost 206.171.50.50>
DocumentRoot /www/apachebible/public/htdocs
ServerName  www.apachebible.com
</VirtualHost>
```

The first line marks the start of a virtual host (www.idgbooks.com) configuration. The enclosed IP address needs to be a valid IP for www.idgbooks.com. If a nonstandard (that is, not 80) port address needs to be used, it can be supplied as follows:

```
<VirtualHost IP:port>
```

For example:

```
<VirtualHost 206.171.50.50:8080>
```

You may be wondering if you can use host names instead of IP addresses inside the <VirtualHost> container. Yes, you can, but please don't until the developers of Apache tell you it's okay to do so. If you use a host name instead of an IP address, Apache must do a DNS lookup to determine the IP address of that host. If, for some reason, the DNS lookup fails, the virtual host is likely to be unavailable until you restart Apache. Like many people, I personally do not like to keep hard-coded IP addresses in configuration files, but until Apache developers come up with a better way of handling this situation, hard-coded IP addresses should be used.

Any directive inside a <VirtualHost> container applies only to that virtual host. Any directive that has been used outside the <VirtualHost> directives constitutes the primary server's configuration. Each virtual host inherits the primary server's configuration unless there is a conflict. In a case where the same directive is used both in the main server configuration and in a virtual host configuration (that is, inside a <VirtualHost> container), the directive inside the virtual host configuration overrides the primary server's setting for only that particular virtual host. For example, if you have ServerName set to www.yourcompany.com in your primary server configuration (that is, outside any <VirtualHost> container), and you have a ServerName directive in a <VirtualHost> container set to www.yourclient.com, then obviously you want the virtual host to respond to www.yourclient.com, right? That's exactly what happens; the directive within the virtual host section overrides the main server's corresponding directive. It may be easier to think of the main server configuration as the global default configuration for all virtual hosts that you create using the <VirtualHost>. So, when configuring virtual hosts, you need to decide what changes need to be made in each of the virtual host configurations.

The directives either override the configuration given in the primary server or supplement it, depending on the directive. For example, the DocumentRoot directive in a <VirtualHost> section overrides the primary server's DocumentRoot, whereas AddType supplements the main server's MIME types.

Now, when a request arrives, Apache uses the IP address and port on which it arrived to find a matching virtual host configuration. If no virtual host matches the address and port, it is handled by the primary server configuration. If it does match a virtual host address, Apache uses the configuration of that virtual server to handle the request.

In the previous example, the virtual host configuration used is the same as the primary server, except that the DocumentRoot is set to /www/apachebible/public/htdocs, and the ServerName is set to www.apachebible.com. Directives commonly set in <VirtualHost> containers are DocumentRoot, ServerName, ErrorLog, and TransferLog.

You can put almost any configuration directive in the VirtualHost directive, with the exception of ServerType, StartServers, MaxSpareServers, MinSpareServers, MaxRequestsPerChild, BindAddress, Listen, PidFile, TypesConfig, ServerRoot, and NameVirtualHost. User and Group may be used inside VirtualHost containers if the suEXEC wrapper is used (see Chapter 12 for more details).

You can have as many <VirtualHost> containers as you want. You can choose to have one or more of your virtual hosts handled by the primary server, or have a <VirtualHost> for every available address and port and leave the primary server with no requests to handle.

At this point, you may be wondering how Apache knows which virtual host configuration to use if more than one non-IP-based virtual host is using the same IP address. Well, Apache is smart enough to look up the ServerName directive to match the requested host found in the Host: header sent by HTTP/1.1-compliant browsers. By matching the ServerName to the requested host, it can decide which virtual non-IP host is being requested, and then services it.

Note that Apache version 1.3 or above requires an additional directive called NameVirtualHost before the actual <VirtualHost> directive that specifies the name-based virtual host configurations. For example:

```
NameVirtualHost 206.171.50.50

<VirtualHost 206.171.50.50>
ServerName www.client1.com
DocumentRoot /www/client1
</VirtualHost>

<VirtualHost 206.171.50.50>
ServerName www.client2.com
DocumentRoot /www/client2
</VirtualHost>

NameVirtualHost 206.171.50.56

<VirtualHost 206.171.50.56>
ServerName www.client3.com
DocumentRoot /www/client3
</VirtualHost>
```

The NameVirtualHost directive specifies an IP address that should be used as a target for name-based virtual hosts. In the preceding example you have two virtual hosts, www.client1.com and www.client2.com, both of which are serviced by the same IP address (206.171.50.50). The third virtual host, www.client3.com, is serviced by a different IP (206.171.50.56), so the second non-IP VirtualHost directive is placed just before the virtual host configuration. You only need a single NameVirtualHost directive for all the non-IP virtual host configurations if you group them as they appear in this example.

Once you have created the virtual host configuration for Apache, you can start (or restart) the Apache server so the configuration can take effect. Do not forget to create the directory structure before you do this final step.

As mentioned earlier, some clients still do not send the required data enabling the name-based virtual hosts to work properly. These clients are always sent the pages from the first virtual host appearing in the configuration file for a specific IP address. In the following section, I discuss a commonly used workaround for this problem.

Common Virtual Host Examples

Now that you know how to set up DNS and configure Apache for your virtual sites, let's take a look at a few common scenarios to help you understand the various aspects of hosting virtual Web sites.

The IP addresses (111.222.333.x) used in the following examples are intentionally invalid.

IP-based virtual hosting on a server with multiple IP addresses

In this example, you want to configure an IP-based virtual host, www.myclient.com, on a host called webserver.mycompany.com. This host also needs to host a main server called www.mycompany.com. Figure 6-9 shows a diagram of what this example discusses. As you can see, the Web server machine has two IP addresses which have the following DNS records:

```
www.mywebserver.com    IN A       111.222.333.1
www.myclient.com       IN A       111.222.333.2
www.mycompany.com      IN CNAME   webserver.mycompany.com.
```

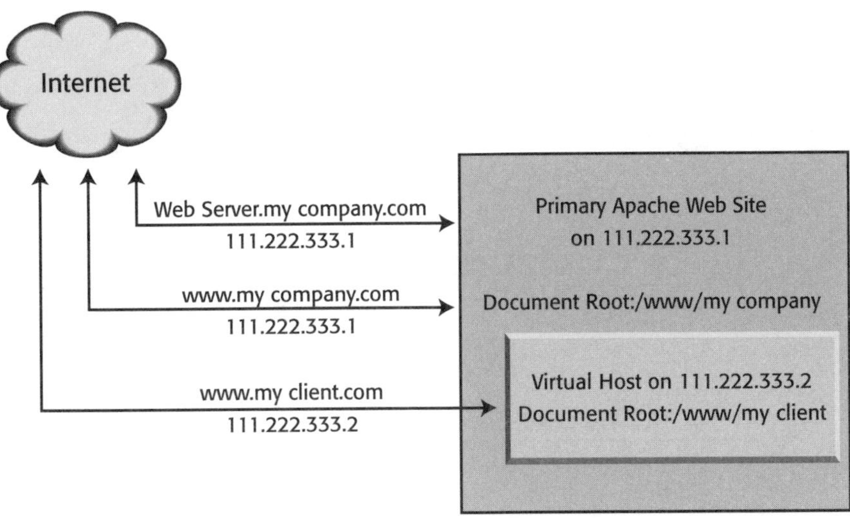

Figure 6-9: Example of IP-based virtual hosting on a multi-IP server

The simplified httpd.conf configuration file looks like this:

```
...
Port 80
DocumentRoot /www/mycompany
ServerName www.mycompany.com

<VirtualHost 111.222.333.2>
DocumentRoot /www/myclient
ServerName www.myclient.com
...
</VirtualHost>
```

The host www.myclient.com can only be reached through the address 111.222.333.2, while the server www.mycompany.com can only be reached through the 111.222.333.1 address.

IP-based virtual hosting without a main server

This example is similar to the previous one; the difference is that only the local users (that is, users who are running their Web browsers on the webserver.mycompany.com machine) can see the main server pages. In other words, there will be no dedicated main server. Figure 6-10 shows the logical diagram for this example.

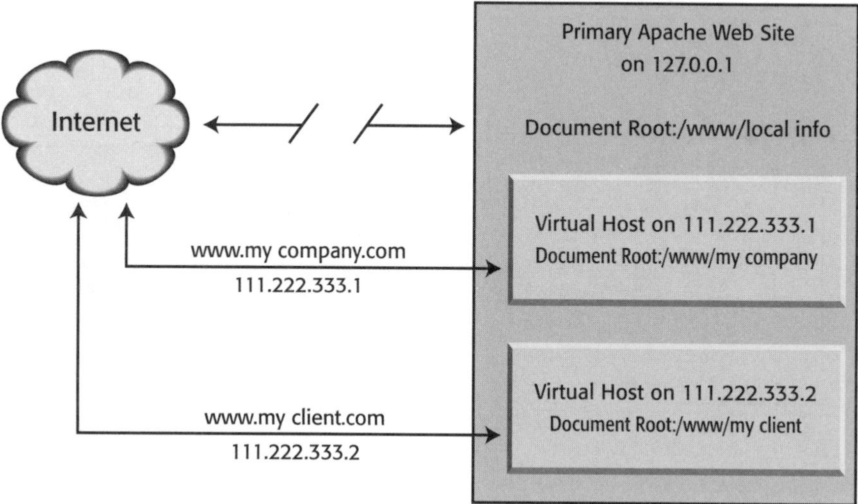

Figure 6-10: Example of IP-based virtual hosting without a main server

The simplified httpd.conf configuration file looks like this:

```
...
Port 80
ServerName webserver.mycompany.com
DocumentRoot /www/localinfo

<VirtualHost 111.222.333.1>
DocumentRoot /www/mycompany
ServerName www.mycompany.com
...
</VirtualHost>

<VirtualHost 111.222.333.2>
DocumentRoot /www/myclient
ServerName www.myclient.com
...
</VirtualHost>
```

In such a setup, the main server can only service the requests of local users who are running their Web browsers on this machine. So, when a local user enters http://localhost/, he or she will be able to access the main server pages stored in /www/localinfo. Calls such as www.mycompany.com/ and www.myclient.com/, however, are serviced by their respective virtual servers.

IP-based virtual hosts on different ports

This example uses the same hosts as in the previous two examples, but this time I want to show how you can configure Apache to have one virtual host listening to one port and another to a different port. Figure 6-11 shows the logical diagram of this example.

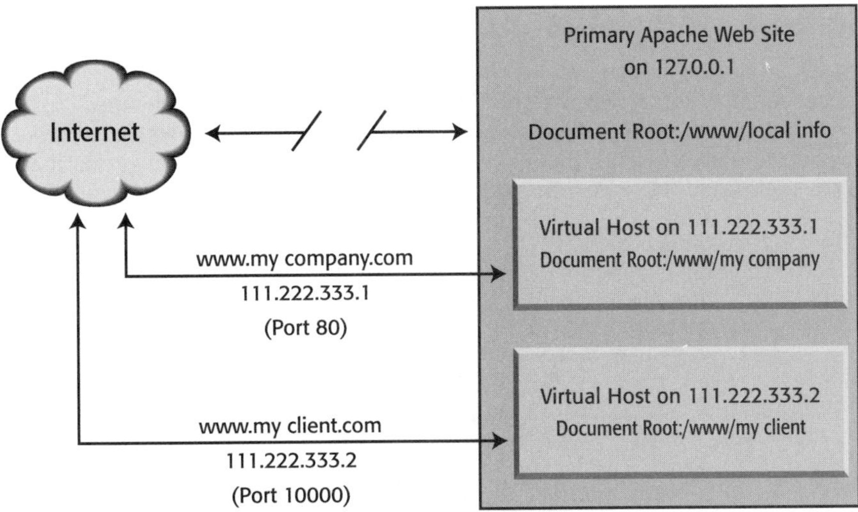

Figure 6-11: Example of IP-based virtual hosting on different ports

The simplified httpd.conf configuration file looks like this:

```
...
Listen 111.222.333.1:80
Listen 111.222.333.2:10000
ServerName webserver.mycompany.com
DocumentRoot /www/localinfo

<VirtualHost 111.222.333.1>
DocumentRoot /www/mycompany
ServerName www.mycompany.com
...
</VirtualHost>

<VirtualHost 111.222.333.2>
DocumentRoot /www/myclient
ServerName www.myclient.com
...
</VirtualHost>
```

As in the example before this one, the main server can only catch the requests from the local users. The www.mycompany.com server can be reached via the standard port (valid URLs are www.mycompany.com/ and www.mycompany.com:80/). The www.myclient.com site, however, can only be reached through the port 10000. Therefore, to access this site the following URL needs to be used:

```
http://www.mycompany.com:10000/
```

Now lets look at a name-based example configuration.

Name-based virtual hosts

This example shows you how to configure a single-IP-based host, webserver.mycompany.com, to host two name-based virtual Web sites: www.mycompany.com and www.myclient.com. Figure 6-12 shows a simplified diagram of what this example discusses. As you can see, the Web server machine has a single IP address with the following DNS records:

```
www.mywebserver.com    IN A        111.222.333.1
www.mycompany.com      IN CNAME    webserver.mycompany.com.
www.myclient.com       IN CNAME    webserver.mycompany.com.
```

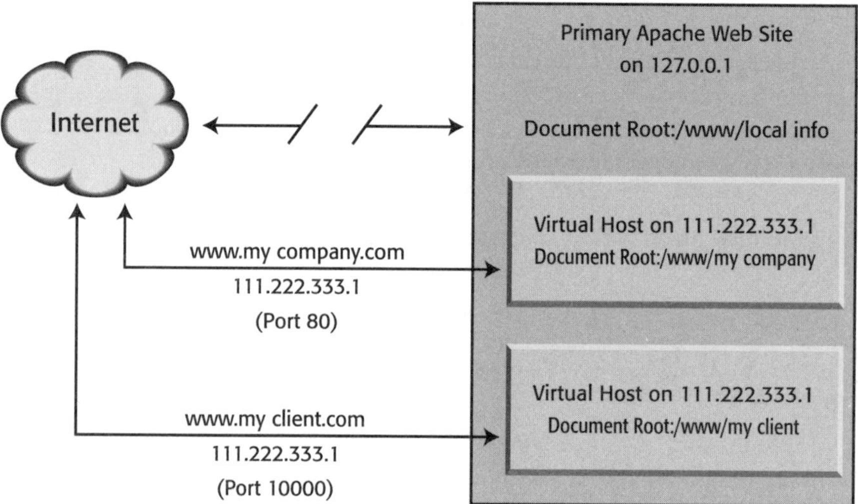

Figure 6-12: Example of name-based virtual hosting

www.mycompany.com and www.myclient.com are two aliases (CNAME records) for webserver.mycompany.com.

The simplified httpd.conf configuration file looks like this:

```
...
Port 80
ServerName webserver.mycompany.com

#Following NameVirtualHost directive is only needed for Apache
versions 1.3 or later
NameVirtualHost 111.222.333.1

# first (or primary) virtual server
<VirtualHost 111.222.333.1>
DocumentRoot /www/mycompany
ServerName www.mycompany.com
```

```
...
</VirtualHost>

<VirtualHost 111.222.333.1>
DocumentRoot /www/myclient
ServerName www.myclient.com
...
</VirtualHost>
```

The main server only services the local users on the system. The first virtual host is what users with non-HTTP/1.1-compliant browsers see. Other than that, all HTTP/1.1-compliant browsers can request the proper virtual host, and the server services them according to the virtual host settings found in the configuration file. Now lets look at a mixed (IP-based and name-based) virtual server example.

Mixing IP-based and name-based virtual hosts

Now lets take a look at an example where both IP-based and name-based virtual hosts are configured. In this example, I use the following DNS records.

```
www.mywebserver.com    IN A        111.222.333.1
www.myclient.com       IN A        111.222.333.2
www.mycompany.com      IN CNAME    webserver.mycompany.com.
www.mycompany.com      IN CNAME    webserver.mycompany.com.
```

The simplified httpd.conf configuration file looks like this:

```
...
Port 80
ServerName webserver.mycompany.com
#Following NameVirtualHost directive is only needed for Apache
versions 1.3 or later
NameVirtualHost 111.222.333.1

<VirtualHost 111.222.333.1>
DocumentRoot /www/client1
ServerName www.client1.com
...
</VirtualHost>

<VirtualHost 111.222.333.1>
DocumentRoot /www/client2
ServerName www.client2.com
...
</VirtualHost>

<VirtualHost 111.222.333.2>
DocumentRoot /www/mycompany
ServerName www.mycompany.com
...
</VirtualHost>
```

When you are combining both IP-based and name-based virtual hosts, remember to use the NameVirtualHost directive before all the name-based virtual hosts with the same IP. If you want to keep your configuration files readable, simply enter the NameVirtualHost once per IP and list all the name-based virtual hosts using that IP afterward, as I did in the preceding example.

Using _default_ virtual hosts

This example shows how to catch every request to any unspecified IP address and port — that is, an address/port combination that is not used for any other virtual host.

The simplified httpd.conf configuration file looks like this:

```
...
<VirtualHost _default_:*>
DocumentRoot /www/default
...
</VirtualHost>
```

Using such a default virtual host with a wildcard port effectively prevents any request from going to the primary server. A default virtual host never serves a request that was sent to an address/port that is used for name-based Virtual Hosts. If the request contains an unknown or no Host: header, it is always served from the primary name-based virtual host (with the virtual host for that address/port appearing first in the configuration file).

If you want to provide a different default for different port addresses, however, you can do that as well. See the following example.

The simplified httpd.conf configuration file looks like this:

```
...
<VirtualHost _default_:80>
DocumentRoot /www/default80
...
</VirtualHost>

<VirtualHost _default_:*>
DocumentRoot /www/default
...
</VirtualHost>
```

The default virtual host for port 80 (which must appear before any default virtual host with a wildcard port) catches all requests that were sent to an unspecified IP address. The primary server is never used to serve a request. If you want to provide a default virtual host only for port 80, then do not provide a wildcard port virtual host.

Migrating a name-based virtual host to an IP-based virtual host

In this example, let's assume that a name-based virtual host, www.myclient1.com, has been assigned the IP address 111.222.333.3. In order to reflect the changes in the Apache configuration, you need to modify the virtual host setting for www.myclient1.com as follows:

```
...
...
NameVirtualHost 111.222.333.1

<VirtualHost 111.222.333.1 111.222.333.3>
DocumentRoot /www/client1
ServerName www.myclient1.com
...
</VirtualHost>
```

Notice that the VirtualHost directive now has both the old IP 111.222.333.1 and the new IP 111.222.333.3. This is done so that both name-based and IP-based requests for this virtual host can be serviced. It is not advisable to remove the old IP right away, because many name servers and proxies could have cached the old IP and might fail to find the site until they update their DNS data. The virtual host www.myclient.com can now be accessed through the new address (as an IP-based virtual host) and through the old address (as a name-based virtual host).

The Limiting Factor for Virtual Hosting

Now let's take a look at an issue that could affect servers with a large number of virtual hosts. UNIX operating systems limit the number of file descriptors (also known as file handles) a process can use. Typically this limit is 64, and may be increased to a large hard-limit. When using a large number of virtual hosts, Apache may run out of available file descriptors.

Apache uses one file descriptor for each log file it opens, and about 10 to 20 additional file descriptors for its internal use. If Apache approaches the limit set on your system, it may try to allocate more file descriptors for itself. This attempt could fail, however, if your system does not provide the setrlimit() system call, if the call does not work on your system, if the needed number of descriptors exceeds the maximum allowance on your system, or if your system has other limits that affect the number of file descriptors.

If you are faced with such a situation, you can try two options to resolve this:

✦ Reduce the number of log files Apache uses; you may want to look at your VirtualHost entries and remove individual log features for each virtual host.

✦ On most UNIX systems, you could try to set the file descriptor limits manually before running Apache. Use the ulimit command as follows:

```
ulimit -S -n 100
```

to set the limit to 100 descriptors. Try different numbers based on your needs. Consult the ulimit man pages for details.

So far I have discussed various aspects of Apache virtual host configurations, which should enable you to set up your own virtual Web sites. I will now switch gears and focus on another aspect of virtual hosting that is not directly linked with Apache, but still is very important for systems with many virtual Web sites.

Sendmail Configuration for Your Virtual Web Site

As I mentioned earlier, virtual Web sites are economical for the service providers as well as the customers. Instead of having a dedicated server system on the Internet, an organization (or even an individual) can have a virtual Web site on an ISP and look exactly like the big players. The virtual Web site is really the entrée for a professional Internet presence. In order to look really professional, most organizations also want their e-mail addresses to reflect their virtual Internet domain name. For example, if you had to guess a Microsoft programmer's e-mail address, you would probably guess that it ends with @microsoft.com and not @aol.com, right? The same is expected from any modern company with Internet access. So, there's a great need for supporting a virtual Internet domain with both a virtual Web site and a virtual e-mail server. Since this is a common requirement for a virtual Internet domain, I will now discuss the configuration changes you need to make to create a virtual SMTP e-mail server.

Because sendmail is the most popular (ever wonder why it is still so cryptic to configure?) SMTP mail server, I use it for all the examples in this section.

To keep things simple, let's assume you want to set up a virtual SMTP mail server for the virtual Internet domain milkyweb.com on nitec.com. We'll also assume that nitec.com's mail server is mail.nitec.com, which will be used as the virtual mail server for milkyweb.com.

DNS configuration for your virtual SMTP mail server

Before you can configure the mail server (sendmail), you need to make sure that proper DNS settings for mail service exist. The DNS records that dictate where mail arrives are called MX records.

In the virtual domain's DNS database file (milkyweb.db), you enter the following line:

```
IN      MX    10 mail.nitec.com.
```

This line goes right after the NS record lines. It states that the SMTP mail server for milkyweb.com is mail.nitec.com, and that it has a priority setting of 10. If nitec.com had multiple mail servers and they were all configured to receive milkyweb.com's mail, then you could add multiple MX records where the priority number and the mail host differ. For example, if you had another mail host called postoffice.nitec.com in nitec.com that was capable of accepting milkyweb.com's mail, you could add:

```
IN      MX      10 mail.nitec.com.
IN      MX      20 postoffice.nitec.com.
```

Notice the priority numbers 10 and 20. They are arbitrary, but there is a scheme: the lower the number, the higher the priority. So, for the preceding example, an Internet mail server wanting to send mail to milkyweb.com will first try the mail.nitec.com host to deliver the mail. If, for some reason, mail.nitec.com is unavailable, it will then try the postoffice.nitec.com server.

Using the nslookup utility, you can ensure that the MX records are configured correctly. The following command entered in the nslookup prompt does just that:

```
set q=mx
milkyweb.com
```

Once the DNS configuration is completed, the next step in setting up the virtual mail support is to edit the /etc/sendmail.cw file of the mail.nitec.com system. Because sendmail configuration might vary between versions, though, you may first want to consult documentation found at the following URL before proceeding to the following section:

```
www.sendmail.org/
```

The following configuration has been tested on sendmail: 8.8.5/8.8.5.

Configuring /etc/sendmail.cw

The /etc/sendmail.cw file contains names of domains that a sendmail daemon services. In this case, you add the milkyweb.com domain in this file:

```
# sendmail.cw - include all aliases for your machine here.
nitec.com
milkyweb.com
```

The next step is to create a virtual user for the physical user translation table.

Creating a virtual user table database

A virtual user table database maps virtual addresses into real addresses. You create a text file where each line has a key/value pair, separated by a tab. For example:

```
info@milkyweb.com            jgunchy
webmaster@milkyweb.com       kabir
@milkyweb.com                jenny.gunchy@aol.com
```

In this example, the address info@milkyweb.com will be mapped to the local user jgunchy, webmaster@milkyweb.com will be mapped to the local user kabir, and anything else coming in to milkyweb.com will go to remote user jenny.gunchy@aol.com. If milkyweb.com had real users on another domain (such as hotmail.com) then you could replace the last line with:

```
@milkyweb.com         %1@hotmail.com
```

This line maps all milkyweb.com users to real users with the same name on hotmail.com. The idea is to map virtual users to some real accounts on either a local or remote system. Once this text file is created, you can use it to create a database file using the makemap utility that comes with standard sendmail distribution:

```
makemap <database type> /etc/virtusertable <  <text file
containing the virtual user map>
```

If the preceding virtual user table text file is called /etc/virtusertable.txt, and you are using the dbm database type, then use the makemap command as follows:

```
makemap dbm /etc/virtusertable < /etc/virtusertable.txt
```

This actually creates one or more non-text files (typically, /etc/virtusertable.dir and /etc/virtusertable.pag, or /etc/virtusertable.db), but does not actually change the /etc/virtusertable.txt file itself. Note that on systems where dbm is not available, you can try the hash option as follows:

```
makemap hash /etc/virtusertable < /etc/virtusertable.txt
```

If you would like to reverse-map local users for outbound mail, you should consult the Masquerading and Relaying page for sendmail at www.sendmail.org/m4/masquerading.html.

The next step is to configure the /etc/sendmail.cf file.

Configuring /etc/sendmail.cf

In the /etc/sendmail.cf file, locate the following lines:

```
# Virtual user table (maps incoming users)
#Kvirtuser dbm /etc/virtusertable
```

Uncomment the second line by removing the leading # sign; replace dbm with **hash -o** if you used the hash method instead of dbm. So for hash method the line would look like this:

```
Kvirtuser hash  -o /etc/virtusertable
```

and for the dbm method, it would be:

```
Kvirtuser dbm /etc/virtusertable
```

Now, locate rule set S98 and uncomment the rules so they look similar to the following:

```
S98
# addresses sent to foo@host.REDIRECT will give a 551 error code
R$* < @ $+ .REDIRECT. >         $: $1 < @ $2 . REDIRECT . > < ${opMode} >
R$* < @ $+ .REDIRECT. > <i>     $: $1 < @ $2 . REDIRECT. >
R$* < @ $+ .REDIRECT. > < $- >  $# error $@ 5.1.1 $: "551 User has moved;
please try " <$1@$2>
```

Note that the rules may be written differently in a newer version of the sendmail distribution, so you should uncomment them first before attempting to make any modifications.

Testing virtual e-mail service

Once the preceding steps are completed, you can restart the sendmail server and test your changes.

You do not need to restart sendmail when you change the virtual user (or generic tables for reverse-map) – only when you change /etc/sendmail.cf or class files such as /etc/sendmail.cw.

Sendmail provides a method for testing the rules in the configuration files. Using the following command:

```
/usr/sbin/sendmail -bt
```

you can enter into an interactive ruleset test mode in sendmail. In Figure 6-13, I perform one such test for the e-mail address webmaster@milkyweb.com; notice that sendmail goes through all the necessary rule translation and finally decides to deliver mail to my account called kabir on the local system. Note that to test an address, all you need to enter in the interactive test mode is:

```
0 user@host
```

```
Telnet - blackhole
Connect Edit Terminal Help
#sendmail -bt
ADDRESS TEST MODE (ruleset 3 NOT automatically invoked)
Enter <ruleset> <address>
> 0 webmaster@milkyweb.com
rewrite: ruleset   0   input: webmaster @ milkyweb . com
rewrite: ruleset  98   input: webmaster @ milkyweb . com
rewrite: ruleset  98 returns: webmaster @ milkyweb . com
rewrite: ruleset  97   input: webmaster @ milkyweb . com
rewrite: ruleset   3   input: webmaster @ milkyweb . com
rewrite: ruleset  96   input: webmaster < @ milkyweb . com >
rewrite: ruleset  96 returns: webmaster < @ milkyweb . com . >
rewrite: ruleset   3 returns: webmaster < @ milkyweb . com . >
rewrite: ruleset   0   input: webmaster < @ milkyweb . com . >
rewrite: ruleset  98   input: webmaster < @ milkyweb . com . >
rewrite: ruleset  98 returns: webmaster < @ milkyweb . com . >
rewrite: ruleset  97   input: kabir
rewrite: ruleset   3   input: kabir
rewrite: ruleset  96   input: kabir
rewrite: ruleset  96 returns: kabir
rewrite: ruleset   3 returns: kabir
rewrite: ruleset   0   input: kabir
rewrite: ruleset  98   input: kabir
rewrite: ruleset  98 returns: kabir
rewrite: ruleset   0 returns: $# local $: kabir
rewrite: ruleset  97 returns: $# local $: kabir
rewrite: ruleset   0 returns: $# local $: kabir
rewrite: ruleset  97 returns: $# local $: kabir
rewrite: ruleset   0 returns: $# local $: kabir
>
```

Figure 6-13: Testing the sendmail ruleset for a virtual domain

If the testing reveals any problems, make sure you review the changes you made. You should also check the log file for sendmail on your mail server to see if you notice any errors. If all is well, you should try sending mail from another domain and check to see if you receive mail. Note that if you make any DNS changes to get the mail service set up, the DNS update for your site may take some time to propagate to other name servers on the Internet.

Summary

Virtual Web sites are everywhere. These days, most ISPs are using virtual Web hosting service to place both personal and business Web sites on the Internet. In this chapter, I covered all the details of how Apache can be used to create these virtual Web sites. I also discussed the necessary information for turning sendmail into a mail server for your virtual hosts. Being able to provide both virtual Web and mail service can greatly enhance any Apache administrator's marketability, and not to mention his or her satisfaction.

In the next chapter, you learn about Server Side Includes.

✦ ✦ ✦

CHAPTER 7

Server Side Includes for Apache

✦ ✦ ✦ ✦

In This Chapter

What are Server Side Includes?

How to set up Apache for SSI

How to use SSI commands

✦ ✦ ✦ ✦

In Chapter 8, you will learn that dynamic Web content can be created using CGI programs; however, there are tasks that may not call for the development of full-blown CGI programs but still require some dynamic intervention. For example, say you want to add a standard copyright message to all your HTML pages; how would you go about implementing this? Well, you have two solutions: Either add the content of the copyright message in each HTML page, or write a CGI program that will add the message to each HTML page. Neither of these options is elegant. The first option requires that anytime you make a change to the copyright message, you manually update all your files. The second option requires that you have some way of getting your CGI program running before each page is sent out to the Web browser. This would also mean that every link on each page has to call this CGI program so it can append the message to the next page. Situations like these demanded a simpler solution: Server Side Includes (SSI), which is the topic of this chapter.

What Are Server Side Includes?

A Server Side Include (SSI) page is typically an HTML page with embedded command(s) for the Web server. The Web server normally does not parse HTML pages before delivery to the Web browser (or any other Web clients). However, an SSI-enabled HTML page is always parsed by the Web server before delivery, and if any special SSI command is found in the page, it is executed. Figure 7-1 shows the simplified delivery cycle of an HTML page and an SSI-enabled HTML page from a Web server.

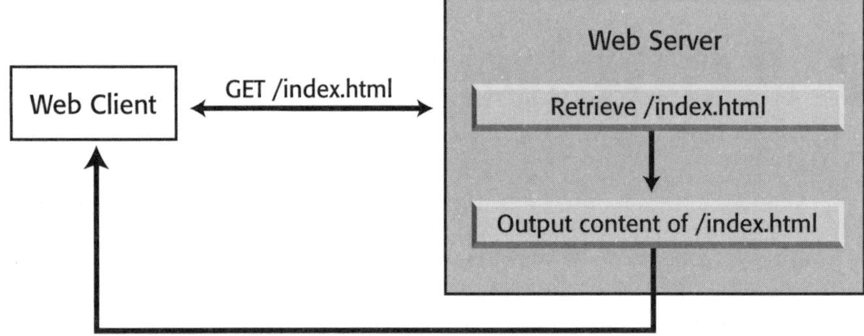

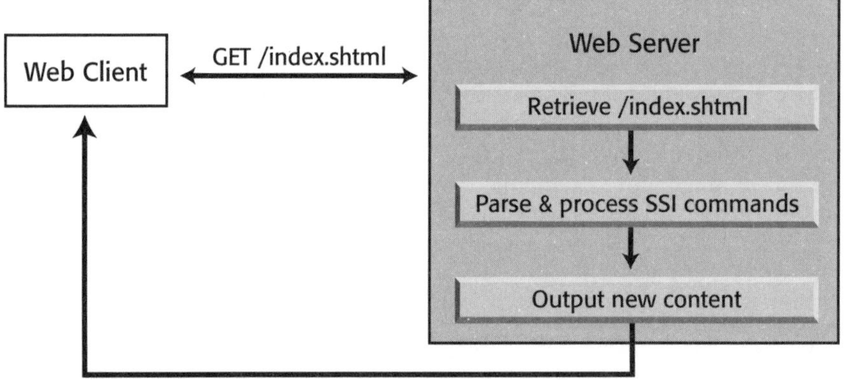

Figure 7-1: Simplified delivery cycle diagram for an HTML page and an SSI-enabled HTML page

As you can see, the SSI version of the HTML page is first parsed for SSI commands. These commands are executed, and finally the new output is delivered to the Web browser (that is, the Web client.)

Apache has supported SSI for a long time. The module that is responsible for SSI is called mod_include, and it is part of the standard Apache distribution. For a while, an optional Apache module package called eXtended Server Side Includes (XSSI) provided an enhanced set of functionality. The XSSI package, written by Howard

Fear, has now been incorporated into the standard distribution, and the standard module now provides support for all the SSI and XSSI commands.

If you are still using a very old version of Apache (that is, prior to 1.2*x*), you need to install the XSSI module, which can be found at www.pageplus.com/~hsf/xssi/.

Fear's XSSI code added more programming language-like functionality such as variables and flow control to the standard SSI command set of the Apache server. Before you can use SSI in your HTML pages, however, you need to configure the Apache server.

Configuring Apache for SSI

Before you can configure Apache for SSI, you need to check your current Apache executable (httpd) to make sure the mod_include module is included in it. To do this, run the following command:

```
httpd -l
```

This enables you to see the list of all modules used in building your Apache executable. By default, you should have this module compiled; if not, you need to add it to the Configuration file using the following line:

```
AddModule modules/standard/mod_include.o
```

Then, you need to run Configure and the make utility, respectively.

Although the mod_include module is compiled by default in the standard Apache distribution, the parsing of HTML pages is not enabled by default. To enable SSI support for Apache (versions 1.2 or above) you need to perform the following steps:

1. Add a new handler for SSI/IXSSI HTML pages.
2. Add a new file extension for SSI/IXSSI HTML pages.
3. Enable SSI parsing for a directory.

When these steps are completed for a directory called chapter 07, under a virtual host called apache.nitec.com, the configuration appears as shown below:

```
<VirtualHost 206.171.50.50>

ServerName apache.nitec.com
DocumentRoot /data/web/apache/public/htdocs
ScriptAlias /data/web/apache/public/cgi-bin
```

```
<Directory /data/web/apache/public/htdocs/chapter_07>
AddHandler serer-parsed .shtml
AddType text/html .shtml
Options +Include
</Directory>

</VirtualHost>
```

The use of Include in the Options directive enables all SSI commands. If you plan on disabling execution of external programs via SSI commands, you can use IncludesNOEXEC instead. This disables execution of external programs. However, it also disables loading of external files via the SSI command Include.

Now let's take a closer look at each step involved in enabling SSI support.

Add a new handler for SSI HTML pages

By default, Apache does not parse HTML files when requested. If it did, the HTML pages that do not have SSI commands in them would still need to be parsed, and the unnecessary parsing would make the delivery of these pages slower. The solution to this problem is to identify pages that do have SSI commands with a different file extension than the typical HTML file extensions (.html or .htm). Let's say you want to use .shtml as the SSI file extension for all HTML pages that will contain one or more SSI commands. You need to tell Apache that the file extension .shtml should be treated as an SSI-enabled page. You can do that using the AddHandler directive as follows:

```
AddHandler server-parsed .shtml
```

The AddHandler directive tells Apache that an .shtml file needs to be handled by the server-parsed handler, which is found in the mod_include module.

If, for some reason, you have to use .html and .htm extension as the SSI extension, do not use:

```
AddHandler server-parsed .html
AddType text/html .html

AddHandler server-parsed .htm
AddType text/html .htm
```

This would degrade your server performance. Apache would process all the .html and .htm files, which would mean that files without any SSI commands would be parsed, therefore increasing the delay in file delivery. You should try hard to avoid using the .html or .htm extensions for SSI; if you must use them, however, then use the XbitHack directive found in the mod_include module.

The XBitHack directive

The XBitHack directive controls server parsing of files associated with the MIME-type text/html.

```
Syntax: XBitHack on | off | full
Default: XBitHack off
Context: server config, virtual host, directory, .per-directory
access control file (.htaccess)
Override: Options
Module: mod_include
```

Typically, only .html and .htm files are associated with text/html. The default value "off" tells the server not to parse these files. When this is set to "on," any HTML file that has execute permission for the file owner is considered an SSI file and is parsed. When the directive is set to "full," it makes the server check the owner and the group executable bits of the file permission settings. If the group executable bit is set, then Apache sets the last-modified date of the returned file to be the last modified time of the file. If it is not set, then no last-modified date is sent. Setting this bit enables clients and proxies to cache the result of the request. Use of the value "full" is not advisable for SSI pages that produce a different output when parsed and processed.

Note that you will still have to perform the third step (Options +Includes) when using this directive.

Add a new file extension for SSI HTML pages

Although Apache now knows how to handle the .shtml file, it needs to be told what to tell the Web browser about this file. Web servers send header information for each request to tell the Web browser what type of content is being sent as the response. Therefore, you need to tell Apache that when responding to an .shtml file request, it should tell the browser, by setting the content type, that the information being sent is still an HTML document. This way, the Web browser will render the content onscreen as usual. The MIME type for HTML content is text/html. The following line shows how Apache can be told to generate text/html content-type header when transmitting the output of an .shtml page:

```
AddType text/html     .shtml
```

For backward compatibility, documents with the MIME-type text/x-server-parsed-html or text/x-server-parsed-html3 will also be parsed (and the resulting output is given the MIME-type text/html).

Enable SSI parsing for a directory

Both Apache and Web browsers know how to handle the new .shtml files; however, Apache is still not ready to parse the .shtml pages.

Using the Options directive, you need to tell Apache that you want to enable Includes support. First, however, you need to determine where to put this Options directive.

If you want to enable SSI support in the entire (primary) Web site, add the following directive in one of the global configuration files (such as access.conf):

```
Options +Includes
```

If you want to enable SSI support for a virtual Web site, you need to put the preceding directive inside the appropriate <VirtualHost ...> container. Or, if you want to be able to control this option from directory to directory, you can put this directive inside a <Directory ...> container or in the per-directory access control file (.htaccess).

If you use per-directory access control file (.htaccess) to enable SSI support, make sure the AllowOverride directive for the site owning that directory allows such an operation. The AllowOverride directive for such a site must allow the Includes option to be overridden. For example, if the AllowOverride is set to None for a site, no SSI parsing will occur.

If you do not use the + sign in the Options line in the preceding example, all the options except Includes will be disabled.

Now that you know how to enable SSI support in Apache, let's discuss the SSI commands in detail.

Using SSI Commands

SSI commands are embedded in HTML pages in the form of comments. The base command structure looks like this:

```
<!—#command argument1=value argument2=value argument3=value …>
```

The value is often enclosed in double quotes; many commands only allow a single attribute-value pair. Note that the comment terminator (➪) should be preceded by white space to ensure that it isn't considered part of the SSI command.

Now, let's examine all the available SSI commands.

config

The config command enables you to configure the parse error message that appears, and the formatting that is used for displaying time and file size information. This is accomplished with the following lines of code:

- `config errmsg="error message"`
- `config sizefmt=["bytes" | "abbrev"]`
- `config timefmt=format string`

The first syntax shows how to create a custom error message:

```
config errmsg="error message"
```

This error message is displayed when a parsing error occurs. For example, Listing 7-1 shows a file called config_errmsg.shtml.

Listing 7-1: config_errmsg.shtml

```
<HTML>
<HEAD><TITLE> Apache Server Bible - Chapter 7 </TITLE></HEAD>
<BODY BGCOLOR="white">

<FONT SIZE=+1 FACE="Arial"> Simple SSI Example #1</FONT>
<HR SIZE=1>

<P> Example of the SSI <STRONG>config errmsg</STRONG> command:
</P>
<P> Embedded commands: <BR><BR>

<CODE>
       &lt;!–#config errmsg="This is a custom SSI error
message." –&gt; <BR>
       &lt;!–#config errmsg_typo="This is a custom SSI error
message." –&gt;
</CODE>

</P>

<P> Result: <BR>

<!–#config errmsg="This is a custom SSI error message." -->
<BR>
<!–#config errmsg_typo="This is a custom error message." -->

</P>

</BODY>
</HTML>
```

In this example file, there are two SSI commands. They are:

```
<!—#config errmsg="This is a custom SSI error message." -->
```

and

```
<!—#config errmsg_typo="This is a custom error message." -->
```

The first one is a valid config errmsg command that sets the error message to the string "This is a custom SSI error message." The second one is an invalid SSI command which I intentionally entered into this file to show you what happens. Figure 7-2 shows what is returned to the browser when this page is requested from an Apache server called apache.nitec.com.

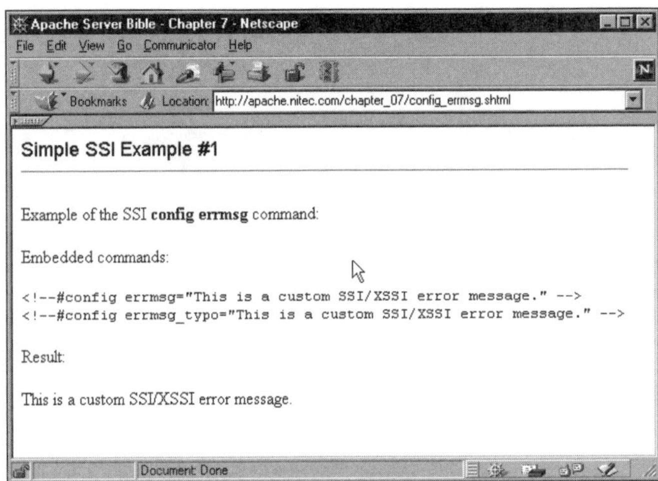

Figure 7-2: Example of config errmsg command

As you can see, the second command caused a parse error, and the error message is displayed as a result. The message appears where the command is found. It is possible to enter HTML tags or even insert client-side script in the string of the error message. For example, the following displays a pop-up JavaScript alert window with an error message:

```
<!— config errmsg="<SCRIPT LANGUAGE=JavaScript> alert('An error
occurred. \n Please report to webmaster@nitec.com');</SCRIPT>" -->
```

The second syntax enables you to choose the output format for the file size:

```
config sizefmt=["bytes" | "abbrev"]
```

Acceptable format specifiers are "bytes" or "abbrev." For example:

```
<!— config sizefmt="bytes" -->
```

This shows file sizes in bytes. To show files in kilobytes or megabytes, use:

```
<!— config sizefmt="abbrev" -->
```

The final syntax enables you to choose the display format for time:

```
config timefmt=format string
```

The commonly used value of the format string can consist of the following identifiers:

%a	The abbreviated weekday name according to the current locale
%A	The full weekday name according to the current locale
%b	The abbreviated month name according to the current locale
%B	The full month name according to the current locale
%c	The preferred date and time representation for the current locale
%d	The day of the month as a decimal number (range 01 to 31)
%H	The hour as a decimal number using a 24-hour clock (range 00 to 23)
%I	The hour as a decimal number using a 12-hour clock (range 01 to 12)
%j	The day of the year as a decimal number (range 001 to 366)
%m	The month as a decimal number (range 01 to 12)
%M	The minute as a decimal number
%p	Either a.m. or p.m., according to the given time value or locale
%S	The second as a decimal number
%w	The day of the week as a decimal, Sunday being 0
%x	The preferred date representation for the current locale without the time
%X	The preferred time representation for the current locale without the date
%y	The year as a decimal number without a century (range 00 to 99)
%Y	The year as a decimal number including the century
%Z	The time zone name or abbreviation
%%	A literal % character

Consider this example:

```
<!—#config timefmt="%c" -->
```

This shows the time as Tue May 20 00:54:07 1998.

And the following example:

```
<!—#config timefmt="%m/%d/%Y" -->
```

This shows the time as 05/20/1998.

echo

The echo command prints one of the Include variables (defined later) or any of the CGI environment variables. The syntax is:

```
echo var="variable name"
```

If the value of the variable is not available, it prints (none) as the value. Any dates printed are subject to the currently configured timefmt. For example:

```
<!—#config timefmt="%m/%d/%Y" -->
<!—#echo var="DATE_LOCAL" -->
```

This prints a date such as 05/20/1998, due to the specified timefmt string.

exec

The exec command enables you to execute an external program. The external program can be a CGI program or any other type of executable such as shell scripts or native-binary files. The syntax for CGI programs is:

```
exec cgi="path/to/cgi/program"
```

The syntax for other programs is:

```
exec cmd="path/to/other/programs"icon-note
```

If you used the IncludesNOEXEC value for the Options directive, this command is disabled.

Let's look at how to use each of these options.

cgi

The cgi value specifies a (%-encoded) URL relative path to the CGI script. If the path does not begin with a slash (/), then it is taken to be relative to the current document. The document referenced by this path is invoked as a CGI script, even if the server would not normally recognize it as such. However, the directory containing the script must be enabled for CGI scripts (with ScriptAlias or the ExecCGI Option).

The CGI script is given the PATH_INFO and query string (QUERY_STRING) of the original request from the client; these cannot be specified in the URL path. The Include variables will be available to the script in addition to the standard CGI environment.

If the script returns a Location: header instead of output, this is translated into an HTML anchor. For example, the following code shows a simple Perl CGI script that prints out a Location: header as the output:

```
#!/usr/local/bin/perl
print "Location: http://apache.nitec.com/\\n\\n\";
exit 0;
```

When the exec_cgi.shtml file, shown in Listing 7-2, is requested by a Web browser, the server turns the Location header into an HTML anchor instead of redirecting the browser to the http://apache.nitec.com site.

Listing 7-2: **exec_cgi.shtml**

```
<HTML>
<HEAD> <TITLE> Apache Server Bible - Chapter 7 </TITLE></HEAD>

<BODY BGCOLOR="white">
<FONT SIZE=+1 FACE="Arial"> Simple SSI Example #2</FONT>
<HR SIZE=1>

<P> Example of the SSI <STRONG>exec cgi</STRONG> command: </P>
<P> Embedded commands: <BR><BR>

<CODE> &lt;!—#exec cgi="/cgi-bin/loc.cgi" —&gt; <BR> </CODE>
</P>
<P> Result: <BR>  <!—#exec cgi="/cgi-bin/loc.cgi" --> </P>

</BODY>
</HTML>
```

As you can see in the listing, the only SSI call in the file is:

```
<!—#exec cgi="/cgi-bin/loc.cgi" —>
```

The output of this is an HTML anchor, as shown in Figure 7-3.

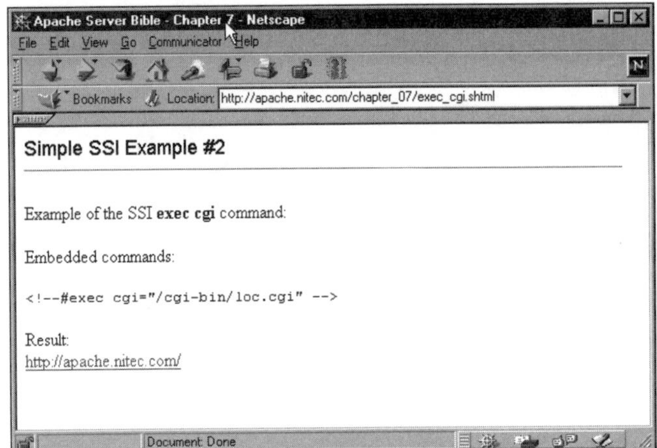

Figure 7-3: Output of exec_cgi.shtml

cmd

When calling a program other than a CGI program, you can use the cmd version of the exec call. The server executes the given string using the sh shell (/bin/sh) on most UNIX systems. The Include variables are available to this command. For example, Listing 7-3 shows a file called exec_cmd.shtml.

Listing 7-3: exec_cmd.shtml

```
<HTML>
<HEAD> <TITLE> Apache Server Bible - Chapter 7 </TITLE></HEAD>
<BODY BGCOLOR="white">

<FONT SIZE=+1 FACE="Arial"> Simple SSI Example #3</FONT>
<HR SIZE=1>

<P> Example of the SSI <STRONG>exec cmd</STRONG> command: </P>
<P> Embedded commands: <BR><BR>

<CODE>
&lt;!—#exec cmd="/bin/date +%m/%d/%y" —&gt; <BR>
&lt;!—#exec cmd="/bin/ls -l ./" —&gt; <BR>
</CODE>

</P>
<P> Result: <BR>

<!—#exec cmd="/bin/date +%m/%d/%y" --> <BR>

<PRE>
```

```
<!-#exec cmd="/bin/ls -l ./*.html" --> <BR>

</PRE>

</P>
</BODY>
</HTML>
```

This file has two cmd calls:

```
<!-#exec cmd="/bin/date +%m/%d/%y" -->
<!-#exec cmd="/bin/ls -l ./*.html" -->
```

The first one calls the UNIX /bin/date utility with the argument +%m/%d/%y, and the second one calls the UNIX ls utility with ./*.html as the argument. The output of this file is shown in Figure 7-4.

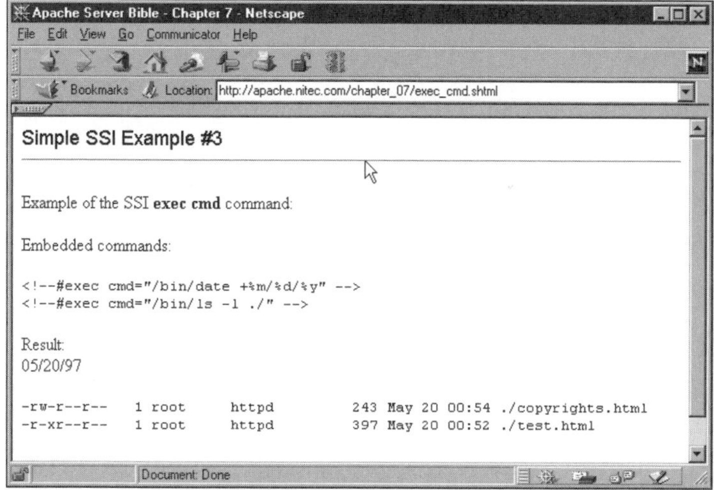

Figure 7-4: Output of exec_cmd.shtml

Notice that the ls output is nicely formatted using the <PRE> and </PRE> pair. If you want to output something that uses new lines, you may have to use <PRE> tags to keep the output readable, as shown in the preceding figure.

fsize

This command prints the size of the specified file. The syntax you use for this depends on whether the path to the directory is relative or virtual:

✦ `fsize file="path"`

✦ `fsize virtual="URL"`

When the first syntax is used, the path is assumed to be relative to the directory containing the current SSI document being parsed. You cannot use ../ in the path, nor can absolute paths be used. You cannot access a CGI script in this fashion. You can, however, access another parsed document. For example:

```
<!—#fsize file="download.zip">
```

If the second syntax is used, the virtual path is assumed to be a (%-encoded) URL path. If the path does not begin with a slash (/), then it is taken to be relative to the current document. You must access a normal file this way, but you cannot access a CGI script in this fashion. Once again, however, you can access another parsed document. For example:

```
<!—#fsize virtual="/download/free_software.zip">
```

Note

The output format is subject to the sizefmt format specification. See the config command for details.

flastmod

The flastmod command prints the last modification date of the specified file. Again, there are two syntax options depending on the path to the directory:

✦ `flastmod file="path"`

✦ `flastmod virtual="URL"`

The output is subject to the timefmt format specification. For example:

```
<!—#flastmod file="free_software.zip">
<!—#flastmod virtual="/download/free_software.zip">
```

Note

If you are unclear about the syntax difference, see the fsize command as an example. To control how the modification date is printed, see the config command.

include

The include directive inserts the text of a document into the SSI document being processed. The syntax depends on the path to the directory:

✦ `include file="path"`

✦ `include virtual="URL"`

Note: See the fsize command for the difference between file and virtual mode.

Any included file is subject to the usual access control. If the directory containing the parsed file has the Option IncludesNOEXEC set, and including the document would cause a program to be executed, then it is not included. This prevents the execution of CGI scripts. Otherwise, CGI scripts are invoked as they normally are, using the complete URL given in the command, including any query string. For example:

```
<!—#include file="copyrights.html" -->
```

This includes the copyrights.html file in the current document. This command is useful for adding repeatable HTML code in files. Many sites use a standard menu bar on each page; if this menu bar is put in an HTML file called menu.html, it can be called from all SSI pages using a similar include file call, as in the preceding example. In the future, when changes need to be made to the menu, the site administrator only needs to update the menu.html page. This will save a lot of work if there are many files in the site.

Recursive inclusions are detected and an error message is generated after the first pass. For example, if a.shtml has an SSI call such as:

```
<!—#include file="b.shtml" -->
```

and b.shtml has a call such as:

```
<!—#include file="a.shtml" -->
```

then Apache logs and displays an error stating that a recursive include has been detected.

printenv

The printenv command prints out a listing of all existing variables and their values. The syntax is:

```
printenv
```

For example:

```
<!—#printenv -->
```

This prints all the Include and CGI environment variables available. Note that in order to make the output more readable, use of the <PRE> tag pair is recommended.

set

The set command sets the value of a user-defined variable. The syntax is:

```
set var="variable name" value="value of the variable"
```

For example:

```
<!-#set var="home" value="index.shtml" -->
```

SSI Variables

The SSI module makes a set of variables, in addition to the CGI environment variables (see Chapter 8), available to all SSI files. These variables are called the include variables. These can be used by SSI commands (echo, if, elif, and so on) and by any program invoked by an SSL command. The include variables are:

DATE_GMT	The current date in Greenwich Mean Time
DATE_LOCAL	The current date in the local time zone
DOCUMENT_NAME	The current SSI filename
DOCUMENT_URI	The (%-decoded) URL path of the document
LAST_MODIFIED	The last modification date of the current file. The date is subject to the config command's timefmt format.

The include variables and the CGI variables are preset and available for use. Any of the variables that are preset can be used as arguments for other commands. The syntax for using defined variables is as follows:

```
<!-#command argument1="$variable1" argument2="$variable2" ...-->
```

As you can see, the variable name is prefixed by a $ sign. Here's another example:

```
<!-#config errmsg="An error occurred in $DOCUMENT_NAME page." -->
```

Note

When using variables in a var="variable" field, the $ sign is not necessary. For example:

```
<!-#echo var="DOCUMENT_NAME" -->
```

If you need to insert a literal dollar sign into the value of a variable, you can insert the dollar sign using backslash quoting. For example:

```
<!-#set var="password" value="\$cheese" -->
<!-#echo var="password" -->
```

This prints $cheese as the value of the variable "password."

Also, if you need to reference a variable name in the middle of a character sequence that might otherwise be considered a valid identifier on its own, use a pair of braces around the variable name. For example:

```
<!—#set var="uniqueid" value="${DATE_LOCAL}_${REMOTE_HOST}" -->
```

This sets uniqueid to something like Tue May 20 06:47:48 1998_206.171.50.51, depending on the timefmt setting.

Flow Control Commands

Like programming languages, flow control is also available in the SSI module. Using flow control commands, you can conditionally create different output. The simplest flow control (that is, conditional) statement is:

```
<!—#if expr="test_expression" -->
<!—#endif -->
```

Here, the test_expression is evaluated, and if the result of the test is true, then all the text up to the endif command is included in the output. The test_expression can be one of the following:

```
string
```

which is true if string is not empty, or

```
string1 comparison_operator string2
```

Here, the comparison_operator can be =, !=, <, >, <=, or >=.

If string2 has the form /string/, then it is compared as a regular expression. See Appendix C for details on regular expressions.

Let's look at an example of a string by itself:

```
<!—#if expr="foobar" -->
This test is successful.
<!—#endif -->
```

This syntax always prints "This test is successful" because the expression is true when the test_expression is a non-null string. If expr="foobar" is changed to expr="" or expr="''", however, then the text within the if-endif block will never be part of the output.

Now let's look at an example of a string equality test:

```
<!—#set var="quicksearch" value="yes" -->

<!—#if expr="$quicksearch = yes" -->
Quick search is  requested.
<!—#endif -->
```

Here, the variable called quicksearch is being set with the value yes, and is later being compared with yes. Since the set value and the comparison value are equal, the "Quick search is requested" line will be the output.

Using logical operators such as !, &&, and ||, you can create more complex test_expressions. For example:

```
<!—#if expr="${REMOTE_HOST} = /206\.171\.50/ &&
${DOCUMENT_NAME} = /${DATE_LOCAL}/" -->
<!—#exec cmd="/usr/local/build/timesheet/timecalc.pl">
<!—#endif -->
```

Here, the test_expression is composed of two smaller expressions. The first subexpression, ${REMOTE_HOST} = /206\.171\.50/, is evaluated to see if the server-defined variable REMOTE_HOST matches the 206.171.50 network address. Note that the address is written using the simple regular expression /206\.171\.50/, where each . (period) is escaped using a \ (backslash) character. This was necessary to undo the . character's special meaning in regular expressions. See Appendix C for more details on regular expressions.

The second subexpression, ${DOCUMENT_NAME} = ${DATE_LOCAL}, is evaluated to see if the current SSI file being processed has a name that matches today's date (this really depends on how timefmt is setup). And finally, the && (logical AND) requires that both subexpressions be true for the entire expression be true. If the final expression is true, then the timecalc.pl script is run using the exec cmd command.

Other logical operations you can perform on the test_expression are:

```
<!—#if expr="! test_expression" -->
This is printed only when the test_expression is false.
<!—#endif -->
```

and

```
<!—#if expr="test_expression1 || test_expression2" -->
This is printed when at least one of the test_expressions is
true.
<!—#endif -->
```

The = (equal) and != (not equal) operators have higher precedence then the && (and) and the || (or) operators. The ! (not) operator has the highest priority. Note that you can use a pair of parentheses to increase priority. For example:

```
<!—#if expr="($win = yes && $loss = false) != ($profit = yes)" -->
```

Here, the ($win = yes && $loss = false) is evaluated before the != operator.

Anything that is not recognized as a variable or an operator is treated as a string. Strings can also be quoted, like this: 'string'. Unquoted strings cannot contain white space (blanks and tabs) because they are used to separate tokens such as variables. If multiple strings are found in a row, they are concatenated using blanks.

If you require more complex flow control constructs, you can use the following

```
<!—#if expr="test_condition1" -->

<!—#elif expr="test_condition2" -->

<!—#else -->

<!—#endif -->
```

The elif enables you to create an else-if condition. For example:

```
<!—#if expr="${HTTP_USER_AGENT} = /MSIE/" -->

      <!—#set var="browser" value="IE" -->
      <!—#include flie="vbscript.html" -->

<!—#else -->

      <!—#set var="browser" value="Navigator" -->
      <!—#include flie="javascript.html" -->

<!—#endif -->
```

Here, the HTTP_USER_AGENT variable is checked to see if it contains the string MSIE (a string used by Microsoft Internet Explorer browser). If it does contain this string, then the browser variable is set to "IE", and a file named vbscript.html is inserted in the current document. On the other hand, if the HTTP_USER_AGENT does not contain the MSIE string, it is assumed to be the other leading browser (Netscape Navigator), and thus the browser variable is set to "Navigator" and the javascript.html file is inserted in the current document. By using the if-then-else construct, this example sets a different value to the same variable and loads different files.

Summary

In this chapter you learned that Server Side Includes (SSI) and eXtended Server Side Includes (XSSI) add dynamic content to otherwise static Web pages. Once enabled, SSI commands are easy to use. It would be unwise, however, to use the exec command on all of your Web pages, because this command imposes a processing load on the server. The best way to use SSI commands is to map a single file extension as an SSI extension, and only enable the commands in needed directories. Moreover, if you do not need the execution of external programs or CGI scripts, you should disable the exec SSI command. You also learned that SSI provides you with flow control commands and the capability to set new variables for later use.

In the next chapter, you learn about Common Gateway Interface (CGI) configuration.

✦ ✦ ✦

CGI Configuration

In This Chapter

Basics of Common Gateway Interface (CGI)

How to configure Apache for CGI

How to provide cgi-bin access for individual users

Commonly used CGI applications

How to configure Apache to debug CGI applications

A Web server's primary job is to deliver requested contents to a client, such as a Web browser. In most cases, the requested content is stored in a file of some kind and readily accessible to the server. The server retrieves the file and transmits its contents to the requesting client system; however, what happens when the content is not readily available and needs to be generated from an application? The Web server must run the application and return the output. This is where Common Gateway Interface (CGI) comes to play.

CGI specification tells a Web server how to interact with an external application. A Web server that runs CGI applications practically enables anyone to run an external application on the server. This is a scary thought for many people who are not well informed about CGI.

In this Chapter, I discuss the basics of CGI to give you a clear understanding of it, and I also cover the details of setting up Apache to support CGI executions.

What Is CGI?

Chances are you have already used one or more CGI applications on the Web. In order to provide dynamic, interactive contents on the Web, a lot of popular Web sites use CGI applications. Of course, as more and more Web technologies emerge, new means of delivering dynamic contents over the Web are becoming available. Most of these solutions are either language specific, or operating-system or commercial-software dependent. CGI, on the other hand, is a language-independent gateway interface specification that can be implemented using virtually any widely popular application development language, including C, C++, Perl, shell scripting languages, and even Java.

Let's take a look at how a CGI program works (see Figure 8-1). The basic idea is that the Web server gets a certain URL that magically—at least for now—tells the Web server that it must run an external application called *helloworld.cgi*. The Web server launches the application; waits for it to complete and returns output. Then, it transmits the application's output to the Web client on the other side.

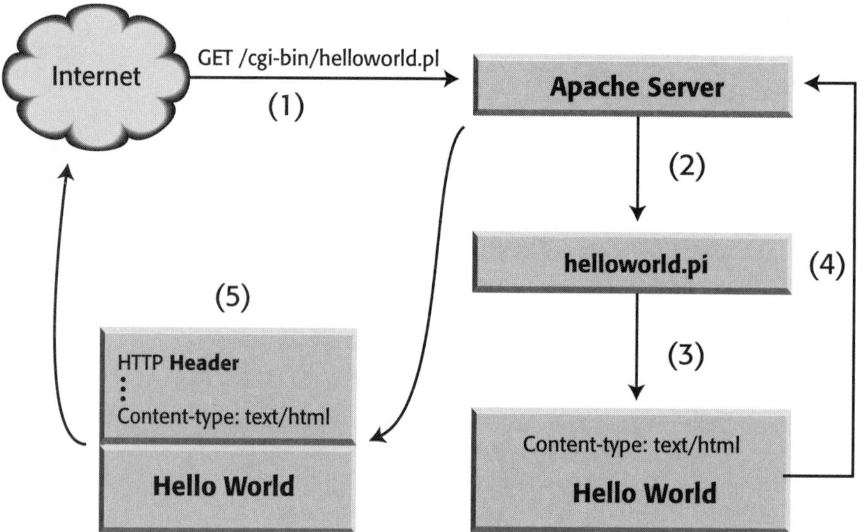

Figure 8-1: This is how a CGI program works.

What happens when you want the client to be capable of interacting with the application? Well, input data from the client must be supplied to the application. Similarly, when an application produces output, how does the server or client know what type of output to return? A program can produce a text message, an HTML form for further inputs, an image, and so on. As you can see the output can vary a lot from application to application; so there must be a way for applications to inform the Web server and the client about the output type.

CGI defines a set of standard means for the server to pass client inputs to the external applications, and it also defines how an external application can return output. Any application that adheres to these defined standards, can be labeled as a CGI application/program/script. For simplicity, I use the term *CGI program* for anything (such as a Perl script or a C program) that is CGI-specification compliant. In the following section, I discuss how the input/output process works.

CGI input and output

There are many ways a Web server can receive information from a client (such as a Web browser). The HTTP protocol defines the way in which a Web server and a client can exchange information. The most common methods of transmitting request data to a Web server are GET requests and POST requests.

GET requests

The GET request is the simplest method. Whenever you enter a Web site address in your Web browser, it generates a GET request and sends it to the intended Web server. If you enter the following:

```
www.idgbooks.com
```

your Web browser sends:

```
GET /
```

to the www.idgbooks.com Web server. This GET request asks the IDG Web server to return the top-level document of the Web document tree. This document is often called the home page, and usually refers to the index.html page in the top-level Web directory. Furthermore, HTTP enables you to encode additional information in a GET request. For example:

www.mycompany.com/cgi-bin/search.cgi?books=cgi&author=kabir

Here, the GET request is as follows:

```
GET www.mycompany.com/cgi-bin/search.cgi?books=cgi&author=kabir
```

This tells the server to execute /cgi-bin/search.cgi CGI program and pass it the books=cgi and author=kabir input data.

When a CGI-compliant Web server, such as Apache, receives this type of request, it follows the CGI specifications and passes the input data to the application (in this case, the search.cgi in the cgi-bin directory). When a CGI resource is requested via an HTTP GET request method, Apache does the following:

1. Sets the environment variables for the CGI program, which includes storing the HTTP request method name in an environment variable called REQUEST_METHOD, and the data received from the client in an environment variable called QUERY_STRING.
2. Executes the requested CGI program.
3. Waits for the program to complete and return output.
4. Parses the output of the CGI program if it is not a nonparsed header program. (A nonparsed header CGI program creates its own HTTP headers so the server does not need to parse the headers.)

5. Creates necessary HTTP header(s).
6. Sends the headers and the output of the program to the requesting client.

Figure 8-2 illustrates this process.

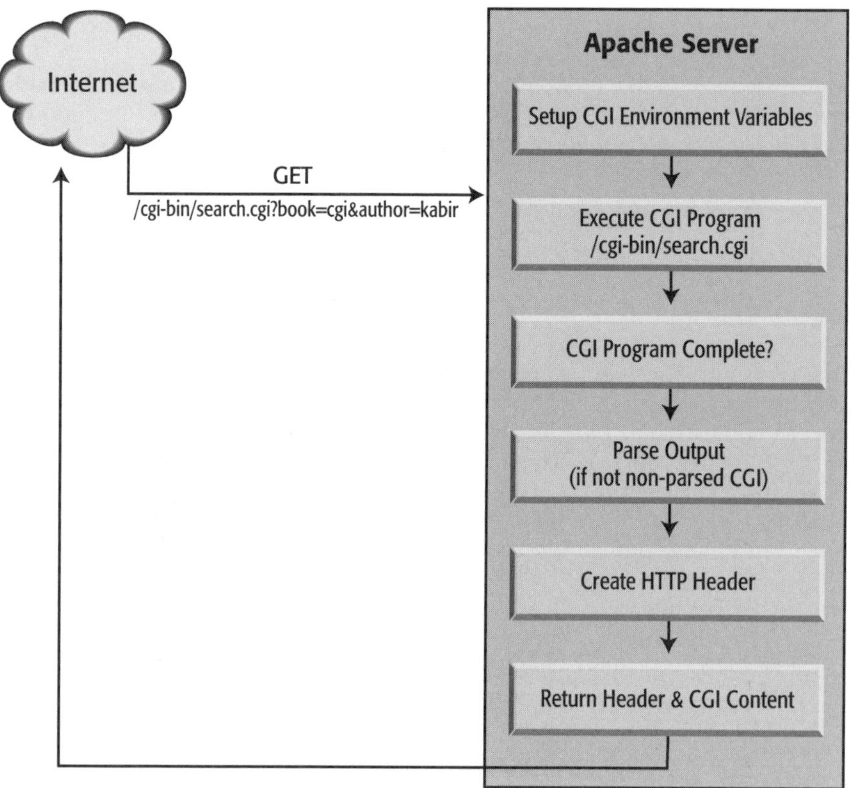

Figure 8-2: CGI Server Processing Diagram

Now let's look at what a CGI program has to do to retrieve the input and use it for its internal purposes.

As you can see in Figure 8-3, a CGI program does the following:

1. Rreads the REQUEST_METHOD environment variable.
2. Determines if GET method is used or not by using the value stored in the REQUEST_METHOD variable.
3. Retrieves the data stored in the QUERY_STRING environment variable, if GET method.
4. Decodes the data.

5. At this point, the CGI program can process the decoded data as it pleases.
6. After processing is complete, it writes the Content-Type of the output to its standard output device (STDOUT).
7. Finally, it writes the output data on the STDOUT and exits.

The Web server reads the STDOUT of the application and parses it to locate the Content-Type of the output. It then transmits appropriate HTTP headers and the Content-Type before transmitting the output to the client. The CGI program is exited and the entire CGI transaction is completed.

Figure 8-3 illustrates the processing diagram for a CGI program.

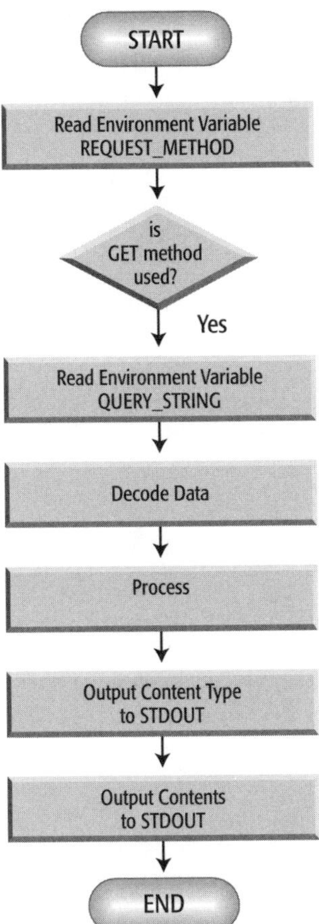

Figure 8-3: CGI Program Processing Diagram

Note that if a CGI program is to provide all of the necessary HTTP headers and Content-Type information itself, its name has to be prefixed by nph (which stands for nonparsed header). An nph CGI program's output is not parsed by the server and transmitted to the client directly; most CGI programs let the server write the HTTP header and are, therefore, parsed header programs.

Using the GET request method to pass input data to a CGI program is limiting in many ways, including the following:

- ✦ The total size of data that can be transmitted as part of a URL is limited by the client's URL-length limit. Many popular Web browsers have hard limits for the length of a URL, and therefore, the total data that can be sent via an encoded URL is quite limited. However, on occasion it might be a good idea to pass data to CGI programs via a URL. For example, if you have an HTML form that uses the GET method to send data to a CGI program, the submitted URL can be bookmarked for later use without going through the data-entry form again. This can be a user-friendly feature for database-query applications.
- ✦ The length of the value of a single environment variable (QUERY_STRING) is limiting. Many — if not all — operating systems have limits on the amount of bytes an environment variable's value can contain. This will effectively limit the total bytes that can be stored as input data.

These limits are probably not of concern for CGI programs that require little or no user input. For programs that require a large amount of user input data, however, another HTTP request method — POST — is more applicable. The POST request method is discussed in the following section.

POST requests

The HTTP POST request method is widely used for passing data to CGI programs. Typical use of this method can be found in the many HTML forms you fill out on the Web. For example, Listing 8-1 shows one such form.

Listing 8-1: An HTML Form Using HTTP POST Request Method

```
<HTML>
        <HEAD>
        <TITLE> Apache Server Bible - Chapter 8 Listing 8-1
</TITLE>
       </HEAD>

<BODY>
<H1>Listing 8-1</H1>
<H2>An Example HTML Form Using the HTTP POST Request
Method</H2>
<HR>
<FORM ACTION="/cgi-bin/search.cgi" METHOD="POST">

<PRE>
 Type of Book <INPUT TYPE="TEXT" NAME="book" SIZE="10"
MAXSIZE="20">
```

```
Author's Name <INPUT TYPE="TEXT" NAME="author" SIZE="10"
MAXSIZE="20">
</PRE>
<INPUT TYPE=SUBMIT VALUE="Search Now">

</FORM>

</BODY>
</HTML>
```

Notice that there is a <FORM ...> ... </FORM> section in the listing. An HTML form usually has a starting <FORM> tag that defines the ACTION and the request METHOD for the form. In the example above, the action is the /cgi-bin/search.cgi CGI program and the method is POST.

Following the starting <FORM> tag, there is usually one or more INPUT entity; INPUT entities might include text input boxes, drop-down menus, and lists. In our example, there are three input entities. The first one enables the user to enter a value for the book variable. The next one is similar, enabling the user to enter a value for the author variable. The third one is a bit special; it enables the user to submit the form. When the user submits the form, the client software transmits a POST request to the server for the ACTION (that is, /cgi-bin/search.cgi) resource, and also transmits the book=<user entered value> and author=<user entered value> in an encoded format.

Comparing GET and POST

What is the difference between the GET and the POST requests? The POSTed data does not get stored in the QUERY_STRING environment variable of a CGI program. Instead, it is stored in the standard input (STDIN) of the CGI program. The REQUEST_METHOD variable is set to POST, while the encoded data is stored in the STDIN of the CGI program, and a new environment variable called CONTENT_LENGTH is set to the number of bytes stored in the STDIN.

The CGI program must now check the value of the REQUEST_METHOD environment variable. If it is set to POST for HTTP POST requests, the program should first determine the size of input data from the value of the CONTENT_LENGTH environment variable and then read the data from the STDIN. Note that the Web server is not responsible for inserting an End-of-File (EOF) marker in the STDIN, which is why the CONTENT_LENGTH variable is set to the length of data, in bytes, making it easier for the CGI program to determine the data's total byte count.

It is possible to use GET and POST at the same time. Here is a sample HTML form that officially uses the POST method, but also sneaks in a query string, username=joe, as part of the CGI ACTION.

```
<FORM ACTION="/cgi-bin/edit.cgi?username=joe" METHOD=POST>
  <INPUT TYPE=TEXT NAME="PhoneNumber">
  </FORM>
```

In this sample, the username=joe query would be part of the URL, but the other field (PhoneNumber) would be part of the POST data. The effect: The end-user can bookmark the URL and always run the edit.cgi script as joe without setting values for any of the other fields. This is great for online database applications and search engines.

Whether you use GET or POST, or both, the data is encoded and it is up to the CGI program to decode it. In the following section, I discuss what is involved in decoding the encoded data.

Decoding of input data

The original HTTP protocol designers planned for easy implementation of this protocol on any system. In addition, they made the data encoding schemes simple.

The scheme defines certain characters as special characters. For example, the equals sign (=) facilitates the making of key=value pairs; the plus sign (+) replaces the space character, and the ampersand character (&) separates two key=value pairs.

If the data itself contains characters with special meaning, you might wonder what is transmitted. In this case, a three-character encoding scheme is used, which can encode any character. A percent sign (%) indicates the beginning of an encoded character sequence that consists of two hex digits.

Hex is a base 16 number system where 0–9 represents the same value as the decimal 0–9, but it also has an extra set of digits. Those are A (=10), B (=11), C (=12), D (=14), and F (=15). For example, 20 in hex is equal to 32 in a decimal system. The conversion scheme is as follows:

$$20 = 2 \times (16^1) + 0 \times (16^0)$$

These two hex digits consist of the value that can be mapped into the ASCII (for English language) table to get the character. For example, %20 (hex) is 32 (decimal) and maps to the space character in the ASCII table.

CGI Support in Apache

There are two ways Apache can implement support for CGI. The standard Apache distribution includes a CGI module that implements the traditional CGI support; however, there is a new module (FastCGI) that implements support for high-performance CGI applications. In this section, I discuss the standard CGI support issues.

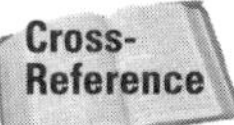

See Chapter 9 for more information on FastCGI.

In the previous sections, you learned that a CGI-compliant Web server uses environment variables, standard input (STDIN) and standard output (STDOUT) to transfer information to and from CGI programs. Apache provides a flexible set of environment variables for the CGI program developers. Using these environment variables, a CGI program not only retrieves input data but also recognizes the type of client and server it is dealing with.

In the following sections, I discuss the environment variables that are available from the standard CGI module compiled into Apache.

Server variables

These variables are set by Apache to inform the CGI program about Apache. Using server variables, a CGI program can determine various server-specific information, such as a version of the Apache software, administrator's e-mail address, and so on.

SERVER_SOFTWARE

SERVER_SOFTWARE is set by Apache, and the value is usually in the following form:

```
Apache/Version
```

Here, Apache is the name of the server software running the CGI program, and the version is the version number of the Apache. A sample value is as follows:

```
Apache/1.3
```

This is useful when a CGI program is to take advantage of a new feature found in a newer version of Apache, and still be capable of performing in older versions.

GATEWAY_INTERFACE tells the CGI program what version of CGI specification the server currently supports. A sample value is as follows:

```
CGI/1.1
```

A CGI program can determine the value of this variable and conditionally make use of different features available in different versions of CGI specifications. For example, if the value is CGI/1.0, the program may not use any CGI/1.1 features, or vice versa.

The first integer before the decimal point is called the *major number,* and the integer after the decimal point is called the *minor number*. Because these two integers are treated as separate numbers, CGI/2.2 is an older version than CGI/2.15.

SERVER_ADMIN

If you use the ServerAdmin directive in the httpd.conf file to set the e-mail address of the site administrator, this variable will be set up to reflect that. Also, note that if you have a ServerAdmin directive in a virtual host configuration container, the SERVER_ADMIN variable is set to that address if the CGI program being accessed is part of the virtual host.

DOCUMENT_ROOT

This variable is set to the value of the DocumentRoot directive of the Web site being accessed.

Client request variables

Apache creates a set of environment variables from the HTTP request header it receives from a client requesting a CGI program. It provides this information to the CGI program by creating the following set of environment variables.

SERVER_NAME

This variable tells a CGI program which host is being accessed. The value is either an IP address or a fully qualified host name, as follows:

```
SERVER_NAME = 206.171.50.51
SERVER_NAME = www.nitec.com
```

HTTP_HOST

See SERVER_NAME variable.

HTTP_ACCEPT

This variable is set to the list of MIME types that the client is capable of accepting, including the following:

```
HTTP_ACCEPT = image/gif, image/x-xbitmap, image/jpeg,
image/pjpeg, image/png, */*
```

Here, the client claims to be capable of handling GIF, JPEG, PNG, and other images. This enables the CGI program to determine what output will be ideal for the client. For example, a CGI program could produce either GIF or JPEG and receive an HTTP_ACCEPT as follows:

```
HTTP_ACCEPT = image/gif,  */*
```

Then, it can send GIF output instead of JPEG because it is not preferred by the client.

HTTP_ACCEPT_CHARSET

This variable specifies which character set is acceptable to the client, for example:

```
HTTP_ACCEPT_CHARSET = iso-8859-1,*,utf-8
```

HTTP_ACCEPT_LANGUAGE

This variable specifies which language is acceptable to the client, for example:

```
HTTP_ACCEPT_LANGUAGE = en
```

In this case, the client accepts en (English) language contents.

HTTP_USER_AGENT

This variable specifies what client software the requesting system is running and what operating system it is running on, for example:

```
HTTP_USER_AGENT = Mozilla/4.04 [en] (WinNT; I)
```

Here the information is equivalent to:

- ✦ Client Software = Netscape Navigator (as Mozilla is a keyword used by Netscape)
- ✦ Client Software Version = 4.04 (English version)
- ✦ Operating System = Windows NT (Intel)

Note that although the word Mozilla was used exclusively by Netscape browsers, many other vendors started using it as part of the HTTP header. For example, Microsoft IE 4.0 produces the following HTTP_USER_AGENT data when run from the same machine:

```
HTTP_USER_AGENT = Mozilla/4.0 (compatible; MSIE 4.0; Windows
NT)
```

This user agent information is used heavily by many Web sites. A site that is optimized for Netscape Navigator (that is, it uses a feature of HTML or JavaScript or a plug-in, that works well in Netscape Navigator) might use the HTTP_USER_AGENT information to return a different page for Microsoft IE, or any of the other less popular browsers. However, I recommend you stick to standard HTML (HTML specification for the current standard is available at www.w3.org), and not implement browser-specific features at all. Although optimizing your pages for a single browser might make them look cool on that browser — not everybody is using that particular browser. This means that your browser-specific HTML tags or plug-ins may make it harder for others (who do not use your preferred browser) to visit your Web site.

HTTP_REFERER

This variable is set to the URI that forwarded the request to the CGI program being called. Using this variable, you can tell if a request is coming from a link on one of your Web pages or a remote URI.

HTTP_CONNECTION

This variable is set to the type of connection being used by the client and the server, for example:

```
HTTP_CONNECTION = Keep-Alive
```

This states that the client is capable of handling persistent connections using Keep-Alive and currently using it.

SERVER_PORT

The value of this variable tells a CGI program which server port is currently being used to access the program. A sample of this is as follows:

```
SERVER_PORT = 80
```

If a CGI program creates URLs that point back to the server, it might be useful to include the port address, which is found as the value of this variable in the URL.

REMOTE_HOST

This variable tells a CGI program about the IP address or IP name of the client, as follows:

```
REMOTE_HOST = ppp-007.speedlink.net
```

Note that if the Apache server is compiled with the MINIMAL_DNS option, this variable is not set.

REMOTE_PORT

This port number was used by the client to originate the connection to request the CGI program.

```
REMOTE_PORT = 1163
```

I have not yet seen any use for this variable.

REMOTE_ADDR

This is the IP address of the client system:

```
REMOTE_ADDR = 206.171.50.51
```

Note that if the client is behind a firewall or a proxy server, the IP address stored in this variable may not be the IP address of the client system.

REMOTE_USER

This will be set only when access to the CGI program requires HTTP basic authentication. The username used in the basic authentication is stored in this variable for the CGI program. The CGI program, however, will have no way of identifying the password used to access it. If this variable is set to an username, the CGI program can safely assume that the user supplied the appropriate password to access it.

SERVER_PROTOCOL

This is the protocol and version number the client used to send the request for the CGI program:

```
SERVER_PROTOCOL = HTTP/1.1
```

REQUEST_METHOD

This variable is set to the HTTP request method used by the client to request the CGI program. The typical values are: GET, POST, HEAD, and so on.

```
REQUEST_METHOD=GET
```

The input is stored in the QUERY_STRING variable when the request method is GET. When the method is POST, the input is stored in the STDIN of the CGI program.

REQUEST_URI

This variable is set to the URI of the request.

```
REQUEST_URI = /cgi-bin/printenv2
```

REMOTE_IDENT

This will only be set if the IdentityCheck directive is set. This variable stores the user identification information returned by the remote identd (identification daemon).Because many systems do not run this type of daemon processes, it should not be considered a reliable means for identifying users.

I recommend using this in an intranet or an extranet environment where you or your organization is running identd server.

AUTH_TYPE

If the CGI program is stored in a section of the Web site where authentication is required to gain access, this variable is set to specify the authentication method used.

CONTENT_TYPE

This variable specifies the MIME type of any data attached to the request header. For example:

```
CONTENT_TYPE = application/x-www-form-urlencoded
```

When using HTML form and the POST request method, you can specify the content type in the HTML form using the TYPE attribute of the <FORM> tag, as follows:

```
<FORM ACTION="/cgi-bin/search.cgi" METHOD="POST" TYPE=
"application/x-www-form-urlencoded">
```

CONTENT_LENGTH

When HTTP POST request method is used, Apache stores input data (attached to the request) in the STDIN of the CGI program. The server does not, however, insert an End-of-File (EOF) marker in the STDIN. Instead, it sets the total byte-count as the value of this variable. For example, if

```
CONTENT_LENGTH = 21
```

then the CGI program should read 21 bytes of data from its STDIN.

SCRIPT_NAME

This is the URI of the requested CGI program:

```
SCRIPT_NAME = /cgi-bin/search.cgi
```

SCRIPT_FILENAME

This is the physical, fully qualified path name of the requested CGI program:

```
SCRIPT_FILENAME = /www/kabir/public/cgi-bin/search.cgi
```

QUERY_STRING

If the client uses the HTTP GET request method and provides input data after a question mark (?), the data is stored as the value of this variable. For example, a request for the following CGI program:

http://apache.nitec.com/cgi-bin/search.cgi?key1=value1&key2=value2

will make Apache set:

```
QUERY_STRING = key1=value1&key2=value2
```

which the CGI program /cgi-bin/search.cgi can read and decode before use.

PATH_INFO

If input data for a CGI program is part of the URI, the extra path (which is really some data for the program being called) is stored as the value of the variable. For example:

```
http://apache.nitec.com/cgi-bin/search.cgi/argument1/argument2
```

will have Apache set:

```
PATH_INFO = /argument1/argument2
```

Note that PATH_INFO will not have anything that is part of the query string. In other words, if the URI includes a query string after a ?, this part of the data will be stored in the QUERY_STRING variable. For example:

http://apache.nitec.com/cgi-bin/search.cgi/CA/95825?book=apache&author=kabir

this will have Apache set the following variables:

```
PATH_INFO = /CA/95825
QUERY_STRING= book=apache&author=kabir
```

PATH_TRANSLATED

This is the absolute path of the requested file.

Configuring Apache for CGI

In this section I discuss how to configure Apache to process CGI requests. The configuration process includes telling Apache where you store your CGI programs, setting up CGI handlers for specific file extensions, and indicating which file extensions should be considered CGI programs. It is a good idea to keep your CGI programs in one central directory. This permits better control of your CGI programs. Keeping CGI programs scattered all over the Web space might make such a Web site unmanageable, and it could also create security holes that would be hard to track.

Aliasing your CGI program directory

Making a central CGI program directory is just the beginning to setting up a secured CGI environment. It is best to keep this central CGI program directory outside of your DocumentRoot directory so CGI programs cannot be accessed directly. Why? Well, when it comes to CGI programs, you want to provide as little information as possible to the outside world. This will ensure better security for your site(s). The less someone knows about where your CGI programs are physically located, the less harm that person can do.

The first step is to create a directory outside of your DocumentRoot directory. For example, if /www/mycompany/public/htdocs is the DocumentRoot directory of a Web site, then /www/mycompany/public/cgi-bin is a good candidate for CGI program directory. To create the alias for your CGI program directory, you can use the ScriptAlias directive.

If you are setting up CGI support for the primary Web server, edit the httpd.conf file and insert a ScriptAlias line with the following syntax:

```
ScriptAlias  /alias/  /path/
to/the/CGI/program/directory/ending/with/
```

For example:

```
ScriptAlias /cgi-bin/ /www/mycompany/public/cgi-bin/
```

If you are setting up CGI support for a virtual site, add a ScriptAlias line in the <VirtualHost . . . > container that defines the virtual host. For example:

```
NameVirtualHost 206.171.50.60
<VirtualHost 206.171.50.60>
ServerName blackhole.nitec.com
ScriptAlias /apps/    /www/nitec/blackhole/public/cgi-bin/
</VirtualHost>
```

Here the /apps/ alias is used to create a CGI program directory alias. If there is a CGI program called feedback.cgi in the /www/nitec/blackhole/public/cgi-bin directory, it can ONLY be accessed via the following:

```
http://blackhole.nitec.com/apps/feedback.cgi
```

After you set up the ScriptAlias directive, make sure that the directory permission permits Apache to read and execute files found in the directory.

The directory pointed by ScriptAlias should have very strict permission settings. No one but the CGI program developer or the server administrator should have full (read, write, and execute) permission for the directory. Note that you can define multiple CGI program directory aliases, and the ScriptAlias specified directory is not browseable (by default) for security reasons.

When requested, Apache will attempt to run any executable (file permission-wise) file found in the ScriptAliased directory. For example:

```
http://blackhole.nitec.com/apps/foo cgi
http://blackhole.nitec.com/apps/foo.pl
http://blackhole.nitec.com/apps/foo.bak
http://blackhole.nitec.com/apps/foo.dat
```

All of the above URL requests will prompt Apache to attempt running the various foo files.

I am not particularly fond of the idea that any file in the ScriptAlias specified directory can be run as a CGI program. I prefer a solution that enables me to restrict the CGI program names such that only files with certain extensions are treated like CGI programs. The following section discusses how you can implement this using an Apache Handler found in mod_cgi module.

Choosing specific CGI file extensions

In this section I provide a sample configuration, in which I enable a select set of file extensions to be treated as CGI programs. This is accomplished with the AddHandler handler.

Let's assume that the Apache server name is www.nitec.com, and it's DocumentRoot directory is set to /www/nitec/public/htdocs; the CGI program directory is /www/nitec/public/cgi-bin. Notice that the CGI program directory is kept outside of the DocumentRoot specified directory intentionally. This ensures that the directory is not browseable by anyone, as Apache can only see it via the alias.

STEP 1: Removing/disabling ScriptAlias

The first thing to do is disable any existing ScriptAlias directive by either removing it completely from the configuration file (httpd.conf), or making it a comment line by inserting a pound sign (#) as the first character in that line.

STEP 2: Creating an alias for CGI program directory

There is no way to access the CGI program directory without an alias (or a symbolic link), as it resides outside the document tree. You can define an alias using the Alias directive which has the following syntax:

```
Alias /alias/ /path/to/cgi/dir/outside/doc/root/
```

Following this syntax, the needed alias directive looks like the following:

```
Alias /cgi-bin/ /www/nitec/public/cgi-bin/
```

Now you must instruct Apache to execute CGI programs from this directory. In order to do so, you need to define a <Directory . . . > container for this special directory.

Step 3: Defining a directory container for the CGI program directory

The directory container definition that is needed to make it all happen (i.e. turn the directory into a CGI program directory) follows:

```
<Directory /path/to/cgi/dir/outside/doc/root>
Options ExecCGI
AddHandler cgi-script .extension .extension ...
</Directory>
```

This directory container gives Apache instructions. First, the Options ExecCGI tells Apache to permit CGI program execution from within this directory. Second, AddHandler cgi-script .extension .extension . . . handler tells Apache to treat the list of extensions as CGI program extensions (in other words, whenever Apache encounters a URL requesting a file that has an extension listed in this directive, it must execute it as a CGI program).

The actual container definition looks like the following:

```
<Directory /www/nitec/public/cgi-bin>
Options ExecCGI
AddHandler cgi-script .cgi  .pl
</Directory>
```

Here, you have enabled .cgi and .pl as valid CGI program extensions and, therefore, when requests, such as the following:

```
www.nitec.com/cgi-bin/anything.cgi

www.nitec.com/cgi-bin/anything.cgi.pl
```

are made, Apache will attempt to execute these files as CGI programs. Of course, if these files are not really executables, Apache will display (and possibly log) error messages.

The CGI program directory permission settings mentioned earlier still apply to this configuration. The same configuration also applies to virtual host sites.

Enabling cgi-bin access for your users

Many Internet Service Providers (ISP) offer Web sites with user accounts. These Web sites usually have URLs, such as:

```
http://www.isp.net/~username
```

They often get requests for cgi-bin access from the users. The term cgi-bin access is a general one that is used by many to indicate CGI facility on a Web server. Traditionally, the CGI program directory has been aliased as /cgi-bin/ and, hence, this term was created. The other common term that became very popular is home page, which refers to the top-level index page of a Web directory of a user.

In this section, I discuss the two ways to providing cgi-bin access for users on a Apache Web server. You only need to implement one of the following methods.

Using Directory or DirectoryMatch containers

When the UserDir directive is set to a directory name, Apache considers it as the top-level directory for a user Web site, for example:

```
ServerName www.yourcompany.com
UserDir public_html
```

Now when a request for www.yourcompany.com/~username comes, Apache locates the named user's home directory (usually by checking the /etc/passwd file on UNIX systems), and then appends the UserDir specified directory to create the path name for the top-level user Web directory. For example:

```
www.yourcompany.com/~joe
```

This makes Apache look for /home/joe/public_html (assuming /home/joe is joe's home directory.) If the directory exists, the index page for that directory will be sent to the requesting client.

One way to add CGI support for each user is to add the following configuration in one of your Apache configuration files:

```
<Directory ~ "/home/[a-z]+/public_html/cgi-bin">
Options ExecCGI
AddHandler cgi-script .cgi .pl
</Directory>
```

Or, if you are using the latest Apache server, you can use the following configuration:

```
<DirectoryMatch  "/home/[a-z]+/public_html/cgi-bin">
Options ExecCGI
AddHandler cgi-script .cgi .pl
</DirectoryMatch>
```

In both methods, Apache translates www.yourcompany.com/~username/cgi-bin/ requests to /home/username/public_html/cgi-bin/ and permits any CGI program with the proper extension (.cgi or .pl) to execute.

Note that all usernames must be lowercase characters in order for this to work. If you have usernames that are alphanumeric, you have to use a different regular expression.

Using ScriptAliasMatch directive

Using ScriptAliasMatch directive, you can also support CGI program directories for each user. For example:

```
ScriptAliasMatch ~([a-z]+)/
cgi-bin/(.*)/home/$1/public_html/cgi-bin/$2
```

This directive matches username to $1, where $1 is equal to ~([a–z]+), and matches everything followed by /cgi-bin/ to $2, where $2 is equal to (.*).Then, it uses $1 and $2 to create the actual location of the CGI program directory. For example:

```
http://www.yourcompany.com/~joe/
cgi-bin/feedback.cgi?book=dummies&author=kabir
```

Here ~([a–z]+) will map one or more lowercase characters following the tilde mark (~) to $1. In other words, the (and) pair enables us to capture everything between the tilde (~) and the trailing forward slash (/) after the username. So, $1 is set to kabir and (.*) maps everything following the cgi-bin/ and the parenthesis pair in this regular expression, and enables us to put everything in $2. So $2 is set to search.cgi?book=dummies&author=kabir.

Now Apache can create the physical path of the CGI program directory using:

```
/home/$1/public_html/cgi-bin/$2
```

This regular expression results in the following path for the previous example:

```
/home/kabir/public_html/
cgi-bin/search.cgi?book=dummies&author=kabir
```

Because this is where the CGI program search.cgi is kept, it executes.

If you are like me — not fond of having the CGI program directory under public_html (i.e. UserDir specified directory) — you can keep it outside by removing the public_html part of the expression as follows:

```
ScriptAliasMatch ~([a-z]+)/cgi-bin/(.*)    /home/$1/cgi-bin/$2
```

This will map the example call:

```
www.yourcompany.com/~joe/
cgi-bin/feedback.cgi?book=dummies&author=kabir
```

To the following physical file:

```
/home/kabir/cgi-bin/search.cgi?book=dummies&author=kabir
```

Of course, if you are not too fond of keeping a user subdirectory world readable (that is, public_html), you can remedy this by creating a Web partition (or a directory) for your users and giving them individual directories to host their home pages. If you need help with regular expressions, see Appendix B.

Creating new CGI extensions using the AddType Directive

You learned how to create CGI program extensions using the AddHandler directive previously; however, if you want to create new CGI program extensions in a particular directory, you can also use the .htaccess (or file specified by the AccessFileName directive).

Before you can add new extensions using the per-directory access control file (.htaccess), you will have to create a <Directory> container as follows:

```
<Directory /path/to/your/directory>
Options ExecCGI
AllowOverride FileInfo
</Directory>
```

The first directive inside the above directory container tells Apache that you want to enable CGI program execution in this directory. The second directive tells Apache to enable the FileInfo feature in the per-directory access control file (.htaccess). This feature enables you to use AddType directive in the per-directory access control file.

To add a new CGI program extension (.wizard), all you need to do is create an .htaccess (or whatever you specified in AccessFileName directive) file in the directory with the following:

```
AddType application/x-httpd-cgi .wizard
```

Now, rename an existing CGI program in that directory to have the .wizard extension, and request it via your browser. Make sure all of the file permission settings for the directory and the CGI programs are set to read and execute by Apache.

Running CGI Programs

So far, I have discussed the basics of CGI specification, how Apache provides support to it, and how to configure Apache to run CGI programs. Chances are that if you are an Apache administrator, you will have to set up CGI programs, or you may even have learn to write them. In this section, I discuss the basics for creating very simple CGI programs. Note that this is a not a CGI programming book and, hence, it is not appropriate for in-depth coverage of CGI programming. My focus in this section, therefore, is to reveal things about CGI programs that will help an Apache administrator manage her CGI-capable Web sites better.

Many of the examples in this section use Perl. If you do not have Perl on your system, you can obtain the source, or possibly the binaries, from www.perl.com. Note that, whenever possible, it is good to compile binaries for a system rather than trusting binaries that have been created by someone else.

A simple CGI program

Perl is used heavily in developing CGI programs. Because Perl is an interpreted language, it creates files that are called *scripts*; hence, Perl-based CGI programs are called CGI scripts. Listing 8-2 shows a very simple Perl script.

Listing 8-2: helloworld.pl

```
#!/usr/local/bin/perl

print "Content-type: text/html\n\n";
print <<HTML;

<HTML>
<HEAD>
<TITLE>Listing 8-2: Simple Perl-based CGI Program</TITLE>
</HEAD>
<BODY>
<CENTER>
<H1> Hello World </H1>
</CENTER>
</BODY>
</HTML>

HTML
```

When this program is run, the output appears as shown in Figure 8-4.

Figure 8-4: Output of helloworld.pl

If you look at the helloworld.pl script carefully, you will notice that most of the script is plain HTML text. The script can be simplified further for analysis, as follows:

```
#!/usr/local/bin/perl

print "Content-type: text/html\n\n";

print <<HTML
HTML TEXT GOES HERE
HTML
```

The first line is very important. When Apache runs this Perl script, the first line tells the system that it is a Perl script, and the Perl interpreter is /usr/local/bin/perl. This enables the system to run the interpreter and pass it the script file. Note that this method of informing the system about the interpreter is standard for all scripting languages. The following example shows the simplified helloworld.pl script as a C Shell script:

```
#!/bin/csh
echo "Content-type: text/html"
echo ""
echo "<HTML>"
echo "HTML TEST GOES HERE"
echo  "</HTML>"
```

As you can see the first line is similar to the Perl script. Here, the interpreter path is /bin/csh, so when you download a free script from the Web, make sure that the first line correctly points at the path of the interpreter on your system. This is the first thing to check typically.

Now look back on the Perl script listing and you will see that the first print statement prints out Content-type: text/html\n\n, which really prints the Content-type: text/html in a line and prints a blank line (\n in Perl means new line). This is absolutely necessary. Remember from earlier discussions that parsed CGI scripts must supply header information for Apache so it can create appropriate HTTP header. The Content-type header tells Apache that the output contains text data of HTML type. The blank line separates this declaration from the rest of the data, and it is required. The C Shell script does the same but with the help of an empty echo statement. What follows after this Content-type header is HTML text.

Caution

Keeping an interpreter, such as Perl, Web accessible from any directory is a bad idea. Many people suffered for this mistake. Because Perl and many other scripting language interpreters have powerful features that involve system command execution, a system abuser can attack a system if the interpreter is directly accessible from the Web. So, keep them away from your Web directories in general.

A useful CGI script

I showed you a simple CGI program that does just about anything. In this section, I cover a useful CGI script that you should be able to use with little modification.

Before I continue further, however, I want to point out what makes a good CGI program. A good CGI program has the following features (at least in my opinion):

- It uses HTML templates instead of hard-coded HTML in the code. An HTML template is typically a text file with HTML tags and some custom tags. The custom tags get replaced with data by the CGI program. Using the HTML template is a desirable because it enables HTML authors and graphics designers to make a great deal of modification to the look and feel of an application without requiring the assistance of the CGI developer.
- It uses the proper mechanism to permit multiple instances of the application to run simultaneously. For example, if a CGI program writes a file in a certain location, it must take into account that more than one copy of the CGI program could be running and, therefore, must handle the situation with care. File-locking techniques should be used when applicable.
- It uses routines from external libraries and packages. This makes the programs easy to maintain.

Although you may or may not be responsible for creating the CGI programs, as an Apache administrator, you might be required to maintain them. This means working at a level that involves modification of CGI programs, their configuration, and installation. I have worked with many Apache administrators who are professionally responsible for all aspects of their organization's Web sites. I found that their insight on CGI helped them greatly in making good decisions about outsourcing and in-house development of CGI programs.

Now let's take a look at a CGI program you can examine and modify. Because most CGI programs process user input returned by HTML forms, I'll show you an example of a reasonably good, general purpose HTML form-processor CGI program written in Perl. Listing 8-3 shows one such program.

Listing 8-3: wizform.cgi

```
#!/usr/local/bin/perl
#
# Script Name: wizform.cgi
#
# Purpose: this is a general purpose HTML form
# processor script that processes data found in
# one or more HTML forms and stores then in a file
# and/or sends them one or # more persons via email.
#
```

```
# Requirements: the HTML form must have a
# HIDDEN variable called conf_file set to
# the name of the of the configuration file
# that MUST be stored in the same file as the script.
# See docs for details.
#
# Version Control Information:
# $Id$
# $Author$
# $Revision$
# $Status$
# $Lock$
#
# Copyright (C) 1997 Mohammed J. Kabir (kabir@nitec.com)
#
##############################################################################
# Tell Perl that we want to use the CGI.pm package
# in this script.
use CGI;

# Create a global CGI object called $cgi
local $cgi = new CGI;

# Get the name of the HTML form configuration file
# and store it in a variable called
# $conf_file.
my $conf_file = $cgi->param('conf_file');

# Get the name of the next HTML form page (if any)
# and store it in a variable called
# $next_template.
my $next_template = $cgi->param('next_form');

# Other (local) variable declarations
my $key;
my $value;

# we will store configuration data in this
# associated array (hash).
local %conf;

# Print the necessary Content-Type header.
# Since we only output HTML text, it
# should be the default text/html.
print $cgi->header();

# Read the configuration file pointed by the $conf_file
variable and store the config. file
# in the %conf associated array.
#
&readConf($conf_file);
```

(continued)

Listing 8-3 *(continued)*

```
# If the $next_tempate variable (which holds the
# file name of the next HTML form)
# is empty then we have no more HTML forms to
# process and therefore we should complete processing
# for this HTML form by calling the processData
# sub routine.
if($next_template eq  ''){
    &processData;
    }

# We do have one or more HTML forms to process
# so lets show the next HTML form and
# get more input data by calling the getInput
# sub routine.
else {
    &getInput($next_template);
    }

# We are done; exit the script.
exit 0;

sub processData{
   # Purpose: this subroutine does all the data processing.

   # an array to hold the saving order of data fields.
   my @saving_order = split(/\,/,$conf{'saving_order'});

   # a variable to hold a data field's value or name
   my $datam;

   # an array to hold all the errors.
   my @errors;

   # a variable to hold a record that gets written to file.
   my $record;

   # a variable to hold the mail message
   my $mail_msg;

   # keeps count of the number of output methods
   # that are successful.
   my $output_successful = 0;

   # keeps count of the number of output methods
   # that are requested.
   my $output_type = 0;

   # Check the inputs for missing (required) inputs
   # by calling the checkInputs sub routine
   # which returns a list of HTML form variable names
   # that are missing.
```

```
    # Store the list in @errors array.
    @errors = &checkInputs;

    # If we have errors (i.e. missing inputs) then
    # we need to show the error message page
    if( $#errors > -1){
        &showErrors(@errors);
        return 1;
        }

    # Lets create the mail message and the data
    # record that we need to send and store
    # respectively. So cycle through all the in
    # @saving_order and add them to the $record
    # variable and the $mail_msg  variable in that
     # order. Use the separator specified in the
    # configuration file.
    foreach $datam (@saving_order){
         $record .= $cgi->param($datam) .
$conf{'field_separator'};
         $mail_msg .= ucfirst($datam) . "\t=\t" . $cgi-
>param($datam) . "\n";
        }
     # Remove the last field separator that got inserted
     # in the loop.
     $record =~ s/$conf{'field_separator'}$//;

     # If output by mail is requested in the configuration
     # file, then send a mail message to
     # specified list of people (found in the configuration
     # file.)
     # Store 1 or 0 (depending on success of the sendMail
     # routine) in the
     # $output_successful variable.
     # Also increment number of output types we have
     # processed so far.
     if($conf{'output_method'} =~ /mail/i){
          $output_successful = &sendMail($mail_msg);
         $output_type++;
        }

     # If output is to be stored in a file (specified
     # in the configuration file) then store the
     # newly created  record in the specified file.
     # Increment the $output_successful variable with
     # whatever value returned by the
     # appendFile. Also increment number of output
     # types we have processed so far.
     #
     if($conf{'output_method'} =~ /file/i){
        $output_successful +=
&appendFile($record,$conf{'data_file'});
```

(continued)

Listing 8-3 *(continued)*

```
        $output_type++;
        }

    # Now in order to figure out if we are successful
    # in producing all requested types of output,
    # we must  compare the $output_successful variable
    # with $output_type variable. An equal
    # count will indicate that  we are completely
    # successful. If we are not, then the
    # $output_type will have a higher value and there
    # we must report a failure by showing the
    # failure page (specified in configuration file.)
    #
    if($output_successful >0 && $output_successful ==
$output_type){
        &showPage($conf{'success_template'});
        }
    else{
        &showPage($conf{'failure_template'});
        }

    # Finally, write the log file.
    &writeLog;
    }

sub writeLog{
    # Purpose: this sub routine writes a log file which
    # records the IP address of the client
    # along with time, date, referrer URL etc.

   # Local variable declarations
   my $log_file;
   my $record;
   my $status;

   # We need to create a string containing current
   # date and time using localtime() function.
   my (↓tefields) = localtime(time);
   my $sec          = $datefields[0];
   my $min          = $datefields[1];
   my $hr           = $datefields[2];
   my $mday         = $datefields[3];
   my $mon          = $datefields[4]  + 1;
   my $year         = $datefields[5];
   my $today = sprintf("%02d:%02d:%02d
%s/%s/%s",$hr,$min,$sec,$mon,$mday,$year);

   # Create the record we want to store in the log file
   $record = sprintf("%s, %s, %s, %s, %s",
                        $today,
```

```
                        $ENV{'SERVER_NAME'},
                        $ENV{'REMOTE_ADDR'},
                        $ENV{'HTTP_USER_AGENT'},
                        $ENV{'HTTP_REFERER'}
                      );

   # Write the log entry to the log file specified
   # in the configuration file.
   $status = &appendFile($record,$conf{'log_file'});

   # Return the success or failure status of the
   # log entry attempt.
   return ($status);
   }

sub sendMail{
   # Purpose: this sub routine sends an email message
   # to the list of addresses specified in the
   # configuration file.

   # Get the data (body of the email) from the
   # passed parameter list.
   my $data = shift;

   # Get the FQPN of the mail daemon program from
   # the configuration file.
   my $sendmail = $conf{'mail_daemon'};

   # Get the list of recepients from the configuration file.
   my $to = $conf{'mail_to'};

   # Get the name of the sender from the configuration file.
   my $from = $conf{'mail_from'};

   # Get the subject name from the configuration file.
   my $subject = $conf{'mail_subject'};

   # Open a PIPE to the mail daemon program.
   # if we fail to connect to the daemon, return
   # failure status.
   open(MAIL,"|$sendmail -t") || return 0;

   # Write the mail message to the pipe
   print MAIL <<DATA;
To: $to
From: $from
Subject: $subject


   $data
DATA
```

(continued)

Listing 8-3 *(continued)*

```
   # Close the pipe
   close(MAIL);

   # We have completed the mail transaction so return the
success status.
   return 1;
   }

sub showPage{
   # Purpose: this sub routine shows an HTML page

  # Get the page file name from the parameter list
   my $file = shift;

   # Local variables
   my @html;
   my %vars;
   my $key;
   my $value;

   # Create an associated array of all the HTML
   # form inputs that we have value for.
   foreach $key ($cgi->param()){
      $value = $cgi->param($key);
      $var{$key} = $value;
      }

   # Create the FQPN for the HTML page we want to display.
   $file =
sprintf("%s/%s/%s",$conf{'base_dir'},$conf{'template_dir'},
$file);

   # Read the page text into a local buffer (an array)
   @html = &readFile($file);

   # Before printing out each line found in the
   # HTML page, replace any custom
   # replaceable data  that is usually in the
   # <VISITOR-STRING> format.
   foreach $line (@html){
     $line =~ s/<(VISITOR-\w+)>/ucfirst($var{$conf{$1}})/eg;
     print $line ,"\n";
     }

   }

sub appendFile{
    # Purpose: this sub routine appends a line in a file.
```

```
    # Get the record, from the parameters, we want
    # to append in the file.
    my $record = shift;

    # Get the file name from the parameters.
    my $filename = shift;

    # Create the FQPN of the file
    $datafile =
sprintf("%s/%s/%s",$conf{'base_dir'},$conf{'data_dir'},$filenam
e);

    # Open the file in append mode. If we fail
    # send the failure status (0)
    open(FP,">$datafile") || return 0;

    # ***  Critical Zone ***
    # Try to get an exclusive lock for the file
    flock FP, 2;

    # Write the record in the file.
    print FP $record, "\n";

    # Release the lock for the file
    flock FP, 8;

    # ** end of Critical Zone ***

    # Close the file.
    close(FP);

    # we successfully wrote to the file so return
    # success status.
    return 1;
    }

sub checkInputs{
  # Purpose: check the inputs for missing fields.
  # The required fields are specified in the
  # configuration file.

# Get the list of the required fields from the
# configuration file.
  my @required_data = split(/\,/,$conf{'required_fields'});

  # Local variables
  my $datam;
  my $key;
  my $value;
  my @errors;
```

(continued)

Listing 8-3 (continued)

```
    # Go through each required field and check to see if
    # we have received a value of it
    # If not, put the variable name in the error list array.
    foreach $datam (@required_data){
       $value = $cgi->param($datam);
       if($value eq ''){
         push(@errors,$datam);
         }
       }

    # Return the error list.
    return (@errors);
    }

sub getInput{
    # Purpose: Show an HTML form but before that insert all the
    # inputs we have gathered from other forms so far by making
    # hidden HTML form variables.

    # Get the name of the HTML form file we want to show
    my $html_template = shift;

    # Local variables
    my $hidden_data;
    my $key;
    my $value;
    my @html;

    # Create FQPN for the template file
    $html_template = sprintf("%s/%s/%s",$conf{'base_dir'},
    $conf{'template_dir'},$html_template);

   # Create hidden data list;
      foreach $key ($cgi->param()){
          next if ($key =~ /next_form/i);
          $value = $cgi->param($key);
          $hidden_data .= <<HIDDEN;
          <INPUT TYPE="HIDDEN" NAME="$key" VALUE="$value">
HIDDEN
          }

    # Get the page text by reading the file and store the
    # data in a buffer.
    @html = &readFile($html_template);

    # if the buffer is not empty we have page text.
    # So print the page text and replace
    # the <HIDDEN-DATA> tag with value of $hidden_data variable.
    if($#html > -1){
       foreach $line (@html){
          $line =~ s/<HIDDEN-DATA>/$hidden_data/g;
```

```
            print $line,"\n";
            }
        }

    # On the other hand, if we don't have any text in
    # this page, we have some sort of access problem to the
    # page so show a general failure message using the
    # failure_template value found in the configuration.
    else{
        &showPage($conf{'failure_template'});
        }
    }

sub readConf{
  # Purpose: this sub routine reads the configuration file
  # and stores the configuration data in an associated array.

  # Get the name of the configuration file
  my $conf_file = shift;

  # Local variables
  my @buffer;
  my $line;

  # Get the data from the file and store it in a local buffer.
  @buffer = &readFile($conf_file);

  # Cycle through the lines in the buffer and locate valid
  # configuration data while
  # ignoring empty blank lines and comment lines that
  # starts with a '#' sign.
  foreach $line (@buffer){
      $line =~ s/  */ /g;
      next if ($line =~ /^#/ || $line =~ /^$/ || $line !~ /=/);
      ($key, $value) = split(/=/,$line);

    # Remove white space characters from configuration
    # option name and value
      $key =~ s/\s//g;
      $value =~ s/\s//g;

    # Store the configuration key=value pair in the
    # %conf associative array (hash.)
      $conf{$key} = $value;
      }
  }

sub readFile{
  # Purpose: read a file and return the lines.

  # Get the file name from the parameter list
  my $file = shift;
```

(continued)

Listing 8-3 *(continued)*

```
  # Local variables
  my @buffer;
  my $line;

  # If file exits then open it and read the lines in a
  # buffer. However remove the
  # newline character from each line before storing it
  # in the buffer. After file is
  # read, close it.
  if(-e  $file){
     open(FP,$file) || die "Can not read $file \n";
     while($line = <FP>){
       chomp($line);
       push(@buffer,$line);
       }
     close(FP);
     }

  # Return the buffer.
  return (@buffer);
  }

sub showErrors{

  # Purpose: this sub routine shows error message page

  # Get the error list from the parameter list and
  # store them in a local list.
  my @fields = @_;

  # Local variables
  my $err_template;
  my @html;
  my $line;
  my $errorlist;

  # Get the FQPN of the error template file.
  $err_template =
sprintf("%s/%s/%s",$conf{'base_dir'},$conf{'template_dir'},
$conf{'input_error_template'});

  # Create an HTML list to display the fields that are
  # in error.
  $errorlist = "<UL>";
  foreach (@fields){
     $errorlist .= "<LI> $_ ";
     }
  $errorlist .= "</UL>";

  # Read the error message template file and store the
  # page text in a local buffer.
```

```
    @html = &readFile($err_template);

    # Cycle through the page text and replace
    # the <ERROR-LIST> variable with the
    # error list created earlier.  Print the page.
    foreach $line (@html){
      $line =~ s/<ERROR-LIST>/$errorlist/g;
      print $line;
      }
  }
```

The best way to understand this script involves looking at a sample application of the script. In the following section, I show you how to create a sample application, called the On-line Newsletter Signup Tool, using this general purpose form-processor script.

A sample application

The purpose of this application is to permit site visitors to sign up for a newsletter that the site owner offers periodically. The sign-up tool must gather the visitor's name and e-mail address,and store them in a file that enables the site owner to use the data to send out the newsletter later.

In the following sections, I show you how to create the configuration file and HTML templates needed for this application. For this example, I will assume the following:

```
DocumentRoot = /www/nitec/public/htdocs
```

The first step is to create a configuration file for the sign-up tool. Using a text editor, create a configuration file called signup.conf. Enter the following configuration lines:

```
base_dir=/www/nitec/public
template_dir = htdocs
```

The base_dir line tells the script which directory is used as the base directory for the script. Because this directory has to be one level outside of the DocumentRoot (/www/nitec/public/htdocs) directory, it is set to /www/nitec/public directory. The template_dir line tells the script the name of the directory where the HTML template files will be stored. In this example, the top-level Web directory (DocumentRoot) is used for this purpose. Note that the template_dir value has to be a relative path to the base_dir.

You need to specify input-related configuration information in the same file as follows:

```
input_fields=firstName,lastName,emailAddress,companyName,office
Phone
required_fields=emailAddress,firstName,lastName
```

Here, the firstName, lastName, e-mailAddress, companyName, and officePhone are the input field names in the HTML form for this application. Note that each field in the list has to be separated by a comma. The second line tells the script about the required fields. In the previous example, the required fields are: e-mailAddress, firstName, and the lastName fields. In other words, if the user does not enter these fields, the script will show an error message page.

Now you need to tell the script where to write the data gathered from a visitor. The following lines need to be added in the configuration file:

```
data_dir=data
data_file=newsletter.cvs
field_separator=,
saving_order=emailAddress,firstName,lastName,companyName,office
Phone
```

The first line specifies the directory name where the data files should be written. This directory name is appended to the base_dir value to get the fully qualified directory name. Note that data_dir line sets the directory to be /www/nitec/public/data, which is outside the DocumentRoot specified directory. Make sure this directory is read/write-able by the Web server. This directory should be kept outside of the regular Web document space for security reasons. The second line is used to specify the name of the data file to be written. The third line is used to specify a field separator for data fields that are written to the newsletter.cvs file. The example uses a comma(,)character as the field separator. The forth line is used to specify the order in which data fields are written to the data file.

Now you need to tell the script about the HTML templates that you want to use. This is done by the following lines:

```
input_error_template = newsletter.err.html
success_template = newsletter.success.html
failure_template = newsletter.failed.html
```

The first line specifies the template file name that is used to display a custom error message when an input error occurs. The fully qualified path to this file is /www/nitec/public/htdocs/newsletter.err.html (that is, base_dir/template_dir/input_error_template.)The newsletter.success.html file, specified in the second line, is displayed when the script completes its task successfully. This serves as an acknowledgment for the user.

The fully qualified path to this file is /www/nitec/public/htdocs/newsletter.success.html (i.e. base_dir/template_dir/success_template.)

The newsletter.failed.html file, specified in the third line, is displayed when an internal error (such as failure to send mail, or a write file due to permission error) occurs.

The fully qualified path to this file is /www/nitec/public/htdocs/newsletter.failed.html (that is, base_dir/template_dir/failure_template).

Next, tell the script to write the output in a file, and also e-mail it using the following lines:

```
output_method=file,email
mail_to=newsletter@nitec.com
mail_from=signup@nitec.com
mail_subjaect=New-registration
mail_daemon=/usr/sbin/sendmail
```

The first line tells the script to write the data file, and also to e-mail the data. The second line specifies the e-mail address to which the data will be sent. The third line specifies the sender's address that the program will use to send the e-mail. The forth line specifies the subject header for the e-mail. The fifth line specifies the fully qualified path of the mail daemon program. Note that this version of the program only supports the widely used Sendmail mail daemon. If you use a different mail server program, you might have to modify the CGI program. The script enables you to create a log of each successful data-entry operation by a visitor. You can specify the log file name as follows:

```
log_file=newsletter.log
```

The log file is written in the data_dir directory; so, the fully qualified path name is constructed using base_dir/data_dir/log_file.

The script also permits the success template to be customized. It uses a custom tag definition to find and replace data values. These custom tags all start with VISITOR- prefix. For example:

```
VISITOR-LAST=lastName
```

Setting this in the configuration file means that the script will look for a custom tag called <VISITOR-LAST> in the success message template (set by success_template) and replace it with the value of input variable lastName. Note that the VISITOR- variable names must be in capital letters in both the configuration file and in the actual HTML message file.

The final configuration file with some additional comment lines (lines that start with # signs) is shown in Listing 8-4.

Listing 8-4: signup.conf

```
#
# signup.conf
#
# Purpose: this file is used by the general purpose
#          form processor script.
#
# Application: Newsletter sign-up tool example.
# $Author$
# $Id$
# $Version$
# $Status$
#######################################################


# base and template directory
base_dir=/www/nitec/public
template_dir = htdocs

#input requirements
input_fields=firstName,lastName,emailAddress,companyName,office
Phone
required_fields=emailAddress,firstName,lastName

# data
data_dir=data
data_file=newsletter.cvs
field_separator=,
saving_order=emailAddress,firstName,lastName,companyName,office
Phone

# response template
input_error_template = newsletter.err.html
success_template = newsletter.success.html
failure_template = newsletter.failed.html

# output
output_method=file,email
mail_to=newsletter@ nitec.com
mail_from=signup@nitec.com
mail_subject=New-registration
mail_daemon=/usr/sbin/sendmail

# Logging
log_file=newsletter.log

# common variables
VISITOR-LAST=lastName
VISITOR-FIRST=firstName
VISITOR-EMAIL=emailAddress
VISITOR-HOMEADDR1=homeAddress1
VISITOR-HOMEADDR2=homeAddress2
```

```
VISITOR-HOMEPHONE=homePhone
VISITOR-OFFICEPHONE=officePhone
```

Save this file in the same directory of the script (that is, in the cgi-bin directory of the Web server.) Then create an HTML form as shown in Listing 8-5.

Listing 8-5: newsletter.html

```
<HTML>
<HEAD>  <TITLE> On-line Newsletter Sign-up Form </TITLE>
</HEAD>

<BODY BGCOLOR="white">
<TABLE BORDER=1>
<TR BGCOLOR="#abcdef">
<TD>

<FORM ACTION="/cgi-bin/wizform.cgi" METHOD="POST">

<TABLE BORDER=0 CELLPADDING=6 CELLSPACING=0>

<TR> <TD BGCOLOR="#abcdef" ALIGN="LEFT" COLSPAN="2">
     <FONT FACE="Arial Bold"> Newsletter Sign-up Form
</FONT><BR>
     </TD>
</TR>

<TR> <TD BGCOLOR="#abcdef" ALIGN="RIGHT"> First Name * </TD>
     <TD BGCOLOR="#aabbcc"> <INPUT TYPE="TEXT" NAME="firstName"
SIZE="20" MAXSIZE="30"> </TD>
</TR>

<TR> <TD BGCOLOR="#abcdef" ALIGN="RIGHT"> Last Name * </TD>
     <TD BGCOLOR="#aabbcc"> <INPUT TYPE="TEXT" NAME="lastName"
SIZE="20" MAXSIZE="30"> </TD>
</TR>

<TR> <TD BGCOLOR="#abcdef" ALIGN="RIGHT"> Email * </TD>
     <TD BGCOLOR="#aabbcc"> <INPUT TYPE="TEXT"
NAME="emailAddress" SIZE="20" MAXSIZE="30"> </TD>
</TR>

<TR> <TD BGCOLOR="#abcdef" ALIGN="RIGHT"> Company </TD>
     <TD BGCOLOR="#aabbcc"> <INPUT TYPE="TEXT"
NAME="companyName" SIZE="20" MAXSIZE="20"> </TD>
</TR>

<TR> <TD BGCOLOR="#abcdef" ALIGN="RIGHT"> Office Phone </TD>
```

(continued)

Listing 8-5 *(continued)*

```
     <TD BGCOLOR="#aabbcc"> <INPUT TYPE="TEXT"
NAME="officePhone" SIZE="20" MAXSIZE="15"> </TD>
</TR>

<TR> <TD BGCOLOR="#abcdef" ALIGN="RIGHT">   </TD>
     <TD BGCOLOR="#aabbcc"> <INPUT TYPE="RESET" VALUE="Clear
All">     <INPUT TYPE="SUBMIT" VALUE="Submit"> </TD>
</TR>

<TR> <TD BGCOLOR="#abcdef" ALIGN="LEFT" COLSPAN="2">
      <FONT SIZE="-1"> * Required field.</FONT>
      </TD>
</TR>

</TABLE>

<INPUT TYPE=HIDDEN NAME="conf_file" VALUE="newsletter.conf">

</FORM>

</TD>
<TD BGCOLOR="#abcdef" VALIGN="TOP">
<FONT SIZE="+2">W</FONT>e send out a monthly newsletter to all
on-line subscribers. If you would like to subscribe, please
sign up here.
</TD>
</TR>

</TABLE>
</BODY>
</HTML>
```

There are several things worth noting in the HTML form. The first thing to notice is the following line:

```
<FORM ACTION="/cgi-bin/wizform.cgi" METHOD="POST">
```

Here, the ACTION of the form is set to the wizform.cgi script stored in the cgi-bin directory. The method is POST. Notice that all of the data-entry fields have the same name (such as lastName or firstName) as specified in the configuration file. This is a requirement of the script. If the field names are not same, the script will not function as intended.

The other thing to notice is that there is a hidden input field as follows:

```
<INPUT TYPE=HIDDEN NAME="conf_file" VALUE="newsletter.conf">
```

This specifies the configuration file name.

After creating this form, store it in the htdocs directory. The following listings, Listing 8-6, Listing 8-7, and Listing 8-8, shows the simple HTML pages that you can create to customize the input error message, the acknowledgment (success message) page and an internal failure message page. These are simple HTML pages. The newsletter.success.html page (Listing 8-11) has a few VISITOR tags to give the page a little custom feel.

Listing 8-6: **newsletter.success.html**

```
<HTML>
<HEAD>
<TITLE> On-line Newsletter Sign-up Form (Success) </TITLE>
</HEAD>

<BODY BGCOLOR="#abcdef">
<BLOCKQUOTE>

<HR>
<FONT FACE="Arial Bold">
Hello <VISITOR-FIRST> <VISITOR-LAST><BR><BR>
</FONT>

Thank you for subscribing our newsletter. We will send you the
latest copy of our newsletter
via the email address (<STRONG><VISITOR-EMAIL></STRONG>) you
provided here. Have a nice day.
<BR>

<FORM ACTION="/" METHOD="GET"> <INPUT TYPE=SUBMIT VALUE="Return
to Index"> </FORM>
<HR>
</BLOCKQUOTE>
</BODY>
</HTML>
```

The newsletter.err.html file is shown when a visitor forgets to submit all of the required data. The custom tag <ERROR-LIST> is replaced with name(s) of all the fields that are missing from visitor's submission.

Listing 8-7: newsletter.err.html

```
<HTML>
<HEAD>
<TITLE> On-line Newsletter Sign-up Form (Error) </TITLE>

</HEAD>

<BODY BGCOLOR="#abcdef">
<BLOCKQUOTE>
<FONT FACE="Arial Bold" SIZE="+1">Incomplete Subscription
Request</FONT><BR>
<HR>

Your newsletter subscription request could not be processed
since one or more of the listed
information are missing.
<BR>
<ERROR-LIST>
<BR>
Please try again.
<BR>

<FORM ACTION="/newsletter.html" METHOD="GET"> <INPUT
TYPE=SUBMIT VALUE="Try Again"> </FORM>
</BLOCKQUOTE>
</BODY>
</HTML>
```

The newsletter.failure.html is shown when the script detects a file-access problem, such as a failure to write the data file due to a file permission problem.

Listing 8-8: newsletter.failure.html

```
<HTML>
<HEAD>
<TITLE> On-line Newsletter Sign-up Form (Internal Error)
</TITLE>

</HEAD>

<BODY BGCOLOR="#abcdef">
<BLOCKQUOTE>
<FONT FACE="Arial Bold" SIZE="+1">Internal Subscription
Error</FONT><BR>
<HR>
Sorry, we are unable to process your subscription request at
this time.
```

```
<BR>
<BR>

<FORM ACTION="/ newsletter.html" METHOD="GET"> <INPUT
TYPE=SUBMIT VALUE="Try Again"> </FORM>
</BLOCKQUOTE>
</BODY>
</HTML>
```

Keep these pages (templates) in the directory specified by the tempate_dir variable in the configuration file. At this point, make sure the script and the CGI.pm package file (included in the CD-ROM) are in cgi-bin directory and the permissions are set properly for Apache to read and execute the files.

Testing newsletter sign-up tool

Now let's test the newsletter sign-up tool. Figure 8-5 shows how the newsletter.html page looks like in a Web browser. Once this page is filled out and submitted by a visitor, the script runs. First, it checks to see if any of the input fields, required by the configuration file, are missing.

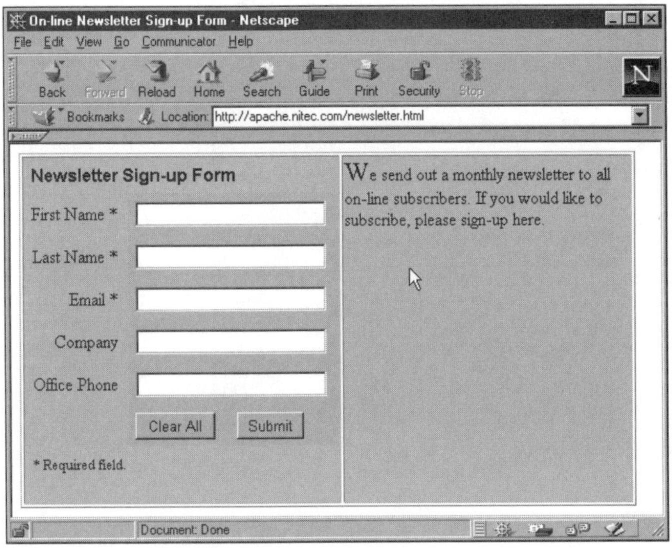

Figure 8-5: newsletter.html page

If any required field is missing, it shows the error page shown in Figure 8-6.

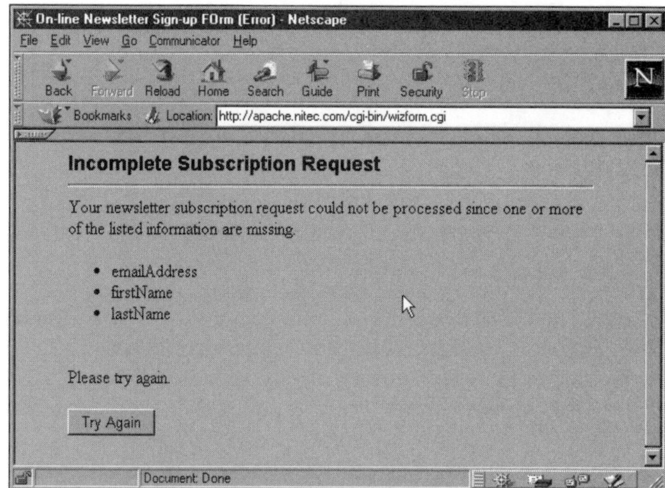

Figure 8-6: Input error

Or else, the acknowledgment message page is displayed as shown in Figure 8-7.

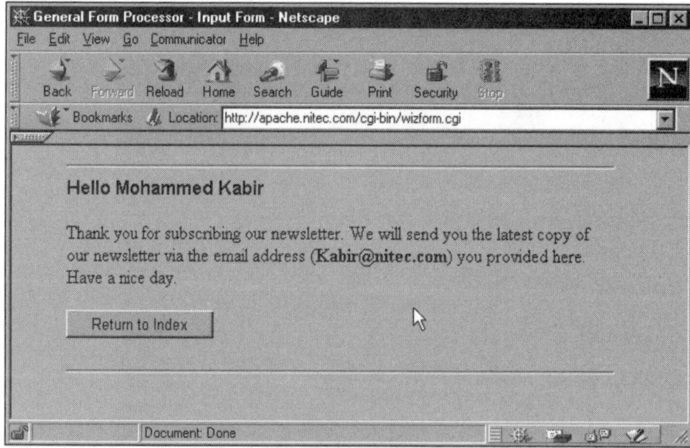

Figure 8-7: Acknowledgment page

After submitting a couple of newsletter requests, the data file newsletter.cvs looks like the following:

```
kabir@nitec.com,Mohammed,Kabir,Nitec,555-1111
joe@gunchy.org,Joe,Gunchy,Gunchy Inc,555-2222
someone@somewhere.net,First,Last,Company Name,555-3333
```

The newsletter.log file looks like the following:

```
11:26:00 4/1/98, apache.nitec.com, 206.171.50.51, Mozilla/4.04
[en]
(WinNT; I)
11:27:00 4/1/98, apache.nitec.com, 206.171.50.51, Mozilla/4.04
[en]
(WinNT; I)
11:30:35 4/13/98, apache.nitec.com, 206.171.50.51, Mozilla/4.0
(compatible; MSIE 4.01; Windows NT)
```

As you can see everything is working just fine. If there was a permission problem in writing the data file, the failure message would have looked like the one shown in Figure 8-8.

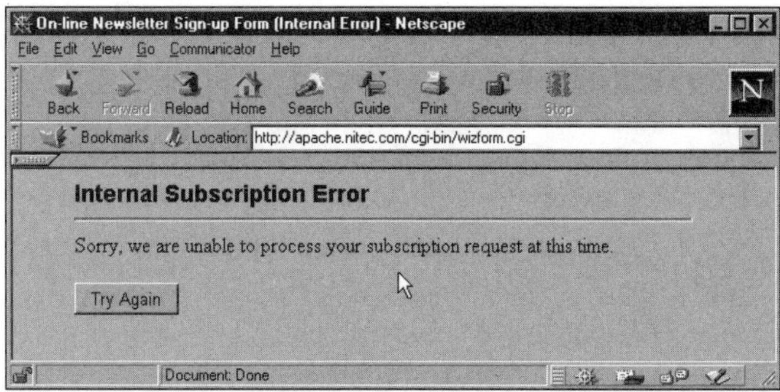

Figure 8-8: Failure message

Modifying the newsletter sign-up tool

Now, you might be wondering if you can use this script for a multiform application where you have more than one HTML forms for the visitor to fill out. Sure, you can.

All you need to do is add a new hidden variable in the all of the HTML forms except for the last one that looks like the following:

```
<INPUT TYPE=HIDDEN NAME="next_form" VALUE="nextform.html">
```

Here, the nextform.html is the HTML form after first form and so on. For example, if I had three forms for an application, I could have the following.

In first HTML form:

```
<INPUT TYPE=HIDDEN NAME="next_form" VALUE="2ndform.html">

second HTML form:
<INPUT TYPE=HIDDEN NAME="next_form" VALUE="lastform.html">
```

The last form would not have this hidden variable. Note that all of the forms will have to be in the template_dir specified directory. Using this general purpose form processor you can create a variety of commonly used applications for your Web site. Examples of such applications are: FeedBack Script, GuestBook, and Mailing List Sign-up Script.

Using widely used CGI modules for Perl

In the previous form generator script, I used the widely used CGI.pm package created by Lincoln D. Stein. Few other useful Perl packages can be used to do rapid Perl-based CGI script development. Let's look at a few of the popular development packages for Perl language:

✦ CGI.pm This is a great Perl package to develop CGI scripts quickly and cleanly. It enables you to create CGI objects that can access the CGI query strings, create appropriate headers, read/write cookies, and write HTML forms without actually using any HTML in the script. You can find this package at:

```
www-genome.wi.mit.edu/ftp/pub/software/WWW/cgi_docs.html
```

✦ Libwww — If you interested in developing powerful user agents, robots, mini Web servers, do not bother writing code from scratch. Use Libwww's eight modules: HTML, LWP, MIME, WWW, HTTP, URL, File and Font, to do it all. You can find these packages at:

```
www.perl.com/CPAN-local/modules/by-module/LWP/
```

✦ cgi-lib.pl — If you are not yet ready for object-oriented Perl programming (both CGI.pm and libwww modules are object oriented), you can try out a simpler library called cgi-lib.pl. This library has routines to parse form inputs and create headers. You can find it at:

```
www.bio.cam.ac.uk/cgi-lib/
```

Debugging CGI Programs in Apache

When you write or install someone else's CGI program, there is a chance that it might not run the right way. Debugging a CGI program is often difficult because, in most cases, you can not just run the program from the command line and feed it inputs.

If you use CGI.pm package in your Perl-based CGI scripts, you can do a great deal of debugging from the command line. The package permits interactive mode where you can enter key=value input pairs as if the data is coming from an HTML form.

In order to help CGI developers, Apache has logs for CGI output. For each CGI program error the log file contains a few lines of log entries. The first two lines contain the time of the request, request URI, HTTP status, CGI program name and so on. If the CGI program can not be run, two other additional lines contains information about the error. Alternatively, if the error is the result of the script returning incorrect header information, the information is logged in as follows: all HTTP request headers, all headers outputted by CGI program, STDOUT and STDIN of the CGI program. Note that if the script failed to output anything the STDOUT will not be included.

To log CGI output in Apache, use the following directives, which are found in the mod_cgi module (part of standard distribution).

ScriptLog

```
Syntax: ScriptLog filename
Default: none
Context: resource config
```

This directive sets the log file name for CGI program errors. If the log file name is relative (that is, it does not start with a leading /) it is taken to be relative to the server root directory set by ServerRoot directive.

When you use this directive, make sure that the log directory is writeable by the user specified by UserDir directive. Note that using this directive on a daily basis might not be a good idea as far as efficiency or performance goes. I recommend using it when needed and turning it off when the debugging is completed.

ScriptLogLength

```
Syntax: ScriptLogLength size
Default: 10385760
Context: resource config
```

This directive limits the size of the log file specified by the ScriptLog directive. The script log file can log a lot of information per CGI error and, therefore, can grow rapidly. Using this directive, you can limit the log so that once the file is at the maximum length, no more information will be logged.

ScriptLogBuffer

```
Syntax: ScriptLogBuffer size
Default: 1024
Context: resource config
```

This directive limits the size of POST or PUT data that is logged.

Using these directives you can set up the logging of CGI programs that you are developing or attempting to install on your system.

Summary

In this chapter, I covered CGI. You learned how CGI programs make use of different HTTP request methods, such as GET and POST. I showed you how to configure Apache to create a secure CGI environment for your Web sites; how to provide individual users on multiuser system with frequently requested cgi-bin access.

I provided an example of a highly configurable CGI program and showed you how to make useful CGI applications with this program. I also discussed configuring Apache to provide CGI debugging support that CGI developers greatly appreciate. Next, you will learn how to speed up your CGI scripts using FastCGI.

✦ ✦ ✦

FastCGI

✦ ✦ ✦ ✦

In This Chapter

What is FastCGI?

Setting up Apache for FastCGI

Configuring Perl for FastCGI

✦ ✦ ✦ ✦

Common Gateway Interface (CGI) has been the de facto standard for server-side application development for years. Over time, many have discovered that Web server systems under heavy CGI loads perform less desirably. Investigations exposed the bottleneck in the CGI specification: Every time a CGI application is requested by a client system, the Web server must launch a new CGI process; the process then performs its tasks and terminates. This works fine when the load is low. However, at a high load, process setup and initialization time become a performance bottleneck.

New standards are now emerging to fix this situation. Although still in an early stage of acceptance, FastCGI is one such promising open standard. In this chapter, I discuss the details of this standard and how to implement FastCGI in Apache.

FastCGI as a New Alternative

Simply speaking, a FastCGI application acts like a server application. Unlike a CGI application, it stays alive and services incoming requests from the Web server. This is the advantage of FastCGI; unlike CGI, there is no overhead in starting up a new process and doing application initialization (for example, connecting to a database) each time a request needs to be processed. It is a high-performance alternative to CGI for writing Web server applications in a variety of languages, including Perl, C, C++, Java, and Python.

You should note that FastCGI is a proposed open standard, and there is a good chance it will become accepted as a Web standard in the near future. However, a few major server vendors are still not sold on the FastCGI concept. They have their own standards, which allow somewhat similar functionality and a great deal of server-specific features. These standards can be categorized as server application programming interfaces (APIs). For example, major server vendors such as Netscape and Microsoft have their own server APIs: NSAPI and ISAPI, respectively. Even Apache has an API of its own.

If you are interested in receiving the latest information on FastCGI, you can subscribe to the mailing list fastcgi-developers@openmarket.com. Note that this mailing list is used by FastCGI developers and may not be appropriate for asking low-level questions. To join the list, send a message to fastcgi-developers-request@openmarket.com with a message body consisting of the word *subscribe*. Mail sent to this list is archived and available on the World Wide Web at

```
www.fastcgi.com/mail/
```

The existence of CGI, FastCGI, and the Server API creates a great deal of confusion for developers and server administrators. To shed some light on this murky subject, Table 9-1 provides some key feature comparisons among these technologies.

Table 9-1
Comparing CGI, Server API, and FastCGI

Feature	*CGI*	*Server API*	*FastCGI*
Programming language dependency	Language independent. CGI applications can be written in almost any programming language.	Applications have to be written in a language supported by the vendor API (usually C/C++).	Language independent. Like CGI, FastCGI applications can be written in any programming language.
Process isolation	Supported. Applications run as separate processes; buggy applications cannot crash the Web server or access the server's private internal state.	No process isolation. Because the applications run in the server's address space, buggy applications can corrupt the core server and compromise security, and bugs in the core server can corrupt applications.	Supported. A buggy FastCGI application cannot crash or corrupt the core server or other applications.
Type of standard	Open standard. Some form of CGI has been implemented on every Web server.	Proprietary. Coding your application to a particular API locks you into a particular vendor's server.	Nonproprietary, proposed open standard. Support is under development for other Web servers, including commercial servers from Microsoft and Netscape. Apache currently supports FastCGI as a third-party module.

Feature	*CGI*	*Server API*	*FastCGI*
Platform dependency	Platform independent. CGI is not tied to any particular server architecture (single-multithreaded, threaded, and so on).	Tie-in to server architecture. API applications have to share the same architecture as the server. If the Web server is multithreaded, the application has to be thread safe. If the Web server has single-threaded processes, multithreaded applications don't gain any performance advantage.	Platform independent. The FastCGI is not tied to any particular server architecture. Any Web server can implement the FastCGI interface.
Performance	A new process is created for each request and thrown away whenthe request is done;efficiency is poor.	Applications run in the server process and are persistent across requests. The CGI startup/initialization problem is absent.	FastCGI processes are persistent; they are reused to handle multiple requests. The CGI startup/ initialization problem is absent.
Complexity	Easy to understand.	Very complex. Vendor APIs introduce a steep learning curve, with increased implementation and maintenance costs.	Simple, with easy migration from CGI.
Distributed architecture	Not supported. To run CGI applications on a remote system, a Web server is needed on that system, as CGI applications are run by Web servers.	Depends on vendor.	Supported. FastCGI applications can be on any host supporting TCP/IP.

Now that you know your options, and you still want to give FastCGI a try, you are in the right place. Let's take a look at the benefits of using FastCGI.

Benefits of FastCGI

Let's first consider the benefits of using FastCGI over CGI or even server API.

High performance through caching

How fast is FastCGI? The answer depends on the application. If an application reads data from files and the data can be cached into memory, the FastCGI version of this application will provide better performance than either CGI or an API-based Web server application. A CGI application by specification cannot make use of in-memory cache because a new instance of the application runs per request and exists after request processing is complete. Similarly, most widely used API-based Web server applications run on child processes that do not share memory, and therefore no caching can be applied there as well. Even if in-memory caching is implemented per child process in this model, it work very poorly because each child process has to have a copy of the cache in memory, which wastes a great deal of memory.

FastCGI is designed to enable effective in-memory caching. Requests are routed from any child process to a FastCGI application server. The FastCGI application process maintains an in-memory cache. Note that in some cases a single FastCGI application server would not provide enough performance. With multithreading you run an application process designed to handle several requests at the same time. The threads handling concurrent requests share process memory, so they all have access to the same cache.

The developer of FastCGI performed some tests using three versions of an application (based on CGI, FastCGI, and a popular Web server–based API specification) that interacted with a database server. What they found out was that when the FastCGI version of the application used in-memory caching and persistent connection to the database server, it outperformed both CGI and the API-based versions of the application by a large margin.

When the in-memory cache was disabled for the FastCGI application, and persistent connection was used for the API-based application, the API-based application performed slightly better than the FastCGI version. This means that only when a level playing field is used (that is, FastCGI advantages such as the in-memory caching feature are disabled) does the API version win. But why would you disable caching? In other words, as long as you do not write a crippled FastCGI application, it is likely to outperform both CGI and API versions.

The tests demonstrated that the FastCGI-based application's architectural advantage resulted in a performance that was three times better than the API counterpart. This factor is likely to be more dramatic if the applications have to connect to remote resources such as a remote database server. However, they also point out that a multithreaded Web server capable of maintaining cache and persistent connections for its API application threads is likely to outperform FastCGI applications. This is due to the absence of interprocess communication overhead in a threaded environment. However, you should note that developing multithreaded applications requires very careful design and programming, as a single faulty thread can shut down the entire Web server system.

On the other hand, FastCGI processes take advantage of the process isolation model, where they run as external processes. This provides a safety net for the Web server system. In case of a faulty FastCGI application, the Web server will still function. If you just love multithreading and can't live without it, you can always write your FastCGI applications in a multithreaded model, which still takes advantage of the process isolation model.

Scalability through distributed applications

Unlike CGI applications, FastCGI applications do not get the CGI environment variables from their process environment table. Instead, a full-duplex connection between the application and the Web server is used to communicate the environment information, standard input, output, and errors. This enables FastCGI applications to run on remote machines using TCP/IP connections to the Web server, as shown in Figure 9-1.

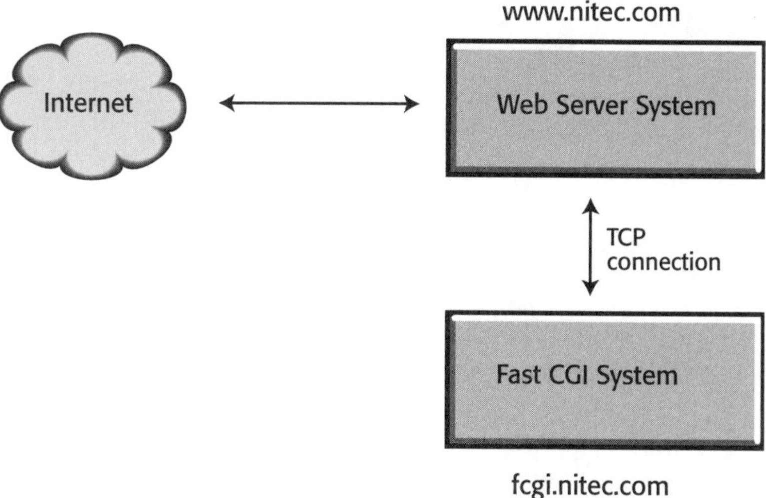

Figure 9-1: FastCGI on a remote machine

When CGI- and API-based applications become the performance bottlenecks due to heavy load; the typical solution is to get either a more powerful Web server or more Web servers to run them. Using FastCGI, this problem can be dealt with in a different manner. The FastCGI applications can be run on dedicated application servers on the network, thus freeing the Web server for what it does the best—service Web requests. The Web server(s) can be tailored to do Web service better and at the same time the FastCGI application server can be tailored to run applications efficiently. The Web administrator will never have to worry about how to balance the resource requirements of the Web server and the applications on the same machine. This will provide for a more flexible configuration on the Web server side as well as the application side.

Many organizations want to provide database access on their Web sites. Due to the limitations of CGI and vendor APIs, however, they must replicate a limited version of the database on the Web server to be able to provide this service. This creates considerable work for the administrator. With remote FastCGI, the applications can run on the internal network, simplifying the administrator's job. When used with appropriate firewall configuration and auditing, this approach provides a secure, high-performance, scalable way to bring internal applications and data to the Internet.

Remote FastCGI connections have two security issues: authentication and privacy. FastCGI applications should only accept connections from Web servers that they trust (the application library includes support for IP address validation). Future versions of the protocol will include support for applications authenticating Web servers, as well as support for running remote connections over secure protocols such as Secured Socket Layer (SSL).

Understanding FastCGI

FastCGI applications use a single connection to communicate with a Web server. The connection is used to deliver the environment variables and STDIN data to the applications and the STDOUT and the STDERR data to the Web server.

Use of this simple communication protocol also permits FastCGI applications to reside on a different machine (or different machines) from the Web server, enabling applications to scale beyond a single system and providing easier integration with existing systems. For local applications, the server uses a full-duplex pipe to connect to the FastCGI application process. For remote applications, the server uses a TCP/IP connection.

The FastCGI Protocol used to communicate between the Web server and the applications employs a simple packet record format. Most application developers will use the FastCGI application library and won't have to worry about the protocol details. However, specialized applications can implement the FastCGI protocol directly.

Because CGI is very similar to FastCGI, let's review the CGI request process. Figure 9-2 shows the simplified CGI request processing model.

For each CGI request, the Web server creates a new CGI process and the process initializes itself. The Web server passes various request-related information to the program via environment variables. Depending on the request method (GET or POST), the user data is stored in either an environment variable called QUERY_STRING or put in the process's standard input.

The CGI application performs its tasks and sends all its output to the standard output, which the Web server reads and parses (with the exception of nonparsed header applications). The CGI program exits, and the server returns the CGI output to the client.

FastCGI processes are persistent: After finishing a request, they wait for a new request instead of exiting, as shown in Figure 9-3.

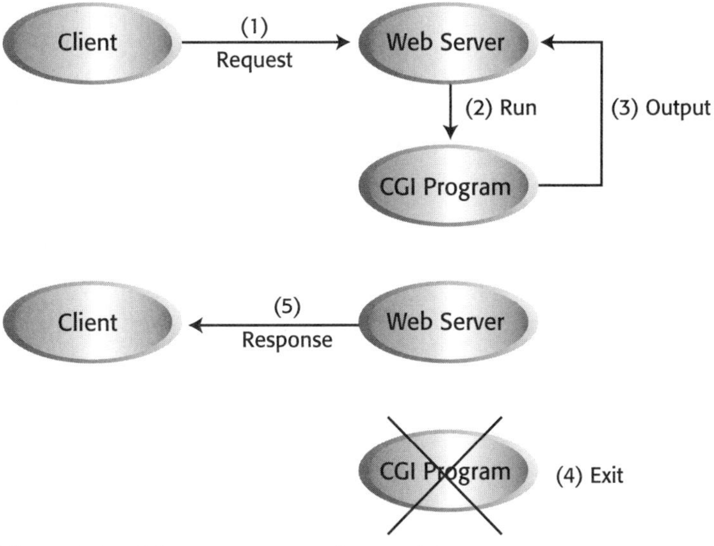

Figure 9-2: CGI request processing model

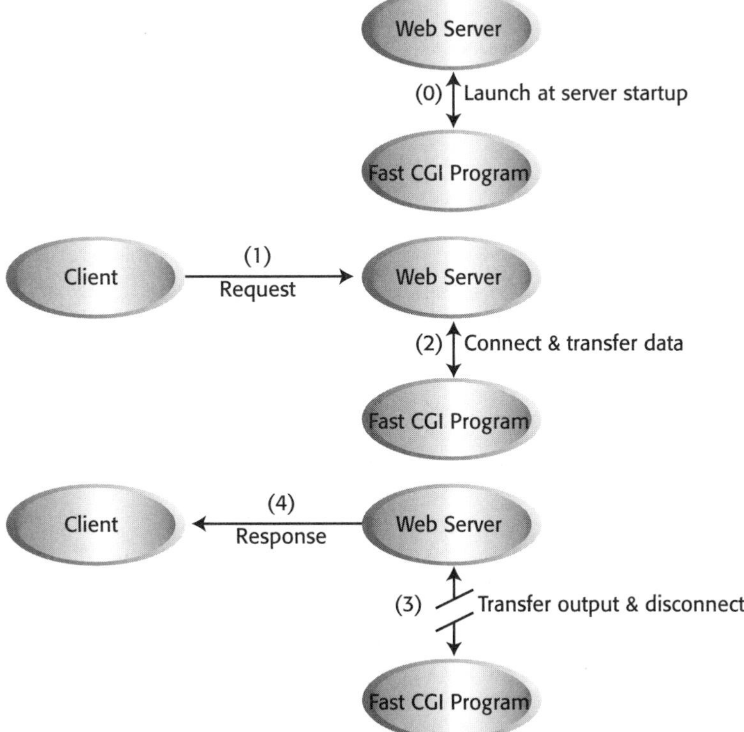

Figure 9-3: FastCGI request processing model

In case of nonparsed header applications, the CGI application is responsible for producing appropriate HTTP headers, and in all other cases the Web server produces appropriate HTTP headers based on the content type found in the STDOUT of the program. Any error information written to the CGI program's standard error is logged by the Web server.

Client request processing in a single-threaded FastCGI application proceeds as follows:

1. The Web server creates FastCGI application processes to handle requests. The processes may be created at startup or on demand.
2. The FastCGI program initializes itself and waits for a new connection from the Web server.
3. When a client request comes in, the Web server opens a connection to the FastCGI process. The server sends the CGI environment variable information and standard input over the connection.
4. The FastCGI process sends the standard output and error information back to the server over the same connection.
5. When the FastCGI process closes the connection, the request is complete. The FastCGI process then waits for another connection from the Web server.

Basic Architecture of a FastCGI Application

As you already know, unlike a CGI program, a FastCGI program keeps on running after it processes a request. This allows it to process future requests as soon as they come. This also makes the architecture of the FastCGI program different from a CGI program. A CGI program executes sequentially and exits, whereas a FastCGI program executes sequentially and loops forever. Figure 9-4 shows the basic architecture of a FastCGI application.

As you can see in the figure, a FastCGI program typically has an initialization code segment and a response loop segment that encapsulates the body of the program. The initialization code is run exactly once, when the application is initialized. Initialization code usually performs time-consuming operations such as opening databases or calculating values for tables.

The response loop runs continuously, waiting for client requests to arrive. The loop starts with a call to FCGI_Accept, a routine in the FastCGI library. The FCGI_Accept routine blocks program execution until a client requests the FastCGI application. When a client request comes in, FCGI_Accept unblocks, runs one iteration of the response loop body, and then blocks again, waiting for another client request. The loop terminates only when the system administrator or the Web server kills the FastCGI application.

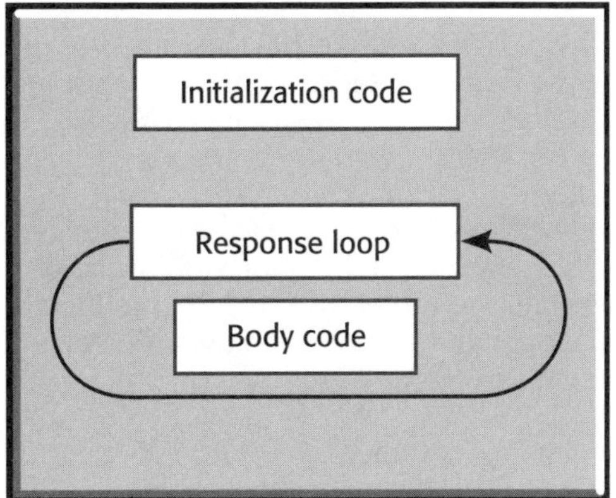

Figure 9-4: Basic architecture of a FastCGI application

The body of the program is executed in each iteration of the response loop. In other words, for each request, the body is executed once. FastCGI will set up the request information, such as environment variables and input data, before each iteration of the body code. Note that when the body code is executed, a subsequent call to FCGI_Accept informs the server that the program has completed a request and is ready for another. At this point FCGI_Accept blocks the execution until a new request is received.

FastCGI applications can be single-threaded or multithreaded. For single-threaded applications, the Web server maintains a pool of FastCGI processes (if the application is running locally) to handle client requests. The size of the pool is user configurable. Multithreaded FastCGI applications may accept multiple connections from the Web server and handle them simultaneously in a single process.

Different Types of FastCGI Applications

Another important aspect of FastCGI is that it supports roles for applications. Unlike a CGI application, a FastCGI application is persistent, and therefore it can be used for purposes that are not practical in CGI-based applications. Let's take a look at the different types of applications FastCGI supports.

Obviously, a FastCGI application can do all that a CGI application can. So the typical applications will be the same as their CGI counterparts. The new type of applications that are now possible and practical with FastCGI support are filters and external authentication applications.

You can create a FastCGI filter application to process a requested file before it is returned to the client. For example, say you want to apply a standard set of headers and footers for each HTML (.html) page returned by the Web server. This is possible using a FastCGI filter application. When a request for an .html file comes to the server, it sends the file request to the FastCGI filter responsible for adding the header and footer. The FastCGI application returns the resulting HTML page to the server, which in turn is transmitted to the client.

FastCGI filter applications can significantly improve performance by caching filter results (the server provides the modification time in the request information so that applications can flush the cache when the server file has been modified). Filter applications can be useful in developing parsers for HTML pages with embedded SQL statements, on-the-fly file format converters, and so on.

Other new types of applications that can be developed using FastCGI support include external authentication programs and gateways to third-party authentication applications. For example, if you use an external database server to store authentication information such as user name, passwords, or other permission-specific data, you can create a FastCGI application to keep a persistent connection to the database server and perform queries to authenticate access requests. Can this be done with a CGI application? Yes, with the exception that a CGI application will have to open the connection to the database server each time it is run. This could become expensive in terms of resource (CPU, network) utilization.

On the other hand, the FastCGI version of the same application will maintain a single connection to the database server, perform queries, and return appropriate HTTP status code based on the results of the queries. For example, when an access request is accompanied with a valid user name/password pair, the FastCGI application will query the database server to find out if the pair is allowed access to the requested resource. If the database server returns a specific value indicating that access should be allowed, the FastCGI application will return a "200 OK" HTTP status code; when authorization fails, it can send a different HTTP status code, such as "401 Unauthorized".

Now that you are aware of the types of FastCGI applications, let's take a look at how you can migrate existing CGI programs to FastCGI.

Migrating from CGI to FastCGI

Yet another advantage of FastCGI is the migration path from CGI to FastCGI is reasonably simple. In this section I demonstrate how to migrate a simple CGI application (written in Perl), fontsize.cgi, which is listed in Listing 9-1.

Listing 9-1: fontsize.cgi

```
#!/usr/local/bin/perl

# Variables
my $MAX = 10;
my $i;

# Content Header
print "Content-type text/html\n\n";

# Main loop
for ($i=0; $i < $MAX; $i++){
print "<FONT SIZE=$i>Font Size = $i</FONT><BR>";
}
exit 0;
```

This CGI application produces the output shown in Figure 9-5.

Now let's convert this to a FastCGI application. For simplicity, I will assume that the FastCGI version of Perl is installed on the system. Read the FastCGI Developer Kit documentation on the CD-ROM to get the FastCGI version of Perl compiled and installed on your system. The following line tells the shell to load the Perl interpreter:

```
#!/usr/local/bin/perl
```

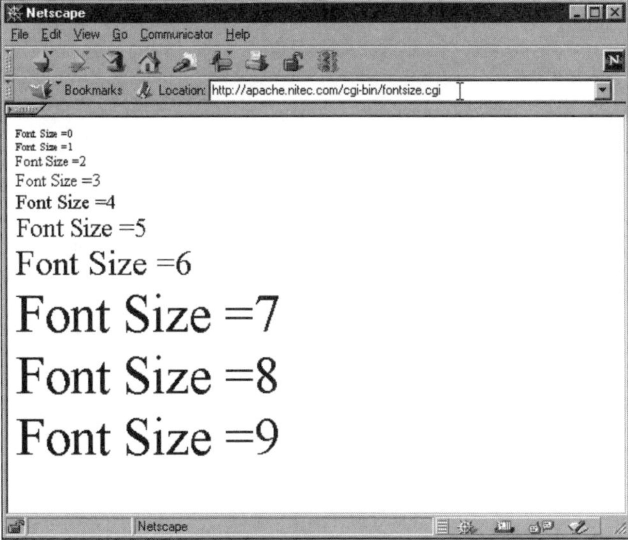

Figure 9-5: Output of fontsize.cgi CGI application

If the FastCGI version of the Perl interpreter has a different name or location, this line needs to be changed to point to the FastCGI-savvy Perl interpreter. I will keep this as it is because on my system perl (the Perl interpreter) is the FastCGI-savvy version.

To use the FastCGI package for Perl, add the following line:

```
Use FCGI;
```

Next, identify the initialization block of the CGI application. For this script the initialization block will consist of the following two variable declarations:

```
my $MAX = 10;
my $i;
```

Now you need to identify the response loop and body blocks of the CGI application. Because every request must be responded to with an appropriate Content-type header, the body of the main code will begin with this line:

```
print "Content-type text/html\n\n";
```

The for loop responsible for the actual processing is the rest of the body. Now that the body code has been identified, you need to put the response loop around it. This is done using the following code:

```
while(FCGIaccept() >= 0) {
# body code goes here
    }
```

Now the body looks like this:

```
while(FCGI::accept() >= 0) {
print "Content-type text/html\n\n";

for ($i=0; $i < $MAX; $i++){
       print "<FONT SIZE=$i>Font Size = $i</FONT><BR>";
}
    }
```

FastCGI applications act like server applications, so the following line will only be executed if the application was sent a signal to terminate by the Web server or administrator:

```
exit 0;
```

The FastCGI version of the entire application is listed in Listing 9-2.

Listing 9-2: fontsize.fcgi

```
#!/usr/local/bin/perl

# Tell Perl that we want to use FastCGI package
use FCGI;

# Variables
my $MAX = 10;
my $i;

# FastCGI Loop
while(FCGI::accept() >= 0) {

# Content Header
print "Content-type text/html\n\n";

# Main Loop
for ($i=0; $i < $MAX; $i++){
        print "<FONT SIZE=$i>Font Size = $i</FONT><BR>";
}
    }

exit 0;
```

To ease migration to FastCGI, executables built with the FastCGI application library (provided in the FastCGI Development Kit) can run as either CGI or FastCGI programs, depending on how they are invoked. The library detects the execution environment and automatically selects FastCGI or regular I/O routines, as appropriate.

An important thing to remember when migrating CGI applications to FastCGI is that many CGI applications are written so that they do not attempt to perform any memory management operations. This is due to CGI applications exiting after execution, and in most cases the operating system is able to restore memory for other use. On top of that, many CGI applications do not even attempt to close files, as the responsibility is handed over to the operating system at exit.

In such a case, it is very important that these types of applications be fixed while migrating to the FastCGI version. Remember, FastCGI applications reside in memory as long as the Web server or the administrator do not kill them. If a CGI application that leaked memory is converted to FastCGI without anyone dealing with the memory issue, the FastCGI version might leak memory over time and eventually causing a resource fault. To avoid long weekends in the office, it might be a good idea to take a look at this issue beforehand. If the CGI application is very complex, and fixing it to behave nicely (memory usage-wise) is too expensive in terms of time and efforts, another solution is available to you.

You can keep a count of how many times this memory-leaking application has serviced requests and kill it programmatically. Listing 9-3 shows a simple example of how request-processing count is kept in a simple C-based FastCGI application.

Listing 9-3: memory_hog.c

```
#include <fcgi_stdio.h>
void main(void){
int maxRequests = 100;         // maximum num of request before
exiting.
int requestCount = 0;          // used to keep count of requests
processed so far.

while(FCGI_Accept() >= 0) {    // start of response loop
/* body code */

printf("Content-type: text/html\r\n");
printf("\r\n");
printf("Number of requests processed so far is %d.",
requestCount++);

/* some memory leaking code could go here */


/* end of application's reall processing code */

if(requestCount >= maxRequests) {
  /* clean-up code goes here */
  exit 0;
  }

/* end of body code */

}
/ * termination or clean-up code (if any) */
exit(0);
}
```

As you can see in the preceding source code, when the maximum number of requests have been processed the FastCGI application exits.

Another issue to be aware of is this: If the CGI application being migrated has code that might interfere with a second run of the body code, it has to be fixed. The solution to this problem could be as simple as adding code to reinitialize some variables, arrays and so on. The application must ensure that any state it creates in processing one request has no unintended effects on later requests.

Finally, you should be aware that it is a common practice among CGI developers to break down a large application into smaller CGI applets. This is done to compensate for the initialization penalty associated with CGI applications. With FastCGI, it's better to have related functionality in a single executable so that there are fewer processes to manage and applications can take advantage of sharing cached information across functions.

The developer of FastCGI specifications provides a freely available software development kit to help ease the process of FastCGI application development. The kit can be obtained from the FastCGI Web site at the URL:

```
www.fastcgi.com/applibs
```

It is also included in the CD-ROM. This kit, provided as a compressed tar file, will help you write FastCGI applications in C, C++, Perl, Tcl, and Java. When you uncompress and untar the file, it will create a fcgi-devel-kit directory. You will find an index.html file that provides information on what is available in the kit.

FastCGI for Apache

Like many other features, FastCGI is supported on Apache by adding a module. If you do not plan to add the mod_fastcgi.c module in your Apache Web server, you can still run FastCGI applications using a traditional CGI application called cgi-fcgi. This application is included in the developer's kit.

The program cgi-fcgi enables you to run FastCGI applications using Apache or any Web server that supports CGI. This is a CGI program that uses a UNIX domain or TCP/IP sockets to communicate with a FastCGI application. The cgi-fcgi program takes the path name or host/port name of a listening socket as a parameter and connects to the FastCGI application listening on that socket. It then forwards the CGI environment variables and STDIN data to the FastCGI application and passes the STDOUT and STDERR data from the FastCGI application to the Web server. When the FastCGI application signals the end of its response, cgi-fcgi flushes its buffers and exits.

Note that using cgi-fcgi is not as good as having an Apache server with integrated FastCGI support. Because the CGI application (cgi-fcgi) has to be launched for each request, the fork/exec call overhead is part of each request. It also does not perform any application management, so you need to provide this yourself. However, cgi-fcgi does allow you to develop applications that retain state in memory between connections, which often provides a major performance boost over normal CGI. And all the applications you develop using cgi-fcgi will work with Web servers that have integrated support for FastCGI. The file examples/tiny-fcgi.cgi demonstrates a way to use cgi-fcgi to run a typical application, in this case the examples/tiny-fcgi application:

```
#!/path/to/cgi-fcgi/cgi-fcgi -f -connect sockets/tiny-fcgi
tiny-fcgi
```

On most UNIX platforms, executing this command-interpreter file runs cgi-fcgi with arguments -f and examples/tiny-fcgi.cgi.

On some UNIX platforms, including HP-UX, the first line of a command-interpreter file cannot contain more than 32 characters, including the new-line character. You may need to install the cgi-fcgi application in a standard place like /usr/local/bin or create a symbolic link to the cgi-fcgi application in the directory containing your application.

I highly recommend that if you want to test out FastCGI's capabilities, use the mod_fastcgi.c module instead of the cgi-fcgi CGI application. This module is not part of the standard Apache distribution. The mod_fastcgi.c module provides the following directives.

AppClass directive

```
Syntax: AppClass <path to FastCGI application> [-processes N]
[-listen-queue-depth N]
[-restart-delay N] [-priority N] [-port N] [-socket sock-name]
[-initial-env key=value]
Context: server config
```

This directive enables you to start FastCGI applications. For example:

```
AppClass /www/development/fcgi-devel-kit/echo.fcg -port 9000
```

This directive will enable mod_fastcgi to load the /www/development/fcgi-devel-kit/echo.fcg FastCGI application. The application will listen on port 9000. When a FastCGI application loaded by this directive dies, mod_fastcgi will restart the application and write a log entry in the error log file. The optional parameters to the AppClass directive are as follows:

- processes — This option specifies how many FastCGI processes to create. On a high-load scenario, loading multiple instances of the same FastCGI application can provide better performance. The default value is 1.
- listen-queue-depth — This option specifies how deep the listen queue is for the FastCGI application(s) loaded with the directive. The default value is sufficient in most cases, but in a high-load scenario, you can increase the depth of the queue. This will decrease chances of a request being rejected due to application(s) being busy. However, if you expect a high load, and your server is capable of running a few extra FastCGI processes, increase the number of processes instead of the depth of the listen queue. The default value is 5.
- restart-delay — This option specifies the number of seconds that will be used to delay a restart of a dead FastCGI process. This is only useful when you are using multiple instances of the same FastCGI application. In the case of a single FastCGI application, it is restarted immediately, and this option has no effect. The default value is 5.

You might wonder why this delay is needed. Normally, a FastCGI application should not die; if it is dying, there is chance that something is wrong with it. In such a case, this delay will at least allow your server to do other useful tasks besides restarting a faulty application again and again.

- Priority — This option sets the process priority of a FastCGI application. The default value enables a FastCGI application to have the same priority as the Apache server itself. Other appropriate values are defined by your operating system's setpriority system call. In a RedHat Linux system, the setpriority system call permits a value in the range of -20 to 20. The lower the number, the more favorable the scheduling used for the process. However, mod_fastcgi does not allow a negative value, which means you cannot set a FastCGI process to have higher priority than the Apache server itself. So all you can do is use a positive integer number to lower the priority of the application. The default value is 0.
- Port — This option specifies the TCP port that the FastCGI application will listen on. Because ports lower than 1024 are used for standard services, you will have to use a higher port number. Use of this option enables you to access the application from another system. No environment variable is provided by default.
- Socket — This option specifies the path name of the UNIX domain socket that the application will listen on. The module creates this socket within the directory specified by the FastCgiIpcDir directive. The default value is Default Socket.

  If you do not provide either the port or socket option, the module creates a Unix domain socket for the application by itself.
- initial-env — This option can be used to insert an environment variable (with value) in the FastCGI application's environment table. You can use this option multiple times to insert more than one key=value pair in the environment of the application. No environment variable is provided by default.

Note that the -socket and -port options are mutually exclusive. Path-name must not equal the path name supplied to an earlier AppClass or ExternalAppClass directive.

ExternalAppClass directive

```
Syntax: ExternalAppClass <FastCGI-application-name> [-host
host:port] [-socket sock-name]
Context: server config
```

Use this directive when you have a FastCGI application running on another system. For example:

```
ExternalAppClass echo.fcg    -host fcgi.nitec.com:9090
```

Here, the echo.fcg application is running on a host called fcgi.nitec.com and listening to port 9090. The <FastCGI-application-name> is just an identifier that can be used to describe the application running on the remote host, so it can be any name you want. Make sure the name you choose is not already used in another AppClass or ExternalAppClasss directive. The optional parameters to the ExternalAppClass directive are listed here:

- ✦ host—This option enables you to specify the host and the TCP port number of the FastCGI application running on another system. Use host:port format to specify the host and port. You can use either a host name or an IP address.
- ✦ socket—This option enables you to specify the path name of the UNIX domain socket being used by a FastCGI application.

FastCgiIpcDir directive

```
Syntax: FastCgiIpcDir path
Default: FastCgiIpcDir /tmp
Context: server config
```

This directive specifies the default path for UNIX domain sockets created by the module. The default /tmp location is fine as long as you do not have cron jobs set up to clean up your /tmp directory from time to time. The socket name has the following format:

```
OM_WS_n.pid
```

Here, *n* is a number and *pid* is the process ID of the main Apache process. If you do set this directive to a path, make sure only Apache has read and write access to the directory.

Compiling mod_fastcgi into Apache

Adding FastCGI support in Apache is quite easy. The first step is to get the latest FastCGI module for Apache. You can find the latest FastCGI module for Apache at the following site:

```
www.fastcgi.com
```

The latest version of this module is also included in the CD-ROM that comes with this book.

Next, you need to configure the Apache configuration file. Copy the module file (mod_fastcgi.c) to a subdirectory in the src/modules directory of your Apache source tree. I like to keep all modules in src/modules/standard. Once the module file is under the Apache source tree, add the following line to your Configuration file, located under the src directory.

```
AddModule modules/standard/mod_fastcgi.o
```

If you keep the module in a different directory, make sure to substitute your path for modules/standard/.

Now you are ready to compile Apache with the FastCGI module. Run the Configure script and the make utility. You should have a new Apache executable (httpd) in the source directory. To make sure the module is used in the building of the new Apache executable, run the ./httpd -l command from the source directory. If you see mod_fastcgi.c listed in the output, you have successfully added the module in Apache.

If your system supports stripping of binaries, you can make your Apache executable a bit lighter in size. For example, on a RedHat Linux system you can use the strip httpd command to remove unnecessary symbolic information from the Apache binary.

Replace your existing httpd with the new executable. To configure FastCGI applications, you need a combination of mod_fastcgi directives and other directives provided by the Apache server.

Use the AppClass directive to start the FastCGI applications that you want to be managed by this Web server. The applications are managed in the sense that the server (a) logs an error message when a managed process dies and (b) attempts to restart managed processes that die.

Use one or both of the AppClass and ExternalAppClass directives to define an association between a path name and the connection information for a FastCGI application. Connection information is either the path name of a UNIX domain socket or the IP address and port number of a TCP port. The difference between the two directives is as follows: A single AppClass directive both starts an application and sets up the association for communicating with it, whereas ExternalAppClass only defines the association. In the case of AppClass, the path name used in the association is always the path name of the application's executable; with ExternalAppClass, the path name is arbitrary.

For an HTTP request to be processed by mod_fastcgi, the request's handler must be fastcgi-script or the request's MIME type must be application/x-httpd-fcgi. Apache provides several ways to set the handler and MIME type of a request:

- SetHandler (in the context of a Location or Directory section or per-directory access control file) can associate the handler fastcgi-script with a specific file or all the files in a directory.
- AddHandler can associate the handler fastcgi-script with files based on file extension.
- ForceType (in the context of a Location or Directory section or .htaccess file) can associate the MIME type application/x-httpd-fcgi with a specific file or all the files in a directory.
- AddType can associate the MIME-type application/x-httpd-fcgi with files based on file extension.

Once the mod_fastcgi module is configured, it is ready to handle requests as follows:

1. The connection information associated with the requested path name is retrieved. If no connection information is associated with the path name, the server returns the error code "404 Not Found."
2. The mod_fastcgi module connects to the FastCGI application process. If the connection attempt fails, the server returns "500 Server Error."
3. The request is transmitted to the FastCGI application process, which generates a response.
4. The application's response is received and transformed into an HTTP response. The server sends this response back to the client.

Example Configuration File

I recommend that you back up your existing httpd.conf file but not use the example configuration file right away. I've provided a minimal configuration using only the httpd.conf file in Listing 9-4 for testing purposes. Use this configuration for initial testing with FastCGI and, when you've verified that this configuration works, merge the FastCGI-specific aspects of this configuration with your own configuration.

Listing 9-4: Example httpd.conf configuration

```
# httpd.conf-minimal for mod_fastcgi
#
# One config file
#
ResourceConfig /dev/null
AccessConfig   /dev/null

# The port number below is above 1024 because we don't want to
# confuse this server with some other standard service
#
Port 9999

# You should replace the User/Group directive with appropriate
# user/group name
User $HTTP_USER
Group $HTTP_GROUP

# Configure just one idle httpd child process, to simplify
# debugging
StartServers 1
MinSpareServers 1
MaxSpareServers 1
```

```
# Tell httpd where it should live, turn on access and error
# logging
#ServerRoot     $APACHE
ErrorLog       logs/error.log
TransferLog    logs/access.log
ScoreBoardFile logs/httpd.scoreboard

# Tell httpd where to get documents
#
#DocumentRoot $FASTCGI

# This is how you'd place the Unix-domain socket files in the
# logs directory (you'd probably want to create a subdirectory
# for them.)
# Don't do this until you've verified that everything works
# with the socket files stored locally, in /tmp!
# FastCgiIpcDir $APACHE/logs
# Start the echo app
#
AppClass $FASTCGI/examples/echo -initial-env SOMETHING=NOTHING

# Have mod_fastcgi handle requests for the echo app #
# (otherwise the server will return the app's binary as a file!)
#
<Location /examples/echo>
SetHandler fastcgi-script
</Location>

# Start a FastCGI application that's accessible from other
# machines
AppClass $FastCGI/examples/echo.fcg -port 8978
<Location /examples/echo.fcg>
SetHandler fastcgi-script
</Location>

# Connect to "remote" app started above. Since the app is
# actually local, communication will take place using TCP
# loopback.
# To test true remote operation, start one copy of this # Web
# server on one machine, then start another copy with
# "localhost" in the line below changed to the host name of the
# first machine.
#
#ExternalAppClass remote-echo -host localhost:8978
<Location /examples/remote-echo>
SetHandler fastcgi-script
</Location>

# This is how you'd have mod_fastcgi handle any request for a file
# whose name  ends in .fcg:
# AddHandler fastcgi-script fcg
# End of httpd.conf
```

Make sure you have built the new httpd with the mod_fastcgi module and that the FastCGI Developer's Kit is built properly. Here I will make use of the echo program that comes with FastCGI Developer's Kit in the example directory. Do not forget to restart Apache after you have placed the new httpd.conf file from Listing 9-4 in the $APACHE/conf directory. Use a browser to access the following URL:

```
http://$YOUR_HOST:9999/examples/echo
```

where $YOUR_HOST is the IP address of the host running httpd. Look for SOMETHING=NOTHING in the initial environment that echoes displays. The request counter should increment each time you reload the page. Before you can use this configuration, you will have to make some substitutions, as shown in Table 9-2.

Table 9-2
Substitution for Example Configuration

Keyword	*Replace With*
$APACHE	Path name of the directory containing Apache
$FASTCGI	Path name of the directory containing your FastCGI Developer's Kit
$HTTP_USER	User name you use for the User directive
$HTTP_GROUP	Group name you use for the Group directive

Summary

In this chapter you learned about how FastCGI solves the performance problems inherent in CGI, without introducing the overhead and complexity of proprietary APIs. It is fast, open, and maintainable. It offers features such as in-memory caching, persistent connections, and distributed architecture. The migration path from CGI to FastCGI is reasonably simple. However, it is still a proposed open standard and therefore not yet widely used.

In the next chapter you will learn about basic HTTP authentication.

✦ ✦ ✦

P A R T

Playing It Safe

✦ ✦ ✦ ✦

In This Part

✦ ✦ ✦ ✦

Basic Authentication

In This Chapter

What basic HTTP authentication is

How secure basic HTTP authentication is

How to restrict certain hosts from accessing your Web pages

How to require a user name and/or password for access

How to use external authentication programs

What host-base and digest authentication are

In general, when a client logs on to a network, that session is maintained between that client and the server until the client logs off. On the Web, that client is typically a Web browser and the server a Web server. The HyperText Transport Protocol (HTTP), however, is stateless, and therefore sessions are not maintained between the Web browser and a Web server such as Apache. As soon as a URL request has been serviced by the Web server, the connection is terminated. Apache is capable of using the Keep-Alive facility to keep the connection open for future request processing, but not all Web browsers support the Keep-Alive facility yet.

This facility is also not used for maintaining authenticated sessions. In other words, the only authentication mechanism guaranteed to be available on the Web is what is provided by HTTP itself. Everything else is specific to a certain server; in other words, other authentication mechanisms are host-based or require custom programming. One such authentication scheme, implemented in the standard Apache server, enables control over which hosts can access a particular site or a portion of it.

Host-based authentication, however, is limiting in many ways. It becomes unusable if you are trying to authenticate users who access the Web via a proxy server or a firewall. Because the user host IP is never revealed to the Apache server, the server is unable to differentiate among the users. Most people on the Internet use dynamically allocated IP addresses from their Internet service provider (ISP), and therefore host-based authentication might not always be appropriate. A more traditional user name/password-based authentication is desirable in most cases. Basic HTTP authentication provides such a facility.

Authenticated login is poorly supported on the Web, because HTTP provides a very minimal support for authenticated access. If you are interested in highly secured authentication architecture, consider authentication based on the Secured Socket Layer (SSL). Except for SSL-based authentication, almost all other currently available Web-based authentication schemes are considered basic authentication.

In this chapter, I discuss two basic authentication schemes: host-based authentication and basic HTTP authentication.

The Host-based Authentication Process

In this authentication scheme, access is controlled by the host name or the host's IP address. When a request is made for a certain resource, the Web server checks to see if the requesting host is allowed access to the resource and takes action based on the findings.

The standard Apache distribution includes a module called mod_access, which enables access control based on the Internet host name of a Web client. The host name can be either a fully qualified domain name (FQDN), such as blackhole.nitec.com, or an IP address, such as 206.171.50.50. The module provides this access control support using the following Apache directives: allow, deny, order, allow from env=variable, and deny from env=variable.

allow directive

```
Syntax: allow from host1 host2 host3 …
Context: directory, location, per-directory access control file
Override: Limit
```

This directive enables you to define a list of hosts (containing one or more hosts or IP addresses) that are allowed access to a certain directory. When more than one host or IP address is specified, they should be separated with space characters. Table 10-1 shows the possible values for the directive.

Table 10-1
Possible Values for the allow Directive

Value	*Example*	*Description*
All	allow from all	This reserved word allows access for all hosts. The example shows how to use this option.

Value	Example	Description
A fully qualified domain name (FQDN) of a host	allow from wormhole.nitec.com	Only the host that has the specified FQDN is allowed access. The allow directive in the example only allows access to wormhole.nitec.com. Note that this compares whole components; toys.com would not match etoys.com.
A partial domain name of a host	allow from .mainoffice.nitec.com	Only all the hosts that match the partial host name are allowed access. The example permits all the hosts in .mainoffice.nitec.com network to access the site. For example, developer1.mainoffice.nitec.com and developer2.mainoffice.nitec.com have access to the site. However, developer3.baoffice.nitec.com is not allowed access.
A full IP address of a host	allow from 206.171.50.50	Only the specified IP address is allowed access. The example shows a full IP address (all four octets of IP are present), 206.171.50.50, that is allowed access.
A partial IP address	Example 1: allow from 206.171.50 Example 2: allow from 130.86	When not all four octets of an IP address are present in the allow directive, the partial IP address is matched from left to right, and hosts that have the matching IP address pattern (that is, it is part of the same subnet) are allowed access. In the first example, all hosts with IP addresses in the range of 206.171.50.1 to 206.171.50.255 have access. In the second example, all hosts from the 130.86 network are allowed access.
A network/ netmask pair	allow from 206.171.50.0/255.255.255.0	This enables you to specify a range of IP addresses using the network and the netmask address. The example allows only the hosts with IP addresses in the range of 206.171.50.1 to 206.171.50.255 to have access. This feature is available in Apache 1.3 or above.

(continued)

Table 10-1 (continued)		
Value	***Example***	***Description***
A network/nnn CIDR specification	allow 206.171.50.0/24	Similar to the previous entry, except the netmask consists of nnn high-order 1 bits. The example is equivalent to allow from 206.171.50.0/255.255.255.0. This feature is available in Apache 1.3 or above.

deny directive

```
Syntax: deny from host1 host2 host3 ...
Context: directory, location, per-directory access control file
Override: Limit
```

This directive is the exact opposite of the allow directive. It enables you to define a list of hosts that are denied access to a specified directory. Like the allow directive, it can accept all the values shown in Table 10-1.

order directive

```
Syntax: order deny, allow | allow, deny | mutual-failure
Default: order deny, allow
Context: directory, location, per-directory access control file
Override: Limit
```

This directive controls how Apache evaluates both allow and deny directives. For example:

```
<Directory /mysite/myboss/rants>
order deny, allow
deny from myboss.mycompany.com
allow from all
</Directory>
```

This example denies the host myboss.mycompany.com access and allows all other hosts to access the directory. The value for the order directive is a comma-separated list, which indicates which directive takes precedence. Typically, the one that affects all hosts is given lowest priority. In the preceding example, because the allow directive affects all hosts, it is given the lower priority.

Although allow, deny and deny, allow are the most widely used values for the order directive, you can use another value, mutual-failure, to indicate that only those hosts appearing on the allow list but not on the deny list are granted access.

Note that in all cases every allow and deny directive is evaluated.

allow from env=variable directive

```
Syntax: allow from env=variable
Context: directory, location, per-directory access control file
Override: Limit
```

This directive, a variation of the allow directive, allows access when the named environment variable is set. This is only useful if you are using other directives such as BrowserMatch to set an environment variable. For example, say you want to allow Microsoft Internet Explorer 4.01, the latest version of Internet Explorer, to access a directory where you stored some HTML files with embedded VBScript. Because the other leading Web browser, Netscape Navigator, does not support VBScript directly, you'd rather not have Navigator users go into the directory. In such a case, you can use the BrowserMatch directive to set an environment variable when Internet Explorer 4.01 is detected. The directive would be as follows:

BrowserMatch "MSIE 4.01" ms_browser

Now you can use a <Directory> container to specify the allow directive, as follows:

```
<Directory /path/to/Vbscript_directory >
order deny,allow
deny from all
allow from env=ms_browser
</Directory>
```

Here the Apache server will set the ms_browser environment variable for all browsers that provide the "MSIE 4.01" string as part of the user-agent identifier. The allow directive will only allow browsers for which the ms_browser variable is set.

deny from env=variable

```
Syntax: deny from env=variable
Context: directory, location, per-directory access control file
Override: Limit
```

This directive, a variation of the deny directive, denies access capability for all hosts for which the specified environment is set. For example, if you want to deny all hosts using Microsoft Internet Explorer access, you can use the BrowserMatch directive to set a variable called ms_browser whenever a browser identified itself to the server with the string "MSIE".

```
BrowserMatch "MSIE" ms_browser
```

Now you can use a <Directory> container to specify the deny directive, as follows:

```
<Directory /path/to/Vbscript_directory >
order deny,allow
```

```
allow from all
deny from env=ms_browser
</Directory>
```

If you are interested in blocking access to a specific HTTP request method, such as GET, POST, and PUT, you can use the <Limit> container to do so. For example:

```
<Location /cgi-bin>
<Limit POST>
order deny,allow
deny from all
allow from yourdomain.com
</Location>
```

This example allows POST requests to the cgi-bin directory only if they are made by hosts in the yourdomain.com domain. In other words, if this site has some HTML forms that send user input data via the HTTP POST method, only the users in yourdomain.com will be able to use these forms effectively. Typically, CGI applications are stored in the cgi-bin directory, and many sites feature HTML forms that use the POST method to dump data to CGI applications. Using the preceding host-based access control configuration, a site can allow anyone to run a CGI script but only allow a certain site (in this case, yourdomain.com) to actually post data to one or more CGI scripts. This gives the CGI access in such a site a bit of read-only character. Everyone can run applications that generate output without taking any user input, but only users of a certain domain can provide input.

The Basic HTTP Authentication Process

Basic HTTP authentication is really quite simple. When a Web browser requests a URL that is protected by the HTTP authentication scheme, the Web server returns a 401 status header along with a WWW-Authenticate response header, which implies that authentication is required to access the URL (see Figure 10-1). The header contains the authentication scheme being used (currently only basic HTTP authentication is supported) and the realm name.

At this point, a Web browser dialog box appears, asking the user to enter a user name and a password. Once the user enters the required user name and password, the browser sends the user name and password along with the previous URL request to the server. The server checks to see if the user name and password are valid. If they are valid, the server returns the requested page. If the user name and password are invalid, the server responds with a 401 status and sends the same WWW-Authenticate response header.

In each subsequent call to the same server, the browser will send the user name and password pair so that the server does not have to generate a 401 status header for calls that fall in the same area of the site. For example, if the URL http://apache.nitec.com/protected/ requires basic HTTP authentication, subsequent calls to http://apache.nitec.com/protected/a_page.html and http://apache.nitec.com/protected/b_page also require the user name/password pair. This is why the browser sends the pair before another authentication challenge — that is, the 401 status header and the WWW-Authenticate response header — is issued by the server. This is faster and more practical than generating a challenge for each request and having the user enter the user name/password pair again and again.

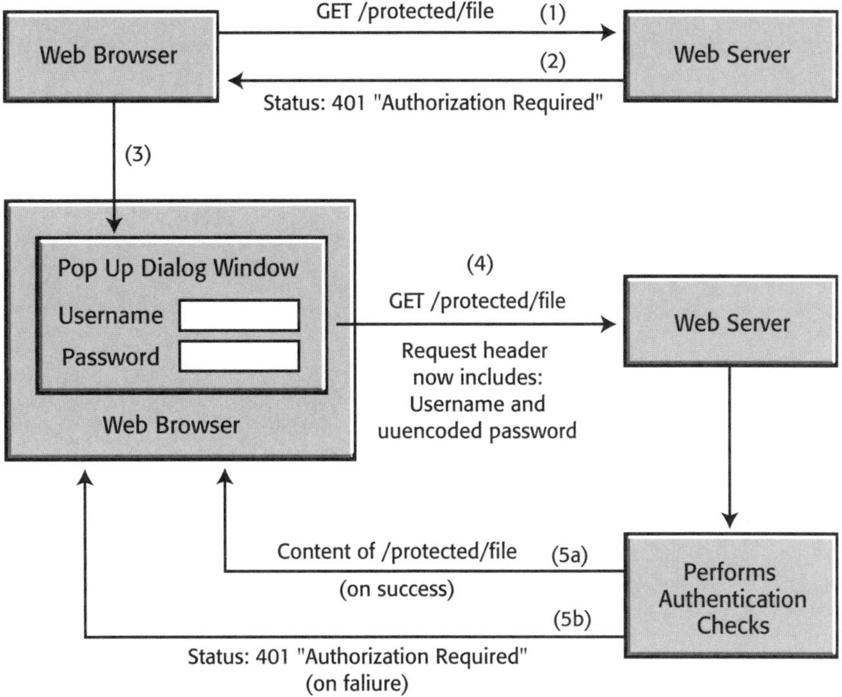

Figure 10-1: The basic HTTP authentication process

When the password is sent from the client system (the host running the Web browser), it is neither sent in clear text nor encrypted. Instead, it is Uuencoded and transmitted over the Internet. This is a disadvantage for this method of authentication, because anyone armed with network traffic sniffer hardware and software might be able to retrieve the IP packet carrying the Uuencoded password. As Uuencode is a widely used data encoding scheme, the decoder, Uudecode, is also widely available, thus enabling practically anyone to decode a Uuencoded password and possibly abuse it. It is true that the packet sniffer has to be able to find the right packet to be able to do the decoding, but technically it is possible.

This is why I want to emphasis that you should never use basic HTTP authentication for any critical application. Do not protect your nation's secrets using this scheme. At the same time, if you are already allowing Telnet or ftp access to your system, you are already using authentication methods (in these services) that are very similar to basic HTTP authentication. If you trust your machine to be on the Internet, open to attempts to Telnet in by anyone who wants to try, then you have no reason not to trust this method.

Support for basic HTTP authentication in Apache has been around for quite a while. Many modules have been written to provide basic HTTP authentication in Apache.

It is fairly simple to create a restricted area on a Web site using one or more of the authentication modules available for Apache. Along with authentication-module-specific directives, you need to use the following core directives:

- AccessFileName
- AllowOverride
- AuthType
- AuthName
- Satisfy
- Require

Each of these directives are discussed in Chapter 4. In the following sections, I discuss the common basic authentication modules currently available for Apache.

Using standard mod_auth module

This module is compiled by default in the standard distribution. Standard mod_auth-based basic HTTP authentication uses user names, groups, and passwords stored in text files to confirm authentication. This works well when dealing with a small number of users. However, if you have a lot of users (thousands or more), use of mod_auth might have a performance penalty. In such a case you can use something more advanced, such as DBM files, Berkeley DB files, or even a SQL database. (These are discussed later in the chapter.)

The standard mod_auth module offers the Apache directives AuthUserFile, AuthGroupFile, and AuthAuthoritative. Let's take a closer look at these directives and some examples that use this module.

AuthUserFile directive

```
Syntax: AuthUserFile filename
Context: directory, per-directory access control file
Override: AuthConfig
```

This directive sets the name of the text file that contains the user names and passwords used in the basic HTTP authentication. You must provide a fully qualified path to the file to be used. For example:

```
AuthUserFile /www/nitec/secrets/.htpasswd
```

This file is usually created using an utility called htpasswd, which is available as a support program in the standard Apache distribution. The format of this file is very simple. Each line contains a single user name and an encrypted password. The password is encrypted using the standard crypt() function.

It is important that the AuthUserFile-specified file resides outside the document tree of the Web site. Putting it inside a Web-accessible directory might enable someone to download it.

AuthGroupFile directive

```
Syntax: AuthGroupFile filename
Context: directory, per-directory access control file
Override: AuthConfig
```

This directive specifies a text file to be used as the list of user groups for basic HTTP authentication. The file name is the absolute path to the group file.

You can create this file using any text editor. The format of this file is as follows:

```
groupname: username username username ...
```

For example:

```
startrek: kirk spock picard data
```

This creates a group called startrek, which has four users: kirk, spock, picard, and data.

The warning for the AuthUserFile directive also applies to this directive.

AuthAuthoritative directive

```
Syntax: AuthAuthoritative  on | off
Default: on
Context: directory, per-directory access control file
Override: AuthConfig
```

If you are using more than one authentication scheme for the same directory, you can set this directive to on so that when a user name/password pair fails with the first scheme, it is passed on to the next (lower) level.

For example, if you are using mod_auth_db (discussed in a later section) and the standard mod_auth module to provide authentication services, and a user name/password pair fails for one of them, the next module is used to authenticate the user, if possible. Which module is considered as a lower- or higher-level authentication module is determined by its appearance in the Configuration file. Say the Configuration file looks like this:

```
AddModule modules/standard/mod_auth.o
AddModule modules/standard/mod_auth_db.o
```

The mod_auth_db will have higher priority because the modules in the Configuration file are listed in reverse priority order.

In any case, when a user name/password pair fails all modules, the server reissues a 401 status header and sends the WWW-Authenticate response header for reauthentication. However, if a user name/password pair is successfully authenticated by a particular module, the lower-level modules never receive the user name/password pair.

Example 1: Requiring user name and password

This example shows you how to create a restricted directory that requires a user name and a password for access. To simplify the example, I will assume the following are settings for a Web site called apache.nitec.com:

```
DocumentRoot   /data/web/apache/public/htdocs
AccessFileName .htaccess
AllowOverride  All
```

Now let's also assume that you want to restrict access to the following directory, such that only a user named "reader" with the password "bought-it" is able to access the directory:

```
/data/web/apache/public/htdocs/chapter_10/
```

Follow these steps to create the restricted access.

STEP 1: Creating a user file using htpasswd

Standard Apache distribution comes with a utility program called htpasswd, which creates the user file needed for the AuthUserFile directive. Use the program as follows:

```
htpasswd -c /data/web/apache/secrets/.htpasswd reader
```

The htpasswd utility asks for the password of "reader." Enter "bought-it" and then re-enter the password again to confirm that you didn't make a typo. After you re-enter the password, the utility creates a file called .htpasswd in the /data/web/apache/secrets directory. Note the following:

- ✦ Use the -c option to tell htpasswd that you want to create a new user file. If you already had the password file and wanted to add a new user, you would not need this option.

✦ Place the user file outside the document root directory of the apache.nitec.com site, as you do not want anyone to download it via Web.

✦ Use a leading period (.) in the file name so that it will not appear in ls output on your UNIX system. This really does not provide any real benefits but is more of a traditional UNIX habit. Many configuration files (such as .login and .profile) in UNIX systems have leading periods.

To save future headaches, execute the following command:

```
cat /data/web/apache/secrets/.htpasswd
```

This should show a line similar to the following (the password won't be exactly the same as this example):

```
reader:hulR6FFh1sxK6
```

This confirms that you have a user called "reader" in the.htpasswd file. The password "bought-it" is encrypted by the htpasswd program using the standard crypt() function.

STEP 2: Creating a .htaccess file

Using a text editor, add the following lines to a file named /data/web/apache/public/htdocs/chapter_10/.htaccess:

```
AuthName Apache Server Bible Readers Only
AuthType  Basic
AuthUserFile /data/web/apache/secrets/.htpasswd
require user reader
```

The first directive, AuthName, sets the realm of the authentication. This is really just a label that is sent to the Web browser so that the user will be provided with some clue about what he or she is about to access. In this case, the "Apache Server Bible Readers Only" string indicates that only readers of *Apache Server Bible* can access this directory. The second directive, AuthType, specifies the type of authentication to be used. Because only basic authentication is supported, AuthType is always set to "Basic." The next directive, AuthUserFile, specifies the file name for the user file. The path to the user file is provided here. The last directive, require, specifies that a user named "reader" is allowed access to this directory.

STEP 3: Setting file permissions

After the .htaccess and the .htpasswd files are created, it is important to make sure that only Apache can read the files. No users except the file owner and Apache should have access to these files.

STEP 4: Testing

Next, use a Web browser to access the following URL:

```
http://apache.nitec.com/chapter_10
```

Apache will send the 401 status header and WWW-Authenticate response header to the browser with the realm (set in AuthName) and authentication type (set in AuthType) information. The browser will display a pop-up dialog box that requests a user name and password, as shown in Figure 10-2.

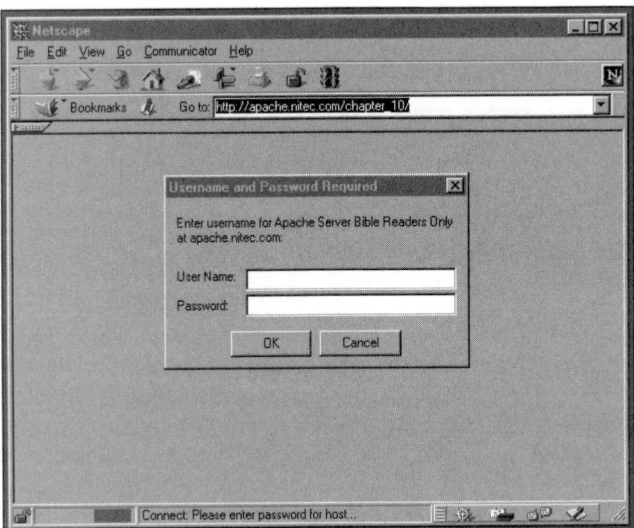

Figure 10-2: Browser requests user name and password.

It is a good idea to see if one can get in without a user name or password, so enter nothing in the entry boxes in the dialog and press the OK button. This should result in an authentication failure. The browser receives the same authentication challenge again, so it displays another dialog box, as shown in Figure 10-3, to ask if you want to retry.

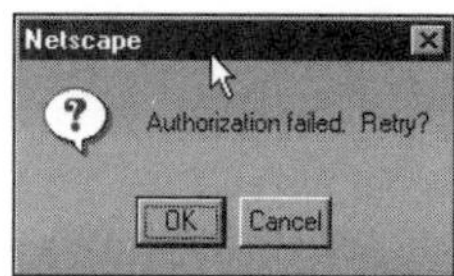

Figure 10-3 Browser shows retry message dialog box.

Choosing the Cancel button results in the browser showing the standard "Authentication Required" error message from Apache, as shown in Figure 10-4.

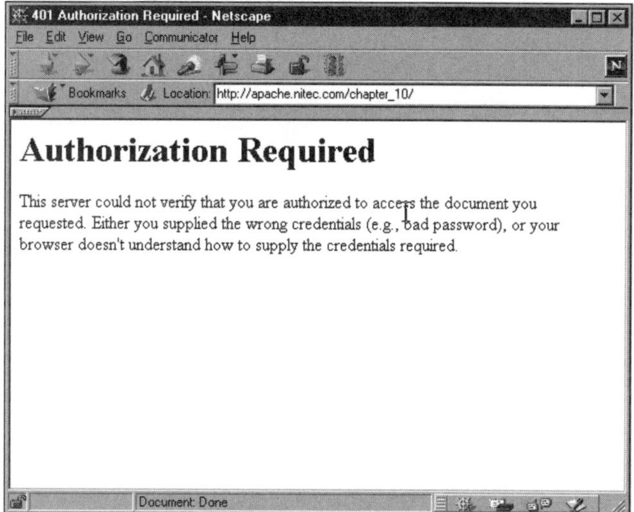

Figure 10-4 Failed authentication message displayed on the browser

Pressing the Reload button on the browser requests the same URL again, and the browser receives the same authentication challenge from the server. This time enter "reader" as the user name and "bought-it" as the password and press the OK button. Apache will now allow you to access the directory.

You can change the "Authentication Required" message if you want by using the ErrorDocument directive:

```
ErrorDocument 401 /nice_401message.html
```

Insert this line in your srm.conf file and create a nice message in the nice_401message.html file to make your users happy.

Example 2: Allowing a group of users to access a directory

Instead of allowing a single user called "reader" to access the restricted area, as demonstrated in the previous example, here you will allow anyone belonging to group named asb_readers to access the same directory. Let's also assume that you want to create the user table shown in Table 10-2.

Table 10-2
User Table

Group	*User Name*	*Password*
asb_readers	pikejb	Red#hat
asb_readers	bcaridad	Net#rat

Follow these steps to give the users in Table 10-2 directory access.

STEP 1: Creating a user file using htpasswd

Using the htpasswd utility, create the users pikejb and bcaridad.

STEP 2: Creating a group file

Using a text editor such as vi (available on most UNIX systems), create a file named /data/web/apache/secrets/.htgroup. This file has a single line, as shown below:

```
asb_readers: pikejb bcaridad
```

STEP 3: Creating a .htaccess file in /data/web/apache/public/htdocs/chapter_10

Using a text editor, add the following lines to a file called /data/web/apache/public/htdocs/chapter_10/.htaccess:

```
AuthName Apache Server Bible Readers Only
AuthType  Basic
AuthUserFile /data/web/apache/secrets/.htpasswd
AuthGroupFile /data/web/apache/secrets/.htgroup
require group  asb_readers
```

This is almost the same configuration that I discussed in the previous example, but with two changes. The first change is the addition of a new directive, AuthGroupFile, which points to the .htgroup group file created earlier. The next change is in the require directive line, which now requires a group called "asb_readers." In other words, Apache will allow access to anyone that belongs to the said group. Note that you could have just as easily used the following line:

```
require user pikejb bcaridad
```

instead of:

```
require group asb_readers
```

However, listing all users in the require line could become cumbersome and cause unnecessary headaches. Using group, one can easily add or remove multiple users.

STEP 4: File permissions

As in the previous example, it is important to make sure.htaccess, .htpasswd, and .htgroup files are only readable by Apache, and no one but the owner has write access to the files.

STEP 5: Testing

Testing the new setting is quite similar to the previous example, so I won't repeat that process here.

Example 3: Mixing host-based access control with basic HTTP authentication

In this example, you will see how you can mix the host-based access control scheme with the basic HTTP authentication method found in Apache. For simplicity, let's assume you want to allow the "asb_readers" group to access the same directory as they do in Example 2, and you also want to allow anyone coming from a domain called apache-training.nitec.com, without a user name/password, to have access to the same directory.

In other words, if a request for the URL http://apache.nitec.com/chapter_10 comes from a domain named apache-training.nitec.com, the request is processed without HTTP authentication by using the following steps.

STEP 1: Modifying .htaccess file

Modify the .htaccess file (from Example 2) to look like the following:

```
AuthName Apache Server Bible Readers Only
AuthType  Basic
AuthUserFile /data/web/apache/secrets/.htpasswd
AuthGroupFile /data/web/apache/secrets/.htgroup
require group  asb_readers
order deny, allow
deny from all
allow from apache-training.nitec.com
```

This adds three host-based access control directives discussed in earlier sections. The first one is the order directive, which tells Apache to evaluate the deny directive before it does the allow directive. The deny directive tells Apache to refuse access from all hosts. The allow directive tells Apache to allow access from the apache-training.nitec.com domain. This effectively tells Apache that any hosts in the apache-training.nitec.com domain are welcome to this directory.

STEP 2: Testing

Using a Web browser from a host called user01.apache-training.nitec.com, if you try to access the URL http://apache.nitec.com/chapter_10, your browser will display the user name/password authentication dialog box. In other words, you are required to authenticate yourself. This is not what you want to happen. So what is going on? Well, Apache assumes that both host-based and basic HTTP authentication are required for this directory, thereby not allowing access to the directory without passing both methods. A satisfactory solution to this problem can be implemented using the satisfy directive, as follows:

```
AuthName Apache Server Bible Readers Only
AuthType  Basic
AuthUserFile /data/web/apache/secrets/.htpasswd
AuthGroupFile /data/web/apache/secrets/.htgroup
require group  asb_readers
order deny, allow
deny from all
allow from apache-training.nitec.com
satisfy any
```

The satisfy directive takes either the all or the any value (discussed in Chapter 4). Because you only want the basic HTTP authentication to be activated if a request comes from any host other than the apache-training.nitec.com domain, specify “any” for the satisfy directive. This effectively tells Apache to do the following:

```
If request comes from any host in the apache-training.nitec.com
domain then
```

```
    No need for basic HTTP authentication
  Else
    Require  basic HTTP authentication
  End
```

If you change your mind and want to allow only users of apache-training.nitec.com domain to access the directory with basic HTTP authentication, specify "all" for the satisfy directive; this tells Apache to enforce both authentication methods for all requests.

Using mod_auth_dbm

As mentioned before, .htpasswd and .htgroup text files are inefficient for high-speed processing and could negatively affect a Web server's performance when thousands of users (or more) need authenticated access to restricted areas. The mod_auth_dbm module is a better choice in such a case. This module uses DBM files instead of text files to store data. A DBM file stores data records in a key=value pair and keeps a computed index table for the keys in the file. Using the index table in a DBM file, it is possible to retrieve the record associated with the key faster than the time needed to parse a large text file with tens of thousands of records.

Many DBMs are available, the most common being GDBM, NDBM, SDBM, and Berkeley DB (BSD-DB). Table 10-3 shows a list of features for these DBMs.

Table 10-3
DBM Features

Features	*NDBM*	*SDBM*	*GDBM*	*BSD-DB*
Licensing restrictions	Unknown	No	Yes	No
Byte-order independent	No	No	No	Yes
Default size limits	4K	1K	None	None
Creates FTP-safe files	No	Yes	Yes	Yes
Speed	Unknown	Slow	Medium	Fast
Database size	Unknown	Small	Large	Medium
Code size	Unknown	Small	Large	Large
Source comes with Perl	No	Yes	No	No

This table is based on the information found in Perl 5 documentation. Before you can use any DBM with Apache, you will have to make sure the DBM you choose to use is already installed in your system. Do this by confirming that the DBM library files are located in your system's default library directory. You are also likely to need Perl with the same DBM support. Make sure you have the latest version of Perl compiled with the chosen DBM support.

Tip

> You can get Perl from http://www.perl.com. Configuring Perl for DBM support is quite easy. Just run the configuration script, and it will prompt you for the DBM support. For example, if you choose NDBM or GDBM as your desired DBM and have these installed on your system, the Perl configuration script should ask you if you want to compile Perl with -lndbm, -lgdbm, and library flags.

Once you have installed the appropriate DBM libraries on your system, you then need to configure Apache for support of DBM files, because the standard Apache distribution does not enable DBM support. Before you recompile, check your Apache executable (httpd) to see if you already have this module precompiled. The following command displays all the compiled modules in a httpd executable file:

```
/usr/sbin/httpd -l
```

If you do not see mod_auth_dbm.c in the listing produced by the preceding command, you need to reconfigure and recompile Apache. To add the DBM authentication module, edit your Configuration file in the Apache source directory. Uncomment the following line:

```
#AddModule modules/standard/mod_auth_dbm.o
```

This is done by deleting the # sign. Save the file and run the Configure script to create a new Makefile. Once you have a new Makefile, run the make utility to create a new Apache executable (httpd).

> If you have trouble compiling, try adding the -l<your dbmname> to EXTRA_LIBS in the Configuration file. For example, if you are using GDBM, you can add -lgdbm so that EXTRA_LIBS=-lgdbm. Make sure you rerun the Configure script and run make again afterwards. In case of problems, it might be best to try GNU GDBM because it is heavily used by many different systems and you are likely to get help on the USENET.

Once you have the new httpd executable, run the httpd -l command to verify that the mod_auth_dbm.c is a listed module. You can now strip off the symbols from the executable by running the strip command, as follows:

```
strip httpd
```

Replace your old httpd with the new one.

> Before you replace your working httpd, you might want to rename it just in case the new one causes a problem. In such a case, you can quickly go back to your old httpd without holding up your Web service.

Once Apache is properly compiled for DBM files, you can use dbmmanage to create a DBM user file. Begin by using the dbmmanage script found in the support directory of the standard Apache distribution for creating a DBM-based user file. The dbmmanage Perl script is able to create many popular DBM files such as NDBM, GDBM, and Berkley DB files. This script can be used to create a new DBM file, add users and passwords, change passwords, delete users, or view user information. Before you use the script, you should modify the following line in the script such that the DBM you want to use is listed as the first item in the ISA array:

```
BEGIN { @AnyDBM_File::ISA = qw(DB_File, NDBM_File, GDBM_file) }
```

For example, if you plan on using GDBM files, change the line to the following:

```
BEGIN { @AnyDBM_File::ISA = qw(GDBM_file , DB_File, NDBM_File)
}
```

To find out what options the script provides, run it as follows:

```
./dbmmanage
```

This will show you a syntax line with all the possible options. To create a new DBM file, called /www/secrets/myuserdbm, by adding a user named "reader," enter the following command:

```
dbmmanage /www/secrets/myuserdbm adduser reader
```

The script will ask you to enter (and re-enter) a password for the user "reader." Once you have done so, it will add the user name and encrypted password to the myuserdbm DBM file.

Tip

Do not use the add option to add a user as it does not encrypt the password.

To see a list of all users in a DBM file, use the following script:

```
dbmmanage /path/to/your/dbmfile view
```

Once you have recompiled Apache with DBM support, you can use the module mod_auth_dbm to provide DBM-based basic HTTP authentication. Note that for Berkeley DB you will have to use mod_auth_db instead of mod_auth_dbm.

The mod_auth_dbm module provides the directives AuthDBMUserFIle, AuthDBMGroupFile, and AuthDBMAuthoritative. Let's take a look at each of these directives and examples using the mod_auth_dbm module.

AuthDBMUserFile directive

```
Syntax: AuthDBMUserFile filename
Context: directory, per-directory access control file
(.htaccess)
Override: AuthConfig
```

This directive sets the fully qualified path name of a DBM file to be used as the user file for DBM authentication. The file contains a key=value pair per record, where the user name is the key and the crypt()-encrypted password is the value. Note that each field in the record is separated by a colon, and arbitrary data can be appended after the initial user name and password fields.

Tip: Never store user database files inside your Web document tree.

AuthDbmGroupFile directive

```
Syntax: AuthDBMGroupFile filename
Context: directory, per-directory access control file
(.htaccess)
Override: AuthConfig
```

This directive sets the fully qualified path name of the group file that contains the list of user groups. Each record in the file is a key=value pair, where the key is the user name and the value is a comma-separated list of group names to which the user belongs.

If you prefer not to use a separate group file, you can use a single DBM file to provide both password and group information. The format of the file is as follows:

```
username: encrypted password: comma-separated group list
```

Here, username is the key, and the password and group lists are two fields of the value. Other data may be left in the DBM file after another colon, if desired; it is ignored by the authentication module. If you use a single DBM to provide both group and password information, you will have to point both AuthDBMGroup and AuthDBMUserFile directives to the same file.

AuthDBMAuthoritative directive

```
Syntax: AuthDBMAuthoritative  on | off
Default: on
Context: directory, .per-directory access control file
(.htaccess)
Override: AuthConfig
```

When using multiple authentication schemes such as mod_dbm and standard mod_auth in the same directory, you can use this directive to define whether mod_auth_dbm is the authoritative authentication scheme.

The default value of the directive enables mod_auth_dbm to become the authoritative authentication for the directory. What this means is if the DBM-based authentication fails for a particular user, the user's credentials will not be passed on to a lower-level authentication scheme. When set to the off value, the credentials of a failed authentication will be passed on to the next authentication level.

A common use for this is in conjunction with one of the basic auth modules, such as mod_auth.c. Whereas this DBM module supplies the bulk of the user credential checking, a few (administrator) related accesses fall through to a lower level with a well-protected .htpasswd file.

Example: Requiring a DBM user name and password

Now that you have the user DBM file created, you are capable of restricting access to any Web directory you want. In the following example, let's assume that the user DBM file is /www/secrets/myuserdbm. You can add the authentication scheme to your global or virtual server using a <Directory> container, or you can use the .htaccess file — there is no difference. The example configuration looks like this:

```
AuthName Apache Server Bible Readers Only
AuthType  Basic
AuthUserDBMFile /www/secrets/myuserdbm
require valid-user
```

Now Apache will use the mod_auth_dbm module for authentication in the directory where this configuration applies.

Make sure that only Apache and the owner can read the dbm file. No one but the owner of the dbm file should be able to write to it.

Using mod_auth_db

If your system is not capable of using DBM, but Berkeley DB file support is available, you can use mod_auth_db to use DB files instead. Like the DBM module, this module is not compiled in the standard Apache distribution. You will have to recompile your Apache server with this module support to use it. However, before you recompile, you might want to check your Apache executable (httpd) to see if you already have this module precompiled. The following command displays all the compiled modules in a httpd executable file:

```
/usr/sbin/httpd -l
```

If you do not see mod_auth_db.c in the listing produced by the preceding command, you need to reconfigure and recompile Apache.

However, first make sure you know where the DB library files are stored on your system. For example, on a Linux system, the files are in the standard /usr/lib directory. If your system does not have the DB libraries, you will have to get the source code and compile DB support first. You can find DB library information at the following URL:

```
www.sleepycat.com/
```

Once you have made sure your system has DB libraries, you can proceed with reconfiguring and recompiling Apache. First you will have to uncomment the following line in the Configuration file:

```
#AddModule modules/standard/mod_auth_db.o
```

Remove the # symbol and then run the Configure script to create a new Makefile. Once you have done that, run the make utility. This should create a new httpd file. Using the -l command line argument, verify that you have the mod_auth_db module built into the new httpd. You can now replace the old httpd with the new one.

At this point, you should be ready to use the mod_auth_db module. This mod_auth_db module provides the directives AuthDBUserFile, AuthDBGroupFile, and AuthDBAuthoritative.

AuthDBUserFile

```
Syntax: AuthDBUserFile filename
Context: directory, .per-directory access control file
(.htaccess)
Override: AuthConfig
```

This directive sets the fully qualified path name of the user DB file that contains the list of users and encrypted passwords.

Like the DBM counterpart, the DB user file is also keyed using the user name and the value is the crypt()-encrypted password.

Always make sure your user files are kept outside the Web document tree and are only readable by Apache. No one but the owner should have write access to these files.

AuthDBGroupFile

```
Syntax: AuthDBGroupFile filename
Context: directory, .per-directory access control file
(.htaccess)
Override: AuthConfig
```

This directive sets the fully qualified path name of the group DB file, which contains the list of user groups for user authentication. Like the DBM counterpart, the group file uses the user name as the key and the comma-separated group list is treated as the value. There must be no white space within the value, and it must never contain any colons.

If you do not prefer to use a separate group file, you can use a single DB file to provide both password and group information. The format of the file would be as follows:

```
username: encrypted password: comma-separated group list
```

where username is the key, and the password and group lists are two fields of the value. Other data may be left in the DB file after another colon; it is ignored by the authentication module. If you use a single DB to provide both group and password information, you will have to point both AuthDBGroup and AuthDBUserFile directives to the same file.

AuthDBAuthoritative

```
Syntax: AuthDBAuthoritative  on | off
Default: on
Context: directory, . .per-directory access control file
(.htaccess)
Override: AuthConfig
```

When using multiple authentication schemes such as mod_db, mod_dbm, and standard mod_auth in the same directory, you can use this directive to define whether mod_auth_db is the authoritative authentication scheme. The default value of the directive allows mod_auth_db to become the authoritative authentication for the directory. What this means is if the DB-based authentication fails for a particular user, the user's credentials will not be passed on to a lower-level authentication scheme. When set to the off value, the credentials of a failed authentication will be passed on to the next authentication level.

Although using DBM or DB files makes it easier to administer a large user base, they are often not suitable for organizations that have the user information already stored in a relational SQL database. A SQL database provides a great deal of functionality that is not available to either DBM or DB files. Apache also provides support for a popular SQL database called mSQL.

Using mod_auth_msql module

Using the mod_auth_msql module you can implement basic HTTP authentication such that the user name/password data resides in an mSQL database server. You will need to create an mSQL database containing the user name/password information.Creating an mSQL database is beyond the scope of this book; look at your mSQL documentation for details. When you do create the user database to be used with the mod_auth_msql module, however, make sure you take the following under consideration:

- ✦ The user name field should not be longer than 32 characters. Many browsers do not allow users to enter more than 32 characters in the pop-up authentication dialog box's user name field.
- ✦ A user name should not include any white space characters.

The password field has the same restriction has the user name field, but you probably do not want to make passwords any smaller than five characters, as small passwords are easy to break.

mSQL

The term mSQL stands for mini-SQL. It is a lightweight Structured Query Language (SQL) database engine developed by David J. Hughes at the Bond University, Australia. Although mSQL provides only a subset of ANSI SQL, it is designed for fast access and low memory requirements. It supports various popular platforms such as Sun OS 4.1.1, Solaris 2.*x*, Ultrix 4.3, Linux, OSF/1, most BSD-derived systems, SVR4-based systems or POSIX O/Ss, HP-UX, NeXT, SCO, Sequent, Cray, Tandem, and *BSD.. The database source can be downloaded from the following URL: `ftp://ftp.bond.edu.au/pub/Minerva/msql`.

Like the DB or DBM authentication modules, this module is not standard in Apache distribution. You will have to add the module to the configuration file as follows:

```
AddModule modules/standard/mod_auth_msql.o
```

This assumes you will keep the mod_auth_msql files in the modules/standard directory of the Apache source distribution. Once you have added the line, run the Configure script and the make utility, in that order. Use the httpd -l command to make sure the httpd has the mod_auth_msq.c code in it.

Now let's take a look at an example access control configuration (shown in Listing 10-1). For this example, I will make the following assumptions:

- ✦ The mSQL server is on the same machine as the Apache server.
- ✦ The name of the mSQL database containing the user information is called asb_readers_db.
- ✦ The name of the mSQL table containing the user information is called asb_users_table.
- ✦ The name of the mSQL field containing the user name field is called Uname.
- ✦ The name of the mSQL field containing the password field is called Passwd.
- ✦ The name of the mSQL table containing the group information is called asb_group_table.
- ✦ The name of the mSQL field containing the group field is called asb_readers.

Listing 10-1: Example access control configuration

```
Auth_MSQLhost localhost
Auth_MSQLdatabase asb_readers_db.
Auth_MSQLpwd_table asb_users_table
Auth_MSQLuid_field Uname
Auth_MSQLpwd_field Passwd
```

```
Auth_MSQLgrp_table asb_group_table
Auth_MSQLgrp_field  asb_readers
Auth_MSQL_nopasswd off
Auth_MSQL_Authoritative on
Auth_MSQL_EncryptedPasswords on
AuthName Apache Server Bible Readers Only
AuthType  Basic
require valid-user
```

I used the default value for Auth_MSQL_nopasswd, Auth_MSQL_Authoritative, and Auth_MSQL_EncryptedPasswords.

Note

Make sure the access control file for mSQL (msql.acl) allows the effective user ID (UID) of Apache read access to the database.

After this, you should be ready to use the mod_auth_msql module, which has the following directives.

Auth_MSQLhost directive

```
Syntax: Auth_MSQLhost  hostname | IP address
Context: directory, per-directory access control file
(.htaccess)
Override: AuthConfig
```

This directive sets the host name of the system running the mSQL server (daemon). If the directive is not set or is set to localhost, it forces the module to use /dev/msql instead of a socket connection to the mSQL server. If the mSQL server is on localhost, the use of /dev/msql is encouraged. Note that the Apache server (UID) must be allowed to access the mSQL server.

Auth_MSQLdatabase mSQL directive

```
Syntax: Auth_MSQLdatabase mSQL name of database
Context: directory, per-directory access control file
(.htaccess)
Override: AuthConfig
```

This directive sets the name of the database, served by the mSQL server, which contains the user information.

Auth_MSQLpwd_table mSQL directive

```
Syntax: Auth_MSQLpwd_table mSQL mSQL name of the table
containing user information
Context: directory, per-directory access control file
(.htaccess)
Override: AuthConfig
```

This directive sets the name of the table that contains at least the user name and the encrypted password. The user name should be set up as the primary key for the table.

Auth_MSQLgrp_table mSQL directive

```
Syntax: Auth_MSQLgrp_table mSQL name of the table containing
group information
Context: directory, per-directory access control file
(.htaccess)
Override: AuthConfig
```

This directive sets the name of the table that contains group information. The table must have at least a user name and a group name field. Note that if you have a user who belongs to multiple groups, you will have multiple entries for the user in the table.

Auth_MSQLuid_field mSQL directive

```
Syntax: Auth_MSQLuid_field mSQL name of the field, which holds
the username
Context: directory, per-directory access control file
(.htaccess)
Override: AuthConfig
```

This directive sets the name of the field in the Auth_MSQpwd_table-specified table, which contains the user name information. If you create a group table using the Auth_MSQLgrp_table directive, this directive will also specify the name of the field for the group table. In other words, you will have to have the same field names for both the Auth_MSQLpwd_table and the Auth_MSQLgrp_table tables.

Auth_MSQLpwd_field mSQL directive

```
Syntax: Auth_MSQLpwd_field mSQL name of the field, which holds
the password
Context: directory, per-directory access control file
(.htaccess)
Override: AuthConfig
```

This directive sets the name of the field in the Auth_MSQpwd_table-specified table, which contains the password.

Auth_MSQLgrp_field mSQL directive

```
Syntax: Auth_MSQLgrp_field mSQL name of the field, which holds
the group name
Context: directory, per-directory access control file
(.htaccess)
Override: AuthConfig
```

This directive sets the name of the field in the Auth_MSQgrp_table-specified table, which contains the group name.

Auth_MSQL_nopasswd directive

```
Syntax: Auth_MSQL_nopasswd on | off
Default: off
Context: directory, per-directory access control file
(.htaccess)
Override: AuthConfig
```

When set to the on value, the mod_auth_msql module will not perform password comparisons if the password field in the database's table is empty. The default value ensures that an empty field in the mSQL table does not allow people with any password in by default.

Auth_MSQL_Authoritative directive

```
Syntax: Auth_MSQL_Authoritative on | off
Default: on
Context: directory, per-directory access control file
(.htaccess)
Override: AuthConfig
```

The default value makes the mod_auth_msql module the authoritative authentication module. In other words, when a user-supplied credential (user name/password pair) fails to pass with this module, it is not passed on to a lower authentication module such as the standard mod_auth module.

Auth_MSQL_EncryptedPasswords directive

```
Syntax: Auth_MSQL_EncryptedPasswords on | off
Default: on
Context: directory, per-directory access control file
(.htaccess)
Override: AuthConfig
```

The default value of this directive tells the mod_auth_msql module that the password is encrypted using the standard crypt() function. If the value is set to off, the password is assumed to be plain text.

Using mod_auth_anon

This module allows anonymous access to authenticated areas. If you are familiar with anonymous FTP servers, this is very similar to such a setup. All users can use a user ID called "anonymous" and their e-mail addresses as the password to get access. The e-mail address entered is stored in log files and can be used to perform user tracking or even creation of a mailing list of prospective clients.

Like the DBM modules discussed earlier, you will have to add this module to the Configuration file as follows:

```
AddModule modules/standard/mod_auth_anon.o
```

Next, run Configure and the make utility to create the new httpd executable.

After this, you should be ready to use the mod_auth_anon module. Let's take a closer look at the directives for this module and an example using the module.

Anonymous directive

```
Syntax: Anonymous user user ...
Default: none
Context: directory, per-directory access control file
(.htaccess)
Override: AuthConfig
```

Using this directive you can specify one or more user names that can be used to access the restricted area. It is a good idea to keep the user name "anonymous" in your chosen list because it is widely associated with anonymous access. If the user name you choose has a space character in it, make sure the user name is surrounded by quotation marks. For example:

```
Anonymous "Unregistered User" anonymous
```

or

```
Anonymous 'Unregistered User' anonymous
```

The strings are not case sensitive.

Anonymous_Authoritative directive

```
Syntax: Anonymous_Authoritative on | off
Default: Anonymous_Authoritative off
Context: directory, per-directory access control file
(.htaccess)
Override: AuthConfig
```

When set to on, the anonymous authentication becomes the authoritative authentication scheme for a directory. In other words, there will be no fall-through to other authentication methods.

Anonymous_LogEmail directive

```
Syntax: Anonymous_LogEmail on | off
Default: Anonymous_LogEmail on
Context: directory, per-directory access control file
(.htaccess)
Override: AuthConfig
```

When this directive is set to on, whatever is entered in the password field of the browser's pop-up authentication window will be logged in the Apache access log file.

Anonymous_MustGiveEmail directive

```
Syntax: Anonymous_MustGiveEmail on | off
Default: Anonymous_MustGiveEmail on
Context: directory, per-directory access control file
(.htaccess)
Override: AuthConfig
```

When set to on, this directive enables the module to reject access requests that do not provide passwords in the form of e-mail addresses. However, you should not trust the e-mail addresses that people will enter when this directive is set to on, as there is no way of checking who entered whose e-mail address.

Anonymous_NoUserID directive

```
Syntax: Anonymous_NoUserID on | off
Default: Anonymous_NoUserID off
Context: directory, per-directory access control file
(.htaccess)
Override: AuthConfig
```

If you want the users to leave the user name field of the pop-up window empty, set this directive to on; otherwise, a user name that matches the values provided in the Anonymous directive is required.

Anonymous_VerifyEmail directive

```
Syntax: Anonymous_VerifyEmail on | off
Default: Anonymous_VerifyEmail off
Context: directory, per-directory access control file
(.htaccess)
Override: AuthConfig
```

When this directive is set to on, it requires that the password be a valid e-mail address. However, the validity check is limited. The module only checks for an @ symbol and a period (.) in the password field. If the entered password has either of these symbols in it, it is accepted.

Example: Anonymous access restriction

The following configuration shows how the preceding directives can be used to provide anonymous access to a directory.

```
Anonymous_NoUserId off
Anonymous_MustGiveEmail on
Anonymous_VerifyEmail on
Anonymous_LogEmail on
Anonymous anonymous guest "I do not know"
AuthName Use 'anonymous' & Email address for guest entry
AuthType basic
require valid-user
```

Using mod_auth_external

So far, I have talked about various authentication methods using authentication code found in a module. What if you needed to use a third-party authentication scheme? In such a case, the solution is to use the mod_auth_external module to enable access to external authentication. Apache can use external authentication programs if the mod_auth_external module is compiled into the server executable.

To install moc_authe_external, you need to add the module to the Configuration file. Using a text editor, add the following line to the Apache Configuration file:

```
AddModule modules/standard/mod_auth_external.o
```

Note that if you plan to keep the module in any directory other than the modules/standard in the Apache source tree, you will have to change the preceding path as appropriate.

Now, run the Configure script to create a new Makefile and then run the make utility to create a new httpd executable. Once the new executable is created, use the following command to list the modules:

```
httpd -l
```

If you see the mod_auth_external.c in the list, you have successfully installed the module.

If you prefer to write your own hard-coded C function for this module, use the following steps (skip these steps if you are not interested in writing your own function).

STEP 1: Enable hard-coded function support in the module

Edit the mod_auth_external.c file and uncomment appropriate lines so that you end up with the following:

```
#define _HARDCODE_
#ifdef HARDCODE
#include "your_function_here.c"
#endif
```

Replace "your_function_here.c" with your authentication function's header file. For example, if you call your authentication function source file my_auth.c and have the function's prototype in my_auth.h, you have to have the following lines in mod_auth_external.c:

```
#define _HARDCODE_
#ifdef HARDCODE
```

```
#include "my_auth.h"
#endif
```

Make sure your source code is in the same directory as the mod_auth_external.c file.

STEP 2: Hard-coding your function in the module

Go down to the large commented section in the middle of mod_auth_external.c and follow the instructions there. Your function should start something like this:

```
int
function_name (char *user_name,char *user_passwd,char
*config_path) {
The function call in mod_auth_external.c should look something
like:

if (strcmp(check_type,"<type>")==0) {
            code = function_name(c->user,sent_pw,config_file);
}
```

Do not use exit() or other such calls that will cause your function to exit abnormally or dump core. It will take the entire httpd with it and display a "no data" message to your browser. Use return() instead of exit().

STEP 3: Save and compile Apache

Run the make utility in the Apache source directory. If you do not get a clean compilation of code, debug your code. Any time you make modifications to your code file (such as my_auth.c) and do not make any changes to the mod_auth_external.c, you should use the touch utility to touch mod_auth_external.c.

If things go well, you will have successfully compiled Apache and replaced your old version.

Once mod_auth_external is installed, you will have access to three external authentication mechanisms.

The first external authentication mechanism is a system() call. This is the default method. In this mode the module calls a user-defined (that is, Apache administrator) authentication program and passes it two environment variables—

USER and PASS. The client-entered user name and password are passed using these two variables, respectively. The external authentication program can read its environment and perform whatever checking is necessary to determine if the client should be allowed access. The module requires that the external authentication program return an exit code of 0 for success and 1 for failure.

Note that on most UNIX systems it is possible to determine what environment variables are available to run processing using the ps utility. For example:

```
ps -auxwe
```

This shows the environment of all the running programs on a Linux system. This could allow someone on the system to see what USER and PASS variables are set to when the authcheck program is running. This could be considered a security hole.

The second external authentication method is the pipe() call. This is similar to the system() call, but in this mode the module writes the user name and the password gathered from the client on the external authentication program's standard input (STDIN). The data is stored in a key=value pair, where USER=user name and PASS=password.

The third external authentication method is a hard-coded function call. In this mode, the module calls a user-defined C function and passes it the user name, password, and a configuration filename. This method will allow developers to write custom gateway interfaces to existing or new authentication applications. Examples of such code are already available, two of which include the following:

- ✦ mod_auth_external_radius.c — A Radius client using code from the publicly available Merit Radius source code.
- ✦ mod_auth_external_sybase.c — A function that queries a sybase database and compares the passwords for said user.

Now that you know what external authentication methods are available to you, let's look at the directives that this module provides and an example that uses the module.

AddExternalAuth directive

```
Syntax (system call and pipe version): AddExternalAuth keyword
path/to/authenticator
Syntax (function version): AddExternalAuth keyword type:
path/to/configuration
Context: server config
```

This directive associates the keyword with the specified user authenticator. For example:

```
AddExternalAuth archive_auth /usr/local/bin/authcheck
```

This associates archive_auth with an external authentication program called /usr/local/bin/authcheck. An example of the directive for a hard-coded function would look like:

```
AddExternalAuth archive_auth RADIUS:
```

where RADIUS is the name of the hard-coded function. If the function requires a configuration file, the file can be passed to it as follows:

```
AddExternalAuth archive_auth RADIUS:/usr/local/raddb
```

External user authentication programs are passed the client-entered user name, the password, and, optionally, a configuration filename (only for hard-coded function-based authentication). By default the external authentication program receives the user name and password as USER and PASS environment variables, respectively. If pipe mode is specified in the SetExternalAuthMethod directive, the user name and password are passed as key=value pairs in the form of USER=user name and PASS=password. For the hard-coded function version, the data is passed as C function parameters.

If the external user authentication program exits with an exit code of 0, authentication is assumed to be successful. A nonzero value indicates either a failure to authenticate or a failure to execute the authenticator.

Note that you can use multiple types of authentication in one server by providing multiple directives in the srm.conf file. Just make sure each group has a different keyword.

AddExternalGroupAuth directive

```
Syntax (system call and pipe version): AddExternalGroupAuth
keyword path/to/authenticator
Syntax (function version): AddExternalGroupAuth keyword type:
path/to/configuration
Context: server config
```

This directive associates the keyword with the specified group authenticator. For example, the following associates archive_auth with an external authentication program called /usr/local/bin/groupcheck:

```
AddExternalGroupAuth archive_auth /usr/local/bin/groupcheck
```

External group authentication programs are passed the user name, the group, and, optionally, a configuration filename (only for hard-coded function-based authentication). By default the external authentication program receives the user name and group as USER and GROUP environment variables, respectively. If pipe mode is specified in the SetExternalGroupMethod directive, the user name and password are passed as key=value pairs in the form of USER=user name and GROUP=group. For the hard-coded function version, the data is passed as C function parameters.

If the external group authentication program exits with an exit code of 0, authentication is assumed to be successful. A nonzero value indicates either a failure to authenticate or a failure to execute the authenticator.

SetExternalAuthMethod directive

```
Syntax: SetExternalAuthMethod keyword method
Context: server config
```

This directive sets the method for passing data to the external user authentication program. Currently there are three methods available:

The first method is environment. In this method, the user name and password is passed via the method environment. The USER variable contains the user name, and the PASS variable contains the password. This is the default method.

Consider the following example:

```
AddExternalAuth archive_auth /usr/local/bin/authcheck
SetExternalAuthMethod archive_auth environment
```

Here, the /usr/local/bin/authcheck program will receive the client-entered user name and password via environment variables USER and PASS.

The second method is function. This method is used when a hard-coded function is defined to handle the authentication.

Take a look at the following:

```
AddExternalAuth archive_auth /usr/local/bin/authcheck
SetExternalAuthMethod archive_auth pipe
```

Here, the /usr/local/bin/authcheck program will receive the client-entered user name and password via a pipe to its standard input device (STDIN), where USER=user name and PASS=password.

The third method is pipe. This method sends the data via a pipe to the external authenticator's standard input device (STDIN). The data is passed as key=value pairs, where USER=user name and PASS=password.

Let's look at the following example:

```
AddExternalAuth archive_auth RADIUS:
SetExternalAuthMethod archive_auth function
```

Here, the hard-coded function RADIUS is used, and the function receives the data as function parameters.

SetExternalGroupMethod directive

```
Syntax: SetExternalGroupMethod keyword method
Context: server config
```

This directive sets the method, which is to be used for passing data to the external group authentication program. Currently three methods are available: environment, function, and pipe. See SetExternalAuthMethod for examples and more details.

AuthExternal directive

```
Syntax (system call and pipe version): AddExternalAuth keyword
Syntax (function version): AddExternalAuth function name:
path/to/configuration file
Context: directory, per-directory access control file
(.htaccess)
```

This directive is used in the directory context or per-directory access control file (.htaccess) to tell Apache which external user authenticator program to use for authentication. The server matches the keyword or the function name (in the case of hard-coded function) to determine what to do.

For example:

```
AuthExternal archive_auth
```

If this line is found in a .htaccess file, Apache will run the user authenticator associated with that keyword.

GroupExternal directive

```
Syntax (system call and pipe version): GroupExternal keyword
Syntax (function version): GroupExternal function name:
path/to/configuration file
Context: directory, per-directory access control file
(.htaccess)
```

This directive is used in the directory context or per-directory access control file (.htaccess) to tell Apache which external group authenticator program to use for group authentication. The server matches the keyword or the function name (in the case of hard-coded function) to determine what to do.

For example, if the following line is found in an .htaccess file, Apache will run the group authenticator associated with that keyword:

```
GroupExternal archive_auth
```

Example: Using a Perl script as an external user authenticator

In this example, you'll see how a simple Perl script can be used to provide user authentication service. To make the example a bit interesting (and perhaps controversial), let's use a Perl script that employs the /etc/passwd and /etc/group files found in most UNIX systems to perform the authentication.

Many will claim that the use of /etc/passwd and /etc/group in any Web-based authentication is not a bright idea, and I tend to agree; however, for a well-protected intranet environment (better if it is not even connected to the Internet at all), it seems very cool. Anyone who has a UNIX account on the Web server machine can authenticate using the Perl script shown in Listing 10-2.

Listing 10-2: **authcheck Script**

```
#!/usr/local/bin/perl

  #
  # Script Name: authcheck
  # Purpose: a simple /etc/passwd and /etc/group based
  # authenticator script
  #
  # Chapter 10 Listing 10-2
  ##############################################################

  #  Variables and assignments
  my $LOG_FILE = '/tmp/authcheck.log';       # log file  to be
  used
  my $this_user = $ENV{USER};          # get username from %ENV
  my $this_pwd = $ENV{PASS};           # get password from %ENV

  # If the user does not enter a username or password exit
  # with a non-zero value to let the mod_auth_external
  # know that the authentication has failed.
  #
  exit 1 if($this_user eq "" || $this_pwd eq "");

  # We only want to allow users of a certain group to be able
  # to authenticate via Web When creating this group in
  # your /etc/group, remember to keep power users out
  # of it. For example NEVER put the 'root' user in
  # this group!
  #
  my $WEB_USER_GROUP = 'web-users';

  # Get the current time and store it in variables
  my ($sec,$min, $hr, $mday, $mon, $year, $wday, $yday, $isdst) =
  localtime(time);

  # Increment month to take care of the 0-11 range used by
  localtime
  $mon++;
```

```
# If the user is a member of the specified Web user group,
# and her password is valid then we will consider the
# authentication to be a success
#
if(isMember($this_user,$WEB_USER_GROUP) &&
validPassword($this_user,$this_pwd)){

   # Log the successful authentication even. However note
   # that since each request from a user will go through
   # this authentication code, logging successful
authentication
   # might create a performance issue. If you do not want
   # to log successful logins, comment the following line
   #
    &log("$mon/$mday/$year $hr:$min:$sec - $this_user login
successful.");

   # Exit with the success code value so that mod_auth_external
   # will consider the authentication to be a complete success.
   exit 0;
   }
else{
     # Well, the user didn't pass the checks so log
     # the attempt.
       &log("$mon/$mday/$year $hr:$min:$sec - $this_user login
failed: invalid password ($this_pwd) .");

    # Exit with a non-zero code to tell mod_auth_external
    # that the user has failed authentication
       exit 1;
       }

sub validPassword{
   #
   # Purpose: this sub routine checks the user's password
   # against the password stored in the /etc/passwd file.

  # Get the username and the user entered password
  # from the subroutine parameter list.
   my $this_user = shift;
   my $guess = shift;

  # Get the user's real password record from /etc/passwd.
   my (@pwdfields) = getpwnam($this_user);

  # Use the crypt() to encrypt the user entered password
  # and compare it with the encrypted password found
  # in the password record in /etc/passwd.

   if(crypt($guess, $pwdfields[1]) eq $pwdfields[1]) {
```

(continued)

Listing 10-2 (continued)

```
    # User has entered a valid password so return a
    # non-zero value to caller routine.
  return 1;
  }
  # Opps! user has entered an invalid password so return 0.
   return 0;
   }

sub isMember{
   #
   # Purpose: this sub routine checks the /etc/group file to
   # determine if a user belongs to a certain group
   #

   # Get the username and the group name from the
   # parameter list.
   my $this_user = shift;
   my $web_group = shift;

  # Get the member list for the group from the
  # /etc/group file
   my ($groupName, $passwd, $gid, $memberList) =
getgrnam($web_group);

  # If the user is a member of this group return a non-zero
  # value or else return 0.
   return 1 if ($memberList =~ /$this_user/);
   return 0;
   }

sub log{
   #
   # Purpose: to provide a simple log
   #

  # Get the log entry from the parameter list
   my $entry = shift;

  # Append the entry in the log file.
   open(FP,">>$LOG_FILE") || die "Can't open $LOG_FILE file";
   print FP $entry, "\n";
   close(FP);
          }
```

This script gets a user name from its USER environment variable and a password from its PASS environment variable. It then checks to see if the USER belongs to a certain group (web-users) defined in /etc/group. If the user belongs to the group, it checks to see if the password is valid. If both conditions are met, the script returns a zero value or else it returns 1. Thus the script meets the mod_auth_external module's requirements for an external user authenticator. The checking of the group is added to make sure only users in a certain group (defined in /etc/group) can be authenticated. If you use this script, make sure you never add power users (such as root) in this group.

Now let's see how this script can be used with the mod_auth_external module using the following steps.

STEP 1: Associating the authcheck authenticator with a keyword

In the srm.conf file, add the following line:

```
AddExternalAuth myauth /usr/local/bin/authcheck
```

This tells Apache that myauth (keyword) is associated with the Perl script authcheck.

STEP 2: Creating the directory access configuration

To restrict access to a directory using the external authenticator, add the following configuration in an .htaccess file:

```
AuthType Basic
AuthName Access for Everyone
AuthExternal myauth
SetExternalAuthMethod myauth environment
require valid-user
```

The AuthExternal directive tells Apache that the authenticator for this directory is identified by the keyword myauth (which refers to the authcheck script). The SetExternalAuthMethod tells Apache to use environment to pass data to the authenticator associated with myauth. Finally, the require line tells Apache to allow valid users who pass the authentication.

STEP 3: Testing

Trying to access the protected directory causes the authentication dialog box to pop up. Entering a valid UNIX account user name/password pair that belongs to the group web-user allows access to the directory.

(continued)

STEP 3: *(continued)*

Tip

If you use this script, you can monitor user logins and attempts using the tail command, as follows:

```
tail -f /tmp/authcheck.log
```

Digest Authentication

As you know, basic HTTP authentication is not secured and should never be used for sensitive applications. Better methods are available, but it is not just up to the server designers to implement new methods. The browser developers must also adapt the new methods. This is where things get slowed down. One authentication method that is likely to replace the basic HTTP authentication is the digest authentication. The spread of digest authentication will depend on whether browser authors incorporate it into their products. Apache already supports digest authentication via the mod_digest module.

The problem with basic HTTP authentication is that the password is transmitted over the network in a simple Uuencoded form, which makes the whole process less secure. In digest authentication, passwords never cross the wire! Instead, a series of numeric values are generated based on the user-entered password (on the browser end) and other information about the request. These numbers are then hashed using a well-known encryption method called MD5. The resulting entity is called a digest and is sent over the network; it is then combined with other items on the server to test against the saved digest on the server. If a match is found, the user is either allowed or denied access.

Although this digest-based authentication is more secure than the basic HTTP authentication, it requires that the server be extremely secure because the server will have to store the digests used for comparisons.

Summary

In this chapter, you learned about many ways of implementing basic HTTP authentication. I discussed many ways of storing the authentication data in text files, db files, dbm files, and even in a SQL database server. The important thing to remember is that the basic authentication scheme transmits passwords across the Internet in an unencrypted manner, so they could be intercepted. Do not use it in sensitive applications. In the future, other authentication schemes such as the digest authentication will likely be supported in all popular browsers. You know Apache is ready for it!

In the next chapter, you will learn about server status and logging.

✦ ✦ ✦

Server Status and Logging

In This Chapter

At this point, hopefully you have your Apache Web site up and running, and you've told the world about its existence. What's next? Well, have you ever wondered who is accessing your cool site? If you are like most people, you probably have. You may also wonder how your Apache server is performing on your system. In this chapter, I show you how to use monitoring and logging techniques to satisfy your need to know.

Monitoring Apache

Apache enables you to monitor two types of information via the Web. They are as follows:

- Server configuration information
- Server status

Server configuration information is static. Being able to quickly access a running server's configuration information can be very useful, however. Server status information, on the other hand, is dynamic. Using Apache's Web-based server status monitoring capabilities, you can monitor information such as the server's uptime, total requests served, total data transfer, status of child processes, and system resource usage. Both types of information are quite valuable, so I discuss them both in the following sections, starting with how to monitor configuration information.

Accessing configuration information

This can be done using the mod_info module. This module provides a comprehensive overview of the server configuration, including all installed modules and directives in the configuration files. This module is contained in the mod_info.c file. It is not compiled into the server by default. You have to compile it by the usual process of adding the module to the Configuration file, and then running the Configure script and the make utility.

The mod_info module provides the AddModuleInfo directive:

```
Syntax: AddModuleInfo module-name descriptive text
Context: server config, virtual host
```

This directive enables you to add descriptive text in the module listing provided by the mod_info module. The descriptive text could be anything including HTML text. For example:

```
AddModuleInfo mod_auth.c 'See <A
HREF="http://www.apache.org/docs/mod/mod_auth.html">http://www.
apache.org/docs/mod/mod_auth.html</A>'
```

This will show an HTML link next to the listing of mod_auth.c. This link provides a quick way to get more information on the module from the Apache Web site. To view server configuration information via the Web, add the following to your access.conf file:

```
<Location /server-info>
SetHandler server-info
</Location>
```

You may wish to add a <Limit> clause inside the location directive to limit access to your server configuration information. Once configured, the server information is obtained by accessing:

```
http://your.host.dom/server-info
```

This returns a full configuration page for the server and all modules.

To return server configuration only, use:

```
http://your.host.dom/server-info?server
```

To return configuration for a single module, use:

```
http://your.host.dom/server-info?module_name
```

To return a quick list of included modules, use:

```
http://your.host.dom/server-info?list
```

Now, lets look at how you can monitor the status of a running Apache server.

Enabling status pages

The module mod_status enables Apache administrators to monitor the server via the Web. An HTML page is created with server statistics. It also produces another page that is machine-readable (which we'll discuss later in the chapter). The information displayed on both pages includes:

- ✦ Current time on the server system
- ✦ Time when the server was last restarted
- ✦ Time elapsed since the server was up and running
- ✦ Total number of accesses served so far
- ✦ Total bytes transferred so far
- ✦ The number of children serving requests
- ✦ The number of idle children
- ✦ The status of each child, the number of requests that child has performed, and the total number of bytes served by the child
- ✦ Averages giving the number of requests per second, the number of bytes served per second, and the average number of bytes per request
- ✦ The current percentage CPU used by each child and used in total by Apache
- ✦ The current hosts and requests being processed

If you do not see all the mentioned fields in the page shown by the status module, you need to add the -DSTATUS option to the AUX_CFLAGS option in the Configuration file, and then reconfigure and remake Apache. Note that on some machines, there may be a small performance loss if you do this.

This module is not compiled by default in the standard Apache distribution, so you need to add it to the Configuration file, run the Configure script, and later run the make utility to create a new Apache executable. Make sure you use httpd -l to verify that mod_status is part of your executable.

Viewing status pages

Once you have the mod_status module compiled and built into your Apache server, you need to define a URL location, which Apache should use to display the information. In other words, you need to tell Apache which URL will bring up the server statistics on your Web browser.

Let's say that your domain name is yourdomain.com, and you want to use the following URL:

```
www.mydomain.com/apache-status
```

Using the <Location ...> container, you can tell the server that you want it to handle this URL using the server-status handler found in the mod_status module. The following will do the job:

```
<Location /apache-status>
SetHandler server-status
</Location>
```

Here, the SetHandler directive sets the handler (server-status) for the previously mentioned URL. This configuration segment should typically go in the access.conf file, but it really can go inside any of the three configuration files. Once you have added the configuration in one of the three files, you can restart the server and access the preceding URL from a browser. An example of such a page is shown in Figure 11-1.

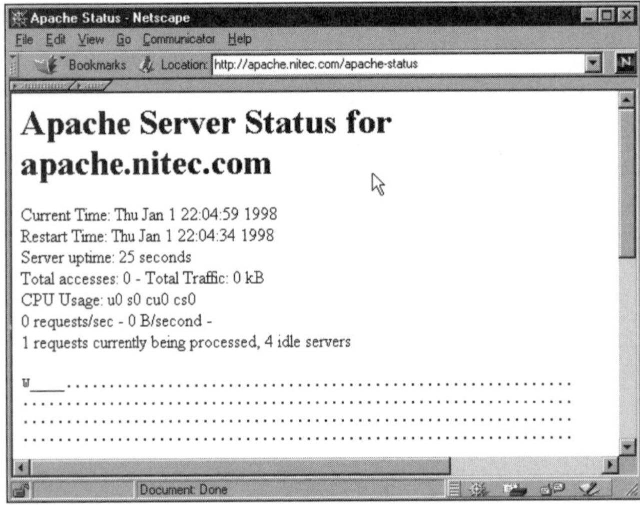

Figure 11-1: Example of Apache status page

The <Location ...> container in Figure 11-1 enables anyone to see the server status using this URL; this may not be a good thing as far as security is concerned. To make sure that only machines on your domain can access the status page, you can replace the preceding configuration with the following:

```
<Location /apache-status>
SetHandler server-status
order deny, allow
deny from all
allow from .yourdomain.com
</Location>
```

where yourdomain.com should be replaced with your own domain name. If you want only one or more selected hosts to have access to this page, you can simply list the host names in the allow directive line.

You can have the status page update itself automatically if you have a browser that supports the refresh command. Access the page http://www.yourdomain.com/server-status?refresh=N to refresh the page every N seconds.

Simplifying the status display

The status page displayed by the module provides extra information that makes it unsuitable for using as a data file for any data analysis program. For example, if you wanted to create a graph from your server status data using a spreadsheet program, you would need to clean up the data manually; however, the module provides a way for you to create machine-readable output from the same URL.

To simplify the status display, add ?auto at the end of the URL. This query string tells Apache to display simplified output, as shown in Figure 11-2.

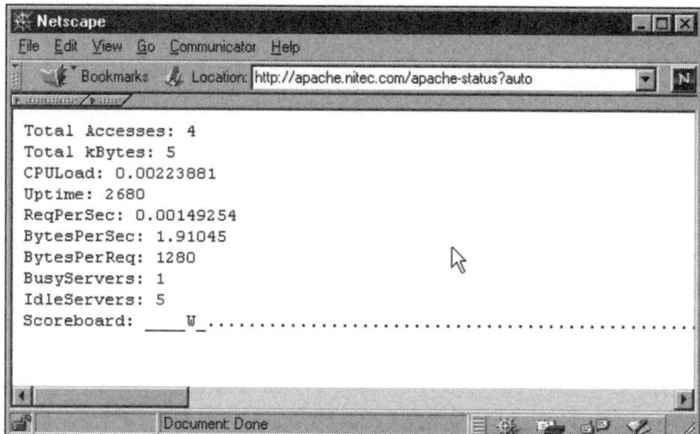

Figure 11-2: Machine-readable status output

Storing server status information

Apache comes with a Perl script (found in the support directory of the source tree) called log_server_status, which can be used to periodically store server status information (using ?auto) in a plain text file.

You can run this script as a cron job to grab the status information on a desired time frequency. Before you can use the script, however, you may have to edit the script source to modify the value of the following configuration variables:

```
$wherelog
$port
$server
$request
```

Change the value of $wherelog to a path where you would like to store the file created by the script. The $port variable value should be the port number of the server you want to monitor. The default value of 80 is fine if your server is running on this standard HTTP port. The $server variable should be assigned the host name of your server. The default value localhost is fine if the script and the server run on the same system. If the server is on another machine, however, specify the fully qualified host name (for example, www.mydomain.com) as the value. The $request variable should be set to whatever you used in the <Location ...> directive plus the ?auto query string.

If you do not like the record format the script uses, you can modify the following line to fit your needs:

```
print OUT "$time:$requests:$idle:$number:$cpu\n";
```

Note: The script uses a socket connection to the Apache server to send the URL request; therefore, you need to make sure you have socket support for Perl.

Creating Log Files

Knowing the status and the configuration information of your server is helpful in managing the server, but knowing who or what is accessing your Web site(s) is also very important, as well as exciting. You can learn this information by using the logging features of Apache server. In the following sections, I discuss the details of how logging works and how to get the best out of Apache logging modules.

As Web server software started appearing in the market, many Web server log analysis programs started appearing as well. These programs became part of the everyday work life of many Web administrators. Along with all these came the era of log file incompatibilities, which made log analysis difficult and cumbersome; a single analysis program didn't work on all log files. Then came the Common Log Format (CLF) specification. This enabled all Web servers to write logs in a reasonably similar manner, thus making log analysis easier from one server to another.

By default, the standard Apache distribution includes a module called mod_log_config, which is responsible for the basic logging, and it writes CLF log files by default. You can alter this behavior using the LogFormat directive. However, CLF covers logging requirements in most environments. The contents of each line in a CLF file are explained as follows.

The CLF file contains a separate line for each request. A line is composed of several tokens separated by spaces:

```
host ident authuser date request status bytes
```

If a token does not have a value, then it is represented by a hyphen (-). Tokens have the following meanings:

✦ Host — The fully qualified domain name of the client, or its IP address.

✦ Ident — If the IdentityCheck directive is enabled and the client machine runs identd, then this is the identity information reported by the client.

✦ Authuser — If the requested URL required a successful Basic HTTP authentication, then the user name is the value of this token.

✦ Date — The date and time of the request.

✦ Request — The request line from the client, enclosed in double quotes (").

✦ Status — The three-digit HTTP status code returned to the client.

✦ bytes — The number of bytes in the object returned to the client, excluding all HTTP headers.

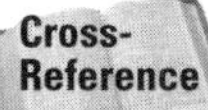

See Appendix B for a list of all HTTP/1.1 status codes.

The date field can have the following format:

```
date = [day/month/year:hour:minute:second zone]
```

For example:

```
[02/Jan/1998:00:22:01 -0800]
```

The field sizes are given in Table 11-1.

Table 11-1
Date Field Sizes

Fields	*Value*
Day	2 digits
Month	3 letters
Year	4 digits
Hour	2 digits
Minute	2 digits
Second	2 digits
Zone	('+' | '-') 4*digit

Now let's take a look at the directives that can be used with mod_log_config. There are four directives available in this module.

TransferLog directive

```
Syntax: TransferLog filename | "| /path/to/external/program"
Default: none
Context: server config, virtual host
```

This directive sets the name of the log file or program where the log information is to be sent. By default, the log information is in the Common Log File (CLF) format. This format can be customized using the LogFormat directive (discussed in the next section).

Note that when the TransferLog directive is found within a virtual host container, the log information is formatted using the LogFormat directive found within the context. If a LogFormat directive is not found in the same context, however, the server's log format is used.

The TransferLog directive takes either a log file path or a pipe to an external program as the argument. The log filename is assumed to be relative to the ServerRoot setting if no leading / character is found. For example, if the ServerRoot is set to /etc/httpd, then the following tells Apache to send log information to the /etc/httpd/logs/access.log file:

```
TransferLog logs/access.log
```

When the argument is a pipe to an external program, the log information is sent to the external program's standard input (STDIN).

Note that a new program is not started for a VirtualHost if it inherits the TransferLog from the main server. If a program is used, then it is run under the user who started httpd. This will be the root if the server was started by the root. Be sure that the program is secure.

LogFormat directive

```
Syntax: LogFormat format [nickname]
Default: LogFormat "%h %l %u %t \"%r\" %s %b"
Context: server config, virtual host
```

This directive sets the format of the default log file named by the TransferLog directive. If you include a nickname for the format on the directive line, you can use it in other LogFormat and CustomLog directives rather than repeating the entire format string. A LogFormat directive that defines a nickname does nothing else— that is, it only defines the nickname, it doesn't actually apply the format.

See the "Customizing Your Log Files" section later in this chapter for details on the formatting options available.

CustomLog directive

```
Syntax: CustomLog file-pipe format-or-nickname
Context: server config, virtual host
```

Like the TransferLog directive, this directive enables you to send logging information to a log file or an external program. Unlike the TransferLog directive, however, it enables you to use a custom log format that can be specified as an argument.

The argument format specifies a format for each line of the log file. The options available for the format are exactly the same as for the argument of the LogFormat directive. If the format includes any spaces (which it will do in almost all cases), it should be enclosed in double quotes.

Instead of an actual format string, you can use a format nickname defined with the LogFormat directive.

Nicknames are only available in Apache 1.3 or later. Also, note that the TransferLog and CustomLog directives can be used multiple times in each server to cause each request to be logged to multiple files.

CookieLog directive

```
Syntax: CookieLog filename
Context: server config, virtual host
```

The CookieLog directive sets the filename for the logging of cookies. The filename is relative to the ServerRoot. This directive is included only for compatibility with mod_cookies, and is deprecated — therefore, use of this directive is not recommended. Use the user-tracking module's directive instead. The user-tracking module mod_usertrack is discussed later in this chapter.

Customizing Your Log Files

Although CLF meets most log requirements, sometimes it is useful to be able to customize logging data. For example, you may want to log the type of browsers that are accessing your site, so your Web design team can determine what type of browser-specific HTML to avoid or use. Or, perhaps you want to know which Web sites are sending (that is, referring) visitors to your sites. All this is accomplished quite easily in Apache. The default logging module, mod_log_config, supports custom logging.

Custom formats are set with the LogFormat and CustomLog directives of the module. The format argument to LogFormat and CustomLog is a string. This format string can have both literal characters and special % format specifiers. When literal values are used in this string, they are copied into the log file for each request. The

% specifiers, however, are replaced with corresponding values. The special % specifiers are:

%b	Bytes sent, excluding HTTP headers
%f	The filename of the request
%{variable}e	The contents of the environment variable VARIABLE
%h	The remote host that made the request
%{ IncomingHeader }i	The contents of IncomingHeader — that is, the header line(s) in the request sent to the server. The i character at the end denotes that this is a client (incoming) header.
%l	If the IdentityCheck directive is enabled and the client machine runs identd, then this is the identity information reported by the client.
%{ Foobar }n	The contents of the note Foobar from another module
%{ OutgoingHeader }o	The contents of OutgoingHeader — that is, the header line(s) in the reply. The o character at the end denotes that this is a server (outgoing) header.
%p	The port to which the request was served
%p	The process ID of the child that serviced the request
%r	The first line of the request
%s	Status returned by the server in response to the request. Note that when the request gets redirected, the value of this format specifier is still the original request status. If you want to store the redirected request status, use %..>s instead.
%t	Time of the request. The format of time is the same as in CLF format.
%{format}t	The time, in the form given by format. (See Chapter 7 for formatting details. You can also look at the man page of strftime on UNIX systems.)
%t	The time taken to serve the request, in seconds
%u	If the requested URL required a successful Basic HTTP authentication, then the user name is the value of this format specifier. The value may be bogus if the server returned a 401 status (Authentication Required) after the authentication attempt.
%u	The URL path requested
%v	The name of the server or the virtual host to which the request came

It is possible to include conditional information in each of the preceding specifiers. The conditions can be presence (or absence) of certain HTTP status code(s). For example, let's say you want to log all referring URLs that pointed a user to a nonexistent page. In such a case, the server produces a 404 status (Not Found) header. So, to log the referring URLs you can use the format specifier:

```
'%404{Referer}i'
```

Similarly, to log referring URLs that resulted in an unusual status, you can use:

```
'%!200,304,302{Referer}i'
```

Notice the use of the ! character to denote the absence of the server status list.

Similarly, to include additional information at the end of the CLF format specifier, you can extend the CLF format, which is defined by the format string:

```
"%h %l %u %t \"%r\" %s %b"
```

For example:

```
"%h %l %u %t \"%r\" %s %b \"%{Referer}i\" \"%{User-agent}i\"".
```

This format specification logs CLF format data and adds the Referer and User-agent information found in client-provided headers in each log entry.

You learned about adding non-CLF data in the log file, but what if you need to store this data in more than one log file? In the next section, I discuss how to use multiple log files to store CLF and non-CLF data.

Creating Multiple Log Files

Sometimes, it is necessary to create multiple log files. For example, if you are using a log analysis program that cannot handle non-CLF data, you may want to write the non-CLF data to a different file. You can create multiple log files very easily using the TransferLog and/or the CustomLog directive of the mod_log_config module. Simply repeat these directives to create more than one log file.

If, for example, you want to create a standard CLF access log and a custom log of all referring URLs, then you can use something like the following:

```
TransferLog logs/access_log
CustomLog   logs/referrer_log     "%{Referer}i"
```

When you have either TransferLog or CustomLog defined in the primary server configuration, and you have a virtual host defined, the virtual host-related logging is also performed in those logs. For example:

```
TransferLog logs/access_log
CustomLog   logs/agents_log     "%{User-agent}i"
<Virtual Host 206.171.50.51>
ServerName reboot.nitec.com
DocumentRoot  /www/reboot/public/htdocs
ScriptAlias /cgi-bin/ /www/reboot/public/cgi-bin/
</VirtualHost>
```

Here, the virtual host reboot.nitec.com does not have a TransferLog or CustomLog directive defined within the virtual host container tags. All logging information will be stored in the log/access_log and the logs/agents_log. Now, if the following line is added inside the virtual host container:

```
TransferLog vhost_logs/reboot_access_log
```

then all logging for the virtual host reboot.nitec.com is done in vhost_logs/reboot_access_log file. None of the log/access_log and logs/agents_log files will be used for reboot.nitec.com.

Storing Specific Information

This section introduces you to a few more logging-specific modules that provide features that are already available from the default logging module (mod_log_config). The information is provided for completeness and backward compatibility purposes.

Storing user agent information

Apache provides another module called mod_log_agent to enable you to store user agent (Web browsers, robots) information in a separate log file. This module is not compiled into standard Apache distribution, so you need to add it to your Apache executable as usual. The module provides a single directive, the AgentLog directive:

```
Syntax: AgentLog filename | "| /path/to/external/program"
Default: AgentLog logs/agent_log
Context: server config, virtual host
```

This directive tells Apache the file or program name to be used to send the UserAgent header for incoming requests. As with the TransferLog directive, you can provide either a log filename or a fully qualified path name to a program.

Note that when using the CustomLog directive, you can add the %{User-agent}i format specifier to log the UserAgent header without the use of this module. In other words, this module does not provide any functionality that is not present in the standard mod_log_config module. If this module had a way of ignoring local accesses made by you and people on your network, then the data would be more interesting.

Next, let's look at a module that enables you to store the referrer information in a log file.

Storing referrer information

Knowing who referred a visitor to your Web site is helpful because it gives you an idea of who your friends are on the Web. It may also help you decide where you should spend your advertising dollars.

Being able to tell who forwarded a request to your Web site is a great advantage in establishing Web relationships with others. If you are receiving many referrals from a particular Web site, you may want to be courteous and provide a link from your Web site to theirs. Remember to ask their permission first, however. On the other hand, if you are getting referrals from Web sites that you do not care for, or do not want to be associated with, you can determine these Web sites from your log and politely request that they remove references that point to your site.

The mod_log_referer provides you with the facility to log the incoming Referer headers from requests. Of course, the standard mod_log_config with the CustomLog directive enables you to do the same using the %{Referer}I format specifier. So, what's the advantage of using this module? Well, this module, unlike mod_log_config, enables you to ignore certain hosts. This way, you can log only your real users and not references from your own host(s).

You need to compile this module into your Apache executable by yourself. It provides the following directives.

RefererLog directive

```
Syntax: RefererLog filename | "| /path/to/external/program"
Default: RefererLog logs/referer_log
Context: server config, virtual host
```

This directive sets the name of the log file or program that receives the Referer headers of incoming requests.

See the TransferLog details in this chapter for more information about the path restrictions and how to use the external program.

RefererIgnore directive

```
Syntax: RefererIgnore string string ...
Context: server config, virtual host
```

The RefererIgnore directive adds to the list of strings to be ignored in Referer headers. If any of the strings in the list are contained in the Referer header, then no referrer information will be logged for the request. For example:

```
RefererIgnore yourcompany.com
```

This avoids logging references from yourcompany.com. If yourcompany.com is the domain name for your internal network, you will be able to ignore all references that have been generated from within your network.

The log file format is quite simple. It contains a separate line for each referral. Each line has the following format:

```
uri -> document
```

where uri is the (%-escaped) URI for the document that references the one requested by the client, and document is the (%-decoded) local URL to the document being referred to.

Storing cookies

So far, I have talked about quite a few logging options. None of these enable you to uniquely identify visitors. This is important, because if you know which requests are made by which visitor, it gives you a better idea of how your content is being used. For example, say that you have a really cool page on your Web site somewhere, and you have a way to identify the visitors in your logs. If you look at your log and see that many visitors have to go from one page to another to find the cool page at the end, you might reconsider your site design and make that cool page available sooner in the click stream. Apache has a module called mod_usertrack that enables you to track your Web site visitor by logging HTTP cookies.

HTTP Cookies

An HTTP cookie is not made with cookie dough. It is simply a piece of information that the server gives to the Web browser. This information is usually stored in a key=value pair and can be associated with an entire Web site or a particular URL on a Web site. Once a cookie is issued by the server and accepted by the Web browser, the cookie resides in the Web browser system. Every time the Web browser requests the same URL, or any URL that falls under the realm of the cookie URL, the cookie information is returned to the server. When setting the cookie, the server can tell the Web browser to expire the cookie after a certain time. The time can be specified so that the cookie is never used in a later session, or it can be used for a long period of time.

There has been much controversy over the use of cookies. Many consider cookies as a intrusion of privacy. Using cookies to track user behavior has become widely popular. In fact, several advertisement companies on the Internet make heavy use of cookies to track users. It should be stressed that cookies themselves cannot cause any harm. The cookie data is usually written in a text file in a directory of your browser software.

Before I get into the mod_usertrack details, I want to clarify a few things. There used to be a module called mod_cookies, which is now known as mod_usertrack. However, the previous version of the module performed its own logging using the CookieLog directive, which is no longer supported in this module. Instead, a much better way of logging cookies is available in the standard mod_log_config module.

For example, using the CustomLog directive in the standard logging module, you can store the cookies in a separate file:

```
CustomLog logs/clickstream "%{cookie}n %r %t"
```

For backward compatibility, the configurable log module implements the old CookieLog directive, but this should be upgraded to the preceding CustomLog directive. Now, lets take a look at the new mod_usertrack module.

Remember that mod_usertrack does not save a log of cookies; it just generates unique cookies for each visitor. You can use CustomLog (as shown earlier) to store these cookies in a log file for analysis.

The mod_usertrack directive is not compiled into the standard distribution version of Apache, so you need to compile it before you can use it. The module provides the following directives.

CookieExpires directive

```
Syntax: CookieExpires expiry-period
Context: server config, virtual host
```

This directive is used to set the expiration period of the cookies that are generated by the module. The expiration period can be defined in terms of number of seconds, or in a format such as "1 month 2 days 3 hours." For example:

```
CookieExpires 3600
CookieExpires "2 days 3 hours"
```

Here, the first directive defines the expiration period in seconds, and the second one defines the expiration period using the special format. Note that when the expiration period is not defined in a numeric form, the special form is assumed. However, the special format requires that you put double quotes around the format string. If this directive is not used, cookies last only for the current browser session.

CookieTracking directive

```
Syntax: CookieTracking on | off
Context: server config, virtual host, directory, per-directory
configuration file ( .htaccess)
Override: FileInfo
```

This directive enables or disables the generation of automatic cookies. When it is set to on, Apache starts sending a user-tracking cookie for all new requests. Figure 11-3 shows an example of such cookie.

Figure 11-3: Apache sends a user-tracking cookie to the browser.

The CookieTracking directive can be used to turn this behavior on or off on a per-server or per-directory basis. By default, compiling mod_usertrack does not activate cookies.

Using Error Logs

In this chapter I have talked about many ways of logging various interesting data. However, one important logging feature you must enable on your Web site is error logs. Without logging errors, you will be unable to determine what's wrong and where the error occurs.

Interestingly, error logging is supported in the core Apache. The ErrorLog directive enables you to log all types of errors that Apache encounters.

For more details, look for this directive in Chapter 4.

In this section, we look at how you can incorporate your Apache error logs into the widely used syslog facility found on almost all UNIX platforms.

Syslog is the traditional way of logging messages sent out by daemon (server) processes. You may ask, "Apache is a daemon, so why can't it write to syslog?" It can, actually. All you need to do is replace your existing ErrorLog directive in the configuration file with:

```
ErrorLog syslog
```

and then restart Apache. Using a Web browser, access a nonexistent page on your Web server and watch the syslog log file to see if it shows an httpd entry. You should take a look at your /etc/syslog.conf file for clues about where the httpd messages will appear.

For example, Listing 11-1 shows /etc/syslog.conf for a Linux system.

Listing 11-1: /etc/syslog.conf

```
# Log all kernel messages to the console.
# Logging much else clutters up the screen.
#kern.*                        /dev/console

# Log anything (except mail) of level info or higher.
# Don't log private authentication messages!
*.info;mail.none;authpriv.none            /var/log/messages

# The authpriv file has restricted access.
authpriv.*                          /var/log/secure

# Log all the mail messages in one place.
mail.*                  /var/log/maillog

# Everybody gets emergency messages, plus log them on another
# machine.
*.emerg                        *

# Save mail and news errors of level err and higher in a
# special file.
uucp,news.crit                      /var/log/spooler
```

There are two important lines (as far as Apache is concerned) in this listing. They are:

```
*.info;mail.none;authpriv.none       /var/log/messages
*.emerg                        *
```

The first line tells syslog to write all messages of the info type (except for mail and private authentication) to the /var/log/messages file, and the second line states that all emergency messages should be written to all log files. Using the LogLevel directive, you can specify what type of messages Apache should send to syslog. For example:

```
ErrorLog syslog
LogLevel debug
```

Here, Apache is instructed to send debug messages to syslog. If you want to store debug messages in a different file via syslog, then you need to modify /etc/syslog.conf. For example:

```
*.debug          /var/log/debug
```

Adding this line in /etc/syslog.conf and restarting syslogd (kill -HUP syslogd PID) and Apache will enable you to store all Apache debug messages to the /var/log/debug file. There are several log level settings:

- Emerg — Emergency messages
- Alert — Alert messages
- Crit — Critical messages
- Error — Error messages
- Warn — Warnings
- Notice — Notification messages
- Info — Information messages
- Debug — Messages logged at debug level will also include the source file and line number where the message is generated, to help debugging and code development.

If you want to see updates to your syslog or any other log files as they happen, you can use the tail utility found on most UNIX systems. For example, if you want to see updates for a log called /var/log/httpd_errors as they occur, use:

```
tail -f /var/log/httpd_errors
```

Analyzing Your Log Files

So far, you learned about creating standard CLF-based logs and custom logs. Now, you need a way to analyze these logs to make use of the recorded data. Your log analysis needs may vary. Sometimes you may need to produce extensive reports, or maybe you just want to do a simple checking on the logs. For simple tasks, it is best to use whatever is available at hand. Most UNIX systems have enough utilities and scripting tools available to do the job.

Let's take a look at using a UNIX utility to get a list of all the hosts. If you use the default logging facility or a custom log with CLF support, you can find a list of all the hosts quite easily. For example:

```
cat /path/to/httpd/access_log | awk '{print $1}'
```

prints out all the host IP addresses (if you have DNS lookup enabled, then host aliases are shown). The cat utility lists the access_log file, and the resulting output is piped to the awk interpreter, which prints out only the first field in each line using the print statement. This prints all the hosts — but what if you wanted to exclude the hosts on your network? In that case, you would use:

```
cat /path/to/httpd/access_log | awk '{print $1}'  | egrep -v
'(^206.171.50)'
```

where 206.171.50 should be replaced with your network address. Note that here, I assume you have a class C network. If you have a class B network, you only need to use the first two octets of your IP addresses. This version enables you to exclude your own hosts using the egrep utility, which is told to display (via -v) only the hosts that do not start with the 206.171.50 network address. This still may not be satisfactory, however, because there are likely to be repeats. Therefore, the final version is as follows:

```
cat /path/to/httpd/access_log | awk '{print $1}'  | uniq |
egrep -v '(^206.171.50)'
```

Here, the uniq utility filters out repeats and show you only one listing per host. Of course, if you want to see the total number of unique hosts that have accessed your Web site, you can pipe the final result to the wc utility with a -l option as follows:

```
cat /path/to/httpd/access_log | awk '{print $1}'  | uniq |
egrep -v '(^206.171.50)' | wc -l
```

This gives you the total line count (that is, the number of unique host accesses).

Using UNIX utilities, you can quickly grab needed information; however, this method requires some UNIX know-how, and is not always convenient because your boss may want a "pretty" report instead of some dry textual listing. In such a case, you can either develop your own analysis programs or use third-party analysis tools.

Many third-party Web server log analysis tools are available. Most of these tools expect the log files to be in CLF format, so make sure you have CLF formatting in your logs. Table 11-2 shows a listing of some of such tools and where to find them.

Table 11-2
Third-Party Log Analysis Tools

Product Name	***Product URL***
WebTrends	www.webtrends.com/
Wusage	www.boutell.com/wusage/
wwwstat	www.ics.uci.edu/pub/websoft/wwwstat/
http-analyze	www.netstore.de/Supply/http-analyze/
pwebstats	www.unimelb.edu.au/pwebstats.html
WebStat Explorer	www.webstat.com/
AccessWatch	http://netpressence.com/accesswatch/

The best way to find out which one will work for you is to try them out, or at least visit their Web sites for feature comparisons. Two utilities that I find very useful are Wusage and wwwstat.

Wusage is my favorite commercial log analysis application. It is highly configurable and produces great graphical reports using the company's well-known GD graphics library. Wusage is distributed in a binary format. Evaluation copies of wusage are provided free for many UNIX and Windows platform.

wwwstat is one of the freely available analysis programs that I prefer. It is written in Perl, so you need to have Perl installed on the system on which you want to run this application. wwwstat output summaries can be read by gwstat to produce fancy graphs of the summarized statistics.

By now, you're probably aware that creating logs in Apache is easy and useful. Doing this enables you to learn more about what's going on with your Apache server. Logs can help you detect problems, identify your site's problems, find out about your site's best features, and much more. Can something so beneficial come without a catch? If you said no, you guessed right. Log files take up a lot of valuable disk space, so they must be maintained regularly.

Log Maintenance

By enabling logging, you may be able to save a lot of work, but the logs themselves do add some extra work for you: they need to be maintained. On Apache sites with high hit rates or many virtual domains, the log files can become huge in a very short time, which could easily cause a disk crisis. When log files become very large, you should rotate them.

You have two options for rotating your logs: you can use a utility that comes with Apache called rotatelog; or you can use logrotate, a facility that is available on most Linux systems.

Using rotatelog

Apache comes with a support tool called rotatelog. You can use this program as follows:

```
TransferLog "| /path/to/rotatelogs <logfile> <rotation time in
seconds>"
```

For example, if you want to rotate the access log every 86,400 seconds (that is, 24 hours), use the following line:

```
TransferLog "| /path/to/rotatelogs /var/logs/httpd 86400"
```

You will have each day's access log information stored in a file called /var/logs/httpd.nnnn, where nnnn represents a long number.

Using logrotate

The logrotate utility rotates, compresses, and mails log files. It is designed to ease the system administration of log files. It enables the automatic rotation, compression, removal, and mailing of log files on a daily, weekly, or monthly basis, or on a size basis. Normally, logrotate is run as a daily cron job. Read the man pages for logrotate to learn more about it.

If your system supports the logrotate facility, you should have a configuration similar to what is shown in your /etc/logrotate.conf file:

```
/path/to/httpd/access_log {
compress
rotate 5
mail {hyperlink mailto:webmaster@yourdomain.com}
errors {hyperlink mailto:webmaster@yourdomain.com}
size=1024K
postrotate
         kill -HUP 'cat /path/to/httpd.pid'
endscript
}
```

This configuration specifies that the /path/to/httpd/access_log file be rotated whenever it grows over one megabyte (1024K) in size, and that the old log files be compressed and mailed to webmaster@yourdomain.com after going through five rotations, rather than being removed. Any errors that occur during processing of the log file are mailed to root@yourdomain.com.

Summary

In this chapter, you learned how to monitor and log information on an Apache server. You discovered how to get quick access to server configurations, how to monitor the status of a running Apache server, and how to create log files in both CLF and custom formats. You also learned how to analyze the log files using third-party applications. Monitoring and logging provides you with a great deal of information that is vital to the smooth system administration of the Web servers, and it also helps the marketing aspects of your site.

In the next chapter, you learn about Web server security.

✦ ✦ ✦

CHAPTER 12

Web Security

Ever lose sleep worrying about your Web server's security? If so, you are not alone — many Web administrators do the same. Many of the new Web administrators started their jobs as Local Area Network (LAN) administrators; and, a few years back, most companies didn't understand the Internet. Company LANs were isolated then, running protocols that would not deliver a single packet on the Internet.

In last few years, this scene has changed dramatically. Most companies are now considering a direct link to the Internet as part of their network design. Connecting a LAN to the Internet has become an easy task, but many LAN administrators still don't grasp the inner workings of the Internet; therefore, they are not comfortable — or even aware of — the security issues.

Unfortunately, a detailed discussion of Internet security is beyond the scope of this book. However, in this chapter, I provide an overview of the security model in question, as well as a detailed discussion of how it impacts your Web service. You learn where security risks lurk, and how to take preventive measures to reduce new risks.

✦ ✦ ✦ ✦

In This Chapter

Understanding Web Security

Knowing the overall security model

Recognizing potential CGI and SSI security risks

Minimizing CGI and SSI security risks

Protecting your Web content

Setting up an administrative security policy

✦ ✦ ✦ ✦

Understanding the Need for Web Security

The need for security is often unclear to novice administrators. Many administrators think about security only after a breach of security has occurred. This passive approach is not wise, but it is understandable. It is difficult for an administrator to worry about something he knows nothing about. Here, I provide some idea of the hidden risks out there.

The moment you got your Web server up and running and available to the rest of the world, you opened a window for others to get into your network. You did intend to do this, right? Most people will use what you provide on your Web site, but some may look for holes in this window to get to the information they are not supposed to access. Some of these people are vandals who want to create embarrassing situations, and some are information thieves. Either way, if anyone succeeds in finding that hole, you may find your Web sites mutilated with obscene materials, or you might even loose confidential data. Sometimes the attacks may not affect your site directly. The infiltrators may use your server and other resources to get to another network and, thus, put you at legal risk. None of these scenarios is desirable.

In order to avoid such risk and embarrassment, make sure you have created security requirements for your Web services. In this chapter, I assume you have the following security requirements for your Web site:

- ✦ Maintaining the integrity of the information you publish on the Web.
- ✦ Preventing the use of the Web server host as a point for break-ins into your organization's network (which could result in breaches of confidentiality, integrity, or availability of information resources).
- ✦ Preventing the use of the Web server host as a staging area for intrusions into other networks (which could result in your organization being held liable for damages).

Most Web security incidents occur because confidential information is made vulnerable by improperly configured software. The software could be the Web server itself, or applications (such as CGI programs, Server Side Includes, and Server API applications). that are run by the Web server. This can result in the inadvertent disclosure of confidential information. Subsequent attacks can be launched by exploiting the confidential information.

If you make sure your Web server configuration is tight and the applications run by the Web server are fairly secured — are you done? No, because the attacks could be targeted to the Web server via different routes. Your Web server might get compromised by way of totally unrelated applications, or by a bug in the operating system, or even by poor network architecture.

To be secure, you have to look at each and every detail. This can become an impossible task but, keep in mind, it is impossible to have a completely secured environment. There is never a foolproof solution to all security issues, as all issues are not known. Your goal should be to improve your security as much as possible, at all times.

The Security Checkpoints

To improve the security of your public Web server, there are a few security checkpoints you need to follow. Figure 12-1 shows the overall security checkpoint diagram. This diagram identifies the security checkpoints that must be examined thoroughly before considering an Internet-connected network secure.

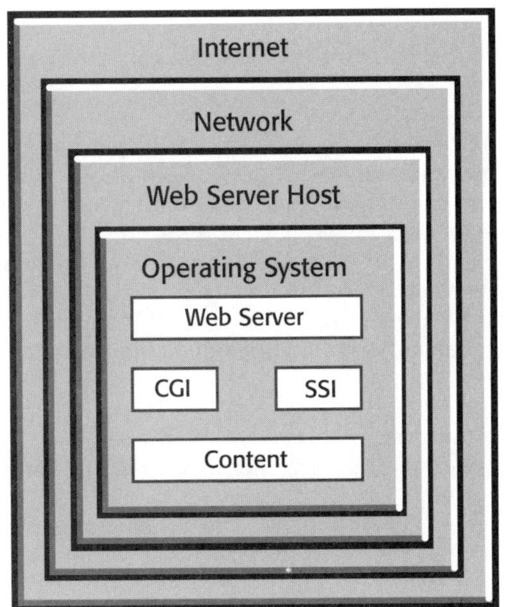

Figure 12-1 Security check points

Your network

The first checkpoint to consider is your network, and how it is connected to the Internet. The real issue is where you place your Web server. If you have a network configuration, such as the one shown in Figure 12-2, your network is virtually unprotected.

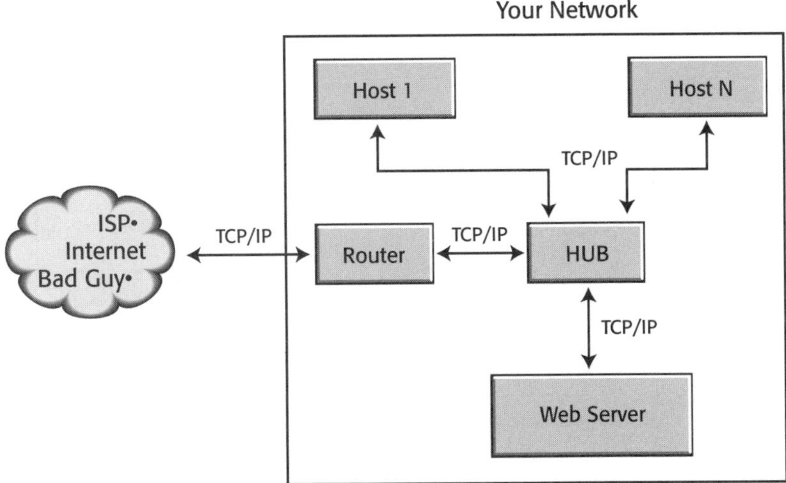

Figure 12-2 A simple network with an Internet connection

To keep things simple, let's assume that you only have a single connection to the Internet.

In this network model, all Internet traffic can be routed to and from your network. In other words, anyone on the Internet can reach any host on your network and vice versa. This also means that a hacker on the Internet must find a weak point in one of the many hosts that you have on your network. Of course, not all of these hosts will be servers with services enabled for others to use; but, even if you have a Windows machine with file sharing enabled, it could be a potential target. Because the entire network uses TCP/IP, a simple file-sharing option on a Windows workstation machine can lead to a break-in. This network almost invites criminals who want to break in.

If you have this configuration, check your router documentation to see if you can enable IP-based restrictions. I recommend this configuration be avoided at all costs.

The next configuration to look at is shown in Figure 12-3. This is called the Sacrificial Lamb configuration.

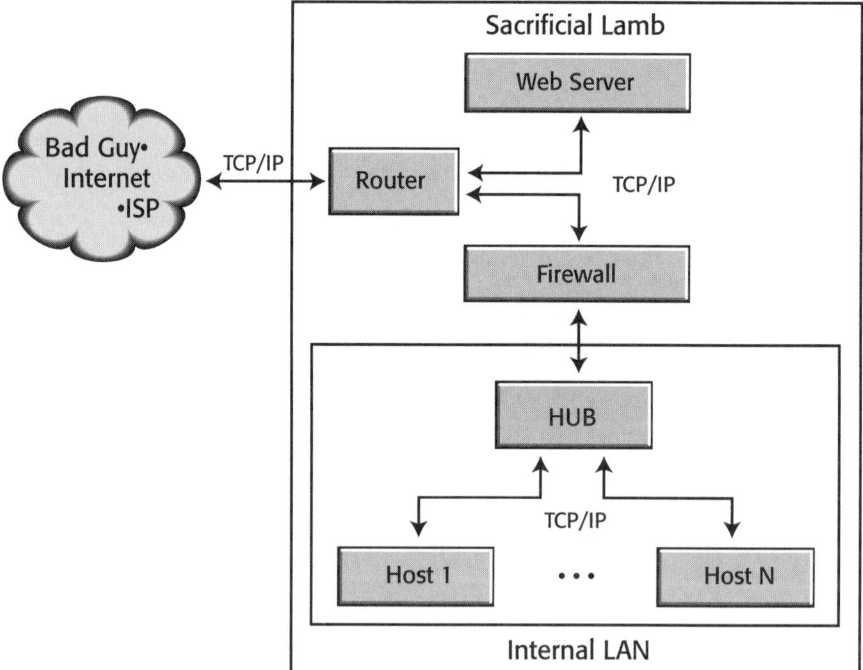

Figure 12-3 The Sacrificial Lamb network configuration

The Web server is kept outside of the firewall and the internal LAN. The hosts in the internal LAN receive or transmit Internet packets through a firewall host. This way, the internal hosts are protected from outside attack — at least in theory).The Web server, on the other hand, is completely open to attack; which is why the configuration is called a Sacrificial Lamb configuration. In this configuration, the following is true:

✦ The intruder cannot observe or capture network traffic flowing between internal hosts. Such traffic might include authentication information, proprietary business information, personnel data, and many other kinds of sensitive data.

✦ The intruder cannot get to internal hosts, or obtain detailed information about them.

The Sacrificial Lamb configuration guards against these two threats, and keeps the Web server isolated from the internal network and its traffic.

Tip

In a Sacrificial Lamb configuration, it is wise to turn off source routing at the router. This way, the Web server host cannot be used to forward packets to hosts in the internal network.

Some people like putting the Web server behind the firewall, as well. In such a configuration, the firewall becomes the gateway for both the internal LAN and Web traffic, and the firewall configuration becomes complex. I believe that such complexity can lead to security holes in the firewall and, therefore, defeats the purpose.

The general idea is to isolate your internal network, keeping it away from prying eyes as much as possible. Definitely consider installing a firewall in your Internet-to-LAN route. If a firewall is not an option, you can consider the proxy-server option. A proxy server takes one network's request to another network without ever connecting the two. This might be a good solution, as it provides an excellent logging facility as well.

As you can see, you should be more concerned about your internal network than the Web server, itself. Because networks introduce Internet-accessible Web server(s) within the network, they are likely to get broken into by way of exploiting a security hole in the Web server software or an application (such as a CGI program) running on the Web server. The chances of this occurring are reduced by choosing a network architecture that isolates the LAN from the Web server.

Although the Web server should be kept out of the secured part of the network, you should protect it to circumvent any open invitations to hackers. In the next section, I discuss securing your operating system and Web server software. After that, I cover the different measures that can be taken to strengthen security on the server.

The operating system

Apache runs on virtually all UNIX platforms, and it is already starting to run on Windows NT, Windows 95, and even on the new Macintosh operating system. Just because it runs on virtually any platform does not mean you should use any operating system to run Apache. Choosing the right operating system (OS) can be a significant factor in system security. Well-known UNIX and UNIX-like operating systems, such as BSDI, FreeBSD, SunOS, Solaris, HP-UX, Digital UNIX, and Linux are big favorites among Internet server administrators. Although the quality and reliability may vary among these operating systems, all are deigned for use as server operating systems.

If you do not shop UNIX, you might want to look into the Windows NT server platform. Windows NT is a very powerful UNIX competitor, likely to give UNIX a run for its money in the future; however, Windows NT is new to the Internet game. Most UNIX and UNIX-like operating systems have been around long enough to suffer numerous hacks and attacks. They stand as the survivors and — though never completely hack-proof — still remain tall.

Once you have chosen an operating system, you should disable any extra features that you don't intend to use on the Web server machine running that OS. For example, if you do not need SMTP/POP mail or FTP services, disable them or completely remove the mail server programs from the system. If you don't need a lot of powerful system utilities, delete them. Make certain that your Web server is just a Web server and has only the services it needs.

You can learn about vulnerabilities that exist in your operating platform by browsing: www.cert.org. CERT (Computer Emergency Response Team) works with the Internet community to facilitate awareness of, and response to, security issues. It also conducts research targeted at improving the security of computer systems.

Web server software

Obviously, you will use Apache as the Web server software or else you would not be reading this book. Make sure you use the latest Apache for your system. It is a good idea to compile your own Apache binaries instead of using those of any binary distribution.

See Chapter 2 to learn about how to configure and compile your very own Apache binaries.

Apache is freely available software, so it is important that you obtain it from a reliable source. Do not ever download Apache binaries or source code from just any Web or FTP site. Always check with the official site, www.apache.org, first. In the future, Apache source will be PGP (Pretty Good Privacy) signed. In fact, the current Apache distribution includes a PGP key-ring file containing the PGP keys of most active Apache developers. You can use this file to authenticate future releases of Apache that are PGP signed. E-mail announcements or security advisories sent out by Apache developers are also likely to be signed with PGP to guarantee authenticity.

The Apache group PGP signatures are in the file KEYS in the top-level distribution of Apache. If you trust the site where you obtained your distribution, you can add these keys to your own key ring. If you do not how to use PGP on your system, learn about it at the following Web site URL:

```
www.pgp.com
```

Some of the distributions are accompanied by a file containing a PGP signature for that distribution. These signatures are stored in files with an .asc extension (for example, the signature for apache_1.3.0.tar.gz is stored in apache_1.3.0.tar.gz.asc). These can be used to check the validity of the distribution if you have added the KEYS file contents to your key ring.

The latest version of Apache doesn't not have any known bugs; however, its capability to incorporate external modules brings up another security issue. Many of the Apache modules are written by people all over the world. Make sure that you only use modules that are available on the official Apache Web site or registered in the Apache module registry located at the URL:

```
www.covalent.net/module_registry/
```

Also never use experimental modules in your production sites. In fact, it is a good idea to determine which modules you really need, and then configure and compile Apache accordingly. This way you have a smaller, faster server with potentially better security.

When configuring Apache, pay a great deal of attention to security configuration issues that follow. The basic idea is to disable anything you do not use. This way, you are taking preventive security measures and are likely to reduce risks.

User and group for Apache

As you already know Apache can be run as a standalone, or as an inetd daemon-run service. If you choose to run Apache as an inetd service, you do not have to worry about the User and Group directives. If you run Apache as a standalone server, however, make sure you create a dedicated user and group for Apache. Do not use the nobody user or the nogroup group, especially if your system has already defined these. Chances are there are other services or other places where your system is using them. This might lead to administrative headaches. Instead, create a fresh new user and group for Apache, and use them with the directives mentioned.

When you use a dedicated user and group for Apache, permission-specific administration of your Web content is simple. All you need to do is ensure that only the Apache user has read access to the Web content. If you need to create a directory to which some CGI applications might write data, you need only enable write permissions for the Apache user.

Protect ServerRoot and log directories

Make sure that the ServerRoot directories are not writable by anyone but the root user (especially the log directories and files). You do not need to give Apache user/group read or write permission in log directories. Enabling anyone other than the root user to write files in the log directory could lead to a major security hole.

Disable default access

The strict security model dictates that there be no default access; so, you should get into the habit of permitting no access at first. Only permit specific access to specific locations. To implement no default access, you can use the following configuration segment in one of your Apache configuration files:

```
<Directory />
     Order deny,allow
     Deny from all
 </Directory>
```

This disables all access first. Now, if you need to enable access to a particular directory, use the <Directory ..> container again to open that directory. For example, if you want to permit access to /www/mysite/public/htdocs add the following configuration:

```
<Directory /www/mysite/public/htdocs>
     Order deny,allow
     Allow from all
 </Directory>
```

This method — opening only what you need — is a preventive security measure, and is highly recommended.

Disable user overrides

If you don't want users to override server-configuration settings using the per-directory configuration file (.htaccess) in a directory, disable this feature as follows:

```
<Directory />
     AllowOverride None
     Options None
     allow from all
</Directory>
```

This disallows user overrides and, in fact, speeds up your server. The server speed increases because it no longer looks for the per-directory access control files (.htaccess) for each request.

Your contents

Anyone concerned about Web security needs to evaluate the means and ways of protecting the contents that make up her Web. When determining how to protect contents, you can use the following guidelines:

- Web content files, such as HTML, images, and sound and video clips should only be readable by the Web server; no one but the content owner should be permitted write access to the files and directory.
- Any file or directory that cannot be displayed on the Web should not reside under the content directories. It should be removed or relocated because even if there is no link to these files from any other viewable content, it may still be accessible to others.
- Any temporary files created by dynamic-content generators, such as CGI applications, should reside in a single subdirectory where the generators have write access. This directory must be kept outside the content area to ensure that a bug in the application does not mistakenly wipe out any existing content file.
- In order to enforce clear copyright on the content, there should be both visible and embedded copyright notices on the content pages. The embedded copyright message should be kept at the beginning of a document, if possible. For example, in an HTML file you can use a pair of comment tags to embed the copyright message at the beginning of the file. If you plan to update your copyright messages often, you might consider an SSI solution using the #include directive. See Chapter 7 for details.
- If you have a great deal of graphical content (images) that you want to protect from copyright theft, you should look into the watermarking technology being introduced currently. This technique invisibly embeds information in images to protect the copyright. The idea is that if you detect some site using your graphical contents without permission, you might be able to verify the theft by looking at the hidden information. If the information matches your watermark ID, you can clearly identify the thief and proceed with legal action. Note that the strength of the currently available watermarking tools are questionable, as many programs can easily remove the original copyright owner's watermarks. This technology is worth investigating, however, if you are concerned about your graphical content.

Aside from these guidelines you should also be aware of Web spiders and robots. All search engines, such as Yahoo!, AltaVista, Excite, and Infoseek use automated robot applications that search Web sites and index contents. This is usually desirable, but on occasion, you might find yourself wanting to stop these robots from accessing a certain part of your Web site(s).

If content in a section of your Web site expires on a high frequency (daily, for example), you do not want the search robots to index them. Why not? Well, when a user at the search engine site finds a link to the old content and clicks it to find out the link is not existent, your customer will not be happy. That user might then go to the next link without going to your site again.

There will be other times when you want to disable indexing of your content (or part of it.) These robots can have intended and unintended effects on the network and Web sites they traverse. On occasion, search robots have overwhelmed Web sites by requesting too many documents too rapidly. Efforts are under way to create Internet standards of behavior for Web robots. The current version, the Robot Exclusion Protocol, enables Web site administrators to place a robots.txt file on their Web site indicating where robots should not go. For example, a large archive of bitmap images would be useless to a robot that is trying to index HTML pages. Serving these files to the robot is a needless use of resources both on your server and at the robot's end.

The current protocol is a voluntary one for the moment, and an etiquette is evolving for robot developers as experience is gained through their deployment. Most popular search engines abide by the Robot Exclusion Protocol.

When a compliant Web robot visits a site called www.somesite.com, it first checks for the existence of the URL:

```
http://www.somesite.com/robots.txt
```

If this URL exists, the Robot parses its contents for directives that instruct the robot how to index the site. As a Web Server Administrator, you can create directives that make sense for your site. Note that there can only be a single /robots.txt on a site. This file contains records that may look like the following:

```
User-agent: *
Disallow: /cgi-bin/
Disallow: /tmp/
Disallow: /~sam/
```

The first directive tells the robot the following directives should be considered by any robots. The following three directives (Disallow) tell the robot not to access the directories mentioned in the directives. Note that you need a separate Disallow line for every URL prefix you want to exclude — you cannot use the following:

```
Disallow: /cgi-bin/ /tmp/ /~sam/
```

Also, you may not have blank lines in a record because they are used to delimit multiple records. Note that regular expressions are not supported in either the User-agent or Disallow lines. The * in the User-agent field is a special value meaning any robot. Specifically, you cannot have lines like these:

```
Disallow: /tmp/*
```

or

```
Disallow: *.gif
```

Everything not explicitly disallowed is considered accessible by the robot (some examples follow).

To exclude all robots from the entire server, use the following configuration:

```
User-agent: *
Disallow: /
```

To permit all robots complete access, use the following configuration:

```
User-agent: *
Disallow:
```

You can create the same effect by deleting the robots.txt file. To exclude a single robot called WebCrawler:

```
User-agent: WebCrawler
Disallow: /
```

To allow a single robot called WebCrawler to access the site, use the following configuration:

```
User-agent: WebCrawler
Disallow:
User-agent: *
Disallow: /
```

To disallow a single file called /daily/changes_to_often.html from being indexed by robots, use the following configuration:

```
User-agent: *
Disallow: /daily/changes_to_often.html
```

Currently, there is no Allow directive.

CGI Risks and Solutions

The biggest security risk on the Web comes in the form of CGI applications. CGI (Common Gateway Interface) is not inherently insecure, but poorly written CGI applications are a major source of Web security holes. Actually, the simplicity of the CGI specification makes it easy for many inexperienced programmers to write CGI applications. These inexperienced programmers, being unaware of the security aspects of Internetworking, create applications that work but also create hidden back doors and holes on the system the applications run on.

Following are the three most common security risks that CGI applications may create:

- ✦ Information leaks — Such leaks help hackers break into a system. The more information a hacker knows about a system, the better he gets at breaking into the system.
- ✦ Execution of system commands via CGI applications — In many cases remote users have succeeded in tricking an HTML form-based mailer script to run a system command or give out confidential system information.
- ✦ Consumption of system resources — A poorly written CGI application can be made to consume system resources such that the server becomes virtually unresponsive.

Of course, you should take careful steps in developing or installing CGI applications when your Apache server will run these applications as an unprivileged user, but even carefully written applications can be a security risk. Next, let's talk about potential dangers and how to guard against them.

Protecting against user input

Most of the security holes created by CGI applications are caused by user input. In the following sections, I look at how user input can create security risks, and how you can protect your CGI applications against them.

User input crashes the CGI application

The biggest danger comes from user inputs. One type of user-input problem occurs when coding practices permit buffers to overflow when reading input. This can create a major security hole, as a program that overflows a buffer will crash and many expert hackers are able to take advantage of a crashed program and gain access to a system. Character buffer overflow is actually more common in languages such as C, and C++.

Here is a sample C code that makes an assumption that user input can only be up to 1,024 characters (that is, bytes long) and, therefore, is sufficient to declare an array of size 1,024. This wrong assumption forces this program to crash or behave wildly when a user enters a great deal of data in the input.

```
#include <stdio.h>
#include <stdlib.h>
static char query_string[1024];

char* POST() {
#
# Function to read input that has been POSTED from an HTML
# form.

# Local integer variable
```

```
int size;

# use getenv() function to get the value of the environment
# variable
# CONTENT_LENGTH which holds the byte count for the form input
# data stored in
# the STDIN. Convert the resulting string value of genet() to
# an integer using
# the atoi() function and return the value to the size
# variable.
size=atoi(getenv("CONTENT_LENGTH"));

# Read the input data from the standard input.
fread(query_string, size,1,stdin);

# Return the string buffer holding the data.
return query_string;
}
```

When a user enters data over 1,024 bytes this routine will break the program and increase the possibility of a major security hole. In some circumstances, the crash can be exploited by the hacker to execute commands remotely.

This problem can be removed by making sure the memory allocation for the data storage (query_string) happens dynamically using a call to malloc() or calloc() function.

User input makes system calls unsafe

Another user-input problem results when a user makes a request in which a system call opens subshells to process a command. For example, in Perl (a widely used CGI programming language) such a call could be made using system(), exec(), piped open() function, and eval() functions. Similarly, in C the popen(), and system() functions are potential security hazards. All of these functions/commands typically invoke a subshell (such as /bin/sh) to process the user command.

Note that even shell scripts using system(), exec() calls are likely to open portals of entries for hackers. Note that backtick quotes, available in shell interpreters and Perl for capturing the output of programs as text strings, are also dangerous.

To illustrate the importance of careful use of system calls, take a look this innocent-looking Perl code segment:

```
#!/usr/local/bin/perl
#
# Purpose: to demonstrate security risks in poorly written CGI
# scripts
#

# Get the domain name from query string environment variable
#
```

```
my $domain = $ENV{'QUERY_STRING'};

# Print the appropriate content type. Since whois output is in
# plain text
# we choose to use text/plain as the content-type here.
#
print "Content-type: text/plain\n\n";

# Here is the bad system call
system("/usr/bin/whois $domain");

# Here is another bad system call using back-ticks.
#
# my $output = `/usr/bin/whois $domain`;
#
# print $output;
exit 0;
```

This little Perl script is supposed to be a Web-based WHOIS gateway. If this script is called whois.pl, and it is kept in the cgi-bin directory of a Web site called www.notsecured.com, a user can call this script as follows:

http://domain/cgi-bin/script.pl?domain anydomain.com

The script will take the anydomain.com as the $domain variable via the QUERY_STRING variable, and launch the /usr/bin/whois program with the $domain value as the argument. This will return the data from the WHOIS database that InterNIC maintains. This is all very innocent and good, but the script is a disaster waiting to happen.

Consider the following line:

http://domain/cgi-bin/script.pl?domain nitec.com;ps

This does a WHOIS lookup on a domain called nitec.com and also provides the output of the UNIX ps utility that shows process status. This reveals information about the system that should not be available to the requesting party. Using this technique, anyone can find out a great deal about your system, which might not be a good thing. For example, replacing the ps command with df (a common UNIX utility that prints a summary of disk space) will enable anyone to determine what partitions you have and how full they are. I will leave to your imagination the real dangers this security hole could pose.

What is the lesson here? The lesson is not to trust any input, and not to make system calls an easy target for abuse. Next, I show you how you can achieve these goals.

There are two approaches in making sure user input is safe. One of these approaches is to scan the input for illegal characters and replace or remove them. For example, for the above whois.pl script, you can add the following line:

```
$domain =~ s/[\/ ;\[\]\<\>&\t]//g;
```

This will remove illegal metacharacters. This is a common but inadvisable approach, as it requires that the programmer be aware of all possible combinations of characters that could cause trouble. If the user uses input not predicted by the programmer, there is the possibility that the program may be used in a manner not intended by the programmer.

A better approach is to define a list of acceptable characters and replace or remove any character that is NOT acceptable. The list of valid input values is typically a predictable, well-defined set of manageable size.

This approach does not require the programmer to trap all characters that are unacceptable, leaving no margin for error. In the recommended approach, a programmer must only ensure that acceptable characters are identified, thus she can be less concerned about the characters an attacker may try in an attempt to bypass security checks.

Building on this philosophy, the Perl program presented earlier could be sanitized to contain ONLY those characters allowed, for example:

```
#!/usr/local/bin/perl
#
# This is a better version of the previous whois.pl script
#
# Assign a variable the acceptable character set for domain
# names
#
my $DOMAIN_CHAR_SET='-a-zA-Z0-9_.';

# Get the domain name from query string environment variable
#
my $domain = $ENV{'QUERY_STRING'};

# Now remove any character that does not belong to the
# acceptable character set.
$domain =~ s/[^$DOMAIN_CHAR_SET]//g;

# Print the appropriate content type. Since whois output is in
# plain text we choose to use text/plain as the content-type
# here.
#
print "Content-type: text/plain\n\n";

# Here is the system call
system("/usr/bin/whois $domain");

# Here is another system call using back-ticks.
#
# my $output = `/usr/bin/whois $domain`;
#
```

```
# print $output;
exit 0;
```

The $DOMAIN_CHAR_SET variable holds the acceptable character set, and the user-input variable $domain is searched for anything that does not fall in the set. The unacceptable character is removed.

The best way to go about user input is to establish rules for each input (that is, what you expect and how you can determine what you have received is acceptable). If you are expecting an e-mail address as input (rather than just scanning it blindly for shell metacharacters) for example, use a regular expression such as the following to detect the validity of the input as a possible e-mail address:

```
$email = $input{'email-addr'};
if ($email=~ /^[\w-\.]+\@[\w-\.]+$/) {
        print "Possibly valid address."
        }
else {
        print "Invalid email address.";
        }
```

Just sanitizing user input is not enough. You need to be careful about how you invoke external programs (for example, there are many ways you can invoke external programs in Perl). Some of these methods include:

Using backticks, you can capture the output of an external program, such as:

```
$list = '/bin/ls -l /etc';
```

This captures the /etc directory listing. Or, you can open a pipe to a program, such as:

```
open (FP, " | /usr/bin/sort");
```

You can also invoke an external program and wait for it to return with system():

```
system "/usr/bin/lpr data.dat";
```

or you can invoke an external program and never return with exec():

```
exec "/usr/bin/sort < data.dat";
```

All of these constructions can be risky if they involve user input that may contain shell metacharacters. For system() and exec(), there's a somewhat obscure syntactical feature that enables you to call external programs directly rather than going through a shell. If you pass the arguments to the external program (not in one long string, but as separate elements in a list), Perl will not go through the shell and shell metacharacters will have no unwanted side effects, as follows:

```
system "/usr/bin/sort","data.dat";
```

You can take advantage of this feature to open up a pipe without going through a shell. By calling open the character sequence -| , you fork a copy of Perl and open a pipe to the copy. Then, the child copy immediately forks another program using the first argument of the exec function call.

To read from a pipe without opening up a shell, you can do something similar with the sequence -|:

```
open(GREP,"-|") || exec "/usr/bin/grep",$userpattern,$filename;
while (<GREP>) {
  print "match: $_";
  }
close GREP;
```

These forms of open()s are more secure than the piped open()s and, therefore, you should use these whenever applicable.

Note that there are many other obscure features in Perl that enable you to call an external program and lie to it about its name. This is useful for calling programs that behave differently depending on the name by which they were invoked. The syntax is as follows:

```
system $real_name "fake_name","argument1","argument2"
```

One trick used by hackers is to alter the PATH environment variable so it points to the program they want your script to execute — rather than the program you're expecting. You should invoke programs using full pathnames rather than relying on the PATH environment variable. That is, instead of this fragment of Perl code:

```
system("cat /tmp/shopping.cart.txt");
```

use this:

```
system "/bin/cat" , "/tmp/shopping.cart.txt ";
```

If you must rely on the PATH, set it yourself at the beginning of your CGI application, as follows:

```
$ENV{'PATH'}="bin:/usr/bin:/usr/local/bin";
```

Even if you don't rely on the path when you invoke an external program, there's a chance that the invoked program will; therefore, you need to include the previous line towards the top of your script whenever you use taint checks. Note that you will have to adjust the line as necessary for the list of directories you want searched. Also note that in general, it's not a good idea to put the current directory (.) into the path.

Perl can Deal with Tainted Input

One of the most frequent security problems in CGI applications is inadvertently passing unchecked user variables to the shell. Perl provides a *taint-checking* mechanism that prevents you from doing this. Any variable assigned data from outside the program (including data from the environment, from standard input, and from the command line) is considered tainted and cannot be used to affect anything else outside your program. The taint can spread. If you use a tainted variable to set the value of another variable, the second variable also becomes tainted. Tainted variables cannot be used in eval(), system(), exec() or piped open() calls. If you try to do so, Perl exits with a warning message. Perl will also exit if you attempt to call an external program without explicitly setting the PATH environment variable. You turn on taint checks in Perl 5 by using a -T flag in the interpreter call line:

```
#!/usr/local/bin/perl -T
```

As mentioned before, once a variable is tainted, Perl won't permit you to use it in a system(), exec(), piped open, eval(), or backtick command (or any other function that affects something outside of the program, such as unlink). You can't use it even if you scan it for shell metacharacters or use the tr/// or s/// commands to remove metacharacters. The only way to untaint a tainted variable is to perform a pattern-matching operation on it and extract the matched substrings. For example, if you expect a variable to contain an e-mail address, you can extract an untainted copy of the address in this way:

```
$e-mail=~/([\w-\.]+\@[\w-\.]+)/;
$untainted_address = $1;
```

Therefore, turning on taint checking in Perl is a good idea.

The rule of thumb is to avoid passing direct user input to external programs, as they might contain hidden commands that do harm. Try to avoid using system calls that open subshells to do the work. Always scan the input for shell metacharacters and remove them from the input.

User sees HIDDEN data

There is one more form of input-related danger that you should be aware of, and it has to do with the misconception about the HIDDEN HTML input fields. CGI applications that require a lot of user input often ask the user for a few inputs, do some processing based on the input, and later ask for another set of inputs. Because CGI applications are run per request, they are unable to maintain what the user has entered in the last invocation. To solve this problem many CGI programmers store the previous input data in the output HTML using HIDDEN input fields. An HTML hidden-input record looks like the following:

```
<INPUT TYPE=HIDDEN NAME="variable" VALUE="value">
```

There is nothing wrong with using this method but beware that, although supposedly hidden, they are not. Any user can see these using the View Source option found in many browsers. Make sure that the data you store to maintain the state between CGI application invocations is not sensitive. In other words, do not store any PATH, filename, username, or password in these fields.

After taking care of user input properly, and ensuring that system calls are used in a manner that poses minimal threat, you might be wondering if that's all there is to do. No. As mentioned before, ensuring security is never complete. It is an ongoing learning experience. As you learn to cope with one problem, another appears on the horizon. In the following section, I discuss a few common abuses of CGI applications.

User input causes a denial of service

The most common type of security attack is the denial of service (DOS) attack. This type of attack makes a system unavailable or nonresponsive to honest users or paying customers. Such an attack can be mounted on CGI applications, as well.

Most CGI applications take user-input data, perform some processing, and later return some output. Because these programs can be run by anyone via the Web, they are game for DOS attacks. An ill-minded user need only call a CGI application on your Web server with whatever input it needs to process and get it started. Then she can make repetitive calls to the same, or other, CGI applications to make your Web server launch many CGI processes along with child server processes.

This can potentially consume a lot of resources on your server system and make it less responsive to the good-natured users. Unfortunately, this type of attack is easy to launch from an university computer laboratory where there are a lot of computers and a great deal of bandwidth is available. A small Perl script can launch an HTTP request to your server and keep repeating the same request over and over. If this is done from multiple machines, it can bring the Web server system to a crawl. How can you correct this situation?

Unfortunately, there is not much you can do to prevent this; however, once such an incident takes place, you can ban the hosts that were responsible. You can use Apache's <Limit ..> container to deny access to these hosts.

You can also use the RLimitCPU and RLimitMEM directives to fine-tune Apache's CPU and memory usage.

See Chapter 10 for details on using the <Limit ..> container and Chapter 4 for details on the RLimitCPU and RLimitMEM directives.

User input gets posted to your site

Another common form of CGI vandalism rampant on the Web is seen on Web sites that enable any user to write texts that later get posted on the Web site. For example, Web sites that use Web-based CGI discussion groups, or CGI guest books are likely to fall victim to vandalism. If any of your CGI applications enable users to write anything that gets posted on your Web site, make sure you have disabled

HTML tag entries in any input a user can enter. The simplest way to disable HTML in Perl is to replace the less-than symbol (<) with <. This way, when rendered on a Web browser, the actual HTML tag appears instead of it being interpreted by the browser. Following Perl code segment does exactly that:

```
$user_input=~ s/</&lt;/g;
```

Many vandals finds sites that permit writing to guest books, usually entering HTML tags that link to obscene sites or a large image to make each real user suffer the time it takes to load the page. It is also possible to embed a JavaScript in a guest book entry, which could cause serious annoyance to a good user. Replacing the < character with < will take care of all these nuisances.

Reducing CGI risks with wrappers

The best way to reduce CGI-related risks is not to run any CGI applications at all; however, in the days of dynamic Web content, this could be suicide! Perhaps you can centralize all CGI applications in one location and closely monitor their development to ensure they are well written.

In many cases, especially on Internet Service Provider systems, all of the users with Web sites want CGI access. In this case, it might be a good idea to run CGI applications under the user ID of the user who owns the CGI application. By default, CGI applications that Apache runs use the Apache user ID. If you run these applications using the owner's user ID, all possible damage is limited to what the user ID is permitted to access. In other words, a bad CGI application run with a user ID other than the Apache server user ID, can only damage the user's files. This has twofold advantages: the user responsible for the CGI application will now be more careful because the possible damage will affect her content solely. In one shot you get increased user responsibility and awareness and, at the same time, a limited area for potential damage. To run a CGI application using a different user ID than the Apache server, you need a special type of program called a wrapper. A wrapper program will enable you to run a CGI application as the user who owns the file rather than the Apache server user. Some CGI wrappers do other security checks before they run the requested CGI applications. In the following sections, I cover two popular CGI wrappers.

suEXEC

Apache comes with a support application called suEXEC that provides Apache users the ability to run CGI and SSI programs under user IDs that are different from the user ID of Apache.

Note that suEXEC may work only on UNIX or UNIX-like platforms.

suEXEC is a setuid wrapper program that is called when an HTTP request is made for a CGI or SSI program that the administrator designates to run as a user ID other than that of the Apache server. When such a request is made, Apache provides the suEXEC wrapper with the program's name and the user and group IDs. suEXEC runs the program using the given user and group ID.

Before running the CGI or SSI command, the suEXEC wrapper performs a set of tests to ensure that the request is valid. Among other things, this testing procedure ensures that the following things are considered:

✦ It was called with appropriate number of arguments.

✦ It is being executed by a valid user who is permitted to run the wrapper. Typically, only the Apache user will be permitted to run the wrapper.

✦ It passed a CGI application or SSI command (target of the exec command) that resides within Apache Web space. The requested application must reside within the current site's DocumentRoot-specified directory. This directory, or the application itself, cannot be writable by anyone but the owner. The application cannot be a setuid or setgid program, as these types of applications will change the user ID or group ID when run.

✦ It is asked to run the CGI application or SSI command (target of the exec command) using a user ID and group ID that are valid. Note that suEXEC does not permit root user or root group to execute any program. Both the user ID and group ID must be below the user ID and group ID numbers specified during configuration. This allows blocking of system accounts and groups.

Once the above checks are successful, the suEXEC wrapper changes user ID and group ID to the target user and group ID via setuid and setgid calls. The group-access list is also initialized with all groups of which the user is a member. suEXEC cleans the process' environment by establishing a safe execution PATH (defined during configuration), as well as only passing through those variables whose names are listed in the safe environment list (also created during configuration). The suEXEC process then becomes the target CGI application or SSI command and executes.

This may seem like a lot of work — and, it is; but this provides a greater security coefficient as well.

Configuring and installing suEXEC

You will find the suexec.c and suexec.h files in the support subdirectory of the source distribution of Apache. In order to configure and compile suEXEC you will have to follow the steps in the next section.

STEP 1: Edit the suEXEC header file

Edit the suexec.h file as follows:

```
#define HTTPD_USER "www"
```

Change the www to the user ID you use for the User directive in Apache configuration file. This is the only user that will be permitted to run the suEXEC program.

The following macro defines the lowest user ID permitted to be a target user:

```
#define UID_MIN 100
```

In other words, user IDs below this number will not be able to run CGI or SSI commands via suEXEC. You should take a look at your /etc/passwd file and make sure the range you chose does not include the system accounts that are usually lower than 100.

The following macro defines the lowest group ID permitted to be a target group:

```
#define GID_MIN 100
```

In other words, group IDs below this number will not be able to run CGI or SSI commands via suEXEC. You should take a look at your /etc/group file and make sure that the range you chose does not include the system account groups that are usually lower than 100.

The following macro defines the subdirectory under users' home directories where suEXEC executables are be kept:

```
#define USERDIR_SUFFIX "public_html"
```

Note

If the UserDir directive points to a location that is not inside the user home directory pointed by /etc/passwd file, suEXEC does not work.

If you have virtual hosts with a different UserDir for each, you must define all of them to reside in one parent directory, and then name that parent directory here:

```
#define LOG_EXEC "/usr/local/apache/logs/cgi.log"
```

This tells suEXEC where to log each call and error message.

The following macro defines the DocumentRoot for Apache:

```
#define DOC_ROOT "/usr/local/apache/htdocs"
```

All suEXEC executable CGI applications and SSI commands must reside within this directory hierarchy unless they are part of a directory specified by the UserDir directive.

The following macro defines the PATH environment variable that gets executed by suEXEC for CGI applications and SSI commands:

```
#define SAFE_PATH "/usr/local/bin:/usr/bin:/bin"
```

STEP 2: Compile and install suEXEC and Apache

Once the suexec.h file is properly edited, you can compile the suexec program as follows:

```
gcc suexec.c -o suexec
```

This creates the suexec executable. If you plan to keep this executable in any location other than /usr/local/apache/sbin, you have to compile Apache as well. In such a case, edit the httpd.h file and change the macro to point to the fully qualified path of the new suexec location, as follows:

```
#define SUEXEC_BIN "/usr/local/apache/sbin/suexec"
```

Now compile Apache and place the new Apache executable and the suexec executable in proper locations.

STEP 3: Set suEXEC file permissions

Because only the programs run by root user are capable of changing their user IDs, you must set suexec executable's ownership to root as follows:

```
chown root /path/to/suexec
```

It must also have the setuserid bit set as follows:

```
chmod 4711 /path/to/suexec
```

That completes your suEXEC installation. Now let's discuss how you can use it.

Enabling and Disabling suEXEC

Once you have installed both the suexec wrapper and the new Apache executable in the proper location, restart Apache. Do not use the HUP (–1) signal to restart; kill using the TERM signal (–9), and then start Apache again. If Apache is configured properly, you will see a message such as the following on the console:

```
Configuring Apache for use with suexec wrapper.
```

If you do not see this message, makes sure you have installed the wrapper in the appropriate location specified by the SUEXEC_BIN macro in httpd.h file.

On the other hand, if you do see the message, you are all set for suEXEC. Now if you want to try out suEXEC, just put a CGI application in a user's cgi-bin directory and access the application via a URL, such as:

```
http://www.yourdomain.com/~user/cgi-bin/scriptname
```

Apache uses suEXEC for all CGI and SSI commands, such as exec requests, that have the tilde character (~)in them.

Following is an example scenario to help you understand how suEXEC setup works. For the following example, let's assume that on an Apache server called wormhole.nitec.com, UserDir is set to public_html and a user name kabir has a home directory /home/kabir where the public_html directory exists. Let's also assume that test.cgi is in the ~kabir/public_html directory.

```
#!/usr/local/bin/perl
print "Content-type: text/html\n\n";
print "Test of  suEXEC<BR>";
print "PATH = $ENV{PATH}";
exit 0;
```

Now. when I access the following URL:

```
http://wormhole.nitec.com/~kabir/test.cgi
```

it runs as expected. The cgi.log file (specified by LOG_EXEC macro in suexec.h) shows the following:

```
[00:50:15 12-01-98]: uid: (kabir/kabir) gid: (kabir/kabir)
test.cgi
```

This is good. Now let's take a look at what ls –l shows for ~kabir/public_html/test.cgi:

```
-rwxr-x-r-x  1 kabir   kabir  85 Jan 12 00:50 test.cgi
```

Let's see what happens when I change the ownership of the script to root user using the following command:

```
chown root test.cgi
```

If I try to run the script again I get a server error and the log file shows the following line:

```
[01:01:30 12-01-98]: target uid/gid (500/500) mismatch with
directory (500/500) or program (0/500)
```

Here the program is owned by user ID 0, and the group is still kabir (500) so the suEXEC refuses to run it. As you can see, suEXEC is doing what it is supposed to do. To ensure that suEXEC is going to run the test.cgi program in other directory, I created a cgi-bin directory in ~kabir/public_html and put test.cgi in that directory. After determining that the user and group ownerships of the new directory and file are set to user ID kabir and group ID kabir, I accessed the script using:

```
http://wormhole.nitec.com/~kabir/cgi-bin/test.cgi
```

It runs as expected. Note that this little script permitted me to do the value of the PATH variable as another check. . Because I have set up the value of safe path using SAFE_PATH macro in suexec.h, I can ensure that PATH is set exactly as I intended. It is. You should do similar checks to make sure your suEXEC setup is working.

If you have virtual hosts and want to run the CGI programs and/or SSI commands using suEXEC, you must use User and Group directives inside the <VirtualHost ...> container. Set these directives to user and group IDs other than those the Apache server is currently using. If only one, or neither, of these directives is specified for a <VirtualHost> container, the server user ID or group ID is assumed.

For security and efficiency reasons, all suexec requests must remain within either a top-level document root for virtual host requests, or one top-level personal document root for userdir requests. For example, if you have four virtual hosts configured, you would need to structure all of your virtual host document roots off of one main Apache document hierarchy to take advantage of suEXEC for virtual hosts.

Now let's take a look at another popular CGI wrapper called CGIWrap.

CGIWrap

CGIWrap is like the suEXEC program in that it permits users to use CGI applications without compromising the security of the Web server. CGI programs are run with the file owner's permission. In addition, CGIWrap performs several security checks on the CGI application, and will not be executed if any checks fail.

CGIWrap is written by Nathan Neulinger and the latest version of CGIWrap is available from the primary ftp site on ftp://ftp.cc.umr.edu. The CD-ROM accompanying this book includes the latest version of the CGIWrap distribution as well.

CGIWrap is used via a URL in an HTML document. As distributed, CGIWrap is configured to run user scripts that are located in the ~/public_html/cgi-bin/ directory.

Configuring and installing

CGIwrap is distributed as a gzip compressed tar file. You can uncompress it using gzip, and extract it using the tar utility.

Run the Configure script, and it will prompt you to answer many questions. Most of these questions are self-explanatory; however, there is a feature in this wrapper that differs from suEXEC. It enables you to create allow and deny files that can be used to restrict access to your CGI applications. Both of these files have the same format, as shown in the following:

```
User ID
mailto:Username@subnet1/mask1,subnet2/mask2...
```

You can either have a single username (not numeric user ID), or a user mailto:ID@subnet/mask line where one or more subnet/mask pairs can be defined, for example:

```
mailto:Myuser@1.2.3.4/255.255.255.255
```

If this line is found in the allow file (file name is specified by you), the user kabir's CGI applications are permitted to be run by hosts that belong in the 206.171.50.0 network with netmask 255.255.255.0. This is much like the host-based access control discussed in Chapter 10.

Once you run the Configure script, you must run the make utility to create the CGIWrap executable.

Enabling CGIWrap

To use the wrapper application, copy the CGIWrap executable to the user's cgi-bin directory. Note that this directory must match what you have specified in the configuration process. The simplest way to get things going is to keep the ~username/public_html/cgi-bin type of directory structure for the CGI application directory.

Once you have copied the CGIWrap executable, change the ownership and permission bits as follows:

```
chown root CGIWrap
chmod 4755 CGIWrap
```

Create hard link or symbolic link nph-cgiwrap, nph-cgiwrapd, cgiwrapd to CGIWrap in the cgi-bin directory as follows:

```
ln [-s] CGIWrap cgiwrapd
ln [-s] CGIWrap nph-cgiwrap
ln [-s] CGIWrap nph-cgiwrapd
```

Note that on my Apache server, I only specify .the cgi extension as a CGI application and, therefore, I renamed my CGIWrap executable to cgiwrap.cgi to get it working. If you have similar restrictions you might try this approach or make a link instead.

Now you can execute a CGI application as follows:

www.yourdomain.com/cgi-bin/cgiwrap/username/ scriptname

To access user kabir's CGI application test.cgi on the wormhole.nitec.com site, for example, I would have to use the following:

```
http://wormhole.nitec.com/cgi-bin/cgiwrap/kabir/test.cgi
```

If you wish to see debugging output for your CGI, specify cgiwrapd instead of CGIWrap, as in the following URL:

```
http://www.yourdomain.com/cgi-bin/cgiwrapd/username/scriptname
```

If the script is an nph- style script, you must run it using the following URL:

```
www.yourdomain.com/cgi-bin/nph-cgiwrap/username/scriptname
```

Server Side Includes Risks and Solutions

Many administrators consider Server Side Includes (SSI) as much a security risk as CGI applications. This is true in some ways, and in some ways it is not.

If you run external applications using SSI commands such as exec, the security risk is virtually the same as the CGI applications. However, you can disable this command very easily under Apache, using the Options directive as follows:

```
<Directory />
Options IncludesNOEXEC
Order deny,allow
Deny from all
</Directory>
```

This disables exec and includes SSI commands everywhere on your Web space; however, you can enable these commands whenever necessary by defining a narrower-scoping directory container. Following is an example:

```
<Directory />
Options IncludesNOEXEC
Order deny,allow
Deny from all
</Directory>

<Directory /risky>
Options Include
Order deny,allow
Deny from all
</Directory>
```

This configuration segment disables the exec command everywhere but the /risky directory.

Basic HTTP Authentication Risks

Another inherent security risk is in the HTTP protocol and basic authentication. Passwords used in this type of authentication travel the network in Uuencoded format. Because Uuencoding is not an encryption scheme, it does not make the password safe to travel over networks and that is where the risk emerges.

In order for a hacker to decode a Uuencoded password, a network packet sniffer must find the exact packet containing the password among all of the IP packets. Although this is not something that a casual hacker would want to undertake, it is not impossible.

The current form of HTTP authentication, therefore, should be considered insecure, and it is not recommended for critical authentication. If you need strong authentication, you will likely have to develop custom solutions that encrypt the password before it travels from the user to the server. You might want to look into Secured Socket Layer (SSL) for such purposes. SSL is covered in Chapter 15.

Security Policy Considerations

An administrative security policy identifies practices that are vital to achieving robust network security. If you do not yet have one, consider adding some of the following things to an administrative security policy to will help you get started.

Log everything

The server log files record information on the server's behavior in response to each request. Analysis of the log can provide both business information (for instance which Web pages are most popular) and security information. Make sure you set up Apache to log both access and errors. With the help of log files you will be able to track who is accessing what. Get in the habit of browsing logs whenever you can — if you notice anything unusual, take a closer look. Your error log is probably the most important log to monitor closely.

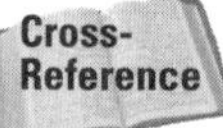

For more information on logging, see Chapter 11.

Maintain an authoritative copy of your Web site(s)

Keep the authoritative copy of your Web site on a more secure host. If the integrity of the public information on your Web server is ever compromised, you need an authoritative copy from which to restore it. Typically, the authoritative copy is kept on a host that is accessible to the Web site administrator (and, perhaps, to the people in your organization who are responsible for the creation and maintenance of Web content). This is likely on your organization's internal network.

In order to ensure security, you might use robust cryptographic-checksum technologies to generate a checksum for each file. Keep authoritative copies of files and checksums on write-protected or read-only media stored in a physically secure location. You can use MD5 encryption to generate cryptographic checksums for your files.

Administer your site from the Web host console

You should administer your Web site from the Web host console. Doing this eliminates the need for network traffic between the Web server and the administrator's workstation. There are, however, many situations when this is not feasible (such as in organizations where the Web server is not easily accessible by the administrator). When you must do remote administration, make sure you use a strong authentication scheme to login to the Web server. If you use a Web-based administrative tool, make sure it does not use basic HTTP authentication. In other words, you want to make sure the passwords are not traveling from your workstation to the Web server in any nonencrypted format. Also, you need to configure the Web server system to accept connection from a single host within your internal network.

Be aware of public domain CGI applications

Whenever using a public domain CGI, make sure you or someone in your organization (or an outside consultant) has complete understanding of the code. Never get a copy of an application from a nonauthentic source. Search USENET to see if anyone has discovered problems with the application you intend to install on your Web server. If possible, install the application in a staging server and test it yourself. Keep monitoring your log files during the test period. If the application uses mail services, monitor the mail log as well.

Compare contents

Intruders often substitute, modify, and damage files on the systems to which they have gained access. In order to gain illegal access to the system again, they often modify system programs that appear to function normally but also include back doors for the intruders. They also modify system log files to remove traces of their activities. Intruders may even create new files on your systems.

It is, therefore, a good idea to compare the attributes and contents of files and directories to the authoritative copy. If you have created cryptographic checksums for files, you can compare the checksums of the current and authentic copy to determine if any difference exists.

Using MD5 to verify the integrity of file contents

The MD5 program generates a unique, 128-bit cryptographic message-digest value derived from the contents of a file. This value is considered a highly reliable fingerprint that can be used to verify the integrity of the file's contents. If even a single bit value in the file is modified, the MD5 checksum for the file will change. Forgery of a file, in a way that causes MD5 to generate the same result as that for the original file, is considered extremely difficult.

A set of MD5 checksums for critical system, application, and data files provides a compact way of storing information for use in periodic integrity checks of those files.

Details for the MD5 cryptographic-checksum program are provided in RFC 1321. Source code and additional information are available via FTP from the following site:

ftp://info.cert.org/pub/tools/md5

Tip

Do not use the UNIX sum program to generate checksum because it is not reliable.

If any changes cannot be attributed to authorized activity, you should consider your system compromised and take prompt actions. In case the change is found to be valid, re-create your authoritative copy and checksum.

Is There Hope?

In the midst of all this discussion of security and risks, it is easy to become depressed, considering there is no clear-cut answer to the security question. I personally feel that, with an appropriate dose of awareness and the ability to undertake countermeasures, it is possible to win the battle.

According to Dr. John D. Howard, author of An Analysis of Security Incidents on the Internet 1989-1995, with the exception of denial-of-service attacks, security incidents were found to be decreasing relative to the size of the Internet. His research is based on the incidents reported to CERT. It was estimated that the probability of server security incidents that go unreported is anywhere between 0 to 4 percent. His research also indicates that a typical Internet domain is involved in no more than one incident per year.

A total of 4,567 incidents over this 7-year period was taken into account. Out of the total reported incidents, 5.9 percent were false alarms. Most of the incidents (89.3 percent) were unauthorized-access incidents that included 27.7 percent root account break-ins, 24.1 percent user account break-ins, and 37.6 percent access attempts.

Relative to the growth in Internet hosts, each of these access categories was found to be decreasing over the period of this research: root-level break-ins at a rate around 19 percent less than the increase in Internet hosts, account-level break-ins at a rate around 11 percent less, and access attempts at a rate around 17 percent less.

Summary

You should have enough know-how to tackle Web security risks. In this chapter, I discussed various risks and pointed out a few solutions; however, as you might have already realized, Web security risks won't ever be tamed to the point that we all (except for the bad guys, hackers, and crackers) feel so comfortable we let some magic security software take care of it all.

Web security is an ongoing fight against the bad guys — the software bugs, the password thugs, and many other nasty entities. So be it, as long as you have your side prepared, you will not lose the fight. You also have organizations, such as CERT, out there on your side. The best defense against security risks is to be prepared and increase awareness of the risks involved.

In the next chapter, you learn how to use a popular CGI scripting language, Perl, with Apache.

✦ ✦ ✦

Implementing Advanced Features

P A R T

IV

✦ ✦ ✦ ✦

In This Part

✦ ✦ ✦ ✦

CHAPTER 13

The Perl in Apache

In This Chapter

What is mod_perl?

Using mod_perl

Writing Perl module for mod_perl

Porting existing CGI scripts for mod_perl

Integrating mod_perl with server side include (mod_include)

Configuring Apache using Perl

What you should know about using mod_perl

Over the years, Perl has become the most popular programming language for developing custom programming solutions for the Web. It is used heavily in developing CGI scripts. However, because it is an interpreted language, it inherits the start-up penalties of an interpreter. The Perl interpreter, perl, must be loaded for each invocation of a Perl script. This makes Perl scripts' start-ups a bit slower then applications that are compiled binary executables.

In Chapter 9, I discuss how you can use FastCGI to speed up Perl-based CGI scripts. Another way to solve the same problem would be to use mod_perl — the fruit of the Apache/Perl integration project. mod_perl offers a lot more functionality than just speeding up CGI scripts. In this chapter I will primarily discuss how you can use mod_perl with your Apache server.

Understanding mod_perl

One of the primary goals of the Apache/Perl integration project was to bring the full power of the Perl programming language into the Apache server. This resulted in the development of mod_perl. It is compiled and linked together with Apache and Perl to provide an object-oriented Perl interface to the server's C language API. This allows Perl programmers to write Apache modules in Perl. An Apache-Perl module may step in during the handler, header parser, URI translation, authentication, authorization, access, type check, fix-up, logger, and cleanup stages of a request.

As mentioned before, when you use mod_perl, you have the full power of the Apache API in your hand. Now let's explore how this power comes down to your hand.

When you update Perl and install mod_perl on your system, you actually create an object-oriented Perl interface for the Apache server API. According to the Apache API, the Apache request object holds all the information needed by the server to service the request. How does your script get ahold of such an important object? It is handed down to the PerlHandler as a parameter. For example:

```
<Location /perl/>
SetHandler  perl-script
PerlHandler Apache::Registry
Options ExecCGI
</Location>
```

In the above configuration the PerlHandler is the Apache::Registry module. This module must implement a method called handler, which will receive the Apache request object as a reference. This allows the module to do anything that could be done using Apache server API.

Apache modules written in mod_perl can do just about anything Apache modules written in C can. In addition, the persistent interpreter embedded in the server avoids the overhead of starting an external interpreter program and the additional Perl start-up time. For example, it is not necessary to start a separate process, as is often done with Web-server extensions. Extension mechanisms such as the Common Gateway Interface (CGI) can be completely replaced with Perl code that handles the response generation phase of request processing. Mod_perl includes a general-purpose module for this purpose (Apache::Registry) that can run existing perl CGI scripts transparently.

Now that you know what mod_perl can do for you, I'll mention the modules available for mod_perl and then tell you how to set up mod_perl.

Installing mod_perl

Many Apache/Perl modules are being developed by developers all around the world; you can keep track of the latest modules at http://perl.apache.org/src/apache-modlist.html. Here's a list of a few Apache/Perl modules currently available for mod_perl:

- ✦ Apache::Registry — Runs unaltered CGI scripts
- ✦ Apache::Status — Embedded interpreter runtime status
- ✦ Apache::Embperl — Embeds Perl code in HTML documents
- ✦ Apache::SSI — Implements server-side includes in Perl
- ✦ Apache::DBI — Maintains persistent DBI connections
- ✦ Apache::DCELogin — Obtains a DCE Login context
- ✦ Apache::AuthenDBI — Authenticates via Perl DBI/DBD::*

- Apache::AuthzAge — Authorizes based on age
- Apache::AccessLimitNum — Limits user access by number of requests
- Apache::Constants — Constants defined in httpd.h
- Apache::MsqlProxy — Translates URIs into mSQL database queries

mod_perl is not distributed with the standard Apache distribution. You will have to install it. But before you can install it, make sure you have met the following requirements.

Installation requirements

You will need to have the Apache source code, Perl version 5.003 or higher, and the latest mod_perl source code. You can get the latest Perl source distribution from www.perl.com. If you haven't installed the latest Perl already, you should do that before you proceed any further.

Installing Perl is as easy as uncompressing the source and running the Configure script. The Configure script will prompt you for a lot of information; if you are unsure, just accept the defaults. Once you have compiled the latest Perl using the command:

```
make install
```

make sure you test the version number using the following command:

```
perl -v
```

If the version number matches the version you just compiled, you are all set.

You should already have the Apache source from the Apache Web site and the mod_perl source is available from http://perl.apache.org.

I have also included the latest (at the time of this writing) mod_perl source distribution in the CD-ROM. However, make sure that you are using the latest release version of all software.

Once you have obtained the mod_perl source distribution, install the source in the same directory level as your Apache source distribution. For example, if you have installed the Apache source in the /usr/local/src/Apache directory, then install mod_perl source in /usr/local/src such that you end up with a directory called /usr/local/src/mod_perl_directory.

Then uncompress the mod_perl-1_10.tar.gz source in the /usr/local/src directory using the following command:

```
zcat mod_perl_1_10.tar.gz | tar xf -
```

This creates /usr/local/src/mod_perl-1.10 directory containing mod_perl.

Compiling and installing mod_perl

Now that you have mod_perl on your machine, you are ready to compile and install it. To compile the mod_perl source, change the directory to the mod_perl source directory and run:

```
perl Makefile.PL
```

If you have installed the mod_perl source at the same directory level as the Apache source, you should accept the default answers to all the questions as it prompts you. This will create the Makefiles for both mod_perl and Apache. The next step is to run the make command as follows:

```
make
```

Once make is done building the new Apache binary, you can test it by running the following command:

```
make test
```

This starts an Apache server on port 8529 which runs under the UID and GID of the perl Makefile.PL process. If for any reason this port is already used on your system, you should run the perl Makefile.PL command with a port address as follows:

```
perl Makefile.PL PORT=nnnn
```

Here nnnn is a port number (greater than 1024) not used currently.

If the tests are successful, you will see a message such as "All tests successful." You are now ready to install mod_perl using the following command:

```
make install
```

You will now need to replace your existing httpd executable with the latest mod_perl version of httpd, which is sitting in your Apache source directory. From the Apache source directory, run the following command:

```
./httpd -v
```

This should provide you with the version number of the Apache server and it should mention the mod_perl version as well. If it does not, try the following command to see if mod_perl.c is listed in the output:

```
./httpd -l
```

If it is not, you will have to carefully start over with your installation procedure.

It might be a good idea to rename your existing httpd to something like httpd.old and then move the new httpd in its place. This way, if anything goes wrong you can always restore the previous version.

Running Perl CGI Scripts via mod_perl

Now you are ready to make use of mod_perl. Let's first discuss how you can take advantage of mod_perl to speed up your existing Perl-based CGI scripts.

You might remember from earlier chapters that to get CGI scripts running, you needed to define a script alias directory using the ScriptAlias directive. However, when using mod_perl to run CGI scripts you cannot use ScriptAlias. Instead, you will need to create a regular alias using the Alias directive. For example, for a Web site called apache.nitec.com with CGI scripts in the /www/apache/public/cgi-bin directory, you can create an Alias called /perl/ as follows:

```
Alias /perl/ /www/apache/public/cgi-bin/
```

Now using the <Location . . . > container, you need to set up the following:

```
<Location /alias-to-cgi-script/>
SetHandler  perl-script
PerlHandler Apache::Registry
Options ExecCGI
</Location>
```

For our example, this would look like:

```
<Location /perl/>
SetHandler  perl-script
PerlHandler Apache::Registry
Options ExecCGI
</Location>
```

You should also have a ScriptAlias directive as follows:

```
ScriptAlias /cgi-bin/  /www/apache/public/cgi-bin/
```

Then you can access an application called printenv.cgi either through the traditional CGI method using the URL:

```
http://apache.nitec.com/cgi-bin/printenv/cgi
```

or you can use mod_perl's Apache::Registry module using the URL:

```
http://apache.nitec.com/perl/printenv.cgi
```

You might wonder how you can tell the difference between the two calls. In the mod_perl version the standard CGI variable GATEWAY_INTERFACE prints "CGI-Perl/1.1" instead of "CGI/1.1." Also a new variable MOD_PERL is set in the mod_perl version of the call. This variable is set to the value of the version of mod_perl being used. So if you needed to detect how your Perl script is being run by Apache, you can use a code segment such as the following:

```
If(exists $ENV{'MOD_PERL'}){
        print "Running as a mod_perl application";
      }
else{
        print "Running as a CGI script";
      }
```

The Apache::Registry module is used to run unaltered CGI scripts under mod_perl. When the following URL is requested, this module reads the printenv.cgi script and inserts it into the body of a Perl subroutine and executes it:

```
http://apache.nitec.com/perl/printenv.cgi
```

Each Apache child server process will compile the subroutine once and store it in memory for future use. If the script gets changed in the meantime, it will be reloaded and compiled and stored in memory again.

However, you can preload your Perl scripts at server start-up. mod_perl provides you with two directives: PerlModule and PerlScript. You can use these two directives to load scripts at start-up.

To load a Perl module at server start-up you can use:

```
PerlModule ModuleName . . .
```

For example:

```
PerlModule Apache::SSI  Foo::Bar Some::Other
```

This loads the SSI, Bar, and Other modules from the Apache, Foo, and Some modules. Note that using the PerlModule directive you can only load up to 10 modules. If you need more, you can use the PerlScript directive.

The PerlScript directive has the following syntax:

```
PerlScript /path/to/a/Perl/script
```

This will load a Perl script at server start-up. If you needed to load a lot of modules at start-up you can write a script such as:

```
use CGI;
use LWP::UserAgent ();
1;
```

This script loads the CGI and UserAgent modules. If you keep your modules in a location other than the default Perl module directory, you will have to specify the module location using:

```
use lib qw(/path/to/your/modules);
```

Here /path/to/your/modules should be replaced with the appropriate fully qualified path name of the module directory.

To make use of your Perl module you will have to use the PerlHandler directive as shown earlier. For example, say you have a PerlModule line as follows:

```
PerlModule Apache::Test
```

You want to use this module for servicing the URL:

```
http://www.myserver.com/test/
```

You can then define an Alias as follows:

```
Alias /test/    /somewhere/some/directory/
```

Then you can define a <Location . . .> container as follows:

```
<Location /test>
SetHandler perl-script
PerlHandler Apache::Test
</Location>
```

This tells mod_perl that you want to use the Apache::Test module for handling all requests that come for the specified URL.

How does mod_perl know what method to call in the Test.pm module? By default the PerlHandler directive expects a subroutine name as the argument. If the argument is not a subroutine name, it assumes it is a module name and calls a special method called handler. So for the PerlHandler line, when a request comes for the specified URL, mod_perl will call the method Apache::Test::handler. If this method is not defined in the module, there will be an error.

You can always use a different method name as long as you specify it in the PerlHandler line. For example, if you had a method called doit in the Test.pm module and wanted to invoke this method instead of handler, you can set the PerlHandler line as follows:

```
PerlHandler Apache::Test::doit
```

This will have mod_perl invoke the doit method instead of handler.

Previously, when I showed you how to use the Apache::Registry module to turn your CGI scripts into mod_perl-based scripts, for each request mod_perl launched the Apache:Registry:handler method, which in turn runs the script requested.

Issues with Porting Perl CGI scripts

When porting an existing Perl-based CGI script to mod_perl, make sure you pay attention to the following issues.

If you are using the latest Perl (version 5.004 or above) interpreter, it is likely that most of your CGI scripts can run under mod_perl without any major modifications. However, if you are using an older version of Perl, you might have trouble using the built-in print and read functions. I strongly suggest that you upgrade Perl.

By default, mod_perl does not send any HTTP headers; however, you can use the following directive to change this:

```
PerlSendHeader On
```

Now the response line and HTTP headers will be sent. However, your script will still have to send the following content-type header:

```
print "Content-type: text/html\n\n";
```

If you are using CGI.pm or CGI::Switch and printing the header using the $query➪header() method, you do not need to set the PerlSendHeader to On.

On the other hand, when converting non-parsed header Perl scripts (scripts with the nph- prefix) to mod_perl based scripts, you will need to force an output flush after every write or print on the output file-handle. This can be done by setting the $| variable to a nonzero value as follows:

```
local $| = 1;
```

Note that if you normally set the PerlSendHeader to On, you will have to disable it for nph- files. You can use the following configuration to do that.

```
<FilesMatch */nph-*>
PerlSendHeader Off
</FilesMatch>
```

Writing a Perl Module for mod_perl

Now that you are aware of the issues involved in using existing CGI scripts in mod_perl, you can start developing new mod_perl-based scripts. In order to keep the example simple, I will show you how to create a very simple Perl module (an object-oriented Perl script) that really doesn't do anything but print out the environment variables. This Perl module is called Test.pm and is shown in Listing 13-1.

Listing 13-1: **Test.pm**

package Apache::Test;

```
# Tell Perl to show warning when a variable is used without
# a declaration. This is done using 'use strict.'
use strict;


sub handler {
#
# Purpose: this method gets called by mod_perl. So this is
# really the entry point into this module. In other words,
# this is the traditional main function.
#

# Assign the request object (passed as a parameter) to a
# local variable.
    my $r = shift;

# Local temporary variable
    my $key;

# Assign a local associative array variable to the hash
# returned by the request object variable's cgi_env()
# method
#
    my %ENV = $r->cgi_env;

# Set the content-type of the output to text/html
#
    $r->content_type("text/html");

# Print out the HTTP headers
    $r->send_http_header;

# Now loop through the %ENV array and print out the
# key=value  pair for each environment variable.
#
    foreach $key (keys %ENV){
      $r->print("$key = $ENV{$key} <BR>.");
      }

# Done
    return 1;
}
```

(continued)

Listing 13-1 (continued)

```
# The following line is required for a Perl module.
1;
__END__
```

In this example there is only one subroutine called handler. When you specify a configuration line such as the following:

```
<Location /test>
SetHandler perl-script
PerlHandler Apache::Test
</Location>
```

the handler method gets called whenever Apache receives a request containing /test/. If you plan on messing around with Apache request processing, make sure that you have a clear understanding of the Apache API. There are several stages of a request where the Apache API allows a module to step in and do something. The Apache documentation will tell you all about those stages and what your modules can do. By default, these hooks are disabled at compile time; see the INSTALL document for information on enabling these hooks.

There are some special programming concerns for CGI programmers developing mod_perl scripts. First let's look at why mod_perl scripts require careful programming, and then we'll look at some special programming issues for writing mod_perl scripts.

Many CGI developers do not spend time cleaning up their code. This is because a CGI script runs for a short time and disappears after the request is complete. But mod_perl run scripts stay cached in memory for a long time, and therefore better programming practices are needed in developing these scripts. Here are some guidelines that might help you in this regard.

Always write script in strict mode using use strict. This will allow you to write clean scripts that do not have undefined variables lying around wasting memory or creating other confusion. Also do not forget to use the -w switch. If you do not yet know why you should use -w, I suggest you read the man page for Perl itself. You will notice that it is suggested over and over again. Here is a quote from the Perl man page:

> Whenever you get mysterious behavior, try the -w switch!!! Whenever you don't get mysterious behavior, try using -w anyway.

While it is not required, it is highly recommended; it will save you more time in the long run.

You should also be vary careful about using user input data. You can turn on Perl's taint checking using the -T switch or you can set the PerlTaintCheck directive to On in one of the Apache configuration files. Read the cgi_to_mod_perl man page that comes with the mod_perl distribution.

Also note that system calls such as system(), exec(), open PIPE, |program, and so on will not work by default. If you want to use these calls, you will have to have sfio support in Perl. Also, the exit() function cannot be used. Instead, you can use the Apache::exit() method. Apache::exit() automatically overrides the built-in exit() for Apache::Registry scripts.

Apart from these general pointers, there are some programming practice related issues that need to be considered when developing scripts for mod_perl. These issues are discussed in the following sections.

Using CGI.pm and CGI::* modules

If you use the CGI.pm module in your CGI scripts, make sure you have the very latest version. Versions earlier than 2.36 will not work with mod_perl. If you have the latest Perl version and the latest CGI.pm, you can use the use CGI command to make use of the module in your CGI script as usual. However, if you are using an older version of Perl, you will have to use the use CGI::Switch() command so that the I/O is handled via the Apache class methods.

The other CGI modules (CGI::*) can only be used with the latest version of Perl (5.004 or higher.)

Note

> If you use the CGI::Request module and the SendHeaders() method, be sure to call your $req_obj➪cgi➪done when you are finished with a request.

Your script will only work from the command line if you use the latest CGI::Switch or CGI.pm and the latest Perl.

Using Apache DB/DBM authentication modules

If you use mod_auth_dbm or mod_auth_db, you might run into problems if the order in which the dbm libraries are stored in Perl's Config.pm is not appropriate. To determine the order of the libraries, use the following command:

```
Perl -V:libs
```

By default, these libraries are linked with Perl and remembered by the Config module. When mod_perl is configured with Apache, the ExtUtils::Embed module returns these libraries to be linked with httpd so Perl extensions will work under mod_perl. However, the order in which these libraries are stored in Config.pm may confuse Apache DB/DBM modules. If -lgdbm or -ldb is before -lndbm, for example:

```
libs='-lgdbm -ldb -lndbm -ldl -lm -lc'
```

modify Perl's Config.pm module and move -lgdbm and -ldb to the end of the list. If you are not sure which Config.pm to modify, use the following short script to determine the location:

```
#!/usr/local/bin/perl
use Config;
print "Your Config.pm directory is" $Config{archlibexp}\n";
exit 0;
```

The mod_perl interface is smart enough to detect changes in a script after it is loaded. So if you modify a script after you have already loaded it via mod_perl, you do not need to restart Apache. However, if you make changes to a Perl library or a module that has been pulled into your script via the use or require facility, mod_perl will not automatically reload it. In such a case you might want to use the Apache::StartINC module.

Another important note is that when you include the same Perl library (not a Perl module) in multiple scripts that you want mod_perl to run via the Apache::Registry facility, only one of them will work. This is because when a required library is pulled into a script, its subroutines and variables become part of the current package. In a typical CGI environment, this is the package main, however, under the Apache::Registry facility the script is compiled into an unique package name (based on the URL). This means that only one script will be able to use the required library; mod_perl will not compile the same library for all the other scripts that require it.

The easiest way to solve this problem is to rewrite the Perl library into a object-oriented Perl module. Because a Perl module has a package definition that gives it its own name space, the required module (which used to be a Perl library) can be used by any script.

Read the perlmodlib man page, the perlmod man page, and related perl documentation, and rework your required file into a Perl module that defines a method interface. However, if rewriting the library to turn it into an object-oriented Perl module is not possible, look into exporting the functions and variables features of Perl.

Also note that if you wish to use a module that is normally linked static with your Perl, it must be listed in static_ext in Perl's Config.pm to be linked with httpd during the mod_perl build.

mod_perl also restricts the use of special tokens (names). As mentioned before, scripts run under Apache::Registry are not run in the default package (main). The namespace used is based on the requested URI. Therefore, these scripts cannot contain special tokens such as the __END__ token to denote the logical end of the script. The __DATA__ token is also not permitted.

Server Side Include and mod_perl Integration

So far I have talked about how you can develop CGI scripts that can take advantage of mod_perl. How about the Perl scripts that you use as Server Side Include (SSI) scripts? They can also take advantage of mod_perl features.

mod_perl can be well integrated with the SSI module mod_include. All you need to do is either make sure that when you build the Apache binary the following line is present in the configuration file:

```
EXTRA_CFLAGS=-DUSE_PERL_SSI -I. `perl -MExtUtils::Embed -ccopts`
```

or when you build mod_perl, make sure you use the following command:

```
perl Makefile.PL PERL_SSI=1
```

Once you have built Apache, you can take advantage of mod_perl for your Perl SSI scripts. Instead of using an SSI command such as the following:

```
<!—#exec cmd="/some_directory_alias/your_perlscript" —>
```

you can use the following in your SSI page:

```
<!—#perl sub="Apache::Include"
arg="/some_directory_alias/your_perlscript" —>
```

However, you will have to use the following line in the httpd.conf configuration file to pre-load the script:

```
PerlScript /path/to/your_perlscript
```

The value of the sub key in the preceding sample SSI call can be a subroutine name, a module name, a method name of a class, or an anonymous subroutine call (sub {}). For example:

```
<!—#perl sub="Apache::Test" —>
```

This will call the Test::handler method by default as long as the Test.pm is pre-loaded with PerlModule or by some other means at server start-up.

If you wanted to call a method other than the default handler, you should specify the method name as well. For example, if you want to call the doit method instead of the handler method, change the previous SSI call to the following:

```
<!—#perl sub="Apache::Test::doit" —>
```

If arguments need to be passed to the above method, you can use:

```
<!—#perl sub="Apache::Test::doit" arg="argument1"
arg="argument2" —>
```

to pass 'argument1' and 'argument2' as the arguments to the method. Note that the very first argument will always be the request object reference.

Using Perl to Configure Apache

Apart from the usual advantages of having mod_perl for your CGI or SSI scripts, there is an unusual feature of mod_perl that devoted Perl programmers and Apache administrators will enjoy—the ability to write Apache server configuration in Perl.

You can include a <Perl> container inside an Apache configuration file as follows:

```
<Perl>
# your Perl code  goes here
1;
</Perl>
```

The very last line (containing the 1;) is required. Your code can be any Perl script. The code in a <Perl> container gets compiled in a special package and mod_perl communicates the configuration information to the Apache core configuration module. Before you can use this feature, you will have to make sure you built Apache and mod_perl properly. To configure this feature for your Apache server, configure mod_perl as follows:

```
perl Makefile.PL PERL_SECTIONS=1
```

Once you have configured and recompiled mod_perl and Apache, you are ready to write Perl code in Apache configuration files. Next I'll discuss the syntax used to describe the configuration.

The directives that take a single value are represented as scalar variables. For example:

```
User httpd
```

This User directive takes a single string value and therefore can be written as:

```
<Perl>
$User = "httpd";
1;
</Perl>
```

Here is an example configuration:

```
<Perl>
$User = "httpd";
$Group = "httpd";
$ServerAdmin = 'kabir@nitec.com';
$MinSpareServers = 5;
$MaxSpareServers = 5;
$MaxClients = 40;
1;
</Perl>
```

The directives that require multiple values can be represented as lists. For example:

PerlModule Apache::TestOne Apache::TestTwo can be represented as:

```
@PerlModule = qw(Apache::TestOne Apache::TestTwo );
```

Containers are represented using hash, for example:

```
<VirtualHost 206.171.50.50>
ServerName www.nitec.com
ServerAdmin kabir@nitec.com
</VirtualHost>
```

this can be represented as the following:

```
$VirtualHost{"206.171.60.60"} = {
        ServerName => 'www.nitec.com',
        ServerAdmin => 'kabir@nitec.com'
       }
```

A slightly more involved example follows:

```
$Location{"/some_dir_alias/"} = {
     AuthUserFile => '/www/nitec/secret/htpasswd',
     AuthType => 'Basic',
     AuthName => 'Subscribers Only Access',
     DirectoryIndex => [qw(welcome.html welcome.htm)],
     Limit => {
         METHODS => POST GET',
         require => 'user reader'
     }
 };
```

You can define other containers such as <Directory>, <Files>, and so on in a similar manner. Note that in order for the <Perl> containers to work, you must define the PerlScript directive in your configuration file. If you do not need to load any Perl scripts, to take advantage of the <Perl> containers you can always set the PerlScript directive as follows:

```
PerlScript /dev/null
```

In my opinion, you should use the <Perl> containers in your configuration files only if you have one or both of the following requirements:

✦ You love Perl so much that you can't imagine not using <Perl> in Apache configuration files now that you know you can.

✦ You run multiple Apache servers and want to create a single set of configuration files that can be used in all of your Apache server systems. (This is where I would use this feature.) A scripted configuration is immensely flexible. It can read external files, use loops to automate configuration, and more. Such a configuration is only limited by the programming ability of the Apache administrator.

If you are doing it for the first reason, you should already be on your way writing fancy Perl scripts in your configuration files. However, if you want to do it for the second reason and are not yet clear how this feature can help you, let's look at an example case.

Let's say that you have three Web server systems: host_a, host_b, and host_c. Let's also say that host_a is more powerful than host_b, and host_b is more powerful than host_c. You want to define a <Perl> container that will allow you to create a single configuration for all three hosts. Here is an example of such a httpd.conf file:

```
<Perl>
# Get the host name using the UNIX hostname utility and store
it
# in the $thisHost variable.
my $thisHost = '/bin/hostname';
if ($thisHost =~ /host_a/) {
      # configuration for host_a goes here
      $MinSpareServers = 10;
      $MaxSpareServers = 20;
      $StartServers   = 30;
      $MaxClients     = 256;
      }
elsif ($thisHost =~ /host_b/) {
      # configuration for host_b goes here
      $MinSpareServers = 5;
      $MaxSpareServers = 10;
      $StartServers   = 10;
      $MaxClients     = 50;
      }
else {
      # configuration for host_c goes here
      $MinSpareServers = 3;
      $MaxSpareServers = 5;
      $StartServers   = 5;
      $MaxClients     = 30;
        }
1;
</Perl>
```

In order to make this example more interesting, let's also say that you have different virtual hosts for each of the three hosts and would like to configure them in an elegant manner. Take a look at this example:

```
<Perl>
# Get the host name using the UNIX hostname utility and store
it in the $thisHost variable.

my $thisHost = '/bin/hostname';
my $thisDomain = 'mydomain.com';
my @vHosts = ();

my $anyHost;

if ($thisHost =~ /(host_a)/) {
        # configuration for host_a goes here
    @vHosts = qw(gaia, athena, romeo, juliet, shazam);
        }
elsif ($thisHost =~ /host_b/) {
        # configuration for host_b goes here
    @vHosts = qw(catbart, ratbart, dilbert);
        }
else {
        # configuration for host_c goes here
    @vHosts = qw(lonelyhost);
    }

for $anyHost (@vHosts) {
        %{$VirtualHost{"$anyHost.$domainName"}} = {
            "ServerName" => "$anyHost.$domainName",
            "ServerAdmin" => "webmaster\@$anyHost.$domainName"
                    }
     }
1;
</Perl>
```

Once you have created a suitable Perl-based configuration for your Apache servers, you can check your code syntax to make sure the code is syntactically correct by using the following command:

```
perl -cx httpd.conf
```

Special Concerns for Using mod_perl

So far I have discussed how wonderful mod_perl is and how to make use of its wonders. Now let's take a look at a couple of issues that you should be aware of. These issues concern your system resources and security.

Memory usage

Mod_perl makes your Perl scripts execute faster by taking advantage of the memory resident interpreter and cached scripts. This is great news, but where's the catch? The catch is that you use a lot of memory when you use mod_perl. Typically, when you run a CGI script in the traditional manner, it runs and disappears after the service. But in the mod_perl version, the script stays resident in memory for future use. This means that the more scripts you want to run under mod_perl, the more memory they will consume.

If your Perl scripts use a lot of common modules, you can pre-load these using a simple Perl script. For example, the following is a script called loader.pl that loads a module called CGI.pm:

```
#!/usr/local/bin/perl
# startup script
use lib qw(/www/perl/modules);
use CGI;
1;
```

To pre-load this commonly used module, load the script via the PerlScript directive as follows:

```
PerlScript /path/to/loader.pl
```

In most modern operating systems, the Apache child processes running mod_perl will be able to share CGI.pm.

In any case, the more scripts you load, the more memory you need. This can become a issue if you have limited memory and need to pay attention to your server's memory consumption. You can easily monitor memory consumption using common UNIX utilities such as ps or top. I use the following command to generate a listing of important httpd-specific information on a Linux system:

```
ps auxw | awk '{print $1, "\t", $2 , "\t", $5 , "\t", $6}' |
egrep '(httpd|SIZE)'
```

This prints out the USER, PID, SIZE(virtual image size; size of text, data, and stack), and RSS (Resident set size; kilobytes of program in memory) of all the httpd child processes.

You can also find out what Perl packages and scripts are currently being cached by mod_perl using the Apache::Status module. However, before you can use this module, you will need to install the Devel::Symdump module. This Perl module provides a convenient way to inspect Perl's symbol table and the class hierarchies within running programs. If you have the CPAN.pm module installed you can use the command:

```
perl -MCPAN -e 'install "Devel::Symdump"'
```

or you can just get the source code from the URL:

```
www.perl.com/cgi-bin/cpan_mod?module=Devel::Symdump
```

Installing the module is quite easy. Just read the README file included in the module. Once you have installed the Devel:Symdump module, you can get information about the modules that have been loaded (in Apache child processes) and their symbol tables. Define the following configuration segment in one of your Apache configuration files:

```
<Location /perl-status>
SetHandler  perl-script
PerlHandler Apache::Status
</Location>
```

and restart the Apache server. You can get status information using a URL such as (see Figure 13-1):

```
http://yourserver/perl-status
```

This is a really cool way of determining what is loaded by the processes.

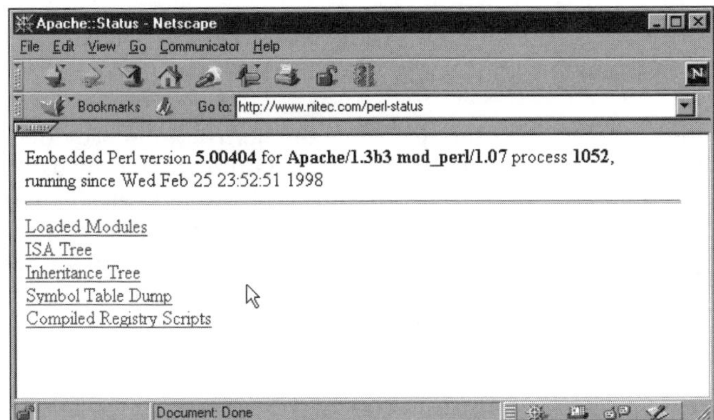

Figure 13-1: Perl status page

Security concerns

Scripts run by mod_perl have the same user and group privileges of the user and group specified by the User and Group directives in the httpd.conf file. Make sure that you keep these user/group privileges very limited.

You should also take care in developing scripts that user input data is checked before use. If you want to enable taint checking in mod_perl, make sure you set the following directive in your httpd.conf file:

```
PerlTaintCheck On
```

the -T switch is usually used to enable taint checking does not work under mod_perl.

Other Embedded Perl for Apache

Now that I've discussed mod_perl, I want to inform you about a few more ways that you can use Perl in Apache. Among the many, there are two are worth mentioning: ePerl and embPerl.

According to the ePerl author, Ralf S. Engelschall, ePerl is the first embedded Perl interpreter ever. ePerl came into being as a stand-alone program that can parse and process Perl scripts embedded in plain ASCII text files. It is usually used in content generation filters but is a good candidate for a Server Side Include language. The ePerl program is a fully functional Perl interpreter that makes use of the original Perl interpreter library (libperl.a.), so the language remains the same and therefore there is nothing new to learn (for a Perl programmer). You can use all modules with ePerl that are normally available to the Perl interpreter. This includes the shared objects that are loaded using the DynaLoader facility. The software can be downloaded for free from the following Web site:

```
www.engelschall.com/sw/eperl/
```

Once you download the software, you should follow the instructions provided with the package to install ePerl on your system. Note that if you plan on only using ePerl in an SSI manner, you do not need to install the stand-alone ePerl. Instead, you can just install the integrated Perl 5 modules into your existing Perl system /path/to/perl/lib/site_perl/{Parse,Apache}/ directories. From your ePerl source directory run the following commands:

```
perl Makefile.PL
make
make test
make install
```

This will install the Apache::ePerl module required for using ePerl in an SSI manner. To quickly test your installation, copy the example script directory (eg) to your Web document tree and modify httpd.conf as follows:

```
Alias /eperl/  /path/to/eg/directory under Web document tree/
<Location /eperl/>
SetHandler perl-script
PerlHandler Apache::ePerl
Options ExecCGI
</Location>
```

Restart Apache and make sure that the example script directory is readable by the Web server. Now you can access the example ePerl scripts. For example, one of the sample scripts provided by the ePerl author is listed in Listing 13-2:

Listing 13-2: demo.env.phtml

```
<!–
##
## demo.env – ePerl demonstration webpage
## Copyright (c) 1996,1997 Ralf S. Engelschall, All Rights
Reserved.
##
–>
<html>
<head>
<title>demo.env</title>
</head>
<body>
<blockquote>
<blockquote>
<h1>demo.env</h1>
<h2>Standard CGI Example: Environment</h1>
<p>

This prints out the CGI environment provided by the Web server
as a sorted list
consisting of key/value pairs.

<p>
<pre>
<? my $key;
   foreach $key (sort(keys(%ENV))) {
       print "$key=$ENV{$key}\n";
   }
!>
</pre>

</blockquote>
</blockquote>
</body>
</html>
```

This script produces the output shown in Figure 13-2.

As you can see in Listing 13-2, the actual Perl code is embedded in the HTML file and is contained in a special tag pair as shown:

```
<?
   # perl code goes here
!>
```

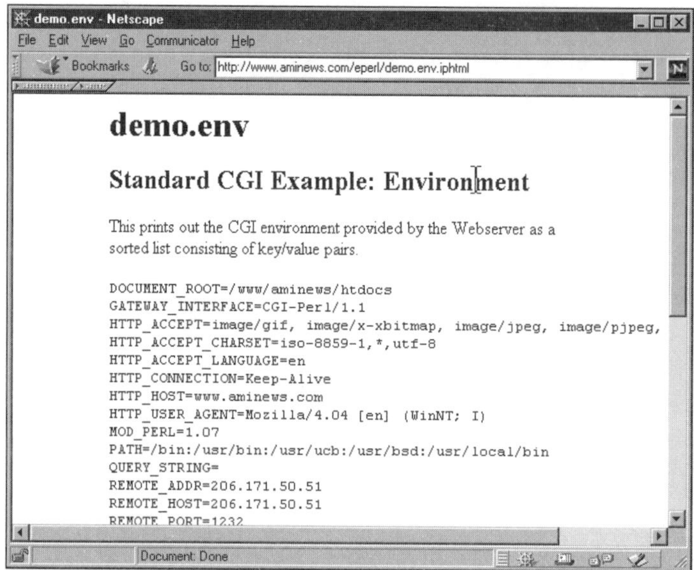

Figure 13-2: Output of demo.env.iphtml

As mentioned before, you can have any valid Perl code in ePerl-based SSI pages, which provides you with a great deal of power. One of the example files shows how the Net::FTP module can be used to obtain a file from a remote FTP server and offer it to the page visitor. There are many other powerful examples that you should take a look at.

The other embedded Perl solution that I like is embPerl by Gerald Richter. You can download embPerl from the following FTP site:

```
ftp://ftp.dev.ecos.de/pub/perl/embperl/
```

embPerl and ePerl are similar in many ways. The real difference is that ePerl is not specific to HTML in any way and embPerl is specific to HTML. embPerl provides some metacommands to do some specific tasks such as filling of HTML tables. It also interprets some HTML tags in a special way. This can be useful on some occasions, but learning the new syntax might appear a bit too much. If you need a general-purpose embedded Perl solution, use ePerl instead.

Summary

In this chapter I discussed how you can use Perl from within Apache by using the mod_perl module. This module provides an easy migration path for turning traditional Perl-based CGI scripts into high-performance mod_perl-based scripts. However, because CGI scripts are often written without a great deal of tender loving care, I recommend rewriting them in object-oriented Perl. I highly recommend using Perl modules in place of traditional scripts to avoid namespace conflicts and save system resources. Along with mod_perl, I provided you a few pointers about other embedded Perl solutions such as ePerl and embPerl.

Next you will learn about Apache proxy service.

✦ ✦ ✦

The Proxy in Apache

✦ ✦ ✦ ✦

In This Chapter

What is a proxy server?

What is a forward proxy server?

What is a reverse proxy server?

Who should use a proxy server?

Using Apache as a proxy server

Configuring Web browsers for proxy

Auto-configuring Web browsers for proxy

What is a mirror and how do you create one with a proxy?

✦ ✦ ✦ ✦

A proxy server is a system that sits between the client hosts and the servers that they need access to. When a client host requests a certain remote resource using a URL, the proxy server receives this request and fetches the resource to fulfill the client's request. In a general sense, a proxy server acts like a server to the client hosts and a client to the remote servers.

In typical proxy scenarios, this process allows the proxy server to store the requested content in a cache. Any new request that asks for information already in the cache no longer needs to be serviced by fetching it from the remote server. Instead, the new request is serviced from the cached data. This allows proxy servers to ease network bottlenecks. However, this is not all that a proxy server does.

In this chapter, you will learn about how you can turn Apache into a proxy server that can perform a multitude of services.

Understanding Proxy Servers

Before we talk about using Apache as a proxy server, let's discuss the types of proxy servers and how they work. There are two types of proxy servers: forward proxy servers and reverse proxy servers.

Forward proxy

A forward proxy server usually sits between the user hosts and the remote resources that they want to access. A resource can be an Internet resource, as shown in Figure 14-1, or it can be an intranet resource. The purpose of this proxy server is to fetch the requested resource from the remote server, return it to the requesting user and typically cache it in local disks. The next request for the same resource will be serviced from the cached data if the data has not expired.

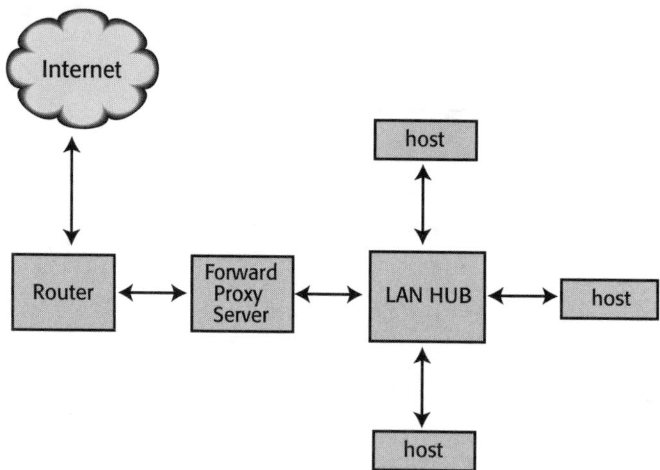

Figure 14-1: A forward proxy server

The user hosts know that they are using a proxy server because each host must be configured to use the proxy server. For example, you must tell a Web browser to use a proxy server before the browser can use it. All remote requests are channeled via the proxy server, providing a manageable and cost-effective solution for reducing bandwidth usage and implementing user access policy.

This type of proxy server is also referred to as a caching proxy server. The reverse proxy server also caches data but it acts in the reverse of the forward proxy server.

Reverse proxy

This type of proxy server sits in front of an Internet resource, as shown in Figure 14-2, or an intranet resource. In such a setup the reverse proxy retrieves the requested resource from the original server and returns it to the user host.

The user hosts who connect to the proxy server are not aware of the fact that they are connecting to a proxy server instead of the resource server itself, unlike a forward proxy server. As far as the end user is concerned, she is accessing the requested resource directly.

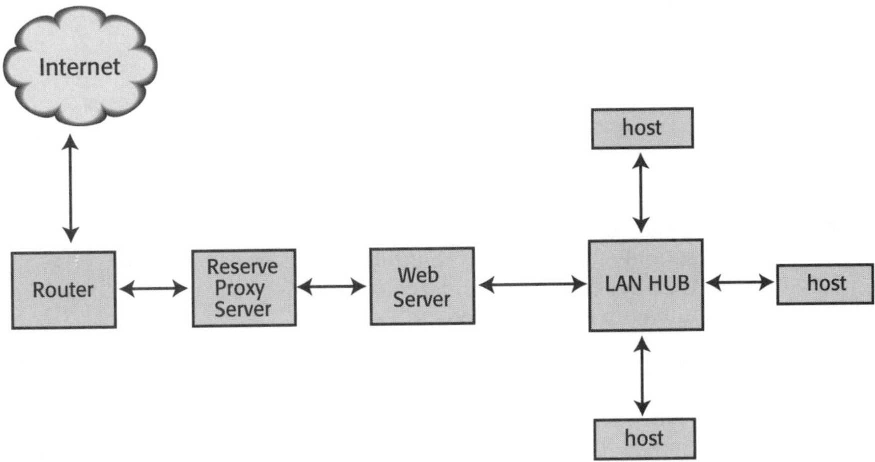

Figure 14-2: A reverse proxy server

For example, if a reverse proxy server is used for a Web site called www.csus.edu, then all a CSUS student has to do is point her browser to www.csus.edu and not tell her browser anything about any proxy configuration. The browser places a request to the server known as www.csus.edu. Little does the browser know that the www.csus.edu server is really a forward proxy server that internally translates the request to a Web server called internal-www.csus.edu to get the content for the request. What does such a setup gain? Because the data is cached from each request, the proxy server can provide some load-balancing support for the real servers behind the scene.

Apache currently does not support reverse proxy service; however, this will soon be implemented in the next version of the Apache server.

Now that you know what proxy servers are all about, let's discuss whether or not a proxy is something you need for your network.

Who Should Use a Proxy Server?

Proxy service is ideal for scenarios where more than one user is accessing the network. Many organizations have several host computers that access the Internet via a single Internet connection such as an ISDN router or other dedicated or on-demand connection. A proxy can be very helpful in such a network.

You can gain the following benefits by using a proxy for both Internet and intranet resources:

✦ Proxying — If the internal network uses non-routable IP addresses for either security or cost reasons, you can use a proxy server to provide Internet resources to hosts that normally cannot access the Internet. In this chapter you will learn about how to do this.

✦ Caching — Using a caching proxy like Apache (with mod_perl), you can provide seemingly faster access to Internet resources to the local users. This will not only enhance the user's perception of network performance but also cut down on bandwidth usage costs.

✦ Logging and Access Control — Using a proxy server you can monitor Internet (or even intranet) usage by employees or students. You can block access to certain Web sites to protect your company from potential lawsuits and stop abuse of company time. By analyzing your proxy server's access and error logs you can identify usage patterns and make better network usage policy in future.

As you can see, there are many benefits of using a proxy server. Now let's look at how you can turn Apache into a proxy server.

Apache as a Proxy Server

The proxy support in Apache comes from the mod_proxy module. This module is not compiled by default. You will have to add the module to the Configuration file in the Apache source directory and recompile Apache. Currently it only implements a caching proxy server in Apache. It is capable of supporting HTTP (HTTP/0.9 and HTTP/1.0), HTTPS (via CONNECT for SSL), and FTP protocols. The module can also be configured to connect to other proxy modules for these and other protocols. It provides the following directives.

ProxyRequests

```
Syntax: ProxyRequests on/off
Default: ProxyRequests Off
Context: server config, virtual host
```

This directive allows you to enable or disable the caching proxy service. However, it does not affect the functionality of the ProxyPass directive.

ProxyRemote

```
Syntax: ProxyRemote <match> <remote-proxy-server-URL>
Default: None
Context: server config, virtual host
```

This directive enables you to interface your proxy server with another proxy server. The value of match can be one of the following:

✦ The name of an URL scheme that the remote server supports

✦ A partial URL for which the remote server should be used

✦ To indicate the server should be contacted for all requests

The <remove-proxy-server-URL> can be http://remove-proxy-hostname:port. Note that, currently, only the HTTP protocol is supported. In other words, you can only specify a proxy server that deals with the HTTP protocol; however, you can forward FTP requests from your proxy server to one that supports both HTTP and FTP protocols as follows:

```
ProxyRemote ftp http://ftp.proxy.nitec.com:8000
```

This will send all FTP requests that come to the local proxy server to ftp://ftp.proxy.nitec.com. The requests will be send via HTTP, so the actual FTP transaction will occur at the remote proxy server.

If you just want to forward all proxy requests for a certain Web site to its proxy server directly, you can do that with this directive. For example:

```
ProxyRemote http://www.bigisp.com/  http://web-
proxy.bigisp.com:8000
```

This will send all requests that match www.bigisp.com to web-proxy.bigisp.com. If you want to forward all of your proxy requests to another proxy, however, you can use the asterisk as the match phrase, for example:

```
ProxyRemote * http://proxy.domain.com
```

This will send all local proxy requests to the proxy server at proxy.domain.com.

ProxyPass

```
Syntax: ProxyPass <relative-URL> <destination-URL>
Default: None
Context: server config, virtual host
```

This directive enables you to map a Web server's document tree onto your proxy server's document space. For example:

```
ProxyPass /internet/microsoft      www.microsoft.com/
```

This directive found in the httpd.conf file of a proxy server called proxy.nitec.com will permit users of the proxy server to access the Microsoft Web site using the URL:

```
http://proxy.nitec.com/internet/microsoft
```

This acts like a mirror of the remote Web site. Any request that uses the <relative-URL> will be converted internally into a proxy request for the <destination-URL>.

If the remote site includes absolute references, images may not appear and links may not work. Also note that currently you cannot use this directive with SSL destination servers.

ProxyBlock

```
Syntax: ProxyBlock  <partial or full host name> . . .
Default: None
Context: server config, virtual host
```

This directive enables you block access to a named host or domain, for example:

```
ProxyBlock gates
```

This will block access to any host that has the word gates in its name. This way, access to http://gates.ms.com or http://gates.friendsofbill.com will be blocked. You can also specify multiple hosts as follows:

```
ProxyBlock apple orange.com bannana.com
```

This blocks all access to any host that matches any of the above words or domain names. The mod_proxy module attempts to determine the IP addresses for these hosts during server start-up, and caches them for matching later.

To block access to all hosts, use:

```
ProxyBlock *
```

This effectively disables your proxy server.

NoProxy

```
Syntax: NoProxy <Domain name|  Subnet | IP Address | Hostname>
Default: None
Context: server config, virtual host
```

This directive gives you some control over the ProxyRemote directive in an intranet environment. You can specify a domain name or a subnet or an IP address or a hostname not to be served by the proxy server specified in the ProxyRemote directive. For example:

```
ProxyRemote  *   http://firewall.yourcompany.com:8080
NoProxy          .yourcompany.com
```

Here all requests for <anything>.yourcompany.com (such as www.yourcompany.com) will be served by the local proxy server and everything else will go to the firewall.yourcompany.com proxy server.

ProxyDomain

```
Syntax: ProxyDomain <Domain>
Default: None
Context: server config, virtual host
```

This directive specifies the default domain name for the proxy server. When this directive is set to the local domain name on an intranet, any request that does not include a domain name will get this domain name appended in the request, for example:

```
ProxyDomain     .nitec.com
```

When a user of nitec.com domain sends a request for an URL such as http://marketing/us.html, the request will be regenerated as the following URL:

```
http://marketing.nitec.com/us.html
```

Note that the domain name you specify must have a leading period.

CacheRoot

```
Syntax: CacheRoot <directory>
Default: None
Context: server config, virtual host
```

This directive allows you to enable disk caching. You can specify a directory name where the proxy server can write cached files. The Apache server running the proxy module must have write permission for the directory, for example:

```
CacheRoot /www/proxy/cache
```

This will tell Apache to write proxy cache data to the /www/proxy/cache directory. Note that you will need to specify the size of the cache using the CacheSize directory before the proxy server can start using this directory for caching. You may also need to use other cache directives (discussed later) to create a useable disk caching proxy solution.

CacheSize

```
Syntax: CacheSize  <n kilobytes>
Default: CacheSize 5
Context: server config, virtual host
```

This directive specifies the amount of disk space (in K) that should be used for disk caching. The cached files are written in the directory specified by the CacheRoot directive. Note that it is possible for the proxy server to write more data than the specified limit but the proxy server's garbage collection scheme will delete files until the usage is at or below this setting. The default setting (5K) is unrealistic; I recommend anywhere from 10MB to 1GB depending on your user load.

CacheGcInterval

```
Syntax: CacheGcInterval <n hour>
Default: None
Context: server config, virtual host
```

This directive specifies the time (in hours) when Apache should check the cache directories for deleting expired files. This is also when Apache will enforce the disk space usage limit specified by the CacheSize directive.

CacheMaxExpire

```
Syntax: CacheMaxExpire <n hour>
Default: CacheMaxExpire 24
Context: server config, virtual host
```

This directive specifies the time (in hours) when all cached documents expire. In other words, if you specify this directive as:

```
CacheMaxExpire 48
```

Then all the cached documents will expire in 48 hours or two days. This directive overrides any expiration date specified in the document itself; so if a document has a expiration date later then the maximum specified by this directive, the document is still removed.

CacheLastModifiedFactor

```
Syntax: CacheLastModifiedFactor <floating point number>
Default: CacheLastModifiedFactor 0.1
Context: server config, virtual host
```

This directive specifies a factor used to calculate expiration time when the original Web server does not supply an expiration date for a document. The calculation is done using the following formula:

```
expiry-period =  (last modification time for the document ) *
(floating point number)
```

So if a document was last modified 24 hours ago, then the default factor of 0.1 will make Apache calculate the expiration time for this document to be 2.4 hours. If the calculated expiration-period is longer than that set by CacheMaxExpire, then the latter takes precedence.

CacheDirLength

```
Syntax: CacheDirLength <length>
Default: CacheDirLength 1
Context: server config, virtual host
```

When disk caching is on, Apache creates subdirectories in the directory specified by the CacheRoot directive. This directive specifies the number of characters used in creating the subdirectory names. You really do not need to change the default for this directive. For curious users who want to know how or why these subdirectories are created, a simplified answer follows.

Apache uses a hashing scheme when creating the path and file name for a URL's data to be cached. For example, when you have caching turned on and access a URL (such as www.microsoft.com) via your proxy Apache server, the server hashes this URL so it can retrieve the data quickly later on. This hash could look like 1YSRxSmB20Q_HkqkTuXeqvw. If the defaults are used for both the CacheDirLength and CacheDirLevels directives, Apache will store the data found on www.microsoft.com in a file called:

```
%CacheRoot%/1/Y/S/RRxSmB20Q_HkqkTuXeqvw
```

Here %CacheRoot% is the directory specified by the CacheRoot directive. The 1/Y/S directories get created because of the default value of the CacheDirLevels directive. When this document is requested again using the same URL, Apache need only recalculate the hash and retrieve the page from the specified path.

CacheDirLevels

```
Syntax: CacheDirLevels <levels>
Default: CacheDirLevels 3
Context: server config, virtual host
```

This specifies the number of subdirectories that Apache will create to store cache data files. See the "CacheDirLength" section for related information.

CacheDefaultExpire

```
Syntax: CacheDefaultExpire <n hour>
Default: CacheDefaultExpire 1
Context: server config, virtual host
```

This directive provides a default time (in hours) that is used to expire a cached file when the last modification time of the file is unknown. CacheMaxExpire does not override this setting.

NoCache

```
Syntax: NoCache <Domain name|  Subnet | IP Address | Hostname>
. . .
Default: None
Context: server config, virtual host
```

The NoCache directive specifies a list of hosts, domain names, and IP addresses, separated by spaces, for which no caching is performed. This directive should be used to disable caching of local Web servers on an intranet. Note that the proxy server also matches partial names of a host. If you want to disable caching altogether, use the following:

```
NoCache *
```

Configuring the Proxy Server

Now that you know which directives you can use to configure the proxy in Apache, let's take at look at some of the configuration details.

To enable the proxy server, you need to set the ProxyRequests to On. After that the additional configuration depends on what you want to do with your proxy server. Whatever you decide to do with it, any proxy configuration that you choose should go inside a special <Directory . . .> container that looks like the following:

```
<Directory proxy:*>
. . .
</Directory>
```

Any directives that you want to use to control the proxy server's behavior should go inside this container. The asterisk is a wild card for the requested URL. In other words, when a request for www.nitec.com is processed by the Apache server, it looks like:

```
<Directory proxy:http://www.nitec.com/>
. . .
</Directory>
```

You can also use the <Directory ~ /RE/> container, which uses regular expressions, for example:

```
<Directory ~ proxy:http://[^:/]+/.*>
. . .
</Directory>
```

Now let's look at a few commonly used proxy configurations.

Connecting a private IP network to the Internet

In this scenario, only one computer on this network has an Internet-routable IP address assigned to it, as shown in Figure 14-3. This computer runs the Apache proxy server with the ProxyRequest set to on, and no additional proxy configuration is needed. All requests are serviced by the proxy server.

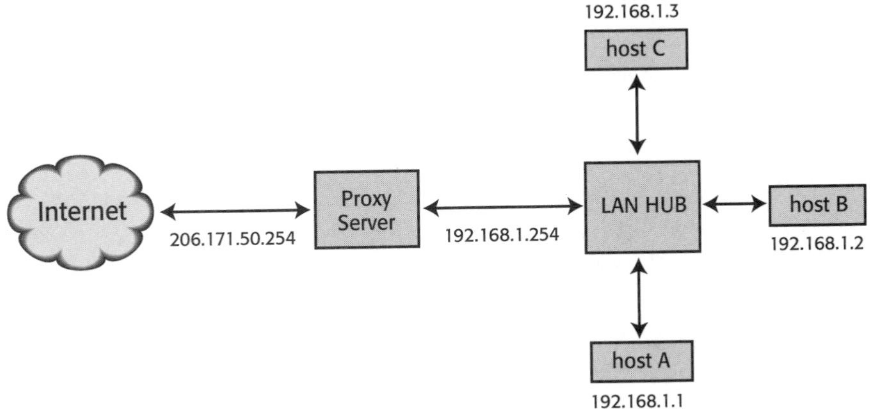

Figure 14-3: Proxy for private IP network to Internet

Note that in such a configuration, the proxy server needs to be multihomed. In other words, it needs to have access to both the nonroutable private network (192.168.1.0) and the routable IP network (206.171.50.0). In a way, this proxy acts like a firewall for the private network although the chosen nonroutable IP pool does that already. The proxy permits the hosts to get access to Internet services, such as the Web, FTP, and so on.

Now let's take a look at a caching proxy server.

Caching remote Web sites

Because a great deal of Web content on both the Internet and intranets is likely to be static, caching them on a local proxy server could save valuable network bandwidth. A cache-enabled proxy server will fetch requested documents only when the cache contains an expired document or when the requested document is not present in the cache. To enable caching on your proxy server, you need to specify caching directives inside the a special directory container, for example:

```
<Directory proxy:*>
CacheRoot /www/cache
CacheSize 1024
CacheMaxExpire 24
</Directory>
```

This configuration defines a caching proxy server that writes cache files to the /www/cache directory. It is permitted to write 1,024K of data (1MB) and the cache must expire after each day (24 hours).

If you do not want to permit outside people to abuse your proxy, you can restrict proxy access either by host or by username/password authentication.

To control which hosts have access to the proxy server, you can create a configuration, such as the following:

```
<Directory proxy:*>

AuthType Basic
AuthName Proxy
order deny,allow
deny from all
allow from myhost.nitec.com

</Directory>
```

This configuration denies access to all but myhost.nitec.com. If you want to use username/password authentication, you can use something similar to the following:

```
<Directory proxy:*>

AuthType Basic
AuthName Proxy
AuthUserFile /path/to/proxy/.htpasswd
AuthName Proxy
require valid-user
</Directory>
```

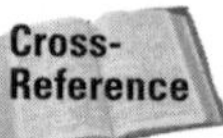

If you are not sure how to create the necessary password files, see Chapter 10.

It is also possible to restrict access for a protocol, for example:

```
<Directory proxy:http:*>
. . .
</Directory>
```

This will enable you to control how HTTP requests are processed by your proxy server. Similarly you can use the following to control how each of these protocols is handled by the proxy server:

```
<Directory proxy:ftp:*>
. . .
</Directory>
```

or

```
<Directory proxy:https:*>
. . .
</Directory>
```

You can also create a virtual host exclusively for proxy server. In that case, the directives should go inside the proxy host's <VirtualHost> container:

```
<VirtualHost proxy.host.com:*>
. . .
</VirtualHost>
```

Mirroring a Web site

A mirror Web site is a local copy of a remote Web site. For example, if you wanted to mirror the www.apache.org Web site so your users can connect to your mirror site for quick access to Apache information, you can use the proxy server to create such a mirror, as follows:

```
ProxyPass /  www.apache.org/
CacheRoot /www/cache
CacheDefaultExpire 24
```

This makes a proxy server a mirror of the www.apache.org Web site. For example, this configuration turns my proxy server blackhole.nitec.com into an Apache mirror as shown in Figure 14-4.

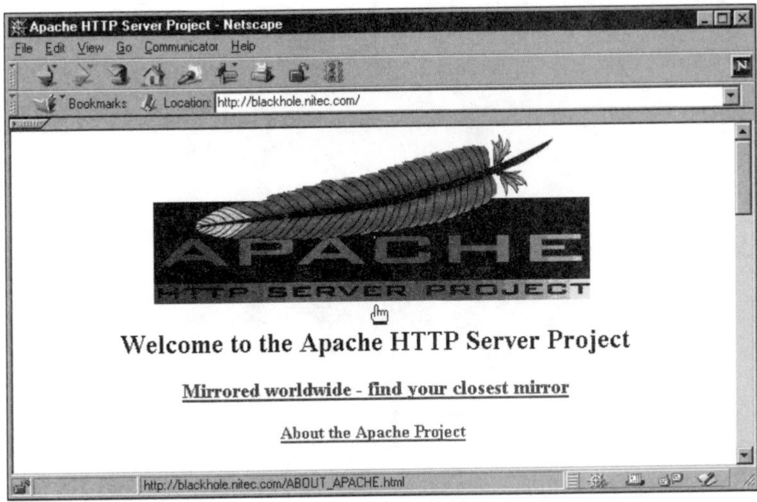

Figure 14-4: Using a proxy server to mirror the Apache Web site

When a user enters http://blackhole.nitec.com as the URL, she receives the Apache mirror's index page as if she had gone to www.apache.org.

Before you mirror someone else's Web site, it is important that you get permission, as there may be copyright issues involved.

Setting Up Web Browsers

Now you are ready to set up Web browsers on your client hosts. The popular Web browsers make it quite easy to use proxy servers. In the following sections I will show you how to configure the latest versions of Netscape Navigator and Microsoft Internet Explorer (IE) for proxy. There are two ways you can set up a proxy server for these browsers: manual or automatic proxy configuration.

You want to do manual proxy configuration in situations where you have only a few clients and your proxy configurations do not change often. If your needs are different, you should skip to the section on "Automatic Proxy Configuration for Web Browsers."

The following steps will guide you through the manual proxy configuration:

1. Select the Preference option under the Edit menu from the Navigator menu bar. You should see a dialog window as shown in Figure 14-5.

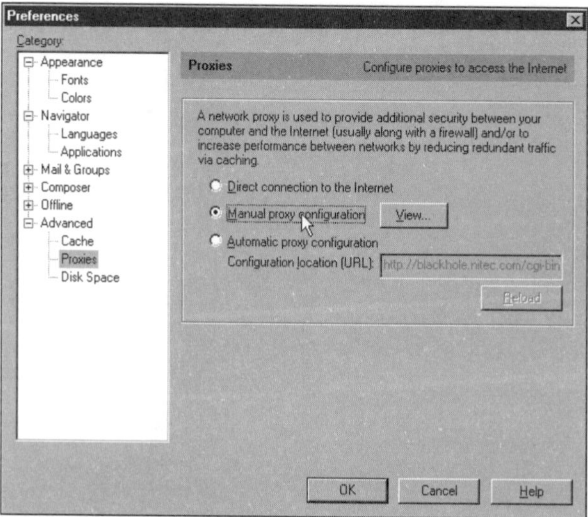

Figure 14-5: Netscape Navigator preference window

2. Click the Advanced category.
3. Click the Proxies category.
4. Select the Manual proxy configuration radio button and click the View button. You will see the window shown in Figure 14-6.

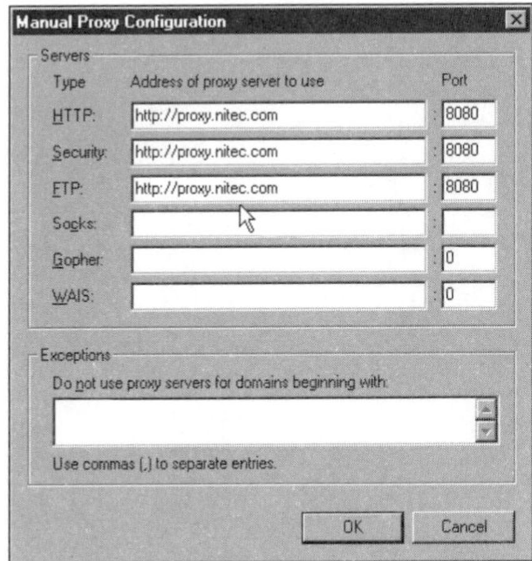

Figure 14-6: Netscape Navigator manual proxy setup window

5. Enter the proxy server URLs for the HTTP, FTP, and Security (HTTPS) data entry fields along with the port information. Because I am using a single proxy server for all of these protocols, the URL (http://proxy.nitec.com/) and the port (8080) are all same. If you have different proxy servers for each of these services, you should specify them accordingly.
6. Once you have entered the information, make a request for a remote document and see if your proxy is working as it should. A good way to determine what's going on is to monitor the proxy server's access and error logs. On most UNIX systems you can use a command such as the following to view log entries as they get written to the file:

   ```
   tail -f  /path/to/access/log
   ```

Now let's configure the other leading Web browser. To configure Internet Explorer for manual proxy, follow these steps:

1. Click the View menu and select Internet options. This brings up the dialog window shown in Figure 14-7.

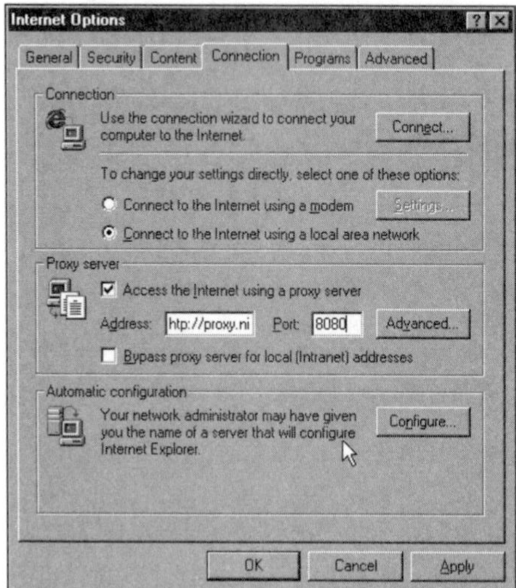

Figure 14-7: Microsoft Internet Explorer manual proxy setup window

2. Select the Connection tab.
3. Select the Access the Internet using a proxy server radio button.
4. Enter the proxy server URL and port number in the fields provided.
5. Click OK to complete configuration.

If you want to specify different proxy server information for different protocols, then you can use the Advanced button to bring up the window shown in Figure 14-8.

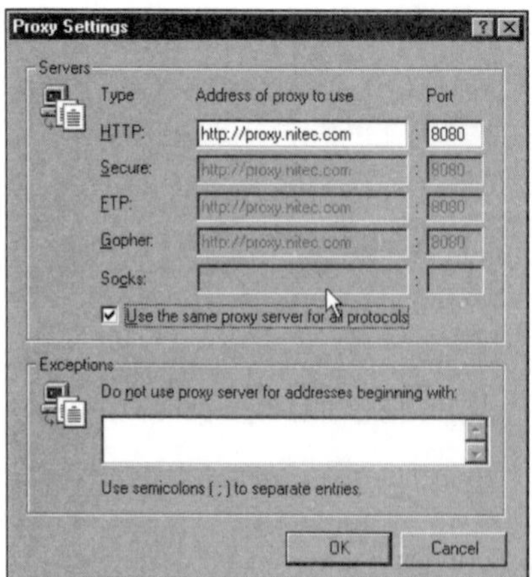

Figure 14-8: Microsoft Internet Explorer advanced proxy setup window

Here, as in Netscape Navigator, you can specify different proxy server settings. Once you click OK and use the Apply button to apply the new settings, your browser is configured to use the proxy server.

As you can see, manually configuring Web browsers for proxy is not that complicated. However, if you have a lot of user computers that need to be configured, this could become a big hassle every time you needed to change your proxy configuration. This is where automatic proxy configuration for browsers comes in handy.

Automatic Proxy Configuration for Web Browsers

The good folks at Netscape thought about the problems involved with manually configuring proxy for several client computers and came up with a way to get around this type of hassle. Microsoft has also caught up with auto-configuring options for Internet Explorer. Unfortunately, they have made auto-configuring a bit harder to incorporate in the browser. You must obtain the Internet Explorer Administrator Kit (IEAK) to create auto-configuration files. Because getting IEAK requires a licensing agreement that asks each IEAK licensee to report quarterly to Microsoft regarding IEAK-related use, this author didn't feel like getting one. However, I have confirmation from a good source that the IEAK documentation discusses a Netscape-like automatic proxy configuration scenario and can even use the same scripts.

This section applies to both IE and Navigator. The only difference is that if you want this to work with IE, you must figure out how to create the appropriate files using IEAK.

The proxy auto-configuration is done using a special JavaScript. This is true for both Netscape Navigator and IE. The special JavaScript has the following requirements:

The proxy auto-config JavaScript must implement a function called FindProxyForURL. This function has the following skeleton:

```
function FindProxyForURL(url, host)
         {
              // java script code goes here

           return "proxy to use for servicing the URL";

         }
```

The arguments that this function receives are url and host. The url is the full URL being requested and the host is the hostname extracted from the URL. For example, when a request for is detected by the Web browser, it will call the function as follows:

```
ret = FindProxyForURL(", )
```

The host argument in the function call is really the sub-string between the :// and the first : or /. The port number is not included in this parameter.

The function must return a string containing the necessary proxy configuration for a particular URL request. The acceptable string values that represent a proxy configuration are:

NULL	When a NULL value (not the string NULL) is returned, it tells the browser not to use any proxy for this request.
DIRECT	Connections should be made directly, without any proxies.
PROXY host:port;	The specified proxy should be used.
SOCKS host:port;	The specified SOCKS server should be used.

Obviously, the real interesting return values are DIRECT and PROXY. When you have multiple proxy or SOCKS servers, you can return a list instead of a single host:port pair. For example:

```
PROXY best-proxy.nitec.com:8080; PROXY good-
proxy.nitec.com:8081; PROXY soso-proxy.nitec.com:8082
```

This proxy configuration will tell the browser to try best-proxy.nitec.com first, and if it fails then try the next one (good-proxy.nitec.com), and so on. Note that each host:port pair is separated by a semicolon and the keyword PROXY is repeated for each pair. If all the proxy servers fail, the user will be asked before attempting a direct connection.

When all proxies fail and there is no DIRECT option specified, the browser will ask the user if proxies should be temporarily ignored, and direct connections attempted.

To avoid user interaction, the configuration can be replaced with the following:

```
PROXY best-proxy.nitec.com:8080; PROXY good-
proxy.nitec.com:8081; PROXY soso-proxy.nitec.com:8082; DIRECT
```

Because direct connection is already specified as the last resort, the user will not be asked before making such a connection in case of total proxy failure. You can also mix PROXY and SOCKS. For example:

```
PROXY best-proxy.nitec.com:8080; SOCKS socks4.nitec.com:1080;
DIRECT
```

Here the SOCKS-based proxy will be used when the primary proxy server best-proxy.nitec.com fails to respond.

When a proxy fails to respond, Netscape Navigator retries the proxy after 30 minutes. Each subsequent time it fails, the interval is lengthened by another 30 minutes.

In order to help Web administrators (who must also know JavaScript programming), a set of pre-defined functions are available. These functions and their descriptions are listed in Table 14-1.

Table 14-1
Pre-defined functions for programming automatic proxy configuration script

Function Name	*Explanation*	*Examples*
isPlainHostName(host)	Returns true if there is no dot in host. In other words, if the domain name is not included.	`isPlainHostName("blackhole")` returns true. `isPlainHostName("blackhole.nitec.com")` returns false.
dnsDomainIs(host, domain)	Returns true if host belongs to the domain. Note that the domain name must contain a leading period.	`dnsDomainIs("www.nitec.com", ".nitec.com")` returns true. `dnsDomainIs("www.apache.org",".nitec.com")` returns false.
localHostOrDomainIs (host, fqdnhost)	Returns true if host part of fqdnhost (fully qualified hostname) matches with host.	`localHostOrDomainIs("a.b.com", "a.b.com")` returns true; `localHostOrDomainIs("a.b", "a.b.com")` returns true; `localHostOrDomainIs("a.b.org", "a.c.com")` returns false;
isResolvable(host)	If DNS server can resolve the hostname to an IP, returns true or else false. Note that use of this function can slow down browsers because a DNS query will be required to perform the test.	`isResolvable("{hyperlink}");` Returns true because {hyperlink} has DNS records.
isInNet(host, IP address pattern, netmask)	Returns true if the IP address of the host matches the pattern specified in the second argument. The match is done using the netmask as follows: if one of the octets of the mask is a 255, the same octet of the IP address of the host must match. If an octet of the mask is 0, the same octet of the IP address of the host is ignored.	If the host has an IP address of 206.171.50.51: `isInNet(host, "206.171.50.50", "255.255.255.0");` returns true because according to the netmask only first three octets must match and the last one should be ignored.

(continued)

Table 14-1 *(continued)*

Function Name	***Explanation***	***Examples***
	Note that use of this function can slow down browsers because a DNS query will be required to perform the test.	
dnsResolve(host)	Returns the IP address of the host if successful. Note that use of this function can slow down browsers because a DNS query will be required to perform the test.	`dnsResolve("proxy.nitec.com")` returns "206.171.50.50"
myIpAddress()	Returns the IP address of the host the Web browser is running. Note that use of this function can slow down e browsers because a DNS query will be required to perform the test.	`var hostIP = myIpAddress()` returns the IP of the Web browser host and stores it in a variable called hostIP.
dnsDomainLevels (host)	Returns number of domain levels in the host name.	`dnsDomainLevels("www.nitec.com")` returns 2.
shExpMatch(string, shellExpression)	Returns true if string matches the shell expression.	`shExpMatch("path/to/dir", "*/to/*")` returns true. `shExpMatch("abcdef", "123")` returns false.
weekdayRange (weekday1, weekday2, gmt)	Only the first argument weekday1 is required. Returns true if the day this function is executed is equal to weekday1 or in the range of weekday1 to weekday2. If the third parameter gmt is "GMT" then GMT time is used instead of local time. Acceptable weekday values for weekday1 or weekday2 are: SUN, MON, TUE, WED, THU, FRI, or SAT.	`weekdayRange("FRI")` returns true if day is Friday in local time. `weekdayRange("MON", "FRI", "GMT")` returns true if day is in the Monday-Friday range in GMT time.

Function Name	*Explanation*	*Examples*
dateRange(day) dateRange(day1, day2) dateRange(month) dateRange(month1, month2) dateRange(year) dateRange(year1, year2) dateRange(day1, month1, day2, month2) dateRange(month1, year1, month2, year2) dateRange(day1, month1, year1, day2, month2, year2) dateRange(day1, month1, year1, day2, month2, year2, gmt)	Returns true if current day, month, year, or all three are in the range. The value of day can be 1–31; month can be JAN, FEB, MAR, APR, MAY, JUN, JUL, AUG, SEP, OCT, NOV, or DEC; year is a four-digit number; gmt is "GMT" or nothing (local time).	`dateRange(31)` returns true if current day is the 31st. `dateRange("JAN", "APR")` returns true if current month is in the January to April range. `dateRange(1995)` returns true if current year is 1995.
timeRange(hour) timeRange(hour1, hour2) timeRange(hour1, min1, hour2, min2) timeRange(hour1, min1, sec1, hour2, min2, sec2) timeRange(hour1, min1, sec1, hour2, min2, sec2, gmt)	Returns true if hour, min, or sec specified is current. If a range is specified, then returns true when the current corresponding unit of time is in the range specified. The value of hour can be 0-23; min can be 0-59, second can be 0-59, and gmt is "GMT" or nothing (local time.)	`timeRange(9, 17)` returns true if current hour is between 9 AM - 5 PM range.

With the help of the pre-defined functions and your custom functions, you can write FindProxyForURL so that it returns appropriate proxy configuration string for each request.

When the Web browser starts, it loads the function from the JavaScript file (how the file is made available to the Web browser will be discussed later) and calls FindProxyForURL for each URL request. The browser supplies the host and URL arguments to the function so that it can return the most appropriate proxy configuration.

Let's take a look at some example scenarios where the FindProxyForURL function can be written in different ways.

Using proxy only for remote URL requests

In this scenario, the idea is to tell the Web browser that proxy should be only for remote URL requests, as shown in Figure 14-9.

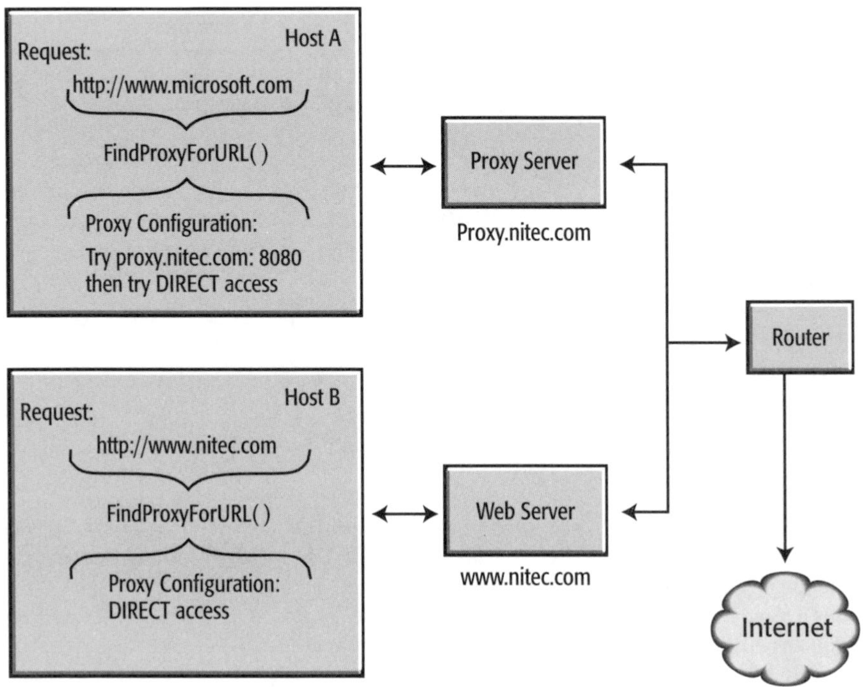

Figure 14-9: Using proxy only for remote URL requests

Listing 14-1 shows a simple example of such a FindProxyForURL function.

Listing 14-1: Using proxy only for remote URL requests

```
function FindProxyForURL(url, host) {

// Check to see if the host is a local host. If it is a local
// host specify DIRECT connection (i.e. no proxy)
// or else use the proxy.
if (isPlainHostName(host) ||
    dnsDomainIs(host, ".nitec.com"))
        return "DIRECT";
else
       return "PROXY proxy.nitec.com:8081; DIRECT";
}
```

When a request for a URL such as is made by the Web browser user, the browser calls FindProxyForURL with the url argument set to and the host set to . The function first calls the isPlainHostName function to see if is a plain host (just www) or not. Because it is not, isPlainHostName returns false. Now the dnsDomainIs function is called to test if is in the .nitec.com domain. This also returns false. Because both of these tests return false, the else part of the conditional statement is executed. In other words, the URL request for returns the following proxy configuration to the Web browser:

```
PROXY proxy.nitec.com:8081; DIRECT
```

This tells the Web browser to use proxy server named proxy.nitec.com on port 8081 if it is not down. In case it is down, the request should be serviced by a direct HTTP request to . For most proxy server installations, this configuration is sufficient. Let's take a look at more complex scenario.

Using multiple proxy severs

In this scenario, there are multiple proxy servers. Figure 14-10 illustrates a network where there are three proxy servers: http-proxy.nitec.com is used for all remote HTTP URL requests, ftp-proxy.nitec.com is used for all remote FTP URL requests, and ssl-proxy.nitec.com is used for all remote HTTPS URL requests. All other remote URL requests using other protocols such as GOPHER, NEWS, and so on are directly connected. All types of local requests are serviced directly as well.

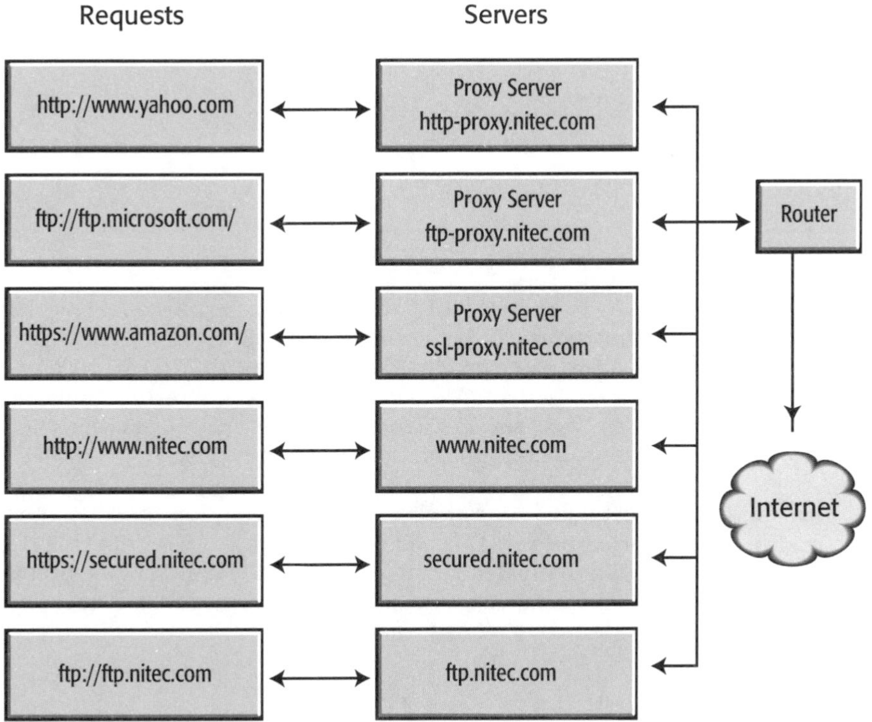

Figure 14-10: Using multiple proxy servers

To implement this configuration, FindProxyForURL becomes a bit complex and looks like Listing 14-2.

Listing 14-2: FindProxyForURL for multiproxy server configuration

```
function FindProxyForURL(url, host) {

  // is the URL local? If it is then use a DIRECT connection
   if (isPlainHostName(host) ||
       dnsDomainIs(host, ".nitec.com")) {
 return "DIRECT";
 }

  // Okay, the URL is remote so check which proxy to use.
  else{
  if (url.substring(0, 5) == "http:") {
        return "PROXY http-proxy.nitec.com:8080";
    }
  else if (url.substring(0, 4) == "ftp:") {
         return "PROXY ftp-proxy.nitec.com:8080";
         }
   else if (url.substring(0, 6) == "https:") {
          return "PROXY ssl-proxy.nitec.com:8080";
        }
   else{
            return "DIRECT";
        }
         }
}
```

This function first checks to see if the URL request is a local one. If it is local, then it is serviced directly. If the request is for a remote server, the URL protocol is matched to locate the appropriate proxy server. However, only HTTP, FTP, and HTTPS protocols are recognized and URLs requesting remote resources using such protocols are directed to proxy servers. When a remote URL request does not match any of the stated protocols, it is connected directly.

It is also possible to customize your proxy server configuration based on the host that is accessing the proxy server. This can be done using a CGI script that outputs the FindProxyForURL differently depending on the REMOTE_HOST (the browser host). Listing 14-3 shows one such script called proxy.pl written in Perl.

Listing 14-3: proxy.pl script

```
#!/usr/local/bin/perl
#
# A Perl script that outputs proxy server configuration.
# $Author$
# $Revision$
# $Id$

# Get the remote host IP from the CGI environment variable
# REMOTE_HOST
my $client = $ENV{REMOTE_HOST};

# Print out the necessary content-type to let the browser
# know that this is a proxy configuration.
print "Content-type: application/x-ns-proxy-autoconfig\n\n";

# If the request came from a host with IP address
# 206.171.50.51 then output proxy configuration
# from subroutine &specialClient
#
if ($client =~ /206\.171\.50\.51/){ &specialClient; }

# If the request came from any other clients, then
# output  proxy configuration from the subroutine
# &otherClients
else { &otherClients; }

exit 0;

sub specialClient{
#
# This subroutine outputs a proxy server configuration
#

print <<FUNC;

     function FindProxyForURL(url, host)
     {
         if (isPlainHostName(host) ||
             dnsDomainIs(host, ".nitec.com"))
             return "DIRECT";
         else if (shExpMatch(host, "*.com"))
             return "PROXY com-proxy.nitec.com:8080; "

         else if (shExpMatch(host, "*.edu"))
             return "PROXY edu-proxy.nitec.com:8080; "

         else
             return "DIRECT";
```

(continued)

Listing 14-3 *(continued)*

```
    }
FUNC

}

sub otherClients{
#
# This subroutine outputs a proxy server configuration
#

print <<FUNC;

    function FindProxyForURL(url, host)
    {
        return "DIRECT";
    }

FUNC

}
```

This script outputs a special proxy server configuration for a host with the IP address 206.171.50.51, and all other hosts get a different configuration. To access this proxy configuration, I can set up the browser (Navigator) to point to this script at . This is done exactly the same way you would specify the .pac file. In this case you are asking the browser to request a CGI script instead of a .pac file. But because the script sends out the content-type of a pac file, the browser has no quarrel about why it got the proxy configuration from a CGI script and not a .pac file. Although the example script does not do much, you can use similar scripts for complex proxy configurations.

Summary

In this chapter you learned about how to turn Apache into a caching (forward) proxy server. Deploying such a server at the network bottleneck can reduce delays in response times, conserve bandwidth, and help reduce your overall communications expense. Because proxy is usually used for networks with large user communities, I also covered various aspects of client configuration including automatic proxy configuration.

Next you will learn about the Secured Socket Layer (SSL).

✦ ✦ ✦

CHAPTER 15

Secured Socket Layer for Apache

◆ ◆ ◆ ◆

In This Chapter

Understanding the need for security on the Internet

What is Secured Socket Layer (SSL)?

Why is SSL not included with Apache?

How to use free Apache-SSL

How to use Stronghold for SSL

◆ ◆ ◆ ◆

Only a few years ago, the Internet was still what it was initially meant to be — a worldwide network for scientists and engineers. By virtue of the Web, however, the Internet is now a network for everyone. These days, it seems as though everyone and everything is on the Internet. It is also the new business frontier; thousands of businesses, large and small, have set up Web sites to open doors to new customers around the world. Customers are being cautious, however, because they know that not all parts of Internet are secured.

To eliminate this sense of insecurity in the new frontier, commercial Web sites must provide a scheme that ensures secured transactions between them and their Web customers. Secured Socket Layer (SSL) is one such technology. In this chapter, I discuss how this new technology plays a considerable role in facilitating business on the Web using Apache server.

The Foundation of SSL: Encryption

When data travels from one point of the Internet to another, it goes through a number of computers such as routers, gateways, and other network devices. For example, when a visitor to a Web site at www.nitec.com/ enters his or her credit card number in an HTML form found on the site, it is quite possible that the information travels on a path like the one shown in Figure 15-1.

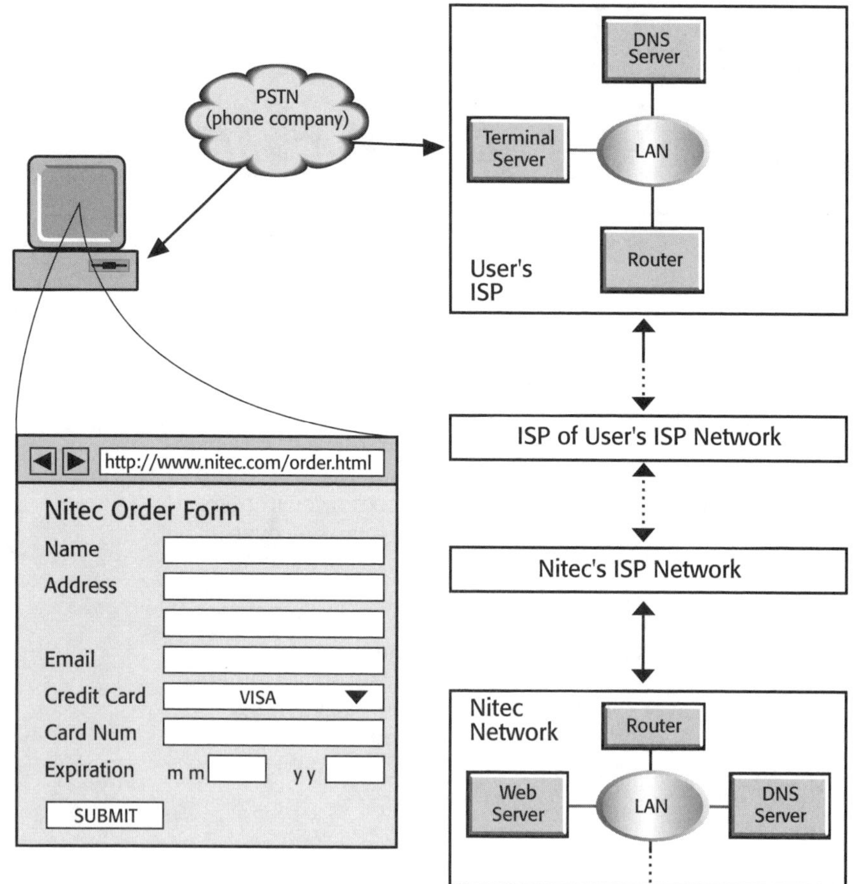

Figure 15-1: Data traveling from one point to another on the Internet

As you can see, the data must travel through many nodes, so there's a chance it can be intercepted by someone at one of these nodes. Although data packets travel at a very high speed (usually milliseconds), interception is still a possibility. This is why we need a secured mechanism for exchanging sensitive data. This security is achieved through encryption.

Technically speaking, encryption is the mathematical encoding scheme that ensures that only the intended recipient can access the data; it hides the data from eavesdroppers. Encryption schemes are widely used to restrict access to resources. For example, if you log onto a UNIX or Windows NT system, the passwords or keys you use are typically stored in the server computer in an encrypted format. On most UNIX systems, a user's password is encrypted and matched with the encrypted password stored in an /etc/passwd file. If this comparison is successful, the user is given access to the requested resource. Two kinds of encryption schemes are available.

Symmetric encryption

This scheme is similar to the keys and locks you probably use on a daily basis. You unlock your car with a key, and also lock it with the same key. Similarly, in symmetric encryption, a single key is used for both locking and unlocking purposes. Figure 15-2 shows an example of such a scheme.

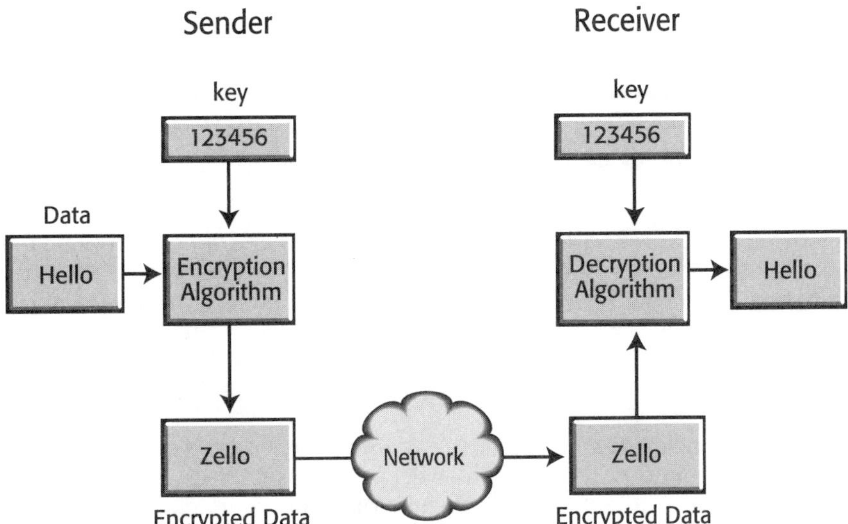

Figure 15-2: Example of symmetric encryption scheme

Because a single key is used in this scheme, all involved parties must know what this key is to make the scheme work. Asymmetric encryption, on the other hand, works a bit differently.

Asymmetric encryption

In this scheme, there are two keys: a public key and a private key. The extra key is the public key—hence this scheme is also known as the public key algorithm. Figure 15-3 shows an example of how this encryption scheme works.

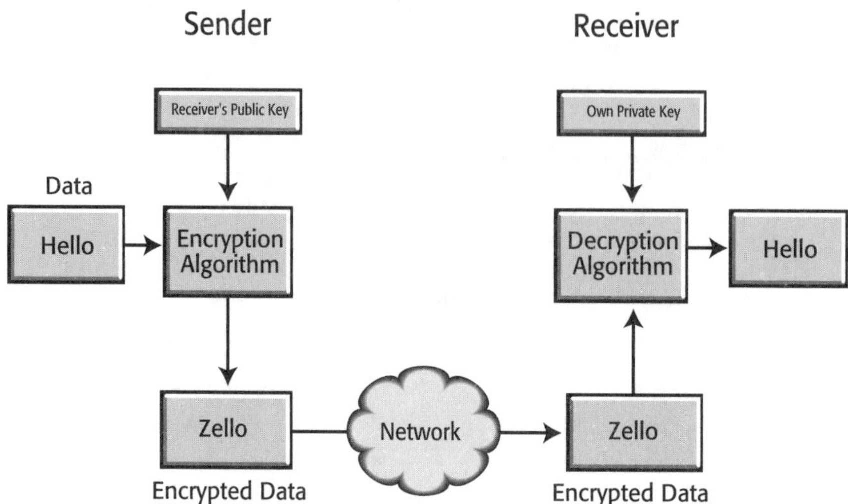

Figure 15-3: Example of the asymmetric encryption scheme

When data is encrypted with the public key, it can only be decrypted using the private key, and vice versa. Unlike symmetric encryption, this scheme does not require that the sender know the private key that the receiver needs to unlock the data. The public key is widely distributed, so anyone who wants to initiate a secure data communication can use it. The private key is never distributed; it is always to be kept secret.

Using both symmetric and asymmetric encryption schemes, Netscape developed an open, nonproprietary protocol called Secured Socket Layer (SSL) to provide data encryption, server authentication, data integrity, and client authentication for TCP/IP-based communication.

Understanding SSL

In an SSL-based transaction, as shown in Figure 15-4, the server sends a certificate to the client system. A certificate is a standard piece of data that contains:

- The certificate issuer's name
- The entity for whom the certificate is being issued
- The public key of the entity
- Other related information

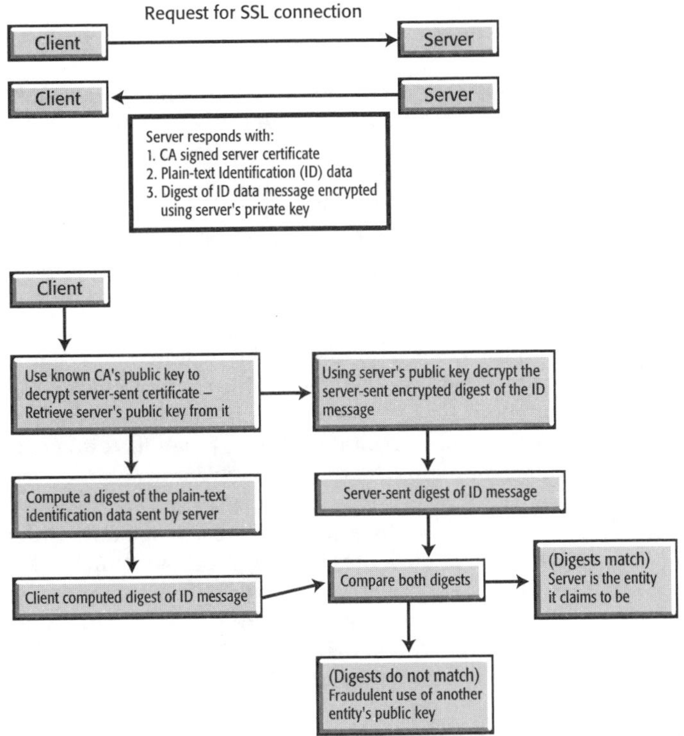

Figure 15-4: An SSL transaction

A certificate is typically issued by a well-known vendor, known as a Certificate Authority (CA). The certificate is encrypted using the Certificate Authority's private key. The client decrypts the certificate using the public key of the Certificate Authority.

Because the certificate contains the server's public key, the client can now decrypt any encrypted data sent by the server. At this point, the server sends a piece of data identifying itself as the entity mentioned in the certificate. It then creates a digest message of the same data it sent to identify itself earlier. The digest is then encrypted using the server's private key. The client now has the certificate from a known CA stating what the server's public key should be, an identity message from the server, and an encrypted digest message of the identity message.

Using the server's public key, the client can decrypt the digest message. The client then creates a digest of the identity message and compares it with the digest sent by the server. If there is a match, this means the server is who it claims to be. Why? Well, the server initially sent a certificate signed by a known CA, so the client is pretty sure to whom this public key belongs. However, the client needed proof that the server that sent the certificate is who it claims to be, so the server sent a simple identification message along with a public key encrypted digest of the same message.

If the server hadn't had the appropriate private key, it would have been unable to produce the same digest that the client computed from the identification message.

If this seems like a complex matter, it is — and it doesn't end here. The client can now send a symmetric encryption key to the server by encrypting it using the server's public key. The server can then use this new key to encrypt data and transmit it to the client. Why do that? Well, it turns out that symmetric encryption is much faster than asymmetric encryption. You can look at it this way: asymmetric encryption (private/public keys) is used to safely transmit a randomly generated symmetric key from the client to the server; this key is later used to provide a fast, secured communication channel.

If an impostor sits between the client and the server system, and is capable of intercepting the data being transmitted, will it be able to do damage? Well, it doesn't know the secret symmetric key that the client and the server are using, so it cannot determine the content of the data; however, it can introduce garbage in the data by injecting its own data into the data packets.

To avoid this, the SSL protocol allows for the use of a message authentication code (MAC). A MAC is simply a piece of data that is computed by using the symmetric key and the data to be transmitted. Because the impostor does not know the symmetric key, it can't compute the correct value for the MAC. For example, a well-known cryptographic digest algorithm called MD5, which was developed by RSA Data Security, Inc., can be used to generate 128-bit MAC values for each data packet to be transmitted. The computing power and time required to successfully guess the correct MAC value this way is almost nonexistent.

SSL makes secure commerce possible on the Internet. Unfortunately, SSL is not readily available in the Apache server, due to a legal dilemma. Current SSL implementation uses algorithms that are patented by RSA. Being a for-profit company, RSA rightfully imposes a restriction on the use of its patented technologies, so if Apache were to include code that used RSA to provide SSL support, it would not remain a free Web server. Another issue is that U.S. government still imposes strict restrictions on the export of software that uses strong cryptography. The government only allows a 40-bit encryption scheme to be exported to rest of the world. But a 40-bit encryption does not provide for adequate security; it has been hacked already. Because Apache is developed by an international group of developers, use of strong cryptography in Apache to support SSL creates all sorts of legal and bureaucratic issues that are unwelcome in such a development project. In light of these issues, it has been decided that Apache will not provide direct support for SSL as long as these issues remain unresolved.

You need not be discouraged by this, however; there are solutions available, both free and commercial. If you want to use SSL for a noncommercial purpose, you can get Apache-SSL. For commercial needs, you can get the commercial Apache derivative called Stronghold from C2Net Technology. In the following sections, I discuss both of these solutions in detail.

Apache-SSL

Apache-SSL is a secure, noncommercial Apache Web server based on Apache and the free implementation of the SSL library called SSLeay. This library supports both SSL versions 2 and 3. Before you explore Apache-SSL any further, make sure you understand the following legal issues.

If you plan on using Apache-SSL outside the United States, you should have no legal restrictions according to the SSLeay documentation. If you use the RSA algorithms provided by RSAREF, however, you can use Apache-SSL for noncommercial purposes. For commercial purposes, you need to make agreements with RSA, because they hold patents in the United States. Also, there may be restrictions on the use of IDEA algorithms in Europe and RC4 in the United States.

If you are still able (legally, that is) and willing to give Apache-SSL a try, the first step is to set up SSLeay in your system. You can get SSLeay at:

```
ftp://ftp.psy.uq.oz.au/pub/Crypto/SSL
```

Setting up SSLeay

First, get the SSLeay compressed tar file from the preceding site. The easiest way to build SSLeay is to run the Perl script called Configure, which is provided in the distribution. You need to specify your operating system name when you run the script. If you run the system without any parameters, you will see a list of supported operating system names.

For example, to create appropriate Makefile configurations for an ELF-based Linux system such as RedHat 5.0, run the script as follows:

```
perl Configure linux-elf
```

Once you have run the configuration script successfully, run the following:

```
make clean
make
make rehash
make test
make install
```

The first make command cleans up any leftover object files from previous compilations. The second make command compiles the library; the third one fixes demo certificates; and the fourth make command tests everything.

If you are on a Windows platform, or are having problems with the installation, you can get more information on how to build SSLeay from the following Web site:

```
www.cryptsoft.com/ssleay/doc/Building.html
```

Once you have tested SSLeay successfully, run the following command to install the software:

```
make install
```

The single executable is called ssleay, and can be found in the apps subdirectory. Run the following to see the version information:

```
ssleay version
```

Now that you have SSLeay support built for your system, you can continue with setting up Apache-SSL.

Setting up Apache-SSL

Getting Apache-SSL files is as easy as going to the www.apache-ssl.org/ site and finding a nearby FTP site. One such site is:

```
ftp://ftp.ox.ac.uk/pub/crypto/SSL/
```

Once you have obtained the Apache-SSL compressed tar file, copy this file to your current Apache distribution directory (that is, the top directory in your Apache distribution) and unpack it. Now you can patch the original Apache files as follows:

```
patch < SSLpatch
```

Change the directory to the Apache src subdirectory and edit the Configuration file. You need to make sure the SSL_BASE value is set to the directory where you unpacked the SSLeay source files. Once you've made sure SSL_BASE points to the right location, run the Apache configuration script Configure as usual, and you should end up with an Apache-SSL executable called httpsd. To verify that the executable is the right version, try:

```
httpsd -v
```

Along with the Apache version, you should also see the Ben-SSL version number. Now you're ready to create a temporary certificate for your secured Apache server.

Creating a temporary certificate

The certificate creation process requires random numbers. To supply some random data for this process, create a file with arbitrary text data. You can simply copy an existing text file from anywhere or type one yourself. Then, set an environment variable called RANDFILE to point to the file you want to use. For example:

```
setenv RANDFILE /tmp/random.txt
```

This command points the RANDFILE environment variable to the /tmp/random.txt file. You should consult your shell documentation regarding how to set environment variables. The preceding command works for the tcsh shell. Once you've set this variable, run:

```
make certificate
```

This prompts you to enter some general information, such as your company's name, your name, and your e-mail address.

While creating your self-generated certificate using the make certificate, you will be prompted to enter something in the Common Name field. You should enter the host name of the machine your server is running as the common name, rather than your own name, as the example in the prompt suggests.

The certificate is stored in the SSLconf/conf/httpsd.pem file.

Directives for configuring Apache-SSL

Now you're almost ready to configure Apache for SSL. First, however, you need to know about the following directives provided by Apache-SSL. You'll use these for the configuration.

SSLDisable

```
Syntax: SSLDisable
Context: server config, virtual host
```

This directive disables SSL. It does not require any arguments.

SSLCertificateFile

```
Syntax: SSLCertificateFile certificate_filename
Default: none
Context: server config, virtual host
```

This directive specifies the certificate filename for a Web site host. Note that you need a separate certificate for each Web site, so if you plan to provide SSL connectivity for a virtual host, you need a separate certificate for the virtual host.

SSLCertificateKeyFile

```
Syntax: SSLCertificateKeyFile certificate_key_filename
Default: none
Context: server config, virtual host
```

This directive specifies the certificate private key file. If you do not use this directive, the key is assumed to be in SSLCertificateFile specified file.

SSLCACertificatePath

```
Syntax: SSLCertificatePath path/to/CA/certificates
Default: none
Context: server config, virtual host
```

This directive specifies the directory in which you keep the Certificate Authority certificate files.

SSLCACertificateFile

```
Syntax: SSLCACertificateFile CA_certificate_filename
Default: none
Context: server config, virtual host
```

This directive specifies the file that contains the Certificate Authority certificate.

SSLVerifyDepth

```
Syntax: SSLVerifyDepth  number
Default: SSLVerifyDepth 0
Context: server config, virtual host
```

Because a CA certificate can be certified by another CA, a chain of CA certificates can be formed. This directive specifies how many CA certificates the server should consult when verifying client certificates. If you are not using client certificates, do not change the default.

SSLVerifyClient

```
Syntax: SSLVerifyClient numeric_option
Default: SSLVerifyClient 0
Context: server config, virtual host
```

This directive sets the client certificate policy for the server. If you require client certificates, set this to 2. If client certificates are optional, set this to 1. If client certificates are not required, use 0.

SSLFakeBasicAuth

```
Syntax: SSLFakeBasicAuth
Context: server config, virtual host
```

This directive translates client X509 to a user name which can be used in authentication. Use of this directive is not recommended.

SSLLogFile

```
Syntax: SSLLogFile log_filename
Context: server config, virtual host
```

This directive specifies where to write information about SSL connections.

SSLRequiredCiphers

```
Syntax: SSLRequiredCiphers cipher1:cipher2:cipher3:...
Context: server config, virtual host, per-directory config
(.htaccess)
```

This directive specifies a colon-separated list of ciphers (cryptographic algorithms such as RC4-MD5 and RC4-SHA).

SSLRequireCipher

```
Syntax: SSLRequiredCipher cipher
Context: per-directory config (.htaccess)
```

This directive adds a cipher to the per-directory list of required ciphers.

SSLBanCipher

```
Syntax: SSLBanCipher cipher
Context: per-directory config (.htaccess)
```

This directive bans a cipher from being used in a per-directory configuration. With this directive, you can disallow clients that want to use the banned cipher.

Configuring Apache for Apache-SSL

Now you are ready to create Apache-like configuration files such as httpd.conf, access.conf, and srm.conf. The author of Apache-SSL, Ben Laurie, provides an example of an httpd.conf file, shown in Listing 15-1. The access.conf and srm.conf files are empty because all the SSL-specific configuration used in the author's example is in httpd.conf.

In this sample configuration, Ben gives an example of how Apache-SSL can be used for both secured and nonsecured document-serving purposes. Instead of the default SSL port 443, he uses port 8887 for secured (https) connection and port 8888 for regular (http) connections. The example configuration is not ready to be tested, since you need to replace directory paths and uncomment a few directives.

Listing 15-1: httpd.conf

```
# This is an example configuration file for Apache-SSL.
# Copyright (C) 1995,6,7 Ben Laurie

# By popular demand, this file now illustrates the way to
# create two web sites, one secured (on port 8887), the
# other not (on port 8888).
```

(continued)

Listing 15-1 *(continued)*

```
# You may need one of these
#User web user

# SSL Servers MUST be standalone, currently.
ServerType standalone

# The default port for SSL is 443...
Port 8887
Listen 8887
Listen 8888

# My test document root
DocumentRoot /u/ben/www/1/docs

# Note that all SSL options can apply to virtual hosts.

# Disable SSL. Useful in combination with virtual hosts.
#SSLDisable

# Set the CA certificate verification path
# (must be PEM encoded).
# (in addition to getenv("SSL_CERT_DIR"), I think).
SSLCACertificatePath /u/ben/apache/apache_1.2.5-
ssl/SSLconf/conf

# Set the CA certificate verification file
# (must be PEM encoded).
# (in addition to getenv("SSL_CERT_FILE"), I think).
#SSLCACertificateFile /some/where/somefile
#SSLCACertificateFile /u/ben/apache/apache_1.2.5-
ssl/SSLconf/conf/httpsd.pem

# Point SSLCertificateFile at a PEM encoded certificate.
# If the certificate is encrypted, then you will be prompted
# for a pass phrase.
# Note that a kill -1 will prompt again.
# A test certificate can be generated with "make certificate".
SSLCertificateFile /u/ben/apache/apache_1.2.5-
ssl/SSLconf/conf/httpsd.pem

# If the key is not combined with the certificate, use this
# directive to point at the key file. If this starts with a '/'
# it specifies an absolute path, otherwise it is relative to
# the default certificate area. That is, it means
# "<default>/private/<keyfile>".
#SSLCertificateKeyFile /some/place/with/your.key
```

```
# Set SSLVerifyClient to:
# 0 if no certificate is required
# 1 if the client may present a valid certificate
# 2 if the client must present a valid certificate
# 3 if the client may present a valid certificate
# but it is not required to have a valid CA
SSLVerifyClient 0
# How deeply to verify before deciding they
# don't have a valid certificate
SSLVerifyDepth 10

# Translate the client X509 into a Basic authorization.
# This means that the standard Auth/DBMAuth methods
# can be used for access control. The user name is the
# "one line" version of the client's X509 certificate.
# Note that no password is obtained from the user.
# Every entry in the user file needs this password:
# xxj31ZMTZzkVA. See the code for further explanation.
SSLFakeBasicAuth

# A home for miscellaneous rubbish generated by SSL. Much
# of it is duplicated in the error log file.
SSLLogFile /tmp/ssl.log

# Custom logging
CustomLog logs/ssl_log "%t %{version}c %{cipher}c
%{clientcert}c"

<VirtualHost scuzzy:8888>
SSLDisable
</VirtualHost>

# New and undocumented directives
#SSLRequiredCiphers
#SSLRequireCipher
#SSLBanCipher

# Experiment with authorization...
#<Directory /u/ben/www/1/docs>
#AuthType Basic
#AuthName Experimental
#AuthGroupFile /dev/null
#AuthUserFile /u/ben/www/1/users
#<Limit PUT GET>
#allow from all
#require valid-user
#</Limit>
#</Directory>

ScriptAlias     /scripts     /u/ben/www/scripts
```

Listing 15-2 shows a functional httpd.conf file for a secured Web server called blackhole.nitec.com with its document root at /www/nitec/secured/htdocs. To provide regular Web service on port 80, I created a virtual host that disables SSL using the SSLDisable directive, and also points to a different document root, /www/nitec/public/htdocs.

Listing 15-2: httpd.conf

```
# User and group for blackhole.nitec.com
User httpd
Group httpd

# SSL Servers MUST be standalone, currently.
ServerType standalone

# Use the default HTTPS port
Port 443

# Also listen to the standard HTTP port
Listen 80

# Document root directory for blackhole.nitec.com
DocumentRoot /www/nitec/secured/htdocs

# The directory where you store CA provided certificate file(s)
SSLCACertificatePath /usr/local/etc/httpd/SSLconf/conf

# The full path of the CA provided certificate file
SSLCACertificateFile /usr/local/etc/httpd/SSLconf/
conf/httpsd.pem

# The full path to the SSL certificate
SSLCertificateFile /usr/local/etc/httpd/SSLconf/conf/httpsd.pem

# Do not require clients to have certificates
SSLVerifyClient 0
SSLVerifyDepth 0

SSLLogFile /logs/ssl.log

# Since I want to have regular (HTTP) web services on
# port 80, here is the virtual host that does that.
<VirtualHost 206.171.50.50:80>
DocumentRoot /www/nitec/public/htdocs
ScriptAlias /cgi-bin/ /www/nitec/public/cgi-bin/
SSLDisable
ServerName blackhole.nitec.com
</VirtualHost>
```

Create a similar configuration for your newly compiled httpsd file. If you are only interested in creating virtual hosts that are secured, and want to leave the main server on port 80 as it is, you can use the following in your main server configuration section (outside a virtual host container):

```
Port 80
SSLDisable
```

To create secured virtual hosts, you use a configuration similar to the following:

```
<VirtualHost host.domain.com:443>
DocumentRoot /path/to/secure/pages
ServerAdmin webmaster@host.domain.com
ServerName host.domain.com
SSLCACertificatePath /usr/local/ssl/certs
SSLCACertificateFile /usr/local/ssl/certs/virtual.host.com.pem
SSLCertificateFile /usr/local/ssl/certs/virtual.host.com.pem
SSLLogFile /path/to/ssl.log
</VirtualHost>
```

The SSLDisable directive in the main server configuration section disables SSL for everything but the virtual hosts that list SSL directives. Now you are ready to test your secured site.

Testing the secured server

Before you start testing, make sure you have the latest Netscape Navigator or Microsoft IE browser. Some of the older browsers do not support SSL.

To test a secured Web site, point your browser to:

```
https://your.secured.web.site.domain/
```

Remember that you must use https:// instead of http:// for all secured server URLs. For the preceding configuration, use the following for secured server access:

```
https://blackhole.nitec.com/
```

For regular Web access, use:

```
http://blackhole.nitec.com/
```

If you created a self-generated certificate by running make certificate earlier, and you try to access your secured site, you will get a warning message from your browser. For example, when you try to access https://blackhole.nitec.com, Netscape Navigator returns the warning screen shown in Figure 15-5.

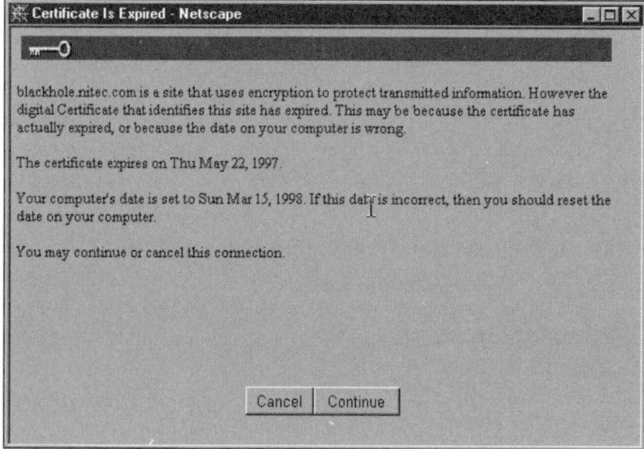

Figure 15-5: Warning message about self-generated certificate

Unless you obtain a certificate from a commercial Certificate Authority that the browsers know, this type of warning message will pop up for each user trying to access the secured site.

Once you get past the warning dialog windows and accept the certificate manually by clicking one or more buttons (OK or Finish), the browser establishes a secured communication channel with the server. Figure 15-6 shows one such session for the blackhole.nitec.com server.

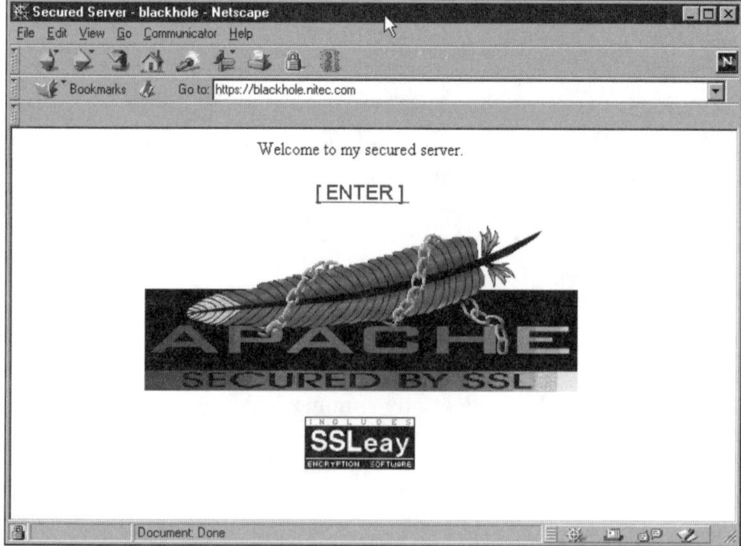

Figure 15-6: A secured session

Notice that the lock icon at the bottom left corner is closed (that is, locked). This means a secured channel has been established.

If you are interested in seeing what happens when a client such as a browser connects to a secured server, you can run the s_client application that comes with the SSLeay package. For the blackhole.nitec.com site, the s_client can be run as follows:

```
ssleay s_client -host blackhole.nitec.com -port 443
```

This produces the output shown in Listing 15-3.

Listing 15-3: **Output of s_client connecting to blackhole.nitec.com on port 443**

```
CONNECTED(00000003)
depth=0
/C=US/ST=California/L=Sacramento/O=Nitec/CN=blackhole.nitec.com
/Email=kabir@nitec.com
verify error:num=18:self signed certificate
verify return:1
depth=0
/C=US/ST=California/L=Sacramento/O=Nitec/CN=blackhole.nitec.com
/Email=kabir@nitec.com
verify return:1
---
Certificate chain
 0
s:/C=US/ST=California/L=Sacramento/O=Nitec/CN=blackhole.nitec.c
om/Email=kabir@nitec.com

i:/C=US/ST=California/L=Sacramento/O=Nitec/CN=blackhole.nitec.c
om/Email=kabir@nitec.com
---
Server certificate
-----BEGIN CERTIFICATE-----
MIICezCCAeQCAQAwDQYJKoZIhvcNAQEEBQAwgYUxCzAJBgNVBAYTAlVTMRMwEQYD
VQQIEwpDYWxpZm9ybmlhMRMwEQYDVQQHEwpTYWNyYW1lbnRvMQ4wDAYDVQQKEwVO
aXRlYzEcMBoGA1UEAxMTYmxhY2tob2xlLm5pdGVjLmNvbTEeMBwGCSqGSIb3DQEJ
ARYPa2FiaXJAbml0ZWMuY29tMB4XDTk3MDQyMjA4NDAwNFoXDTk3MDUyMjA4NDAw
NFowgYUxCzAJBgNVBAYTAlVTMRMwEQYDVQQIEwpDYWxpZm9ybmlhMRMwEQYDVQQH
EwpTYWNyYW1lbnRvMQ4wDAYDVQQKEwVOaXRlYzEcMBoGA1UEAxMTYmxhY2tob2xl
Lm5pdGVjLmNvbTEeMBwGCSqGSIb3DQEJARYPa2FiaXJAbml0ZWMuY29tMIGfMA0G
CSqGSIb3DQEBAQUAA4GNADCBiQKBgQDVuXIKqg7p9eS1xVIRyglaLTSZ+Ge+CESR
HUBUQiGuiU+eo97CaKze4B19AM4ZV3xnloJrS8LKTnLmkJ95A++6ymrhHVIVgmXZ
DgkczjQ2LKInWCJ9QZntoEu/1mPUY2KnXbbQo5v/gtf/J6tbhuRJKtLgz2dK4CWM
/0PQzzrYjQIDAQABMA0GCSqGSIb3DQEBBAUAA4GBAIT2FA3Je7Q+tnu3KjBj7NLT
VDG5YsEyGXZKBEWJEzpAzOywnqndiTwwdUgocYl/EADidHsrgiYDsYPD3oVFkWOw
evHLwxBE++6FIcLkRty3C/bfgrdJWWFsrd14nZq3Vy8y/xFQkZJ9ObOcpo6acOqm
5HrrSatn6DBaWuDXdEI5
-----END CERTIFICATE-----
```

(continued)

Listing 15-3: *(continued)*

```
subject=/C=US/ST=California/L=Sacramento/O=Nitec/CN=blackhole.n
itec.com/Email=kabir@nitec.com
issuer=/C=US/ST=California/L=Sacramento/O=Nitec/CN=blackhole.ni
tec.com/Email=kabir@nitec.com
SSL handshake has read 813 bytes and written 317 bytes
---
New, SSLv3, Cipher is RC4-SHA
SSL-Session:
    Cipher    : RC4-SHA
    Session-ID:
C26196B7FC9C2DBE664FC5C55AD4C89887BC9703B98F9441362853E428C4D67F
    Master-Key:
303EBE61E04175F81C605E02A2CC264022F6E55F7714FA32DB3A37852A4AD6C
85B2748ED3FAD06FDD733CDD098B443D6
    Key-Arg   : None
    Start Time: 861699068
    Timeout   : 7200 (sec)
---
```

The preceding output contains a lot of information. The server provides a distinguished name associated with the output, in abbreviated form. Distinguished names are defined by the X.509 standard, which defines the fields, field names, and abbreviations used to refer to the fields. Table 15-1 lists some of the fields shown in the preceding output.

Table 15-1
Distinguished Name Fields

Field	*Abbreviation*	*Description*	*Example*
Common Name	CN	Name being certified. This is the fully qualified domain name of the system.	CN=blackhole.nitec.com
Organization or Company	O	Name is associated with this organization.	O=Nitec
Organizational Unit	OU	Name is associated with this organizational unit, such as a department.	OU= I didn't specify one.
City/Locality	L	Name is located in this city.	L=Sacramento
State/Province	ST	Name is located in this state/province	ST=California
Country	C	Name is located in this country (ISO code)	C=US

The Certificate Authorities define which fields are required and which are optional. There may be even restrictions on the content of a field. For example, Netscape browsers require that the Common Name field for a certificate be the server name or a regular expression for the domain.

The binary format of a certificate is defined using the Abstract Syntax Notation 1 (ASN.1). This notation defines how to specify the contents, and the encoding rules define how this information is translated into binary form. ASN.1 can be encoded in many ways, but the emerging standard is a very simple encoding scheme called Direct Encoding Rules (DER), which results in a compact binary certificate. For e-mail exchange purposes, the binary certificate is often Base64 encoded, resulting in ASCII text lines such as the one appearing between the ——BEGIN CERTIFICATE—— and ——END CERTIFICATE—— lines.

Information about certificate chains also appears. When a certificate is issued by a CA whose certificate is issued by another CA, a chain is created and the server reveals information regarding the chain so the client can decide to investigate the certificates mentioned in the chain. In this particular example, the chain is not present.

After displaying the output shown in Listing 15-3, the s_client program remains connected to the server. Therefore, if you enter the following HTTP request:

```
GET / HTTP/1.0
```

followed by a blank line, you get the output shown in Listing 15-4.

Listing 15-4: **Output of a GET request on a secured server**

```
HTTP/1.1 200 OK
Date: Tue, 22 Apr 1997 08:51:56 GMT
Server: Apache/1.2.5 Ben-SSL/1.13
Connection: close
Content-Type: text/html

<HTML><HEAD>
<TITLE>Index of /</TITLE>
</HEAD><BODY>
<H1>Index of /</H1>
<UL><LI> <A HREF="/"> Parent Directory</A>
<LI> <A HREF="development"> development</A>
<LI> <A HREF="future"> future</A>
<LI> <A HREF="public"> public</A>
</UL></BODY></HTML>
read:errno=0
```

There was no directory index file in the top-level directory of the secured server blackhole.nitec.com, so a dynamically generated directory listing was produced by the server as usual.

If you've been able to perform similar tests on your Apache-SSL server, you have successfully created a secured Web server.

Getting a CA-signed certificate

Now, all you need to do is get a browser-recognizable certificate from one of the well-known Certificate Authorities. Unfortunately, not all CAs issue server certificates for Apache-SSL, because of policies chosen by their own management.

Here are a few CAs that are likely to provide you with a certificate for Apache-SSL:

✦ Thawte Consulting, at www.thawte.com/certs/server/request.html

✦ CertiSign Certificadora Digital Ltda., at www.certisign.com.br

✦ IKS GmbH, at www.iks-jena.de/produkte/ca/

✦ Uptime Commerce Ltd., at www.uptimecommerce.com

✦ ID-Pro GmbH, CA-Projekt, at www.id-pro.de/security/CA

Only Thawte and VeriSign (which does not provide certificates for Apache-SSL) are supported by all versions of both Netscape Navigator/Communicator and Microsoft Internet Explorer browsers. This situation may change eventually; as more and more people start using Apache-SSL or other Apache-based SSL servers, CAs may feel the business pressure to certify these servers. The best approach for you would be to identify which CAs are currently supported in target browsers, and find out if any of them are willing to sign your certificate. For the time being, Thawte is the only real choice.

Stronghold

If you do not want to go through the trouble of configuring SSLeay, patching Apache source files with Apache-SSL patches and extra source files, and dealing with self-signed certificate issues, your best choice is to get the commercially available Apache derivative server called Stronghold.

Stronghold is developed by C2NET Technology. It is based on the latest Apache server and SSL. Stronghold comes with a nice Web-based Configuration Manager that enables you to administer the server from anywhere on the Web. If you are planning on doing commerce for profit on the Web, you should definitely consider using this product.

You can easily obtain an evaluation copy of this product from C2NET. Go to their Web site at www.c2.net and sign up for an evaluation version of the Stronghold server. When you sign up for the evaluation copy, you are asked to enter the IP address of the host you plan on using as the Stronghold server platform. Once you register, an e-mail message is sent to your e-mail address (which you provide during registration) within minutes. This e-mail message contains the user name/password to download Stronghold. It also contains the license key you will need during installation, as well as a URL to the download site.

I think Stronghold is a great solution for those who want to spend fewer sleepless nights trying to get SSL working with Apache-SSL. The company provides useful documentation and appears to be helpful, in general. If this option seems too expensive for you, but you still don't want to deal with Apache-SSL, try the Raven SSL module for Apache which can be found at the URL:

```
http://raven.covalent.net/
```

Technically speaking, the Raven SSL module, developed by Covalent Technologies, may not be exactly like other Apache modules (such as mod_cgi or mod_rewrite), but it still works like a module from an end-user perspective. The company supplies a precompiled version of the Apache server, which includes the Raven SSL module. The module also comes with prepatched Apache source file, so recompiling a new server with your own modules and configuration while including Raven is as easy as uncommenting a line in the Configuration file. Note that Covalent Technologies does not include sources for the Raven module or RSA cryptography algorithms, because of the distribution restrictions on cryptography code in the United States. Currently, VeriSign does not give out certificates for Raven-based Apache servers, but Thawte Consulting does issue certificate for it — and yes, it is cheaper than Stronghold (at least at the time of writing).

Installing Stronghold

Installing Stronghold is a breeze. Simply unpack the software you downloaded from the Web site and run the INSTALL.sh script. It prompts you for information such as where you want to install Stronghold, which ports you want to use for the HTTP and HTTPS services, and the server name and license key. Most of the prompts include the default value, which should be fine for virtually all scenarios.

You do not need to run a separate Apache server for HTTP services. Stronghold can handle both secure and nonsecure HTTP services.

If you accept the defaults, then the following ports are used:

80	Standard HTTP service. Example: http://yourserver/
443	SSL-based HTTP service. Example: https://yourserver/
444	Configuration Manager. Example: https://yourserver:444/
445	Direct (localhost) Interface. Example: http://localhost:445/

The installation script asks you to add the following to your .cshrc file if you are using csh/tcsh shells:

```
sentenv SSLTOP /path/to/stronghold/dir/ssl
setenv PATH ${SSLTOP}/bin:$PATH
```

If you are using sh/bash shells, add:

```
$ SSLTOP=/path/to/stronghold/dir/ssl
$ PATH=${SSLTOP}/bin:$PATH
$ export SSLTOP PATH
```

The installation script also provides options to either convert an existing Netscape Commerce key/certificate or create a new key/certificate pair. If you never had a secured Netscape commerce server, you should create a new key/certificate pair. In this case, you are asked to select the size of the key in bits. You can choose from 512 to 4096 (4K) bits.

I recommend using 1024 bits as the key size, because lower-sized keys are unsafe and higher-sized keys could make your server slow. Also, some versions of popular browsers are unable to handle larger keys. Once you have chosen the size of the key, you are asked to type random keys on your keyboard. Do not worry about what you type. The real purpose of this is to measure the time differences between your keystroke, without regard to which keys you type. Type away until you hear a beep or the counter counts down to zero. At the end of this interaction, the key is generated.

Now you need to make a major decision: you are asked if you want to request a CA authorized certificate. Note that Stronghold currently bundles a free certificate from Thawte Certificate Authority; however, this certificate can only be obtained after you have paid for the software. If you just want to evaluate the software for a while and then decide whether you want to use it, I recommend not creating the certificate request until you purchase the software. You can always generate a certificate request using the genreq utility provided with Stronghold. For evaluation purposes, answer No; you are then prompted for information needed to create a self-signed certificate for the evaluation period.

The private key that is created in this process can be protected using a password. You are asked to add a password to protect your private key from being compromised after a break-in. If you choose to use a password, however, every time you start the secured server you will be required to enter this password. This means you may not be able to start the server automatically at boot from rc.d or rc.local facilities.

Finally, the installation script starts the secure server, and you should be able to access it right away from the URL:

```
https://yourserver/
```

You are warned by your browser that it does not recognize the self-signed certificate used by the server. When you install a real CA-provided certificate on your server, however, this warning is not displayed. The first page you see on your secured site will look like the one shown in Figure 15-7.

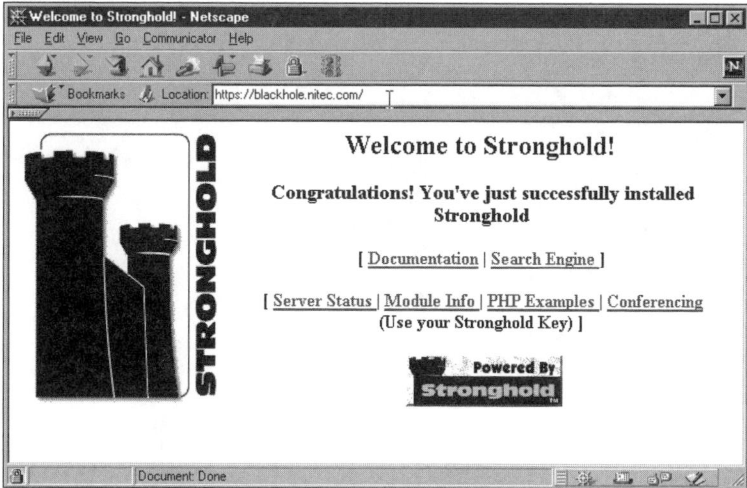

Figure 15-7: The Welcome to Stronghold page

When you install Stronghold using the INSTALL.sh script, it also installs Python, the Focus conferencing system, and the SWISH/WWWWAIS search engine.

Now that you have successfully installed Stronghold, you can go ahead and create contents in your secured Web space. To administer the secured Web server, you can use the Web-based Configuration Manager.

Using the Web-based Configuration Manager

Stronghold can be configured using the Web-based Configuration Manager or the usual configuration files such as httpd.conf, access.conf, and srm.conf. To access the Configuration Manager from anywhere on the Web, point your browser to your secured server URL at port 444. (Use a different port address if you didn't use the default value supplied by the INSTALL.sh script).

For example, my secured Stronghold server's Configuration Manager can be accessed with the following URL:

```
https://secured.nitec.com:444/
```

To protect itself from abuse, the Configuration Manager deploys a user name/password based authentication scheme. You supplied the user name and password at installation so use them when requested. Once you authenticate yourself as the configuration administrator, you see a page similar to the one shown in Figure 15-8.

Figure 15-8: Main page of the Configuration Manager

This is the index page of the Configuration Manager, and it provides quick access to the following:

✦ Global server configuration

✦ Keys and certificate enrollment

✦ Module configuration

✦ Starting, stopping, or reloading the server

You can also click the Enter image, and you'll see a page similar to the one shown in Figure 15-9.

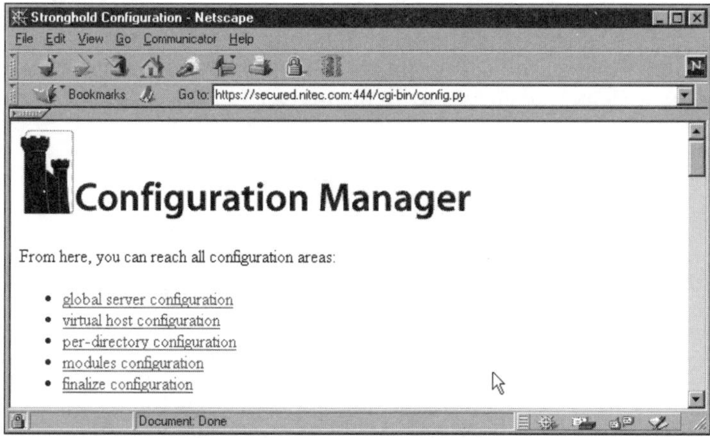

Figure 15-9: Global server page of the Configuration Manager

From here, you can access any of the following:

- ✦ Global server configuration
- ✦ Virtual host configuration
- ✦ Per-directory configuration
- ✦ Modules configuration
- ✦ Finalize configuration

The last option enables you to submit any additions or modifications you make to the server. When you click on this option, you will see a page such as the one shown in Figure 15-10.

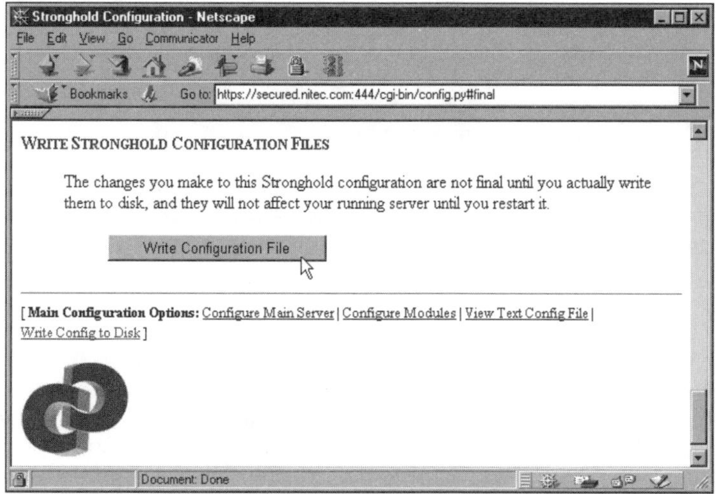

Figure 15-10: Saving changes

When you are ready to submit your new configuration, click the button labeled Write Configuration File to write the changes to disk files. Once you have written the changes, you must restart the server for the changes to be effective. You can use the Start, Stop, or Reload page as shown in Figure 15-11 to restart the server.

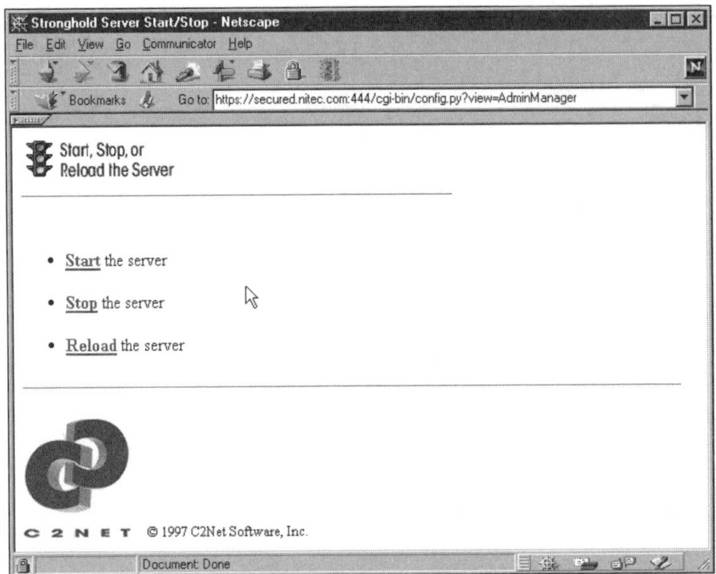

Figure 15-11: Start, Stop, or Reload from the Configuration Manager

If you have an SSL-compliant browser on the secured server system, you can access the Configuration Manager via the direct (localhost) interface using the URL https://localhost:445/. Change the port number if you have chosen a different port at installation. This feature becomes useful when you find yourself running Telnet sessions on the Web server and want to modify some settings quickly. Use an SSL-capable Lynx browser in such a situation.

Getting a CA-signed certificate

When you decide to use Stronghold as your Web server and want to acquire a CA-signed certificate, you can back up your existing key stored in the $SSLTOP/private directory and run:

```
genkey <hostname>
```

This utility generates a key pair for the host name specified, then calls genreq to generate a certificate-signing request (CSR), and finally calls gencert to create a temporary certificate that you can use until your CA responds. The temporary certificate is signed with your site's private key. Before you run this utility, however, you should determine which CA you want to use. Stronghold offers a free certificate from Thawte Consulting (www.thawte.com) when you buy the server package. This bundled certificate should do the job, unless you have a reason for using another CA, such as VeriSign (www.verisign.com/).

If you want to know about pricing differences between the two companies, you can find this information as well. VeriSign publishes its pricing information at www.verisign.com/enroll.s/payment.html and its secure server service agreement at www.verisign.com/enroll.s/legal.html. Thawte provides a rate table at https://www.thawte.com/pricing.html. If you want to use a different CA, make sure you choose one that the clients who access your site can accept.

After you've submitted your CSR to a CA, and provided the CA with requested papers that help authenticate your organization, all you can do is wait for the CA to get back to you with a site certificate. Typically, you will receive this certificate as an e-mail attachment. When you receive it, you must use Stronghold's getca utility to install it.

To install a site certificate, follow these steps:

1. Save the e-mail-attached certificate file in a temporary location, such as /tmp/01.pem.
2. Run getca, specifying the name of the host that owns this certificate and providing the temporary file as input:

   ```
   getca hostname < /tmp/01.pem
   ```

3. Restart the server using the reload script or by entering the command:

   ```
   kill -HUP `cat /path/to/httpd.pid'
   ```

You are required to have a key/certificate pair for each host using SSL. This includes the virtual hosts you run. You have to pay for each certificate you request, so this can be an expensive approach if you have many sites to bring under the SSL umbrella. In such a case, it is wise to organize your virtual sites so they point to a single host, for SSL.

For example, you can create a host called secured.yourdomain.com and just get one key/certificate pair for this host. If you want your virtual site called virtualone.yourdomain.com to perform secured transactions, you can simply create a directory under the document root of secured.yourdomain.com and put the virtual site's files there. The HTML documents in the virtual sites that need to linked to the secured area will now use links such as:

```
<A HREF=https://secured.yourdomain.com/virtualhost-
directory/filename>A secured Page</A>
```

You just need to make sure that visitors have a way to get back to the nonsecured virtual site after they finish browsing or interacting with the secured documents or scripts. You can ensure this by adding a link back to the virtual site. To reduce confusion among the visitors of the virtual site, you might want to leave optional fields (such as Organizational Unit) blank in your certificate request.

If you are using the server for an intranet or a campuswide network, however, you might consider creating your private Certificate Authority.

Setting up a private Certificate Authority

A private CA allows you to sign your own certificates. There are two reasons why you may want to create a private CA:

- ✦ You just want to satisfy your curiosity.
- ✦ You have considerable need for security within your organization, and need to use SSL heavily between departments.

In the second case, make sure the system on which you decide to build your CA is physically secured and preferably not connected to any network at all. Doing so ensures that your CA is hard to break into. If you do not take steps to protect your CA system, and an intruder gains access to your CA, the intruder can create false certificates and use them to access secured documents or even set up software to impersonate your server.

The Stronghold Web server provides tools for setting up a basic Certification Authority. Note that you can create a private CA using the SSLeay package you installed for Apache-SSL. In the following section, however, I use the Stronghold-installed SSLeay utilities to create a private CA.

Setting up a private CA

The first step in setting up a private CA is to create a key/certificate pair for the CA. You can use the makeca script found in the $SSLTOP/bin directory to create this pair. You will use the private key created for the CA to sign server certificates that your CA offers. Client systems will use the certificate you create for the CA to verify the CA's signature on server certificates it issues.

The makeca script stores the CA certificate it creates in the $SSLTOP/CA/cacert.pem file. Netscape Navigator requires that the CA certificate be in DER format, however. To convert the PEM certificate format to DER format, use the x509 program:

```
x509 -outform DER < $SSLTOP/CA/cacert.pem >
/path/to/document/root/your_organization.cacert
```

The resulting file, your_organization.cacert, is placed in your Web server's document root directory. You can keep it in another location if you want as long as it is accessible by your client browsers. The file's extension, .cacert, is important because it is associated with the MIME-type application/x-x509-ca-cert. Make sure you check the mime.type file on the top-level Stronghold directory for a line such as:

```
application/x-x509-ca-cert   cacert
```

This associates the extension (cacert) with a Certificate Authority certificate, and instructs browsers to download and install the certificate. For example, when a Nitec user points his Netscape Navigator browser to:

```
https://blackhole.nitec.com/nitec.cacert
```

the browser displays a dialog window as shown in Figure 15-12.

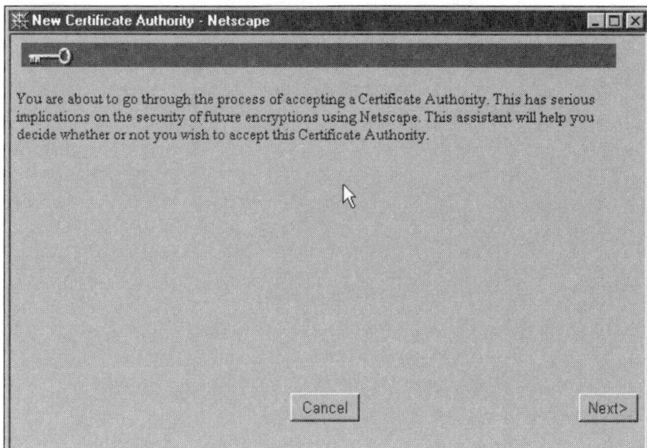

Figure 15-12: Installing a private CA certificate on a browser

A few more dialog windows inform the user about the certificate. The user can view details of the certificate, as shown in Figure 15-13.

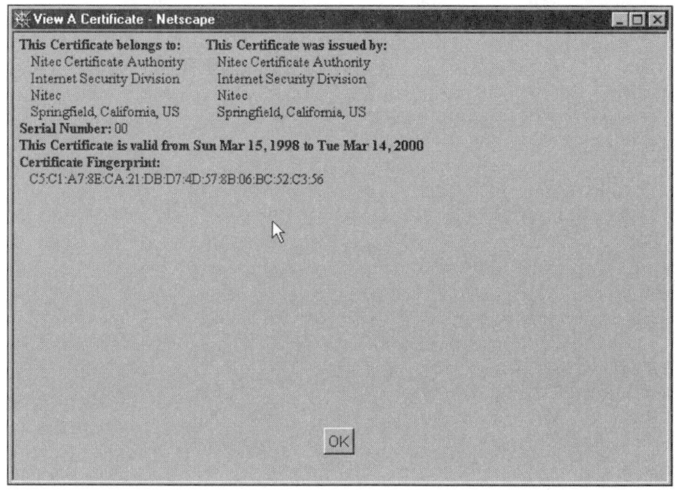

Figure 15-13: Details of Nitec's certificate

In the process, the user is given an opportunity to decide what this private CA can certify. For example, he can decide to allow this private CA to certify other (network) sites, e-mail users, or software developers. Figure 15-14 shows that the user has decided to trust this CA for everything.

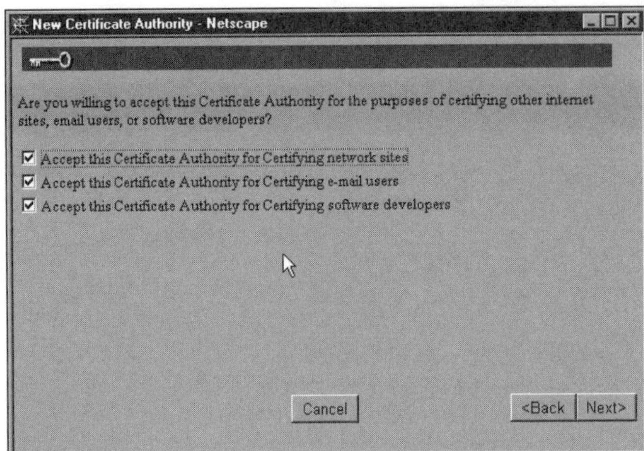

Figure 15-14: The user gets to choose what a private CA can certify.

Finally, when the user accepts the private CA, he must assign a nickname for the CA. In Figure 15-15, the nickname he chooses is Nitec CA.

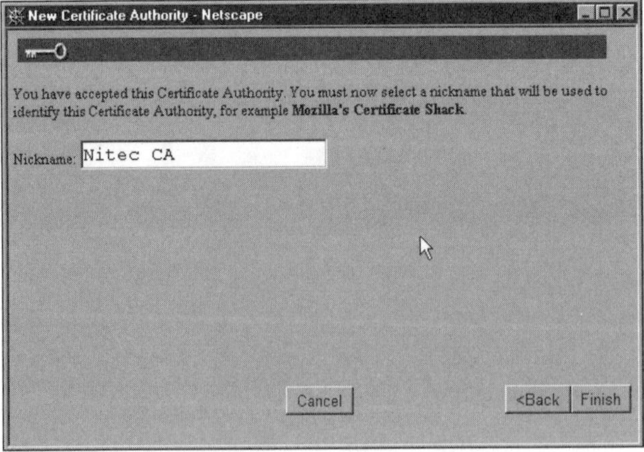

Figure 15-15: Choosing a nickname for the private CA

Once the user has completed these steps, the CA's certificate is listed along with other official CA certificates. Figure 15-16 shows the nickname Nitec CA listed among the many other commercial Certificate Authorities.

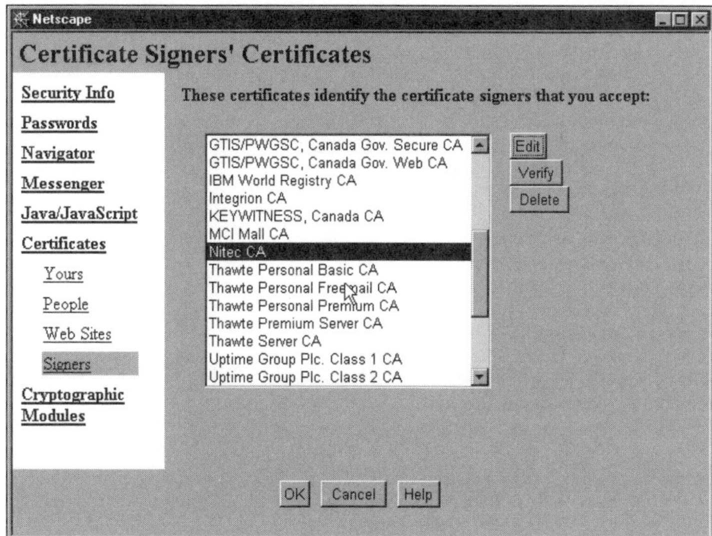

Figure 15-16: Private CA certificate appears along with commercial CA certificates

The user can decide at any time to edit, delete, or verify the CA's certificate and its uses.

Once the CA's certificate is installed on user browsers, the browsers do not warn the users if the CA is unknown (unless the user has chosen to be warned during the certificate installation process).

The next step in creating a private CA is to configure the SSLeay library configuration file.

Configuring SSLeay

By default, the SSLeay security policy may be too loose for your private CA needs. For example, the default SSLeay configuration allows server certificate requests to supply only the CommonName information, and everything else is optional.

If you are using the private CA to provide a strict security environment for your organization, you may want to modify the policy section of the SSLeay configuration file. This file, ssleay.conf, can be found in the $SSLTOP/CA directory.

Locate the line that sets the policy being used. Because the default policy is policy_anything, this line looks like the following:

```
policy = policy_anything
```

Two policies are available in the default configuration file. The default policy is defined as follows:

```
# For the 'anything' policy
 [ policy_anything ]
countryName            = optional
stateOrProvinceName    = optional
localityName           = optional
organizationName       = optional
organizationalUnitName = optional
commonName             = supplied
emailAddress           = optional
```

As you can see, everything but the commonName is optional. The other policy, called policy_match, is defined as follows:

```
# For the CA policy
[ policy_match ]
countryName            = match
stateOrProvinceName    = match
organizationName       = match
organizationalUnitName = optional
commonName             = supplied
emailAddress           = optional
```

This policy requires that the server certificate request match the CA's country name, state or province name, and organization name. It also requires that the commonName be provided in the request. Now you can either modify one of these two policies (policy_anything or policy_match) or create a new policy.

The simplest way to create a new policy is to copy one of the preceding policies and replace the values as needed. The acceptable values are:

- match — The contents of the field must match the same field in the CA certificate.
- optional — The field is not required in the certificate request.
- supplied — The field must be supplied in the certificate request.

Each policy parameter field corresponds to a certificate request field, and must have one of these three values. You should also make sure that your new policy has a new name, which you must provide in the brackets. If you decide to use your policy instead of the default, then also make sure you set the policy to your policy.

If your policy is called my_policy, you set the following line to have your policy section (my_policy) defined:

```
policy = my_policy
```

Normally, the policy parameters are the only fields you need to edit in the ssleay.conf file. If you want to edit other fields, make sure you read the file comments carefully.

Now you are ready to accept certificate requests (CSR) and sign them!

Signing certificates

Actually, you should establish another policy before you start signing server certificates. This policy should indicate which proofs in what format you require for a certificate to be processed. This is to verify the origin of the CSR request.

Once you receive a CSR request via e-mail or via a CGI script your Web site, you can save the content of the CSR in a temporary file and supply it as an argument to the sign_csr script. For example:

```
sign_csr /tmp/a_csr_request_file
```

You are asked to enter your CA password, which you set up when you created the CA using the makeca script. The sign_csr request checks the signature on the request, prints the requested fields, and prompts you to decide whether or not to sign this request. If you feel that all information provided is appropriate and matches with the other forms of authentication (usually paper) that you obtained from the certificate applicant, you can sign the request. The script then prompts you to commit the signature.

When you enter **Y**, the script prints the contents of the new certificate and saves it in the $SSLTOP/CA/new_certs directory.

The new_certs directory was not created in my version of Stronghold, so I created it manually.

The filename of each new certificate is a number in the series of all certificates signed by this CA. For example, the first certificate you sign is 01.pem, the next is 02.pem, and so on. Once you have created the certificate, send it to the applicant, who can then install it.

I created a CSR request for blackhole.nitec.com and signed it using the Nitec CA facility discussed earlier. The resulting certificate was then installed on the Stronghold server. When the server was accessed from a browser that had also installed the Nitec CA certificate (in an earlier example), it didn't display those annoying warning dialog windows stating that the server's certificate was unknown. This was expected, so I selected the Security Info option from a Netscape Navigator menu, clicked the View Certificate button, and was shown the dialog window seen in Figure 15-17.

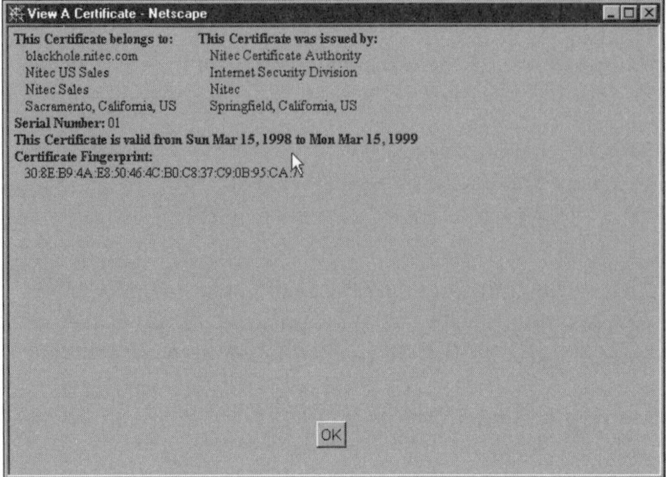

Figure 15-17: blackhole.nitec.com server certified by Nitec CA

So, to create this wonderful self-signing setup, you simply follow these steps:

1. Create a CSR for blackhole.nitec.com.
2. Create a CA called Nitec CA.
3. Have client browsers download and install the Nitec CA certificate.
4. Get the CSR signed by Nitec CA.
5. Install the Nitec CA-signed server certificate on blackhole.nitec.com.

Because all these steps were accomplished within the same organization, the process was virtually painless and was completed in a very short time. In a real-world case, however, you may want to establish a procedure for CSR submission, such as setting up a special e-mail account for receiving CSR requests, and another to send out signed server certificates.

Summary

In this chapter, you learned what SSL is and why Apache does not support SSL by default. You learned how to implement SSL in Apache using noncommercial Apache-SSL and the commercial Apache derivative server called Stronghold. You also learned about certificates, Certificate Authorities, and how to create your own private Certificate Authority.

Next, you learn about URL rewriting tools.

✦ ✦ ✦

Rewriting Your URLs

✦ ✦ ✦ ✦

In This Chapter

The URL rewriting engine for Apache

URL layout

Content handling

Access restriction

✦ ✦ ✦ ✦

A URL brings visitors to your Web site. As an Apache administrator, you will need to make sure that all possible URLs to your Web site are functional. How do you do that? You keep monitoring the server error logs for broken URL requests. If you see requests that are being returned with a 404 Not Found status code, it is time to investigate these URLs. Often, when HTML document designers upgrade a Web site, they forget that renaming an existing directory could cause a lot of visitors' bookmarked URLs to break.

As an administrator, how do you solve such a problem? The good news is that there is a module called mod_rewrite that not only allows you to solve these problems but also lets you create very interesting solutions using URL rewrite rules. In this chapter, I discuss this module and provide practical examples of URL rewriting.

Among all currently available Apache modules, mod_rewrite stands out. This is a very sophisticated module for two reasons:

- ✦ It provides Apache administrators with a degree of URL rewrite flexibility that is very cool and practical.
- ✦ It is a very well-documented module.

Now let's look at how mod_rewrite works.

The URL Rewriting Engine for Apache

When Apache receives a URL request, it processes the request by serving the file to the client (the Web browser). What if you wanted to intervene in this process to map the URL to a different file or even to a different URL? That's where mod_rewrite comes in. It provides you with a flexible mechanism for creating URL rules. An URL rule has the form:

```
regex-pattern-to-be-matched          regex-substitution-pattern
```

However, it is also possible to add conditions (such as more regex-patterns-to-be-matched) to a rule such that the substitution is only applied if the conditions are met. The substituted URL can be handled as an internal subrequest by Apache, or sent back to the Web browser as an external redirect. Let's take a look at an example to understand this a little better. Figure 16-1 shows an example request and the result of a mod_rewrite rule.

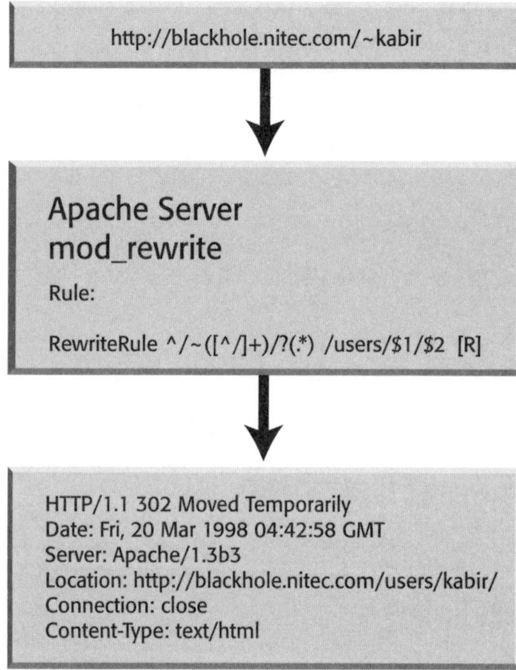
http://blackhole.nitec.com/~kabir
Apache Server
mod_rewrite
Rule:
RewriteRule ^/~([^/]+)/?(.*) /users/$1/$2 [R]
HTTP/1.1 302 Moved Temporarily
Date: Fri, 20 Mar 1998 04:42:58 GMT
Server: Apache/1.3b3
Location: http://blackhole.nitec.com/users/kabir/
Connection: close
Content-Type: text/html

Figure 16-1: Example of a rule-based rewrite URL operation

A request for http://blackhole.nitec.com/~kabir is made to the Apache server. The server receives the request and passes it to the mod_rewrite module at the URL translation stage of the processing of the request. The mod_rewrite module applies the rewrite rule defined by a directive called RewriteRule. In this particular example the rule states that if a pattern such as /~([^/]+)/?(.*) is found, it should be replaced with /users/$1/$2. Because there is a [R] flag in the rule, an external URL redirect should also be sent back to the Web browser. The output shows the redirect location to be http://blackhle.nitec.com/users/kabir/.

As you can see, this sort of redirect can come in handy in many situations. Let's take a look at the directives that give you the power to rewrite URLs. You should also familiarize yourself with the server variables that can be used in many rewrite rules and conditions:

SERVER_NAME	Host name of the Web server
SERVER_ADMIN	Web server administrator's e-mail address
SERVER_PORT	Port address of the Web server
SERVER_PROTOCOL	Version of HTTP protocol being used by the Web server
SERVER_SOFTWARE	Name of the Web server vendor
SERVER_VERSION	Version of the Web server software
DOCUMENT_ROOT	Top-level document directory of the Web site
HTTP_ACCEPT	MIME types that are acceptable by the Web client
HTTP_COOKIE	Cookie received from the Web client
HTTP_FORWARDED	Forwarding URL
HTTP_HOST	Web server's host name
HTTP_PROXY_CONNECTION	The HTTP proxy connection information
HTTP_REFERER	The URL that referred to the current URL
HTTP_USER_AGENT	Information about the Web client
REMOTE_ADDR	IP address of the Web client
REMOTE_HOST	Host name of the Web client
REMOTE_USER	Username of the authenticated user
REMOTE_IDENT	Information about remote user's identification
REQUEST_METHOD	HTTP request method used to request the current URL
SCRIPT_FILENAME	Physical path of the requested script file
PATH_INFO	Path of the requested URL
QUERY_STRING	Query data sent along with the requested URL
AUTH_TYPE	Type of authentication used
REQUEST_URI	Requested URI
REQUEST_FILENAME	Same as SCRIPT_FILENAME
THE_REQUEST	Requested URL
TIME_YEAR	Current year
TIME_MON	Current month

TIME_DAY	Current day
TIME_HOUR	Current hour
TIME_MIN	Current minute
TIME_SEC	Current second
TIME_WDAY	Current weekday
TIME	Current time
API_VERSION	Version of API used
IS_SUBREQ	Set if request is a subrequest

RewriteEngine

```
Syntax: RewriteEngine on | off
Default: RewriteEngine off
Context: server config, virtual host, per-directory config
(.htaccess)
```

This directive provides you with the on/off switch for the URL rewrite engine in the mod_rewrite module. By default all rewriting is turned off. To use the rewrite engine, you must turn the engine on by setting this directive to on.

When enabling URL rewriting per-directory configuration (.htaccess) files, you must enable (set to on) this directive inside the per-directory configuration file and make sure that you have enabled the following directive in the appropriate context for the directory:

```
Options FollowSymLinks
```

In other words, if the directory belongs to a virtual host site, make sure this option is enabled inside the appropriate virtual host container. Similarly, if the directory in question is part of the main server's Web document space, make sure this option is enabled in the main server configuration.

Note that enabling rewrite rules in per-directory configurations could degrade the performance of your Apache server. This is because mod_rewrite employs a trick to support per-directory rewrite rules and this trick involves increasing the server's processing load. Therefore you should avoid using rewrite rules in per-directory configuration files whenever possible.

RewriteOptions

```
Syntax: RewriteOptions option1 option2 ...
Default: none
Context: server config, virtual host, per-directory config
(.htaccess)
```

This directive enables you to specify options to change the rewrite engine's behavior. Currently, the only available option is inherit. By setting this directive to the inherit option, you can force a higher-level configuration to be inherited by a lower-level one. For example, if you set this directive in your main server configuration area, a virtual host defined in the configuration file will inherit all the rewrite configurations, such as the rewrite rules, conditions, maps, and so on.

Similarly, when this directive is set as mentioned in a per-directory configuration file (.htaccess), it will inherit the parent directory's rewrite rules, conditions, and maps. By default, the rewrite engine does not permit inheritance of rewrite configuration, but this directive permits you to alter the default.

RewriteRule

```
Syntax: RewriteRule search-pattern substitution-string [flag
list]
Default: none
Context: server config, virtual host, per-directory config
(.htaccess)
```

This directive enables you to define a rewrite rule. The rule must have two arguments. The first argument is the search pattern that must be met to apply the substitution string. The search pattern is written using regular expression (see Appendix B for basics of regular expression). The substitution string can be constructed with plain text, back-references to substrings in the search pattern, values from server variables, or even map functions. The flag list can contain one or more flag strings, separated by commas, to inform the rewrite engine about what to do next with the substitution. Let's take a look back at the previous example:

```
RewriteRule /~([^/]+)/?(.*)  /users/$1/$2 [R]
```

Here, the search pattern is /~([^/]+)/?(.*) and the substitution string is /users/$1/$2. Notice the use of back-references in the substitution string. The first back-reference string $1 corresponds to the string found in the first set of parentheses (from the left). So $1 is set to whatever is matched in ([^/]+) and $2 is set to the next string found in (.*). When a URL request is as follows:

```
http://blackhole.nitec.com/~kabir/welcome.html
```

The value of $1 is kabir, and $2 is welcome.html; so the substitution string looks like:

```
/users/kabir/welcome.html
```

When you have more than one RewriteRule specified, the first RewriteRule operates on the original URL and if a match occurs, the second rule will no longer operate on the original URL. Instead, it gets the URL substituted by first rule as the URL on which to apply rules. In a scenario where a match occurs at every step, a set of three rewrite rules will function as follows:

```
RewriteRule  search-pattern-for-original-URL     substitution-
string-1  [flags]
RewriteRule  search-pattern-for-substitution-string-1
substitution-string-2  [flags]
RewriteRule  search-pattern-for-substitution-string-2
substitution-string-3  [flags]
```

Is it possible to apply more than one rule to the original URL? Yes, you can use the C flag to instruct the rewrite engine to chain multiple rules. In such a case, you may not want to substitute until all rules are matched so you can use a special substitution string to disable a substitution in a rule.

The details of the possible flags are as follows:

C | chain	This flag specifies that the current rule be chained with the next rule. When chained by a C flag, a rule is looked at if and only if the previous rule in the chain results in a match. Each rule in the chain must contain the flag, and if the first rule does not match, the entire chain of rules is ignored.
E=var:value | env=var:value	You can set an environment variable using this directive. The variable is accessible from rewrite conditions, Server Side Includes, CGI scripts, and so on.
F | forbidden	When a rule using this flag is matched, an HTTP response header called FORBIDDEN (status code 403) is sent back to the browser. This effectively disallow the requested URL.
G | gone	When a rule using this flag is matched, a HTTP response header called GONE (status code 410) is sent back to the browser. This informs the browser that the requested URL is no longer available on this server.
L | last	This tells the rewrite engine to end rule processing immediately so that no other rules are applied to the last substituted URL.
N | next	This tells the rewrite engine to restart from the first rule. However, the first rule no longer tries to match the original URL, because it now operates on the last substituted URL. This effectively creates a loop. You must have terminating conditions in the loop to avoid an infinite loop.
NS | nosubreq	Use this flag to avoid applying a rule on an internally generated URL request.
P | proxy	Using this flag will convert a URL request to a proxy request internally. This will only work if you have compiled Apache with the mod_proxy module and configured it to use the proxy module.

PT | passthrough	This is a hack and likely to disappear in a later version of Apache. This flag forces the rewrite engine to modify the internal request record structure such that the URL member variable of the structure is set to the value of the filename member variable. Use this directive only when you are using directives from mod_rewrite with other modules that contain URL-to-filename translators. An example of such module is the mod_alias module.
QSA | qsappend	This flag allows you to append data (such as key=value pairs) to the query string part of the substituted URL.
S=n | skip=n	Skips n rules.
T=mime-type | type=mime-type	Forces the specified MIME-type to be the MIME-type of the target file of the request.

Note that you can add conditions to your rules by preceding them with one or more RewriteCond directives, which are discussed in the following section.

RewriteCond

```
Syntax: RewriteCond test-string  condition-pattern [flag list]
Default: none
Context: server config, virtual host, perl-directory config
(.htaccess)
```

This directive is useful when you want to add an extra condition for a rewrite rule specified by the RewriteRule directive. You can have several RewriteCond directives per RewriteRule. All rewrite conditions must be defined before the rule itself.

The test string may be constructed with plain text, server variables, or back-references from both the current rewrite rule and the last rewrite condition. To access the first back-reference from the current RewriteRule directive, use $1, and to access the first back-reference from the last RewriteCond directive, use %1.

To access a server variable, use the %{variable name} format. For example, to access the REMOTE_USER variable, specify %{REMOTE_USER} in the test string.

There are a few special data access formats:

%{ENV:variable}	Use this to access any environment variable that is available to the Apache process.
%{HTTP:header}	Use this to access the HTTP header used in the request.
%{LA-U:variable}	Use this to access the value of a variable that is not available in the current stage of processing. For example, if you need to make use of the REMOTE_USER server variable in a rewrite condition stored in the server's

	configuration file (httpd.conf), you cannot use %{REMOTE_USER} because this variable is only defined after the server has performed the authentication phase, which comes after mod_rewrite's URL processing phase. To look ahead at what the username of the successfully authenticated user is, you can use %{LA-U:REMOTE_USER} instead. However, if you are accessing the REMOTE_USER data from a RewriteCond in a per-directory configuration file, you can use %{REMOTE_USER} because the authorization phase has already finished and the server variable has become available as usual. The lookup is performed by generating a URL-based internal subrequest.
%{LA-F:variable}	Same as the %{LA-U:variable}in most cases, but lookup is performed using a filename-based internal subrequest.

The condition pattern can also use some special notations in addition to being a regular expression. For example, you can perform lexical comparisons between the test string and the condition pattern by prefixing the condition pattern with a <, >, or = character. In such a case the condition pattern is compared with the test string as plain text string.

Also note that there may be times when you want to check if the test-string is a file, directory, or symbolic link. In such a case, you can replace the condition pattern with the following special strings:

-d	Tests if the test-string specified directory exists or not
-f	Tests if the test-string specified file exists or not
-s	Tests if the test-string specified non-zero size file exists or not
-l	Tests if the test-string specified symbolic link exists or not
-F	Tests the existence and accessibility of the test-string specified file
-U	Tests the validity and accessibility of the test-string specified URL

The optional flag list can consist of one or more comma-separated strings as follows:

NC | nocase	Performs a case-insensitive condition test.
OR | ornext	Normally, when you have more than one RewriteCond for a RewriteRule directive, these conditions are ANDed together for the final substitution to occur. However, if you need to create an OR relationship between two conditions, use this flag.

RewriteMap

```
Syntax: RewriteMap name-of-map type-of-map:source-of-map
Default: none
Context: server config, virtual host
```

This directive facilitates a key-to-value lookup through the use of a map. Think of a map as a table of data where each row has a key and a value. Typically, a map will be stored in a file. However, the map can be either a text file, a DBM file, internal Apache functions, or an external program. The type of the map corresponds to the source of the map. The applicable types are:

txt — Plain text file that has key value lines such that each key and value pair are on a single line and are separated by at least one white space character. The file can contain comment lines starting with # characters or can have blank lines. Both comments and blank lines are ignored. For example:

```
Key1    value1
Key2    value2
```

defines two key value pairs. Note that text file-based maps are read during Apache startup and only reread if the file has been updated after the server is already up and running. The files are also reread during server restarts.

rnd — A special plain text file which has all the restrictions of txt type but allows a flexibility in defining the value. The value for each key can be defined as a set of ORed values using the | (vertical bar) character. For example:

```
Key1    first_value_for_key1 | second_value_for_key1
Key2    first_value_for_key2 | second_value_for_key2
```

this defines two key value pairs where each key has multiple values. The value selected is decided randomly.

int — The internal Apache functions toupper(key) or tolower(key) can be used as a map source. The first function converts the key into all uppercase characters and the second one converts the key to lowercase characters.

dbm — A DBM file can be used as a map source. This can be very useful and fast (compared to text files) when you have a large number of key value pairs. Note that DBM-file-based maps are read during Apache startup and only reread if the file has been updated after the server is already up and running. The files are also reread during server restarts.

prg An external program can generate the value. When a program is used, it is started at the Apache startup and data (key, value) is transferred between Apache and the program via standard input (stdin) and standard output (stdout). Make sure you use the RewriteLock directive to define a lock file when using an external program. When constructing such a program, make sure you read the input from the stdin and write it on stdout in a nonbuffered I/O mode.

RewriteBase

```
Syntax: RewriteBase <base URL>
Default: current directory path of per-directory config
(.htaccess)
Context: per-directory config (.htaccess)
```

This directive is only useful if you are using rewrite rules in per-directory configuration files. It is also only required for URL paths that do not map to the physical directory of the target file. Set this directive to whatever alias you used for the directory. This will ensure that mod_rewrite will use the alias instead of the physical path in the final (substituted) URL. For example, when an alias is set as follows:

```
Alias /icons/   /www/nitec/htdocs/icons/
```

and rewrite rules are enabled in the /www/nitec/htdocs/icons/.htaccess file, the RewriteBase directive should be set as follows:

```
RewriteBase /icons/
```

RewriteLog

```
Syntax: RewriteLog path/to/logfile
Default: none
Context: server config, virtual host
```

If you want to log the applications of your rewrite rules, use this directive to set a log filename. Like all other log directives, it assumes that a path without a leading slash (/) means that you want to write the log file in the server's root directory, for example:

```
RewriteLog logs/rewrite.log
```

This will write a log file in the logs subdirectory under your server's root directory. As mentioned before, a log written by server should be only writable by the server user.

RewriteLogLevel

```
Syntax: RewriteLogLevel level
Default: RewriteLogLevel 0
Context: server config, virtual host
```

This directive allows you to specify what gets logged in the log file. A default value of 0 means that nothing will be logged. In fact, a log level of 0 means no log-related processing is done inside the module. Therefore, if you wanted to disable logging, keep it set to 0.

Note that if you set the RewriteLog directive to /dev/null and the RewriteLogLevel to a non-zero value, the internal log-related processing will still be done but no log will be produced. This is a waste of your system's computing resources, so if you don't want logging, keep this directive set to its default value. You have a choice between 0 and 9 for log levels. The higher the level, the more logging data is written.

RewriteLock

```
Syntax: RewriteLock filename
Default: none
Context: server config, virtual host
```

If you use an external mapping program for creating rewrite maps, you will need to specify a filename with this directive. This file is used as a lock file for synchronizing communication with external mapping programs.

URL Layout

In this section you will find examples of URL rewrites that deal with the layout of URLs. Often you will need to redirect or expand a URL request to another URL. In the following examples you will see how mod_rewrite can help in such cases.

Expanding requested URL to canonical URL

Web sites that offer user home pages usually support an URL scheme such as:

```
http://hostname/~username
```

This is a shortcut URL and needs to be mapped to a canonical URL. You may also have other shortcuts or internal URLs that need to be expended to their canonical URLs. In this example, you will see how the ~username gets translated to /u/username. Figure 16-2 illustrates what needs to happen.

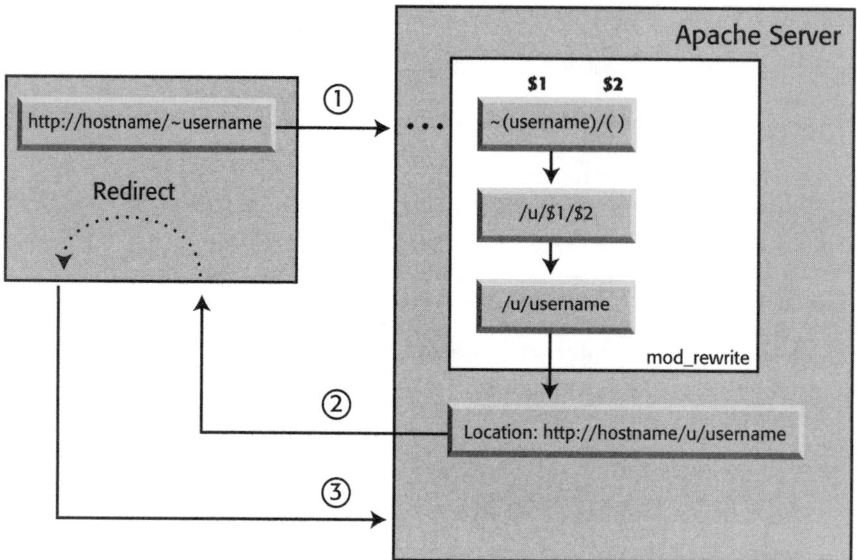

Figure 16-2: Expanding requested URL to canonical URL

When a request for http://hostname/~username is received, the rewrite rule will translate that into /u/username and redirect the new URL to the browser. The browser then rerequests the http://hostname/u/username URL and the usual Apache request processing completes the request.

The external HTTP redirect is necessary because any subsequent requests must also use the translated canonical URL instead of ~username. The rule needed to do this is:

```
RewriteRule   ^/~([^/]+)/?(.*)     /u/$1/$2  [R]
```

Many ISP sites with thousand of users use a structured home directory layout; that is, each home directory is in a subdirectory that begins, for instance, with the first character of the username. So, /~foo/anypath is /home/f/foo/www/anypath while /~bar/anypath is /home/b/bar/www/anypath. To implement a translation scheme from shortcut URLs to canonical URLs in this case the following rule can be used:

```
RewriteRule   ^/~(([a-z])[a-z0-9]+)(.*)  /home/$2/$1/www$3
```

Redirecting a user home directory to a new Web server

If you had a lot of user home pages on a Web server and needed to move them to a new machine for some reason, you would need to have a redirect rule as shown in Figure 16-3.

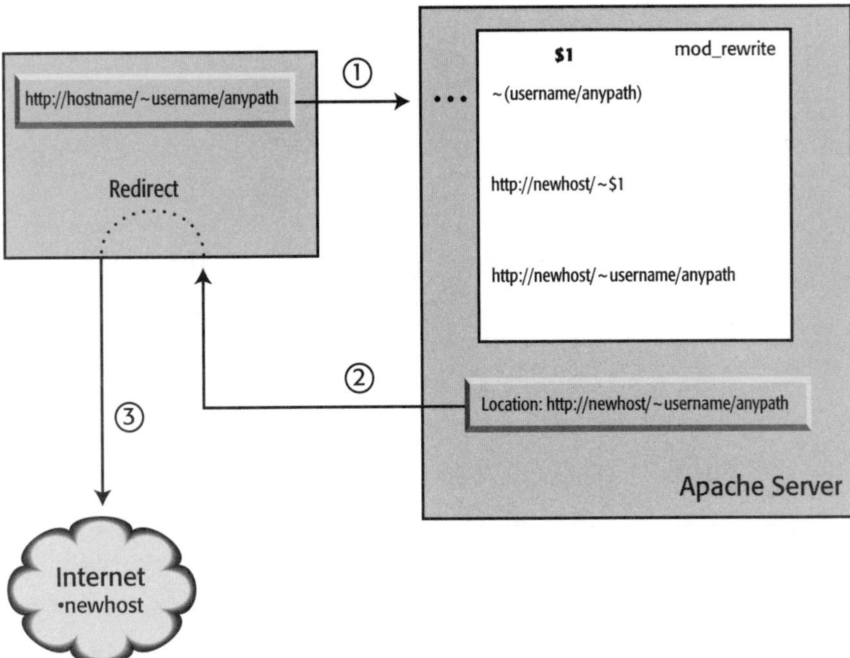

Figure 16-3: Redirecting user home directories to a new Web server

The solution is simple with mod_rewrite. On the old Web server just redirect all /~user/anypath URLs to http://newserver/~user/anypath as follows:

```
RewriteRule   ^/~(.+)  http://newserver/~$1  [R,L]
```

Note that the L flag is used to indicate that no other rewrite rule can be applied to the substituted URL.

Searching for a page in multiple directories

Sometimes it is necessary to let the Web server search for pages in more than one directory. Here MultiViews or other techniques cannot help. For example, say you want to handle a request for http://hostname/filename.html such that if filename.html is not present in the dir1 directory of your Web server, you want the server to try a subdirectory called dir2. Figure 16-4 illustrates what needs to happen.

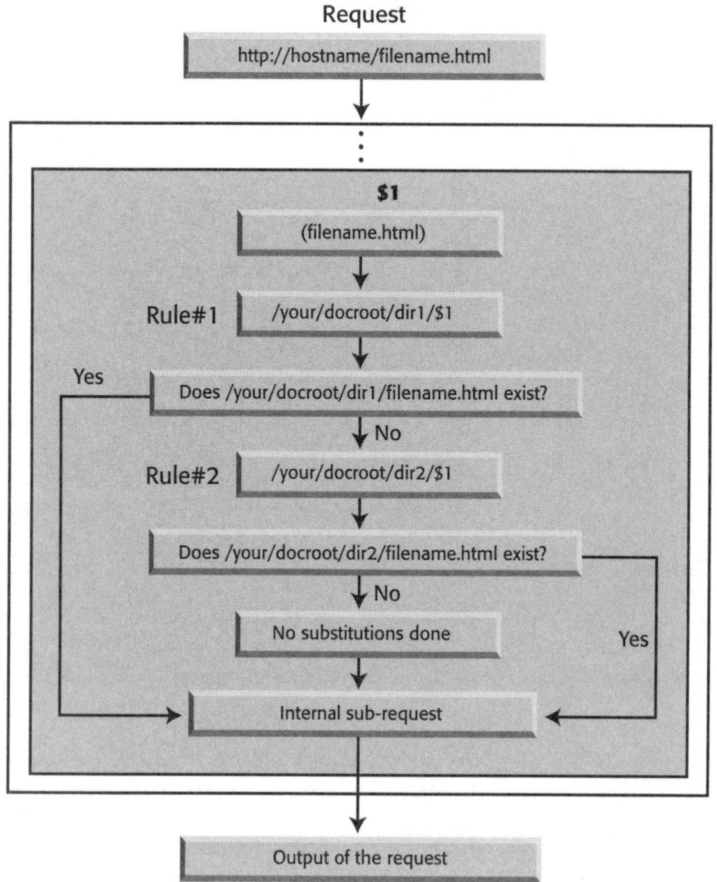

Figure 16-4: Searching for a page in multiple directories

The rules needed to implement this are as follows:

```
RewriteCond          /your/docroot/dir1/%{REQUEST_FILENAME}   -f
RewriteRule  ^(.+)  /your/docroot/dir1/$1  [L]

RewriteCond          /your/docroot/dir2/%{REQUEST_FILENAME}   -f
RewriteRule  ^(.+)  /your/docroot/dir2/$1  [L]

RewriteRule   ^(.+)  -  [PT]
```

The first rule substitutes the requested URL with /your/docroot/dir1/$1 (where $1 is the target file in the request) only if the requested file exists in your/docroot/dir1/ subdirectory. If the condition is met, this is the last rule applied to this URL. However, if no match is found then the next rule applies. This rule does the same thing as the first one but this time a subdirectory dir2 is used for the path. This rule is also final if a match is found. In the event that none of the rules match, the request is not substituted and is passed on to Apache as usual.

Setting an environment variable based on a URL

You might want to keep status information between requests and use the URL to encode it. But you don't want to use a CGI wrapper script for all pages just to strip out this information. You can use a rewrite rule to strip out the status information and store it via an environment variable that can be later dereferenced from within XSSI or CGI. This way a URL /foo/S=java/bar/ gets translated to /foo/bar/ and the environment variable named STATUS is set to the value java. Figure 16-5 illustrates what happens.

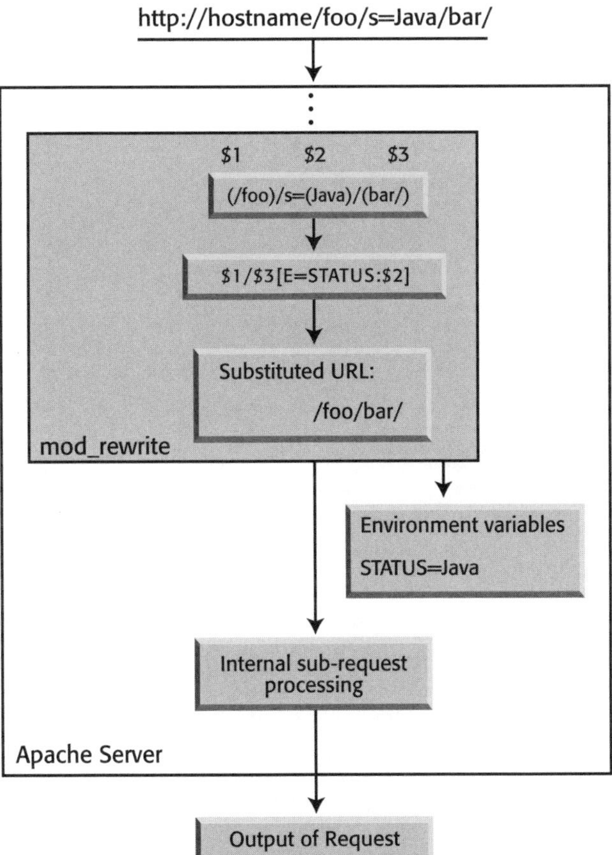

Figure 16-5: Setting an environment variable from a URL

The URL rewriting steps shown in Figure 16-5 can be implemented using the following rewrite rule:

```
RewriteRule    ^(.*)/S=([^/]+)/(.*)     $1/$3 [E=STATUS:$2]
```

Here value of $3 gets stored in the environment variable called STATUS using the E flag.

Creating www.username.host.com sites

Assume that you want to provide www.username.host.com for the home page of username via just DNS address (A) records to the same machine and without any virtual hosts on this machine. For HTTP/1.0 requests there is no solution, but for HTTP/1.1 requests that contain a Host: HTTP header you can use the following rule set to rewrite http://www.username.host.com/anypath internally to /home/username/anypath:

```
RewriteCond   %{HTTP_HOST}            ^www\.[^.]+\.host\.com$
RewriteRule   ^(.+)          %{HTTP_HOST}$1            [C]
RewriteRule   ^www\.([^.]+)\.host\.com(.*)        /home/$1$2
```

Figure 16-6 illustrates how this works.

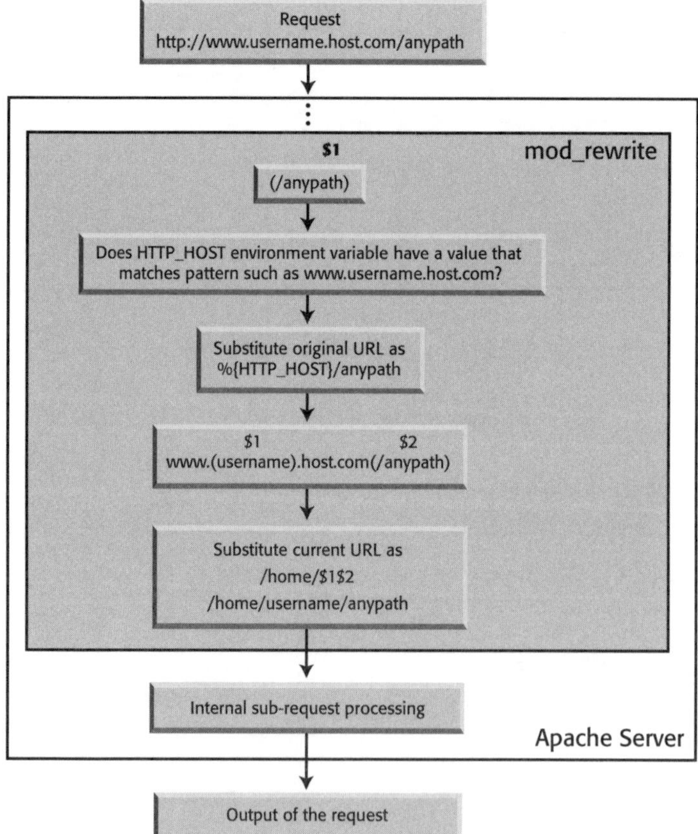

Figure 16-6: Virtual hosts for each username

This is an example of a chained rule set. The first rule has a condition that checks to see if the environment variable HTTP_HOST matches a pattern such as www.username.host.com. If it does, the rule is applied. In other words, a request such as www.username.host.com/anypath gets substituted with www.username.host.com/anypath. This could be a bit confusing because the substitution is not quite obvious. This is needed so that the username can be extracted using the second rule. The second rule extracts the username part from the substituted request and creates a new URL /home/username/anypath for an internal subrequest.

Redirecting a failing URL to another Web server

If you have a multiserver Web network and often move contents from one server to another, you might face a problem where you need to redirect failing URL requests to from Web server A to another Web server B. There are many ways of doing this: you can use the ErrorDocument directive (see Chapter 4), write a CGI script to handle this, or use mod_rewrite to rewrite the failing URLs to the other server. Note that using this mod_rewrite based solution is less preferable than using an ErrorDocument CGI-script. The first solution has the best performance, but less flexibility and is less error-safe:

```
RewriteCond   /your/docroot/%{REQUEST_FILENAME} !-f
RewriteRule   ^(.+)                             http://Web
serverB.dom/$1
```

The problem here is that this will only work for pages inside the DocumentRoot. While you can add more Conditions (to also handle home directories, for example), there is a better variant:

```
RewriteCond   %{REQUEST_URI} !-U
RewriteRule   ^(.+)          http://Web serverB.dom/$1
```

This uses the URL look-ahead feature of mod_rewrite, and will work for all types of URLs. This does have a performance impact on the Web server, however, because for every request there is one more internal subrequest. If your Web server runs on a powerful CPU, use this one. If it is a slow machine, use the first approach, or better, an ErrorDocument CGI-script.

Creating an access multiplexer

This example will show you how to create a rule set to redirect requests based on a domain type, such as .com, .net, .edu, .org, .uk, .de, and so on. The idea is to redirect the visitor to the geographically nearest Web site. This technique is employed by many large corporations to redirect international customers to an appropriate Web site or FTP server.

The first step in creating such a solution is to create a map file. For example, the following shows a text-based map file called site-redirect.map:

```
com      http://www.mydomain.com/download/
net      http://www.mydomain.com/download/
edu      http://www.mydomain.com/download/
org      http://www.mydomain.com/download/
uk       http://www.mydomain.uk/download/
de       http://www.mydomain.de/download/
ch       http://www.mydomain.ch/download/
```

When a request is received for http://www.mycompany.com/downlod/anypath from a host called dialup001.demon.uk, the request needs to be redirected to the Web site www.mydomain.uk/download/ and similarly any request from hosts that belong to the top-level domains (TLD) .com, .net, .edu, and .org is routed to the www.mycompany.com/download/ site.

Here are the rules that are needed for the above setup:

```
RewriteMap    sitemap              txt:/path/to/site-
redirect.map
RewriteRule   ^/download/(.*)      %{REMOTE_HOST}::$1
[C]
RewriteRule   ^.+\.([a-zA-Z]+)::(.*)$
%{sitemap:$1|www.mydomain.com/download/}$2  [R,L]
```

Figure 16-7 illustrates the use of this rule.

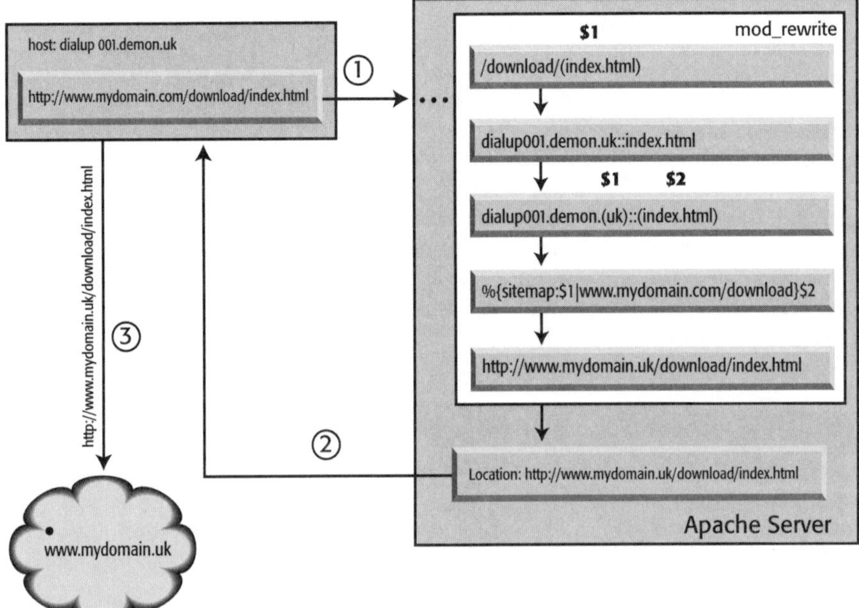

Figure 16-7: URL-based access multiplexer

As you can see in Figure 16-7, when a host such as dialup001.demon.uk requests the www.mydomain.com/download/index.html page, the first rule rewrites the request using the hostname of the requesting host as follows:

```
dialup001.demon.uk::index.html
```

Then the next rule in the chain is applied. This rule gets applied when the search pattern matches and the substitution URL is created by looking up the map file for the TLD. If no matches are found, the default www.mydomain.com is used. This is done by the | (or) operator in the substitution URL string. Perhaps it is easier to understand the second rule using the algorithm shown in Listing 16-1.

Listing 16-1: Algorithm for the second rewrite rule

```
if(current URL matches a fully-qualified-hostname::anything)
then

# substitute the current URL using the domain type information
stored in $1 perform a
#  lookup in the map file.

If  (map file has a key that matches the domain type) then
#use the key's value as follows:

       Substituted URL = value-of-the-key$2      #where $2 is
anything after

#fully-qualified-hostname::  pattern


Else
       # Use default value www.mydomain.com/download/$2

       Substituted URL = www.mydomain.com/download/$2
endif

Endif
```

The R flag makes this a external URL redirect and the L flag makes this the last rule for the substituted URL.

Creating time-sensitive URLs

Ever wonder if it would be possible to have a URL that would point to different files based on time? Well, mod_rewrite makes it easy to create such an URL. There are a lot of variables named TIME_xxx for rewrite conditions. Using the special lexicographic comparison patterns <STRING, >STRING, and =STRING you can do time-dependent redirects, for example:

```
RewriteCond   %{TIME_HOUR}%{TIME_MIN} >0700
RewriteCond   %{TIME_HOUR}%{TIME_MIN} <1900
RewriteRule   ^foo\.html$             foo.day.html
RewriteRule   ^foo\.html$             foo.night.html
```

This provides the content of foo.day.html under the URL foo.html from 07:00 to19:00 and the remaining time provides the contents of foo.night.html.

Content Handling

The examples in this section deal with content-specific rewriting rules. You will learn how to create backward-compatible URLs, browser-based content rewriting, end-user transparent HTML to CGI redirects, and more.

Adding backward compatibility in URLs

Assume that you have recently renamed the page bar.html to foo.html and now you want to provide the old URL for backward compatibility. Additionally, you do want the users of the old URL to even not recognize that the page was renamed. How can this be done? Here is how:

```
RewriteRule    ^foo\.html$  bar.html
```

If you want to let the browser know about the change, you can do an external rewrite so the browser will display the new URL. All you need to do is add the R flag as follows:

```
RewriteRule    ^foo\.html$  bar.html [R]
```

Creating browser-matched-content URLs

You can use rewrite rules to dish out different contents (using internal subrequests) to different browsers. You cannot use content negotiation for this because browsers do not provide their types in that form. Instead you have to act on the HTTP header User-Agent. For example, if a browser's User-Agent header matched Mozilla/3 then you can send out a Netscape Navigator 3 (or above) features-friendly page or you can send out a different page if the browser is an older version of Navigator or if it is another type of browser.

If the HTTP header User-Agent begins with Mozilla/3, the page foo.html is rewritten to foo.NS.html and the rewriting stops. If the browser is Lynx or Mozilla version 1 or 2 the URL becomes foo.20.html. All other browsers receive the page foo.32.html. This is done by the following rules:

```
RewriteCond %{HTTP_USER_AGENT}  ^Mozilla/3.*
RewriteRule ^foo\.html$         foo.3x.html          [L]

RewriteCond %{HTTP_USER_AGENT}  ^Lynx/.*         [OR]
RewriteCond %{HTTP_USER_AGENT}  ^Mozilla/[12].*
RewriteRule ^foo\.html$         foo.2x.html          [L]
```

When a request for an URL such as http://hostname/foo.html is received, the first condition tests to see if the environment variable HTTP_USER_AGENT has a value that contains the string Mozilla/3. or not. If it does, the first rule is applied. This rule substitutes foo.3x.html for the original URL and all rewriting is complete, however, when the first rule is not applied, the second rule is invoked. There are two conditions that are ORed. In other words, one of these conditions must match before this rule can be applied.

The first condition is to test the same environment variable for the substring Lynx/, and the second condition tests the same environment variable for the substring Mozilla/1 or Mozilla/2. If any of these conditions are met, the rule is applied. The rule substitutes foo.2x.html, the original URL. The substituted URL is turned into a subrequest and processed by Apache as usual.

Creating an HTML to CGI gateway

You may want to transform a static page foo.html into a dynamic variant foo.cgi in a seamless way, that is, without informing the browser or user. Here is how:

```
RewriteRule    ^foo\.html$  foo.cgi  [T=application/x-httpd-cgi]
```

The rule rewrites a request for foo.html to a request for foo.cgi. It also forces the correct MIME-type so it gets run as a CGI-script. A request, such as http://hostname/foo.html, is internally translated into a request for the CGI script. The browser does not know that its request has been redirected.

Access Restriction

These examples deal with access control issues. You will learn about how to control access to certain areas of your Web site using the URL rewrite module.

Blocking robots

It's easy to block an annoying robot from retrieving pages of a specific Web site. You might try a /robots.txt file containing entries of the Robot Exclusion Protocol but that is typically not enough to get rid of such a robot. A sample solution, as follows:

```
RewriteCond %{HTTP_USER_AGENT}   ^NameOfBadRobot.*
RewriteCond %{REMOTE_ADDR}       ^123\.45\.67\.[8-9]$
RewriteRule ^/not/to/be/indexed/by/robots/.+    -    [F]
```

This rule has two conditions, as follows:

```
If  (HTTP_USER_AGENT of the robot matches a pattern
"NameOfBadRobot" ) and
     (REMOTE_ADDR of the requesting host is 123.45.67.8 to
123.45.67.9) then
       No substitution but send a HTTP "Forbidden" header
(status code 403)
endif
```

As you can see, the robot's User-Agent header is matched, along with the IP address of the host it uses. The above conditions allow for multiple IP addresses (123.45.67.8 and 123.45.67.9) to be checked.

Creating an HTTP referer-based URL deflector

You can program a flexible URL deflector that acts on the Referer HTTP header and configure it with as many referring pages as you like. Here is how:

```
RewriteMap   deflector              txt:/path/to/deflector.map
RewriteRule  ^/(.*)
${deflector:%{HTTP_REFERER}|/$1}
RewriteRule  ^/DEFLECTED       %{HTTP_REFERER}
[R,L]
RewriteRule  .*                -       [PT]
```

This is used in conjunction with a corresponding rewrite map such as:

```
http://www.badguys.com/bad/index.html     DEFLECTED
http://www.badguys.com/bad/index2.html    DEFLECTED
http://www.badguys.com/bad/index3.html    http://somewhere.com/
```

This automatically redirects the request back to the referring page if the URL matches the DEFLECTED value in the map file. In all other cases, the requests are redirected to specified URLs.

Summary

In this chapter, you learned about the powerful URL rewriting engine, mod_rewrite. You also learned how to use URL rewriting rules to create many practical solutions; however, writing URL rewrite rules can be challenging for administrators who are new to regular expressions. I recommend that if you are new to regular expressions, use rewriting rules with care.

Next, you learn how to fine-tune everything that affects your Web site.

✦ ✦ ✦

PART

V

Using Apache Today and Tomorrow

✦ ✦ ✦ ✦

In This Part

✦ ✦ ✦ ✦

CHAPTER 17

Performance Tips

In This Chapter

Fine-tuning your Apache computer

Streamlining Apache and its configuration

Getting better performance out of your network

Developing high-performance content

To get the maximum performance out of your Apache server you need to constantly monitor four things: the computer, the network, the content, and the people involved. In this chapter, I discuss some of the issues that can cause performance bottlenecks, and tell you how to cure them.

I must warn you that if you're someone who hacks operating system kernels regularly to get maximum performance, this chapter probably won't teach you anything that you don't know already. This chapter is for people who are just beginning to look at performance as an issue. Also, you may get the feeling that I am primarily dealing with PC-based Apache installations. This is due to the assumption that most people using Apache are running it on PC-based systems. However, most of what I discuss here still applies to all Apache platforms.

The Apache Computer

Apache runs on a variety of computers. Although the architecture may vary greatly, the hardware components that cause performance bottlenecks are virtually the same.

Note

By the way, since you're reading a chapter on performance, I will assume that your current Apache system is a modern machine. If you told me that you use a PC clone as your Web server and were concerned about performance, I would assume that you have a Pentium class computer and not an i386-based system.

When analyzing your performance needs, the very first question you should ask yourself is: "Do I need a fast CPU for my Apache computer?" The answer depends on how you use your Apache server.

If the server serves mostly static HTML pages, chances are your CPU will not be a significant performance factor. On the other hand, if you generate a lot of dynamic content using Server Side Includes, CGI scripts, and so on, your Apache server is likely to make good use of a fast processor. In such a case, getting a faster processor is advisable.

How fast is fast enough? Nothing is enough! The faster the better. You should know, however, that just getting a fast CPU won't do you any good if you deal with dynamic content in high volume. The most likely candidate for performance bottleneck in such a scenario is RAM.

You can never get enough RAM. But RAM is not cheap, so how much is going to give you better performance? Only you can answer this question by monitoring your system on a regular basis during load. For example, on most UNIX systems you can run utility programs to monitor your system performance. Figure 17-1 shows the output of one such widely available UNIX utility called top.

```
/bin/csh (ttyp2)
  9:35pm  up 10 days,  6:48,  1 user,  load average: 0.06, 0.05, 0.01
48 processes: 47 sleeping, 1 running, 0 zombie, 0 stopped
CPU states:  0.3% user,  0.5% system,  0.0% nice, 99.2% idle
Mem:  257068K av, 251984K used,   5084K free,  26556K shrd, 129220K buff
Swap: 128484K av,      0K used, 128484K free                 96820K cached

  PID USER     PRI  NI  SIZE  RSS SHARE STAT  LIB %CPU %MEM   TIME COMMAND
22679 kabir     13   0   588  588   456 R       0  0.7  0.2   0:00 top
22548 httpd      1   0  1024 1024   876 S       0  0.1  0.3   0:00 httpd
    1 root       0   0   404  404   340 S       0  0.0  0.1   0:03 init
    2 root       0   0     0    0     0 SW      0  0.0  0.0   0:00 kflushd
    3 root     -12 -12     0    0     0 SW<     0  0.0  0.0   0:00 kswapd
22546 httpd      5   0  1048 1048   880 S       0  0.0  0.4   0:00 httpd
  304 root       0   0   316  316   260 S       0  0.0  0.1   0:00 mingetty
  305 root       0   0   316  316   260 S       0  0.0  0.1   0:00 mingetty
   23 root       0   0   380  380   328 S       0  0.0  0.1   0:00 kerneld
  209 root       0   0   448  448   372 S       0  0.0  0.1   5:56 syslogd
  218 root       0   0   556  556   340 S       0  0.0  0.2   0:00 klogd
  229 daemon     0   0   408  408   332 S       0  0.0  0.1   0:00 atd
  240 root       0   0   480  480   400 S       0  0.0  0.1   0:00 crond
  251 bin        0   0   408  408   328 S       0  0.0  0.1   0:14 portmap
  263 root       0   0   404  404   336 S       0  0.0  0.1   0:04 inetd
  286 root       9   0   844  844   772 S       0  0.0  0.3   0:01 httpd
```

Figure 17-1: Output of the top program

A program such as top shows a great deal of information about a running system. In this particular sample output, the computer is using almost all of its physical memory (256MB), but has not yet used any of its virtual memory.

> **Note** If you are running Apache on a Windows platform, use the Task Manager program to monitor memory, virtual memory, and CPU usage.

Another program you can use on most UNIX systems to check on your system's virtual memory use is called vmstat. Figure 17-2 shows a sample output of a vmstat session on the same computer as the last example. When you see your Web server computer making use of virtual memory—that is, swap space—you have a memory shortage! This is a good time to invest in RAM.

```
/bin/csh (ttyp2)
[kabir@www1 ~]$ vmstat 1
 procs                  memory    swap          io     system          cpu
 r b w   swpd   free   buff cache  si  so    bi    bo   in    cs  us  sy  id
 0 0 0      0  5232 129220 96912   0   0     1     5   35    15   1   4  47
 0 0 0      0  5232 129220 96912   0   0     0     0  107    10   0   2  98
 0 0 0      0  5232 129220 96912   0   0     0    10  115    10   0   2  98
 0 0 0      0  5156 129220 96916   0   0     1     0  133    87   1   4  95
 0 0 0      0  5204 129220 96916   0   0     0     0  137    24   0   2  98
 0 0 0      0  5224 129220 96916   0   0     0     0  112    24   0   2  98
 0 0 0      0  5228 129220 96916   0   0     0     0  107    10   0   2  98
 0 0 0      0  5228 129220 96916   0   0     0     6  112    12   1   1  98
 0 0 0      0  5232 129220 96916   0   0     0     0  113     8   0   2  98
 0 0 0      0  5232 129220 96916   0   0     0     0  110     8   0   2  98

[kabir@www1 ~]$
```

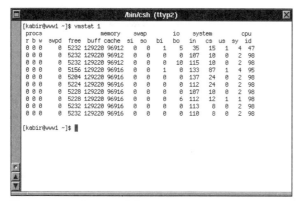

Figure 17-2: Output of the vmstat program

If buying more memory is not an option, or you think you already have plenty, then you need to look at a way of reducing your RAM usage. You can do this using some of the software tips that are included in the software section of this chapter.

The next piece of hardware you should consider as a major factor in your Web server's performance is the hard disk. A Web server spends a great deal of time accessing disk drives, and since disk drives are still very slow, they are often the primary cause of lousy performance.

Make sure your Web server is using a high-end SCSI disk controller with a set of high-end SCSI disk drives. The latest ultra-wide SCSI disks are your best choice. It's a good idea to use multiple disks on your Web server — for example, you shouldn't keep your operating system and Web data on the same disk. Use at least two disks: one for the operating system and another for data. Keeping operating-system-specific software out of the way of the Web server is a good security measure as well.

Disks are also a common point of failure. If you are concerned about disk failure, consider backing up your data on a regular basis. If you can afford to get Redundant Array of Inexpensive Disks (RAID) subsystems, it's worth looking into. RAID is essentially a group of smaller drives acting in concert to mimic a larger drive. If one of the drives fails, the others take up the slack until the failed drive can be replaced. Using RAID subsystems could mean high performance disk I/O and reasonable data security for your Web server.

Many people buy their PC servers from vendors who lure them into package deals that tend to feature a large IDE or EIDE disk. I highly recommend that you avoid using IDE/EIDE disks for your Web server, if you expect the server to function as more than a toy.

The last piece of hardware that resides in your computer system and can have an impact on your server performance is the network adapter card. I assume that your Web server is going to be connected to an Ethernet somewhere. The adapter card you use should be reasonably high-quality and fast. For example, if the Ethernet to which you are hooking up your Web server handles either 10Mbps or 100Mbps nodes, get a 100Mbps adapter card from a brand-name vendor.

The rest of the hardware that may become a factor in your server performance is discussed in the network section of this chapter.

After you've made sure your Apache server hardware surpasses all the issues discussed here, you are ready to tame the beasts in the software.

The Software

The type of operating system you use for Apache can make a great difference in your server's performance. For example, if you are trying out the early Windows version of Apache and are wondering why it's so slow, then all you can do is wait for Apache to mature in this platform.

Currently, Apache shines on most UNIX platforms. However, it is a common belief among the fans of Apache, a free and open source server, that most Apache servers are also run on free UNIX clones such as FreeBSD and Linux. If you are using one of these operating systems, you are already in good shape. If you are using one of the different flavors of UNIX operating systems, you may want to ensure that the networking aspects of your operating system are built for today's TCP/IP needs. Check the server documentation at www.apache.com/ for more specific information on your operating system.

It's always advisable to get the latest patch or upgrade for your operating systems. Many of the operating system updates remove security holes or enhance network support — so keep your eyes and ears open for those upgrades.

When you're sure you have a lean and mean operating system running on your powerful hardware, you can start looking at other software "places" for performance bottlenecks. How about the Apache server itself? Could it be the bottleneck? It sure can.

As mentioned earlier in this book, there are two ways to get Apache. You can either download a binary distribution and install it onto your system, or you can compile your own Apache binary and install it. The latter method is highly recommended because it enables you to fine-tune Apache from the start. Look at the binary you currently have, and determine whether you need all the things it has to offer. Run a command such as:

```
httpd -l
```

This reveals all the modules that have been built into your current Apache executable. If you see something you don't need, remove it by editing the configuration file and then recompiling and reinstalling it. If your operating system allows you to remove unnecessary symbolic information from executables, then strip them off. For example, the following command:

```
strip httpd
```

discards symbols from httpd under Linux. This makes the size of the executable a bit smaller, which results in RAM savings for each httpd.

Because many of you are likely to be using Linux, I though I should warn you that if you have a lot of RAM, you should make sure programs such as top are reporting all the physical memory available to your system. Many (if not all) Linux distributions come with kernels that don't use more than 64MB of RAM, due to some BIOS settings. This can easily be remedied, however, by adding a line such as the following in the /etc/lilo.conf file:

```
append = "mem=256M"
```

Here, the limit is set to 256 megabytes. Don't forget to run lilo after modifying its configuration file.

If you think your Apache executable (httpd) is as lean and mean as it can be, but you still suspect the bottleneck is within Apache, then take a close look at your Apache configuration files. Some Apache directives are expensive in terms of performance, and they are usually the ones that require domain name resolution, system calls, disk I/O, and process manipulation. You can use the following rules of thumb in creating Apache configuration files:

- ✦ Use less DNS
- ✦ Reduce disk I/O
- ✦ Limit the child processes

Using less DNS

If you are using directives that can take either host names or IP addresses, use an IP address to avoid a domain name resolving penalty. For example, if you use directives such as the following:

```
allow from .nitec.com
```

or

```
deny from .nitec.com
```

each of these directives will be very expensive as far as performance is concerned. The server will perform multiple name resolution calls to determine the validity of each host request that falls into the directive's realm. On a busy server, this could be quite unwelcome, so use the host IP address list instead of the domain name. Using the IP address means that no name resolutions have to be performed. The downside of this is that your server configuration becomes less easy to manage as you add more IP addresses to it. Who said performance comes cheap?

Many novice Apache administrators turn on HostnameLookups to record host names in the log files. This is a bad idea because each request needs to resolve a host name, which is a slow process.

Reducing disk I/O

If you do not use a per-directory configuration file, then you should tell Apache not to look for one. Otherwise, Apache will check for it in every directory that falls in the realm of a URL request, which means a lot of unnecessary disk I/O will be performed. You can disable this function by setting the AllowOverride directive to none.

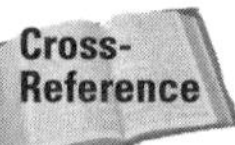

See Chapter 4 for details on how to tell Apache not to look for per-directory configuration files.

Using new concepts such as FastCGI, or the embedded Perl module for Apache (mod_perl), you can write Web applications that use in-memory caching, which reduces disk I/O. For high-traffic sites, this caching can effectively reduce the load on the Web servers.

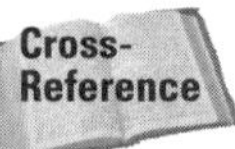

See Chapter 9 and Chapter 13 for more details on how to use FastCGI and embedded Perl modules.

Limiting child processes

Under the UNIX implementation of Apache, a main server process creates child processes to handle the requests. There are directives you can use to manipulate how many child processes are used and how long they hang out after a request. If you experience a considerable load, you may get better results by changing directives such as MinSpareServers, MaxSpareServers, MaxRequestsPerChild. You can also limit the quantity of system resources used by Apache and its child when it processes directives such as RLimitCPU, RLimitMEM, RLimitNPROC.

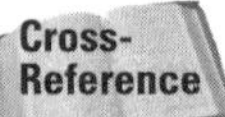

All the preceding directives are discussed in detail in Chapter 4.

Once you have fine-tuned the Apache configuration, make sure you've removed all unnecessary software. On UNIX and NT server systems, many software programs (called servers/daemons on UNIX and services on NT) are run in the background, so you should be able to determine which should remain and which should be removed. For example, if you find that your server is running a print server (lpd), you might want to disable this print server. In addition to killing the running process, you should also make sure the process will not start up next time you boot your server.

It's a good idea to reboot the machine after software changes. This enables you to check whether the machine still operates as expected. This is especially helpful if you have removed or disabled one or more daemon programs from being loaded. Make sure your computer is working as you want it to be by checking the services you usually need. For example, if you have a mail server running on this system, you might try sending and receiving e-mails after the reboot, or at least check to see if the mail server daemon is up and running.

The Network

A Web server resides on a network, so the network configuration has a significant impact on how a Web server performs. Depending on how you are using your Web server, you can probably make some adjustments to the network hosting the Web server. The typical Web server network installations are:

- In-house Internet Web server
- ISP colocated Web server
- Intranet Web server
- Distributed Web network

In-house Internet Web server

Many organizations are getting connected to the Internet and installing their Web servers on their own network. Typically, these connections are low-bandwidth connections ranging from a dedicated ISDN link to a fractional T-1 (DS-1). This may not be a problem if the content you provide on your Web server is not in high demand. All you want to do is give existing customers and potential customers a way to obtain useful information about your company.

If your content is rich and demand is heavy, though, you obviously need to get more bandwidth. In my experience, many people responsible for getting bandwidth do not perform any calculations to determine what they need, but rather rely on guesses or hearsay. You can actually do some simple calculations to get a good idea of your bandwidth needs.

Figure out your average Web page size, and identify your peak hours per day and peak hits per day. Determine your average byte transfer from this formula: (peak hits per day × average page size) ÷ total peak hours per day. Once you know your average byte transfer requirements for a peak hour, you can easily calculate your average bandwidth requirement as the following: (average byte transfer for a peak hour ÷ 3600 seconds). This gives you the average bytes/sec rate for peak hours. If you see that your current bandwidth can meet this peak bytes/sec reasonably well, you'll be fine.

Most bandwidth information is presented in kilobits/sec (Kbps) or megabits/sec (Mbps), and you can do the same for your peak bytes/sec rate. To convert bytes/sec to Kbps or Mbps, use the following:

```
Kbps = (bytes / sec) * ( 8 bits / byte) * ( 1 Kilobits /
1024 bits)
Mbps = (bytes / sec) * ( 8 bits / byte) * ( 1 Kilobits /
1024 bits)  * ( 1 Megabits / 1024 Kilobits)
```

It is generally a good idea to have two times the current bandwidth needs. Once you're sure that your Internet connection has enough bandwidth, you want to focus on how your Web server is placed on your network. Figure 17-3 shows a Web server on an organization's LAN that is connected to the Internet via a router.

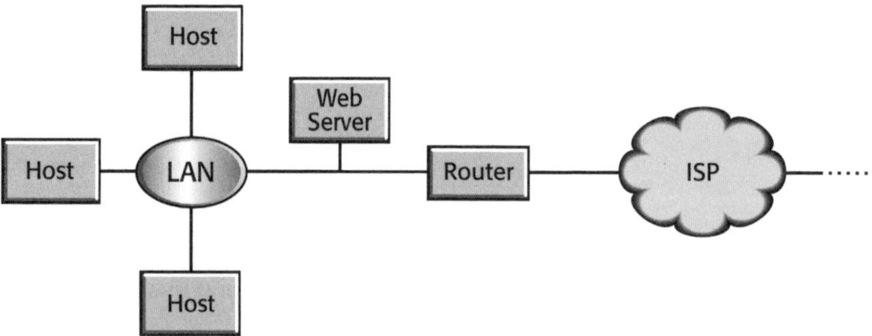

Figure 17-3: Web server on a LAN connected to the Internet

What's wrong with this setup? Well, as you can see from the figure, all LAN (Ethernet) traffic is seen by the Web server. This means that on a busy LAN, the Web server will perform like one of the PC hosts because it shares the Ethernet with many. This is also a very high-risk network design because the entire LAN is visible from the Internet via the router. Hopefully, all users have the sense never to do this. It's bad for performance and even worse for network security. To enhance both performance and security, the LAN should be segmented as shown in Figure 17-4.

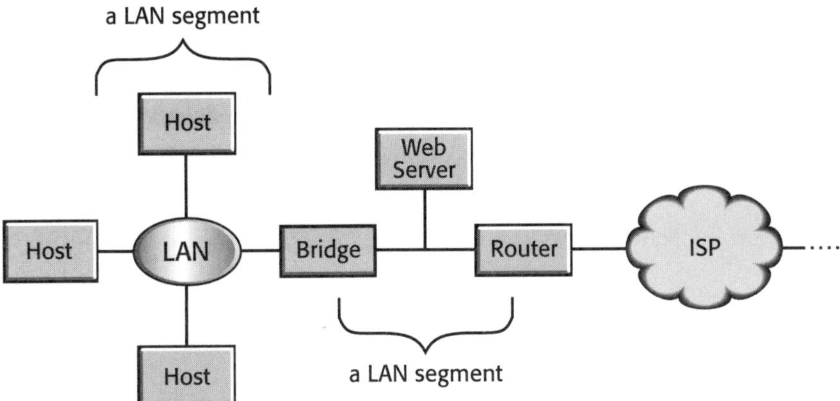

Figure 17-4: Web server on a segmented LAN connected to the Internet

Now the LAN traffic stays in the first segment, and the Web server does not see this traffic on its Ethernet. In fact, the only traffic the Web server sees is incoming or outgoing Internet traffic to and from the router. This makes the Ethernet on the Web server's side free from LAN traffic, and thus maximizes the server's chance to receive and transmit packets efficiently. The bridge can be implemented with bridge hardware, or simply a multihomed PC running an operating system that can forward IP traffic from one network to another.

So, the key things to remember when you host your Web server on your own network is that the connection to the Internet must have an appropriate amount of bandwidth to handle peak loads, and your network (LAN) traffic should never interfere with the Web server.

Hosting a Web server in-house is not always financially possible or desirable. If you do not have knowledgeable staff members who can manage server systems and handle network issues, I highly recommend you install your Web server on an ISP network. This type of server installation is often called a colocated server.

ISP colocated Web server

Having a colocated Web server offers many benefits. If you choose the right ISP, you shouldn't need to worry about network design or bandwidth congestion. The ISP should be able to handle all this for you. A number of ISPs are currently hosting colocated servers, though, so make sure you choose a good one. Before signing contracts with an ISP, visit its location and ask questions.

Ask your potential ISP how it will isolate your server from rest of the colocated servers. Also, ask if the ISP will put you on your own network segment. This should be a requirement for you, because you don't want other people on the same segment to be able to sniff your packets whenever they want to. If an ISP tells you that your server system will share an Ethernet segment with other colocated servers, this means anyone from one of those servers may be able to monitor your server packets using a program such as tcpdump and other network packet sniffing tools. This is totally unacceptable, for both performance and security reasons. Ask the ISP how it is connected to the Internet, and what level of network redundancy it claims to have. ISPs with multiple upstream providers (that is, the ISP of the ISP in question) probably have more than one way to route packets to the Internet, which is a plus.

You should do your homework, as well. You can perform a simple investigative analysis with easy-to-use TCP/IP tools. For example, you can ping the potential ISP's Web site using the ping program. Ping gives you an idea of how long it takes for a packet to travel to and from the destination network. The less time it takes, the better the connection from the pinging host to the host being pinged.

If you have access to the traceroute program (called tracert under Windows NT), trace the route to the ISP Web server. Count the number of hops (the number on the left column of the output) from your machine to the ISP Web site. Try to do this from more than one point on the Internet. You can ask a few friends who live in different cities to help you out with the traceroute or pings. Collect this data as much as possible.

If you do the same experiments for your current ISP, you can get a comparison on how your Web server ISP performs. These are crude methods, but they do provide some valuable information about how well an ISP is connected to the Internet. I recommend doing these experiments with more than one ISP at a time to get a better understanding of each ISP's performance. Also, try to do your experiments at different times, not just early in the morning or late in the evening. Collecting data at different times of the day will give you more realistic data.

By doing your homework, you increase your chances of choosing an ISP that will provide you with a higher network performance.

Intranet Web server

If you are using a Web server on your intranet, you should seldom need to worry about network performance, unless your network is heavily congested. If that's the case, put your Web server in a less busy segment, or create a new segment and isolate the Web server so it sees only the traffic that is meant for it.

If the Web becomes an important way for you to do business, chances are that your Web server will become quite busy due to the load. A single server may not be able to do the job your load places on it. In such a case, you'll want to consider distributing the load among two or more Web servers.

Distributed Web network

When your Web sites turn into high-traffic hot spots, you're likely to face an issue that many Web administers face on a daily basis: load balancing. If you have implemented all or many of the performance tips discussed in earlier sections of this chapter, your single Web server is probably performing at an optimal level. However, a single high-performance Web server may not be enough for a highly loaded Web site. In such a case, you need to look into distributing your load to other systems. You can distribute your Web load among many servers in two ways. Let's take a closer look at these two load-balancing methods, and then we'll look at potential problems with these setups.

Off-loading tasks to specialized servers

This method can be done when your Web server is being loaded with tasks that can be off-loaded onto other systems. For example, if you run a number of CGI applications and find out that your Web server is having problems keeping up with CGI requests, you may want to create one or more CGI servers and off-load CGI tasks to them. Figure 17-5 shows an example of such a network.

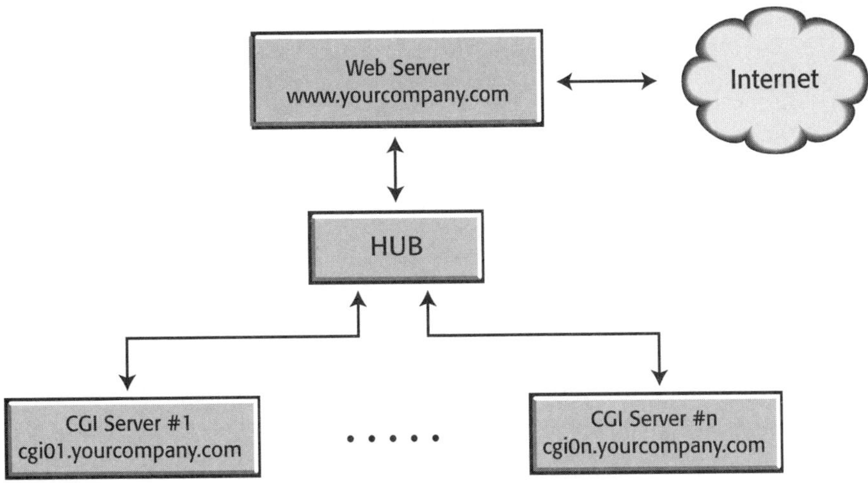

Figure 17-5: Off-loading the CGI load to external CGI servers

In this figure, the Web server host www.yourcompany.com is connected to one or more CGI servers, such as cgi01.yourcompany.com. To make use of the CGI servers, the HTML pages that have links to the CGI scripts, or the HTML forms that call the CGI scripts, must be updated. For example, Listing 17-1 shows an HTML form that resides on www.yourcompany.com.

Listing 17-1: Order.html

```
<HTML>
<HEAD>
<TITLE> Order Form </TITLE>
</HEAD>
<BODY BGCOLOR="white">
<H1> Order Form </H1>
<HR>
<PRE>

<FORM ACTION="/cgi-bin/takeorder.pl" METHOD="POST">
  Last  Name <INPUT TYPE=TEXT NAME="LastName" SIZE="30">
  First Name <INPUT TYPE=TEXT NAME="FirstName" SIZE="30">
  Email Addr <INPUT TYPE=TEXT NAME="EmailAddr" SIZE="30">
  Product    <INPUT TYPE=TEXT NAME="Product" SIZE="30">
  Quantity   <INPUT TYPE=TEXT NAME="Qty" SIZE="3">

  <INPUT TYPE=SUBMIT VALUE="Order Now">

  <INPUT TYPE=RESET VALUE="Clear All">

</BLOCKQUTE>
</PRE>
</FORM>
</BODY>
</HTML>
```

In a single Web server scenario, this order form can be accessed using this URL:

```
www.yourcompany.com/order.html
```

The visitor can enter order information in the form and click the Order Now button to get the order processed. At this point, the www.yourcompany.com server receives a request for the takeorder.pl CGI script as follows:

```
www.yourcompany.com/cgi-bin/takeorder.pl
```

The data the visitor entered is submitted via the HTTP POST request method to the same server.

To make use of the external CGI server (cgi01.yourcompany.com), the HTML form needs to be changed. The ACTION for the order form needs to changed from /cgi-bin/takeorder.pl to http://cgi01.yourcompany.com/cgi-bin/takeorder.pl so that the CGI server host cgi01.yourcompany.com receives the order processing request. This off-loads the CGI request to the CGI server, and the primary Web server can serve other pages in the meantime.

One issue needs to be addressed in such a setup, however. Most CGI scripts perform a task and generate output pages. The output pages need to be constructed so that all links on the output page point to the www.yourcompany.com server. Every link on the output page must use absolute references; no relative URL references can be made. For example, if the takeorder.pl script (on a single server configuration) prints out an HTML page that has the source shown in Listing 17-2, it needs to be changed.

Listing 17-2: **HTML output of takeorder.pl**

```
<HTML>
<HEAD>
<TITLE> Successful Order</TITLE>
</HEAD>
<BODY BGCOLOR="white">

<IMG SRC="/images/header.gif" HEIGHT=50 WIDTH=500 BORDER=0>

<P> Thank you for your order Moahmmed Kabir</P>
<HR>
<BLOCKQUTE>
We have already sent an order confirmation number at your
email address (kabir@nitec.com) for your future reference.
<P>
Click <A HREF="/index.html">here</A> to return to home page.
</P>
</BLOCKQUTE>
<CENTER>
<IMG SRC="/images/copyright.gif" HEIGHT=20 WIDTH=400 BORDER=0>
</CENTER>
</FORM>
</BODY>
</HTML>
```

The URL link and the image sources will have to be changed from:

```
<A HREF="/index.html">here</A>
```

to

```
<A HREF="http://www.yourcompany.com/index.html">here</A>
```

Similarly, the image source attribute of the image tags needs be www.yourcompany.com/images/ instead of just /images/. You may wonder what would happen if you keep copies of all files on the primary Web server and the CGI Web servers. Well, in this case a visitor remains in a CGI server after the first CGI script has been executed, and it will be confusing to the visitor to see cgi01.yourcompany.com in the URL location of the Web browser. In addition, some frequent visitors may bookmark areas of your Web site on the CGI server and go there directly. If you have only one CGI server, chances are it is bogged down at this point by both CGI requests and regular file requests. This defeats the purpose of having two servers.

Besides that, the real reason for having an external CGI server may be that you have a very CPU-intensive or I/O CGI application. Therefore, making sure your CGI output pages have appropriate links to go back to the primary server makes a lot of sense. Note that you can make use of the HTTP redirect header Location: URL to automatically redirect visitors to files on your primary server from a CGI script. For example, the following CGI script, goback.pl, illustrates a Perl-based CGI script:

```
#!/usr/local/bin/perl
#
print "Location:
www.yourcompany.com/thanks_for_order.html\\n\\n\";
exit 0;
```

Whenever this script runs using the URL http://cgi01.yourcompany.com/cgi-bin/goback.pl, it returns the visitor to the thanks_for_order.html page on the www.yourcompany.com server. This technique can be used in order form processing scripts to redirect the visitor automatically to the primary Web server. This way, the visitor has little chance of getting confused about where he or she is. If the takeorder.pl uses a redirect such as the one shown in goback.pl, most visitors will not even know (unless they look into the source of the HTML order form) that the CGI was processed by a different machine.

As you can see, this type of distributed Web network can become quite a performance advantage for a busy Web site. Note that the distributed design of such a network not only helps the performance of your Web, but also enables you to create a more secure environment. For example, say you have a database server that you would like to connect to your Web server, so visitors can interact with the database applications. If you are concerned about the server's safety, you can implement a network such as the one shown in Figure 17-6.

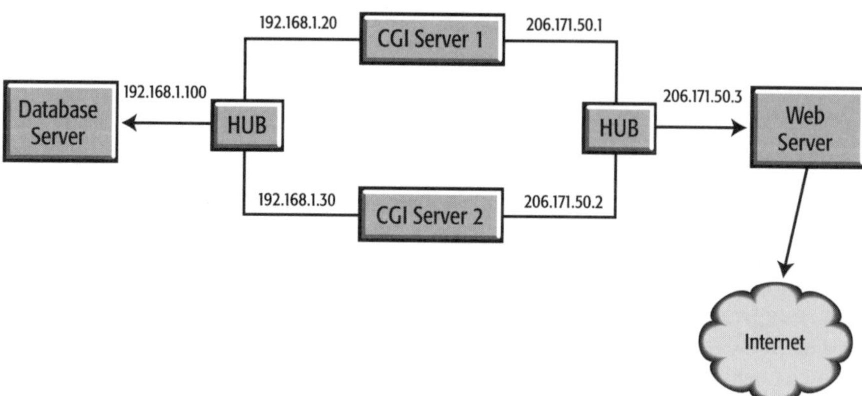

Figure 17-6: Secured and high-performance Web network

Here, the database server system resides in a nonroutable IP network (192.168.1.0), which is only connected to the two multihomed CGI servers. These CGI servers are also connected to the Internet routable network (206.171.50.0), so they can function as described previously. All you need to do is install database client software on the CGI servers so that they can access the database server in the nonroutable network. This enables you to distribute your load to three external systems, and therefore provides a very high-performance yet secured solution.

Note that the degree of security depends on how well-protected your CGI servers are, because anyone who can break into one of these two systems is likely to interact with or even break into your database server. Since the database server resides totally behind the scenes, however, it is highly unlikely that the network configuration will be revealed that easily.

Replicating Web servers for load balancing

If your Web site contains a large number of static documents and a moderate number of CGI script-generated documents or other dynamic documents, and you are experiencing high load, you may want to consider replicating the Web network for balancing this load over multiple identical Web servers.

For example, let's take three Web servers, each with the same host name (www.yourcompany.com) but different IP addresses. How is that possible? The answer lies in DNS setup.

Using a DNS trick called round-robin name resolution, it's possible to assign the same name to multiple IP addresses. The DNS configuration for the network in this example is as follows:

```
www    IN A  206.171.50.1
www    IN A  206.171.50.2
www    IN A  206.171.50.3
```

This address (A) records tells the DNS server to give out each IP address in listed order for a host called www (for example, www.yourcompany.com). The DNS server gives out the first IP address (206.171.50.1), then the second one, and then the third one. It recycles the list repeatedly.

As long as you keep all the Web servers identical, the visitors won't notice any differences, and the load will be balanced in some manner. Note that when a visitor points to www.yourcompany.com/, the DNS server will give out the IP address that is next on the list at that time. The browser will then use the same Web server for the entire session. Thus, load balancing is achieved by redirecting different clients to different servers.

Two problems quickly appear in such a setup. The first one is how to keep the servers in synchronization. If you try to do this manually, you need to update files, possibly via FTP, on all three servers. This is very cumbersome. The solution is to use one of the servers as the staging area and use a software program such as rdist to update the other servers automatically and periodically.

Cross-Reference

You can learn more details about this setup in Chapter 19.

The second problem appears when you have some CGI scripts that write data files, as well the data later searched by another CGI script, to locate records. For example, say you have a promotional lottery application for your Web sites that enables visitors to sign up and get an HTTP cookie as an identifier. You have devised a way for the visitors to collect points by visiting some of your special pages. The points are written to a disk so you can accumulate them later and figure out which visitor came to your site the most. The visitors can also view their total points through a CGI script that reads the points data file. Because you use a replicated Web network, your CGI scripts reside in each server, and they create and read from the data files that reside on that particular server.

Therefore, when a visitor visits a Web site and signs up for your promotional lottery, everything may be fine, but when he comes back another day and is directed to a server where his points are not stored, he will be shocked to know that he has collected no points at all. How do you take care of this problem? Well, you can solve this by introducing the Network File System (NFS) into the picture. By mounting an area of a disk from one server to the others and making necessary changes to CGI scripts for writing files in the NFS-mounted location, you can have all servers share data.

Cross-Reference

See Chapter 19 to learn more about configuring NFS for such a setup.

Round-robin DNS configuration enables you to create a replicated Web server network that offers load balancing, and thus provides better performance than a large single server. One of the big pluses for this type of configuration is that it's inexpensive; however, the round-robin setup has a few known downsides of which you should be aware. Anytime you want to make a change to your DNS setup, it takes time for it to propagate over the Internet. This could cause a problem if one of your servers goes down, and you want to redirect requests for the down server to another working server. There's also a limit on how many entries you can have per DNS record. The current limit is 32, which means you can have a maximum of 32 replicated servers at this time. If you are looking for a better solution, the price goes up to thousands or even tens of thousands of dollars. A possible solution lies in the use of hardware packages.

Problems with load balancing

One of the problems, both with off-loading tasks to multiple servers or with round-robin DNS distributed Web networks, is that neither provides true load balancing. In either configuration, you can't tell which server is busy and which is not. To achieve true load balancing based on a server's availability, you must buy some extra hardware.

Load-balancing hardware components are now appearing on the market. Some of these are called Web multiplexers, and some are just smart Ethernet switches with load-balancing algorithms that detect server loads from the outside. These hardware components often come with many extra features, which makes them expensive. However, these features, which include detection of failure and rerouting of HTTP requests to a functional Web server, are probably things you should consider if you have a decent budget. If you decide this option is affordable, you can look for information on load-balancing products from vendors such as CISCO (www.cisco.com/) and HydraWeb (www.hydraweb.com/).

The Content

Once you are absolutely sure that your Apache computer, software, and the network have been tuned to their fullest, you can concentrate on tuning your content.

Static content such as HTML pages and images does not create as much load as dynamic content that needs to be created by applications such as CGI scripts, Java servlets, and databases. To reduce the load on your Web server, you should look into speeding up dynamic content production. For example, if you use Perl for CGI scripts, you should look into mod_perl, or consider FastCGI.

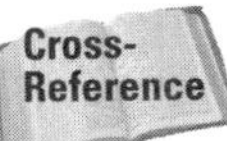

See Chapter 13 for more information on mod_perl, and Chapter 9 to learn about FastCGI.

You can also reduce dynamic content load on the Web server by creating applications that use client-side scripts or applets; this gets a good amount of work done before communicating with the Web server. For example, using Java scripts or Java applets, you can off-load user input validation tasks at the browser end. Also, using Java applets, you can reduce most of the work from your server side to the client.

In the same spirit, you should reduce the use of Server Side Includes (SSI) as much as possible. Be careful about what you choose as an SSI filename extension, because the server treats all files like this as something that needs to be parsed for possible SSI calls. For example, making .html your SSI filename extension will degrade server performance heavily if you have a great deal of non-SSI HTML pages with the .html extension.

Although dynamic content creates the most load on a server, static content can also be streamlined in many ways to get the maximum performance out of your server. Following are some guidelines to use in developing static content:

✦ Using appropriate HTML metatags, encourage clients and proxy servers to cache pages that do not change often.

✦ Use HEIGHT and WIDTH attributes in IMG tags to give visitors an impression of speedier page downloads.

- Use small images.
- Use client-side image maps to reduce server load in processing server-side image maps.

The People

A Web site's performance depends heavily on the people who manage and develop it. Therefore, you should note that simply tuning the hardware, software, and network will not turn your Web server into a high-performance machine; the human factor must be considered. Here are some of my recommendations:

- Enforce the CGI development guidelines found in Chapter 18.
- Discourage people from logging on to Web servers and then running user processes or doing development work on them.
- Provide your Web development team with access to the latest tools and technology. Offer training opportunities.
- Tell everyone that better performance is welcome, but not at the cost of lowered standards. For example, you don't want your HTML developer to insert IP addresses in links to reduce DNS requests on the browser side. A visitor may feel that your pages are downloading faster, but when you change IP addresses for your servers, you don't want to be left with the mess of many IP address changes in links everywhere.

Your performance goal for your Web servers should be like the goal the Apache Group set for Apache: correct first, then fast.

Summary

In this chapter, you learned how to get better performance out of your Web server computer, Apache and its configuration, the network, the content, and the people involved. This chapter really gets you thinking in the right direction about improving performance.

Next, you learn how to create a perfect Web site.

✦ ✦ ✦

CHAPTER 18

Running Perfect Web Sites

✦ ✦ ✦ ✦

In This Chapter

Creating a Web cycle for your organization

Standardizing your standards

Making your Web user-friendly

Promoting your Web site on the Web

✦ ✦ ✦ ✦

By now, you probably have one or more Web sites up and running on your new Apache Web server. Everyone in your organization is crediting you for a wonderful job. You are in Web heaven, right? Wrong! Pretty soon, many of your fellow colleagues will be asking you how to update their pages on the Web site. For example, the marketing department will call and ask how to update the pricing information, or the legal department may ask how they can add more legal content in one of the Web sites.

This is what happens to Web administrators of medium-to-large organizations. Soon, you will find yourself in the midst of a mass of update requests and wish lists. How do you manage your Web now? In this chapter, you learn how to create a professional Web management environment that will keep you and your Web developers sane and in sync with the Web.

Creating a Web Cycle

Unfortunately, typical Web development projects do not start with the design of a manageable Web. In the most projects, much of the time is spent getting the servers running and the content developed; it is rarely spent worrying about the long-term management aspects of the Web. Ironically, as soon as everything seems to be working, things start falling apart due to the lack of a clear, maintainable cycle. In this section, you learn about something I call the Web cycle, which enables you to create a highly manageable Web solution.

A Web cycle consists of three phases: development, staging, and production. By implementing each of these phases, you can create a maintainable, manageable Web. Figure 18-1 shows a high-level diagram of a Web cycle.

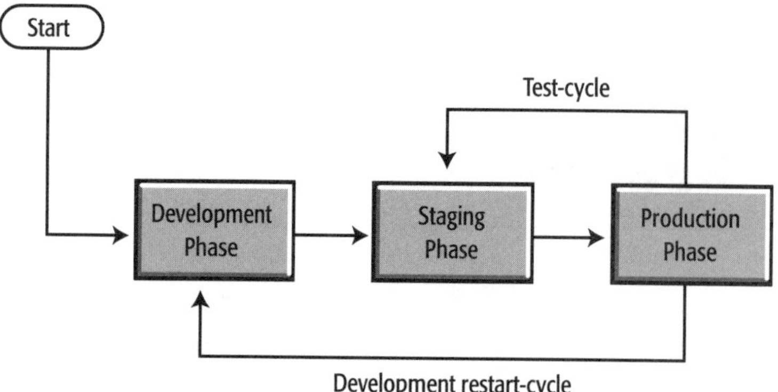

Figure 18-1: High-level diagram of a Web cycle

As you can see in this figure, a Web cycle starts at the development phase, continues to the staging phase, and ends in the production phase. When it restarts, however, it starts from the production phase and repeats the previous cycle path. You may be wondering what all this means; well, let's take a look at each phase:

- ✦ Development phase — In this phase, you start developing your Web content. The content, be it HTML documents or CGI scripts, is completely developed and tested in this phase. Once the developers are absolutely sure that their work is ready for integration with the Web site(s), the newly developed content moves to the next phase.
- ✦ Staging phase — The purpose of this phase is to allow integration of the newly developed content with the existing content, and to perform testing cycles. Once in the staging phase, developers no longer participate in the staging process. In this process, you introduce testers who are not developers, in order to remove developer bias — in other words, developers may not test the content completely, due to overconfidence. At this point, you either see problems or you end up with a successful set of tests. In the latter case, you are ready to move the newly developed, staged, and tested content to the production phase. If problems are created by the new content, you will need to restart from the development phase after the developers have fixed the problem in the development area. Do not allow the developer(s) to fix problems in the staging area.
- ✦ Production phase — This phase consists of content backup and content deployment tasks. First, you back up your existing (functional) content and then move the staging content to your production Web space. The switchover has to happen in the least amount of time to reduce disconnects from potential visitors and prevent any loss of data collected via the Web.

When you are ready to begin another development cycle (to restart the entire process), you copy content from the production phase and make it available in the development phase, so developers can work on it. The cycle continues in the same manner whenever needed.

What does all this buy you? It buys you reliability and management options. For example, if you are currently developing content and dumping it directly on your production system before a full suite of tests, you are living dangerously. In most cases, content developers claim to have tested their new content in their local environment, and are quick to apply the seal of completion. Since a developer's local environment typically lacks the integration of current content with the new content, the tests are not always realistic. Only by integrating existing and new content together can you detect possible incompatibilities. For example, without the staging phase, a direct dump on the production system from the development phase is likely to cause any of the following errors:

- Files in the production system could get overridden by the new contents. This typically happens with image files, due to the lack of a standard file naming convention or the use of common directories of image files.
- Data files on the live (production) system could get overridden, because the CGI developers used old data files when developing the content.
- When multiple developers are involved, some old files may reappear on the production server, because each developer may have started working with a copy at a different time. One developer dumps his copy, and then another developer dumps his, and the result is a mess.

Many other problems could appear if several developers are involved and their projects are interconnected. If you cannot risk having such problems on your production server, you need the staging phase. Let's look at how Apache can help you implement these phases.

Putting the Web Cycle into Action

Now you are ready to put your Web cycle into action.

First, you need to set up your server(s) for the Web cycle. There are many ways to do this, but I discuss only three here. Of the three methods, two are for organizations with a single Apache server machine, and one is for organizations with multiple Apache server machines.

Ideally, you do not want to perform any development work on the production server system. If your budget does not permit deployment of multiple machines for your Web, however, you should use your lone server to implement the cycle.

Once you've set up your server(s), you are ready to implement the Web cycle.

Setting up for the Web cycle

You can set up for the Web cycle in two ways: you can either use two new virtual hosts to implement the development and staging sites on your production server, or you can create three separate Apache configurations for the production server, the development server, and the staging server.

If your development work includes tweaking Apache configuration files or testing a newly released Apache server, you should use separate configuration files for the production Apache server and the other two Apache servers. If your normal Web development does not include Apache-related changes, however, you can use the virtual host approach.

Before going into the details of setting up the Web cycle, I would like to point out that a good Web cycle requires a well-planned Web directory structure. Figure 18-2 shows one such directory structure for a Web cycle.

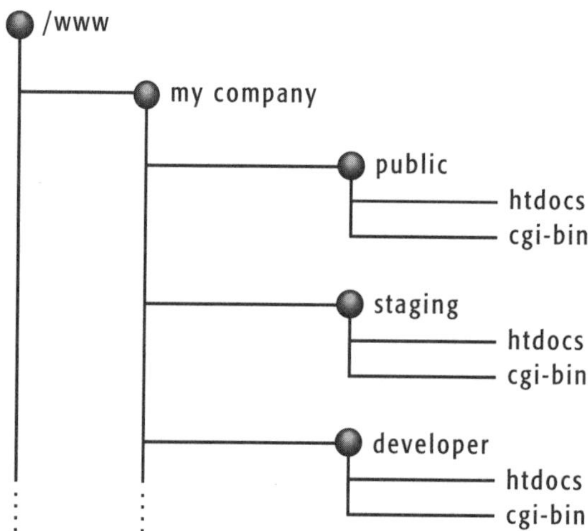

Figure 18-2: Directory structure used for public, staging, and developer sites for my company

This is a good example of a directory structure because it enables you to keep the public, staging, and developer sites for each Web site under a single top-level directory (in this case, mycompany). Adding a new Web site means creating a similar directory structure for it.

In the example configurations discussed in the following sections, I assume that you have the preceding directory structure in place. I also assume that your Web server host is called www.mycompany.com, and that it has the IP address 206.171.50.50. Make sure you replace these values with whatever is appropriate for your own configuration.

Creating a virtual host for each phase

If you decide that you do not need to make Apache-related changes, you can create a virtual host for each phase. To do so, you should create two virtual hosts that have the same ServerName but run on different port addresses. Table 18-1 shows a sample port assignment for such a setup.

Table 18-1
Port assignments for Apache servers for Web cycle

Port	*Server Type*
80	Production server (main server)
1080	Staging server (virtual host)
8080	Development server (virtual host)

You can choose any other port assignments you wish, as long as you don't use a port address that is already being used or is greater than 65535. The production server port should not be changed from 80, because default HTTP requests are sent to this port address.

To create these virtual hosts per the port assignment shown in Table 18-1, you need to edit the Apache server's httpd.conf file as follows.

To make the Apache server listen to these ports, use the Listen directive:

```
Listen 80
Listen 1080
Listen 8080
```

Then, create two virtual hosts as follows:

```
# Do not forget to change the IP address, ServerName,
# DocumentRoot, ScriptAlias,
# TransferLog, and ErrorLog directive values with whatever is
# appropriate for you
# actual configuration setup.
#
<VirtualHost 206.171.50.50:1080>
ServerName
DocumentRoot /www/mycompany/staging/htdocs
ScriptAlias  /cgi-bin/       /www/mycompany/staging/cgi-bin/
TransferLog  logs/staging-server.access.log
ErrorLog     logs/staging-server.error.log
</VirtualHost>

<VirtualHost 206.171.50.50:8080>
ServerName
```

```
DocumentRoot  /www/mycompany/developer/htdocs
ScriptAlias  /cgi-bin/       /www/mycompany/developer/cgi-bin/
TransferLog  logs/developer-server.access.log
ErrorLog     logs/developer-server.error.log
</VirtualHost>
```

Note that in the preceding example, the same IP address is used in both virtual hosts, but different ports are specified in the <VirtualHost . . .> container. The IP address is the same as the main server, www.mycompany.com. The ServerName directive is set to the main server name as well. Your main server configuration will be as usual.

The following URL can be used to access the staging site:

```
www.mycompany.com:1080/
```

To access the developer site, the following URL can be used:

```
www.mycompany.com:8080/
```

If you plan to modify Apache configuration files as part of your development process, do not use the preceding scheme; you only need one set of Apache configuration files in this setup, and changing the files for experimentation can affect your production server. In such a case, you can still use a single machine, but you need to run multiple Apache (main) servers. This approach is described next.

Using multiple Apache (main) server processes

You should use more than one (main) server process if you plan to experiment with Apache itself as part of your Web development phase. To implement the cycle, follow these instructions.

Create two subdirectories in your Apache configuration directory called staging and developer, as follows:

```
mkdir /path/to/Apache/server/root/conf/staging
mkdir /path/to/Apache/server/root/conf/developer
```

Don't forget to replace /path/to/Apache/server/root/conf with the actual path of your server configuration directory. Copy all *.conf files to both the staging and developer subdirectories, as follows:

```
cp /path/to/Apache/server/root/conf/*.conf
/path/to/Apache/server/root/conf/staging/*
cp /path/to/Apache/server/root/conf/*.conf
/path/to/Apache/server/root/conf/developer/*
```

Now, modify the httpd.conf file in the staging subdirectory to listen to port 1080 instead of the default 80. You can either use the Port or Listen directive to do this. Similarly you need to modify the httpd.conf in developer so that the Port or the Listen directive is set to 8080.

You should now modify the srm.conf (or httpd.conf) in staging and developer subdirectories to point their DocumentRoot and ScriptAlias directives to the appropriate path. For example, the changes needed here for the directory structure shown earlier in Figure 18-2 will be:

```
DocumentRoot            /www/mycompany/staging/htdocs
ScriptAlias     /cgi-bin/     /www/mycompany/staging /cgi-bin/
```

for the staging site configuration. For the developer site configuration file, it will be:

```
DocumentRoot            /www/mycompany/developer/htdocs
ScriptAlias     /cgi-bin/     /www/mycompany/developer/cgi-bin/
```

Note that if you use a special configuration for your production server that uses absolute path information, you may have to edit the new configuration files further, for staging and developer.

The idea is to create three sets of configuration files where each points to a different DocumentRoot and ScriptAlias. Once you have done that, you can start up the three Apache (main) server processes as follows:

```
httpd -f /path/to/Apache/server/root/conf/httpd.conf httpd -f
/path/to/Apache/server/root/conf/staging/httpd.conf httpd -f
/path/to/Apache/server/root/conf/developer/httpd.conf
```

When you decide to compile a new version of Apache and run it under the developer server, you can simply feed it the configuration file for the developer server. For example, if you've decided to add a new module and want to see the effect of the module on your content, you can simply run the developer and staging servers using that executable instead of your production server executable (httpd.) After compiling a new executable, it might be a good idea to rename it to something like httpd-xx80, to make sure you do not accidentally overwrite the production server executable with it.

Now, lets look at what it takes to set up multiple hosts for the Web cycle environment.

Using multiple Apache server computers for the Web cycle

If you can afford to have multiple Apache server computers (that is, one for development, one for staging, and one for production) to create the Web cycle environment, you don't need special Apache configuration. You can simply install Apache on all your involved hosts, and treat one them as the developer site host, another as the staging site host, and the third one as the production site. Since you now have Apache servers running on three different hosts, you can run each server on port 80 as well. That's all you need to do for a multihost Web cycle environment.

Implementing the Web cycle

At this point, you should have one of the following three Web cycle environments:

✦ You are using a single computer with two virtual hosts for development and staging. The production server is the main Apache server. Be careful when modifying any Apache configuration in this setup, because changes could affect how your production server behaves.

✦ You are using a single computer with three main Apache servers for development, staging, and production, and you created separate configurations for each (main) Apache server. You created this configuration so you can experiment with Apache configurations in the development site without disturbing the production configuration.

✦ You have set up at least three different computers as development, staging, and production Apache servers. All three computers run Apache servers on port 80.

To initiate your Web cycle, copy your production content from the production server's document root directory to your development site. For example, if your configuration is one of the first two in the above list, you can easily copy your entire Web content to the development site using the following UNIX commands:

```
cd  /path/to/production/docroot/dir
tar cvf  -  .  | (cd /path/to/development/site/docroot/dir ;
tar xvf - )
```

This copies all the files and directories in your production server to the development site's document root. Just make sure you change the path information to whatever is appropriate on your system.

For a multicomputer Web cycle environment, you can create a tar archive of your production server and copy it over to your development site via FTP.

Set the file permissions so Apache can read all files and execute the CGI scripts. If you have directories in which Apache should have write access (for CGI scripts that write data), you should also set those permissions. Once you've done so, start or restart Apache to service the development site.

Now, make sure the development site appears (via the Web browser) exactly the same as the production site. Perform some manual comparisons and spot checks. Make sure the scripts are also working.

If any of your CGI scripts produce hard-coded URLs for your production server, they will keep doing the same for your development site. You can either ignore these URLs or get them fixed so they use the SERVER_NAME environment variable and SERVER_PORT port address.

When everything is working as it should, you have successfully created a Web cycle environment. Now you can ask your developers to put new content and scripts in the development site and test them. Whenever a new content development is completed, you should first test it in the development area. The testing should focus on the following issues:

✦ Does it serve its purpose? In other words, does the functionality provided by the new content meet your specification?

✦ Are there any side effects of the new content? For example, if the new content is really a new CGI script, you should use Apache's script debugging support (see Chapter 8) to monitor how the script works.

Once you are satisfied with the test results, cease any further development on the new content to avoid having to perform another set of functionality tests on it. When it's time for a production site update, make a copy of your production site and place it on your staging site. Make sure the staging site is exactly the same as the production site. Once you've done some manual checking to ensure that everything looks and feels the same, you can move new contents and scripts over to the staging and integrate them.

It's a good idea to move one project at a time so you can find problems in stages. For example, if you added three new CGI scripts to your development system, move one at a time to the staging area. Perform both functional and site integration testing. If the script passes the tests, you can start with the next new item. Once you have moved over all the new content, you can perform site level integration tests. Monitor your staging site logs carefully. See if you notice anything odd in the error logs. If all goes well, you are ready to perform an update to your production site. You have to be very careful in doing so, however. For example, if you have any CGI scripts on the production server that create data files in the production area, you do not want to override any of these data files with what you have in the staging area.

Therefore, the best method for updating your production site would be to do it during a time when you expect the production server to be the least busy. At this time, you can grab the data files from your production server and apply them to the appropriate directories in the staging version of the site. This gets your staging site in sync with the production site. At this point, you have to quickly dump your staging site over to the production area. This could be very tricky because the production site is live, and you never know when a visitor may be accessing a page or using a CGI script that will eventually need to read or write data files.

To minimize the switchover time (at least on a single-server setup) you can create a shell script that does the following:

1. Copies all live data files to appropriate areas of your staging site.
2. Renames your top-level production directory (such as the public directory in Figure 18-2) to something like public.old.
3. Renames your top-level staging directory (such as the staging directory in Figure 18-2) to what you used to call your top-level production directory — for example, public.
4. Renames the old production directory (such as public.old) to what you used to call your staging top-level directory — for example, staging.

This way, the staging site becomes the production site in only a few steps, without a great number of file copy operations. A sample of such a script that corresponds to the environment shown in Figure 18-2 is provided in Listing 18-1.

Listing 18-1: stage2production.sh script

```
#!/bin/sh
# Purpose: a simple shell script to copy live data files
# to staging area and rename the staging area into live
# production site. It also renames the old  production
# area into staging area.
#
# $Author$
# $Revision$
# $Id$
# $Status

# You will need to change these variables to use this script.
DATA_FILES ="/www/mycompany/public/htdocs/cgi-data/*.dat";
TEMP_DIR="/www/mycompany/public.old";
PRODUCTION_DIR="/www/mycompany/public";
STAGE_DIR="/www/mycompany/staging";

# Copy the live data to the staging directory.
/bin/cp $DATA_FILES $STAGE_DIR

# Temporarily rename current production directory to TEMP_DIR
/bin/mv PRODUCTION_DIR       TEMP__DIR

# Now rename the current staging site to production directory
/bin/mv STAGE_DIR            PRODUCTION_DIR

# Now rename the temporary (old) production directory
# to staging directory
/bin/mv TEMP_DIR             STAGE_SITE
```

```
# To be safe lets change the current production directory's
# permission setting such  that the Apache user (httpd)
# and Apache group (httpd) can read all files. Note that
# if you use some other user and group for Apache, you
# will have to modify this command according to
# your setup.

/bin/chown -R httpd.httpd  $PRODUCTION_DIR

# Now lets change the  file permission such that the
# owner (httpd in this case) has  read, write, execute
# permission, the group (httpd in this case) has read,
# execute permission and everyone else has no
# permission to see the production directory files

/bin/chmod - R 750    $PRODUCTION_DIR
```

After running this script, you should perform a quick check to make sure everything is as it should be. In case of a problem, you can rename the current production directory to something else, and change the staging directory name back to your production directory name to restore your last production site.

Once you get used to the cycle, you'll find that it makes it easy to track development and integration problems, and it also ensures that all your production sites are functional at all times. Apart from maintaining a strict Web cycle, you still need to do a few more tasks to keep your Web in perfect shape. These tasks fall into the maintenance category.

Maintenance for Your Web

Once you've implemented the Web cycle, it is important to maintain your Web. The typical Web maintenance tasks include server monitoring, logging, and data backup. The server monitoring and logging aspects of Web site maintenance are covered in Chapter 11. Here, I discuss the data backup. You should have two types of backup, if possible.

Online backup

Online backup is useful in case of an emergency. You can access the backup data fairly quickly and perform necessary restoration tasks in a few minutes, in most cases. To obtain an online backup solution, you can either look for a commercial online backup vendor or talk to your ISP. If you are hosting your Web server(s) on your own network, however, you can keep backups on another host on your network. On most UNIX systems, you can run a program called rdist to create mirror directories of your Web sites on other UNIX hosts (Chapter 19 shows an example of an rdist-based site mirroring application).

It may even be a good idea to keep a compressed version of the Web data on the Web server itself. On UNIX systems, you can set up a cron job to create a compressed tar file of the Web data on a desired frequency. For example:

```
# for system V-ish Unix, weekday range is  0-6 where 0=Sunday
# For BSD-ish system use weekday range 1-7 where 1=Monday
# This example is for a Linux system (System V-ish cornd)
30 2 * * 0,1, 3, 5,     root  /bin/tar czf /backup/M-W-F-Sun.tgz
/www/*
30 2 * * 2, 4, 6        root  /bin/tar czf /backup/T-TH-Sat.tgz
/www/*
```

If these two cron entries are kept in /etc/crontab, then two files will be created. Every Monday, Wednesday, Friday, and Sunday, the first cron job will run at 2:30 a.m. to create a backup of everything in /www and store the compressed backup file in the /backup/M-W-F-Sun.tgz file. Similarly, on Tuesday, Thursday, and Saturday mornings (2:30 a.m.), the second cron entry will create a file called T-TH-Sat.tgz in the same backup directory for the same data. Having two backups ensures that you have at least last two days' backup in two compressed files.

Offline backup

You should also perform backups on removable media and keep them in safe locations. Restoring from this type of backup is usually a time-consuming operation. You can use tape drives, removable hard disks (such as Jaz disks) to perform this backup. I prefer an 8mm tape-based backup because it provides 8GB of data storage capacity; also, 8mm tape drives have been on the market much longer than the new compact removable media.

As your Web sites grow richer in content, you will notice that the Web space is being filled rapidly. This is often due to files that are unused but are never removed for fear that something (such as a link) will break somewhere. If you think this is true for your Web, and you are on a UNIX platform, you may want to consider running the find utility to locate files that have not been accessed for a long time. For example:

```
find /www -name "*.bak" -type f -atime +10 -exec ls -l {} \;
```

This lists all files in /www directories that end with the .bak extension and have not been accessed for the last ten days. If you want to remove these files, you can replace the ls -l command and do a find such as:

```
find /www -name "*.bak" -type f -atime +10 -exec rm -f {} \;
```

If this helps, perhaps you can create a cron entry that runs this command on a desired frequency.

Standardizing Standards

With a Web cycle in place, you have an environment that can accommodate many developers; however, just creating the Web cycle does not ensure high-quality Web production. A high-quality Web requires high-quality content, and there are guidelines you should follow regarding content development. The theme here is to standardize your standards.

Each Web site should offer unique content to make it attractive to potential visitors. All types of Web content can be categorized as either static or dynamic. Static content is typically created with HTML files, and dynamic content is usually the output of CGI or other server-side or client-side applications. Most sites use a mix of both static and dynamic content to publish their information; therefore, standards are needed for both static and dynamic content development.

HTML document development policy

Although you can provide static content in a number of ways, such as a plain text file or PDF file, for example, most Web sites use HTML documents as the primary information repository. To help guide your HTML authors, you should create an HTML development policy. Following are some guidelines that you can adapt for your organization by making any necessary changes or additions.

Always use standard HTML tags

HTML developers should always use standard HTML. Use of browser-dependent HTML may make a page look great on one type of browser, but terrible on another.

For example, the following shows a skeleton HTML document that meets the minimal HTML document standard.

```
<HTML>
<HEAD>
<TITLE> Document title goes here </TITLE>
</HEAD>
<BODY>
Document body goes here
</BODY>
</HTML>
```

Each of your documents should contain at least these HTML tags.

Keep in-line images along with the documents

The in-line images of a document should reside in a subdirectory of the document's directory. There is one exception to this rule, however: if some of your images are reusable, you should consider putting them in a central image directory. An example of such a case would be a standard navigation bar implemented using image files. The navigation bar can be reused in multiple documents, so you may want to store these images in a central directory instead of keeping them with each document. This provides better control and saves disk space. Aside from the noted exception, all other images should reside along with the document that uses them. The source references to these images should be relative, so if the document is moved from one location to another along with the image directory, the image is still rendered exactly the same way it was before. In the following example, I show you how to create a portable HTML document that has multiple graphic files linked to it.

Let say you want to publish two HTML documents (mydoc1.html and mydoc2.html) that contain three images (image1.gif, image2.gif and image3.gif). You can first create a meaningful subdirectory under your document root directory or any other appropriate subdirectories. Let's assume you created this directory under the server's document root directory (/www/mycompany/htdocs) and you called it mydir.

Now, create a subdirectory called images under the mydir directory and store your three images in this directory. Edit your HTML documents so that all links to the images use the SRC attribute as follows:

```
SRC="images/image1.gif"
SRC="images/image2.gif"
SRC="images/image3.gif"
```

An example of an in-line image link for image3 might look like this:

```
<IMG SRC="images/images3.gif" HEIGHT="20" WIDTH="30" ALT="Image
3 Description">
```

Notice that the SRC attributes in the preceding lines do not contain any absolute path information. If the documents were to be moved from mydir to otherdir along with the images subdirectory, there would be no broken images. However, if the links contained path information such as:

```
<IMG SRC="mydir/images/images3.gif" HEIGHT="20" WIDTH="30"
ALT="Image 3 Description">
```

or

```
<IMG SRC="/mydir/images/images3.gif" HEIGHT="20" WIDTH="30"
ALT="Image 3 Description">
```

then these documents would need to be fixed after the move. Many sites keep their images in a central image directory (such as images) under document root and link documents, using IMG tags such as:

```
<IMG SRC="/images/images3.gif" HEIGHT="20" WIDTH="30"
ALT="Image 3 Description">
```

This is fine, but there are two problems:

- ✦ When you want to delete the HTML document, you need to make sure you also delete the appropriate image in the central image directory.
- ✦ If you fail to address the first problem, eventually a lot of disk space will disappear in your image pit.

Therefore, it is not a good idea to keep images in a central directory. You should keep images in a subdirectory with their links.

Display clear copyright messages on each document

Each document should contain an embedded (commented) copyright message that clearly names the owner of the document and all its images. A similar copyright message should also appear on each page. To make it easy to update the copyright message, you may want to consider using an SSI directive as follows:

```
<!—#include file=/copyright.html" -->
```

Now, all you need is to create an HTML page called copyright.html, and place it under your server's document root directory. Note that because the content of this HTML page gets inserted in the SSI-enabled document that makes this call, you should not use the <HTML>, <HEAD>, <TITLE>, or <BODY> tags in this document. If you have many documents that use this SSI call, this will make your life easier when you need to update the year in the copyright message, or make another change.

Dynamic application development policy

The other type of content is dynamic, and it is usually produced by CGI scripts or other applications that implement CGI or some server-side interface. A vast majority of dynamic content is produced using Perl-based CGI scripts. Because CGI scripts and applications usually have a very short life span, many CGI developers do not devote the time to producing a high-quality application.

If you plan to use FastCGI or mod_perl-based scripts and applications, it is important that they be developed in a proper manner. You should consider the following policy when implementing scripts and applications for your dynamic content.

Always use version control

CGI developers must use version control, to enable you to go back to an older version of an application in case the newly developed and deployed version contains a bug. On most UNIX systems, you can use the Concurrent Versions System (CVS) software to implement a version-controlled environment. You can find the latest version of the CVS software at:

```
ftp://prep.ai.mit.edu
```

Do not use absolute path names in CGI scripts or applications

No absolute path names should be used in CGI scripts, to ensure that the scripts can be used from one Web site to another without modifications. If absolute path names are required for some special purpose, a configuration file should be supplied for the script; this way, the paths can be updated by modifying the textual configuration file.

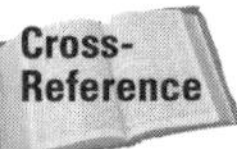

In Chapter 8, I show you how to use a configuration file-based CGI script that can be used for general form processing.

Provide both user and code level documentation

Source code needs to be well documented so future developers can update the scripts without spending a lot of time trying to figure out how it works.

Avoid embedding HTML tags in scripts or applications

The output of CGI scripts should be template-driven. In other words, a CGI script reads an output page template and replaces dynamic data fields (which can be represented using custom tags). This makes output page updating easy for HTML developers, because the HTML is not within the CGI script. In fact, CGI scripts should contain as little HTML as possible.

Do not trust user input data

To reduce security risks, make sure that user input data is checked before it is used.

You can learn more about checking user input in Chapter 12. That chapter discusses input-related security risks and solutions in detail.

Avoid global variables in Perl-based CGI scripts

When developing CGI scripts in Perl, you should avoid global variables. Limiting the scope of a variable is one way to eliminate unpredictable script behavior. Perl programmers should use the following for variable declarations:

```
my $variable;
```

instead of :

```
local $variable;
```

because the latter creates a global variable, whereas the former creates a local variable.

User-Friendly Interface for Your Web site

Using standard HTML and well-written CGI scripts/applications can certainly make your Web site better than many of the sites that exist out there. However, there's another aspect of Web site design that you need to consider: user Interface.

Think of a Web site as an interactive application with a Graphical User Interface (GUI) that is visible in a Web browser. The GUI needs to be user-friendly for people to have a pleasant Web experience while they are visiting your Web site. Having a visitor-friendly user interface (UI) will make your visitors happy.

The key issues in developing a user-friendly GUI are discussed in this section. Along with making your GUI user-friendly, you need to watch out for broken links or requests for deleted files. Use your server error logs to detect these kinds of problems. You should also have a way for visitors to give you feedback. Most sites use a simple HTML form-based feedback CGI script. You can develop one that suits your needs. Gathering feedback is a good way to find out what your visitors think about your Web site.

Make your site easy to navigate

Users must be able to go from one page to another without pulling their hair out. They should be able to locate buttons or menu bars that enable them to move back and forth or jump to related information.

Many Web page designers argue that popular Web browsers already include a Back and Next button, so having a Back or Next button on a page is redundant. Wrong! Imagine that a user lands on one of your pages (other than the home page) from a search engine's output. He simply searched for one or more keywords, and the search engine gave him a URL to a page on your site. He is very interested in knowing more about the topic on your site, so he wants to start from the beginning of the document — but there's no way he can do that, because the browser's Back button takes him back to the search engine output page!

Alas, if only this page had a link (or a button) to a previous page, the user could have gone back easily. The Web page designers who don't like the extra buttons insist that the user should have simply manipulated the URL a bit to go back to the home page and start from there. Well, this assumes that there is a clear link to this page (that matched the search keyword) from the home page. Is that always true? I hope you get my point.

I think it's a good idea to implement a menu bar that enables the user to go back and forth, and also enables the user to jump to a related location or even a home page. Figure 18-3 shows an example of such a page.

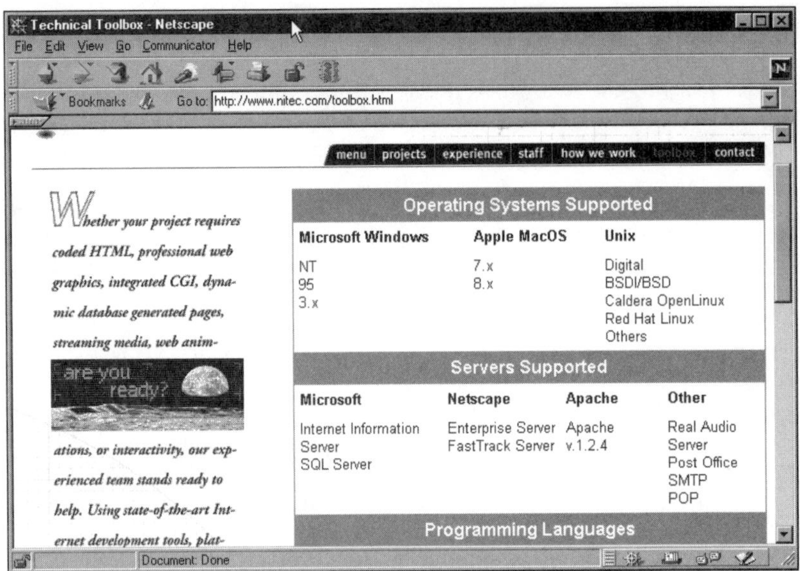

Figure 18-3: Example of a page with a navigational menu bar

Create an appealing design

Think of Web sites as colorful and interactive presentations that are active 24 hours a day. If the look and feel of this presentation is not just right, your visitors will click away from your site(s). Consider the following guidelines for developing an appealing site design.

Appropriate foreground and background colors

Make sure you don't go overboard with your color choices. Use of extreme colors makes your Web site appear unprofessional and dull. Be color-conscious and use an appropriate coloring scheme. For example, if your Web site is about kids' toys, it should be a very colorful site. If your site is about Digital Signal Processor benchmarks, however, you probably don't need many colors or flashy backgrounds.

Appropriate text size

Try to make your primary content appear in normal font. Use of a special font through <FONT FACE="myVerySpecialFont"> may make the page look good on your Web browser (because you happen to have the font), but on someone else's browser the page may look completely different and may be difficult to read. Also, be careful with the size of the text; do not make it too large or too small. Remember, if your visitors can't read what you have to say on your Web page, they won't be able to like what you have to say.

Less use of images

Go easy with unnecessary images on pages. Images make your Web pages download more slowly. Remember that not everyone is connected to an ISDN line; most people still use 28.8K modems for their Internet connection. A slow page download could might make a potential client click away from your pages.

Also, be cautious about using animations. Even the cutest animations become boring after the first few visits, so make sure you are not overcrowding your pages with them.

Remove cryptic error messages

Configure Apache with the ErrorDocument directive, so users do not receive server error messages that are difficult to understand (at least to the average user). For example, when a requested URL is not found on the server, the server may display an error message such as the one shown in Figure 18-4.

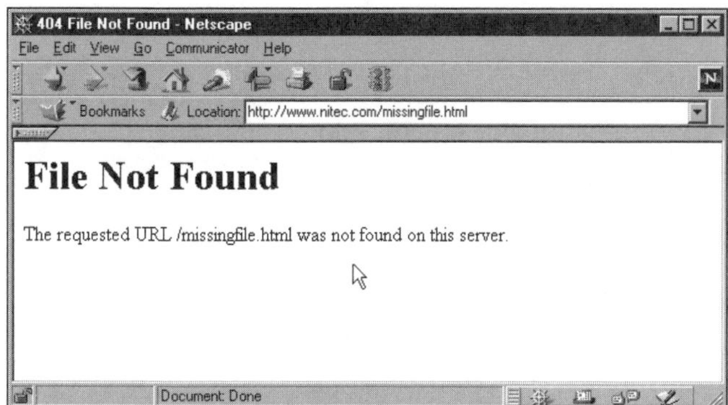

Figure 18-4: Document not found

To make this error message a bit more friendly, you can add an ErrorDocument directive such as:

```
ErrorDocument 404     /sorry.html
```

in one of the Apache configuration files (such as srm.conf), so the error message looks like the one shown in Figure 18-5.

See Chapter 4 for details on how to use this directive for other error messages.

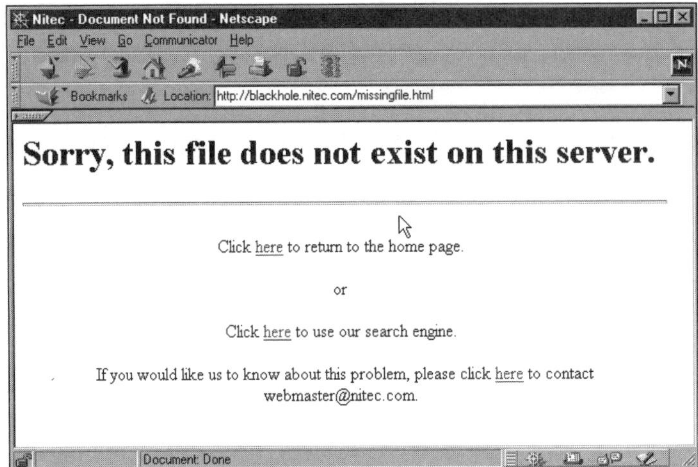

Figure 18-5: Friendly error message

Test your Web GUI

One of the best ways to test your Web interface is to use a system that resembles the average Internet user's computer, or perhaps your potential client's computer. If you think your clients will all have high-performance computers with fast connections, you may not need to worry about using fewer graphics or client-side applications such as Java applets and shockwave animations.

In most cases, you do not know the potential client's computer and network specifications, so you should go with the average user setup. Use a low-end Pentium computer with 16MB of RAM and a 28.8K modem connection to test your Web site from an ISP account. Try low monitor resolutions such as 640 × 480 or 800 × 600 pixels; if your target visitors will be using Web-TV systems, try lower a resolution of 550 × 400 pixels.

If you enjoyed looking through your Web site, others will probably enjoy it too. On the other hand, if you didn't like what you saw, others probably won't either!

If you prefer, you can have a third party test your Web site as well. For example, a company called AtWeb Inc. provides a Web-based, free tune-up service at this URL

```
www.websitegarage.com/
```

Their back-end application can examine any Web site for page download time, quality of the HTML, dead links, spelling errors, HTML design quality, and link popularity. To try it out, just go to the preceding Web site and enter your own Web site address in a text entry window.

For example, I decided to get a free tune-up report for www.nitec.com from their site, so I entered the site URL, as shown in Figure 18-6.

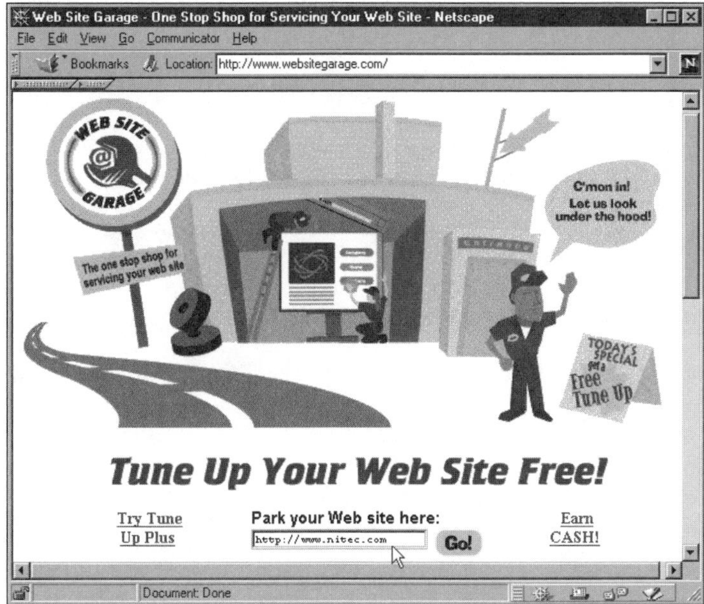

Figure 18-6: Requesting a tune-up report

After clicking the Go icon, I had to wait a few seconds, and then the application produced a report, as shown in Figure 18-7.

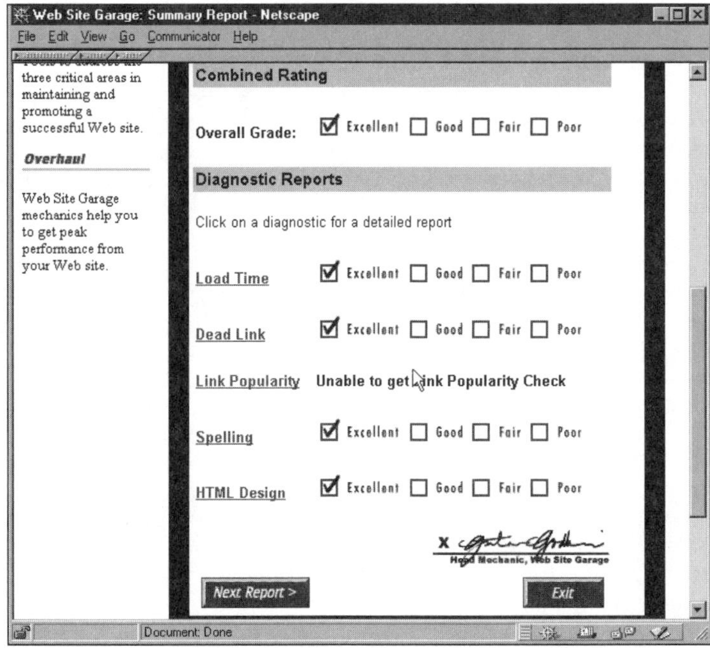

Figure 18-7: A live report from www.websitegarage.com

The application reported how the site measured up to AtWeb's standards. This free version is limited, but the company offers other commercial packages for site tune-ups as well.

Pointers for Promoting Your Web Site

What good is a perfect Web site if nobody knows about it? You should think about promoting your Web site on the Web. You can hire advertising agencies to help you in this regard, although advertising on the Web can be expensive. If your budget gets in the way, you can do some promoting yourself.

Before you do anything to promote your Web site, ask yourself, “How do I find information on the Web?” The answer is: through search engines. Is your company listed in the search engines? If not, this is the first step in promoting your site.

Almost all search engines enable you to submit your URL to their search robot's database so it can traverse your Web in the future. You should make a list of search engines that you consider important, and submit your Web site's URL to these engines. Although this process can take days or even weeks, you can add META information in your content to help your URL appear in a decent position when a potential customer does a search. For example, you can add META information such as:

```
<META NAME="KEYWORD" CONTENT="keyword1 keyword2 keyword3 …">
<META NAME="DESCRIPTION" CONTENT="Description of your company">
```

To increase traffic, you can also participate in link exchanges such as www.linkexchange.com. Link exchanges require that you put a special set of HTML tags in your Web pages; these tags pull advertisement graphic (banner ad) files into your pages. In return, your banner advertisement graphics are also displayed in Web sites operated by others who agreed to show someone else's banner on their pages. This type of advertisement sharing is quite popular among personal and small business sites.

Whether you buy advertisement space on high-profile Web sites such as Yahoo, AltaVista, or Netscape, or you use the link exchange method, you should periodically check your site's standing in the search engines output by generating search queries yourself.

Summary

This chapter dealt with various issues relating to developing a successful Web site. It introduced you to the Web cycle, which requires that you use three phases (development, staging, and production) to manage your Web sites. The chapter discussed how you can improve your static and dynamic content quality by using standards and improved user interfaces. It even provided helpful information on how to get your Web site promoted on the Web. I hope that all the information given in this chapter will help you create perfect Web sites.

In the next chapter, you learn how to create a Web network.

✦ ✦ ✦

CHAPTER 19

Apache for the Web Network

In This Chapter

What is a Web network?

How to implement a multisystem, Apache-based Web network

How to use round-robin DNS in Web networks

How to use NFS to share common data

By now this book has covered a lot about Apache features and functionality that you can put to use. If you already have a machine running Apache, you've surely started playing with all the new things you've learned so far in this book.

If your needs are of small scale, you can install Apache on a machine and set up a few Web sites. But what if you need something of a larger scale — a Web network? If you or your organization needs a Web network, where multiple systems are used to create a reliable and scaleable environment for all the Web sites you host, this chapter will help you create such a network.

The example in this chapter is taken from real-world experiences in deploying Apache-based Web networks.

What Is a Web Network?

First of all, let's understand the need for Web networks. A fictitious company called XC News wants to create a scaleable Web solution in which a form of load balancing is used to distribute requests over two Web server systems.

Note

The name XC News and the IP addresses used in this chapter are purely fictitious, and any resemblance to a real company and its IP addresses is completely unintentional.

Let's look at the specific needs of the project:

✦ **Purpose** — XC News has hundreds of clients who want XC News to host their Web sites and provide access to XC News–developed Web applications and other services. After using a single Windows NT–based server on a colocated environment, XC News now requires a better solution because their future projection shows that growth of the Internet-based services they offer is likely to skyrocket soon. So the company wants to develop a Web network consisting of multiple Web server systems that provide a scaleable and reliable environment for client sites. The network will initially have two Web servers and a monitor server system, but the design and implementation of the network must be flexible enough to add more servers when needed.

✦ **Server platform** — XC News realizes the importance of a distributed network and how such network architecture can be used to provide a scaleable solution. To have the capability of adding new systems quickly to satisfy sudden bursts of traffic on the Web network, the company wants to use Intel-based PC systems running operating systems that offer a great deal of remote administration features. Their past Windows NT experience led them to believe that Windows NT is still hard to manage via the Internet, and virtually no server software can be installed, upgraded, or removed via Internet-based remote access.

✦ **Location of the Web network** — To reduce cost and increase reliability, the XC News company wants to deploy this Web network in a colocation environment with an Internet service provider. This will allow them to take advantage of industry-standard power management facilities and give them instant access to a large bandwidth network.

✦ **DNS server system** — Because XC News wants to have DNS for all client domains along with its own domains, it needs a DNS server. XC News also wants to be able to monitor Web server systems via a system that will run scheduled monitor programs to check on the availability of the Web servers. When a Web server has failed for some reason, the monitor will send out e-mail alert messages or even send alphanumeric pages to individuals responsible for the Web server.

✦ **Secured server system** — XC News would like to provide secured (SSL-based) transaction services for each client site. Neither XC News nor its clients are interested in buying separate certificates for each site. The company also wants to restrict access to secured space in such a way that clients will not be able to create their own secured pages.

✦ **Network design** — The network will be designed such that load will be distributed among the Web servers. The design and implementation must account for Web server failures: it will have to be very easy to either automatically or manually route all requests to the rest of the Web servers. Many of the XC News CGI applications write data to files. These files will have to be synchronized among all the Web servers so that each client site using the files has the latest data.

✦ **Network backup requirements** — The Internet service provider (ISP) chosen by XC News provides a network backup solution using Legato NetWorker server/client architecture. The ISP requires that XC News run a Legato client on the staging system that will dump these files to the ISP NetWorker server via TCP/IP protocol. Note that this backup solution is too specific to a particular commercial software and is not likely to be available from most ISPs. Therefore I do not discuss the backup details. However, I kept the requirements for the sake of completeness and to remind you that backing up is an important aspect of all network solutions.

✦ **Client Web site requirements** — Each XC News client will have a unique domain for which XC News will provide primary Domain Name Service (DNS). The client domain will have a standard www.client-domain.com host, which will be its Web site host. Each client will have FTP access to its Web document root directory. A client might optionally request to get one or more POP3 mail accounts or request that mail for the domain be sent to a outside mail server host.

  Each client's Web site will be allowed to run XC News-developed CGI applications. A client site will not have its own CGI-BIN directory. However, XC News foresees that their policy on CGI-BIN access might change in the future, so they would like the design to be such that local CGI script directory access be implemented but kept disabled at this point in time.

These are the high-level specifications. Read on to make sure you understand what is required to meet these specifications.

Understanding the Requirements

Before designing a project, one must understand its requirements. So let's take a look at the requirements from a network designer's prospective. It seems as though XC News wants to build a network of Web servers, where each server will host all the client Web sites and XC News sites. This network will work such that URL requests will be automatically routed to a different machine running the same Web site. Figure 19-1 shows how this needs to work.

As you can see, a request such as www.xcnews.com has to be magically serviced by either Web server #1 or Web server #2. This "magic" will have to be done using round-robin domain name service. In case of a single Web server failure, it has to be easy to redirect traffic to another functioning server.

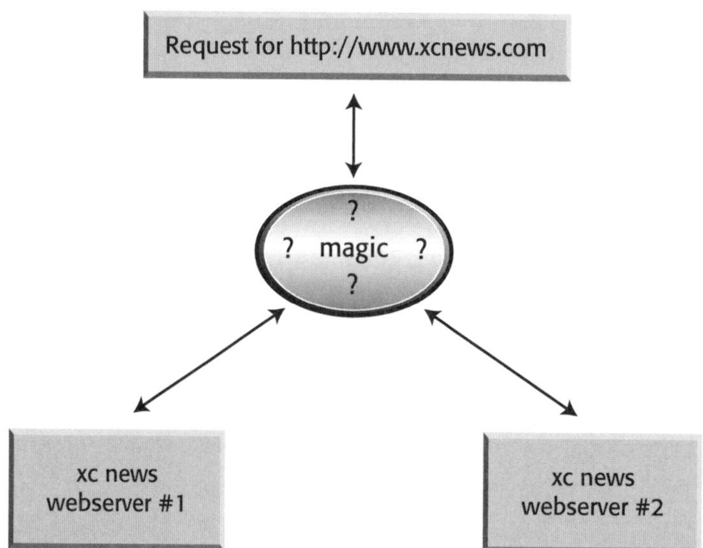

Figure 19-1: How URL requests are distributed

The requirements also state that there has to be a single staging area for clients to FTP files. This staging area has to be distributed to the Web servers so that each of them has all the files needed to service any URL request for all the sites. Where can this staging area reside? Before answering this question, a distinction needs to be made between the server systems. If you carefully read the specifications, you will notice that the XC News company wants to treat the Web servers as production systems. Because it is generally a good idea to minimize user interactions on production systems, the staging area cannot be on the production systems. It has to be on the third system — the DNS and monitoring server. Now all you have to do is create a staging area on the DNS server and have the staging files distributed to the production Web servers.

How do the files get over to the Web servers? Here are a couple of solutions:

✦ Use the Network File System (NFS) to share the staging area with the Web servers.

✦ Use a popular remote distribution software called rdist to distribute files to the Web servers.

If NFS is used for all Web sites, and there are a large number of files, it could become a performance bottleneck because NFS is not as good as a local file system. So rdist appears to be a good choice. Using the cron facility found on UNIX systems together with rdist, you can distribute files on a schedule basis. However, there is still an outstanding issue concerning synchronizing the CGI script written data. If rdist is used to sync the CGI data files, there will be periods when the files will not be in sync among the servers; in addition, multiple copies of the same data file will exist, which is likely to cause all sorts of problems. So it appears the CGI data files should be kept in sync some other way.

The good news is that the CGI data files are all written in the same data directory area, so all you need to do is mount that directory as an NFS-exported directory to the Web servers; as a result, the Web servers can all read and write the same files.

NFS does not provide any file-locking mechanism, so it is important that the CGI scripts themselves implement some sort of file locking.

From the requirements, it is also clear that the secured server has to be run on the DNS server. Table 19-1 shows what services are performed by each system in the network.

Table 19-1
Services on Each System

System	*Services*
DNS server	Domain Name service Monitoring service NFS server for CGI data file directories FTP server for the staging area rdist server for distributing files from staging area Secured server
Web server #1	Apache server NFS Client for CGI data file directories rdist client
Web server #2	Apache server NFS Client for CGI data file directories rdist client

Note that instead of developing an in-house monitoring solution, a simple, Perl-based monitoring package called Spong (included in the CD-ROM) can be used to meet the specified requirements. However, due to the simplicity of its installation and setup process, it is not discussed any further.

Now that the services for each machine have been identified, let's also look at the type of traffic that this network will experience. There are three types of network traffic for XC News:

✦ **The usual Internet traffic** — Each server will communicate with Internet clients.

✦ **rdist file synchronization traffic** — This particular type of traffic will only be experienced by the three machines involved in file distribution. This traffic will not and should not travel to and from any outside hosts.

✦ **NFS traffic** — This particular type of traffic will only be experienced by the three machines involved. The DNS server will act as the NFS server, which will export certain directories to the other two Web servers. The NFS traffic will not and should not travel to and from any other outside hosts.

Now that the services and traffic requirements are identified, it is time to design the network.

Designing the Web Network

The first step in designing a Web network is to picture how the high-level solution will look. Figure 19-2 shows a high-level network diagram. As you can see in this diagram, the Web servers and the DNS server are connected to the ISP network via an Ethernet hub. All traffic to and from the Internet passes through the hub to the systems. This network will do the job, but it is not optimal. Why? If you look closely, the network uses a single Ethernet hub to connect the three machines to the Internet and to each other. This means all the NFS and rdist traffic will have to travel on the same Ethernet hub as the Internet traffic. Because this makes the Ethernet very busy, it is not a good solution.

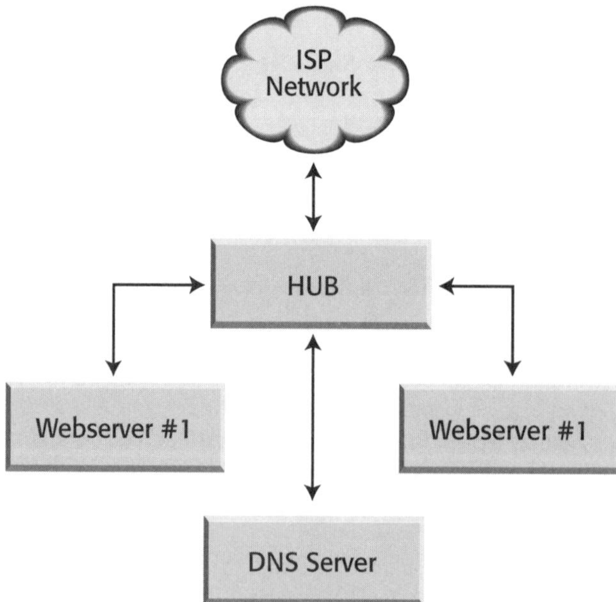

Figure 19-2: A high-level network diagram (single Ethernet)

To solve this problem, you can redesign the network as shown in Figure 19-3. Here you can see two Ethernet hubs being used. One connects the servers to the ISP network, and the second connects the servers with each other. What is so great about this? If I can keep the NFS and rdist traffic on the Ethernet for the servers, the Ethernet connected to the ISP network can only be used for Internet services. In other words, one of the Ethernets will be used as a local area network (LAN) and the other one used for Internet access.

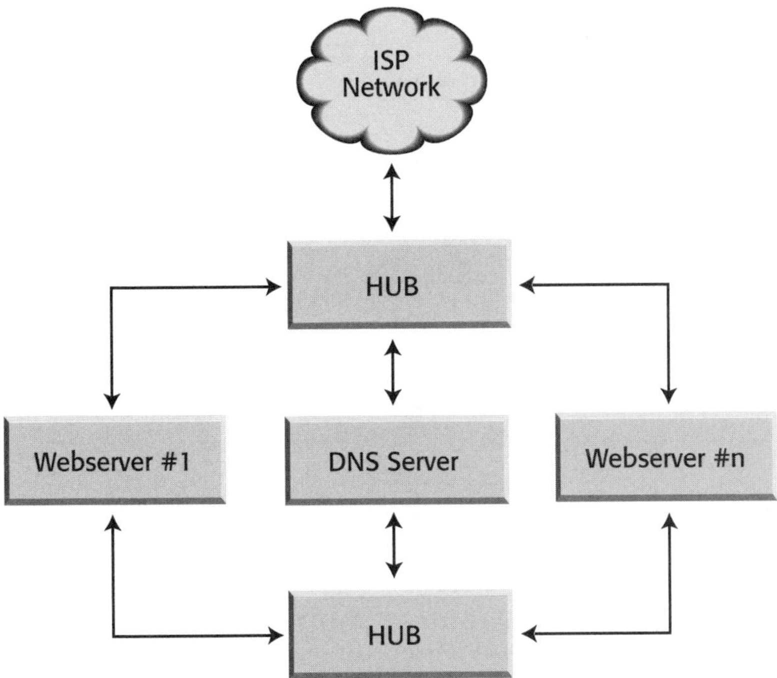

Figure 19-3: A high-level network diagram (multiple Ethernet)

Figure 19-4 shows a high-level network traffic diagram. This is a better solution because both NFS and rdist traffic will only travel across the LAN, thus making the other Ethernet free for Internet connectivity. It also adds more armor to the security of the network. It is a common belief among system administrators that NFS is not as secure as it should be. So if I use a single Ethernet and export the NFS directories to the Web servers, there is a chance that Ethernet could become a point of attack.

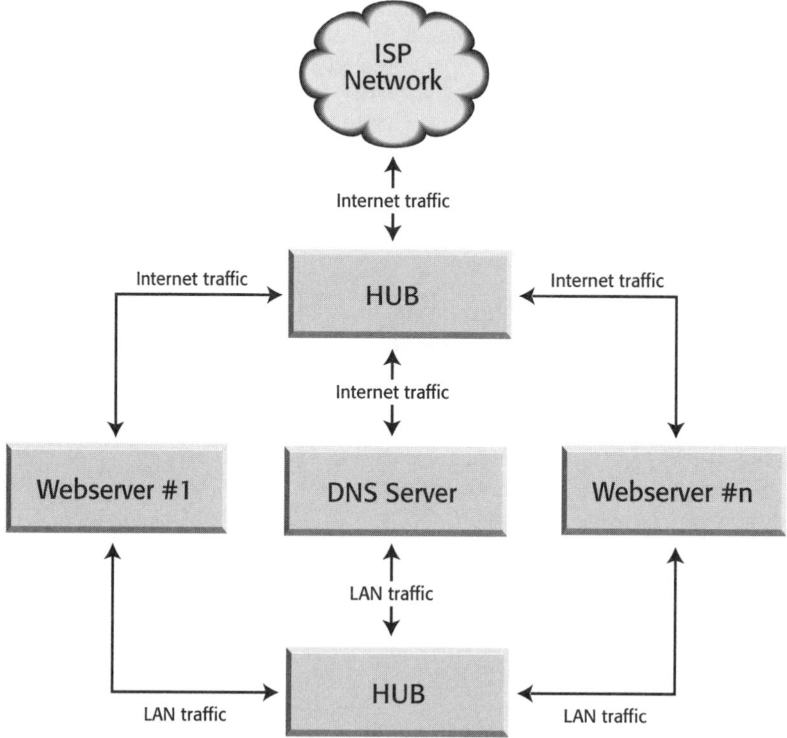

Figure 19-4: A high-level network traffic diagram

Many systems have been hacked via NFS-related security holes, so it is a good idea to avoid making NFS directories available via the Internet. To ensure the LAN is not accessible to any but the three systems, make sure no direct routes exist between the two Ethernets. This will prevent anyone from the Internet accessing the LAN. On top of that, to enhance the security scheme a bit further, I can use nonroutable IP addresses on the LAN. Figure 19-5 shows the IP address assignments for the nodes on both networks. As you can see, the LAN is using a network address, 192.168.1.60, which is nonroutable on the Internet.

You can also use other nonroutable IP addresses from a Class A network, such as 10.0.0.0.

The IP addresses on the Internet side are ISP dependent, as these IP addresses will have to be routable on the Internet.

Now you know enough about the network to get started with a hardware and software list.

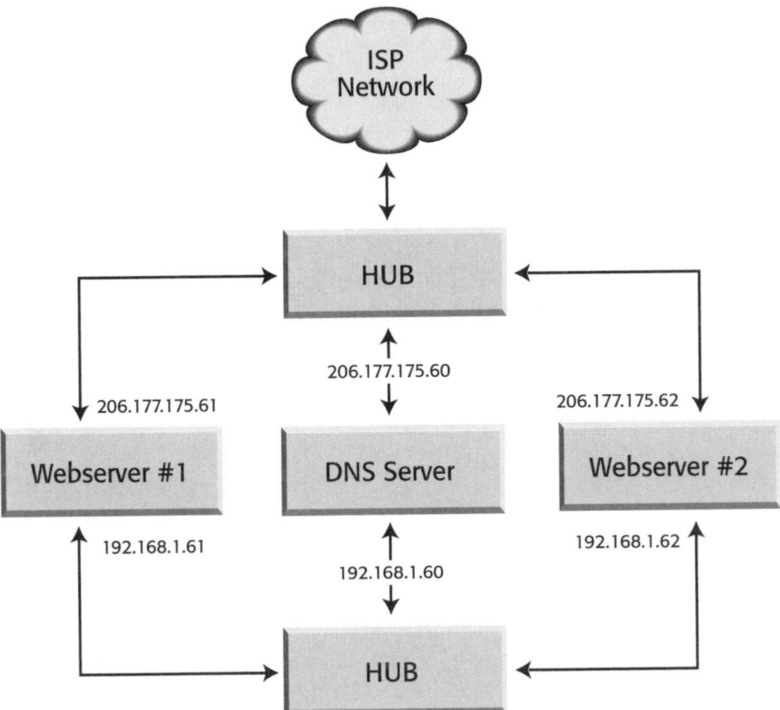

Figure 19-5: IP address assignment for the networks

Choosing the Hardware and Software

As mentioned earlier, the XC News company wants to use PC servers instead of expensive server platforms so that they can easily add servers as their needs grow. In light of that, you can develop a specification for the servers in this network. My personal experience with brand-name PC clones are comparable with non-brand-name ones, so I prefer to use one of the following vendors for server systems:

- ✦ Micron (www.micronpc.com)
- ✦ ASA Computers (www.asacomputers.com)

Now let's look at what hardware is needed for a server system.

Setting up a PC server

It is always good to have a system that you can upgrade easily. Because Intel has decided to use a slot system for its new CPUs, it is not a good idea to get a CPU that uses a socket like socket 7. I suspect that soon these will become hard to find. Besides, the new Pentium II processors are extremely fast and should be considered an integral part of any decent PC server. I recommend a 233MHz Intel processor for each server. The motherboard of the system is very important, so I recommend a high-end motherboard from Intel.

The next item to consider is the amount of RAM. The general rule of thumb is the more RAM the better. However, RAM is very expensive, especially the 10 nanoseconds SDRAM modules. I recommend 256MB of SDRAM on each server system.

Each system should also have two ultra-wide SCSI disks connected to a brand-name SCSI UW controller. Having at least two disks per system is a good idea, because it enables the operating system to be on one disk and data to be on the other. The total data capacity for the data disk can be determined by the company's current and future needs. For XC News, I calculated the total disk space requirements for all XC News sites to be close to 200MB. So having a 4GB disk for data is sufficient for now.

A good thing about having a SCSI-based disk system is you can easily add external disks to the SCSI chain when the need arises. Almost all popular brands of SCSI controllers provide support for a minimum of 7 to a maximum of 15 devices in a daisy chain.

Each system should also have two brand-name 100Mbps PCI-based Ethernet adapter cards, a regular SVGA video card, and a server-class case with dual power supply. The video card will seldom be used, so it does not need to have lots of video RAM.

Similarly, each system should have an IDE CD-ROM drive and a floppy disk drive. A server case needs to be strong and sturdy, and it should have lots of room and a good power supply system. The dual power supply system provides a safety net; if one fails, the other one is there to provide uninterrupted service.

Now, for the XC News network, additional equipment is needed: two 100base-TX Ethernet hubs (as shown back in Figure 19-5), some precut category 5 100base-TX cables, a 9-inch SVGA monitor, and a 101-key keyboard to be stored at the ISP location for any emergency work.

Now that the PC server configuration and additional hardware for XC News has been selected, it's time to consider the software.

Selecting an operating system

A good number of x86 PC-based UNIX operating systems are available — for example, Linux, FreeBSD, BSDI, and Solaris. For XC News, let's use Linux; I've personally used it over and over with many real-world networks and have always had good success with it. Specifically, let's use the RedHat distribution of Linux because it comes with an easy-to-use installer and RedHat keeps their version of Linux up-to-date with the latest developments. The commercially packaged version of RedHat Linux can be ordered from www.redhat.com.

Choosing a Web server

The Web server is an easy choice. Let's use the stable, release 1.2.6 version of Apache instead of the latest beta version. I personally prefer not to run beta software on production systems.

As discussed in Chapter 15, the software program Stronghold is a good choice for securing an Apache-based server, so let's add this program to the list.

Now that the hardware and software has been selected, the systems can now be set up, one by one.

Setting Up the Systems

To set up the systems, RedHat Linux needs to be installed on each system; but before that, a decision needs to be made about how to partition the disks.

Partitioning the disks

Almost all UNIX systems have a number of standard disk partitions, such as the / (root) partition, /usr, and /home. The disks must be divided into partitions so that administration of the operating system and other software can be somewhat standardized. Even a newbie UNIX administrator can tell you that the operating system software resides on the / partition and most other software resides on the /usr partition. This has been the UNIX tradition, and it simply makes system administration easier. Table 19-2 shows the partitions I recommend for the operating system (OS) disk for each XC News system.

Table 19-2
Disk Partitions for the OS Disk

Partition	*Size in MB*	*Explanation*
/	512	Root partition
/usr	1024	Standard partition where various software will be installed
/home	384	User home directories
Swap	128	Swap space

Notice that the /home partition, where user home directives will be located, is not so large. This is because most of the users logging in will not have much in their home directories. In fact, most XC News clients will have their home directories pointed to a Web directory, as discussed in more detail later in this chapter.

Table 19-3 shows the data disk partitions I recommend XC News use for each system. Note that although users are not meant to log in on the Web server system, I kept the partitions the same for the OS disk on all three systems.

Table 19-3
Disk Partition for the Data Disk

Partition	*Size in MB*	*Explanation*
/www	3,072	Web data partition
/log	1,024	Log files space

The log partition needs to be 1GB (1024MB) because a lot of Web sites produce log entries per request.

Installing Linux

Now it's time to install Linux on each XC News system. RedHat Software makes it a breeze to install RedHat. All you have to do is boot the system with the boot disk and partition disks, as desired. There are many ways one can install RedHat, but I prefer to install it from a local CD-ROM because this method seems to take the least amount of time.

Next, install the operating system using the simple menu installation program. When installing a server operating system, you should not install any program that is not going to be needed; restricting installation to necessary programs only reduces disk space use and also enhances the security of the system. For example, the servers for XC News do not need any X Windows software, so X Windows and X Windows–related packages should be excluded from the installation. XC News does need the base operating system and network components such as FTP, NFS, SMTP, and Apache servers for each system. Software such as news servers, news readers, extra editors, support software for Netmanager services, printer daemons, and so on need not be installed on server systems, so I avoid these for each system.

For the DNS server system, I include the Berkeley Internet Domain (BIND) software.

Configuring the networks

Now it's time to configure both networks for each system.

Let's start with the Internet network, which is the network that will be connected to the ISP network. The systems for the Internet network should be configured to use the IP addresses shown in Table 19-4.

Table 19-4
Host Names and IP Address for Internet-Bound Network

Host Name	*IP Address*	*Machine*
ns.xcnews.com	206.177.175.60	DNS server
www1.xcnews.com	206.177.175.61	Web server #1
www2.xcnews.com	206.177.175.62	Web server #2

These IP addresses are not randomly picked. They are assigned by the ISP, which provides the reverse name service for the IP numbers, whereas ns.xcnews.com provides primary name service for itself and all its client domains. The ISP will also furnish secondary DNS service for all domains of XC News.

The ISP provides the netmask (255.255.255.0) and the default gateway IP for this network so that all traffic will go to their gateway system via the hub.

Now let's choose a fictitious domain name for the LAN, such as xcnews-lan.com, and assign the nonroutable IP addresses, as shown in Table 19-5.

Table 19-5
Host Name and IP Address Assignments for xcnews-lan.com

Host Name	*IP Address*	*Machine*
ns.xcnews-lan.com	192.168.1.60	DNS server
www1.xcnews-lan.com	192.168.1.61	Web server #1
www2.xcnews-lan.com	192.168.1.62	Web server #2

I made the host part of the IP address (60-62) the same as the other network to keep things easy to remember for the system administrator. The netmask for this network is also 255.255.255.0 because I used a class C network address (192.168.1.0), and the default gateway for this network is the name server system — ns.xcnews-lan.com.

Once the operating system is installed and the networks are all configured, use the ping program to test the network.

To test the Internet-bound network, send ping requests from one host to another, each time using the appropriate IP address. For example, to ping the www1.xcnews.com system from ns.xcnews.com, use the following command:

```
ping 206.177.175.61
```

It's not possible to ping using host names yet because the name server is not set up. When you ping one host from another, notice the LED display of the Internet-bound hub blink rapidly and the other one remain steady. This is a visual assurance that the ping packets are going through the right hub. Pinging IP addresses on the xcnews-lan.com network makes the other hub's LED blink. Of course, you can determine the routes the packets took from the route table as well. The command to do this is as follows:

```
/sbin/route -n
```

This displays the routing table shown in Listing 19-1.

Listing 19-1: Routing table of the name server

```
Kernel IP routing table
Destination    Gateway         Genmask         Flags Metric Ref Use
Iface
206.177.175.0 0.0.0.0          255.255.255.0 U       0         0
179 eth0
192.168.1.0    0.0.0.0         255.255.255.0 U       0         0
23 eth1
127.0.0.0      0.0.0.0         255.0.0.0     U       0         0
2 lo
0.0.0.0        206.177.175.1  0.0.0.0       UG      0         0 53116
  eth0
```

Next, the DNS server software called BIND should be set up.

Setting Up DNS Server

The Web network DNS for XC News is going to make use of a DNS trick known as round-robin DNS. In this setup, a DNS server is configured in such a way that it gives out different IP addresses for a single host. Because XC News wants to make all its Web servers service the same set of domains in a distributed manner, each host name must point to two IP addresses. Figure 19-6 illustrates this point.

The /etc/named.boot file for the DNS server is listed in Listing 19-2. Notice that the DNS server is configured as the primary for both xcnews.com and xcnews-lan.com. Because the ISP does the primary reverse DNS, this server is set up as the secondary for the 175.177.206.in-addr.arpa domain. For the 1.168.192.in-addr.arpa reverse domain, however, it is set up as the primary.

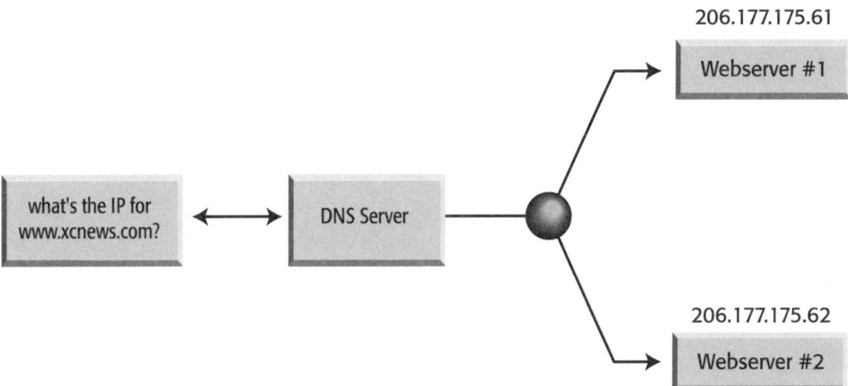

Figure 19-6: Two IP addresses per Web host

Listing 19-2: /etc/named.boot file

```
Directory                                       /var/named
Cache                                           named.ca
Primary           0.0.127.in-addr.arpa          named.local
;
; XC News domains
;
primary           xcnews.com                    xcnews.db
secondary     175.177.206.in-addr.arpa          xcnews.rev
;
; This domain is used for internal LAN that is not routed on
; the Internet.
;
primary           xcnews-lan.com                xcnews-lan.db
primary           1.168.192.in-addr.arpa        xcnews-lan.rev
```

Now if you look at the xnews.com DNS database file called xcnews.db, listed in Listing 19-3, you will see that, along with the usual SOA, NS, MX, A, and CNAME records, there are two special CNAME (Canonical Name)records.

Listing 19-3: /var/named/xcnews.db

```
@ IN    SOA  xcnews.com.     hostmaster.xcnews.com. (
             19980205000     ; serial YYYYMMDDXXX
             7200            ; refresh
             3600            ; (1 hour) retry
             1728000         ; (20 days) expire
             3600)           ; (1 hour) minimal TTL
```

(continued)

Listing 19-3 *(continued)*

```
; Name server and Mail eXchange records
            IN   NS   ns.xcnews.com.
            IN   MX   5 mail.xcnews.com.

; A records
ns          IN   A    206.177.175.60

www1        IN   A    206.177.175.61
www2        IN   A    206.177.175.62

; CNAME records
mail        IN   CNAME     ns
ftp         IN   CNAME     ns
www         IN   CNAME     www1
www         IN   CNAME     www2
secured     IN   CNAME     ns
```

The special CNAME records are as follows:

```
www         IN   CNAME     www1
www         IN   CNAME     www2
```

These records indicate that www.xcnews.com is a CNAME for www1.xcnews.com and www2.xcnews.com. So what does the name server do when a client queries about the address of www.xcnew.com? It gives you either www1.xcnews.com or www2.xcnews.com. Actually, this happens in a round-robin fashion: The DNS server returns 206.177.175.61 (www1.xcnews.com) to the first request for www.xcnews.com and 206.177.175.62 (www2.xcnews.com) for the next request. This trick enables a requesting client to be directed towards one of the Web servers. The reverse database record for xcnews.com is listed in Listing 19-4.

Listing 19-4: /var/named/xcnews.rev

```
@ IN    SOA   xcnews.com.      hostmaster.xcnews.com. (
              19980205000      ; serial YYYYMMDDXXX
              7200             ; refresh
              3600             ; (1 hour) retry
              1728000          ; (20 days) expire
              3600)            ; (1 hour) minimal TTL

; Name server and Mail eXchange records
            IN   NS   ns.xcnews.com.
            IN   MX   5 mail.xcnews.com.
```

```
; PTR Records
60          IN    PTR   ns.xcnews.com.
61          IN    PTR   www1.xcnews.com.
62          IN    PTR   www2.xcnews.com.
```

Notice that there is no need to create the PTR records for the CNAME records, since they are just aliases to records that must have PTR records. So when a client wants to perform reverse name lookup, it gets the canonical name www1.xcnews.com or www2.xcnews.com, each of which has a PTR record.

The DNS records for xcnews-lan.com, shown in Listing 19-5, are straightforward.

Listing 19-5: /var/named/xcnews-lan.db

```
@ IN    SOA   xcnews-lan.com.      hostmaster.xcnews-lan.com. (
              19980205000    ; serial YYYYMMDDXXX
              7200           ; refresh
              3600           ; (1 hour) retry
              1728000        ; (20 days) expire
              3600)          ; (1 hour) minimal TTL

; Name server and Mail eXchange records
        IN    NS    ns.xcnews.com.

; A records
ns      IN    A     192.168.1.60
www1    IN    A     192.168.1.61
www2    IN    A     192.168.1.62
```

Notice that no mail exchange (MX) record is provided because there is no need for one. The reverse DNS records for xcnews-lan.com, shown in Listing 19-6, are equally simple.

Listing 19-6: /var/named/xcnews-lan.rev

```
@ IN    SOA   xcnews-lan.com.      hostmaster.xcnews-lan.com. (
              19980205000    ; serial YYYYMMDDXXX
              7200           ; refresh
              3600           ; (1 hour) retry
              1728000        ; (20 days) expire
              3600)          ; (1 hour) minimal TTL
```

(continued)

Listing 19-6 *(continued)*

```
; Name server and Mail eXchange records
            IN   NS   ns.xcnews-lan.com.

; PTR Records
60          IN   PTR  ns.xcnews-lan.com.
61          IN   PTR  www1.xcnews-lan.com.
62          IN   PTR  www2.xcnews-lan.com.
```

The key thing here is to make it very easy for XC News to add a new Web server and provide round-robin name service. If the system administrators for the company decided to add a new Web server system called www3.xcnews.com (206.177.175.63) to the network, all they need to do is make the following additions to the /var/named/xcnews.db file:

```
www3   IN   A          206.177.175.63
www    IN   CNAME      www3
```

Then they would have to add a new PTR entry in the /var/named/xcnews.rev file, as follows:

```
63     IN   PTR        www3.xcnews.com.
```

They would also have to update /var/named/xcnews-lan.db, as follows:

```
www3   IN   A    192.168.1.63
```

Finally, they would need to update /var/named/xcnews-lan.rev, as follows:

```
63     IN   PTR        www3.xcnews-lan.com.
```

Once these changes are made, the name server can be restarted, and www.xcnews.com will now be directed to all three Web servers.

This is all well and good, but how are the client sites going to take advantage of this round-robin DNS scheme? Let's take a look at an example. Say that XC News client client-one.com needs to be setup on this network. In such a case, a line to the /etc/named.boot file would be added, as follows:

```
primary              client-one.com              client-one.db
```

Then, in /var/named, a file called client-one.db would need to be created as shown in Listing 19-7.

Listing 19-7: client-one.db

```
@ IN   SOA  client-one.com.      hostmaster. client-one.com. (
            19980205000    ; serial YYYYMMDDXXX
            7200           ; refresh
            3600           ; (1 hour) retry
            1728000        ; (20 days) expire
            3600)          ; (1 hour) minimal TTL

; Name server and Mail eXchange records
            IN    NS  ns.xcnews.com.

; CNAME records for www.client-a.com
www         IN    CNAME    www.xcnews.com.
```

This sets up ns.xcnews.com as the DNS server for client-one.com and makes its www.client-a.com host point to www.xcnews.com. Because www.xcnews.com is a nickname for www1.xcnews.com and www2.xcnews.com, the DNS server will give out www1.xcnews.com and www2.xcnews.com host IP addresses for ww.client-a.com as well. This basically employs the round-robin DNS scheme, as desired. Now if XC News adds a new Web server, the client-a.com DNS records don't need to be changed as long as www.xcnews.com is a nickname for the new Web server.

What if one of the Web servers becomes unavailable? For example, say that www1.xcnews.com needs to be serviced. As a result, what needs to be changed in the DNS? The /var/named/xcnews.db file can be modified such that the following entry

```
www       IN    CNAME      www1
```

is commented out, as follows:

```
; www     IN    CNAME      www1
```

After making this change, the DNS server will need to be restarted to effect the change. Due to the nature of DNS, however, the change will still take some time to propagate.

Although the XC News client–related DNS setup is made to be quite simple, there's room for human error in the setup process. For example, if a period is not present at the end of a line, as shown in the following line, the setup won't work:

```
www       IN    CNAME      www.xcnews.com
```

To reduce the chances of human error, it is necessary to create a Perl script that uses a template (such as the one shown in Listing 19-8) to create the new client DNS database file; in addition, the template modifies the /etc/named.boot file such that the ns.xcnews.com is set up as the primary DNS server for the client domain.

Listing 19-8: named.template

```
@       IN    SOA        <DOMAIN>. hostmaster.<DOMAIN>. (
                         19980205000     ; serial YYYYMMDDXXX
                         7200            ; refresh
                         3600            ; (1 hour) retry
                         1728000         ; (20 days) expire
                         3600)           ; (1 hour) minimal TTL

; Name Servers
        IN    NS         ns.xcnews.com.
        IN    MX         10 mail.xcnews.com.

; CNAME records
mail         IN    CNAME          ns.xcnews.com.
ftp          IN    CNAME          ns.xcnews.com.
www          IN    CNAME          www.xcnews.com.
```

Notice that in this template file the domain name is specified as a tag called <DOMAIN>. This tag gets replaced by the script with the domain name of the client. Also, XC News will require additional Apache configuration per new client. Because this process also includes room for human error, let's make the Perl script create the necessary <VirtualHost …> container configuration using another template file, shown in Listing 19-9.

Listing 19-9: httpd.template

```
# Domain Configuration for <WWW-SITE>
#
<VirtualHost REPLACE-THIS-WITH-WEB-SERVER-IP-ADDR>
ServerAdmin webmaster@<DOMAIN>
DocumentRoot     <HTDOCS-DIR>
#ScriptAlias     /cgi-bin/      <CGI-BIN-DIR>/
ScriptAlias      /cgi-bin/      /www/xcnews/cgi-bin/
Alias            /cgi-data/     /www/cgi-data/
ServerName       <WWW-SITE>
ErrorLog         logs/<WWW-SITE>.error.log
TransferLog      logs/<WWW-SITE>.access.log
</VirtualHost>
#
# End of Domain Configuratin for <WWW-SITE>
```

The Perl script, called makesite, replaces the <WWW-SITE> tag with www.client-domain-name. The script is shown in Listing 19-10.

Listing 19-10: The makesite script

```
#!/usr/local/bin/perl
#
# Purpose: makesite creates virtual sites. It uses set
# of templates to create DNS, HTTPD, and SMTP
# configurations and appends these configuration data
# to appropriate configuration files.
#
# $Author$ (kabir@nitec.com)
# $Version$
# $Id$
# $Status
#
##############################################################

# You might need to change some of these values before
# you can use this script on your system
#

# Directory where the script is stored
my $MAKESITE_DIR = '/usr/local/build/makesite';

# The username which owns the newly created client
# directory
my $USER = 'httpd';

# The group which owns the newly created client
# directory
my $GROUP = 'httpd';

# Default file permission for $USER.$GROUP
my $PERMISSION = '2770';

# The Web partition directory
my $BASE_DIR = '/www';

# Document Root directory (relative to
# /$BASE_DIR/<CLIENT-DOMAIN-DIR>)
my $HTDOCS = 'htdocs';

# CGI program directory (relative to
# /$BASE_DIR/<CLIENT-DOMAIN-DIR>)
my $CGIBIN = 'cgi-bin';

# FQPN of BIND DNS record directory
my $NAMED_PATH = '/var/named';
```

(continued)

Listing 19-10 *(continued)*

```
# File extension for each domain record file
my $NAMED_FILE_EXT = '.db';

# FQPN of the BIND DNS record template file
my $NAMED_TEMPLATE_FILE = "$MAKESITE_DIR/named.template";

# FQPN of BIND named.boot file
my $NAMED_ETC_FILE = '/etc/named.boot';

# FQPN of the Apache httpd.conf file
my $HTTPD_CONF_FILE = '/www/apache/conf/httpd.conf';

# FQPN of the virtual host template file
my $VIRTUAL_HOST_TEMPLATE = "$MAKESITE_DIR/httpd.template";

# FQPN of the log file
my $LOG_FILE = "$BASE_DIR/makesite.log";

# FQPN of the 'date' program in back-ticks.
my $date = `/bin/date`;

# Remove the newline character from date.
chomp($date);

# Get the first argument passed to the script.
my $site = $ARGV[0];

# The arugment is the site name (such as nitec.com)
# So assign it to a variable called $dir.
my $dir = $site;

# Store the allowed domain types in an array
my @domain_types = (com,net,org,edu);

my $domain_ext;        # used to store domain extension
my $thesite_dir;       # used to store site's dir. name
my $htdocs_dir;        # used to store DocumentRoot dir. name
my $cgibin_dir;        # used to store cgi-bin dir. name
my $named_file;        # used to store site's DNS file name
my $dir_len;           # length of dir. name
my $temp_len;          # temp. variable

# Lowercase the site name supplied by user.
$site =~ y/[A-Z]/[a-z]/;

# If no arguments to the script was suppplied
# then $site will be empty show syntax in such a case
&syntax if($site eq '');
```

```
# Get the lenght with the EXT
$dir_len = length($dir);

# Remove the domain extension from the supplied name
foreach $domain_ext (@domain_types){
   $dir =~ s/\.$domain_ext//g;
   }

# Get the new length without the EXT
$temp_len = length($dir);

# If the user has not entered an extension then show syntax.
&syntax if($temp_len == $dir_len);

# Create FQPN names
$named_file = $NAMED_PATH . '/' . $dir . $NAMED_FILE_EXT ;
$thesite_dir = $BASE_DIR . '/' . $dir;
$htdocs_dir = $BASE_DIR . '/' . $dir . '/' . $HTDOCS;
$cgibin_dir = $BASE_DIR . '/' . $dir . '/' . $CGIBIN;

# If this site's dir. Already exists show error msg and exit
if(-e $thesite_dir){
   print "$thesite_dir already exist! No action taken for
$thesite_dir\n";
   exit 0;
   }

# OK. It is time to create the necessary directories.
system("mkdir $thesite_dir");
system("mkdir $htdocs_dir");
system("mkdir $cgibin_dir");

# Create the DNS record file for this site
&createNamedFile($named_file,$site,"$dir$NAMED_FILE_EXT");

# Create the dummy index file in the DocumentRoot dir.
&createIndexFile($htdocs_dir,$site);

# Create the virtual host configuration in httpd.conf
&createVirtualHostConf(domain=>$site,website=>"www.$site",cgibi
n=>$cgibin_dir,htdocs=>$htdocs_dir);

# Change ownership and access permissions for site dirs.
system("chown -R $USER.$GROUP $thesite_dir");
system("chmod -R $PERMISSION $thesite_dir");

# Write log file
open(FP,">$LOG_FILE") || die "Can't write to log file.\n";
print FP "Date: $date created www.$site [$htdocs_dir] \n";
close(FP);
```

(continued)

Listing 19-10 *(continued)*

```
# Done!
exit 0;
sub createNamedFile{
#
# Purpose: create the DNS record file in BIND file format
#

# Get passed parameters
   my $file = shift;
   my $domain = shift;
   my $database = shift;
   my $line;

# Open the DNS record file for writing
   open(OUT,">$file") || die "Can't write $file\n";

# Open the named template for reading
   open(FP,$NAMED_TEMPLATE_FILE) || die "Can't open
$NAMED_TEMPLATE_FILE\n";

# Read each line in the template file and replace
# the <DOMAIN> tag with user specified site name
# which is passed to $domain variable
#
   while($line=<FP>){
     $line =~ s/<DOMAIN>/$domain/g;
     print OUT $line;
     }
# Close all files opened here
  close(FP);
  close(OUT);

# Open the named.boot file and add the site in the
# file to setup primary DNS for it.

   open(FP,">$NAMED_ETC_FILE") || die "Can't open
$NAMED_ETC_FILE\n";

# Write the record
   print FP "primary\t\t$domain\t\t$database\n";

# Close the file
   close(FP);
   }

sub createIndexFile{
#
# Purpose: create a dummy index.html file in the
# new site's DocumentRoot directory.
```

```
# Get the arguments passed to this sub routine
  my $htdocs = shift;
  my $domain = shift;
   # Write the index.html file.
  open(FP,">$htdocs/index.html") || die "Can't write index.html
\n";
  print FP <<INDEX_PAGE;
  <HTML>
  <HEAD> <TITLE> $domain </TITLE> </HEAD>
  <BODY BGCOLOR="white">
  <CENTER> This is $domain </CENTER>
  </BODY>
  </HTML>
INDEX_PAGE

# Close file
  close(FP);
  }

sub createVirtualHostConf{
#
# Purpose: create the virtual host configuration
# using the template file and store the configuration
# in the httpd.conf file.

# Get all parameters passsed to this sub routine
  my %params = @_;

# Temp. variable
  my $line;

# Open httpd.conf for appending data
  open(OUT,">$HTTPD_CONF_FILE") || die "Can't open
$HTTPD_CONF_FILE\n";

# Open virtual host template file for reading
  open(FP,$VIRTUAL_HOST_TEMPLATE) || die "Can't open
$VIRTUAL_HOST_TEMPLAT\n";

# Read each line of template file and replace
# special tags with values
  while($line=<FP>){
    $line =~ s/<DOMAIN>/$params{domain}/g;
    $line =~ s/<CGI-BIN-DIR>/$params{cgibin}/g;
    $line =~ s/<HTDOCS-DIR>/$params{htdocs}/g;
    $line =~ s/<WWW-SITE>/$params{website}/g;
    print OUT $line;

    }
```

(continued)

Listing 19-10 *(continued)*

```
# Close all files
  close(FP);
  close(OUT);
  }
sub syntax{
#
# Purpose: to display script's syntax.
#
    print <<SYNTAX;

    makesite <virtual Internet domain>

    Example: makesite nitec.com

    Do not confuse the domain name with host name such as
www.nitec.com.
    This script will create www.<virtual Internet domain> host
automatically.

SYNTAX

# Exit after showing the syntax.
   exit 0;
   }
```

This script can be run as follows:

```
./makesite client-domain-name
```

For example:

```
./makesite client-a.com
./makesite client-b.org
```

This will create DNS and Apache configuration for client-a.com and client-b.org. The DNS configuration files will be stored in /var/named/client-a.db and /var/named/client-b.db. The Apache configuration will be stored in a file called /www/apache/conf/httpd.conf. This script will also create the directory structure for each of these client sites. For example, client-a.com will have a directory structure such as the one shown in Figure 19-7.

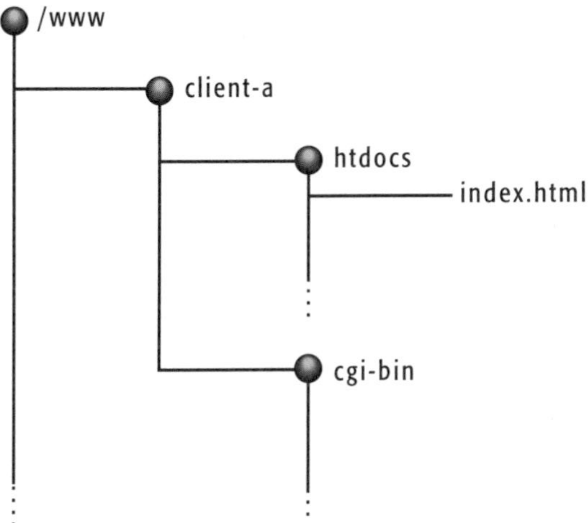

Figure 19-7: Web directory structure for www.client-a.com site

The makesite script will also create an index.html page to make it easy to test the newly created site. After running the makesite script for each new client domain, restart the name server and append the Apache configuration (that is, the new <VirtualHost >container sections in the /www/apache/conf/httpd.conf file) to each Web server's httpd.conf file. For example, when makesite client-a.com is run, the Apache configuration shown in Listing 19-11 gets appended to the /www/apache/conf/httpd.conf file.

Listing 19-11: /www/apache/conf/httpd.conf file

```
# Domain Configuration for www.client-a.com
#
<VirtualHost REPLACE-THIS-WITH-WEB-SERVER-IP-ADDR>
ServerAdmin webmaster@www.client-a.com
DocumentRoot      /www/client-a/htdocs
#ScriptAlias      /cgi-bin/       /www/client-a/cgi-bin/
ScriptAlias       /cgi-bin/       /www/xcnews/cgi-bin/
Alias       /cgi-data/      /www/cgi-data/
ServerName  www.client-a.com
ErrorLog          logs/cerror.log
TransferLog       logs/ www.client-a.com.access.log
</VirtualHost>
#
# End of Domain Configuratin for www.client-a.com
```

Next, this section must be copied from the /www/apache/conf/httpd.conf file and pasted into the www1.xcnews.com and www2.xnews.com Apache server httpd.conf configuration files. Note that REPLACE-THIS-WITH-WEB-SERVER-IP-ADDR must also be replaced with the appropriate IP address. For example, when adding this configuration section to www1.xcnews.com Apache server's httpd.conf, the REPLACE-THIS-WITH-WEB-SERVER-IP-ADDR is replaced with 206.177.175.61.

Note that Apache servers should not be restarted until the new directories for the client domain are distributed to the Web servers. This brings us to the file distribution aspects of this project.

Using rdist to distribute files

The rdist program enables you to maintain identical copies of files over multiple hosts. It uses either the rcmd function calls or the remote shell (rsh) to access each of the target host computers.

The easiest way to get rdist working is to create a common account on all the machines involved and create .rhosts files for each target system (www1 and www2) so that the common user on the name server host is allowed to run rsh sessions. For this purpose, create a user called httpd on all three systems involved. On each of the Web server systems, add a .rhosts file in the home directory of the httpd user. This file contains a single line such as the following:

```
ns.xcnews-lan.com
```

This file must be owned by the root user and be read-only for everyone else. This allows a user called httpd on ns.xcnews-lan.com to run remote shell sessions on each Web server system. Notice that the ns.xcnews-lan.com host is used for this purpose. This is because the internal LAN needs to be used for rdist traffic. The next step is to create a distfile for rdist. A distfile is a text file that contains instructions for rdist on how to perform the file distribution task. Listing 19-12 shows one such distfile, rdist_distfile.

Listing 19-12: rdist_distfile

```
#
# Distfile for rdist
#
# This is used to distribute files from ns.xcnews-lan.com
# to www[12].xcnews-lan.com systems
#
# $Author$ (kabir@nitec.com)
# $Version$
# $Date$
# $Id$

# List all the hosts that need to be updated.
```

```
# The list is created using user@hostname entries where each
# entry is separated by a white-space character.
#
HOSTS = (httpd@www1.xcnews-lan.com httpd@www2.xcnews-lan.com)

# List the directories that needs to be updated.
#
FILES = ( /www)

# list the directories that need to be excluded from
# the update process.
EXCLUDE_DIR = (/www/cgi-data/    /www/apache /www/secured)

# Here are the commands:
# Install all directories listed in FILES for all hosts
# listed in HOSTS except for the directories that are
# listed in EXCLUDE_DIR
#
${FILES} -> ${HOSTS}
  install ;
  except ${EXCLUDE_DIR};
```

This is really a very simple distfile. It defines a variable called HOSTS that has two entries as values: httpd@www1.xcnews-lan.com and httpd@www2.xcnews-lan.com. This tells rdist to use the httpd user account on both www1.xcnews-lan.com and www2.xcnews-lan.com for connection. The next variable, FILES, defines the files and directories for rdist to distribute. Because the staging area is /www on ns.xnews-lan.com, there is nothing but a single entry as the value.

The third variable is EXCLUDE_DIR. This variable is set to list all the files and directories that we want to exclude from getting distributed. The values that you see in the example are important. The first directory, /www/cgi-data/, is the CGI data directory where all CGI scripts write their data. This directory will be exported to the Web server hosts via NFS, so it does not need to be copied onto each Web server via rdist. The /www/apache directory is where makesite writes the /www/apache/conf/httpd.conf file, which needs to be copied because each Web server has its very own Apache configuration file in the local /www/apache directory. The final value is /www/secured, which is used by the secured server as the document root and needs to be copied onto the Web servers. The rest of the file describes a simple command:

```
${FILES} -> ${HOSTS}
  install ;
  except ${EXCLUDE_DIR};
```

This command takes all the files and directories that the FILES variable points to and installs them on the hosts indicated by the HOSTS variable. It also tells rdist to exclude the files and directories specified by the EXCLUDE_DIR variable. To run rdist (as httpd), use the following command from the command line:

```
/usr/bin/rdist -p /usr/sbin/rdistd -oremove,quiet -f
/usr/local/rdist/ rdist_distfile
```

The -p option specifies the location of the rdistd program needed by rdist; the -o option specifies that one or more options are to follow — in this case, remove and quiet. The remove option tells rdist to remove any extraneous files found in the target system in target directories. This provides an easy method for maintaining an identical copy of the staging area on each Web server. The quiet option tells rdist to be as quiet as possible during the operation. The final option, -f, specifies the location of the distfile.

To reduce human error in running this command, create an sh script called rdistribute.sh, as shown in Listing 19-13.

Listing 19-13: rdistribute.sh script

```
#!/bin/sh
#
# This script runs rdist to update Web servers via the
# non-routable lan xcnews-lan.com. The script is run
# by cron at a fixed interval.
#
# /etc/rc.d/rc.local starts the script to clean up
# left-over tempfiles that might have been left
# at shutdown. This process also removes the
# log file.
#
# $Author$ (kabir@nitec.com)
# $Version$
# $Id$
# $Date$
# $Status
##################################################################

# If the script is called with an argument then
case "$1" in
  boot)
  # since the argument is 'boot' the script is being
  # called at system start-up so remove all old lock
  # files and logs.
  echo -n "Cleaning up rdistribute.sh tmp files: "
     rm -f /tmp/rdist.lck
        rm -f /tmp/rdist.log
  echo "complete."
  exit 0;
  ;;

  # since the argument is 'restart' the script
  # needs to clean up as if the system just booted.
  restart)
  $0 boot
  ;;

esac
```

```
# If the lock file exists then don't do anything.
if [ -f /tmp/rdist.lck ]; then
   exit 0
fi

# Otherwise create the lock file using /bin/touch
/bin/touch  /tmp/rdist.lck

# Run rdist
/usr/bin/rdist -p /usr/sbin/rdistd -
oremove,nochkgroup,nochkmode,nochkowner,quiet -f
/usr/local/rdist/rdist_distfile

# Remote the lock file
rm -f /tmp/rdist.lck

# Write the time and date in the log file
echo `date` >> /tmp/rdist.log

# Exit the script
exit 0
```

This script is smart enough to detect in progress the rdistribute.sh process by using a lock file, which can tell when a previous rdistribute.sh is already in progress and continuing. This can happen when a great deal of files are being updated over multiple servers. The script also accepts an argument called boot that can be used to clean up the lock file and the log file it creates during the boot process. The script should be called from /etc/rc.d/rc.local as follows:

```
/usr/local/rdistribute.sh boot
```

This script can be scheduled to run by a cron entry in /etc/crontab. For example, to run this script at 10-minute intervals, the following cron entry can be added in /etc/crontab:

```
0,10,20,30,40,50 * * * * httpd  /usr/local/rdistribute.sh >
/dev/null
```

The cron daemon will run the script as httpd.

Using NFS for an internal network

So far, the DNS and the file distribution are set up, but the Web servers still have not been restarted. Before doing that, the CGI data area /www/cgi-data directory needs to be NFS mounted on the Web hosts to make Web service fully functional. To make the CGI data directory (/www/cgi-data/) available to the Web servers, set up the name server host as an NFS server and the Web servers as NFS clients.

Setting up an NFS server

An NFS server needs to run a program called portmapper, (also called portmap or rpc.portmap), which is usually started by an rc script. To check if the portmapper is already running, use the following command:

```
ps auxw | grep portmap
```

It turns out that under RedHat Linux, portmapper is automatically started by the /etc/rc.d/rc3.d/S40portmap script (that is, the /etc/rc.d/init.d/portmap.init script) so there is no need to manually start it for XC News.

The next step is to modify the /etc/exports file to tell the system what file systems or directories need to be exported to NFS clients. Because XC News only needs the /www/cgi-data directory exported to the Web servers, the export file on the ns.xcnews-lan.com host looks like this:

```
/www/cgi-data       www1.xcnews-lan.com(rw) www2.xcnews-
lan.com(rw)
```

This line tells the NFS server to allow both www1.xnews-lan.com and www2.xcnews-lan.com read and write access to the /www/cgi-data directory.

The syntax for the exports file may not be the same for all brands of UNIX.

The next programs needed to run are mountd (rpc.mountd) and nfsd (rpc.nfsd). These two programs are also started automatically from rc scripts in /etc/rc.d/rc3.d. Whenever a change is made to the /etc/exports file, however, these two program need to be told about this change. A script called exportfs can be used to restart these to programs, as follows:

```
exportfs
```

If exportfs is missing on a system, then a script such as the following can be used instead:

```
#!/bin/sh
killall -HUP /usr/sbin/rpc.mountd
killall -HUP /usr/sbin/rpc.nfsd
echo re-exported file systems
```

This script uses the killall program found on most Linux systems such as RedHat; if it is not available, you can always run a ps command, find the PID for these processes, and manually perform a kill -HUP for each process. Now to make sure both mountd and nfsd are running properly, run a program called rpcinfo, as follows:

```
rpcinfo -p
```

The output looks like this:

```
program vers     proto     port
100000    2      tcp       111        rpcbind
100000    2      udp       111        rpcbind
100005    1      udp       635        mountd
100005    2      udp       635        mountd
100005    1      tcp       635        mountd
100005    2      tcp       635        mountd
100003    2      udp       2049       nfs
100003    2      tcp       2049       nfs
```

This shows that portmapper, mountd, and nfsd have announced their services and are working fine. Before setting up the client side of NFS on the Web servers, it is important to make sure the following security issues are addressed.

Server security issues

The portmapper, in combination with nfsd, can be fooled, making it possible to get to files on NFS servers without any privileges. Fortunately, the portmapper Linux uses is relatively secure against attack, and can be made more secure by adding the following line in the /etc/hosts.deny file:

```
portmap: ALL
```

The system will deny portmapper access for everyone. Now the /etc/hosts.allow file needs to be modified as follows:

```
portmap: 192.168.1.0/255.255.255.0
```

This will allow all hosts from the 192.168.1.0 network to have access to portmapper-administered programs such as nfsd and mountd.

Never use host names in the portmap line in /etc/hosts.allow because use of host name lookups can indirectly cause portmap activity, which will trigger host name lookups in a loop.

One other security issue on the server side is whether to allow the root account on a client to be treated as root on the server. By default, Linux prohibits root on the client side of the NFS to be treated as root on the server side. In other words, an exported file owned by root on the server cannot be modified by the client root user. To explicitly enforce this rule, the /etc/exports file can be modified as follows:

```
/www/cgi-data    www1.xcnews-lan.com(rw, root_squash)
www2.xcnews-lan.com(rw, root_squash)
```

Now, if a user with UID 0 (the root user) on the client attempts to access (read, write, or delete) the file system, the server substitutes the UID of the server's "nobody" account. This means the root user on the client can't access or change files that only the root on the server can access or change.

To grant root access to an NFS file system, use the no_root_squash option instead.

At this point the NFS server is set up and secure, so now let's set up the NFS client hosts.

Setting up an NFS client

RedHat by default supports NFS file systems, so there is no need to mess around with the kernel. To mount the /www/cgi-data directory exported by the ns.xnews-lan.com host, add the following line to the /etc/fstab file for both of the Web servers:

```
ns.xcnews-lan.com:/www/cgi-data          /www/cgi-data       nfs
```

The preceding line automatically mounts the /www/cgi-data directory when any of the Web servers are rebooted. Next, create the /www/cgi-bin directory on both systems and manually mount the directory using the mount command, as follows:

```
ns.xcnews-lan.com:/www/cgi-data          /www/cgi-data       nfs
```

One typical NFS mounting problem occurs because many forget to run exportfs (that is, restart rpc.mountd and rpc.nfsd) after they modify the /etc/exports file on the NFS server.

Unmounting an NFS file system is exactly the same as unmounting the local file system. Note that it is also possible to enhance NFS client security by not trusting the NFS server too much. For example, you can disable suid programs to work off the NFS file system with a nosuid option. This means the server's root user cannot make a suid-root program on the file system, log in to the client as a normal user, and then use the suid-root program to become the root on the client, too. It is also possible to forbid execution of files on the mounted file system altogether with the noexec option. You can enter these options in the options column of the line that describes your NFS mount point in the /etc/fstab file.

At this point the file distribution scheme and the NFS-based CGI data directory are both ready. It is time to configure Apache and make sure it is secured.

Apache Server Configuration

Apache server configuration is as usual. There are no special requirements to meet for XC News.

The <VirtualHost> container sections produced by the makesite script need to be added to each Web server's httpd.conf file. As discussed earlier, these virtual hosts specify IP addresses specific to each Web server. Using a /etc/rc.d/rc3.d/S85httpd script (that is, a /etc/rc.d/init.d/httpd script), check to make sure the Apache server will start up at the end of the boot process.

For secured Web service, I recommend Stronghold on secured.xcnews.com, which is just another CNAME for ns.xcnews.com. As mentioned before, XC News does not want a setup where each virtual host (client site) is required to pay for a certificate from a CA, so setting up Stronghold on the secured .xcnews.com makes good sense. In such a configuration, the Stronghold server points to /www/secured as the document root directory. This way XC News can create subdirectories under /www/secured to enable clients to store files that need to be accessed via SSL-based secured communication channels. For example, if client site www.client-a.com needs to have a secured order form called order.html installed, the first thing they have to do is ask XC News to create a directory under /www/secured for them and get the file stored there. XC News can create a subdirectory called /www/secured/client-a/ and store the order.html file in this directory. Now the client can make sure all references (A HREF links) to order.html point to the URL https://secured.xcnews.com/client-a/order.html.

Because XC News also wants the CGI scripts in www.xcnews.com (/www/xcnews/cgi-bin) to be accessed via the secured server, a ScriptAlias directive needs to be added to Stronghold's httpd.conf, as follows:

```
ScriptAlias /cgi-bin/   /www/xcnews/cgi-bin/
```

This permits the secured server to run the same CGI scripts.

Client documents should include a link back to the original client site. For example, if the XC News order form was processed by a CGI script, the output page should include a link to the original client page. This makes the configuration a little more user friendly.

Whenever an XC News client–generated HTML page is put on a subdirectory under the secured server's document root, it should be checked for a return link back to the original client Web site. If a page does not have such a link, visitors might get confused.

For all HTML form processing or possibly other CGI scripts, XC News should make sure that the scripts are written so that they have a way to return the visitor to the original Web site. For example, an HTML form can contain a hidden variable such as the following:

```
<INPUT TYPE=HIDDEN NAME="return-url" VALUE="http;//www.client-
a.com/thanks_for_the_order.html" >
```

This should be used by the form-processing CGI script to either redirect the visitor to the URL provided as the value of the return-url variable or create an output page that has a link clearly marked as "Return to Our Site" or something similar.

FTP User Accounts for Clients

XC News wants to enable clients to update their Web files via FTP so accounts don't need to be created on the ns.xcnews.com server. Because the ftp.cxnews.com alias is already set up in the DNS for xcnews.com, it can be used as the official FTP server IP alias.

RedHat provides a program called /usr/sbin/adduser (or /usr/sbin/useradd) that is used to create new users from the command line. The program uses a default configuration stored in the /etc/default/useradd file. This file contains the following setting for the home directory:

```
HOME=/home
```

Change this to HOME=/www so that each client user account will have it's Web directory as the home directory as long as the account name is the same as the client's domain.

The /www directory is in each user's home directory path, so it needs to be readable to and executable by everyone.

For example:

```
adduser client-a
```

This creates a user called client-a that has a home directory /www/client-a. Recall that makesite run as makesite client-a.com creates /www/client-a directory, so the user's home directory matches the Web directory. When such a user uses FTP to get into ftp.xcnews.com, she automatically starts her session in her home directory (that is, the Web site top-level directory.)

The adduser program by default creates a new group per user, and the group is added to the /etc/group file. Therefore, it is necessary to change permission for the home directory. For example, after running the command adduser client-a it is necessary to run the following permission setting commands:

```
chown -R client-a.httpd /www/client-a/
chmod -R 750 /www/client-a/
```

The first command makes sure the /www/client-a/ directory and all its subdirectories are owned by client-a and its group, called client-a. The second command sets permissions for all files and directories in /www/client-a/ so that the owner (client-a) has read, write, and executable permissions, the group (httpd group) has read and executable permissions, and everyone else has no permissions. The httpd group should contain the httpd user, which is used by rdist and any technical support account. Because no one but the owner and the group is allowed access to the home directory, a client cannot see the content of another client's site via FTP. Passwords for each user are set using the /usr/bin/passwd utility, as usual. After each account is created, it should be tested via FTP for upload and download permissions.

Testing the New Systems

At this point, all the services needed on the new systems are up and running, so the testing phase can begin. To test the new system from remote hosts, change the name server on the remote host to be the IP address of the ns.xcnews.com. This enables the remote test hosts to query ns.xcnews.com, which has the appropriate DNS settings for the new sites. This enables the testers to continue testing without affecting anything on the live sites.

The first set of tests are done using simple TCP/IP tools such as ping, nslookup, and traceroute. For example, using nslookup from the command line, the testers can find out if the ns.xnews.com DNS server is giving out appropriate information regarding xcnews.com or any of its client sites.

A lot of domains need to be tested, so it is necessary to come up with at least some crude methods to reduce the human interactivity needed to perform simple tests. Let's create a text file containing a list of domain names, as follows:

```
xcnews.com
client-a.com
client-b.com
...
...
client-z.org
```

Now it is easy to use various UNIX tools to create batch text-command files. For example, to test the DNS information for each domain, use commands such as the following:

```
cat ./domain-list.txt | awk '{printf("nslookup -query=ns -
timeout=3 %s\n",$1);}' > ./ns_test
chmod 750 ./ns_test
./ns_test
```

The first line creates a file called ns_test, which contains lines such as the following:

```
nslookup -query=ns -timeout=3 xcnews.com
nslookup -query=ns -timeout=3 client-a.com
```

The second line turns the ns_test script into an executable script, and the third line runs it. This tests each domain for name server information. Now the first line can easily be changed to test mail exchange records for each domain by modifying -query=ns to -query=mx, as shown below:

```
cat ./domain-list.txt | awk '{printf("nslookup -query=mx -
timeout=3 %s\n",$1);}' > ./mx_test
```

Now mx_test can be made into an executable script like ns_test and run to test MX records. Similarly, scripts can be run to test Web sites via HTTP. Here is an example of such a test script:

```
cat ./domain-list.txt | awk '{printf("lynx -dump -head
www.%s\n",$1);}' > ./www_test
chmod 750 ./www_test
./www_test > /tmp/www_problems
```

Here I use the text-based Web browser called lynx to make HTTP HEAD requests for each Web host on my domain list. When the resulting www_test script is run as shown in the preceding example, a file called www_problems is created in /tmp. If lynx fails to access a Web site host because it is not configured properly, an error message such as the following appears in the www_problems file:

```
lynx: Can't access start file http://www.some-client-site.com
```

Because all sites are created using makesite, there are no human errors in site configuration.

Along with these type of tests, you should also test the sites via Web browsers. Because none of the sites have any real content, they just display the default index.html page created by makesite to identify each site.

After all the preceding tests are completed successfully, it is time to transfer contents from the live system to the new system.

Going Live!

As soon as files are moved into the new staging area, some problems will likely surface. For example, many of the XC News and client pages use Server Side Include (SSI) directives to run scripts that display banner advertisements. Although the Apache servers were configured properly to support SSI calls, the banners are not displayed; instead, an error message appears on each page that called the banner advertisement script.

The problem appears to be due to the way Microsoft IIS Server runs SSI scripts. One such SSI call that works fine on the live NT-based server but doesn't work on the Apache server is this:

```
<!—#exec cmd="perl.exe d:/var/www/xcnews/cgi-
bin/rotate_banner_ad.pl d:/var/www/xcnews/banners/giflist.txt"
—>
```

SSI calls like this need to be converted as follows:

```
<!—#exec cmd=" /www/xcnews/cgi-bin/rotate_banner_ad.pl
/www/xcnews/banners/giflist.txt" —>
```

A Perl script called rotate_banner_ad.pl also needs to be updated so that it uses the #!/path/to/perl line as the first line, which is something not required under NT. It also needs to be checked for any reference to d:/var/www or any other DOS-style path info. Once the SSI call is converted to a standard SSI call, and the script is executable by the Apache server, it works.

Similar problems can be found for SSI calls that use the DOS-style path. These paths need to be translated into UNIX-style path names. Because hundreds of files need to be fixed, let's write a simple script, like the one shown in Listing 19-14, to fix all the files automatically.

Listing 19-14: fixssi

```
#!/bin/csh -f
#
# This script should be removed after AMINEWS sites
# have completely moved away from NT (BVS)
# Kabir

set thisdir = `/bin/pwd`;

echo "fixssi will translate NT SSI calls to Apache SSI calls."
echo "Current directory: $thisdir";
echo -n "Replacing perl.exe d:/var/www/htdocs/cgi-bin :"

/usr/bin/find . -type f -exec /usr/local/bin/fgres "perl.exe
d:/var/www/htdocs/cgi-bin "  "/www/xcnews/cgi-bin" {} \;

echo "done."
```

When fixssi is run from /www, it fixes all sites that had the broken SSI calls.

Tip: Fgres is a utility you can get from most comp.unix.source archives, which can be found via Web search engines.

All the Perl CGI scripts are modified to use the #!/usr/bin/perl line to invoke the Perl interpreter. All the file permissions are set up so that the httpd process on each Web server can run CGI scripts and write data to /www/cgi-bin directory.

With these problems solved, it's time to make the transition from the old system to the new Web network. Just to be safe, I run another round of tests to make sure the Web sites are set up properly and the CGI scripts are all working fine. The tests show that some CGI scripts e-mail data when collected from HTML forms to client e-mail addresses. These need to be fixed so that they use the sendmail mail daemon. After a final set of tests on the CGI scripts and other content files, everything appears to be functional and ready to go live!

By the virtue of InterNIC's Web-based DNS record update pages, a request is submitted to change the primary and secondary name server for all the domains involved. In a short while, the DNS changes propagate all around the Internet. Yes, there will be times when some clients cannot access their Web sites, but there is nothing that you can do to help the DNS propagation over the Internet. After a couple of days, the propagation is complete, and all the sites are up and running on the new systems.

Future Possibilities

Using round-robin DNS is better than using nothing, but it is not the best solution possible. Unfortunately, better solutions cost a lot more than a round-robin DNS scheme implemented in free DNS server software. The potential drawbacks of using round-robin DNS schemes are as listed here:

- The scheme cannot detect a server failure, and therefore it will keep directing client requests to the dead server until the DNS is manually changed by the administrator.
- When a change is made to the DNS records, it is not propagated right away due to caching done by DNS servers to reduce bandwidth use. The propagation can be made speedier using small numbers in TTL values, but this might cause a great deal of DNS-related traffic on the network.

So what could be done to improve the situation? You can deploy an expensive load balancing switch such as the AceDirector from Cisco to handle load balancing at the network level. New hardware solutions for load balancing are just emerging right now to deal with the problems mentioned. The hardware solutions usually operate at a network level, where the special switching hardware detects load via network utilization statistics and other related information. Because this type of technology is just breaking through, the price for it will be high. It is probably a good idea to wait for the prices to drop and deploy such a hardware solution in the future.

Summary

In this chapter, you learned how to create a Web network consisting of multiple Apache Web servers. I used a real-world example so that you could get a good idea about the details that surface in such a project. Note that the real project did include server monitoring requirements, which I decided to exclude here due to space limitations.

Next, you will learn how to get Apache running on Windows 95 and Windows NT systems.

✦ ✦ ✦

CHAPTER 20

Apache for Microsoft Windows 95/NT

✦ ✦ ✦ ✦

In This Chapter

✦ ✦ ✦ ✦

Apache for Microsoft Windows 95/NT is planned for the next major release of Apache. At least that's what Apache Group wants. But because the next major release is going to be a big deal, the group anticipates that it will not happen soon.

One Apache user could not wait that long. He ported the latest Apache beta to Windows and provided Apache Group with a new option: they now have a beta version of Apache for Windows. With their blessings, the beta is now available on all major Apache distribution mirror sites including the official Apache Web site.

In this chapter, I discuss how you can use this beta (version 1.3b3) to preview what is coming for Windows. I must warn you that the beta version is considered unstable and should not be used for anything but experimentation. Do not plan on running your organization's Web site(s) on it. If you are curious about how a UNIX Web server found its way into the Windows market, you can read the following section or skip straight to the Getting Apache for Windows section.

Issues in Porting Apache to Windows

Porting tasks are often hairy; they are not for weak-hearted programmers. The task becomes harder when there are major underlying differences between the operating systems involved, as there are between UNIX and Windows.

Because Apache is a UNIX child (created on the UNIX platform), it inherited all the goodies of UNIX software design. It uses a pre-forking server model that is almost the de facto standard in the UNIX world. The main server process does very little; it forks child processes that do the hard work. This makes the child processes very complicated programs, although the main server code is fairly simple in nature.

Did someone say fork? Fork is not a word in the Windows dictionary. Windows doesn't fork child processes. In fact, Windows doesn't create children at all! A Windows server process uses threads and is called a multi-threaded server. A thread is not a separate process; it is a executable entity that works within the server process space and can perform a task independent from another thread. These threads are often called the worker threads and the server process is called the parent thread (reminds me of worker bees and their queen). So what does all this mean in terms of porting Apache to Windows?

Because forking is not available on Windows, Apache must be run from a single server process that has to launch threads to service requests. Also, the parent thread must do some work before the worker threads can pick up the request. What if something happens to one of the threads? A disaster happens — all the threads die. In Apache's case, this would mean a total shutdown of the Web service. A workaround was developed to solve this problem. The solution is that additional Apache processes are started as standby Apache servers. When the acting Web server process dies, one of the standby servers will take its place. This way the Web service will not totally disappear.

Another requirement in developing multithreaded applications is that the data must be thread-safe. Some Apache modules use global variables that could not be used in a multithreaded version of Apache because the threads might corrupt the data. Special care was needed to ensure that each thread got its own copy of the variables.

Apart from the multithreading issues, one other major difference surfaced quickly. Windows loads its modules via external Dynamically Linked Library (DLL) files, but in UNIX all modules are compiled into a single executable file. A special module called mod_dll had to be written that loads the other modules to be compiled as DLL files.

Note that this is probably not all there is to do for the UNIX to Windows Apache port. The current port does not work much like a Windows-native application because it does not have a graphical user interface (GUI); it is still a command-line application. This will change in a future release version.

Let's get started with what is available, but remember this is just an experimental server, so go easy on it when things don't work exactly the way you want.

Getting Apache for Windows

You have two choices in getting Apache for Windows. You can download either the source code distribution or the binary distribution. Unless you are well versed in Visual C++ or Borland C++ development under Windows, you should not bother with the source distribution. Only get the source if you are anxious to see what the Apache source looks like.

I highly recommend that you get the binary version of the latest distribution. Both the source and the binary distributions are available from the primary Apache Web site at this URL:

```
www.apache.org
```

However, you should probably go to the nearest Apache mirror site to download the software. Note that the binary distribution does not contain any documentation. You will have to download the documentation distribution separately. Both the source and the binary distribution are available on the CD-ROM.

Installing Apache for Windows

The installation process is a typical Windows-based software installation. Here is what you need to do:

1. Run the self-extracting executable that you downloaded from the Apache mirror site. When you run the executable it brings up the dialog window shown in Figure 20-1.

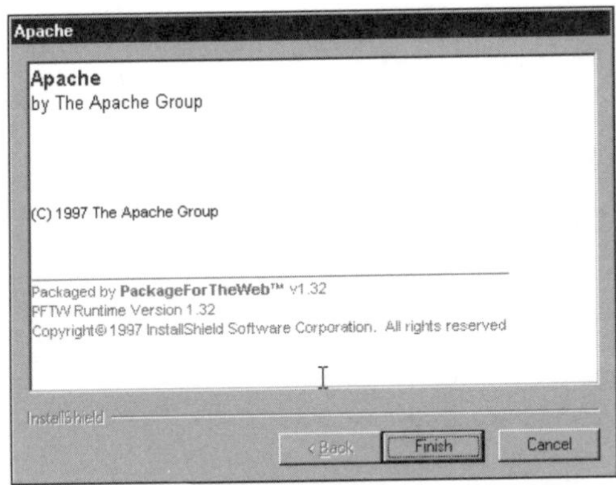

Figure 20-1: First Apache installation screen

This shows the copyright message and tells you that the package is created with the InstallShield software.

2. Click the Finish button to start the software installation (ironically). You will see a Welcome screen, shown in Figure 20-2.

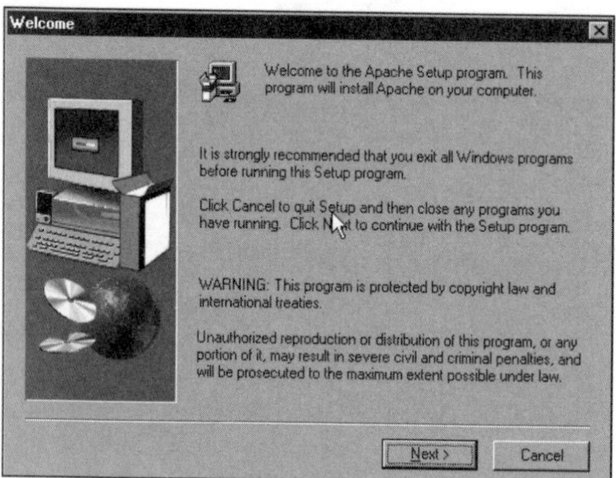

Figure 20-2: Welcome screen

3. Click the next button and you will see the Apache licensing terms, shown in Figure 20-3. If you agree to these terms, click on the Yes button. Otherwise, you should click on the No button to abort the installation.

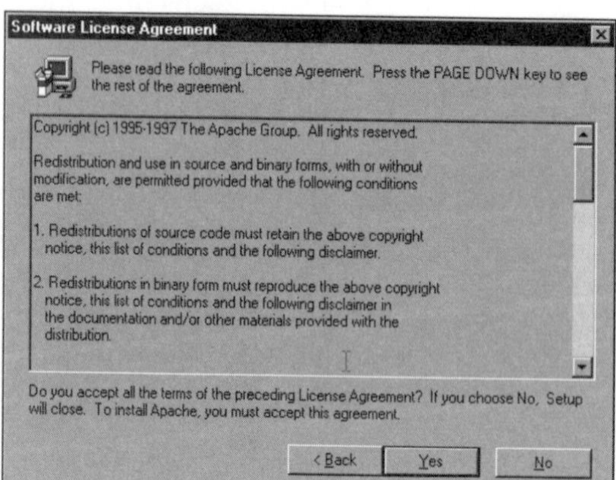

Figure 20-3: Apache license screen

4. Assuming you have said yes, you will see the screen shown in Figure 20-4. Here you will be able to either accept the default folder location (such as C:\Program Files\Apache) or select a folder of your choice. By default, Apache for Windows looks for configuration files in \apache\conf, so if you

install it in the \Apache directory, you will not have to specify the configuration file path when running Apache.

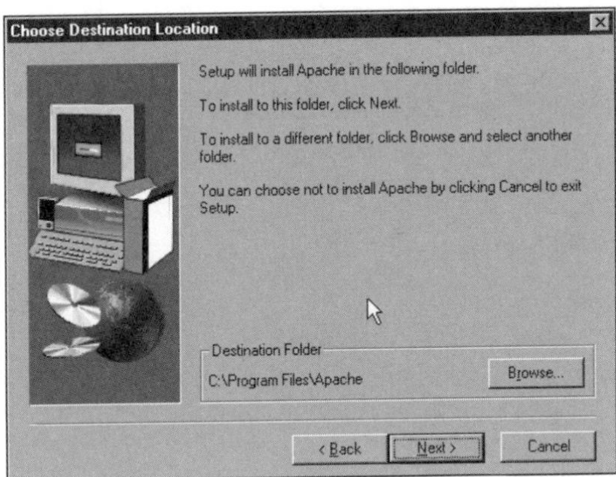

Figure 20-4: Apache installation directory

However, for the sample installation used in the screen shots, I chose to keep the default path as C:\Program Files\Apache. Once you have chosen your path, press the Next button to go forward.

5. Next you will be asked to choose the type of setup you prefer. This window is shown in Figure 20-5.

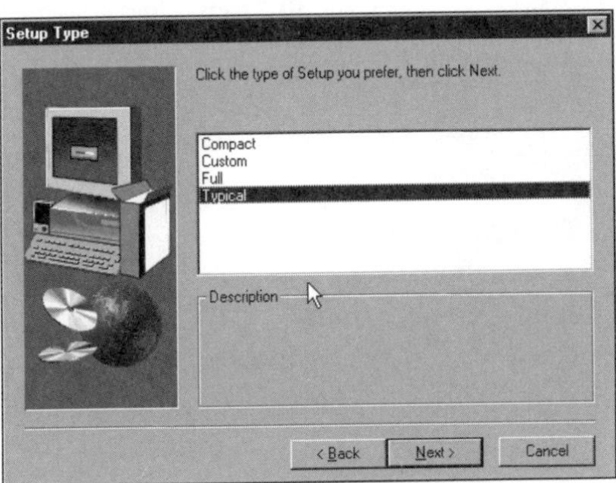

Figure 20-5: Type of Apache installation

Choose typical if you want to get this over quickly. However, I chose the custom option to see any other configuration needed during installation. All I was asked was to choose a folder. After the setup type selection is made, the installer will copy the files to the appropriate location and on success show the window in Figure 20-6.

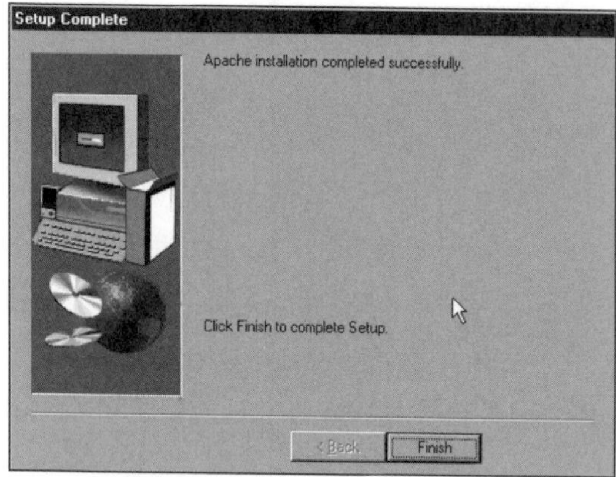

Figure 20-6: Installation complete notice

6. If you decide to install the documentation, make sure you install it under the same directory as your top-level Apache directory. In other words, if you have installed Apache in C:\Program Files\Apache, then install the documentation in the same directory. The installation program for the documentation distribution will ask you to enter the path name as shown in Figure 20-7.

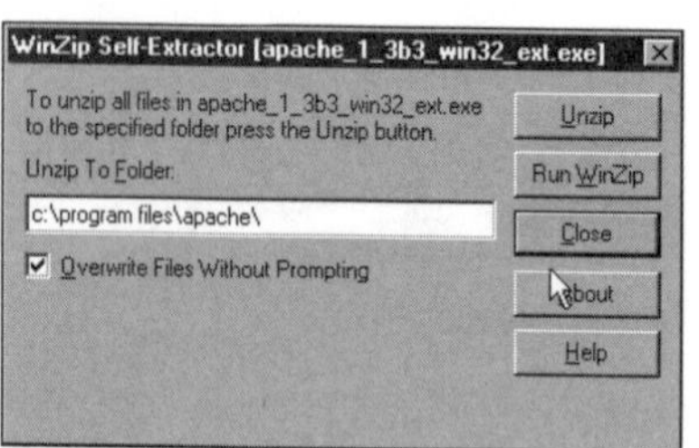

Figure 20-7: Installing documentation for Apache

You have now completed the Apache binary installation and are ready to run it. However, the way you (want to) run it might differ based your flavor of Windows.

Running Apache in Windows 95

In Windows 95, Apache runs as a console application. In other words, either click on it from Windows Explorer (not Internet Explorer) or run it from a DOS box as shown in Figure 20-8.

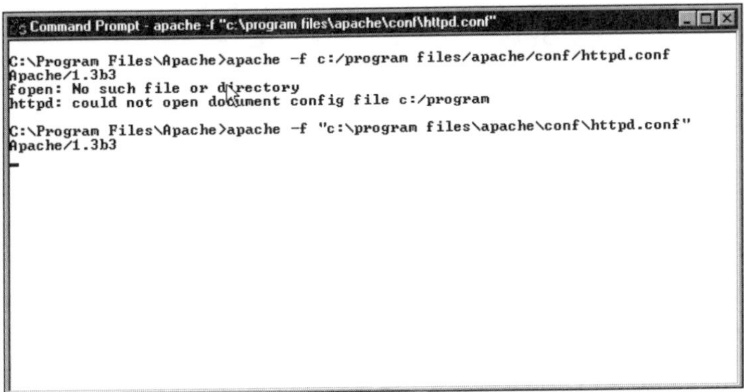

Figure 20-8: Running Apache in Windows 95

Notice that when I tried running the Apache executable from the C:\Program Files\Apache directory as follows:

```
Apache -f c:/program files/apache/conf/httpd.conf
```

it did not run, but when I tried the following:

```
Apache -f  "c:\program files\apache\conf\httpd.conf"
```

it worked. The difference is the double quotes I used in this version so that Apache would not confuse the path containing a space character (in `\program files\`) as two command line arguments. Also note that I used the UNIX slash instead of the DOS slash. However, my experiment shows that the following also works:

Apache -f "c:/program files/apache/conf/httpd.conf"

So either slash works from the command line. However, you must use the UNIX slash in all configuration path information used in the configuration files such as httpd.conf, access.conf, or srm.conf. When you run Apache this way, you will notice that it does not display any additional information other than the initial display of the Apache version number.

Tip: You can also start the server from the Start menu shortcut added by the installer.

If you plan to run the Apache server on boot, you can copy the Start menu shortcut created by the installer to the StartUp group on the Start Menu. A DOS window with the Apache server will launch automatically when the computer boots up. This window can be minimized and ignored (which is an option for the DOS box properties).

If you want to stop the server, you will either have to close the DOS shell window or you can press Ctrl+C to stop the server. There is no graceful way of stopping the server yet.

Running Apache in Windows NT as a service

You can run Apache in Windows NT exactly as you run can run it in Windows 95. But you can also run Apache as a service under a Windows NT 4.0 or higher platform. To run Apache as an NT service, you use the command:

```
Apache -i
```

If you have installed the Apache files in any directory other than /Apache you will have to use the -d option to specify the directory. For example:

```
Apache -i -d  "c:/program files/apache"
```

This will install Apache as an NT service and tell Apache to look for configuration files under the C:/program files/apache path. Once you have installed Apache as a service you can control how it is run from the NT Control Panel applet. Select the Services icon from the Control Panel window and you will see a window shown in Figure 20-9.

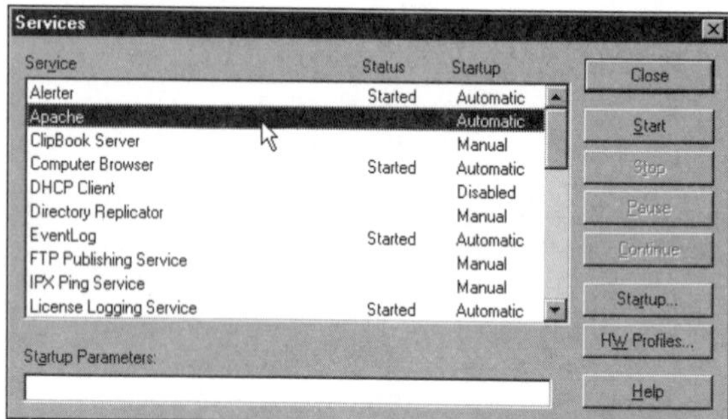

Figure 20-9: Apache as an NT Service

By default Apache is configured to start automatically at NT boot-up time. However, if you want it to run now, select the Apache service from the list and click on the Start button to start it manually.

If you decide to remove Apache from your NT server's services, use the command:

```
Apache -u -d "c:/program files/apache"
```

This will remove it from the service list. This command assumes that the Apache directory is C:/program files/apache; replace it with your custom Apache path if necessary.

Once you get Apache running under either Windows 95 or NT, you should use the Task Manager to verify that it is running. Figure 20-10 shows Apache processes in the Task Manager window.

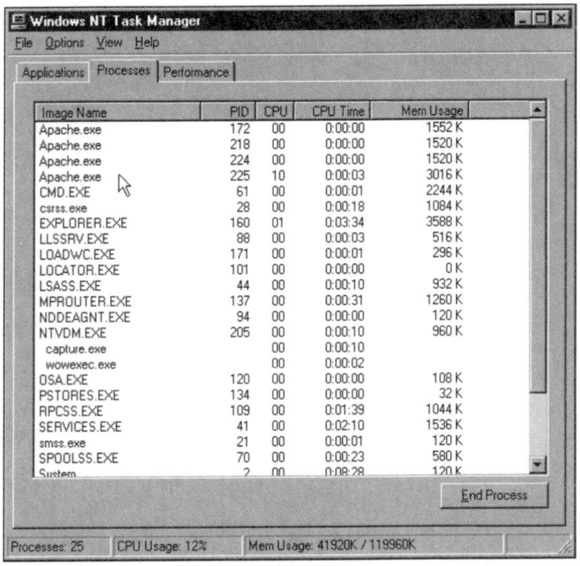

Figure 20-10: Apache server processes in Task Manager

There is really one Apache that is ready to serve. The rest of the Apache processes are just standbys in case the current one dies. You can control how many standby Apache processes are launched using special configuration options discussed below.

Configuring Apache for Windows

Apache configuration under Windows is pretty much the same as the UNIX-based configuration (see Chapters 3, 4, and 5) except for the following.

Any directive that uses path information might need to use the drive:/path/to/something format instead of the /path/to/something format used in UNIX. Note that you must use UNIX slashes in path names. For example, C:/www/mysite is allowed but not C:\www\mysite. If you do not specify a drive letter, the drive where Apache is installed will be assumed.

Apart from the path information differences, there are some directive-related changes. In fact, some old directives have new meanings and other new directives have also been added. These are discussed in the next section, starting with the new directives.

Windows-specific Apache directives

The Windows version of Apache comes with a special module called mod_dll. This module is used to load any external modules that are not already compiled into the Apache server. You can get a list of modules that are compiled into the Apache server using the command:

```
Apache -l
```

The current version of Apache shows the following modules as built into the binary:

- http_core.c
- mod_dll.c
- mod_mime.c
- mod_access.c
- mod_auth.c
- mod_negotiation.c
- mod_include.c
- mod_autoindex.c
- mod_dir.c
- mod_cgi.c
- mod_userdir.c
- mod_alias.c
- mod_env.c
- mod_log_config.c
- mod_asis.c
- mod_imap.c
- mod_actions.c
- mod_setenvif.c
- mod_isapi.c

Notice that the mod_dll module is already built into the binary; it wouldn't be able to do its job otherwise. However, there are other modules that can be found in the modules subdirectory of the Apache server root directory. These modules are listed below:

- ApacheModuleAuthAnon.dll
- ApacheModuleCERNMeta.dll

- ApacheModuleDigest.dll
- ApacheModuleExpires.dll
- ApacheModuleHeaders.dll
- ApacheModuleRewrite.dll
- ApacheModuleStatus.dll
- ApacheModuleUserTrack.dll

If you want to use any of these modules in your Apache server, you will have to use mod_dll-provided directives described in the following sections.

Apart from the new mod_dll functionality, there are some old directives whose meaning has been tweaked a little bit. Except for what is mentioned here, all other directives should work pretty much the same way. However, because the current version is a beta, many other directives may not function yet.

Directives whose meaning has changed include:

- StartServers — This directive specifies the number of standby servers that Apache will start in case one of them needs to take over the Web service when the current server process dies in an accident. If you launch many of these, you will probably be wasting memory for nothing. The default value is recommended.
- MinSpareServers — Because only one server is really used (the others are just standby), there is no need for this directive in Windows.
- MaxSpareServers — Because only one server is really used (the others are just standby) there is no need for this directive in Windows.
- MaxRequestsPerChild — Under Windows, only one process handles all the requests so there are no child processes to remove after the maximum requests specified by this directive. If set to a low number, the server will exit. However, if you set it to 0, the server will not exit at all.

Let's look at the two mod_dll-provided directives and the one new core directive.

LoadModule

```
Syntax: LoadModule module_name  path_to_module_dll
Context: server config
```

This directive allows you to load a DLL file as an Apache module at server start-up time. For example:

```
LoadModule   mod_digest  modules/ApacheModuleDigest.dll
```

This will load the modules/ApacheModuleDigest.dll DLL file as the mod_digest module. If the path to the module file does not have a / prefix, it is assumed to be a subdirectory of the server's root directory.

LoadFile

```
Syntax: LoadFile filename path_to_dll_ file
Context: server config
```

This directive allows you to load a DLL file that is required by a module DLL itself. If path to the file does not have a / prefix, it is assumed to be a subdirectory of the server's root directory.

ThreadsPerChild

```
Syntax: ThreadsPerChild number_of_threads
Default: ThreadsPerChild 50
Context: server config
```

This is a new core directive called ThreadsPerChild that sets the total number of threads that the Windows Apache server can use. Since each thread can process a request, this is the effective limit on the total number of requests that a server can service.

Summary

In this chapter, you learned about the current state of the Windows version of Apache. Hopefully, you were encouraged to learn that the Apache Group is working on covering a great deal of ground to ensure Apache's leadership in all popular platforms. After all, why should all good things only live under UNIX?

✦ ✦ ✦

HTTP/1.1 Status Codes

For each request from a Web client, the Web server must return to the client an HTTP status code, which consists of a three-digit number. A Web client can attempt to understand the server's response by looking at this status code, sent in the HTTP Status-Line header. The code is accompanied by a short phrase, called a reason phrase, which is intended to provide a brief explanation for the user. For example, an HTTP Status-Line header may look like this:

```
HTTP/1.1 404 Not Found
```

Here, "404" is the status code, and "Not Found" is the reason phrase. On a typical Web client, a Web browser will display the "Not Found" phrase in the browser window. Five different classes of status codes are available from the latest HTTP/1.1 specifications; these are discussed in the following sections.

Informational Status Codes (100–199)

The purpose of this type of status code is to let the client know the server is in the process of fulfilling a request. These status codes are only informational; the client does not have to act on any of them. Note that HTTP/1.0 does not define 1*xx* status codes, so 1*xx* status codes must not be sent to HTTP/1.0 clients. The currently defined 1*xx* status codes are as follows:

100 Continue	The server sends this code to let the client know it is ready to receive the rest of the request.
101 Switching Protocols	The server sends this code when it is willing to switch the application protocol to one specified in an Upgrade request header provided by the client. Switching should only take place if the new protocol provides an advantage over the existing one. For example, the client may request that the server use a newer HTTP protocol than what it is currently using. In such a case, the server should switch if possible.

Client Request Successful (200–299)

If the server returns a status code in the range 200– 299, the client's request was successfully received and accepted. The currently defined 2*xx* status codes are as follows:

200 OK	The server has succeeded in processing the request, and the requested document is attached.
201 Created	The server has successfully created a new URI, specified in a Location header.
202 Accepted	The request has been accepted for processing, but the server has not yet completed processing it.
203 Non-Authoritative Information	The metainformation in the response header did not originate with the server; it was copied from another server.
204 No Content	The request is complete, but no new information needs to be sent back. The client should continue to display the current document.
205 Reset Content	The client should reset the current document. This is useful when an HTML form needs to be reset to clear all existing values of input fields.
206 Partial Content	The server has fulfilled the partial GET request for the resource. This code is used to respond to Range requests. The server sends a Content-Range header to indicate which data segment is attached.

Request Redirected (300–399)

Status codes in the range 300–399 are sent to a client to let it know it needs to perform further action to complete the request. The currently defined 3*xx* status codes are as follows:

300 Multiple Choices	The requested resource corresponds to a set of documents. The server can send information about each document with its own specific location and content negotiation information to enable the client choose one.
301 Moved Permanently	The requested resource does not exist on the server. A Location header is sent to redirect the client to the new URL. The client directs all future requests to the new URI.
302 Moved Temporarily	The requested resource has temporarily moved. A Location header is sent to redirect the client to the new URL. The client continues to use the old URI in future requests.
303 See Other	The requested resource can be found in a different location indicated by the Location header, and the client should use the GET method to retrieve it.
304 Not Modified	The server uses this code to respond to the If-Modified-Since request header. This indicates the requested document has not been modified since the specified date, and the client should use its cached copy.
305 Use Proxy	The client should use a proxy, specified by the Location header, to retrieve the requested resource.

Client Request Incomplete (400–499)

The status codes in the range 400–499 are sent to indicate the client request is not complete and more information is needed to complete the resource request. The currently defined 4*xx* status codes are as follows:

400 Bad Request	The server detected a syntax error in the client request.
401 Unauthorized	The request requires user authentication. The server sends the WWW-Authenticate header to indicate the authentication type and realm for the requested resource.
402 Payment Required	This code is reserved for future use.
403 Forbidden	Access to requested resource is forbidden. The request should not be repeated by the client.
404 Not Found	The requested document does not exist on the server.
405 Method Not Allowed	The request method used by the client is unacceptable. The server sends the Allow header stating what methods are acceptable to access the requested resource.

(continued)

406 Not Acceptable	The requested resource is not available in a format that client can accept, based on the accept headers received by the server. If the request was not a HEAD request, the server can send Content-Language, Content-Encoding, and Content-Type headers to indicate which formats are available.
407 Proxy Authentication Required	Unauthorized access request to a proxy server. The client must first authenticate itself with the proxy. The server sends the Proxy-Authenticate header indicating the authentication scheme and realm for the requested resource.
408 Request Time-Out	The client has failed to complete its request within the request timeout period used by the server. However, the client can repeat the request.
409 Conflict	The client request conflicts with another request. The server can add information about the type of conflict along with the status code.
410 Gone	The requested resource is permanently gone from the server.
411 Length Required	The client must supply a Content-Length header in its request.
412 Precondition Failed	When a client sends a request with one or more If. . . headers, the server uses this code to indicate that one or more of the conditions specified in these headers is false.
413 Request Entity Too Large	The server refuses to process the request because its message body is too large. The server can close connection to stop the client from continuing the request.
414 Request-URI Too Long	The server refuses to process the request because the specified URI is too long.
415 Unsupported Media Type	The server refuses to process the request because it does not support the message body's format.

Server Errors (500-599)

The status codes in the range 500–599 are returned when the server encounters an error and cannot fulfill the request. The currently defined 5*xx* status codes are as follows:

500 Internal Server Error	A server configuration setting or an external program has caused an error.
501 Not Implemented	The server does not support the functionality required to fulfill the request.
502 Bad Gateway	The server encountered an invalid response from an upstream server or proxy.

503 Service Unavailable	The service is temporarily unavailable. The server can send a Retry-After header to indicate when the service may become available again.
504 Gateway Time-Out	The gateway or proxy has timed out.
505 HTTP Version Not Supported	The version of HTTP used by client is not supported.

✦ ✦ ✦

APPENDIX B

Basics of Regular Expression

A regular expression is typically composed of both normal and special characters to create a pattern. This pattern is used to match one or more substrings or an entire string, for example:

([a–z]+)\.([a–z])\.([a–z]+)

This regular expression matches www.idgbooks.com, www.apache.org, and so on. The special characters used in a regular expression are often called *metacharacters*. Following are commonly used metacharacters:

.	Matches any character (except Newline)
^	Matches the start of the string
$	Matches the end of the string
\b	Matches a word boundary
x?	Matches 0 or 1 x's, where x is any regular expression
x*	Matches 0 or more x's
x+	Matches 1 or more x's
foo|bar	Matches one of foo or bar
[abc]	Matches any character in the set abc
[A–Z]	Matches any character in the range A to Z.
[^xyz]	Matches any single character not in the set xyz
\w	Matches an alphanumeric character (for instance, [a–zA–Z0–9_])

\s	Matches a white-space character
\t	Tab character
\n	Newline character
\r	Return character
\f	Form feed character
\v	Vertical tab, whatever that is
\a	Bell character
\e	Escape character
\077	Octal char
\x9f	Hex char
\c[	Control char
\l	Lowercase next char
\L	Lowercase till \E
\U	Uppercase till \E
\E	End case modification
\u	Uppercase next char
\Q	Quote metacharacters till \E

If you need to use a metacharacter as a normal character in the regular expression, you can use \metachar format to take away the special meaning. An example of this is \$, which is a regular dollar sign character. The standard quantifiers used in regular expressions are as follows:

*	Match 0 or more times.
+	Match 1 or more times
?	Match 1 or 0 times
{n}	Match exactly n times
{n,}	Match at least n times
{n, m}	Match at least n but not more than m times

Also note that a | character is treated as an OR operator. A pair of parenthesis () enables you to group a character in a regular expression. A pair of square brackets [] creates a character class or range.

Lets revisit the first example again:

```
([a-z]+)\.([a-z])\.([a-z]+)
```

As mentioned before this expression can be used to match strings such as www.idgbooks.com. The first [a–z]+ specifies that one or more characters in the a to z range is needed to match the group specified by first pair of parenthesis. If a match is found, whatever is matched can be accessed using $1. There are three pairs of parenthesis in this expression. The first one (starting from the left) is $1, second on is $2, and the third one is $3. Notice that \ is use to escape the dot (.) metacharacter between the groups.

Here are two more examples:

✦ ^foo\.htm$

  This will match a string foo.htm. It would not match afoo.htm because the ^ metacharacter is used to specify that the matching string must start with the f character. It also would not match foo.html because the $ metacharacter is used to specify that the matching string must end with the m character.

✦ ^www\.([^.]+)\.host\.com(.*)

  This will match a string, such as www.username.host.com STATUS=java and the $1 will be assigned to host and $2 will hold everything followed by the www.username.host.com part of the string. The $2 will hold STATUS=java.

✦ ✦ ✦

Internet Resources for Apache

In this Appendix, you will find a list of Websites, Usenet newsgroups, and mailing-list addresses that you might find useful.

Free Resources

Following are some of the free Internet resources for Apache.

Web Sites

Official Apache Web site `www.apache.org`

Apache Module Registry `http://modules.apache.org/`

Apache-SSL `http://www.apache-ssl.org/`

Apache/Perl Integration Project `http://perl.apache.org/`

Apache GUI Project
`http://butler.disa.mil/ApacheConfig/`

Java-Apache Project `http://java.apache.org/`

Apache for OS/2 `http://www.slink.com/ApacheOS2/`

Apache for Amiga
`http://www.xs4all.nl/~albertv/apache/`

Usenet Newsgroups

You can also find information about World Wide Web topics in 15 distinct newsgroups. They are subdivided for good reason — please use the newsgroup that is most relevant to your topic. Before you post anything make sure you are posting to the right newsgroup(s) and always read the FAQ of the newsgroup, if available.

Web server-related newsgroups

`comp.infosystems.www.servers.unix`

This newsgroup discusses Web servers for UNIX platforms. Possible subjects include configuration questions/solutions, security issues, directory structure, and bug reports.

`comp.infosystems.www.servers.ms-windows`

This newsgroup covers Web servers for the MS Windows and NT platforms. Possible subjects include configuration questions/solutions, security issues, directory structure, and bug reports.

`comp.infosystems.www.servers.mac`

This newsgroup holds discussions of Web servers for the Macintosh (MacOS) platform. Possible subjects include configuration questions/solutions, security issues, directory structure, and bug reports.

`comp.infosystems.www.servers.misc`

This newsgroup discusses Web servers for other platforms, such as Amiga, VMS, and others. Possible subjects include configuration questions/solutions, security issues, directory structure, and bug reports.

`japan.www.server.apache`

This newsgroup covers discussion of Apache in Japanese.

Authoring related newsgroups

`comp.infosystems.www.authoring.cgi`

This newsgroup discusses the development of Common Gateway Interface (CGI) scripts as they relate to Web page authoring. Possible subjects include: how to handle the results of forms, how to generate images on the fly, and how to put together other interactive Web offerings.

`comp.infosystems.www.authoring.html`

This newsgroup covers discussion of HyperText Markup Language (HTML) as it relates to Web page authoring. Possible subjects include HTML editors, formatting tricks, and current and proposed HTML standards.

`comp.infosystems.www.authoring.images`

This newsgroup discusses the creation and editing of images as they relate to Web page authoring. Possible subjects include how best to leverage the image-display capabilities of the Web and common questions and solutions for putting up imagemaps.

`comp.infosystems.www.authoring.misc`

This newsgroup covers miscellaneous Web authoring issues not covered by the other comp.inforsystems.www.authoring.* groups. Possible subjects include the use of audio and video, and so on.

Web-browser related newsgroups

`comp.infosystems.www.browsers.ms-windows`

This newsgroup discusses Web browsers for the MS Windows and NT platforms. Possible subjects include configuration questions/solutions, external viewers (helper applications), and bug reports.

`comp.infosystems.www.browsers.mac`

This newsgroup talks about Web browsers for the Macintosh platform. Possible subjects include configuration questions/solutions, external viewers and bug reports.

`comp.infosystems.www.browsers.x`

This newsgroup discusses Web browsers for the X-Window system. Possible subjects include configuration questions/solutions, external viewers and bug reports.

`comp.infosystems.www.browsers.misc`

This newsgroup covers Web browsers for all other platforms. Possible subjects include configuration questions/solutions, external viewers (helper applications), and bug reports. Included platforms are Amiga, DOS, VMS, and UNIX text-mode.

Announcements newsgroups

`comp.infosystems.www.announce`

This is a newsgroup in which new, web-related resources can be announced. READ THE GROUP FIRST to find the posting guidelines.

Other WWW newsgroups

`comp.infosystems.www.advocacy`

This newsgroup is for comments, arguments, debates, and discussions about which Web browsers, servers, external-viewer programs, and other software is better or worse than any other.

`comp.infosystems.www.misc`

comp.infosystems.www.misc provides a forum for general discussion of WWW-related topics that are not covered by the other newsgroups in the hierarchy. This group is likely to include discussions of the Web's future changes in the structure and protocols of the Web that affect both clients and servers.

Perl newsgroups

`comp.lang.perl.misc`

These newsgroups are devoted to discussions about Perl; they include everything from bug reports to new features, to history, humor and trivia. This is the best source of information about anything Perl related, especially what's new with Perl5.

`comp.lang.perl.announce`

New releases, the FAQ, and new modules, are announced here.

WWW resources for Usenet newsgroups

DejaNews `www.dejanews.com/`

The Reference Archive `www.reference.com/`

American Web Services `www.awebs.com/news_archive`

Critical Mass Communications
`http://www.criticalmass.com/concord/index.htm`

Mailing lists

If you would like to receive Apache-related announcements on a timely basis, you can subscribe to this mailing list. To subscribe, send a message to apache-announce-request@apache.org with the word "subscribe" in the body of the message. Note that this is not a forum for asking questions.

To subscribe for general discussions, send the command "subscribe apache" to majordomo@geek.net. There is also a digested version of the list, which you can subscribe to with the command "subscribe apache-digest."

Commercial Resources

A growing number of Apache users (especially corporate users) are always looking for commercial resources that offer Apache software or services. Following are some well-known commercial resources for Apache:

The Apache Week online free magazine `www.apacheweek.com`

US/Canada Stronghold `www.c2.net`

Outside US/Canada Stronghold `www.uk.web.com`

Covalent Raven `http://raven.covalent.net`

Rovis `www.rovis.com/warpaint/`

Other Related Resources

WWW Consortium `www.w3.org/`

Netcraft Survey Report Web site `www.netcraft.co.uk/Survey/`

All RFC documents `http://ds.internic.net/ds/dspg1intdoc.html`

Server Watch `www.ServerWatch.com`

Search Engine Watch `www.SearchEngineWatch.com`

Browser Watch `www.BrowserWatch.com`

Web Compare `www.WebCompare.com`

Web Developer `www.WebDeveloper.com`

Web Reference `www.WebReference.com`

Electronic Commerce on Internet `http://e-comm.internet.com`

The List `www.TheList.com`

Internet News `www.InternetNews.com`

CGI Specification `http://hoohoo.ncsa.uiuc.edu/cgi/interface.html`

FastCGI Web site `http://www.fastcgi.com`

Perl Language Site `www.perl.com`

✦ ✦ ✦

What's on the CD-ROM?

The accompanying CD-ROM contains the latest Apache source and binary distributions, third-party modules and utilities, and Web-related RFC documents.

The easiest way to browse the CD-ROM content is to use a Web browser. Open the index.html file from the top-level directory in the CD-ROM. This page will provide links to all the software available on this CD-ROM. If you browse the index.html pages using a Web browser as recommended, you will be able to download the software onto your hard disk from the CD-ROM by clicking on the download links. I have also included links to related Internet resources (if available).

You can also access the files in the individual directories by clicking the directory and selecting the software you want to use.

The contents of the CD-ROM are organized as follows:

- /apache — Apache source and binary distributions, plus third-party Apache modules
- /chapters — useful scripts and configuration files from each chapter
- /perl — the latest Perl source and binary distributions, Perl-based CGI modules, ePerl, and embPerl
- /utils — various third-party programs such as Web server log analyzers, Web robots, CGI wrappers, and Web site mirroring software
- /rfc — Web related RFC files that describe the latest Web standards such as HTTP and HTML

Each program is kept in its own subdirectory. You will find an index.html file in each software directory that has links to licensing information, readme files, and documentation.

Note that some software that could not be included on the CD-ROM will have links to the Internet Web or FTP sites from which you can download them. Remember to have your Internet connection up and running before you attempt to download such software.

Apache Software

Here is a list of software you will find in the /apache directory and its subdirectories:

- ✦ Source distributions — The source files are located in the /apache/source directory. I have included the latest released and beta source distributions in common compressed-file formats such as tar.Z and tar.gz. Note that only the latest beta version of Apache can be compiled for the Windows platform.
- ✦ Binary distributions — The binary files are located in the /apache/binaries directory. You will find compiled binaries from many popular operating systems such as AIX 4.1, DUNIX 4.0, FreeBSD 2.x, HP-UX 10.20, SINIX 5.4, IRIX 6.2, Linux 2.x, NetBSD 1.2, OS/2, Solaris 2.5.x, SunOS 4.1.x, Ultrix 4.4, and Windows 95/NT.
- ✦ Featured modules — The nonstandard Apache modules featured in this book are stored in the /apache/featured-modules directory. You will find separate directories for mod_perl, mod_fastcgi, and mod_auth_external.
- ✦ Contributed software — Various contributed Apache software, such as nonstandard modules, patches, and demos, is stored in the /apache/contrib directory. Please be careful when you use these programs because they probably have not been widely tested yet.
- ✦ Official patches — Official patches (issued by the Apache Group) are in the /apache/patches directory.

Perl Software

Perl and Perl-based software is included in the /perl directory. Here is a list of what is available:

- ✦ Source distributions — The latest Perl source distribution is included in the /perl/source directory. If you are installing Perl on a UNIX system, use the latest.tar.gz distribution. If you are installing it on a Windows system, use the Pw32s316.zip distribution from ActiveState. The use of this program is subject to the terms of the GNU General Public License or the Artistic License contained on the CD.

✦ Binary distributions — The only binary distributions I have included on the CD-ROM are for Windows 95 and NT systems. There are two binary distribution for such systems: one (Pw32a316.zip) for Digital Alpha-based systems and the other (Pw32i316.zip) for Intel x86-based systems. These files are located in the /perl/binaries directory.

✦ EPerl — ePerl interprets embedded Perl scripts in ASCII text files. It can run as a stand-alone program or as a Perl 5 module. I discussed this program in Chapter 13. The ePerl distribution is located in the /perl/eperl-2.2.12 directory. The use of this program is subject to the terms of the GNU General Public License or the Artistic License contained on the CD.

✦ Embperl — Embperl interprets embedded Perl scripts in HTML documents; it is like a limited version of ePerl. Embperl can run as a stand-alone program, as a CGI script, or as a module using mod_perl. I briefly discussed this program in Chapter 13 as well. The Embperl distribution is located in the /perl/HTML-Embperl-0.26-beta directory. The use of this program is subject to the terms of the GNU General Public License or the Artistic License contained on the CD.

✦ Web-related Perl modules — I have included two commonly used Perl-based CGI modules on the CD-ROM. They are:

  - CGI.pm — This module enables you to write Perl-based CGI programs using object-oriented techniques. Since I discovered this module a few years ago, I always use it when I write CGI scripts in Perl. The module is located in the /perl/modules/CGI.pm-2.39 directory.

  - libwww-perl — This is a collection of Perl modules that enable you to write Web client applications using a consistent programming interface. The libwww-perl modules are located in the /perl/modules/libwww-perl-5.31 directory. Note that libwww-perl modules require quite a few other Perl modules, which are also included on the CD-ROM. Information about these prerequisite modules are discussed in the following section. The use of this program is subject to the terms of the GNU General Public License or the Artistic License contained on the CD.

✦ Miscellaneous Perl modules — With the exception of the CPAN module, all the miscellaneous Perl modules included on the CD-ROM are required by the libwww-perl modules.

✦ HTML-Parser module — This is a collection of modules that parse HTML text documents. These modules are located in the /perl/modules/misc/HTML-Parser-2.16 directory. The use of this program is subject to the terms of the GNU General Public License or the Artistic License contained on the CD.

✦ MD5 module — This module provides an interface to RSA's Message Digest algorithm, called MD5. The module is located in the /perl/modules/misc/MD5-1.7 directory. The use of this program is subject to the terms of the GNU General Public License or the Artistic License contained on the CD.

✦ MIME-Base64 module — This module contains a base64 encoder/decoder. The module is located in the /perl/modules/misc/MIME-Base64-2.05 directory. The use of this program is subject to the terms of the GNU General Public License or the Artistic License contained on the CD.

✦ libnet modules — This is a collection of Perl modules that provide application programming interface (API) to the client side of various protocols used on the Internet. The modules are located in the /perl/modules/misc/libnet-1.0605 directory. The use of this program is subject to the terms of the GNU General Public License or the Artistic License contained on the CD.

✦ CPAN module — This module allows you to query, download, and build Perl modules from CPAN sites. This module is located in the /perl/modules/misc/CPAN-1.36 directory. The use of this program is subject to the terms of the GNU General Public License or the Artistic License contained on the CD.

Web Server Log Analyzers

I've included three products to help you analyze your server logs:

✦ Wusage — Wusage is a commercial Web-based statistics program that can analyze your Apache server log files (in CLF format). The latest version of the software is really a server application that has a Web-based user interface. The software is located in the /utils/wusage-6.0 directory. Note that the evaluation copy included on the CD-ROM expires after a certain number of days. If you plan on using this software after the evaluation period expires, you will have to purchase the software from the vendor.

✦ WebTrends Professional Suite — WebTrends Professional Suite is also a commercial log analyzer program. The evaluation version of this software is located in the /utils/webtrends directory.

✦ Wwwstat — Wwwstat is a freely distributed log analyzer program that can analyze Web server logs in CLF format. You can use it with your Apache server. The software is located in the /utils/wwwstat-2.0 directory. The software was developed in part by the University of California, Irvine.

Useful Utilities

I have also included a few useful Web and network programs that may come in handy. Here is a list of what is included:

✦ CGIWrap — This is a CGI wrapper program discussed in chapter 12. It provides a secure way of running CGI programs. It is located in the /utils/cgiwrap-3.6 directory.

✦ MOMspider — This is a Web robot that will help you find broken links. It is located in the /utils/MOMspider-1.00 directory. The software was developed in part by the University of California, Irvine.

- w3mir — This is a Web site mirroring program. It is located in the /utils/w3mir-1.0.1 directory.
- Spong — This is a monitoring utility written in Perl. It allows you to monitor various network services such as HTTP, FTP, and DNS. When a problem is detected, it can e-mail or page an on-call administrator. It also provides a CGI script that shows monitoring reports and system status on the Web. It is located in the /utils/spong-1.1 directory.

Protocols and Standard Documents

Various RFC documents for standards such as HTTP/1.1, HTTP/1.0, and HTML. are located in the /rfc directory.

✦ ✦ ✦

Index

B

(continued)

D

(continued)

F

G

H

(continued)

(continued)

N

O

P

Q

R

(continued)

T

(continued)

U

V

(continued)

X

Y

IDG Books Worldwide, Inc. End-User License Agreement

contained in the individual license agreements recorded on the Software Media. These limitations may include a requirement that after using the program for a specified period of time, the user must pay a registration fee or discontinue use. By opening the Software packet(s), you will be agreeing to abide by the licenses and restrictions for these individual programs that are detailed in *Appendix D, What's on the CD-ROM?* and on the Software Media. None of the material on this Software Media or listed in this Book may ever be redistributed, in original or modified form, for commercial purposes.

5. Limited Warranty.

(a) IDGB warrants that the Software and Software Media are free from defects in materials and workmanship under normal use for a period of sixty (60) days from the date of purchase of this Book. If IDGB receives notification within the warranty period of defects in materials or workmanship, IDGB will replace the defective Software Media.

(b) **IDGB AND THE AUTHOR OF THE BOOK DISCLAIM ALL OTHER WARRANTIES, EXPRESS OR IMPLIED, INCLUDING WITHOUT LIMITATION IMPLIED WARRANTIES OF MERCHANTABILITY AND FITNESS FOR A PARTICULAR PURPOSE, WITH RESPECT TO THE SOFTWARE, THE PROGRAMS, THE SOURCE CODE CONTAINED THEREIN, AND/OR THE TECHNIQUES DESCRIBED IN THIS BOOK. IDGB DOES NOT WARRANT THAT THE FUNCTIONS CONTAINED IN THE SOFTWARE WILL MEET YOUR REQUIREMENTS OR THAT THE OPERATION OF THE SOFTWARE WILL BE ERROR FREE.**

(c) This limited warranty gives you specific legal rights, and you may have other rights that vary from jurisdiction to jurisdiction.

6. Remedies.

(a) IDGB's entire liability and your exclusive remedy for defects in materials and workmanship shall be limited to replacement of the Software Media, which may be returned to IDGB with a copy of your receipt at the following address: Software Media Fulfillment Department, Attn.: *Apache Server Bible*, IDG Books Worldwide, Inc., 7260 Shadeland Station, Ste. 100, Indianapolis, IN 46256, or call 1-800-762-2974. Please allow three to four weeks for delivery. This Limited Warranty is void if failure of the Software Media has resulted from accident, abuse, or misapplication. Any replacement Software Media will be warranted for the remainder of the original warranty period or thirty (30) days, whichever is longer.

(b) In no event shall IDGB or the author be liable for any damages whatsoever (including without limitation damages for loss of business profits, business interruption, loss of business information, or any other pecuniary loss) arising from the use of or inability to use the Book or the Software, even if IDGB has been advised of the possibility of such damages.

(c) Because some jurisdictions do not allow the exclusion or limitation of liability for consequential or incidental damages, the above limitation or exclusion may not apply to you.

7. **U.S. Government Restricted Rights.** Use, duplication, or disclosure of the Software by the U.S. Government is subject to restrictions stated in paragraph (c)(1)(ii) of the Rights in Technical Data and Computer Software clause of DFARS 252.227-7013, and in subparagraphs (a) through (d) of the Commercial Computer—Restricted Rights clause at FAR 52.227-19, and in similar clauses in the NASA FAR supplement, when applicable.

8. **General.** This Agreement constitutes the entire understanding of the parties and revokes and supersedes all prior agreements, oral or written, between them and may not be modified or amended except in a writing signed by both parties hereto that specifically refers to this Agreement. This Agreement shall take precedence over any other documents that may be in conflict herewith. If any one or more provisions contained in this Agreement are held by any court or tribunal to be invalid, illegal, or otherwise unenforceable, each and every other provision shall remain in full force and effect.

my2cents.idgbooks.com

Register This Book — And Win!

Visit **http://my2cents.idgbooks.com** to register this book and we'll automatically enter you in our fantastic monthly prize giveaway. It's also your opportunity to give us feedback: let us know what you thought of this book and how you would like to see other topics covered.

Discover IDG Books Online!

The IDG Books Online Web site is your online resource for tackling technology — at home and at the office. Frequently updated, the IDG Books Online Web site features exclusive software, insider information, online books, and live events!

10 Productive & Career-Enhancing Things You Can Do at www.idgbooks.com

- Nab source code for your own programming projects.
- Download software.
- Read Web exclusives: special articles and book excerpts by IDG Books Worldwide authors.
- Take advantage of resources to help you advance your career as a Novell or Microsoft professional.
- Buy IDG Books Worldwide titles or find a convenient bookstore that carries them.
- Register your book and win a prize.
- Chat live online with authors.
- Sign up for regular e-mail updates about our latest books.
- Suggest a book you'd like to read or write.
- Give us your 2¢ about our books and about our Web site.

You say you're not on the Web yet? It's easy to get started with IDG Books' *Discover the Internet,* available at local retailers everywhere.

CD-ROM Installation Instructions

The accompanying CD-ROM contains the latest Apache source and binary distributions, third-party modules, utilities, and Web-related RFC documents.

After you insert the CD in your CD-ROM drive, you can access the files on this CD-ROM in one of two ways: by using a Web Browser or accessing your CD-ROM drive.

The Web browser is the preferred method. Popular browsers, such as Netscape Navigator and Microsoft Internet Explorer, offer an Open Page option, which lets you select a file from a disk (or CD-ROM). Use this feature to open the topmost index.html page on the CD-ROM. You can also enter a file:///location/ type *URL* directly on your browser's window. For example, on a UNIX system that has the CD-ROM mounted on /cdrom, you would load the topmost index.html page by entering file:///cdrom/index.html. On a Windows (95, NT, and so on) system that maps drive letter D to the CD-ROM drive, you would load the topmost index.html page by entering file:///D|/index.html. Once you load the index.html page, you can browse all of the software on the CD-ROM.

You can also access the files in the individual folders by navigating to the folder you want, clicking the folder, and selecting the software you want to use. This is done using the same method used to access files on your hard drive.

Each item on the CD has its own installation requirements and procedures. Make sure you read the appropriate README file and installation instructions before attempting to install any software.

✦ ✦ ✦